Deadly Arsenals

Praise for the First Edition

"As accessible as it is lucid and offers the most comprehensive unclassified assessment available today. In context of the U.S. avowed war on terrorism, *Deadly Arsenals* is an especially timely resource and comprehensive reference for scholars, students, and policy makers interested in weapons of mass destruction."

—CHOICE, Association of College & Research Libraries

"The proliferation of weapons of mass destruction, especially to terrorists groups, ranks today as the number one threat to America's national security. *Deadly Arsenals* is required "reading for those who care about the future of our country and our planet."

—U.S. Senator Joseph R. Biden

"To combat weapons of mass destruction, the United States must strengthen the non-proliferation regime, address regional threats and bolster defenses. *Deadly Arsenals* is an indispensable resource for anyone working in these critical areas."

—Samuel R. (Sandy) Berger, Former U.S. National Security Adviser

"*Deadly Arsenals* is a proliferation encyclopedia. It is a powerful tool for anyone grappling with ways to contain the spread of weapons of mass destruction."

—Susan Eisenhower, President, Eisenhower Institute

"*Deadly Arsenals* provides reliable information, solid analysis, and balanced assessments of those programs that threaten international security, and on efforts undertaken to address those threats."

—Robert L. Gallucci, Dean, School of Foreign Service, Georgetown University

Deadly Arsenals

NUCLEAR, BIOLOGICAL, AND CHEMICAL THREATS

Second Edition

Joseph Cirincione
Jon B. Wolfsthal
Miriam Rajkumar

CARNEGIE ENDOWMENT FOR INTERNATIONAL PEACE
Washington, D.C.

Carnegie Endowment for International Peace
1779 Massachusetts Avenue, N.W., Washington, D.C. 20036
202-483-7600, Fax 202-483-1840
www.CarnegieEndowment.org

The Carnegie Endowment for International Peace normally does not take institutional positions on public policy issues; the views and recommendations presented in this publication do not necessarily represent the views of the Carnegie Endowment, its officers, staff, or trustees.

To order, contact Carnegie's distributor:
The Brookings Institution Press
Department 029, Washington, D.C. 20042-0029, USA
1-800-275-1447 or 1-202-797-6258
Fax 202-797-2960, E-mail bibooks@brook.edu

Composition by Stephen McDougal
Back cover photo by Chad Evans Wyatt
Maps by Dave Merrill
Printed by Automated Graphic Systems

Library of Congress Cataloging-in-Publication data

Cirincione, Joseph.
Deadly arsenals : nuclear, biological, and chemical threats / Joseph Cirincione, Jon B. Wolfsthal, Miriam Rajkumar. — 2nd ed.
p. cm.
Includes bibliographical references and index.
ISBN-13: 978-0-87003-216-5 (isbn-13)
ISBN-10: 0-87003-216-X (isbn-10)
1. Weapons of mass destruction. 2. Nuclear arms control—Verification. 3. Chemical arms control—Verification. 4. Biological arms control—Verification. I. Wolfsthal, Jon B. II. Rajkumar, Miriam. III. Title.

U793.C57 2005
327.1'74—dc22 2005012915

13 12 11 10 3 4 5 1st Printing 2005

Contents

Foreword

In the three years since the first edition of *Deadly Arsenals*, the field of nonproliferation has been through a period of breathtaking change—all of which is reflected in this new volume. The threat brought to life by the attacks of September 11, 2001—that terrorists might seek and one day use nuclear, chemical, or biological weapons—swiftly rose to the top of an agenda that for 40 years had been focused on threats from states. North Korea's violation of its commitments and subsequent announced withdrawal from the Non-Proliferation Treaty (NPT), and its declaration that it had acquired nuclear weapons, underlined the treaty's Achilles heel that allows a state to exploit NPT membership to become a nuclear state.

North Korea's actions emphasized, as did the Iraq conflict, the glaring gaps in the international community's capacity for tough enforcement of nonproliferation commitments. The failure to find nuclear, chemical, or biological weapons in Iraq underlined how little outsiders can know about what happens within member states without inspectors on the ground. In 2003, news emerged that the A. Q. Khan network, based in Pakistan but involving engineers and businesspeople from more than a dozen countries, was able to traverse the world selling nuclear bomb designs and equipment necessary to produce nuclear weapons for years before it was stopped. Buyers included North Korea, Iran, Libya, and perhaps others. Existing laws and export practices proved manifestly inadequate to block these transfers of equipment and know-how. One dangerous consequence of this failure has been the accelerated pace of the Iranian nuclear program, which benefited substantially from partnership with the Khan network.

The news is not all bleak, however. Since the signing of the NPT in 1968, many more countries have given up nuclear weapons programs than have begun them. There are fewer nuclear weapons in the world and fewer nations with nuclear weapons programs than there were 20 years ago. This new edition, for example, does not include a chapter on Algeria, which reflects the international community's greater confidence in the peaceful intentions of that country's nuclear program. The new material in this volume on the United States and Russia reflects the fact that these two countries continue to work cooperatively to dismantle materials left over from the Cold War. The threats posed by weapons programs in the former Soviet republics have diminished considerably. And Libya has become an important success story and a model for other nations to follow as it verifiably dismantles its clandestine nuclear and chemical weapons capabilities.

With the first edition of *Deadly Arsenals*, we set out to produce the most complete and authoritative resource available anywhere from nonclassified sources on the spread of nuclear, chemical, and biological weapons and their means of delivery. The widespread use of that volume and the warm feedback we have received from scholars, government officials, and experts from around the world have reinforced our belief that this project, while highly labor intensive, is well worth the effort. I am confident that this second edition will earn the same reputation for comprehensive coverage, accuracy, clarity, and meticulous attention to detail. Though its content differs substantially from that of the first volume, reflecting the extraordinary pace of change in this field, users will find it to be the same reliable guide that its predecessor proved to be.

We would like to thank the John D. and Catherine T. MacArthur Foundation, the Carnegie Corporation of New York, the Nuclear Threat Initiative, the Prospect Hill Foundation, the Ploughshares Fund, the Ford Foundation, and the New Land Foundation for their generous support of our work.

Jessica T. Mathews
President
Carnegie Endowment for International Peace

Acknowledgments

For this substantially improved second edition of *Deadly Arsenals*, we must acknowledge the international team of experts and scholars who generously gave their time and intellects to review chapters. Our research benefited from extensive private discusions with defense and foreign affairs officials in many nations. We would like to thank publicly Wade Boese, Michael Eisenstadt, Thomas Cochran, Gaurav Kampani, Geoffrey Kemp, John Redick, Paul Walker, Joel Wit, and Frank Pabian, as well as our Carnegie Endowment colleagues, Rose Gottemoeller, Hussein Haqqani, George Perkovich, Hadi Semati, Michael Swaine, and Ashley Tellis, for their valuable amendments and suggestions. Jonathan Tucker, who greatly improved the chemical and biological weapons chapter in the first edition, graciously did the same for this new book. Once again, data and analysis on the nuclear weapon arsenals of the United States and Russia relied heavily on the research and advice of Robert S. Norris and Hans M. Kristensen at the Natural Resources Defense Council.

We are still grateful to those who provided vaulable suggestions for the first edition of this book: Michael Barletta, Avner Cohen, Shai Feldman, Camille Grand, Evan Medieros, Judith Perera, John Russell, Mark Smith, John Simpson, and the dedicated 2002 Carnegie Endowment staff of Marshall Breit, Andrew Krepps, Maya Pilatowicz, and Sarah Schumacher—all of whom have now advanced their careers. Maya coauthored the first edition's chapter on chemical and biological weapons, and Andrew the chapter on missile proliferation.

We could not have produced this second edition without the help of the superb Carnegie Nonproliferation staff: Caterina Dutto, Revati Prasad, Jane Vaynman, and Joshua Williams. They did a fabulous job researching developments, dissecting intelligence assessments, counting missiles, and fact-checking revisions. The Carnegie Endowment's Phyllis Jask patiently shepherded the manuscript through the publications maze to produce the high-quality book you now hold. As always, the library staff of Kathleen Higgs and Chris Henley provided wonderful and timely research. Sally Murray James of Cutting Edge Design gave us a clean, artistic cover and book design; Alfred Imhoff copy edited; and compositor Stephen McDougal produced the book in record time.

The first edition of this book stood on the broad shoulders of those who preceded us at the Carnegie Non-Proliferation Project. We are indebted to the project's founder, Leonard Spector, and to Rodney Jones, the late Mark McDonough, Toby Dalton, and Gregory Koblentz, the authors of *Tracking Nuclear Proliferation* (1998), which formed the basis of our original study.

None of this would have been possible without the guidance and support of the Carnegie Endowment's president, Jessica Mathews, whose suggestion launched the first edition of this book three years ago, and vice presidents George Perkovich, Paul Balaran, and Carmen MacDougall.

We are ever grateful for the faith and generous support of the John T. and Catherine D. MacArthur Foundation, the Carnegie Corporation of New York, the Nuclear Threat Initiative, the Prospect Hill Foundation, the Ford Foundation, the Ploughshares Fund and the New Land Foundation.

With our great appreciation to those who worked to improve the quality of our work also goes our general absolution of any sins; the authors alone accept responsibility for the content and any errors that may remain.

PART ONE

Assessments and Weapons

PREVIOUS PAGE: *The XX-39 CLIMAX, part of Operation Upshot/Knothole, was a 61 kiloton device fired June 4, 1953, at the Nevada Test Site.*
(U.S. DEPARTMENT OF ENERGY, AVAILABLE AT www.nv.doe.gov/news&pubs)

CHAPTER 1

Global Trends

The proliferation of nuclear, biological, and chemical weapons is widely recognized as the most serious threat to the national security of the United States and other nations. Official and public attention to proliferation issues, however, has varied over the years from near hysteria to apathy. During this first decade of the twenty-first century, concern is very high, with passionate international debates over which strategies can best prevent the spread and use of these weapons.

To inform these debates, this second edition of *Deadly Arsenals* revises and updates all the chapters, figures, and tables from the first edition published in 2002. This edition includes new chapters on Iraq, Iran, Libya, North Korea, and new information and analysis on other countries, which are needed to capture the dramatic developments of the past three years. All the parts of the book emphasize factual and historical analysis of weapons programs. The book is intended to serve as a proliferation atlas and ready reference for students, experts, and concerned citizens alike.[1]

One significant change in the new edition is that it no longer employs the term "weapons of mass destruction." Though used widely by officials and the media, this phrase conflates very different threats from weapons that differ greatly in lethality, consequence of use, and the availability of measures that can protect against them. Chemical weapons are easy to manufacture, but they inflict relatively limited damage over small areas and dissipate fairly quickly. Biological weapon agents can be made in most medical laboratories, but it is very difficult to turn these agents into effective weapons, and prompt inoculation and quarantine could limit the number of victims and the areas affected. Nuclear weapons are difficult to produce, but one weapon can destroy an entire city, killing hundreds of thousands instantly and leaving lingering radiation that would render large areas uninhabitable for years. A failure to differentiate these threats can lead to seriously flawed policy. For example, the repeated use of the term "weapons of mass destruction" to describe the potential threat from Iraq before the 2003 war merged the danger that it still had anthrax-filled shells, which was possible, with the danger that it had nuclear bombs, which was highly unlikely. Similarly, saying that Syria has weapons of mass destruction merges the danger that it has chemical weapons, which is almost certainly true, with the danger that it has a nuclear bomb, which is certainly not true. The first threat is real, but its elimination requires an entirely different set of policies than does the second. The term also blurs the possible responses to threats, justifying for some the use of nuclear weapons to prevent a potential chemical weapons attack. This study disaggregates these threats, considering weapons and programs as they actually appear.

The Twentieth Century's Deadly Legacy

Nuclear, biological, and chemical weapons were twentieth-century inventions. There is nothing new, of course, about mass destruction. From ancient times, a military campaign often meant the slaughter of tens of thousands of soldiers and civilians. As the Industrial Revolution mechanized warfare, the industrialized nations sought ways to more efficiently kill armored troops or unprotected populations dispersed over wide areas and to annihilate military and economic targets. Military researchers produced weapons that could deliver poison gas, germs, and nuclear explosions with artillery, aerial bombs, and, later, missiles.

Poison gas was used for the first time during World War I, as both the Central Powers and the Allies tried attacks with chlorine gas, mustard gas, and other agents to break the trench warfare stalemate. Japan inaugurated biological warfare in its attacks against the Chinese at the beginning of World War II, but all the belligerent nations had biological weapon research programs, and Germany invented and used nerve gas to kill millions of Jews and other prisoners in its concentration camps. Nuclear weapons were used for the first and last time at the end of that war, when the United States struck Japanese cities. Global arsenals peaked during the Cold War years of the 1960s, 1970s, and early 1980s, when both the NATO nations and the Warsaw Pact perfected and produced tens of thousands of nuclear, biological, and chemical bombs.

Since then, the absolute numbers of these weapons have decreased dramatically. Even before the end of the Cold War, the United States and the Soviet Union, which had the vast majority of global holdings, agreed to reduce their nuclear arsenals and to eliminate all their chemical and biological weapons. As the threat of global thermonuclear war receded, officials and experts agreed that the acquisition of those weapons by other nations or groups posed the most serious remaining threat. In January 1992, for example, the U.N. Security Council declared that their spread constituted a "threat to international peace and security." In 1998, the U.S. Defense Intelligence Agency concluded in its annual threat assessment, "The proliferation of nuclear, chemical, and biological weapons, missiles, and other key technologies remains the greatest direct threat to U.S. interests worldwide." In early 2001, President George W. Bush said, "The grave threat from nuclear, biological, and chemical weapons has not gone away with the Cold War. It has evolved into many separate threats, some of them harder to see and harder to answer."[2]

This chapter provides a brief overview of global proliferation threats, describes the weapons and the nations that have or wish to have them, and outlines the prospects for the next few years. Chapter 2 details the major elements of the nonproliferation regime, including the international network of treaties and agreements constructed over the past 50 years to prevent and reduce proliferation. Chapters 3, 4, and 5 describe in greater detail the characteristics of the various weapons and the specific national programs that exist or may evolve.

Chapters 6 through 21 review the history and status of the most significant national programs, including those countries that have given up nuclear weapons. (The appendixes to the book include detailed information on the main nonproliferation treaties and nuclear supplier organizations, along with an extensive glossary of nonproliferation and weapons terms; a list of abbreviations and acronyms also appears at the end of the book.)

Updates and expansion of the information in this volume, plus the latest developments, debates, and discussions, are available at the Carnegie Endowment's proliferation web site (www.ProliferationNews.org).

Weapons and Trends

The nations of the world confront serious and immediate threats from the global presence of thousands of nuclear weapons and chemical weapons. They also face the possibility that some nation or group still has or soon could have biological weapons. A wide variety of delivery mechanisms for these weapons exists, including ballistic missiles, cruise missiles, aircraft, artillery, ships, trucks, and envelopes. There is also now the added danger that terrorist organizations could kill thousands with these weapons or by sabotaging critical urban and industrial infrastructures.

Although a terrorist attack on these infrastructures using conventional weapons is the most likely threat—as seen by the terrorist attacks on September 11, 2001, in New York and Washington and on March 11, 2004, in Madrid—the explosion of a nuclear weapon would be the most devastating.[3] This calculation of "risk times consequences" should force us to focus most of our attention on this catastrophic possibility while not neglecting the threats from chemical and biological weapons and doing all we can to prevent conventional attacks.

The development of accurate threat assessments and effective national policies requires understanding the technologies of the various types of weapons, the history of their spread, and the successes and failures of nonproliferation efforts. The sections below give a brief overview, with greater detail provided in the country chapters that follow (see table 1.1). It is followed by a global assessment of the current threats and of past and proposed nonproliferation policies.

Nuclear Weapons

Nuclear weapons are the most deadly weapons ever invented—the only true weapons of mass destruction. A single, compact nuclear device can instantly devastate a midsized city. Nuclear weapons are also the most difficult of the three types of weapons to manufacture or acquire. Today, only eight nations are known to have nuclear weapons. Five nuclear weapon states are recognized by the Treaty on the Non-Proliferation of Nuclear Weapons (NPT) and enjoy special rights and privileges under international law. In order of the size of their nuclear arsenals, they are *Russia*, *the United States*, *China*, *France*, and *the United Kingdom* (see table 1.2). The members of this group acquired their arsenals during the 20 years after World War II, and the group remained remarkably stable

Table 1.1. **A Weapons Guide**

Nuclear Weapons

A nuclear weapon is a device with explosive energy, most or all of which is derived from fission or a combination of fission and fusion processes. Explosions from such devices cause catastrophic damage due both to the high temperatures and ground shocks produced by the initial blast and the lasting residual radiation.

Nuclear fission weapons produce energy by splitting the nucleus of an atom—usually of highly enriched uranium or plutonium—into two or more parts by bombarding it with neutrons. Each nucleus that is split releases energy as well as additional neutrons that bombard nearby nuclei and sustain a chain reaction. Fission bombs, such as those dropped on Hiroshima and Nagasaki, are the easiest to make, and they provide the catalyst for more complex thermonuclear explosions. In such weapons, a fission explosion creates the high temperatures necessary to join light isotopes of hydrogen, usually deuterium and tritium, which similarly liberate energy and neutrons. Most modern nuclear weapons use a combination of the two processes, called boosting, to maintain high yields in smaller bombs.

Biological Weapons

Biological weapons intentionally disseminate agents of infectious diseases and of conditions that would otherwise appear only naturally or not at all. These agents can be divided into bacteria (such as anthrax), viruses (such as smallpox), rickettsiae (such as Q fever), chlamydia, fungi, and toxins (such as ricin). The features of these agents that influence their potential for use as weapons include infectivity, virulence, toxicity, pathogenicity, the incubation period, transmissibility, lethality, and stability. The advent of genetic engineering has had a profound impact on the threat from biological weapons. Agents that are extremely harmful can be modified to increase their virulence, production rate per cell, and survivability under environmental stress, as well as to mask their presence from immune-based detectors.

Because most biological agents are living organisms, their natural replication after dissemination increases the potential impact of a strike, making biological weapons even more attractive. Any country possessing a pharmaceutical or food storage infrastructure already has an inherent stabilization and storage system for biological agents. Though aerosol delivery is optimal, explosive delivery is also effective, but to a lesser extent, owing to the possibility of organism inactivation caused by heat from the blast.

Chemical Weapons

Chemical weapons use the toxic properties, as opposed to the explosive properties, of chemical substances to cause physical or physiological harm to an enemy. Classic chemical weapons, such as chlorine and phosgene, were employed during World War I and consisted primarily of commercial chemicals used as choking and blood agents, which caused respiratory damage and asphyxiation. The advent of such blistering agents as mustard gas and lewisite, which even in low doses cause painful burns necessitating medical attention, marked the first use of chemical weapons to produce a significant military effect. Mustard gas, because of its low cost and ability to produce resource-debilitating casualties, has been a popular weapon; it was used to inflict numerous casualties during the Iran-Iraq War.

Nerve gases, or anti-cholinesterase agents, were discovered by the Germans in the 1930s and represent the beginning of modern chemical warfare. Such agents block an enzyme in the body that is essential for the functioning of the nervous system, causing a loss of muscle control, respiratory failure, and eventually death. These gases, which are all liquids at room temperature, are lethal far more quickly and in far smaller quantities than are classic agents and are effective both when inhaled and when absorbed through the skin. Nerve gases can be classified as either G agents (sarin) or V agents (VX), both of which are exceedingly volatile and toxic.

Other types of chemical weapons include mental and physical incapacitants (such as BZ) and binary systems, both of which have undergone limited military development. Chemical weapons can be delivered through bombs, rockets, artillery shells, spray tanks, and missile warheads, which in general use an explosion to expel an internal agent laterally.

Radiological Weapons

Radiological weapons use conventional explosives such as dynamite and C-4 to disperse radioactive materials over large areas. The most common method for their use is as explosives surrounded by radioactive material in the form of pellets, powder, or even a radioactive gas. The area of dispersal would depend on the size of the explosion. Victims not injured in the explosion would be exposed to life-threatening levels of radiation. This radiation also would inhibit or prevent emergency response teams from aiding the victims and, depending on the size of the explosion, would contaminate large areas for years pending expensive removal operations. Alternatively, a source of radioactive material, such as a nuclear reactor or spent-fuel storage depots, could be targeted with large explosive devices to disperse very high levels of radioactivity into the atmosphere and the surrounding area.

Sources

Federation of American Scientists, *Biological Weapons;* available at www.fas.org/nuke/intro/bw/intro.htm. Federation of American Scientists, *Chemical Weapons Introduction*; available at www.fas.org/nuke/intro/cw/intro.htm. U.S. Department of State, *Biological Weapons Convention;* available at www.state.gov/www/global/arms/treaties/bwc1.html.

Table 1.2. **World Nuclear Arsenals**

Known Programs	Number of Weapons
Russia	16,000
United States	10,300
China	410
France	350
United Kingdom	200
Israel	100–170 suspected
India	75–110 possible
Pakistan	50–110 possible
Suspected Programs	
Iran	
North Korea	

from 1964, when China tested its first nuclear weapon, until 1998, when *India* and *Pakistan* both detonated nuclear devices and declared their intention to deploy weapons. India and Pakistan have not yet openly deployed any weapons, but both are capable of configuring aircraft and missiles with tens of weapons over the next few years, if they so desire. *Israel* is widely believed to have approximately 100 nuclear weapons but neither acknowledges nor denies their existence. India, Pakistan, and Israel are not parties to the NPT.

Apart from these eight countries, two others may be actively pursuing nuclear weapons programs. *North Korea* acknowledges a program and may have accumulated enough material to construct as many as nine weapons. The 1994 agreement that had frozen the nation's plutonium program broke down in 2002, and it soon announced its withdrawal from the NPT. In January 2005, North Korean officials declared publicly for the first time that they had nuclear weapons. *Iran* is slowly but steadily pursuing an open civilian nuclear power program and may be covertly developing expertise for nuclear weapons. Iran is a member state of the NPT and, as such, any nuclear weapons program is illegal and, if proved, could subject it to additional sanctions or even military action through U.N. resolutions.

Since the signing of the NPT in 1968, however, many more countries have given up nuclear weapons programs than have begun them.[4] There are fewer nuclear weapons in the world and fewer nations with nuclear weapons programs than there were 20 or 30 years ago.[5]

In the past 20 years, several major countries have abandoned nuclear programs, including *Argentina* and *Brazil*, and four others have relinquished their nuclear weapons to join the NPT as non-nuclear-weapon states. *Ukraine*, *Belarus*, and *Kazakhstan* gave up the thousands of nuclear weapons deployed on their territories when the Soviet Union dissolved, thanks in great measure to the dedicated diplomacy of the George H. W. Bush and Bill Clinton administrations. Similarly, *South Africa*, on the eve of its transition to majority rule, destroyed the six nuclear weapons its apartheid regime had secretly constructed. President

Nelson Mandela agreed with the decision, concluding that South Africa's security was better served in a nuclear-free Africa than in one with several nuclear nations, which is exactly the logic that inspired the original members of the NPT decades earlier. (Africa is one of several areas of the world that have established nuclear-weapon-free zones, where the use or possession of nuclear weapons is prohibited anywhere on the continent.) *Iraq* gave up its nuclear program after the 1991 Gulf War and subsequent U.N. disarmament efforts, though the United States led a coalition of nations to invade Iraq, claiming that the country still had major programs for nuclear, biological, and chemical weapons. *Libya* gave up its nuclear and chemical weapons programs and long-range missile program in December 2003 after negotiations with the United States and the United Kingdom. *Algeria* showed some interest in nuclear weapons over the years but turned away from these programs in the 1990s and is no longer considered a high-risk state.

Radiological weapons, although not as destructive as nuclear explosive weapons, also pose a serious danger, particularly as a terrorist threat. These are weapons that use conventional explosives, such as dynamite, to disperse radioactive materials, including the highly radioactive waste material from nuclear power reactors or other nonweapon sources. They may be attractive weapons for terrorists owing to the relative ease of their acquisition and use and mass disruption potential. A terrorist act involving the dispersal of radioactive materials would contaminate a wide area, making the treatment of casualties more difficult, exposing many people unhurt in the initial explosion to death and injury from radioactivity and rendering large areas uninhabitable, pending sizable removal and cleansing operations.[6] As with chemical and biological agents, the invisible and uncertain danger from these weapons would cause widespread fear and horror. There is also the risk of a "reverse dirty bomb" that brings the conventional explosive to an existing radioactive source (e.g., storage pools for spent-fuel rods from civilian nuclear reactors), triggering an explosion that could be many times more deadly than the accident at Chernobyl.

Biological Weapons

Biological weapons are weapons that intentionally use living organisms to kill. They are second only to nuclear weapons in their potential to cause mass casualties. Although instances of the deliberate spread of disease go back to the ancient Greeks and Assyrians, the efficient weaponization of biological agents did not occur until the twentieth century. With the exception of the Japanese attacks in China before and during World War II, these weapons have not been used in modern warfare.

During the Cold War, the United States and the Soviet Union perfected biological weapons, each developing arsenals capable of destroying all human life and many food crops on the planet. In 1969, President Richard M. Nixon announced that the United States would unilaterally and unconditionally renounce biological weapons. He ordered the destruction of the entire U.S. biological weapons stockpile and the conversion of all production facilities to peaceful purposes. He reversed 45 years of U.S. reluctance and sought the ratification of the 1925 Geneva Protocol, which prohibited the use of biological and chemical weapons in war (and which was subsequently ratified under President Gerald Ford). Nixon successfully negotiated the Biological and Toxin Weapons Convention (BWC), signed in 1972 and ratified by the Senate in 1975, which prohibits the development, production, stockpiling, acquisition, or transfer of biological weapons. This treaty requires all signatories to destroy all their biological weapons and biological weapon production facilities. The treaty has no verification mechanism, however, and the states that are parties to it have been trying to negotiate a verification protocol and additional measures to strengthen it.

It is often difficult to get a complete picture of which countries or groups have biological weapons or programs. Milton Leitenberg points out that official assessments rarely distinguish between *suspected, capability, developing*, and *weapon*. Worse, nations with such capabilities or programs are often lumped together in lists with countries that have chemical weapons programs or capabilities.[7] This book differentiates the distinct programs and threats. National programs are distinguished by whether they have produced actual weapons, have only research and development programs, or have the basic capability to produce agents. The chapters on specific countries provide the full details of each program.

When the BWC originally entered into force in 1975, 4 nations were thought to have biological weapons: the United States, the Soviet Union, China, and South Africa. By the spring of 2005, 169 nations had signed the treaty; however, seven nations are suspected of having some level of offensive biological warfare research programs: China, Egypt, Iran, Israel, North Korea, Russia, and Syria (table 1.3). U.S. officials have publicly identified many of these nations on several occasions, including at the 1996 and 2001 review conferences for the BWC and in annual reports to Congress. These nations are all suspected of pursuing offensive biological weapons programs prohibited by the BWC, though not all the countries, such as Israel, are members of the BWC. Almost all the programs are research efforts, and only one nation—Russia—is believed to have produced and stockpiled weapon agents; four others—Iran, North Korea, Israel, and China—may have done so.

BIOLOGICAL WEAPONS PRODUCTION. Although the *Soviet Union* claimed that it had ended its extensive bioweapons program when it signed the BWC in 1972, President Boris Yeltsin in 1992 disclosed that work had, in fact, continued at substantial levels. There is still considerable uncertainty surrounding Russian weapon facilities, and the possibility exists that agents and weapons remain in Russia.

BIOLOGICAL WEAPONS PROGRAMS. *Israel* is believed to have a sophisticated biological weapons program; it may have produced anthrax and more advanced agents in weaponized form as well as toxins. U.S. officials believe that *North Korea* has pursued biological warfare capabilities since the 1960s and may have the capability to produce sufficient quantities of biological agents for military purposes within weeks of a decision to do so.[8] *China* has a large, advanced

Table 1.3. **Countries Suspected of Retaining Biological Weapons or Programs**

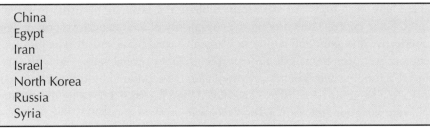

China
Egypt
Iran
Israel
North Korea
Russia
Syria

biotechnical infrastructure that could be used to develop and produce biological agents. Chinese officials have repeatedly asserted that the country has never researched or produced biological weapons. U.S. officials, however, believe that the voluntary BWC declarations submitted by China are inaccurate and incomplete.

POSSIBLE BIOLOGICAL WEAPON RESEARCH PROGRAMS. *Iran* may have an offensive biological weapons program, including the capability to produce small quantities of biological weapons agents. In November 2001, U.S. undersecretary of state John Bolton said that Iran had actually produced agents and weapons,[9] but he had a more cautious assessment in 2004: "I cannot say that the United States can prove beyond a shadow of a doubt that Iran has an offensive biological weapons program. The intelligence I have seen suggests that this is the case."[10] There is considerable evidence that *Egypt* started a program in the early 1960s that produced weaponized agents.[11] In 1996, U.S. officials reported that by 1972 Egypt had developed biological warfare agents and that there was "no evidence to indicate that Egypt has eliminated this capability and it remains likely that the Egyptian capability to conduct biological warfare continues to exist."[12] Egyptian officials assert that Egypt never developed, produced, or stockpiled biological weapons.[13] *Syria* has a biotechnical infrastructure capable of supporting limited agent development but has not begun a major effort to produce biological agents or to put them into weapons, according to official U.S. assessments.[14] *Sudan* is not believed to have a biological weapons program, but U.S. officials have repeatedly warned of Sudanese interest in developing such a program.

Other states of some concern include *South Africa*, which had a bioweapons program that the new unity government says it ended in 1992, and *Taiwan*, which is now rarely mentioned in either official or expert reviews. *India* and *Pakistan* are not believed to have produced or stockpiled offensive biological weapons, although official assessments note that both countries have the resources and capability to support biological warfare research and development efforts.[15] Finally, U.S. officials had long believed that both *Iraq* and *Libya* had biological weapons or programs, but inspections after the 2003 war in Iraq and the 2003 agreement with Libya showed that neither had an active program.

BIOTERRORISM. During the past several decades, terrorist attempts to acquire biological agents have fallen short of successful weaponization. Almost all threats to use biological agents—including hundreds of terrorist anthrax hoaxes against abortion clinics and other targets in the United States—have been false alarms. There have been only two significant biological attacks by terrorists in recent times. Some experts contend that the complexity of a biological weapon design for effective dissemination has by and large thwarted bioterrorism. The Japanese religious sect Aum Shinrikyo, for example, tried for several years, and with considerable funding and expertise, to produce and weaponize botulinum toxin and anthrax. The group's extensive efforts failed, and it resorted to using the chemical agent sarin for attacks in a Tokyo subway in 1994 and 1995. The first successful terrorist incident involving biological agents occurred in 1984 in Dalles, Oregon, when a religious cult, Rajneesh, disseminated salmonella bacteria in ten restaurants, infecting 750 people, but with no fatalities.

When the bioterrorism attack that many had long feared finally came, it was not what the experts had predicted. In the United States in October 2001, someone sent letters containing anthrax to members of Congress and the media. The terrorist either did not realize that sophisticated dispersal mechanisms were required for mass casualties from anthrax or simply did not care. The letters killed five and infected eighteen others. The attack could have been much worse, but this was the first time that a biological warfare agent was used against the U.S. population. Even this limited attack caused mass disruption and cost billions of dollars in decontamination and prevention expenses.

Chemical Weapons

Mass casualties require large amounts of chemical agents relative to either biological or nuclear weapons. Still, 5 metric tons of the nerve gas sarin carried in bombs and dropped by two strike aircraft or the warheads of 36 Scud missiles could kill 50 percent of the people over 4 square kilometers.[16] By comparison, a Hiroshima-size nuclear bomb of 12-kiloton yield would kill 50 percent of the population over 30 square kilometers.

Chemical weapons have been used only in isolated instances of warfare since World War I, despite (or perhaps because of) the substantial numbers of weapons that were in national arsenals. The 1996 Chemical Weapons Convention (CWC) started a process of "deproliferation," whereby most nations declared their holdings (if any) and began eliminating their arsenals and production facilities. The CWC requires all state parties possessing chemical weapons to destroy them in a safe and environmentally friendly manner not later than ten years after the treaty entered into force, or by April 29, 2007, unless special extensions are granted. The treaty also requires all state parties to destroy or convert all present and past capabilities used to produce chemical weapons by that time. The declarations by the United States and Russia account for the vast majority of known chemical weapon stockpiles.

As of the spring of 2005, 168 countries were state parties to the CWC. Four countries—the United States, Russia, India, and South Korea—have declared their possession of chemical weapons stockpiles totaling more than 70,000 metric tons of agents. Russia's 40,000 metric tons is the largest declared stockpile,

Table 1.4. **Countries Suspected of Retaining Significant Chemical Weapons Programs**

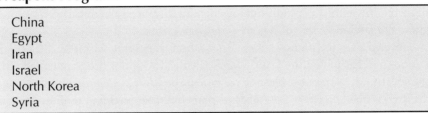

China
Egypt
Iran
Israel
North Korea
Syria

and that nation's financial difficulties make complete elimination of its stockpile by 2007 impossible. Eleven nations have declared their possession of existing or former chemical weapon production facilities: Bosnia and Herzegovina, China, France, India, Iran, Japan, Russia, South Korea, the United Kingdom, the United States, and Yugoslavia. Forty-nine of the 64 declared facilities were destroyed or converted, nearly 10,700 metric tons of chemical agents were destroyed, and one-fourth of the 8.6 million chemical weapons declared by the four possessor states was eliminated through treaty procedures between 1997 and February 2005.[17]

The most significant remaining suspected national programs are those of China, Egypt, Iran, Israel, North Korea, and Syria (table 1.4). The other countries sometimes suspected of conducting chemical weapons research include India, Pakistan, Sudan, and Taiwan, but there is no publicly available evidence of such activity.

SUSPECTED CHEMICAL WEAPONS STOCKPILES. U.S. intelligence assessments state that *North Korea* has had a long-standing chemical warfare program, including the ability to produce bulk quantities of nerve, blister, choking, and blood agents. North Korea is believed to have a large stockpile of these agents and weapons.[18]

Israel is also believed to have an active research and development program for chemical warfare agents and to have produced and stockpiled weapons. *Syria* has not signed the CWC, and U.S. officials believe it has a significant stockpile of the nerve agent sarin. A 1990 intelligence assessment reported that Syria had weaponized these chemicals in 500-kilogram aerial bombs and warheads for its Scud-B missiles.[19] *Egypt* was the first country in the Middle East to obtain chemical weapons and the first to use them. It reportedly employed phosgene and mustard gas against Yemeni royalist forces in the mid-1960s.[20] It is believed still to have a research program and has never reported the destruction of any of its chemical agents or weapons. Israel, Syria, and Egypt are not members of the CWC.

Iran's declaration at the May 1998 session of the CWC conference was the first time that nation had admitted to having had a chemical weapons program, apparently developed in response to Iraqi chemical warfare attacks during the Iran-Iraq War. U.S. officials say that in the past Iran has stockpiled blister, blood, and choking chemical agents and has weaponized some of these agents into artillery shells, mortars, rockets, and aerial bombs.[21] Iranian officials deny these charges.

China has ratified the CWC and has declared that it does not possess an inventory of chemical agents. U.S. officials, however, believe that China has a moderate inventory of traditional agents, an advanced chemical warfare program and a wide variety of potential delivery systems.[22]

Libya gave up its offensive chemical weapons capability with the 2003 negotiations and has joined the CWC. *Iraq*'s chemical weapons program ended after the 1991 Gulf War, but it has not yet joined the CWC. *Albania* discovered and declared a small cache of chemical weapons in 2004, pledging to destroy them by 2006.

CHEMICAL WEAPON RESEARCH PROGRAMS. *Sudan* may have an active interest in acquiring the capability to produce chemical agents but is not believed to have done so. Sudan is a member of the CWC. *Pakistan* sometimes appears on a list of countries with chemical "capabilities" because it has the ability to manufacture chemical weapons should it choose to do so. Though Pakistan has imported a number of dual-use chemicals, they are probably for the development of commercial chemical industrial activities and not for a dedicated warfare program. *India*'s declaration under the CWC in June 1997 was the first time that nation acknowledged it had a chemical warfare production program. Though it has pledged to destroy all agents and production facilities, India's activities and exports of dual-use equipment and chemical precursors cause some concern. *South Korea* ended its weapons program when it ratified the CWC in 1997 and has been destroying its chemical weapons and production facilities.

Missile Proliferation

Much of the proliferation debate over the past few years has centered not on the weapons themselves but on one possible means for delivering them: ballistic missiles (table 1.5). It has become common wisdom and a political habit to refer to the growing threat of ballistic missiles. The threat is certainly changing and is increasing, according to some measures. Yet by several other important criteria, the ballistic missile threat to the United States is significantly smaller than it was in the mid-1980s.

In comparison with the high point of deployments in the mid-1980s, there are now dramatically fewer long-range, intermediate-range, and medium-range ballistic missiles (see chapter 5, "Missile Proliferation"). Most nations that have missiles have only short-range, Scud-type missiles, and many of these arsenals are being retired as they age. The number of countries trying to develop long-range ballistic missiles has not changed greatly in 20 years and is somewhat smaller than in the past. The nations now attempting to do so are also smaller, poorer, and less technologically advanced than were those with missile programs 20 years ago.

Only China and Russia have the capability to hit the mainland of the United States with nuclear warheads on intercontinental land-based ballistic missiles. This has not changed since Russia and China deployed their first intercontinental

Table 1.5. **The Thirty Nations with Ballistic Missiles**

Nineteen countries possess only short-range ballistic missiles (that is, with ranges of less than 1,000 kilometers):		
Afghanistan Armenia Bahrain Belarus Egypt Greece Iraq	Kazakhstan Libya Slovakia South Korea Syria Taiwan Turkey	Turkmenistan Ukraine United Arab Emirates Vietnam Yemen
Seven countries possess medium-range ballistic missiles (with ranges of 1,000–3,000 kilometers):		
China India	Iran Israel	North Korea Pakistan Saudi Arabia
One country possesses intermediate-range ballistic missiles (with ranges of 3,000–5,500 kilometers):		
China		
Five countries possess intercontinental ballistic missiles (with ranges of 5,500+ kilometers):		
China France	Russia	United Kingdom United States

ballistic missiles in 1959 and 1981, respectively. Confusion arises when policy makers speak of missile threats to the United States or to such U.S. interests as forward-deployed troops or allied nations. This merges very-short-range missiles, of which there are many, with long-range missiles, of which there are few.

The greatest programs of concern are those developing medium-range missiles in India, Iran, Israel, North Korea, and Pakistan. None of these nations view their programs as threatening, but their neighbors take a decidedly different view. Though these programs are a cause for serious regional concern and could develop into potential international threats, overall the ballistic missile threat is limited and changing slowly.

A Global Nuclear Threat Assessment

On the basis of the proceeding information, it is reasonable to conclude that of all the potential threats, nuclear weapons pose the greatest risks. We can categorize these threats along four axes, though developments along one axis often influence developments along the others. These four categories of threat are nuclear terrorism, new nuclear weapon states and regional conflict, existing nuclear arsenals, and regime collapse. The greatest concerns are outlined here.

Nuclear Terrorism: The Most Serious Threat

Although *states* can be deterred from using nuclear weapons by fear of retaliation, *terrorists*, who do not have land, people, or national futures to protect, may not be deterrable. Terrorists' acquisition of nuclear weapons therefore poses the greatest single nuclear threat. The gravest danger arises from terrorists' access to state stockpiles of nuclear weapons and fissile materials, because acquiring a supply of nuclear material (as opposed to making the weapon itself) remains the most difficult challenge for a terrorist group. So-called outlaw states are not the most likely source. Their stockpiles, if any, are small and exceedingly precious, and hence well guarded. (Nor are these states likely to give away what they see as the jewels in their security crowns.) Rather, the most likely sources of nuclear weapons and materials for terrorists are storage areas in the former states of the Soviet Union and in Pakistan, and fissile material kept at dozens of civilian sites around the world.

Russia and other former Soviet states possess thousands of nuclear weapons and hundreds of tons of inadequately secured nuclear material. Terrorist organizations and radical fundamentalist groups operate within Pakistan's borders. National instability or a radical change in government could lead to the collapse of state control over nuclear weapons and materials and to the migration of nuclear scientists to the service of other nations or groups.

There is also a substantial risk of terrorist theft from the nuclear stockpiles in more than 40 countries around the world. Many of these caches of materials consist of highly enriched uranium that could be directly used in nuclear weapons or further enriched to weapons grade. There are also significant stockpiles of plutonium that could be used in a weapon, though with more difficulty.

New Nuclear Nations and Regional Conflicts

The danger posed by the acquisition of nuclear weapons by Iran or North Korea is not that either country would likely use these weapons to attack the United States, the nations of Europe, or other countries. States are and will continue to be deterred from such attacks by the certainty of swift and massive retaliation. The greater danger is the reactions of other states in the region. A nuclear chain reaction could ripple throughout a region and across the globe, triggering weapons decisions in several, perhaps many, other states. And along with these rapid developments and the collapse of existing norms could come increased regional tensions, possibly leading to regional wars and to nuclear catastrophe.[23]

New nuclear weapon states might also constrain the United States and others, weakening their ability to intervene to avoid conflict in dangerous regions—as well as, of course, emboldening Tehran, Pyongyang, or other new possessors.

Existing regional nuclear tensions already pose serious risks. The decades-long conflict between India and Pakistan has made South Asia for many years the region most likely to witness the first use of nuclear weapons since World War II. There is an active missile race under way between the two nations, even as China and India continue their rivalry. In Northeast Asia, North Korea's nuclear capabilities remain shrouded in uncertainty but presumably continue to advance. Miscalculation or misunderstanding could bring nuclear war to the Korean peninsula.

In the Middle East, Iran's nuclear program, together with Israel's nuclear arsenal and the chemical weapons of other neighboring states, add grave volatility to an already conflict-prone region. If Iran were to acquire nuclear weapons, Egypt, Saudi Arabia, or others might initiate or revive their nuclear weapons programs. It is possible that the Middle East could go from a region with one nuclear weapon state to one with two, three, or five such states within a decade—with existing political and territorial disputes still unresolved.[24]

The Risk from Existing Arsenals

There are grave dangers inherent in the maintenance of thousands of nuclear weapons by the United States and Russia and the hundreds of weapons held by China, France, the United Kingdom, Israel, India, and Pakistan. Though each state regards its nuclear weapons as safe, secure, and essential to its security, each views others' arsenals with suspicion.

Though the Cold War has been over for more than a dozen years, Washington and Moscow maintain thousands of warheads on hair-trigger alert, ready to launch within fifteen minutes. This greatly increases the risk of an unauthorized launch. Because there is no time buffer built into each state's decision-making process, this extreme level of readiness also enhances the possibility that either country's president could prematurely order a nuclear strike based on flawed intelligence.[25]

Recent advocacy by some in the United States of new battlefield uses for nuclear weapons could lead to new nuclear tests. The five nuclear weapon states recognized by the NPT have not tested since the signing of the Comprehensive Test Ban Treaty (CTBT) in 1996, and no state has tested since India and Pakistan did so in May 1998. New U.S. tests would trigger tests by other nations and cause the collapse of the CTBT, which is widely regarded as a pillar of the nonproliferation regime.

To the extent that the leaders of a given state are contemplating acceding to U.S. or international nonproliferation demands, these leaders may feel a strong need for equity so that they can show their public that giving up nuclear aspirations is fair and in their interest. It is difficult, if not impossible, to demonstrate either positive outcome when immensely powerful nuclear weapon states reassert the importance of nuclear weapons to their own security.

The Risk of Regime Collapse

If U.S. and Russian nuclear arsenals remain at Cold War levels, many nations will conclude that the weapon states' promise to reduce and eventually eliminate these arsenals has been broken. Non-nuclear states may therefore feel released from their pledge not to acquire nuclear arms.

The NPT has already been severely threatened by the development in several states of facilities for enriching uranium and reprocessing plutonium. Although each state has asserted that these facilities are for civilian use only, the resulting supplies of nuclear materials give each country a "virtual" nuclear weapons capability. This situation greatly erodes the confidence that states can have in a neighbor's non-nuclear pledge.

Additionally, there appears to be growing acceptance of the nuclear status of India and Pakistan, with each country accruing prestige and increased attention from leading nuclear weapon states, including the United States. Some now argue that a nuclear Iran or North Korea could also be absorbed into the international system without serious consequence.

If the number of states with nuclear weapons increases, the original nuclear weapon states fail to comply with their disarmament obligations, and states such as India gain status for having nuclear weapons, it is possible that Brazil, Japan, and other major non-nuclear nations will reconsider their nuclear choices. Most nations would continue to eschew nuclear weapons, if only for technological and economic reasons, but others would decide that nuclear weapons were necessary to improve their security or status. There is a real possibility, under these conditions, of a systemwide collapse.

Successes and Failures of the Nonproliferation Regime

Ever since American scientists detonated the first nuclear bomb at Alamogordo, New Mexico, in July 1945, many officials and experts have feared the future. They have worried that proliferation could run out of control, creating a bleak, dangerous world with dozens of nations armed with nuclear weapons. Several times in the past few decades, the public's fear of nuclear war has moved millions of people worldwide to petition for an immediate change in their governments' policies. More than once, the very fate of the Earth seemed to be at stake, as Jonathan Schell titled his book in 1982.

President John F. Kennedy worried that while only the United States, the Soviet Union, the United Kingdom, and France in the early 1960s possessed nuclear weapons, by the end of the decade 15 or 20 nations would have them. The concern was not that developing countries would acquire the bomb but rather that the advanced industrial nations would do so, particularly Japan and Germany. Several European nations were already actively pursuing nuclear weapons programs. Neutral Sweden, for example, was then developing plans to build 100 nuclear weapons to equip its air force, army, and navy.

Kennedy moved aggressively to counter those trends. He created the Arms Control and Disarmament Agency in 1961; began negotiations on a treaty to stop the spread of nuclear weapons; and negotiated the Limited Test Ban Treaty, which ended nuclear tests in the atmosphere, under water, and in outer space.

U.S. diplomacy and international efforts to create legal and diplomatic barriers to the acquisition of nuclear weapons, which were codified in the NPT in 1968, dramatically stopped the rush toward nuclear weapons status. Twenty years after Kennedy's warning, only China (with Soviet help) had openly joined the ranks of the new nuclear nations, whereas India had exploded a so-called peaceful nuclear device and Israel was building a secret nuclear arsenal. All the other nations that had studied nuclear programs in the 1950s and 1960s had abandoned their pursuits. The treaty did little at that time, however, to constrain the nuclear arms race between the two superpowers in the 1960s and 1970s, which was sometimes known as vertical proliferation.

Throughout the 1980s and 1990s, however, proliferation experts were again ringing alarms. As Leonard Spector said in 1984 in *Nuclear Proliferation Today* (the first book in the Carnegie Endowment's series on proliferation): "The spread of nuclear weapons poses one of the greatest threats of our time and is among the most likely triggers of a future nuclear holocaust . . . . The spread of nuclear arms also increases the risk of their falling into the hands of dissident military elements or revolutionaries . . . . The threat of nuclear terrorism is also growing."[26]

Nonproliferation efforts have steadily advanced in the past two decades, but never easily and never without serious setbacks. Though some nations renounced their weapons of mass destruction programs, others started new ones. Often a majority of nations was able to agree on new treaties and new restraints, only to have other nations block their progress or feign compliance.

Since September 11, 2001, few have questioned the need for urgent government action. President Bush said during his meetings with Russian president Vladimir Putin in November 2001, "Our highest priority is to keep terrorists from acquiring weapons of mass destruction. . . . We will strengthen our efforts to cut off every possible source of biological, chemical, and nuclear weapons, material and expertise."[27] These new efforts can be built on the successes of previous actions.

Although nuclear, biological, and chemical arsenals in the United States and the Soviet Union once grew to enormous levels and the technology of these weapons has become increasingly accessible, the world has not been devastated by a thermonuclear war. Moreover, the number of new prospective nuclear nations has shrunk dramatically during the past 20 years, not increased, and the international norm has been firmly established that countries should not, under any circumstances, possess or use either biological or chemical weapons. Global expectations are that the existing stockpiles of nuclear weapons will be greatly reduced, even if their eventual elimination seems but a distant hope.

Since 1964, only four nations are known to have overcome the substantial diplomatic and technical barriers to manufacturing nuclear weapons. The proliferation of biological and chemical weapons is broader, but it is still mainly confined to two regions of the world: the Middle East and Northeast Asia. Most of the world's biological weapons have been destroyed, and the bulk of the global chemical weapons arsenals will likely be eliminated in the next ten years.

Even with all the serious challenges it has faced, the nonproliferation regime has still had a remarkable record of success (see figure 1.1). But can it hold? Or are international conditions so different today that the regime can no longer work?

Twenty-First-Century Proliferation

Some argue that with the end of superpower conflict, the world confronts a fundamentally different proliferation problem. Although the regime may have

Figure 1.1. **Countries with Nuclear Weapons or Programs (number of programs)**

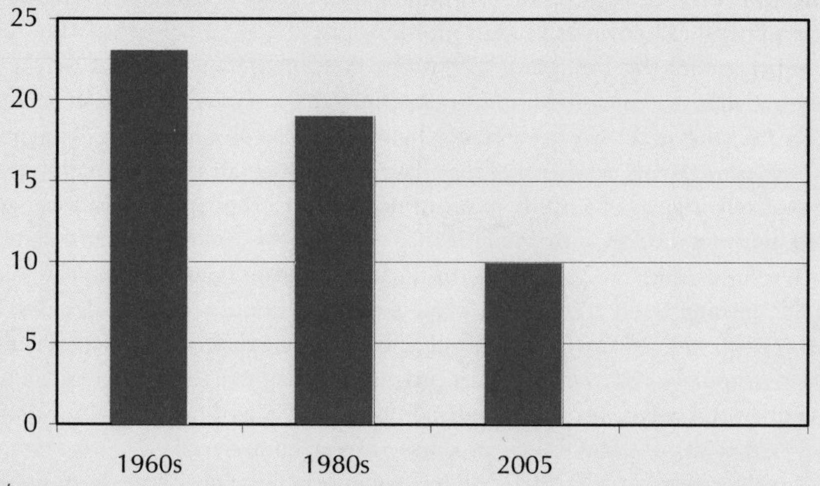

	Number of programs
1960s	23
1980s	19
2005	10

NOTE

In the 1960s, 23 countries had weapons, were conducting weapons-related research, or were discussing the pursuit of weapons: Argentina, Australia, Brazil, Canada, China, Egypt, France, India, Israel, Italy, Japan, Norway, Romania, South Africa, Spain, Sweden, Switzerland, Taiwan, United Kingdom, United States, USSR, West Germany, and Yugoslavia.

In the 1980s, 19 countries had weapons or were conducting weapons-related research: Argentina, Brazil, Canada, China, France, India, Iran, Iraq, Israel, Libya, North Korea, Pakistan, South Africa, South Korea, Taiwan, United Kingdom, United States, USSR, and Yugoslavia.

In 2005, in addition to the 8 states with nuclear weapons, Iran and North Korea are suspected of having active nuclear weapons programs.

worked in the past, they doubt the holdouts can be convinced to adopt the same norms as those held by the regime founders. This inspection regime had failed to independently detect significant hidden programs in Iran, Iraq, and Libya. Many officials in the George W. Bush administration believe that the entire process of negotiating and implementing nonproliferation treaties is both unnecessary and harmful to U.S. national security interests. They argue that some of the treaties—such as the CTBT, the Anti–Ballistic Missile Treaty, and the Landmine Treaty—restrict necessary armaments, thus weakening the principal nation that safeguards global peace and security. Other treaties, such as the CWC and the BWC, promote a false sense of security as some nations sign, then cheat on, the agreements.

The Bush administration therefore has implemented a radically new nonproliferation approach. Previous presidents, as noted above, treated the weapons themselves as the problem and sought their elimination through treaties. President Bill Clinton, for example, warned in November 1998 of the threat "posed by *the proliferation of nuclear, biological, and chemical weapons and the means of delivering such weapons*" (italics added). President Bush framed the issue differently in his 2003 State of the Union address: "The gravest danger facing America and the world is *outlaw regimes that seek and possess nuclear, chemical, and biological weapons*" (italics added). The Bush administration thus has changed the focus from "what" to "who." This corresponds to a strategy that seeks the elimination of regimes rather than weapons. This action-oriented approach has been detailed in two key documents—*The National Security Strategy of the United States of America* (September 2002) and *National Strategy to Combat Weapons of Mass Destruction* (December 2002)—in which the administration states its view that the threat from weapons of mass destruction emanates from a small number of outlaw states and from the nexus of these states, nuclear weapons and materials, and terrorists.[28]

The first direct application of this theory was the war with Iraq. There had been previous applications of military force to deal with proliferation threats, but this was the world's first nonproliferation war, a battle fought primarily over the claimed need to prevent the acquisition or transfer of nuclear, biological, and chemical weapons (see chapter 17, "Iraq").

Three major conclusions can be drawn from the war:

> In 2003, Iraq was not producing and did not have stockpiles of, nuclear, biological or chemical weapons or any Scud missiles or unmanned aerial vehicles designed to deliver such weapons. All active nuclear, chemical, and biological programs ended between 1991 and 1996.
>
> U.N. sanctions and inspections were more effective than most realized in disarming Iraq after the 1991 War. Inspectors in 2003 were finding what there was to find.
>
> In the year prior to the war, U.S. and British officials systematically misrepresented Iraq's weapon capabilities.[29]

This last finding is contested by officials in the U.S. and British administrations but is widely accepted outside these governments. Further, none of these conclusions appear to have diminished the enthusiasm of the proponents of the Iraq war for applying the Iraq model to other problem states. The new strategy, however, has not yet proved superior to the one it replaced.

Since 2000, proliferation problems have grown worse, not better (see table 1.6). Libya has been the only unqualified success, as that nation has abandoned decades of work on nuclear and chemical weapons and missile programs. But Iran has accelerated its program—whether peaceful or not—in the past few years. So has North Korea. That country ended the freeze on its plutonium program, claimed to have reprocessed the plutonium into weapons, withdrew from the NPT, and declared itself a nuclear weapon state. Globally, the threat from nuclear terrorism has grown as U.S. intelligence officials have concluded that the Iraq War made the terrorism problem worse and supplies of weapons and weapons materials remain dangerously insecure.[30] Though U.S. attention focused on the three "axis of evil" states, the nuclear black market of Pakistan's A. Q. Khan spread nuclear weapons technology and know-how around the world. It is not clear if this network has shut down or merely gone further underground.

Meanwhile, the United States and Russia have ended the process of negotiating reductions in their nuclear arsenals, and the reductions themselves are

Table 1.6. **The Fifteen Countries with Nuclear, Biological, or Chemical Weapons or Offensive Research Programs**

Country	Nuclear	Biological	Chemical
Russia	W	W	W*
China	W	W	W
Israel	W	W?	W
United States	W		W*
France	W		
United Kingdom	W		
India	W	R?	W*
Pakistan	W	R?	R?
North Korea	W?	W	W
Iran	R	R?	W?
Egypt		R?	W
Syria		R?	W
South Korea			W*
Libya			W*
Albania			W*

Key: W = has known weapons or agents; R = has known research program; ? = is suspected of having weapons or programs; and W* = possesses chemical weapons but has declared them under the Chemical Weapons Convention and is in the process of eliminating them.

proceeding at a slower pace than previous administrations planned. Programs to secure nuclear materials in the states of the former Soviet Union are also slowing down, though only half the materials have been secured. Finally, there is growing concern that the entire nonproliferation regime is in danger of a catastrophic collapse. (See the chapters on Iran, Libya, North Korea, Pakistan, Russia, and the United States for details.)

Elements of a New Nonproliferation Policy

Some believe that the strategy, or some modified variation, could still prove its worth. Many countries are cooperating in the Proliferation Security Initiative to interdict illegal trade in weapon components (see chapter 2 for more on this initiative). There is a much greater willingness internationally to enforce nonproliferation commitments. The right combination of force and diplomacy could yet result in negotiated solutions to the North Korean and Iranian programs. And prospects for peacefully resolving regional conflicts may have increased through the growing movement for democracy in the Middle East and Central Asia.

A combination of approaches may offer the best chance of success. There is the need for a new strategy that combines the best elements of the United States–centric, force-based approach with the traditional multilateral, treaty-based approach. For example, the European Union has crafted a joint nonproliferation strategy that includes tying all E.U. trade agreements to the observance of nonproliferation treaties and norms. This "soft power" approach could meld with the "hard power" of the United States to replicate the success of the United States and United Kingdom with Libya. The Libyan model could emerge from and prevail over the Iraq model: Change a regime's behavior rather than change the regime.

The theory and practical applications of a new approach have been detailed in a 2005 Carnegie Endowment report, *Universal Compliance: A Strategy for Nuclear Security*.[31] This report analyzes how to end the threat of nuclear terrorism by implementing comprehensive efforts to secure and eliminate nuclear materials worldwide and to stop the illegal transfer of nuclear technology. The strategy would prevent new nuclear weapon states by increasing penalties for withdrawal from the NPT, enforcing compliance with strengthened treaties, and radically reforming the nuclear fuel cycle to prevent states from acquiring dual-use technologies for uranium enrichment or plutonium reprocessing. The threat from existing arsenals would be reduced by shrinking global stockpiles, curtailing research on new nuclear weapons, and taking the weapons off hair-trigger-alert status. Finally, greater efforts would be devoted to resolving the regional conflicts that fuel proliferation imperatives and to bringing the three nuclear weapon states outside the NPT into conformance with a expanded set of global nonproliferation norms.

Tomorrow's solutions, like yesterday's, will not emerge in a diplomatic vacuum. As we struggle to develop new policies, it is worth remembering that the nonproliferation treaties were an integral part of the political and military balance-of-power and alliance systems of the late twentieth century. Alliance security arrangements, including the promise that the United States would extend a "nuclear umbrella" over Europe and Japan, undoubtedly made it easier for several industrial nations to abandon their nuclear weapons programs. The Soviet Union simply forced nonproliferation on its alliance system, whereas the United States was not adverse to using strong-arm tactics to compel South Korea and Taiwan, for example, to abandon nuclear weapons research.

Further thwarting proliferation, many developing nations found that their ambitions ran into formidable financial and technological obstacles to nuclear weapons development, missile engineering, and biological agent weaponization. This is still true today and should give pause to those who predict a smooth and rapid rise to nuclear weapon status for new nations.

These financial, technical, and alliance factors were not, however, sufficient barriers to proliferation. These factors were present in the 1960s and 1970s. But before the signing of the NPT, nuclear proliferation was on the rise; afterward, it was on the decline. The critical importance of the NPT and other treaties is that they provide the necessary international legal mechanism and establish the global norms that give nations a clear path to a non-nuclear future. These historic lessons must be remembered anew, lest in our haste to construct new solutions we tear down the very structures we mean only to repair.

NOTES

1. For a comprehensive study of a new nonproliferation strategy, see George Perkovich, Jessica Mathews, Joseph Cirincione, Rose Gottemoeller, and Jon Wolfsthal, *Universal Compliance: A Strategy for Nuclear Security* (Washington, D.C.: Carnegie Endowment for International Peace, 2005); available at www.ProliferationNews.org.
2. President George W. Bush, "Remarks by the President to the Troops and Personnel," Norfolk Naval Air Station, Virginia, February 13, 2001.
3. For a brief discussion of the threat from conventional attacks on industrial and urban infrastructures, see the first edition of this book: Joseph Cirincione with Jon B. Wolfsthal and Miriam Rajkumar, *Deadly Arsenals: Tracking Weapons of Mass Destruction* (Washington, D.C.: Carnegie Endowment for International Peace, 2002), pp. 16–17.
4. Six nations abandoned indigenous nuclear weapon programs that were under way or under consideration in the 1960s: Egypt, Italy, Japan, Norway, Sweden, and West Germany. Since the late 1970s, Argentina, Australia, Belarus, Brazil, Canada, Iraq, Kazakhstan, Libya, Romania, South Africa, South Korea, Spain, Switzerland, Taiwan, Ukraine, and Yugoslavia have abandoned nuclear weapon programs or nuclear weapons (or both) on their territory. North Korea and Iran are the only two states that began acquiring nuclear weapon capabilities in this later period and have not ceased the effort.
5. In 1970, the year the NPT entered into force, there were about 38,000 nuclear weapons in global arsenals, mostly in the stockpiles of the United States and the Soviet Union; by 1986, the number of weapons had increased to a peak of 65,000 worldwide; in 2004, there were approximately 27,000.
6. National Council on Radiation Protection and Measurements, "Management of Terrorist Events Involving Radioactive Material," Bethesda, Md., October 24, 2001.
7. Milton Leitenberg, "Biological Weapons Arms Control," Center for International and Security Studies, University of Maryland, 1996, p. 20; available at www.ceip.org/files/projects/npp/pdf/leitenberg.pdf.
8. John Bolton, U.S. undersecretary of state for arms control and international security, "Remarks to the Fifth Biological Weapons Convention," Geneva, November 19, 2001.
9. Bolton, "Remarks to the Fifth Biological Weapons Convention."
10. John Bolton, U.S. undersecretary of state for arms control and international security, "Iran's Continuing Pursuit of Weapons of Mass Destruction," statement before the House International Relations Committee Subcommittee on the Middle-East and Central Asia, June 24, 2004.
11. Dany Shoham, "Chemical and Biological Weapons in Egypt," *Nonproliferation Review*, Spring–Summer 1998, pp. 48–58.
12. U.S. Arms Control and Disarmament Agency, "Annual Report to Congress," July 1996.
13. Shoham, "Chemical and Biological Weapons in Egypt," p. 55.
14. U.S. Department of Defense, *Proliferation: Threat and Response* (Washington, D.C.: U.S. Department of Defense, 2001), p. 45.
15. Ibid., pp. 24, 28.
16. Julian Perry Robinson, "Chemical Weapons Proliferation in the Middle East," in *Non-Conventional Weapons Proliferation in the Middle East*, edited by Efraim Karsh, Martin Navias, and Philip Sabin (Oxford: Clarendon Press, 1993), p. 80.
17. Organization for the Prohibition of Chemical Weapons, "Instant Briefing: Results," available at www.opcw.org/ib/.
18. U.S. Department of Defense, *Proliferation: Threat and Response*, p. 11.
19. E. J. Hogendoorn, "A Chemical Weapons Atlas," *Bulletin of the Atomic Scientists*, September/October 1997, p. 37.
20. Ibid., p. 37.
21. Ibid., p. 36.

22. Ibid., p. 15.
23. This is the danger President John Kennedy warned of in 1963: "I ask you to stop and think for a moment what it would mean to have nuclear weapons in so many hands, in the hands of countries large and small, stable and unstable, responsible and irresponsible, scattered throughout the world," he said. "There would be no rest for anyone then, no stability, no real security, and no chance of effective disarmament. There would only be the increased chance of accidental war, and an increased necessity for the great powers to involve themselves in what otherwise would be local conflicts." John F. Kennedy, "Radio and Television Address to the American People on the Nuclear Test Ban Treaty," July 26, 1963; available at www.jfklibrary.org/jfk_test_ban_speech.html.
24. Several countries in the Middle East are capable of pursuing nuclear weapon programs or otherwise acquiring nuclear weapons, including Saudi Arabia, Egypt, and Turkey. Saudi Arabia might seek to purchase nuclear weapons from Pakistan or invite Pakistan to station nuclear weapons on its territory. Other countries have at least the basic facilities and capabilities to mount a nuclear weapon program, albeit not without significant political and economic consequences. Egypt and Turkey could probably acquire enough nuclear material to produce a nuclear weapon within a decade of launching such an effort.
25. Former U.S. senator Sam Nunn argues, "The more time the United States and Russia build into our process for ordering a nuclear strike the more time is available to gather data, to exchange information, to gain perspective, to discover an error, to avoid an accidental or unauthorized launch." Speech to the Carnegie International Non-Proliferation Conference, June 21, 2004, available at www.ProliferationNews.org.
26. Leonard Spector, *Nuclear Proliferation Today* (New York: Vintage Books, 1984), pp. 3–4.
27. "President Announces Reduction in Nuclear Arsenal," press conference by President Bush and Russian president Vladimir Putin, November 13, 2001; available at www.whitehouse.gov/news/releases/2001/11/20011113-3.html.
28. National Security Council, *The National Security Strategy of the United States of America* (Washington, D.C.: White House, 2002); available at www.whitehouse.gov/nsc/nss.pdf. National Security Council, *National Strategy to Combat Weapons of Mass Destruction* (Washington, D.C.: White House, 2002), p. 1; available at www.whitehouse.gov/news/releases/2002/12/WMDStrategy.pdf.
29. For a detailed examination of these issues, see Joseph Cirincione, Jessica Mathews, and George Perkovich, *WMD in Iraq: Evidence and Implications* (Washington, D.C.: Carnegie Endowment for International Peace, 2004); available at www.ProliferationNews.org.
30. See testimony of Central Intelligence director Porter Goss and Defense Intelligence Agency director Admiral Lowell Jacoby before the Senate Intelligence Committee, February 16, 2005.
31. Perkovich et al., *Universal Compliance.*

CHAPTER 2

The International Nonproliferation Regime

The global nonproliferation regime is a network of interlocking treaties, organizations, inspections, and unilateral and bilateral arrangements aimed at halting the spread of nuclear, chemical, and biological weapons. The systems in place to control each type of weapon rely on a central agreement that establishes a norm against the possession of weapons and a set of obligations for treaty members.

At the core of this regime are three key treaties: The Treaty on the Non-Proliferation of Nuclear Weapons (NPT) restrains the spread of nuclear weapons; the Chemical Weapons Convention prohibits the development, possession, or use of chemical weapons; and the Biological and Toxin Weapons Convention bans the development, possession, or use of biological weapons. The nuclear and chemical weapons regimes also involve extensive inspection and verification arrangements and are covered by comprehensive international export control arrangements. An effort to negotiate a verification mechanism for biological weapons continues. (See appendixes A, B, and C for the text of each treaty or for more information.)

The Nuclear Nonproliferation Regime

The nuclear nonproliferation regime is the oldest and most elaborate of the weapon control systems. It is founded on the basis of the NPT and includes additional treaties that limit the testing and geographical spread of nuclear weapons. It provides for a variety of export control and supplier arrangements, the most important of which is the International Atomic Energy Agency (IAEA).

The Nuclear Non-Proliferation Treaty

The NPT helped establish the international norm against proliferation. It was opened for signature in 1968 and entered into force in 1970, and it divides member countries into nuclear weapon states and non-nuclear-weapon states. "Nuclear weapon states" are defined by the treaty as countries that detonated a nuclear explosion before January 1, 1967. These include only the United States (first detonation in 1945), the Soviet Union (1949), United Kingdom (1952), France (1960), and China (1964). Russia succeeded to the Soviet Union's status as a nuclear weapon state under the treaty in 1992; while Ukraine, Kazakhstan, and Belarus, in giving up their nuclear weapons, agreed to become non-nuclear-weapon states. The NPT defines all other countries as non-nuclear-weapon states.[1] Under the NPT:

- Non-nuclear-weapon states pledge not to manufacture or receive nuclear explosives. (Both nuclear weapons and "peaceful nuclear explosives" are prohibited.)
- To verify that they are living up to this pledge, non-nuclear-weapon states also agree to accept IAEA safeguards on all nuclear activities, an arrangement known as full-scope safeguards.
- All countries agree not to export nuclear equipment or material to non-nuclear-weapon states except under IAEA safeguards, and nuclear weapon states agree not to assist non-nuclear-weapon states in obtaining nuclear weapons.
- All countries agree to facilitate the fullest possible exchange of peaceful nuclear technology.
- All countries agree to pursue negotiations in good faith to end the nuclear arms race and to achieve nuclear disarmament under international control.
- A party may withdraw from the treaty on 90 days' notice if "extraordinary events related to the subject matter of the Treaty" have "jeopardized its supreme interests."

The five permanent members of the U.N. Security Council are all members of the NPT. The United States, Russia, and the United Kingdom serve as the treaty's depositary states; China and France did not join until 1992. By the spring of 2005, the treaty had 184 non-nuclear-weapon state parties, including North Korea, for a total of 189 parties. The most recent addition to the treaty is East Timor, which officially became a party on May 5, 2003. Only India, Israel, and Pakistan have yet to sign the treaty, making it the most widely adhered to arms control treaty in history.[2] North Korea announced its withdrawal from the NPT on January 10, 2003. However, the United Nations has not recognized this withdrawal because Pyongyang did not give the three months' advance notice required under article 10 of the treaty.

The original term of the NPT was 25 years, with periodic reviews of the treaty occurring every 5 years. At the NPT Review and Extension Conference held in New York City in April and May 1995, the parties agreed to extend the agreement indefinitely and unconditionally, giving it (for all practical effect) a permanent duration. In addition, the treaty members approved a set of principles and objectives to guide the parties during a strengthened review process in the future. This indefinite extension of the treaty was by no means a foregone conclusion. It was a major victory in international efforts to combat the proliferation of all nuclear, biological, and chemical weapons.

At the May 2000 NPT Review Conference, the participants adopted a program of action (known as the "13 Steps") that included the early entry into force of the second Strategic Arms Reduction Treaty (known as START II), further reductions of both strategic and nonstrategic nuclear arsenals, measures to reduce the operational status of nuclear weapons systems, a diminished role for nuclear weapons in security policies, a moratorium on nuclear testing, and application of the principle of irreversibility to nuclear disarmament, among others (see appendix A).

Since the May 2000 NPT Review Conference, there have been three separate preparatory sessions in anticipation of the seventh NPT review conference, which was scheduled to take place in May 2005. At these preparatory sessions, a number of major themes were sounded, such as

- the importance of taking practical steps to fulfill article 6 of the NPT, which calls for the nuclear weapon states to move toward complete nuclear disarmament;
- the early entry into force of the Comprehensive Test Ban Treaty (CTBT);
- concern over the United States' withdrawal from the Anti–Ballistic Missile Treaty and the potential proliferation effects of the development and deployment of an antimissile system;
- the need for the verifiable and irreversible reductions in nonstrategic nuclear arsenals;
- support for nuclear-weapon-free zones and their accompanying security assurances;
- the need to incorporate the comprehensive safeguard agreements with the Additional Protocol to the IAEA Safeguards Agreement (see below) to create the new NPT safeguards standard;
- support for the IAEA's action plan on protection against nuclear terrorism (see below).
- the feeling that the Moscow Treaty, with its reductions in deployment and operational status, cannot substitute for irreversible cuts in nuclear weapons;
- serious concern regarding the North Korean withdrawal from the NPT and the challenge it represents to the nonproliferation regime;
- the need to consider measures to strengthen control over the most sensitive aspects of the nuclear fuel cycle; and
- the feeling that the next logical step for the nonproliferation regime is a fissile material cutoff treaty.[3]

The International Atomic Energy Agency

The Vienna-based IAEA is a United Nations–affiliated organization with 137 member countries.[4] It was created in 1957, before the NPT had even been negotiated. Its principal mission is twofold: to facilitate the use of nuclear energy for peaceful purposes; and to implement a system of audits and on-site inspections (collectively known as safeguards) to verify that nuclear facilities and materials are not being diverted for nuclear explosions.

The IAEA does not offer physical protection and is not a police force; it cannot prevent states from using nuclear materials under its control for use in nuclear weapons. Instead, its safeguards are designed to provide it and its member states with timely warning should significant quantities of nuclear-weapons-usable materials be diverted to nuclear weapons or for nuclear explosions of any kind. It is then up to the IAEA's Board of Governors (and possibly the U.N. Security Council, to which major safeguard violations are reported) to take appropriate action.[5]

The IAEA's system of inspection was used to form the verification measures of the NPT. Under the NPT, non-nuclear-weapon states must accept "full-scope safeguards" over all nuclear materials—and the facilities that contain those materials—within the jurisdiction of the state in question. A state may declare and exempt nuclear materials from IAEA inspection for narrow military purposes, such as fueling naval nuclear reactors, an exemption pointed to by some as a weakness in the IAEA system of verification.

IAEA officials can monitor only those activities connected with the production or use of nuclear materials. The IAEA does not possess the means or the legal authority to search for or investigate activities related to the development or production of nuclear weapons. The activities outside the IAEA's jurisdiction include the fabrication and testing of non-nuclear components of nuclear weapons, high-explosive testing, and research and development on nuclear weapon design.

In addition to monitoring all peaceful nuclear activities in non-nuclear-weapon states that are parties to the NPT, the IAEA also monitors certain individual facilities and associated nuclear materials in the nuclear weapon states. As of the spring of 2005, Russia was the only nuclear weapon state not to have any facilities or materials under IAEA safeguards. Moreover, the IAEA monitors some nuclear facilities and materials in non-NPT parties at the request of these states or their suppliers. Thus, although India, Israel, and Pakistan are not parties to the NPT, several nuclear facilities in each of those countries are subject to IAEA monitoring and cannot be used to support those nations' nuclear weapons programs without detection by the IAEA.[6]

The Additional Protocol

Until 1991, in non-nuclear-weapon states that are parties to the NPT, the IAEA monitored only those facilities declared by the inspected country and did not seek possible undeclared nuclear installations, lacking a clear political mandate from its members to do so. After the 1991 Gulf War, however, it was learned that Iraq had secretly developed a network of undeclared nuclear facilities as part of an extensive nuclear weapons program. This led the IAEA's Board of Governors in 1991 to reiterate the IAEA's right to exercise its previously unused authority to conduct "special inspections," that is, to demand access to undeclared sites where it suspected nuclear activities were being conducted. This evolved into the voluntary Additional Protocol to the IAEA Safeguards Agreement, which was designed to strengthen and expand existing IAEA safeguards to prevent the development of clandestine weapons programs, such as that in Iraq before 1991.

The Additional Protocol enables the IAEA's inspectors to be proactive in their inspections, by demanding that the state of concern submit a more thorough declaration of its nuclear activities and by giving inspectors greater access to that state's nuclear sites. Subsequent measures, including environmental sampling and other holistic safeguard measures, were adopted under Program 93+2 of the protocol, to be implemented in two installments. Part 1, implemented initially in 1996, consisted of measures that could be traced to existing legal authority. Part 2 consisted of measures whose implementation would require complementary legal authority. The IAEA's Board of Governors approved part 2 measures on May 15, 1997.

The model protocol outlined four key changes that must be incorporated into each NPT state party's safeguards agreement:[7]

- First, the amount and type of information that states will have to provide to the IAEA is greatly expanded. In addition to the current requirement for data about nuclear fuel and fuel-cycle activities, states will now have to provide an "expanded declaration" on a broad array of nuclear-related activities, such as "nuclear fuel cycle–related research and development activities not involving nuclear materials" and "the location, operational status and the estimated annual production" of uranium mines and thorium concentration plants. (Thorium can be processed to produce fissile material, the key ingredient for nuclear weapons.) All trade in items on the Nuclear Suppliers Group (see "Supplier Control Mechanisms" below) trigger list will have to be reported to the IAEA as well.

- Second, the number and types of facilities that the IAEA will be able to inspect and monitor are substantially increased beyond the previous level. In order to resolve questions about, or inconsistencies in, the information a state has provided on its nuclear activities, the new inspection regime provides the IAEA with "complementary," or preapproved, access to "[a]ny location specified by the Agency," as well as all of the facilities specified in the "expanded declaration." By negotiating an Additional Protocol, states will, in effect, guarantee the IAEA access on short notice to all of their declared—and, if necessary—undeclared facilities in order "to assure the absence of undeclared nuclear material and activities."

- Third, the IAEA's ability to conduct short notice inspections is augmented by streamlining the visa process for inspectors, who are guaranteed to receive within one month's notice "appropriate multiple entry/exit" visas that are valid for at least a year.

- Fourth, the Additional Protocol provides for the IAEA's right to use environmental sampling during inspections at both declared and undeclared sites. It further permits the use of environmental sampling over a wide area rather than being confined to specific facilities.

As of the spring of 2005, the Additional Protocol had been signed by 90 nations.[8] Though the Additional Protocol greatly strengthens the IAEA's ability to verify that non-nuclear-weapon states that are parties to the NPT use nuclear materials and facilities only for peaceful purposes, it cannot prevent a determined state from acquiring a nuclear weapons capability. The IAEA's most important recent work under the Additional Protocol has come in Iran and Libya, two states that are headed in opposite proliferation directions.

The IAEA Action Plan

After the September 11, 2001, terrorist attacks in the United States, the IAEA's Board of Governors, in March 2002, agreed on an "action plan designed to upgrade worldwide protection against acts of terrorism involving nuclear and radioactive materials." This action plan to guard against nuclear terrorism is designed "to supplement and reinforce national efforts in areas where international cooperation is indispensable to the strengthening of nuclear security." The plan covers eight areas:

- physical protection of nuclear material and facilities,
- detection of malicious activities involving nuclear and radioactive materials,
- strengthening of state systems for nuclear material accountancy and control,
- security of radioactive sources,
- assessment of safety and security at nuclear facilities,
- response readiness in the case of a malicious event/emergency, and
- enhancement of program coordination and information management for nuclear safety matters.[9]

These important safeguards, however, do not address a fundamental problem in the regime: The same technologies that can enrich uranium to low levels for reactor fuel can enrich it to high levels for nuclear weapons. The same reprocessing facility that separates the plutonium from the spent-fuel rods for reuse as fuel or for disposal can separate it for weapons use. The risk is that if a country builds these facilities—as allowed under article 4 of the NPT—the country could come right up to the edge of nuclear weapons capability. In a worst-case scenario, it could then withdraw from the NPT, having used its rights within the treaty to acquire a nuclear weapons capability.

The Comprehensive Test Ban Treaty

The newest potential element of the nonproliferation regime is the Comprehensive Test Ban Treaty, which is a barrier to vertical as well as horizontal proliferation.

The conclusion of this treaty fulfilled a preambular commitment of NPT parties to fulfill pledges made in the 1963 Partial Test Ban Treaty "to seek to achieve the discontinuance of all test explosions of nuclear weapons for all time." The CTBT, which was opened for signature in New York on September 24, 1996, prohibits nuclear test explosions of any size and establishes a rigorous verification system, including seismic monitoring and on-site inspections, to detect violations. The CTBT was negotiated at the Geneva Conference on Disarmament, where decisions are usually made by consensus. India temporarily blocked approval of the treaty in mid-August 1996; it objected to the fact that the treaty did not include provisions demanded by India prescribing a "time-bound framework" for the global elimination of nuclear weapons. India also opposed the treaty's entry-into-force provision, which, in effect, would require India's ratification to bring the pact into force. To circumvent India's veto, Australia introduced the treaty to the U.N. General Assembly, where decisions are made by majority rather than by consensus. The General Assembly adopted the CTBT on September 10, 1996, by a vote of 158 to 3 (the no votes were from Bhutan, India, and Libya).

The U.S Senate rejected ratification of the CTBT in October 1999, though the United States and all other participating nations continue to voluntarily observe the treaty's ban on further tests. The CTBT's entry-into-force provision requires the ratification of the 44 "nuclear-capable" nations that possess either nuclear power or nuclear research reactors. Of those nations, 3—India, North Korea, and Pakistan—have not signed the treaty; and 8—including China, Israel, and the United States—have yet to ratify it. In total, 175 nations (including the five nuclear weapon states and Israel) have signed the treaty, and 121 have ratified it as of the spring of 2005.[10] (For more on the CTBT, see appendix E.)

Supplier Control Mechanisms

The Zangger Committee and the Nuclear Suppliers Group are two informal coalitions of nations that form a third major element of the nonproliferation regime. Without any legal requirements, these two coalitions consist of nations that voluntarily restrict the export of equipment and materials that could be used to develop nuclear weapons.

Shortly after the NPT came into force in 1970, a number of Western and Soviet-bloc nuclear supplier states began consultations concerning the procedures and standards that would apply to nuclear exports to non-nuclear-weapon states. The group, known as the NPT Exporters Committee (or the Zangger Committee, so named after its Swiss chairman), adopted a set of guidelines in August 1974. These guidelines included a list of export items that would trigger the requirement for the application of IAEA safeguards in recipient states. These procedures and the "trigger list," which have been updated in subsequent years, represented the first major agreement on the uniform regulation of nuclear exports by current and potential nuclear suppliers. China joined the group in October 1997 and participated in trigger-list discussions for the first time in February 1999.

Following India's nuclear test in 1974, an overlapping group of nuclear supplier states—in this case including France, which was not then a party to the NPT—met in London to further develop export guidelines. In January 1976, this London group, which became known as the Nuclear Suppliers Group (NSG), adopted guidelines that were similar to those of the NPT Exporters Committee but also extended to transfers of technology and included an agreement to "exercise restraint" in the transfer of uranium enrichment and plutonium extraction equipment and facilities.

In April 1992, in the wake of the Gulf War, the NSG expanded its export control guidelines, which until then had covered only uniquely nuclear items, to cover 65 "dual-use" items as well. The NSG also added as a requirement for future exports that recipient states accept IAEA inspections on all their peaceful nuclear activities. This rule, which had previously been adopted by only some NSG members, effectively precludes nuclear commerce by NSG member states with India, Israel, and Pakistan.

In addition to agreeing to such full-scope safeguards, all nations importing regulated items from NSG member states must promise to furnish adequate physical security for transferred nuclear materials and facilities; pledge not to export nuclear materials and technologies to other nations without the permission of the original exporting nation or without a pledge from the recipient nation to abide by those same rules; and promise not to use any imports to build nuclear explosives. Finally, in May 2004 the NSG adopted a "catch-all" mechanism, permitting member states to prevent any export that they suspect might be used for a nuclear weapons program, even if the blocked item does not appear on any of the NSG's control lists.[11] Similar rules, apart from the requirement for full-scope safeguards, apply to exports regulated by the Zangger Committee, which continues to function, although it has been partially eclipsed by the NSG, whose export controls are more far reaching. (The members of the two supplier groups are listed, and more detailed discussion is provided, in appendix D in this volume.)

Nuclear-Weapon-Free Zones

Nuclear-weapon-free zones (NWFZs) complement NPT arrangements because they can be geared to specific regional situations. The growing role of NWFZs as part of the nonproliferation regime was reflected in the draft review document of the 1995 NPT Review and Extension Conference: "The establishment of nuclear-weapon-free zones . . . constitutes an important disarmament measure which greatly strengthens the international non-proliferation regime in all its aspects." NWFZs have been established in Latin America (the Treaty of Tlatelolco, 1967), the South Pacific (SPNWFZ, 1996), and Africa (ANWFZ, 1996). The Treaty of Bangkok, which created a Southeast Asian NWFZ, came into force in 1997, despite the fact that it has not yet attained protocol ratification from the five nuclear weapon states. In 2002, Kazakhstan, Kyrgyzstan, Tajikistan, Turkmenistan, and Uzbekistan completed negotiations to establish a Central Asian NWFZ. They are waiting for endorsements from the five nuclear weapon states before the treaty is officially opened for signatures.[12]

The Biological and Chemical Nonproliferation Regime

Global efforts to contain the spread of biological and chemical weapons center on the Biological and Toxin Weapons Convention (BWC) and the Chemical Weapons Convention (CWC). These treaties are not as well developed or long-standing as their nuclear counterparts, but they have made major advances in the past two decades and now establish international norms against the development, possession, and use of such weapons. In addition, efforts to expand and improve the implementation of the regimes continue, as witnessed by efforts to negotiate a verification protocol to the BWC.

The Biological and Toxin Weapons Convention

The Geneva Protocol for the Prohibition of the Use in War of Asphyxiating, Poisonous, or Other Gases, and of Bacteriological Methods of Warfare of 1925 was limited. It symbolically prohibited the use of both poison gases and bacteriological weapons, but it did not restrict the ability of states to acquire and store chemical and biological weapons, nor did it have verification or enforcement provisions.

The Biological and Toxin Weapons Convention was opened for signature in April 1972 and entered into force on March 26, 1975. The BWC prohibits the development, production, stockpiling, acquisition, or transfer of biological agents or toxins in "quantities that have no justification for prophylactic, protective, and other peaceful purposes."[13] The BWC also specifically bans "weapons, equipment or means of delivery designed to use such agents or toxins for hostile purposes or in armed conflict." Russia, the United States, and the United Kingdom are the three depositary governments for the BWC. As of the spring of 2005, the BWC had 169 signatories and 153 member states.[14] Review conferences are held regularly and have taken place in 1980, 1986, 1991, 1996, 2000, 2001, and 2002.

When it entered into force, the BWC was the first international treaty to ban an entire class of weapons. However, the treaty lacked effective verification and enforcement measures to ensure compliance. Recognizing these weaknesses, member states established an ad hoc group in 1994 to draft binding verification guidelines for the convention. The ad hoc group is authorized to review four areas: "Definitions of terms and objective criteria; incorporation of existing and further enhanced confidence building and transparency measures, as appropriate, into the regime; a system of measures to promote compliance with the Convention; and specific measures designed to ensure the effective and full implementation of Article X."[15] Yet the BWC's shortcomings continue to restrict its impact. Violations of the convention by Russia, persistent allegations regarding Iraq's biological weapons activities prior to the spring of 2003, and a doubling of the number of states suspected of pursuing a biological weapons capability since 1975 have raised questions about the BWC's effectiveness.[16] Efforts by the ad hoc group to negotiate a legally binding protocol for verification were severely damaged by the withdrawal from the talks by the United States in July

2001 and by a U.S. proposal on December 7, 2001, the last day of the 2001 Review Conference, to disband the ad hoc group.[17]

The next review conference began on November 11, 2002. No decision was made on the future of the ad hoc group, effectively leaving it in limbo. Instead, Chairman Tibor Tóth proposed the convening of three intersessional meetings between 2003 and 2005 to "discuss" and "promote" actions that could be taken by member states on a voluntary basis to strengthen the BWC and prevent bioterrorism. This proposal was accepted and ensured that no verification protocol would even be discussed until the next review conference in 2006. Due in part to the limited agenda (largely at the United States' behest) of the intersessional meetings, Tóth warned that the meetings could easily become "an empty shell."[18]

The Chemical Weapons Convention

Soon after the entry into force of the BWC, draft efforts began for a ban on chemical weapons. Negotiations stalled, however, in seeking agreement on compliance and verification issues. Progress resumed in 1986, when the Soviet Union accepted provisions for systematic inspections at chemical weapons storage and production facilities, the destruction of production facilities, and declarations and routine inspections at commercial industry sites. A year later, the USSR also agreed to mandatory short-notice challenge inspections—insisting, however, that all facilities and locations be subject to the procedure. The final catalyst for the completion of a chemical weapons treaty was the use of chemical attacks by both sides during the Iran-Iraq War, demonstrating a clear absence of international means to prevent the acquisition and use of chemical weapons for conflict.

The Chemical Weapons Convention entered into force on April 29, 1997. The treaty prohibits the development, production, acquisition, stockpiling, retention or use of chemical weapons, as well as the "transfer, directly or indirectly, [of] chemical weapons to anyone."[19] State parties to the treaty cannot conduct military preparations for the use of chemical weapons, nor can they assist other states in any treaty-banned activity. The CWC also requires members to destroy all chemical weapons and production facilities under its jurisdiction or control, as well as any chemical weapons it may have abandoned on the territory of another state party. Full compliance is expected within ten years of the convention's entry into force. As of the spring of 2005, the CWC had 168 member states.[20]

The CWC includes a number of confidence-building measures and ensures transparency through a verification regime that subjects all declared chemical weapons and chemical weapons production facilities to systematic inspections. The Organization for the Prohibition of Chemical Weapons was established to oversee the inspection and verification proceedings, and it maintains a comprehensive web site with the latest information on treaty membership and activities.[21]

The CWC categorizes chemicals into three "schedules," depending on their applicability for chemical weapons programs and for commercial purposes. Varying levels of control are then applied to the classified chemicals and to their production facilities. Facilities producing chemicals listed in any of the three schedules in quantities in excess of allotted amounts must be declared and will be subject to inspection. The CWC's verification provisions regulate both the military and civilian chemical industries active in the production, processing, and consumption of relevant chemicals. CWC provisions authorize a combination of reporting requirements, the routine on-site inspections of declared sites, and short-notice challenge inspections to ensure compliance. The conditions for challenge inspections of any declared or nondeclared facility are also included. The CWC also contains provisions for assistance in the event that a member state is attacked or threatened with chemical weapons and for promoting trade in chemicals and related equipment between states for peaceful purposes.

The Australia Group

The Australia Group is an informal association of 39 countries that are opposed to the proliferation of chemical and biological weapons (CBW).[22] Its member nations work on the basis of consensus to limit the spread of CBW by the control of chemical weapon precursors, biological weapon pathogens, and CBW dual-use equipment. Measures to address CBW proliferation also include the coordination of national export controls and information sharing on suspicious activities.

The group was established in 1984 after the extensive use of chemical weapons in the Iran-Iraq War. It initially focused on regulating the export of eight dual-use chemical precursors. By 1991, however, the "warning list" of chemicals subject to control had expanded to include 54 materials (chemicals, pathogens and toxins, and dual-use equipment). In 2002, the group took two important steps to strengthen export controls. The first was the "no-undercut" requirement, which stated that any member of the group considering making an export to another state that had already been denied an export by any other member of the group must first consult with that member state before approving the export. The second was the "catch-all" provision, which requires member states to halt all exports that could be used by importers in chemical or biological weapons programs, regardless of whether or not the export is on the group's control lists.[23]

Australia Group member states share the group's "warning list" with chemical industries and scientific communities to promote an awareness of CBW proliferation risks within individual nations. Enterprises are asked to report any suspicious activities. Many substances used in the production of chemical weapons, however, also have legal industrial purposes, which forces control efforts to strike a difficult balance between security concerns and legitimate trade.

Significant Additions to the Nuclear, Chemical, and Biological Nonproliferation Regime since September 11, 2001

The terrorist attacks of 2001 increased the willingness of many countries to take collective action on proliferation. The two most significant multilateral achievements have been the Proliferation Security Initiative and the adoption of U.N. Resolution 1540.

The Proliferation Security Initiative

The United States–led Proliferation Security Initiative (PSI) is a voluntary grouping to block the transfer of weapons and technology by improving information sharing and stepping up interdiction.[24] More than 60 states have pledged their support for this initiative.[25] The PSI has little standing in international law, and therefore does not apply directly to international waters. It encompasses only states that choose to abide by its provisions, and it is limited only to the national territory, airspace, and waterways of participants. Countries under whose flag a ship is traveling can give permission for that ship to be stopped and searched, and the United States has strengthened its ability to use this effectively by working out prior consents arrangements with Liberia and Panama, the two countries most popular with shippers seeking flags of convenience.

PSI-related activities fall into three main areas:

1. enhancing national legislation in participating states to ensure that shipments of controlled items can be searched or seized under national authority,
2. intelligence sharing and law enforcement cooperation to identify illicit transfers, and
3. interdiction training exercises and actual intercepts in nationally controlled areas (land, sea, and air).

The PSI's members include Australia, Canada, France, Germany, Italy, Japan, the Netherlands, Norway, Poland, Portugal, Russia, Singapore, Spain, the United Kingdom, and the United States.[26] Though the PSI is an important addition to the tools of enforcement, still missing is a system that can deal with a legally flagged vessel or aircraft carrying material or technology related to nuclear, chemical, or biological weapons to another country across international territory.

U.N. Security Council Resolution 1540

On April 28, 2004, the U.N. Security Council unanimously adopted Resolution 1540 under chapter 7 of the U.N. Charter, thereby making it legally binding on all member states. Resolution 1540 requires all states to "establish, develop, review and maintain appropriate effective national and trans-shipment controls" and "border controls" to prevent the proliferation of nuclear, chemical, and biological weapons and their means of delivery. States must enact "appropriate laws and regulations to control export, transit, trans-shipment and re-export" of materials that would contribute to proliferation. A Security Council committee was also set up to monitor progress and to receive implementation reports from member states, with a two-year mandate. The primary advantage of the resolution over treaties addressing similar matters is that it is binding on all U.N. member states, including those outside the scope of the nonproliferation regime and those non-nuclear states that serve as reexport and manufacturing points in the proliferation network.[27]

Although there was considerable consternation over the role of the Security Council as a law-making body, widespread recognition of the urgency of enforcement eventually overcame these reservations. In response to these objections, however, Resolution 1540 states that it does not override the existing treaties of the nonproliferation regime. The resolution obliges member states to take action aimed at preventing both the proliferation of nuclear, chemical, and biological weapons and also their means of delivery. In the wake of the unraveling of the A. Q. Khan nuclear black market network (see chapter 12), this resolution focused particularly on member states' responsibilities to actively restrain nonstate actors.

NOTES

1. In this book, Israel, India, and Pakistan are described as non-NPT nuclear weapon states. The NPT and the nonproliferation regime have no legal category and no provision for additional nuclear weapon states.
2. United Nations Department for Disarmament Affairs, "Status of Multilateral Arms Regulation and Disarmament Agreements: View by Country and Treaty," available at http://disarmament2.un.org/TreatyStatus.nsf Site.
3. "Preparatory Committee for the 2005 Review Conference of the Parties to the Treaty on the Non-Proliferation of Nuclear Weapons," First Session, April 8–19, 2002; available at http://disarmament2.un.org/wmd/npt/2005/index-PC1.html. See also "Preparatory Committee for the 2005 Review Conference of the Parties to the Treaty on the Non-Proliferation of Nuclear Weapons," Second Session, April 28–May 9, 2003; available at http://disarmament2.un.org/wmd/npt/2005/index-PC2.html. And see "Preparatory Committee for the 2005 Review Conference of the Parties to the Treaty on the Non-Proliferation of Nuclear Weapons," Third Session, April 26–May 7, 2004; available at http://disarmament2.un.org/wmd/npt/2005/index-PC3.html.
4. IAEA, "IAEA by the Numbers," available at www.iaea.org/About/by_the_numbers.html.
5. IAEA, IAEA Statute, article XII, paragraph C; available at www.iaea.org/About/statute_text.html#A1.12.
6. IAEA, IAEA Annual Report for 2003, table A23, available at www.iaea.org/Publications/Reports/Anrep2003/annex_tables.pdf.
7. Adapted from "The 1997 IAEA Additional Protocol at a Glance," Fact Sheet by the Arms Control Association; available at www.armscontrol.org/factsheets/IAEAProtocol.asp.
8. IAEA, "Strengthened Safeguards System: Status of Additional Protocols," available at www.iaea.org/OurWork/SV/Safeguards/sg_protocol.html.
9. "IAEA Action Plan to Guard against Nuclear Terrorism," Disarmament Diplomacy, no. 64, May/June 2002; available at www.acronym.org.uk/dd/dd64/64nr04.htm.
10. See the web site for the Preparatory Commission for the Comprehensive Test Ban Treaty Organization, www.ctbto.org.
11. Arms Control Association, "The Nuclear Suppliers Group at a Glance," June 2004, available at www.armscontrol.org/factsheets/NSG.asp.
12. Arms Control Association, "Fact Sheet: Nuclear-Weapon-Free Zones (NWFZ) at a Glance," July 2003, available at www.armscontrol.org/factsheets/nwfz.asp.
13. U.N. Conference on Disarmament, text of Biological Weapons Convention, available at www.unog.ch/disarm/distreat/bac_72.htm.
14. See the web site www.opbw.org.
15. United Nations, "Brief Background on the Biological Weapons Convention," available at www.un.org/Depts/dda/WMD/page6.html.
16. Joseph Cirincione, ed., *Repairing the Regime: Preventing the Spread of Weapons of Mass Destruction* (New York: Routledge, 2000).
17. Jenni Rissanen, "Anger after the Ambush: Review Conference Suspended after US Asks for AHG's Termination," BWC Review Conference Bulletin, available at www.acronym.org.uk/bwc/revcon8.htm.

18. Jonathan B. Tucker, "The BWC New Process: A Preliminary Assessment." *Nonproliferation Review*, Spring 2004, pp. 30–34; available at www.cns.miis.edu/pubs/npr/vol11/111/111tucker.pdf.
19. Text of Chemical Weapons Convention, available at www.opcw.org/html/db/cwc/eng/cwc_frameset.html.
20. "States Parties to the Chemical Weapons Convention as of 21 May 2005," available at www.opcw.org/html/db/members_frameset.html.
21. See www.opcw.org.
22. Australia Group, "Australia Group Members," available at www.australiagroup.net/en/agpart.htm.
23. Arms Control Association, "The Australia Group at a Glance," September 2003, available at www.armscontrol.org/factsheets/australiagroup.asp.
24. This section has been adapted from George Perkovich, Jessica Mathews, Joseph Cirincione, Rose Gottemoeller, and Jon Wolfsthal, *Universal Compliance: A Strategy for Nuclear Security* (Washington, D.C.: Carnegie Endowment for International Peace, 2005), pp. 59–60; available at www.ProliferationNews.org.
25. Arms Control Association, "The Proliferation Security Initiative at a Glance," June 2004, available at www.armscontrol.org/factsheets/PSI.asp.
26. Ibid.
27. Adapted from Perkovich et al., *Universal Compliance*, pp. 57–58.

Table 2.1. **Major Treaties and Agreements of the Nonproliferation Regime**

Non-Proliferation Treaty
Entered into force in 1970. A total of 189 member states. Under the treaty, the five "nuclear weapon" states commit to pursue general and complete disarmament, while the remaining "non-nuclear-weapon" states agree to forgo developing or acquiring nuclear weapons.
Additional Protocol to the NPT Safeguards Agreement
Approved on May 15, 1997. Signed by 90 states, in force in 66 states. The Additional Protocol facilitates more robust inspections by requiring states to submit an expanded declaration of their nuclear-related activities, and by giving International Atomic Energy Agency inspectors greater authority to visit both declared and undeclared sites of concern.
Nuclear Suppliers Group
Established in 1975. A total of 44 participants. This is an organization of nuclear supplier states that voluntarily agree to coordinate export controls in order to prevent passing nuclear material and nuclear-related technologies to states that might use them in a nuclear weapons program.
Comprehensive Test Ban Treaty
Opened for signature on September 24, 1996. A total of 121 member states, 175 signatories. The treaty prohibits nuclear test explosions of any size and establishes a rigorous global verification system to detect violations. For the treaty to enter into force, all 44 nuclear-capable states, including the United States, must ratify it.
Chemical Weapons Convention
Entered into force on April 29, 1997. A total of 168 member states, 184 signatories. The treaty prohibits the production, stockpiling, acquisition, and transfer of chemical weapons.
Biological and Toxin Weapons Convention
Entered into force on March 26, 1975. A total of 153 member states, 169 signatories. The treaty prohibits the development, production, stockpiling, acquisition,

(table continues on the following page)

Table 2.1. **Major Treaties and Agreements of the Nonproliferation Regime** (continued)

and transfer of pathogens or toxins in weapons systems or other means of delivery.

Australia Group

Established in 1984.
A total of 39 participants.
This is a voluntary association of states that work cooperatively to limit the spread of chemical weapons precursors, biological pathogens, and dual-use technologies that could be employed in a chemical or biological weapons program.

Missile Technology Control Regime

Announced on April 16, 1987.
A total of 34 participants.
This is an informal export control arrangement designed to regulate the spread of ballistic and cruise missiles capable of delivering a 500-kilogram payload at a range of 300 kilometers.

International (Hague) Code of Conduct

Announced on November 25, 2002.
A total of 114 participants.
This is a voluntary organization meant to supplement the Missile Technology Control Regime (see above). It calls for restraint in domestic ballistic missile programs and for the nonproliferation of any ballistic missiles that can deliver nuclear, biological, or chemical weapons, regardless of range.

U.N. Security Council Resolution 1540

Passed on April 28, 2004.
Legally binding on all U.N. member states.
This resolution obliges member states to take action to prevent the spread of weapons of mass destruction, particularly by nonstate actors, through strengthened border controls, better export controls, and other domestic laws.

Proliferation Security Initiative

Announced May 31, 2003.
Informal arrangement supported by more than 70 states.
This initiative focuses on intelligence sharing and other methods of cooperation to facilitate the interdiction of vessels carrying weapons of mass destruction and related goods and technologies via water, sea, or air.

SOURCES

"Australia Group Members," available at www.australiagroup.net/en/agpart.htm. Austrian Foreign Ministry, "Ballistic Missiles-HCOC," available at www.bmaa.gv.at/view.php3?f_id=54&LNG=en&version. "Fact Sheets," Arms Control Association, available at www.armscontrol.org/factsheets/. "Missile Technology Control Regime," available at www.mtcr.info/english/index.html. Department for Disarmament Affairs, United Nations, "Multilateral Arms Regulation and Disarmament Agreements," available at http://disarmament2.un.org/TreatyStatus.nsf. "Nuclear Suppliers Group: Participants," available at www.nuclearsuppliersgroup.org/member.htm. "Preparatory Commission for the Comprehensive Test Ban Treaty Organization," available at www.ctbto.org. Organization for the Prohibition of Chemical Weapons, "States Parties to the Chemical Weapons Convention," available at www.opcw.org/html/db/members_frameset.html. International Atomic Energy Agency, "Strengthened Safeguards System: Additional Protocol," available at www.iaea.org/OurWork/SV/Safeguards/sg_protocol.html.

CHAPTER 3

Nuclear Weapons and Materials

Nuclear weapons were invented more than 60 years ago. Although the technology required to produce them is complex, nuclear weapon concepts are well understood and widely available. Nine countries (China, France, India, Israel, Pakistan, Russia, South Africa, the United Kingdom, and the United States) and possibly North Korea have produced nuclear weapons. More than 40 other countries could also produce nuclear weapons, if their governments decided to invest the time, money, and political effort to do so. If they first acquired the necessary nuclear materials, even well-organized subnational organizations and terrorist groups with adequate time and resources could produce a nuclear explosive device.

Some nuclear weapon designs are highly complex, while some basic designs are much easier to understand and build. By far the most costly, complicated, and observable part of building nuclear weapons is producing sufficient amounts of weapons-usable nuclear materials needed to fuel a nuclear explosion. The two main elements needed to produce a nuclear explosive device are highly enriched uranium (containing a high percentage of uranium-235, or U-235, and also known as HEU) and plutonium. If these special nuclear materials can be purchased or stolen from existing state stockpiles, it dramatically reduces—but does not totally eliminate—the challenges associated with the production of nuclear weapons or explosive devices.

Producing plutonium requires the construction of large and highly visible facilities, making the clandestine acquisition of nuclear weapons with plutonium extremely difficult, though not impossible. Some uranium enrichment technologies are more easily concealed but are also possible to detect in many cases through national technical means, such as surveillance satellites. The challenge of preventing the spread of nuclear weapons is complicated, however, by the fact that nuclear materials, including weapons-usable materials, have peaceful uses. The same facilities that enrich uranium to low levels for fuel for power reactors can also enrich uranium to the high levels needed for nuclear weapons. The same facilities that reprocess the spent fuel from reactors to separate plutonium for a special type of reactor fuel can also separate the plutonium for use in nuclear weapons (see below for more on these processes). (Some facilities may need to be modified, but the science and engineering required are essentially the same.)

The physical protection of nuclear materials in the civilian sector, therefore, is a critical component of preventing the spread of nuclear weapons. To the extent that weapons-usable materials are used in civilian activities, it is imperative to ensure that they cannot be stolen for use in nuclear weapons, and that any attempt to divert nuclear materials by a non-nuclear-weapon state can be detected in a timely manner, so that it can be halted and the material recovered. Going beyond physical protection and diversion detection, there are also international proposals under discussion that would further control the ability of any state to possess national nuclear material production capabilities.

While pursuing these long-term structural reforms, the international system of safeguards, administered by the International Atomic Energy Agency (IAEA), requires strengthening to provide timely warning of any diversion of nuclear materials or use of civil facilities for weapons material production. The IAEA's ability to detect undeclared facilities also needs to be strengthened as part of broader nonproliferation enforcement efforts.

Basic Nuclear Concepts

Conventional explosives—like dynamite—release energy through rapid chemical reactions involving changes in the structure of molecules. Nuclear explosions harness far greater amounts of energy by splitting or fusing together the nuclei of individual atoms.

An atom consists of a nucleus, or central core, in which there are protons and neutrons surrounded by orbiting electrons. Elements—such as hydrogen, iron, uranium, and plutonium—are distinguished by an atomic number that is equal to the number of protons in their nucleus. All atoms of the same element have the same number of protons in their respective nuclei, but they can exist in different forms called isotopes, which have the same atomic number (that is, the same number of protons) but a different number of neutrons in the nucleus.

For example, three isotopes of the element hydrogen—all with an atomic number of 1—are found in nature. The simplest form has but a single proton in the nucleus and is referred to as hydrogen-1 (abbreviated H-1). A second isotope has one proton and one neutron in the nucleus and is variously referred to as deuterium, hydrogen-2, or H-2. And a third isotope with one proton and two neutrons is called tritium, hydrogen-3, or H-3. Atoms of uranium all have 92 protons in the nucleus. Some of the more common isotopes of uranium are uranium-233, or U-233 (which has 92 protons plus 141 neutrons), U-235 (92 protons plus 143 neutrons), and U-238 (92 protons plus 146 neutrons). Plutonium isotopes (with 94 protons) include Pu-238, Pu-239, Pu-240, Pu-241, and so on.

The various isotopes interact with each other and with other atomic particles (such as other neutrons) differently, and each has properties that can be used in various ways. For example, at very high temperatures some isotopes with low atomic numbers (e.g., H-2 or H-3) fuse together, releasing energy and/or atomic particles. Some isotopes with high atomic numbers (for example, U-235 or Pu-239) split apart into other isotopes after absorbing a neutron. It is this fusing or splitting of atoms that produces the energy released in a nuclear weapon (or a nuclear reactor). The energy and atomic particles released are in the form of alpha particles (subatomic fragments consisting of two protons and two neutrons), beta particles (electrons), neutrons, X-rays, and gamma rays, and are collectively referred to simply as "radiation."

Isotopes of uranium and plutonium are the main materials used in nuclear weapons. Isotopes of some other elements (for example, neptunium) can also be used in weapons, but for a variety of technical reasons they have not been. Some of these isotopes only exist in limited quantities, but they are nonetheless a matter of some proliferation concern.

Isotopes that are readily split, or "fissioned," when a slowly moving neutron is absorbed into the nucleus are referred to as fissile materials. Basic fission weapons (see the discussion below) are made using fissile materials, principally U-235, Pu-239, U-233, or a combination of these and other fissionable isotopes of uranium and plutonium. This fissioning of isotopes is accompanied by the release of energy and additional neutrons that can go on to be absorbed by and split other atoms, which in turn release more energy and more neutrons. This chain reaction is what enables nuclear materials to be harnessed for various purposes, including the production of heat in a nuclear reactor (for creating steam and then electricity) and the explosive power of a nuclear weapon. In a nuclear reactor, the chain reaction is controlled and limited over a long period of time, while in nuclear weapons most of the released energy typically takes place in a very short time (a fraction of a millionth of a second).

Basic Nuclear Weapon Concepts

Some amounts of fissile material are too small to sustain a chain reaction because a large fraction of the neutrons produced are able to escape the confines of the nuclear reaction, making them unavailable to cause fissions in other nuclei. The minimum amount of material necessary to sustain a chain reaction is called a critical mass. The amount of material in a critical mass depends on the exact type of materials present, their density, purity, and geometry. Pu-239 has a smaller critical mass than U-235, and uranium containing 90 percent U-235 will have a smaller critical mass than uranium containing 45 percent U-235.

The amount of fissile material needed to make a nuclear weapon depends on design considerations, such as geometry, the degree to which the fissile material is compressed, and the desired yield. The IAEA publishes figures on the quantities of material required to produce a nuclear weapon—amounts known as a "significant quantity." The significant quantities that the IAEA specifies are 25 kilograms of highly enriched uranium and 8 kilograms of plutonium. The minimum or exact amount of nuclear material needed to produce nuclear weapons is classified information in all nuclear weapon states. The U.S. classification regulation permits cleared individuals to state that a nuclear weapon can be made with as little as 4 kilograms of plutonium. Nongovernment experts claim that a 1-kiloton-yield nuclear explosive device can be achieved using sophisticated designs with as little as 1 to 2 kilograms of plutonium, or approximately 8 to 10 kilograms of highly enriched uranium.

Basic Nuclear Weapon Designs

There are two classical methods for achieving the desired mass and explosive yield of a single-stage nuclear weapon. The first is to rapidly bring together two subcritical masses (the gun assembly technique), and the second is to rapidly compress a single subcritical mass (the implosion technique). The gun design is the least complex of the known nuclear weapon designs. The nuclear weapon that the United States dropped on Hiroshima, Japan, on August 6, 1945, was a gun-type weapon and was so well understood, even at that time, that it was used without being explosively tested beforehand.

An implosion design is more complex but allows for a smaller device, such as those used in today's modern missile warheads. The implosion design was used in the first nuclear explosion (the Trinity test) at Alamogordo, New Mexico, on July 16, 1945, and in the nuclear weapon dropped on Nagasaki, Japan, on August 9, 1945.

Gun-design weapons can only use uranium as a fissile material. The chain reaction in a gun design using plutonium will begin too soon, and the nuclear dissassembly will occur too quickly, before the desired yield can be achieved. Because uranium can be used in the simpler gun design, highly enriched uranium is considered a particularly attractive material for terrorists seeking to acquire nuclear weapons. Either uranium and plutonium or a combination of the two can be used in the more complex implosion design.

Advanced Nuclear Designs

Most advanced weapon designs have two or more separate nuclear components in the same device that are ignited in stages—the energy released in the exploding fission-based "primary" is contained and used to compress and ignite nuclear reactions in the separate fusion-based "secondary," thus further increasing the explosive yield of the nuclear weapon. Such devices are called thermonuclear weapons, because the secondaries (and often the primaries) typically contain lighter isotopes—in the form of lithium deutride, deuterium, or tritium—that are fused by the high temperature produced by a nuclear reaction.

The first multistage thermonuclear device—also referred to as a hydrogen bomb (because it used liquid deuterium, which is an isotope of hydrogen)—was exploded by the United States on November 1, 1952, in the southern Pacific Ocean. The device used a basic fission primary explosive to produce the heat and radiation necessary to ignite the secondary explosive of liquid deuterium. Whereas the first fission nuclear explosions—the Trinity device—had a force of 20,000 metric tons of TNT (that is, 20 kilotons), the first hydrogen explosion had a force of 10,400,000 metric tons of TNT (10.4 megatons).

In advanced nuclear designs, the primary typically relies on a process referred to as "boosting." In a boosted device, fusion materials (such as deuterium and tritium) are located within the atomic device. These materials are typically injected as a gas into the center of the fissile material before initiating the nuclear chain reaction. As the chain reaction releases energy in the initial phase of the explosion, some of the energy is used to compress and heat these lighter atoms, causing then to fuse together. These thermonuclear reactions release additional energy and neutrons, and the neutrons cause additional fission reactions, thereby accelerating the ongoing fission chain reaction, increasing the energy output and efficiency of the boosted device.

The Production of Nuclear Materials

Fortunately, from a nonproliferation perspective, fissile materials are not readily available in nature. U-235 exists in natural uranium, but it makes up only 0.7 percent of all of the uranium that comes out of the ground, and much higher concentrations are required to construct an actual nuclear explosive. The concentration of the desired isotope, U-235, can be increased through a variety of processes, collectively referred to as "enrichment." With some technologies, the U-235 concentration can be increased to almost 100 percent. The uranium used in a fission weapon is typically enriched to above 90 percent U-235, although fission weapons can be made with less concentrated U-235. If the concentration of uraniun-235 is lower, larger amounts of uranium (and the chemical explosive for compressing it) are required to fabricate a nuclear explosive device. So much material is required if the enrichment is below 20 percent U-235 that the international community has adopted a concentration of 20 percent U-235 as a threshold above which additional safeguards and physical security requirements are invoked. All other fissile materials, including plutonium, must be created artificially in a nuclear reactor and subsequently separated in a process referred to as reprocessing or chemical separation.

Uranium Enrichment

Numerous methods have been developed to enrich uranium. All of them ultimately rely on the varying weights of different isotopes. Two principal enrichment techniques used today are the gaseous diffusion method, in which uranium hexafluoride gas is forced through a selectively porous barrier, and the gas-centrifuge method, in which uranium hexafluoride gas is swirled in a cylinder that rotates at extremely high speeds. One other technique, electromagnetic isotope separation, was one of the processes used to enrich uranium for the first U.S. nuclear weapons. This highly inefficient but relatively simple enrichment method was largely abandoned by the United States in the 1950s, but it was adopted by Iraq in its nuclear weapon program in the 1980s (see chapter 17).

Considerable research and development has been conducted on several chemical and laser isotope-separation technologies, but none of these is yet efficient enough to use in the commercial production of enriched uranium. Iran and South Korea have recently been found to have conducted uranium enrichment activities using lasers, causing increased concern about the control of this technology. South Africa used another technology for the production of enriched uranium for weapons—the aerodynamic, or "jet nozzle," enrichment process, which is still a sensitive and controlled technology.

For illustrative purposes, the basic nuclear resources and facilities that are needed to produce weapons-grade uranium include

- uranium deposits;
- a uranium mine;
- a uranium mill, for processing uranium ore, which usually contains less than 1 percent uranium into uranium oxide concentrate, or yellowcake;
- a chemical conversion plant, for purifying yellowcake and converting it into uranium hexafluoride (UF_6) or uranium tetrachloride (UCl_4), the material processed in the enrichment plant;
- an enrichment plant, for enriching the uranium hexafluoride gas or uranium tetrachloride in the isotope U-235; and
- a capability for converting the enriched uranium hexafluoride gas or uranium tetrachloride into uranium metal.

Centrifuges

Considerable attention has been focused on centrifuge enrichment technology in the past few years. Not only do centrifuges offer a highly efficient way to enrich uranium, but the Pakistan-based A. Q. Khan nuclear black market network also made centrifuge technology, equipment, and expertise available to several states, including Iran, Libya, and North Korea, and possibly others that have not yet been identified. Pakistan relies primarily on uranium enrichment for its nuclear weapons program (see chapter 12).

In centrifuge enrichment, natural uranium must first be converted through a chemical process into uranium hexafluoride (figure 3.1). The gaseous form of this chemical is then fed along the axis of cylinders spinning at the rate of several hundred miles per hour. The forces inside the cylinder fling the uranium gas to the exterior wall of the unit, but the weight differential between various uranium isotopes allows collectors at different positions along the centrifuge ends to pick up slightly higher or lower percentages of U-235 or U-238, depending on where they are positioned. Fractional increases in the U-235 percentage can be multiplied by repeating the process thousands of times. Linking together hundreds or thousands of centrifuges into what is known as a "cascade" can thus enrich uranium gas from the natural level to much higher levels, one small step at a time.

Centrifuges are used in a wide variety of legitimate applications, and the basic concepts involved in their use are taught in college-level physics. The enrichment of uranium through centrifuges, however, remains a highly technical and challenging activity that requires extensive experience and expertise to master. The centrifuges must be made from specialized materials, including metal alloys and carbon fibers; must spin at very high speeds (several times the speed of sound);

Figure 3.1. **Diagram of a Centrifuge**

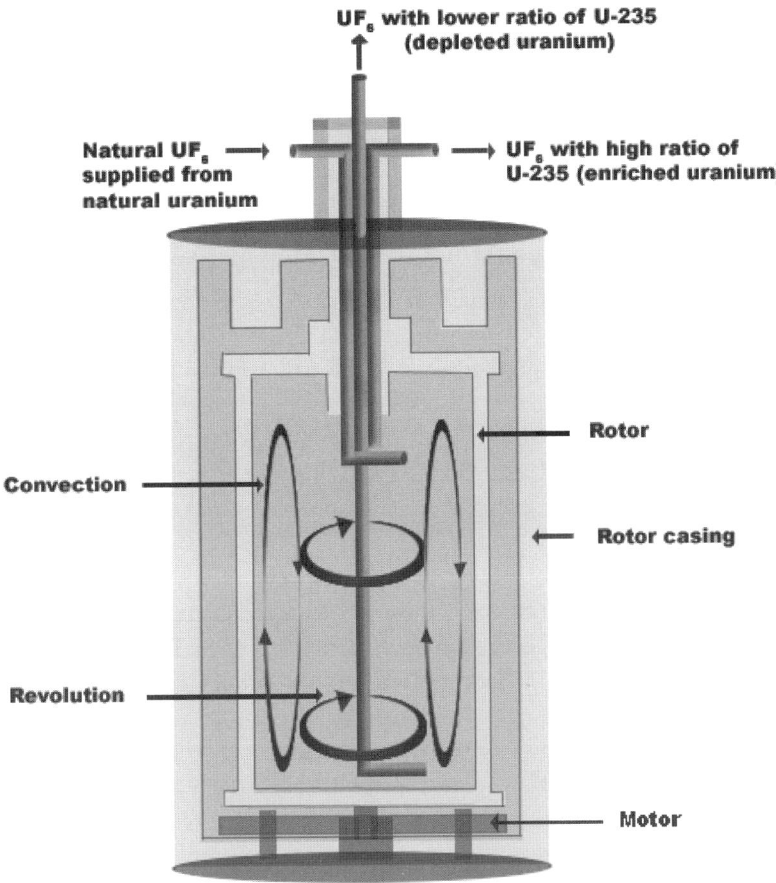

and must be perfectly balanced or they will fly apart. The centrifuge units themselves are surrounded by vacuum-sealed chambers to reduce friction, complicating the industrial process.

Along with these engineering challenges, uranium hexafluoride—the feedstock used in centrifuges—is a highly caustic mixture that must be heated to remain gaseous, and any system breaches can clog the entire centrifuge cascade, requiring complete replacement. Without outside assistance, it can take decades for a state to develop and master uranium centrifuge enrichment. Even with considerable assistance, success is rarely quick and never guaranteed.

Plutonium Production

Plutonium, the other main nuclear material used in weapons, is not available in nature and must be created artificially in nuclear reactors. The United States and several other nuclear weapon states have used dedicated military reactors to produce these weapons-usable materials, but other states (such as India and North

Korea) have used civilian reactors to produce plutonium for weapons. In a reactor, uranium fuel (either natural uranium or slightly enriched uranium, depending on the reactor design) is used to create a controlled nuclear chain reaction. This reaction releases neutrons, some of which are captured by fertile nuclear materials, such as U-238 or thorium-232. Neutron capture produces new isotopes, which—after radioactive decay—can be converted into fissile materials such as Pu-239 or U-233. However, the fuel rods containing these materials also contain other fission products and by-products, many of which are highly radioactive. Some form of chemical separation or other process is required to separate plutonium from the highly radioactive waste materials.

To accomplish this separation, "spent" fuel elements and target materials are taken to a separation or "reprocessing" plant. In a chemical separation plant, spent fuel is dissolved in hot nitric acid, and the plutonium is separated from the solution in a series of chemical processing steps. Because the spent-fuel rods are highly radioactive, heavy lead casks must be used to transport them, and the rooms at the reprocessing plant where the plutonium is chemically extracted must have thick walls, lead shielding, and special ventilation to contain radiation hazards.

Although detailed information about reprocessing was declassified by the United States and France in the 1950s and is generally available, it remains a complex engineering procedure. Indeed, almost every nation that has tried to develop nuclear weapons by the plutonium route—India, Iraq, Israel, and Pakistan—has sought outside help from the advanced nuclear supplier countries. North Korea, however, has apparently succeeded in constructing a reprocessing facility at Yongbyon without, it seems, significant foreign assistance.

Like enrichment facilities, however, reprocessing plants can also be used for legitimate civilian purposes because plutonium can be used as fuel in nuclear power reactors. Indeed, throughout the 1970s, it was generally assumed that because nuclear power use would steadily grow and worldwide uranium resources would be depleted, plutonium would need to be extracted from spent fuel for use as a substitute fuel in conventional power reactors.

In addition, research and development is under way in several nations on a new generation of reactors, known as fast or "breeder" reactors, most notably in France, Japan, and Russia. Fast reactors typically use mixed plutonium-uranium fuel, often surrounded by a "blanket" of natural uranium. As the reactor operates, new plutonium is created in the core and the blanket. In some fast reactors, more plutonium is produced than is consumed in the reactor; hence the name "breeder" reactor. These programs have encountered complex technical and political challenges—not the least of which is related to the proliferation risks caused by the overabundance of plutonium—and also questions about safety and the waste produced from these types of reactors and their spent-fuel handling.

Like plutonium recycling in general, the economic advantages of breeders depend on natural uranium becoming scarce and expensive. During the past three decades, however, new uranium reserves have been discovered, and the improved efficiency in extraction has outpaced the depletion of higher-grade ores; nuclear power has reached only a fraction of its expected growth levels; and spent-fuel reprocessing has proven to be far more expensive and complex than anticipated.

Moreover, concern has grown over the proliferation risks of the wide-scale use of plutonium as a fuel. In the late 1970s, these factors led the United States to abandon its plans to recycle plutonium in light-water reactors and, in the early 1980s, to end its breeder reactor development program. Germany has abandoned its breeder reactor program and is phasing out its recycling of plutonium and nuclear power in general. The United Kingdom has also frozen its program to develop breeder reactors, though it is continuing to reprocess spent fuel on a commercial basis for itself and several industrial nations.

The principal proponents of the use of plutonium for civilian purposes are France, Japan, and Russia, which are all continuing to develop breeder reactors and are moving forward with sizable plutonium recycling programs. Broadly speaking, the proponents of nuclear energy in these countries have maintained support for the civil use of plutonium by arguing that, though it may not be economical, it represents an advanced technology that will pay off in the future and reduce dependence on foreign sources of energy.

Like the production of enriched uranium, the production of plutonium entails many steps, and many installations and capabilities are needed along with the reactor and reprocessing plant. For illustrative purposes, the following facilities and resources are required for an independent plutonium production capability, assuming that a research or power reactor—moderated by either heavy water or graphite and employing natural uranium fuel—is used:

- uranium deposits;
- a uranium mine;
- a uranium mill, for processing uranium ore containing less than 1 percent uranium into uranium oxide concentrate, or yellowcake;
- a uranium chemical conversion plant, to convert the yellowcake into reactor-grade uranium dioxide;
- a fuel fabrication plant, to manufacture the fuel elements placed in the reactor, including a capability to fabricate zircaloy or aluminum tubing;
- a research or power reactor moderated by heavy water or graphite;
- a heavy-water production plant or a reactor-grade graphite production plant; and
- a reprocessing plant.

In contrast to heavy-water and graphite-moderated reactors, which use natural uranium as fuel, a light-water-moderated reactor would necessitate the use of low-enriched uranium, implying that a domestic enrichment capability could be available. If so, highly enriched uranium could, in theory, be produced, obviating the need for plutonium as a weapon material. It is also possible that a state might import fuel for a light-water reactor under IAEA inspection and, after using the material to produce electricity, reprocess it to extract plutonium. Although IAEA rules would require the country involved to place any such plutonium under IAEA monitoring, the state might one day abrogate its IAEA obligations and seize that material for use in nuclear arms.

NUCLEAR WEAPON STATUS 2005

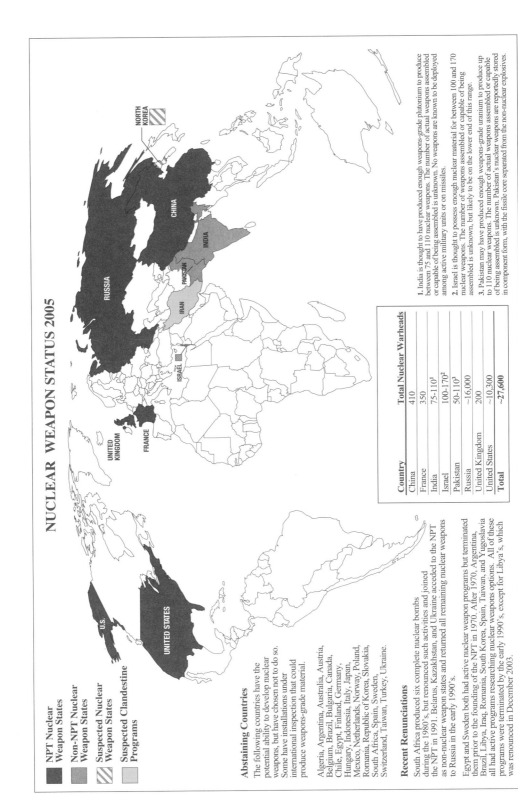

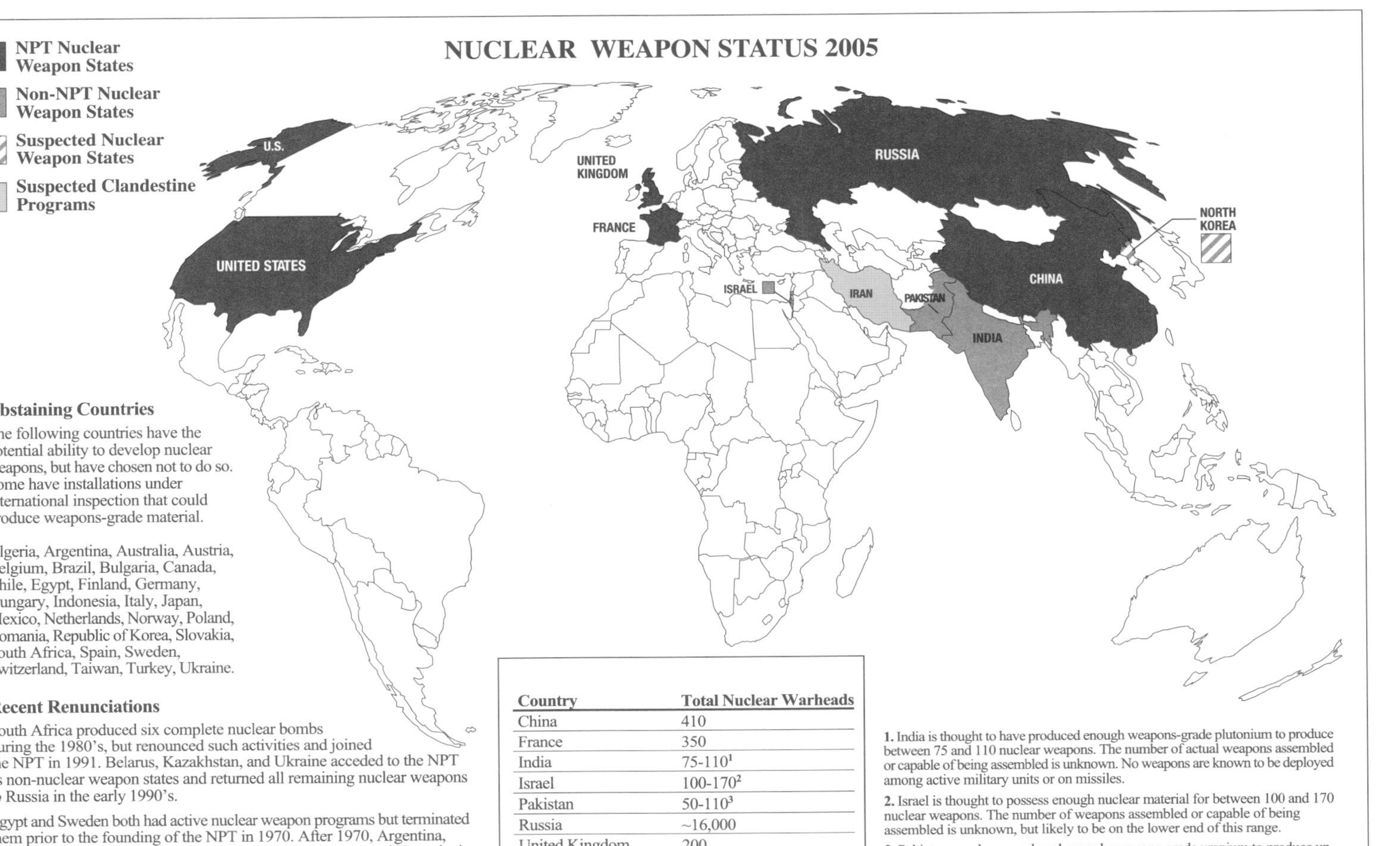

Abstaining Countries

The following countries have the potential ability to develop nuclear weapons, but have chosen not to do so. Some have installations under international inspection that could produce weapons-grade material.

Algeria, Argentina, Australia, Austria, Belgium, Brazil, Bulgaria, Canada, Chile, Egypt, Finland, Germany, Hungary, Indonesia, Italy, Japan, Mexico, Netherlands, Norway, Poland, Romania, Republic of Korea, Slovakia, South Africa, Spain, Sweden, Switzerland, Taiwan, Turkey, Ukraine.

Recent Renunciations

South Africa produced six complete nuclear bombs during the 1980's, but renounced such activities and joined the NPT in 1991. Belarus, Kazakhstan, and Ukraine acceded to the NPT as non-nuclear weapon states and returned all remaining nuclear weapons to Russia in the early 1990's.

Egypt and Sweden both had active nuclear weapon programs but terminated them prior to the founding of the NPT in 1970. After 1970, Argentina, Brazil, Libya, Iraq, Romania, South Korea, Spain, Taiwan, and Yugoslavia all had active programs researching nuclear weapons options. All of these programs were terminated by the early 1990's, except for Libya's, which was renounced in December 2003.

Country	Total Nuclear Warheads
China	410
France	350
India	75-110[1]
Israel	100-170[2]
Pakistan	50-110[3]
Russia	~16,000
United Kingdom	200
United States	~10,300
Total	**~27,600**

1. India is thought to have produced enough weapons-grade plutonium to produce between 75 and 110 nuclear weapons. The number of actual weapons assembled or capable of being assembled is unknown. No weapons are known to be deployed among active military units or on missiles.

2. Israel is thought to possess enough nuclear material for between 100 and 170 nuclear weapons. The number of weapons assembled or capable of being assembled is unknown, but likely to be on the lower end of this range.

3. Pakistan may have produced enough weapons-grade uranium to produce up to 110 nuclear weapons. The number of actual weapons assembled or capable of being assembled is unknown. Pakistan's nuclear weapons are reportedly stored in component form, with the fissile core separated from the non-nuclear explosives.

CHAPTER 4

Biological and Chemical Weapons, Agents, and Proliferation

Since the mid-1990s, governments and the public have grown increasingly concerned over the threats posed by the proliferation of chemical weapons (CWs) and biological weapons (BWs). The fall 2001 anthrax attacks in the United States transformed that concern into a requirement for substantial government action to respond to and prepare for terrorist attacks using chemical or biological warfare agents. Some experts categorize a number of these agents as weapons of mass destruction because of their potential to inflict massive casualties throughout a broad geographical area. More accurately, CWs and BWs have also been called "mass casualty weapons . . . [that] do not destroy buildings, cities or transportation. They unfortunately just destroy human lives."[1] Recent technological developments have contributed to the threat posed by these weapons. The spread of dual-use chemical technologies has facilitated the surreptitious acquisition of indigenous CW programs by potential proliferators, while advances in biotechnology could expand the availability and lethality of common BW agents.

Biological Weapons

BWs deliver pathogenic microorganisms or biologically manufactured toxins to cause illness or death in human, animal, or plant populations (see table 4.1 at the end of the chapter).[2] NATO defines a biological agent as a "microorganism (or toxin derived from it) which causes disease in man, plants or animals, or causes deterioration of material."[3] Unlike normal disease outbreaks, which appear naturally and may spread through contagion, BWs would be used deliberately to infect a target group. The utility of a biological agent as a weapon is determined by its virulence, infectiousness, stability, and ease of production. Biological agents can be grouped in four categories: bacterial agents, viral agents, rickettsial agents, and toxins:

- Bacterial agents, such as those that cause anthrax and tularemia, are single-cell organisms that either invade host tissue or produce nonliving toxins (poisons). Some bacteria cause disease by both means. Bacterial agents can be cultivated in nutrient-rich solutions. Under specific conditions, some bacteria (for example, anthrax bacilli) can transform themselves into spores. Spores are more resistant to environmental stresses, such as temperature and humidity, than are the original bacteria. Spores are "a dormant form of bacterium, and like the seeds of a plant, they can germinate when conditions are favorable."[4] Because of their persistence, spores are often more effective as biological warfare agents.
- Viral agents include smallpox virus, Venezuelan equine encephalitis virus, and various viral hemorrhagic fever viruses. Viruses are microorganisms that can replicate only inside living cells. Viral agents act as intracellular parasites by commandeering the biochemical machinery of the infected cell to produce more virus particles, triggering changes that eventually lead to cell death. The successful cultivation of viruses is more difficult than that of bacteria.
- Rickettsial agents include those that cause Q fever and epidemic typhus. Rickettsiae are parasitic microorganisms that live and replicate inside living host cells. They are often highly susceptible to antibiotic treatments.
- Biological toxins, such as ricin and botulinum toxin, are potent poisons generated by living organisms (that is, bacteria, fungi, algae, and plants). Unlike bacterial or viral agents, toxins are nonliving protein or nonprotein molecules. As nonliving agents, toxins cannot reproduce or spread and are therefore less deadly than living pathogens. Several characteristics, however, differentiate biological toxins from chemical agents. Unlike their chemical counterparts, toxins are of biological origin, although some toxins can be produced by chemical synthesis. Toxins are not volatile and hence are unlikely to penetrate the skin. However, the toxicity of many biological toxins is several orders of magnitude higher than that of the most potent chemical poisons.[5] Like other biological agents, the effective delivery of toxins generally requires their dispersal as an inhalable aerosol, although they can also be used to poison food or beverages.

The level of technical expertise required to acquire a biological warfare capability may vary depending on the sophistication of the weapons being sought. Several key characteristics make pathogens or toxins more or less suitable for use as BWs: the availability of virulent strains; ease of production; lethality; particle size and weight; ease of dissemination; and stability in storage and after release into the environment. To maximize casualties, biological agents must be delivered over a widespread area in a concentration high enough to infect and under atmospheric and weather conditions that ensure agent survival for a period of a few hours or more. Aerosol delivery—the dispersion of microscopic liquid droplets or dry particles of a microorganism or toxin in an airborne cloud—is considered the most effective means of delivery. Precise variables such as particle size and the altitude of dissemination are significant determinants of the range and damage that can be caused by a BW attack. Furthermore, to infect large numbers of the target population, a BW must disseminate a microbial or toxin agent in the appropriate particle size range of 1 to 5 microns (a micron is a thousandth of a millimeter). Agent stability and virulence must also be maintained during production, storage, and dissemination.

Although biological agent production per se is not technically difficult, combining a stable biological agent with an effective dissemination device requires sophisticated technology and expertise. The ability of an agent to survive and maintain its virulence for several hours in aerosol form as it floats downwind is a prerequisite for infecting large numbers of people. This is a challenging task because biological warfare agents are vulnerable to a host of environmental conditions, including desiccation, humidity, and oxidation. Many agents, particularly live organisms, die when exposed to ultraviolet light or oxygen. Other agents require moisture to survive. Most cannot withstand the heat or blast of an explosion. As a result, standard warfare munitions—artillery shells, grenades, rockets, missiles, and bombs—are not effective delivery vehicles for BWs.

The acquisition of an advanced BW capability requires expertise in various disciplines, including microbiology and aerobiology. Recent advances in the biological sciences, often termed the "biotechnology revolution," have increased the availability of dual-use equipment and the number of individuals with the knowledge necessary for BW production. The dissolution of the Soviet Union and the decommissioning of its massive BW program have also increased BW proliferation risks, adding to concerns that rogue states or terrorist organizations may acquire a BW capability. Inadequate security at former BW institutes in Russia that still possess collections of highly virulent pathogen strains, and lay-offs or underemployment of former BW scientists and technicians, increase the risk that BW expertise and materials could leak from Russia to potential proliferators. (See the section on Russian CW and BW programs in chapter 6.)

Once disseminated, aerosols of various pathogenic microorganisms and toxins are invisible, odorless, and tasteless. Because of these characteristics, a BW attack could remain undetected until the victims began to exhibit symptoms of infection. Depending on the number of victims who inhaled the agent, the result could be a massive, simultaneous outbreak of disease.[6] Incubation periods of BW agents vary from several hours to several days, depending on the specific agent and the amount that has been distributed and inhaled. Pathogenic microorganisms are potential mass-casualty weapons because of their ability to multiply within the host. Large quantities of biological agents, effectively distributed, could cause tens to hundreds of thousands of deaths.

BWs are also well suited for covert delivery. As a result, their potential use by terrorists has been identified as a growing threat to international security. Terrorist intentions involving BWs were exposed publicly by the repeated attempts of the Aum Shinrikyo cult to produce and distribute two lethal biological agents in Japan in the early 1990s. Despite sustained and well-funded efforts, the group was ultimately unsuccessful in acquiring and disseminating virulent strains of botulinum toxin and anthrax. The cult's failure demonstrates the significant technical hurdles associated with BW development.[7] It also reveals the terrorists' recognition of the utility of BWs as instruments of mass terror. The potential diversion of biological agents from culture collections in the former Soviet states or from states with covert BW programs has increased concerns that terrorists may be able to acquire these weapons.

The fall 2001 mailings of anthrax bacterial spores in the United States raised widespread speculation about the methods and potential consequences of covert BW use. The attacks exhibited the range of covert delivery options available to bioterrorists, raised questions about the ease and source of acquisition, and exposed the widespread vulnerabilities of population centers to BWs. Recent discussions center on possible methods of protection and appropriate measures for emergency treatment and containment in the event of a large-scale BW attack.

Historical incidents of BW use in warfare have been rare but often dramatic. In the third century B.C., the Carthaginian leader Hannibal filled pots with poisonous snakes and hurled them onto enemy ships. In 1346, the Tartars catapulted corpses of bubonic-plague victims over the walls of enemy fortresses. British officers engaged in biological warfare in eighteenth-century North America by distributing blankets contaminated with the smallpox virus to Native Americans.

In the twentieth century, the sophistication of biological warfare was amplified with the emergence of state-sponsored BW programs. In 1940, residents in Chuhsien, China, reportedly contracted the bubonic plague after the Japanese dropped ceramic bombs containing plague-infected fleas along with rice to attract rodents, which were infected by the fleas and then spread the disease to humans. From 1932 until the end of World War II, Japan developed an extensive BW and CW program, which included experimentation with biological agents on human subjects in the infamous Units 731 and 100.[8]

Growing capabilities sparked recognition of the destructive potential of BWs and were accompanied by international efforts to control their proliferation and use. Nevertheless, the Cold War prompted the development of vast offensive BW programs in the United States and the Soviet Union.

The United States officially ended its offensive BW program in November 1969, when President Richard Nixon unilaterally and unconditionally renounced BWs and ordered the destruction of all U.S. BW stockpiles and the conversion of all production facilities to peaceful purposes.[9] At the time, the U.S. biological warfare capability was formidable. The weapon thought most likely to be used was the E133 cluster bomb, which held 536 biological bomblets, each containing 35 milliliters of liquid-suspension anthrax spores. A small explosive charge would, on impact, turn the slurry of spores into an aerosol to be inhaled by the target population. When the BW program was dismantled, the United States held in storage some 40,000 liters of antipersonnel biological warfare agents and some 5,000 kilograms of antiagriculture agents. All were destroyed in the early 1970s.[10]

The full extent of the Soviet BW program is still being uncovered. Official admission of the program's existence did not occur until 1992, nearly twenty years after the Soviet Union had signed a treaty pledging not to develop or stockpile BWs. The Soviet BW program had two main components: one under the

Ministries of Defense and Agriculture, and the other under an ostensibly civilian pharmaceutical development and production complex known as Biopreparat. During U.S. Senate testimony in 1998, Ken Alibek (a.k.a. Kanatjan Alibekov), the former first deputy director of Biopreparat, described a Soviet bioweapons program that employed a total of more than 60,000 people and included several large-scale production facilities that could be mobilized during a period of crisis or war.[11] At its peak, the Soviet BW program had the capacity to produce massive quantities of several biological agents, including 1,500 metric tons of tularemia bacteria; 4,500 metric tons of anthrax; 1,500 metric tons of bubonic plague bacteria; and 2,000 metric tons of glanders bacteria.[12]

In April 1992, Russian President Boris Yeltsin pledged to halt the further development of offensive BW capabilities. Subsequently, Russia, the United States, and the United Kingdom agreed to a trilateral process of information sharing and reciprocal site visits to verify the end of Russia's illicit BW program. By 1994, however, Russia had refused to extend the site visits to facilities under the auspices of the Ministry of Defense, causing the trilateral process to collapse and raising concerns about the extent of Russia's deactivation of the Soviet BW complex. Despite such concerns, the United States continues cooperative efforts to help secure the former Soviet Union's vast nuclear, chemical, and biological arsenals, and spent over $10 billion on these programs between 1991 and 2004. Of these funds, $300 million was spent directly on BW programs and $985 million was devoted to chemical demilitarization and destruction.[13] As a result, important progress has been achieved in securing collections of biological pathogens at former BW research institutes in the former Soviet Union. Nevertheless, security remains lax at some former Soviet facilities in Russia, Kazakhstan, Uzbekistan, and Georgia that house lethal biological agents, while the underpayment of former Russian BW scientists has increased the threat of diversion of biological warfare agents and technical expertise.[14]

The exact number and identity of all countries having biological warfare capabilities remain uncertain because of the dual-use nature of biotechnology and the ease with which BW development can be camouflaged. In March 2000, the director of the U.S. Central Intelligence Agency stated that "about a dozen states, including several hostile to Western democracies—Iran, Iraq, Libya, North Korea, and Syria—now either possess or are actively pursuing offensive biological and chemical capabilities for use against their perceived enemies . . . Some countries are pursuing an asymmetric warfare capability. . . . Other states are pursuing BW programs for counterinsurgency use and tactical applications."[15] In February 2001, the director of the U.S. Defense Intelligence Agency also told the U.S. Senate that "there are a dozen countries believed to have biological warfare programs."[16]

Although it is difficult to know with any certainty, the figure of a dozen national BW programs appears exaggerated, both because it blurs together biological and chemical programs, and because it counts countries where a BW program is only alleged or suspected. It now seems clear, for example, that neither Libya nor post-1991 Iraq possessed stockpiles of BWs, although many governments and outside experts believed that they did.

Iraq's clandestine program is the one about which the most in known, thanks to U.N. inspections after the 1991 war. The Soviet Union, Iraq, and apartheid South Africa are the only nations known to have produced and stockpiled BWs since the 1980s. Russia may also have done so, even after it claimed to have ended its program (see chapter 6). The most significant remaining suspected BW programs are in Israel and North Korea. Other countries often mentioned by governments or experts as having suspected BW programs include China, Egypt, Iran, and Syria. There is no independent confirmation of these claims, and all the governments concerned deny having any BW programs. The programs, if they exist, are most likely at the research and development stage. Israel may have produced BW agents but is not thought to have stockpiled weapons, and South Africa's BW program reportedly ended in 1992.

Chemical Weapons

CW are lethal, human-made substances that can be disseminated as gases, liquids, or solids (see table 4.2 at the end of the chapter). The U.S. Army defines a chemical agent as "a chemical which is intended for use in military operations to kill, seriously injure, or incapacitate man because of physiological effects."[17] The use of such chemical substances against soldiers or civilians constitutes chemical warfare.[18] CW agents are produced by mixing various chemical ingredients, called precursors, in specific ratios. Despite the abundance of modern-day toxic substances, only a small number of chemicals are considered suitable for chemical warfare. Throughout the twentieth century, approximately 70 different chemical substances were used and stockpiled as CW agents. Such substances must be highly toxic yet not too difficult to handle. CW agents must also be able to withstand prolonged storage without deterioration, and must also be resistant to atmospheric water vapor and oxygen in order to maintain stability and effectiveness during dispersal. Finally, to be effective, CW agents must be able to withstand the high levels of heat that accompany explosive dispersal.

Most substances used in CWs are liquids, although some agents are used in a gaseous form. They may be disseminated by an explosive munitions or a sprayer system. CW agents may also be allowed to evaporate spontaneously. CWs are generally categorized in four groups: blood gases, blistering agents (or vesicants), choking agents, and nerve agents:

- Blood gases, such as hydrogen cyanide, poison cells by blocking the transport of oxygen by red blood cells from the lungs to the tissues. The most serious effects of cyanide poisoning are caused by a lack of oxygen to the brain.
- Blistering agents, such as mustard gas, phosgene oxime, and lewisite, penetrate body tissues and mucous membranes and react with enzymes, proteins, and DNA to destroy cells, producing severe chemical burns and massive, fluid-filled blisters. The skin, eyes, and airways are especially vulnerable.
- Choking agents, such as chlorine and phosgene, damage the membrane of the lungs and ultimately cause suffocation from pulmonary edema. Choking agents must be inhaled to harm the body.

- Nerve agents, such as tabun, sarin, and V nerve agent (VX), disrupt the transmission of nerve impulses in human and animal nervous systems, resulting in death. All nerve agents are chemically categorized as organophosphorus compounds.[19] Such chemical warfare agents are highly toxic and can kill within several minutes after exposure to a lethal dose through skin contact or inhalation.

Effective CW delivery involves disseminating the agent as liquid droplets or an aerosol. When dispersed, the larger droplets fall to earth, causing skin or ground contamination, whereas the smaller, lighter droplets remain airborne as an aerosol that can be inhaled. A chemical cloud is highly susceptible to environmental conditions. Wind velocity necessarily dictates its direction and rate of spread. Rain and low temperatures may reduce agent effectiveness. Conversely, warm temperatures and high humidity can increase the toxic concentration of the chemical cloud.

A wide variety of possible delivery systems exists for CW agents. Typical military devices include "artillery shells, aerial bombs (including cluster bombs), spray tanks, missiles, rockets, grenades, and mines. All of these munitions types are intended to provide an appropriately sized aerosol that will remain suspended in the air close to the ground[,] where it will be readily inhaled."[20] Sophisticated chemical delivery systems were perfected in the 1960s with the development of "binary" munitions. Previously, CWs were of a "unitary" design. The CW agent was manufactured, poured into munitions, and then stored, ready for use. In a binary munition, in contrast, two precursor chemicals of lesser toxicity are reacted together to create the lethal agent only after the munition is fired. By delaying the synthesis of the toxic substance until after the weapon's launch from an aircraft or gun, binary technology ensures greater safety during transportation, handling, and storage of CWs. Crude methods of delivering CW agents are typically less efficient and reliable but can nevertheless be effective. Crop-dusting aircraft, pesticide foggers, and even simple aerosol spray cans offer potential dissemination methods for terrorists.

The use of CW agents in warfare can be traced back to the ancient Greeks, who mixed sulfur and pitch resin to engulf enemy troops in toxic fumes during the Trojan War. CWs have been used or stockpiled by various military forces throughout the twentieth century. The first major instance of chemical warfare occurred on April 23, 1915, when the German army used chlorine gas against Allied troops at Ypres, Belgium. Both the Allies and the Central Powers subsequently employed chemical agents such as phosgene and mustard on a massive scale during World War I. By the war's end, an estimated 124,000 metric tons of chemicals had been used on the battlefield by both sides. Mustard gas alone killed 91,000 and injured 1.2 million.[21] After World War I, a significant use of chemical warfare occurred in 1935–1936, when Fascist Italy employed mustard agent in bombs and aerosols during its invasion of Ethiopia. During World War II, the German CW program stockpiled 78,000 metric tons of agents, including 12,000 metric tons of tabun and 1,000 pounds of sarin, but fortunately did not use them.[22] Japan produced 8,000 metric tons of chemical agents.[23]

Immense quantities of CWs were also produced by both the United States and the Soviet Union throughout World War II and the Cold War. The United States stockpiled an estimated 30,000 metric tons of CW agents. Destruction of U.S. CWs began in 1985 and is still in progress at several CW depots across the nation.

The Soviet Union officially announced its possession of a CW stockpile in 1987. This announcement was followed by the deactivation of its CW production program. In 1989, the United States and the Soviet Union signed the Wyoming Memorandum of Understanding, which entailed an exchange of data about their respective CW stockpiles and production complexes. Official Russian declarations suggest that the country now has 40,000 metric tons of CWs stored at seven sites, concentrated in central Russia and the Urals. (See chapter 6.)

Most major states with known CW stockpiles have pledged to destroy them under the Chemical Weapons Convention (see below).[24] Six member countries have declared the possession of CW stockpiles totaling approximately 70,000 metric tons of agents: Albania, India, Libya, Russia, South Korea, and the United States. Twelve nations have also declared existing or former CW production facilities (CWPFs): Bosnia and Herzegovina, China, France, India, Iran, Japan, Libya, Russia, South Korea, the United Kingdom, the United States and Yugoslavia. Approximately half the 64 declared CWPFs have been destroyed thus far.[25]

The most significant remaining national CW programs are those of Egypt, Israel, North Korea, and Syria, and perhaps China and Iran. Myanmar, Saudi Arabia, South Korea, Taiwan, and Vietnam are also sometimes listed as nations with active CW programs,[26] although these claims are difficult to verify.

Currently, no nonstate actor or substate group is known to possess CWs. Aum Shinrikyo, however, did successfully produce significant amounts of sarin nerve agent. In 1994, the cult released sarin in a residential area of Masumoto, Japan, and it carried out a second attack on the Tokyo subway in March 1995, killing twelve people and injuring about a thousand. These incidents elevated concern over the ability of terrorists to acquire a CW capability.

The September 11, 2001, terrorist attacks raised a new worry: terrorists may not have to produce chemical agents in order to use chemicals to cause mass casualties. An accident or sabotage at the Union Carbide pesticide plant in Bhopal, India, in December 1984 released a cloud of chlorine gas that killed at least 5,000 people immediately and injured tens of thousands more. Intentional destruction or sabotage at chemical plants or involving trucks or trains transporting hazardous chemicals could turn industrial facilities into weapons of chemical terrorism.

Efforts to Control Biological and Chemical Weapons

Global efforts to contain the spread of CWs and BWs center on the Biological and Toxin Weapons Convention (BWC) and the Chemical Weapons Convention (CWC). Initial multilateral efforts to prohibit the use of chemical and biological agents on the battlefield can be traced to the end of the nineteenth century. In 1899, the First Hague Convention on the Laws and Customs of War included a declaration banning "the use of projectiles, the sole object of which is the diffusion of asphyxiating or deleterious gases."

The extensive use of CWs during World War I in violation of the Hague gas projectile declaration led to another attempt by states to establish an international norm against the use of weapons of mass destruction: the 1925 Geneva Protocol. Although this treaty prohibited the use in war of both poison gases and bacteriological weapons, its impact remained limited because it did not restrict the ability of states to acquire or store CWs and BWs, did not have verification or enforcement provisions, and because many states reserved the right to respond in kind to a chemical or biological attack. The U.S. Senate also failed to ratify the Geneva Protocol until January 1975, fifty years after it was concluded.

The BWC was opened for signature in April 1972 and entered into force on March 26, 1975. It prohibits the development, production, stockpiling, acquisition, and transfer of biological agents or toxins in types or "quantities that have no justification for prophylactic, protective, and other peaceful purposes."[27] The BWC also specifically bans "weapons, equipment or means of delivery designed to use such agents or toxins for hostile purposes or in armed conflict."[28] The United States, the United Kingdom, and Russia are the three depositary governments for the BWC. As of Spring 2005, 153 states were members of the treaty. Review conferences of the BWC have taken place about every five years since the treaty entered into force, namely in 1980, 1986, 1991, 1996, and 2001–2002.[29]

The BWC was the first international treaty to ban an entire class of weapons. However, the treaty lacked effective verification and enforcement measures to ensure compliance. Violations of the BWC by the former Soviet Union, persistent allegations regarding Iraq's BW activities, and a doubling of the number of states suspected of pursuing a BW capability since 1975[30] have all raised questions about the BWC's effectiveness. Recognizing these weaknesses, member states established an Ad Hoc Group in 1994 to draft legally binding verification measures for the convention. The Ad Hoc Group was authorized to negotiate in four areas: "Definitions of terms and objective criteria; incorporation of existing and further enhanced confidence-building and transparency measures, as appropriate, into the regime; a system of measures to promote compliance with the Convention; and specific measures designed to ensure the effective and full implementation of Article X."[31]

Efforts by the Ad Hoc Group to negotiate a legally binding protocol for verification ended abruptly in July 2001, when the United States rejected the draft treaty and withdrew from the talks.[32] The United States claimed that the BWC protocol would have jeopardized the security of U.S. biotechnical and pharmaceutical secrets without effectively detecting treaty violations. The terrorist attacks in New York and Washington on September 11, 2001, and the subsequent wave of anthrax attacks gave rise to a renewed U.S. interest in strengthening the BWC, but without resuming multilateral negotiations. To that end, the George W. Bush administration proposed a series of measures that individual countries could adopt and implement to reduce the risk of bioterrorism, including the criminalization of activities prohibited by the BWC, the adoption of regulations to restrict access to dangerous pathogens and toxins, and the strengthening of existing U.N. procedures for investigating suspicious disease outbreaks or allegations of BW use.

Soon after the conclusion of the BWC in 1972, efforts began to negotiate a ban on CWs. These negotiations stalled, however, over compliance and verification issues. Progress resumed in 1986 when the Soviet Union accepted provisions for systematic inspections at CW storage and production facilities, the destruction of production facilities, and declarations and routine inspections at commercial industry sites. A year later, the USSR also agreed to mandatory short-notice challenge inspections, insisting that all facilities and locations be subject to this procedure. The final catalyst for completion of the CWC was the use of CWs by both sides during the Iran-Iraq War (1980–1988), which demonstrated the absence of international means to prevent the acquisition and use of CWs in conflict.

The CWC entered into force on April 29, 1997. This treaty prohibits the development, production, acquisition, stockpiling, retention, or use of CWs, as well as the "transfer, directly or indirectly, [of] chemical weapons to anyone."[33] State parties to the CWC cannot conduct military preparations for the use of CWs, nor can they assist other states in any treaty-banned activity. The CWC also requires members to destroy all CW stockpiles and production facilities under its jurisdiction or control, as well as any CWs abandoned on the territory of another state party. Full elimination of CWs and former production facilities is expected within ten years of the convention's entry into force, with a provision for a one-time, five-year extension in exceptional cases. As of Spring 2005, 168 countries had signed and ratified the CWC.[34] The Organization for the Prohibition of Chemical Weapons (OPCW), headquartered in The Hague, oversees the implementation of the treaty.

The CWC includes an extensive verification regime that subjects all declared CW and weapon production facilities to systematic inspections. The convention categorizes chemicals into three "schedules" depending on their applicability for CWs and for commercial purposes. Varying levels of control are then applied to the listed chemicals and their production facilities. Facilities producing chemicals listed in any of the three schedules in quantities in excess of specified threshold amounts must be declared and are subject to inspection. The verification provisions of the treaty regulate both military and civilian chemical facilities that are active in the production, processing, and consumption of chemicals relevant to the convention. Verification involves a combination of declaration and reporting requirements, routine on-site inspections of declared sites, and short-notice challenge inspections in cases of alleged non-compliance. A member state may request the OPCW international inspectorate to conduct a challenge inspection of any suspect facility, declared or undeclared. The CWC also includes provisions for assistance in the event a member state is attacked or threatened with CWs, and for promoting trade in chemicals and related production equipment among member states for peaceful purposes.

The Australia Group is an informal association of 39 countries plus the European Commission that seeks to prevent the proliferation of CWs and BWs. Member nations work on the basis of consensus to limit the spread of CWs and BWs by "harmonizing" their national export controls on CW precursors, BW pathogens, and CW-BW dual-use equipment. Member states also share intelligence on CW-BW proliferation.[35]

The Australia Group was established in 1985 after the extensive use of CWs in the Iran-Iraq War. The group focused initially on regulating the export of eight dual-use chemical precursors, but by 1991 the "warning list" of chemicals subject to control had been expanded to 54 precursors. The group also began restricting BW-related exports in 1991. Member states share the group's core lists with chemical industries and scientific communities to promote awareness of CW and BW proliferation risks. The fact that many chemicals used in the production of CWs also have legal industrial applications has forced Australia Group members to strike a balance between chemical proliferation concerns and legitimate trade.

NOTES

1. "Biological Weapons in the Former Soviet Union: An Interview with Kenneth Alibek," conducted by Jonathan B. Tucker, *Nonproliferation Review*, Spring–Summer 1999, p. 1.
2. Richard A. Falkenrath, Robert D. Newman, and Bradley A. Thayer, *America's Achilles Heel* (Cambridge, Mass.: MIT Press, 1998), p. 15.
3. U.S. Department of the Army, *NATO Handbook on the Medical Aspects of NBC Defensive Operations* (Washington, D.C.: U.S. Department of the Army, 1966), HQ, DA; AmedP-6(B), part 2, p. 1-1.
4. U.S. Army Medical Research Institute of Infectious Diseases, *Medical Management of Biological Casualties Handbook*, 4th ed. (Maryland: Fort Detrick, Md.: U.S. Army, 2001), p. 13.
5. Organization for the Prohibition of Chemical Weapons, "FOA Briefing Book on Chemical Weapons," available at www.opcw.org/chemhaz/nerve.htm.
6. Falkenrath, Newman, and Thayer, *America's Achilles Heel.*
7. Milton Leitenberg, "Biological Weapons Arms Control," PRAC Paper 16, Center for International and Security Studies, May 1996.
8. Edward Eitzen and Ernest Takafuji, "Historical Overview of Biological Warfare," in *Medical Aspects of Chemical and Biological Warfare, Part I. The Textbook of Military Medicine* (Washington, D.C.: Borden Institute, Office of the Surgeon General, 1997), p. 416–419.
9. Jonathan B. Tucker, "A Farewell to Germs: The U.S. Renunciation of Biological and Toxin Warfare, 1969–70," *International Security*, vol. 27, no. 1, Summer 2002, pp. 107–148.
10. For more information on the U.S. biological weapons program, see Edward Regis, *The Biology of Doom: The History of America's Secret Germ Warfare Project* (New York: Henry Holt and Company, 1999).
11. Joseph Cirincione, ed., *Repairing the Regime: Preventing the Spread of Weapons of Mass Destruction* (New York: Routledge, 2000), pp. 7, 14. See also Kenneth Alibek, "Terrorist and Intelligence Operations: Potential Impact on the U.S. Economy," Statement before the Joint Economic Committee, U.S. Congress, May 20, 1998.
12. Judith Miller, Stephen Engelberg, and William Broad, *Germs: Biological Weapons and America's Secret War* (New York: Simon and Schuster, 2001), p. 254.
13. Nuclear Threat Initiative, "Controlling Nuclear Warheads & Materials Interactive Threat Reduction Budget Database," available at www.nti.org/e_research/cnwm/overview/cnwm_home.asp.
14. "Officials Wary about Soviet Arsenal," Associated Press, October 30, 2001.

15. George Tenet, director of central intelligence, statement to the Senate Foreign Relations Committee, "Worldwide Threat in 2000: Global Realities of Our National Security," March 21, 2000; available at www.cia.gov/cia/public_affairs/speeches/archives/2000/dci_speech_032100.html.
16. V. A. Thomas Wilson, "Global Threat and Challenges through 2015," statement for the record, Senate Select Committee on Intelligence, U.S. Congress, February 7, 2001; available at www.ceip.org/files/projects/npp/resources/dia020701.htm.
17. Excluded from consideration are riot control agents, chemical herbicides, and smoke and flame materials. U.S. Department of the Army, *NATO Handbook on the Medical Aspects of NBC Defensive Operations*, AmedP-6, Part 3; 1-1 Field Manual 8-9.
18. Ibid.
19. Organization for the Prohibition of Chemical Weapons, "FOA Briefing Book on Chemical Weapons."
20. Frederick Sidell, William Patrick, and Thomas Dashiell, *Jane's Chem-Bio Handbook* (Alexandria, Va.: Jane's Information Group, 2000), p. 147.
21. Gert Harigel, "Chemical and Biological Weapons: Use in Warfare, Impact on Society and Environment," Carnegie Endowment for International Peace; available at www.ceip.org/files/_publications/Harigelreport.asp.
22. Jeffrey Smart, "History of Chemical and Biological Warfare: An American Perspective," in *Medical Aspects of Chemical and Biological Warfare*, p. 36.
23. Ibid. p. 37.
24. Organization for the Prohibition of Chemical Weapons, "Chemical Demilitarization," available at www.opcw.org/html/db/chemdemil_frameset.html.
25. Organization for the Prohibition of Chemical Weapons. "Verification Activities, Chemical Demilitarization," available at www.opcw.org/html/db/chemdemil_frameset.html.
26. Office of Technology Assessment, *Proliferation of Weapons of Mass Destruction: Assessing the Risks* (Washington, D.C.: U.S. Government Printing Office, 1993). See also E. J. Hogendoorn, "A Chemical Weapons Atlas," *Bulletin of the Atomic Scientists*, September/October 1997, pp. 35–39.
27. Text of the Biological Weapons Convention, U.N. Conference on Disarmament; available at www.unog.ch/disarm/distreat/bac_72.htm.
28. Ibid.
29. "Status of Multilateral Arms Regulation and Disarmament Agreements, BWC (in Chronological Order by Deposit)," available at http://disarmament.un.org:8080/TreatyStatus.nsf.
30. Cirincione, *Repairing the Regime*.
31. United Nations, "Brief Background on the Biological Weapons Convention," available at www.un.org/Depts/dda/WMD/page6html.
32. "Envoy Tries to Save Pact on Bio-War," *International Herald Tribune*, August 1, 2001. Text of Chemical Weapons Convention, available at www.opcw.nl/cwc/cwc-eng.htm.
33. Text of Chemical Weapons Convention, available at www.opcw.nl/cwc/cwc-eng.htm.
34. "States Parties to the Chemical Weapons Convention as of 19 November 2004," available at www.opcw.org/html/db/members_frameset.html.
35. Daryl Kimball and Celeste Powell, "The Australia Group at a Glance," Arms Control Association Fact Sheet, September 2004, available at www.armscontrol.org/factsheets/australiagroup.asp; see also www.australiagroup.net.

Table 4.1. **Examples of Biological Warfare Agents**

Bacterial Agents						
BW Agent *(causative organism)*	**Lethality**	**Incubation Period (days)**	**Symptoms/ Clinical Manifestations[1]**	**Prophylaxis/Treatment**	**Direct Person-to-Person Aerosol Transmission?**	**Infective Dose**
Anthrax *(Bacillus anthracis)*	High	1–6	Fever, malaise, and fatigue which may be followed by an improvement in symptoms for 2–3 days. Alternatively, initial symptoms may progress directly to severe respiratory distress; shock; pneumonia. Death normally follows within 24–36 hours of initiation of symptoms. >90% fatality if untreated.	Vaccine is available. Treatable with high dose of antibiotics administered before onset of symptoms.	No	8,000–50,000 spores

(table continues on the following page)

Table 4.1. **Examples of Biological Warfare Agents** (continued)

BW Agent *(causative organism)*	Lethality	Incubation Period (days)	Symptoms/Clinical Manifestations[1]	Prophylaxis/Treatment	Direct Person-to Person Aerosol Transmission	Infective Dose
Brucellosis *(Brucella suis)*	Low, incapacitating	5–60	Fever, chills, headache, nausea, weight loss, malaise. Symptoms may last for weeks or months. Fatalities in less than 5% of untreated patients.	No vaccine. Treatable with antibiotics.	No	10–100 organisms
Cholera *(Vibrio cholerae)*	Moderate	1–5	Severe gastroenteritis, diarrhea, vomiting, dehydration. >50% fatality if untreated.	No vaccine. Treatable with antibiotics.	No	10–500 organisms
Glanders *(Burkholderia mallei)*	High	3–5	Fever, sweats, muscle pain, headache, chest pain, and generalized papular/pustular eruptions. >50% fatality rate without treatment. Death in 7–10 days.	No vaccine.	Low	Assumed low

Tularemia *(Francisella tularensis)* (rabbit fever or deer-fly fever)	Moderate	2–10	Fever, exhaustion, headache, muscle ache and weight loss. 30–60% fatality if untreated.	Vaccine is available. Treatable with antibiotics.	No	10–50 organisms
Typhoid fever *(Salmonella typhi)*	Low, incapacitating	7–14	Fever, headache, rose-colored spots on skin, constipation, fatigue. 10–20% fatality if untreated.	Vaccine is available. Treatable with antibiotics.	No	10,000,000 organisms
Plague (Pneumonic) *(Yersinia pestis)*	High	2–3	Pneumonia with malaise, high fever, chills, headache, muscle pain, and productive cough with bloody sputum. Progresses rapidly, resulting in shortness of breath, stridor, bluish discoloration of skin and mucous membranes, and circulatory failure. Death in 1–6 days. 100% fatality if untreated.	Vaccine is available. Treatable if antibiotics are administered within 12–24 hours of onset of symptoms.	Yes, highly infectious	100–500 organisms

(table continues on the following page)

Table 4.1. **Examples of Biological Warfare Agents** (continued)

BW Agent (causative organism)	Lethality	Incubation Period (days)	Symptoms/Clinical Manifestations[1]	Prophylaxis/Treatment	Direct Person-to Person Aerosol Transmission?	Infective Dose
Viral Agents						
Smallpox (*Variola major*)	High to moderate	12, on average	Initial symptoms include fever, malaise, vomiting, headache, and backache. Rash and lesions develop in 2–3 days on face, hands, and forearms, followed by the lower extremities and then centrally. 20–40% fatality in unvaccinated individuals.	Vaccine is available.	Yes	10–100 organisms
Venezuelan equine encephalitis (VEE)	Low, incapacitating	2–6	Initial symptoms include general malaise, severe headache, and fever. Nausea, vomiting, cough, and diarrhea may follow. Full recovery usually occurs within 1–2 weeks. Approximately 4% fatality.	Vaccine is available.	No	10–100 organisms

Viral hemorrhagic fevers (RNA viruses from several families, incl. : *Filiviridae* –Ebola –Marburg *Arenaviridae* –Lassa –Junin –Machupo *Flaviviridae* –Yellow Fever	High	4–21	Fever, muscle aches, and exhaustion, vomiting, diarrhea. Can be complicated by easy bleeding, hypotension, flushing of the face and chest, and edema.	No vaccine[2]	Unclear[3]	1–10 organisms
Rickettsial Agents						
Q Fever *(Coxiella burnetti)*	Low, incapacitating	14–21	Fever, chills, headache, excessive sweating, malaise, fatigue, loss of appetite, nausea, muscle pain, and weight loss. Approximately 1% fatality if untreated.	Vaccine is available. Treatable with antibiotics.	No	1–10 organisms

(table continues on the following page)

Table 4.1. **Examples of Biological Warfare Agents** (continued)

BW Agent *(causative organism)*	Lethality	Incubation Period (days)	Symptoms/Clinical Manifestations[1]	Prophylaxis/Treatment	Direct Person-to Person Aerosol Transmission?	Infective Dose
Epidemic typhus/ Endemic typhus *(Rickettsia typhi/ Rickettsia prowazekii)*	High	6–16	Fever, headache, weakness, pain and delirium. 30% fatality rate if untreated. 10–40% fatality if untreated.	No vaccine	No	
Toxins						
Saxitoxin (paralytic shellfish poisoning)	High	Minutes to hours	Dizziness, numbness, paralysis of respiratory system, followed by death.	No vaccine	No	2–9 micrograms per kilogram of body weight if ingested.
Botulinum toxin *(Clostridium botulinum)*	High	1–3	Ptosis, generalized weakness, dizziness, dry mouth, blurred vision, and difficulty in speaking and swallowing. Interruption of neurotransmission, progression to muscle paralysis and respiratory failure. 65% fatality if untreated.	Vaccine is available. Treatable with antibiotics if administered early.	No	.001 μg/kg of body weight, if inhaled. 1 μg/kg if ingested.

Ricin *(Ricinus communis)* (castor beans)	High	18–24 hours	Weakness, fever, cough, and pulmonary edema. Progression to severe respiratory distress, hemorrhage and death within 36–72 hours.	No vaccine	No	3 µg/kg of body weight, if ingested. (Two castor beans have been fatal to humans.)
Trichothecene (T–2) mcotoxins *(Fusarium tricinetum)*	High to moderate	1–4 hours	Dizziness, nausea, vomiting, blisters, eye pain, necrosis of tissues, hemorrhage, followed by death.	No vaccine	No	25-50 µg/kg of body weight if inhaled. 2.4–8 µg/kg through dermal contact.
Staphylococcal enterotoxin B *(Staphylococcus aureus)*	Low, incapacitating	1–6 hours	Sudden onset of fever, chills, headache, muscle pain, non-productive cough, diarrhea, vomiting, and stomach pain. Fever may last for 2–5 days. Cough may persist for 4 weeks. < 2% fatality rate.	No vaccine	No	.03 µg/kg per person

(table continues on the following page)

Table 4.1. **Examples of Biological Warfare Agents** (continued)

Sources

Centers for Disease Control and Prevention, "Bioterrorism Agents/Diseases," November 19, 2004; available at www.bt.cdc.gov/agent/agentlist.asp. Department of the Army, *Textbook of Military Medicine: Medical Aspects of Chemical and Biological Warfare* (Washington, D.C.: Borden Institute, Office of the Surgeon General, 1997); available at www.vnh.org/MedAspChemBioWar. Departments of the Army, Navy and Air Force, "Annex C: Potential Biological Agents Operational Data Charts," *NATO Handbook on Medical Aspects of NBC Defensive Operations*, AmedP-6(B), part 2, Biological, Washington, D.C., 1996; available at www.fas.org/nuke/guide/usa/doctrine/dod/fm8-9/2toc.htm. Henry L. Stimson Center, "Biological Weapons Agents," available at www.stimson.org/cbw/?sn=cb2001112953. James Chin, ed., *Control of Communicable Diseases Manual*, 17th ed. (Washington, D.C.: American Public Health Association, 2000. Mitretek Systems, "Background on Biological Warfare," May 5, 2004, available at www.mitretek.org/home.nsf/HomelandSecurity/BackgroundBioWar. Office of the Secretary of Defense. "Anthrax Vaccine Immunization Program," available at www.anthrax.osd.mil/Flash_interface/default.html. Frederick R. Sidell, William C. Patrick, and Thomas R. Dashiell. *Jane's Chem-Bio Handbook* (Alexandria, Va.: Jane's Information Group, 1998). U.S. Army Medical Research Institute of Infectious Diseases, *Medical Management of Biological Casualties Handbook*, 4th ed., February 2001; available at www.nbc-med.org/SiteContent/HomePage/WhatsNew/MedManual/Feb01/handbook.htm.

Notes

1. Symptoms and clinical manifestations apply to the inhalation of the causative organism.
2. Licensed vaccine is available for yellow fever. A vaccine for Argentine hemorrhagic fever is available as an Investigational New Drug. This vaccine may provide cross protection against Bolivian hemorrhagic fever.
3. It is unclear how easily filoviruses can be transmitted from human to human. Transmission clearly occurs by direct contact with infected blood, secretions, organs, or semen. Research suggests that the transmission of viruses such as Marburg and Ebola by inhalation is possible, yet consistent evidence has not yet been found.

Table 4.2. **Examples of Chemical Warfare Agents**

Nerve Agents	
NAME AND AGENT IDENTIFICATION	Tabun (GA) Sarin (GB) Soman (GD) Cyclohexyl sarin (GF) V nerve agent (VX)
MECHANISM OF ACTION	These agents can be absorbed through any body surface: eyes, skin, and respiratory tract. The agents effectively prevent the transmission of nerve signals by inhibiting the enzyme cholinesterase. This enzyme normally breaks down acetylcholine, the neurotransmitter at cholinergic receptor sites. Cholinergic receptor sites are found at smooth and skeletal muscles, the central nervous system, and most exocrine glands. Accumulation of acetylcholine leads to continued stimulation and clinical symptoms such as muscle paralysis.
RATE OF ACTION	*Vapor:* Within seconds to several minutes after exposure *Liquid:* Within minutes to an hour after exposure. Commonly, there is an asymptomatic period of 1–30 minutes, which is followed by a sudden onset of symptoms.
EFFECTIVE DOSE	*Skin contact:* Tabun (GA), 1,000 mg; Sarin (GB), 1,700 mg; Soman (GD), 50 mg; Cyclohexyl sarin (GF), 30 mg; VX, 10 mg *Inhalation:* (2–10 minutes' exposure): Tabun (GA), 200 mg; Sarin (GB), 70–100 mg; Soman (GD), 70 mg; Cyclohexyl sarin (GF), 75–120 mg; VX, 30 m
SYMPTOMS	*Vapor:* SMALL EXPOSURE: contraction of pupils, dim vision, headache, mild difficulty breathing LARGE EXPOSURE: sudden loss of consciousness, convulsions, muscular twitching, weakness or paralysis, copious secretions, respiratory failure *Liquid on skin:* SMALL TO MODERATE EXPOSURE: localized sweating, muscle twitching at site of exposure, vomiting, feeling of weakness LARGE EXPOSURE: sudden loss of consciousness, convulsions, muscle twitching, weakness or paralysis, copious secretions, respiratory failure

(table continues on the following page)

Table 4.2. **Examples of Chemical Warfare Agents** (continued)

Vesicants	
NAME AND AGENT IDENTIFICATION	Mustard (H, HD) Lewisite (L) Phosgene oxime (CX)
MECHANISM OF ACTION	Following absorption, the structure of mustard changes. In this form, it is extremely reactive to water and binds with intra- and extracellular enzymes and proteins. Mustard can destroy a large number of cellular substances, thereby influencing numerous processes in living tissue. Lewisite causes an increase in capillary permeability. The exact mechanisms of mustard, lewisite, and phosgene oxime are not known. Phosgene oxime is not a true vesicant; it causes extensive tissue damage and has therefore been called a corrosive agent.
RATE OF ACTION	*Mustard:* Binds irreversibly to tissue within several minutes after contact. Clinical signs and symptoms may appear as early as 2 hours after a high-dose exposure or extend to 24 hours after a low-dose vapor exposure. Exposure does not cause immediate pain. *Lewisite:* Immediate pain or irritation. Lesions develop within hours. *Phosgene oxime:* Immediate burning and irritation.
EFFECTIVE DOSE	*Skin contact:* Mustard (H, HD), 100 mg/kg; Lewisite (L), 2.8 g Inhalation (2–10 minutes exposure): Mustard (H, HD), 1,500 mg; Lewisite (L), 1,200–1,500 mg
SYMPTOMS	*Mustard:* Skin, eyes, and airways most commonly affected. Appearance of redness and blisters on skin, irritation, conjunctivitis and corneal opacity and damage in the eyes, irritation of nares, sinus and pharynx, and increasingly severe productive cough if the lower airways are affected. *Lewisite:* Skin and mucous membranes are immediately affected after contact. Redness and blister formation occur more rapidly than following exposure to mustard. Eye exposure causes pain and twitching of the eyelid. Edema of the conjunctiva and lids follow, and eyes may be swollen shut within an hour. Contact with airways leads to similar signs and symptoms to mustard. Increased permeability of capillaries resulting in low intravascular volume and shock. May lead to hepatic or renal necrosis with vomiting and diarrhea.

	Phosgene oxime: Redness of skin and appearance of elongated, wheal-like lesions on skin. Damage to eyes similar to that caused by lewisite. Causes pulmonary edema. No other chemical agent produces such immediate onset of symptoms followed by rapid tissue necrosis.
Blood Gases	
NAME AND AGENT IDENTIFICATION	Hydrocyanic acid (AC) Cyanogen chloride (CK)
MECHANISM OF ACTION	Blood gases allow red blood cells to acquire oxygen, but prevent the transfer of this oxygen to other cells. Cyanide ion combines with iron in a component of the mitochondrial cytochrome oxidase complex. This complex is necessary for cellular respiration, an energy-providing process using oxygen. The heart and brain rapidly decay from lack of oxygen and a buildup of carbon dioxide.
RATE OF ACTION	Death occurs 6–8 minutes after inhalation.
EFFECTIVE DOSE	*Skin contact:* Hydrocyanic acid (AC), 1.1 mg/kg; Cyanogen chloride (CK), 200 mg/kg *Inhalation* (2–10 minutes exposure): Hydrocyanic acid (AC), 2,500–5000 mg; Cyanogen chloride (CK), 11,000 mg
SYMPTOMS	Central nervous system and heart are most susceptible to cyanide. Fifteen seconds after inhalation of a highly concentrated vapor, there is a period of rapid breathing that is followed in 15–30 seconds by convulsions. Respiratory activity stops 2–3 minutes later, followed by cessation of cardiac activity. Cyanogen chloride also irritates the eyes, nose, and airways.
Pulmonary Agents	
NAME AND AGENT IDENTIFICATION	Chlorine (Cl) Phosgene (CG)
MECHANISM OF ACTION	Pulmonary agents attack lung tissue. Phosgene irritates the alveoli in the lungs and results in the constant secretion of fluids into the lungs. Death results from a lack of oxygen when the lungs are filled with fluid.

(table continues on the following page)

Table 4.2. **Examples of Chemical Warfare Agents** (continued)

RATE OF ACTION	*Chlorine:* Immediate cough and choking sensation. Signs of pulmonary edema may appear within 30 minutes to 4 hours. *Phosgene:* Cough and chest discomfort may appear within 30 minutes of exposure. Pulmonary edema within 2–6 hours. Occasionally, an asymptomatic period can last up to 24 hours.
EFFECTIVE DOSE	*Inhalation* (2–10 minutes exposure): Chlorine (Cl), 6,651 ppm/min; Phosgene (CG), 3,200 mg
SYMPTOMS	Corrosion of the eyes, skin, and respiratory tract. Burning sensation in the lungs, choking, coughing, headache, difficulty breathing, nausea, vomiting, sore throat, skin burns, and blurred vision. Accumulation of fluid in lungs leads to fatal choking and pulmonary edema.

Sources

Centers for Disease Control and Prevention. "Chemical Agents Listing and Information," available at www.bt.cdc.gov/Agent/AgentlistChem.asp. Department of the Army, *Textbook of Military Medicine: Medical Aspects of Chemical and Biological Warfare* (Washington, D.C.: Borden Institute, Office of the Surgeon General, 1997); available at http://ccc.apgea.army.mil/reference_materials/textbook/HTML_Restricted/index_2.htm. Henry L. Stimson Center, "Characteristics of Chemical Warfare Agents," available at www.stimson.org/cbw/?sn=CB2001121892. Organization for the Prohibition of Chemical Weapons, "An Overview of Chemicals Defined as Chemical Weapons," available at www.opcw.org/resp/html/cwagents.html.

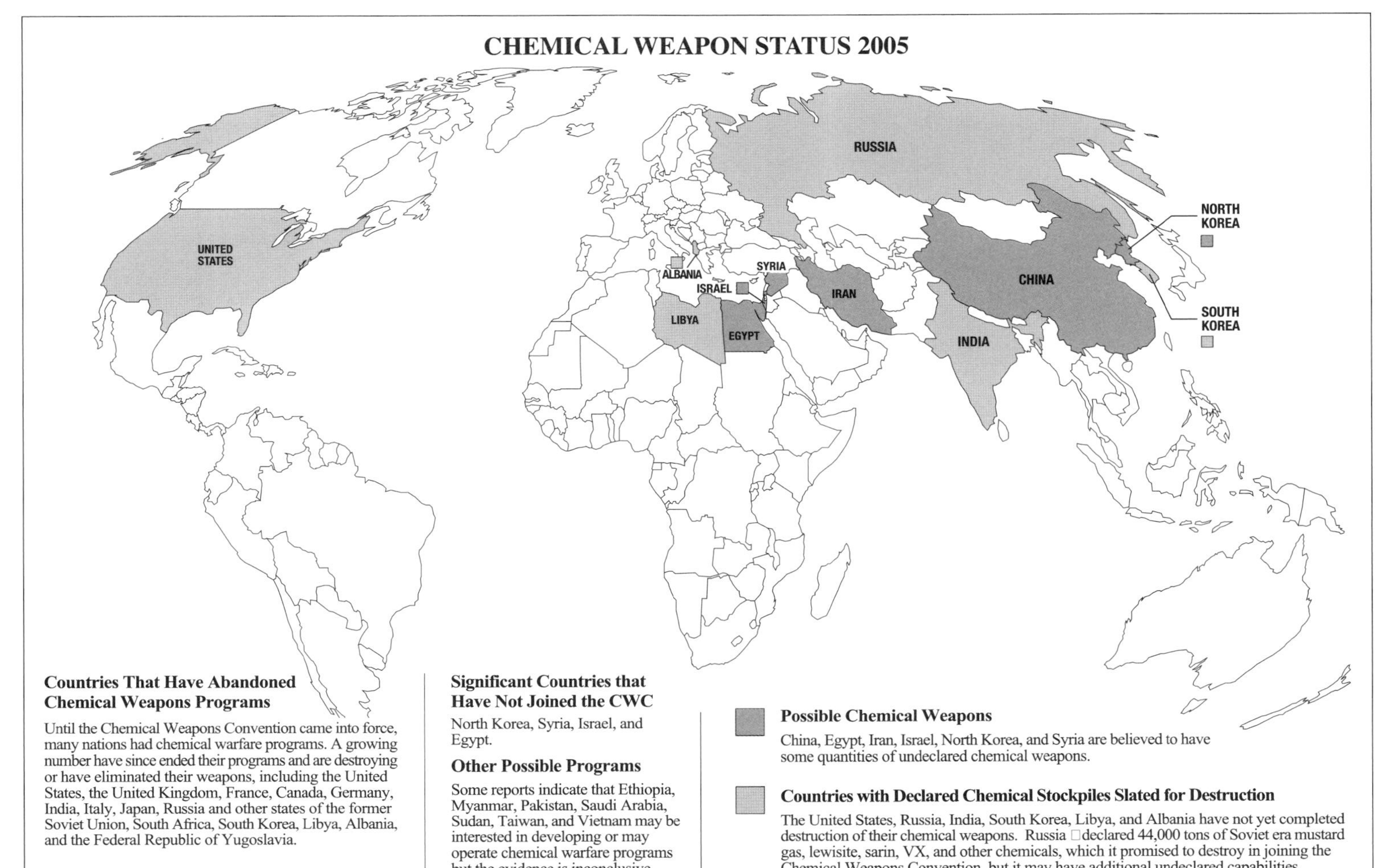
CHEMICAL WEAPON STATUS 2005
RUSSIA
UNITED STATES
NORTH KOREA
SOUTH KOREA
CHINA
INDIA
IRAN
SYRIA
ISRAEL
ALBANIA
LIBYA
EGYPT
Countries That Have Abandoned Chemical Weapons Programs
Until the Chemical Weapons Convention came into force, many nations had chemical warfare programs. A growing number have since ended their programs and are destroying or have eliminated their weapons, including the United States, the United Kingdom, France, Canada, Germany, India, Italy, Japan, Russia and other states of the former Soviet Union, South Africa, South Korea, Libya, Albania, and the Federal Republic of Yugoslavia.
Significant Countries that Have Not Joined the CWC
North Korea, Syria, Israel, and Egypt.
Other Possible Programs
Some reports indicate that Ethiopia, Myanmar, Pakistan, Saudi Arabia, Sudan, Taiwan, and Vietnam may be interested in developing or may operate chemical warfare programs but the evidence is inconclusive.
Possible Chemical Weapons
China, Egypt, Iran, Israel, North Korea, and Syria are believed to have some quantities of undeclared chemical weapons.
Countries with Declared Chemical Stockpiles Slated for Destruction
The United States, Russia, India, South Korea, Libya, and Albania have not yet completed destruction of their chemical weapons. Russia □declared 44,000 tons of Soviet era mustard gas, lewisite, sarin, VX, and other chemicals, which it promised to destroy in joining the Chemical Weapons Convention, but it may have additional undeclared capabilities.

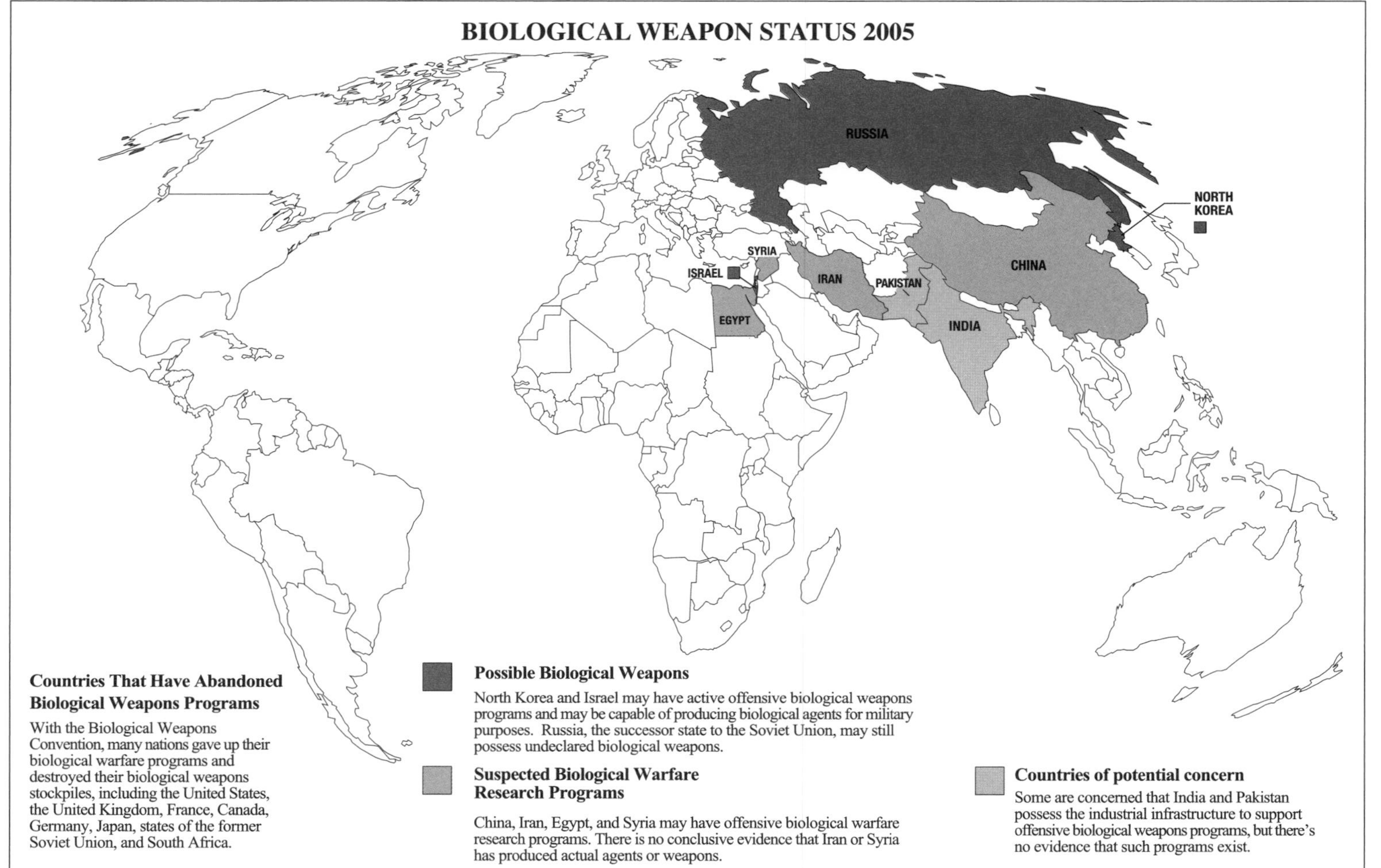
BIOLOGICAL WEAPON STATUS 2005
RUSSIA
NORTH KOREA
CHINA
SYRIA
ISRAEL
IRAN
PAKISTAN
EGYPT
INDIA
Countries That Have Abandoned Biological Weapons Programs
With the Biological Weapons Convention, many nations gave up their biological warfare programs and destroyed their biological weapons stockpiles, including the United States, the United Kingdom, France, Canada, Germany, Japan, states of the former Soviet Union, and South Africa.
Possible Biological Weapons
North Korea and Israel may have active offensive biological weapons programs and may be capable of producing biological agents for military purposes. Russia, the successor state to the Soviet Union, may still possess undeclared biological weapons.
Suspected Biological Warfare Research Programs
China, Iran, Egypt, and Syria may have offensive biological warfare research programs. There is no conclusive evidence that Iran or Syria has produced actual agents or weapons.
Countries of potential concern
Some are concerned that India and Pakistan possess the industrial infrastructure to support offensive biological weapons programs, but there's no evidence that such programs exist.

CHAPTER 5

Missile Proliferation

One of the most contentious proliferation debates of the past ten years has been about assessing the ballistic missile threat and deploying antimissile systems to defeat these weapons. When the end of the Cold War largely eliminated the likelihood (if not the capability) of a global thermonuclear war, policy makers turned their attention to the very real danger that nuclear, biological, or chemical weapons could be used in smaller, but still horrifically deadly, numbers. Ballistic missiles garnered the lion's share of attention, though they constitute only one—and perhaps the most difficult—delivery method for those weapons.

The Proliferation Threat

Many experts and officials view ballistic missiles as a particularly menacing and rapidly proliferating technology. Several threat assessments and reports followed the lead of the 1998 study by the Commission to Assess the Ballistic Missile Threat to the United States (known as the Rumsfeld Commission for its chair, Donald Rumsfeld):

> With the external help now readily available, a nation with a well-developed, Scud-based ballistic missile infrastructure would be able to achieve first flight of a long range missile, up to and including intercontinental ballistic missile (ICBM) range (greater than 5,500 kilometers), within about five years of deciding to do so. During several of those years the U.S. might not be aware that such a decision had been made.[1]

The commission identified two countries—North Korea and Iran—as being particularly dangerous:

> The extraordinary level of resources that North Korea and Iran are now devoting to developing their own ballistic missile capabilities poses a substantial and immediate danger to the U.S., its vital interests and its allies. . . . Each of these nations places a high priority on threatening U.S. territory, and each is even now pursuing advanced ballistic missile capabilities to pose a direct threat to U.S. territory.[2]

The August 31, 1998, North Korean test of a Taepo Dong I missile/space launch vehicle appeared to lend credence to these warnings. The Taepo Dong I failed in its attempt to launch a small satellite into orbit and flew only 1,320 kilometers, but it had an enormous international impact due to the unexpected use of a third stage on the rocket. As a result of this test and the changing

Joshua Williams, a junior fellow with the Nonproliferation Project at the Carnegie Endowment for International Peace, is coauthor of this chapter.

strategic environment, the 1999 National Intelligence Estimate (NIE) for the first time included countries other than Russia and China as ballistic missile threats to the United States. This expanded assessment was also used in the most recent NIE, which was made publicly available in December 2001. It concluded that by 2015 the United States

> most likely will face ICBM threats from North Korea and Iran, and possibly Iraq—barring significant changes in their political orientations—in addition to the strategic forces of Russia and China. One agency assesses that the United States is unlikely to face an ICBM threat from Iran before 2015. The threats to the U.S. homeland, nevertheless, will consist of dramatically fewer warheads than today owing to significant reductions in Russian strategic forces. China has been modernizing its long-range strategic missile force since the 1980s. . . . By 2015, the total number of Chinese strategic warheads will rise several-fold, though it will remain still well below the number of Russian or U.S. forces.[3]

Significantly, the assessment notes that

> U.S. territory is more likely to be attacked with these [chemical, biological, radiological, and nuclear] materials from nonmissile delivery means—most likely from terrorists—than by missiles, primarily because nonmissile delivery means are less costly, easier to acquire, and more reliable and accurate. They can also be used without attribution.[4]

The report also cautioned:

> Our assessments of future missile developments are inexact and subjective because they are based on often fragmentary information. . . . States with emerging missile programs inevitably will run into problems that will delay and frustrate their desired development timelines. The impact of these problems increases with the lack of maturity of the program and depends on the level of foreign assistance. Most emerging missile states are highly dependent on foreign assistance at this stage of their development efforts, and disturbance of the technology and information flow to their programs will have discernible short-term effects.[5]

Still, the Quadrennial Defense Review presented to Congress by the Department of Defense on October 1, 2001, argued that "in particular, the pace and scale of recent ballistic missile proliferation has exceeded earlier intelligence estimates and suggests these challenges may grow at a faster pace than previously expected."[6] This concern persisted in 2002, when Director of Central Intelligence George Tenet reported that "the proliferation of ICBM and cruise missile designs and technology has raised the threat to the U.S. from WMD [weapons of mass destruction] delivery systems to a critical threshold." Tenet's rhetoric was more cautious in 2003, however: "The United States and its interests remain at risk from increasingly advanced and lethal ballistic and cruise missiles."[7] The issue was scarcely mentioned in the 2004 and 2005 assessments, even as funding for antimissile systems increased.

To compare more completely today's ballistic missile threats with those of the past and to perform an accurate net assessment of the global ballistic missile threat, it is useful to evaluate the threat in its component parts.

Global Ballistic Missile Arsenals

The blurring of the short, medium, intermediate, and intercontinental ranges of the world's missile inventory often results in a misinterpretation of the oft-quoted assessment that more than 25 nations possess ballistic missiles. This statement is true. But only China, Russia, and the United States possess the ability to launch nuclear warheads on land-based ICBMs. This has not changed since Russia and China deployed their first ICBMs in 1959 and 1981, respectively.[8] An analysis of global ballistic missile arsenals shows that there are fewer ICBMs, long-range submarine-launched ballistic missiles (SLBMs), and intermediate-range ballistic missiles (IRBMs) in the world today than there were during the Cold War. The total number of medium-range ballistic missiles (MRBMs) has also decreased, though 5 new countries have developed or acquired MRBMs since the late 1980s. The number of countries with short-range ballistic missiles (SRBMs) has increased during the past 20 years.

Thus, the most accurate way to summarize existing global ballistic missile capabilities is to say that there is a widespread capability to launch SRBMs. There is a slowly growing, but still limited, capability to launch MRBMs. Most important, a decreasing number of long-range missiles remain from the stockpile levels of the Cold War, a fact that is often overlooked.

Long-Range Ballistic Missiles

Force reductions in U.S. and Russian arsenals have dramatically decreased the number of long-range ballistic missiles (missiles with a range of greater than 5,500 kilometers) in the world from their Cold War levels (figure 5.1). In 1987, the Soviet Union deployed 2,380 long-range missiles in its combined ICBM and SLBM arsenals.[9] The United States deployed 1,640 long-range missiles.[10] In 2005, Russia had 777 long-range missiles, and the United States had 846.[11] France has reduced its total nuclear arsenal but now has 48 long-range SLBMs that it did not have in 1987.[12] Similarly, the United Kingdom has reduced its arsenal but now holds the title to 58 long-range Trident SLBMs that it did not have in 1987.[13] During this period, China has maintained a force of about 20 Dong Feng–5 ICBMs.[14] No other country has developed an ICBM or long-range SLBM during this time. By the beginning of 2005, the total number of long-range ballistic missiles in the world had decreased 57 percent, to 1,749, from the 4,040 that were deployed in 1987.[15]

Intermediate-Range Ballistic Missiles

IRBM arsenals have undergone even more dramatic reductions (figure 5.2). The Intermediate-Range Nuclear Forces Treaty (INF Treaty), a bilateral agreement between the United States and the USSR, eliminated this entire class of missiles (with ranges of 3,000 to 5,500 kilometers) from the Soviet/Russian arsenal over a three-year period.[16] The final INF Treaty inspections took place on May 31, 2001, verifying the destruction of 660 Soviet IRBMs.[17] In 1987, France

Figure 5.1. **Global Long-Range Ballistic Missile Arsenals (Combined ICBM and SLBM)**

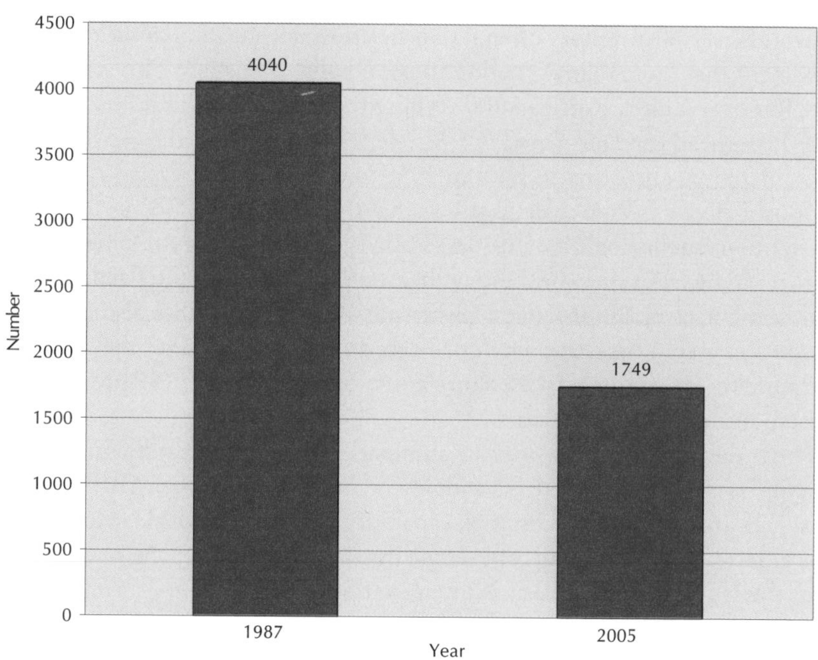

deployed 18 land-based and 32 submarine-based IRBMs, which it has since deactivated and destroyed. China has maintained about 12 DF-4 IRBMs, and no other nation has developed an IRBM, effectively reducing the current number of IRBMs by 98 percent from Cold War levels.[18]

Medium-Range Ballistic Missiles

The broad scope of the INF Treaty also covered MRBMs. Thus, the treaty resulted in the elimination of this class of missile (with a range of 1,000 to 3,000 kilometers) from Soviet/Russian and U.S. ballistic missile arsenals (figure 5.3). A total of 149 Russian SS-4s and 234 U.S. Pershing IIs were destroyed under this treaty.[19] Outside the treaty, France also eliminated 64 medium-range SLBMs that it possessed in 1987.

The most significant proliferation threat comes from the slow but steady increase in the number of states possessing MRBMs, even though Russia and the United States have eliminated their arsenals. This development has attracted great attention and is often cited as evidence of a larger proliferation threat than before. China, India, Iran, Israel, North Korea, Pakistan, and Saudi Arabia all now possess MRBMs. China may also possess a medium-range SLBM capability of 12 Julang I SLBMs.[20] Only India, Iran, North Korea, Pakistan, and Saudi Arabia have developed or obtained their missiles since the late 1980s, and of these countries all but India's missiles are based primarily on assistance or technology received from North Korea or China.

Numerically speaking, even though MRBMs are now in the hands of more countries than in 1987, the total number of MRBMs in existence in 2005 is lower than the 547 MRBMs in the combined Chinese, Russian, French, and

Figure 5.2. **Global Intermediate-Range Ballistic Missile Arsenals**

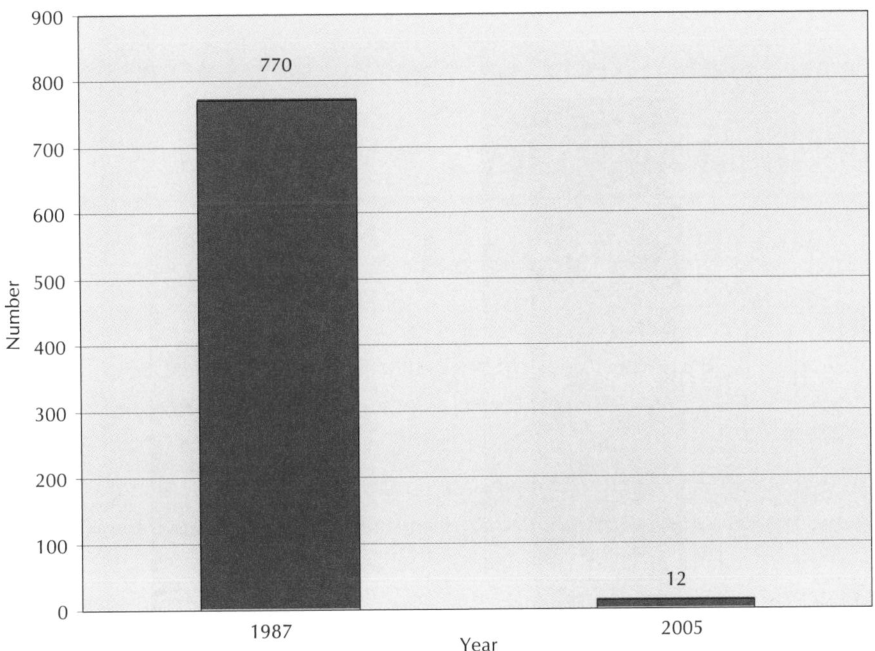

U.S. forces in 1987.[21] Since then, Israel is believed to have deployed 50 operational Jericho IIs,[22] while Saudi Arabia has approximately 40 CSS-2/DF-3As that it purchased from China.[23] North Korea is believed to have deployed close to 100 No Dongs, but it may have produced at least 150 missiles of this type.[24] At least five Iranian Shahab IIIs were deployed in July 2003.[25] MRBMs in India and Pakistan and North Korea's Taepo Dong I are still in operational testing. Assuming that each of these countries could deploy 1 to 5 missiles in a crisis during the next five years, the global total of MRBMs in existence is no more than 417 and possibly as low as 285.[26] This represents a 24 or 48 percent decrease, respectively, in global MRBM arsenals from the 1987 level.

Short-Range Ballistic Missiles

In addition to the five recognized nuclear weapon states, 25 nations have ballistic missiles. Of these 25 nations, 19 only have missiles with ranges under 1,000 kilometers, and 17 only have missiles with a range of about 300 kilometers or less. Many of these missiles are old Scud-B systems that are not well maintained and are declining in military utility.

Countries with Ballistic Missile Programs

Another factor by which proliferation can be measured is the number of states with ballistic missile development programs (see table 5.1; for a detailed, comprehensive listing, also see table 5.2 at the end of the chapter). The number of countries with such programs has also decreased from the number pursuing

Figure 5.3. **Global Medium-Range Ballistic Missile Arsenals**

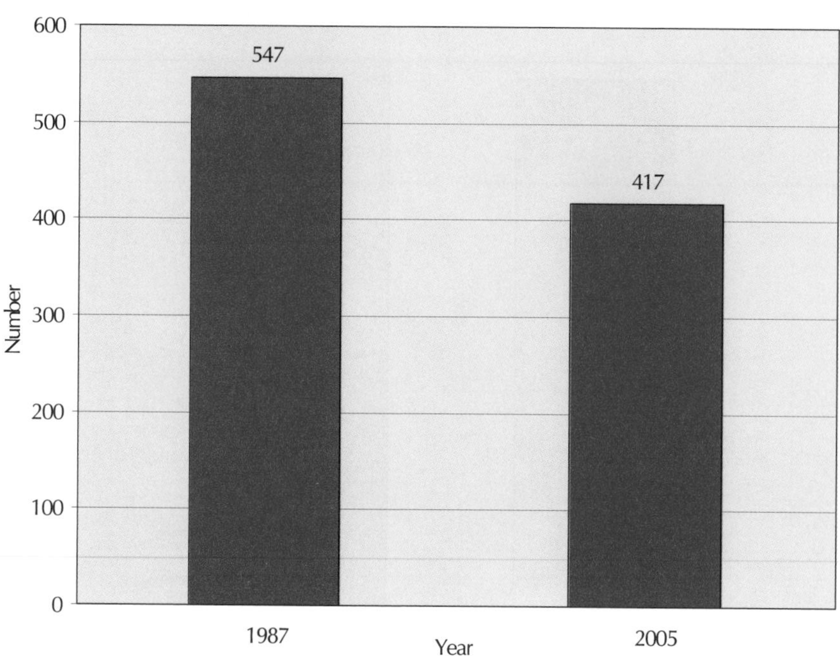

development programs during the Cold War. In addition to the five recognized nuclear weapon states, countries such as Argentina, Brazil, Egypt, India, Iraq, Israel, Libya, and South Africa had programs to develop long-range or medium-range missiles in 1987. By 2005, Argentina, Brazil, Egypt, and South Africa had abandoned their programs, and Libya, through its December 2003 agreement with the United States and the United Kingdom, had scrapped all of its missiles and programs, except for the Al Fatah, which has never traveled more than 200 kilometers in a flight test.[27]

Today, the nations that are pursuing long-range missile development programs are also smaller, poorer, and less technologically advanced than those that had missile programs fifteen years ago. Iran and North Korea currently have active ballistic missile development programs. Syria and South Korea have active SRBM programs but have not yet demonstrated any great interest in, or the capability to produce, MRBMs. The most recent NIE on foreign missile developments confirmed that Syria is unlikely to gain an interest in ICBM development before 2015 but also indicated that strategic imperatives could lead to interest in acquiring an MRBM such as the No Dong.[28] Thus, even with the inclusion of India and Pakistan, this listing highlights the limited nature of the missile proliferation threat, one that is confined to a few countries whose political evolution will be a determining factor in whether they emerge as, or remain, threats to global security.

In South Asia and the Middle East, strategic interest and political dynamics have fueled the continued development of ballistic missile technology as both a means of gaining international prestige and of obtaining a strategic advantage

Table 5.1. **Countries with Active Ballistic Missile Development Programs with a Range of More Than 1,000 Kilometers**

1987	2005
Argentina	India
Brazil	Iran
Egypt	Israel
India	North Korea
Iraq	Pakistan
Israel	
Libya	
South Africa	

Note

This table excludes the NPT nuclear weapon states China, France, Russia, and the United States. All these countries had developed ballistic missiles with ranges greater than 1,000 kilometers by 1987 and were continuing indigenous programs to develop and deploy new missiles that exceeded this range.

vis-à-vis regional rivals and outside powers. Though somewhat limited, this proliferation and the transfer of ballistic missile technology originating in North Korea and China continue to destabilize both regional and global security.

Technical Background

In addition to ballistic missiles, developments in cruise missile technologies and the increasing use of drones, or unmanned aerial vehicles, pose serious threats. This section briefly discusses the various technologies and proliferation prospects.

Ballistic Missiles, Cruise Missiles, and Unmanned Aerial Vehicles

A ballistic missile is a guided rocket that is powered during the initial part of its flight and then coasts without power—mostly above the atmosphere—along a ballistic path to its target. A cruise missile is an aerodynamic system with jet or rocket propulsion that is powered all the way to its target. An unmanned aerial vehicle (UAV) is a remotely piloted or self-controlled aircraft that can carry cameras, sensors, communications equipment, and weapon payloads. UAVs are generally powered either by jet or propeller engines.

Ballistic missiles travel at hypersonic speeds, allowing little warning time and making defense difficult. Since the Cold War, ballistic missiles have been considered the most threatening delivery vehicles for nuclear weapons. The 1988 War of the Cities between Iran and Iraq and the 1991 Gulf War highlighted the threat from Scud ballistic missiles armed with conventional (high-explosive) warheads, and the possible threat of chemical and biological warheads. As a result of their highly visible use, many commentators interpreted the missile threat to be one of *ballistic* missiles alone.

Yet cruise missiles are now recognized as a rapidly growing and particularly dangerous problem. A guidance system enabling cruise missiles to attack distant land targets was once such an expensive and sophisticated technology that, for most countries, cruise missiles could be used only with terminal homing against ships. During the past few years, however, inexpensive satellite navigation (the U.S. Global Positioning System and the Russian Glonass) has become universally available, allowing the most advanced cruise missiles, such as the U.S. Tomahawk, to attack land targets with as much as 6-meter accuracy.[29]

This accuracy greatly exceeds that available from all but the most sophisticated ballistic missiles. The Scud, for example, is accurate on the order of 1,000 meters, making it ineffective against discrete military targets except with nuclear, biological, or chemical warheads, which cause damage over wide areas. With the high accuracy of cruise missiles, which has already been demonstrated by U.S. Tomahawks, even high-explosive warheads are reliable in destroying their targets. Moreover, in comparison with ballistic missiles, cruise missiles are

- cheaper, quicker, and easier to build, and increasingly available on world markets. The Chinese Silkworm, which is already widely disseminated, produced by a number of regional powers, and easily extended in range, may become the Scud of cruise missiles. A proliferator can now acquire many cruise missiles quickly.
- easier to launch from planes and ships. This makes it easier for cruise missiles to reach targets far from an attacker's homeland. It would be possible to use a ship-launched cruise missile to attack North American targets, for example.
- more effective for disseminating chemical and biological agents. Because a cruise missile can release chemical and biological agents in a gradual and controlled fashion (as opposed to a wasteful burst of agent or submunitions with a ballistic missile), each cruise missile can adjust its attack to local conditions, creating a lethal area coverage that is about ten times as great as that from a ballistic missile. With chemical and biological agents being cheaper and more available than nuclear weapons, and with cruise missiles being more affordable than ballistic missiles, cruise missiles with chemical or biological warheads may become more widespread threats than ballistic missiles.
- difficult to defend against. Ballistic missiles (except for the most sophisticated) coast along an observable and predictable path, but cruise missiles can weave around, fly low following the contours of the earth, and attack targets from any direction. Advanced cruise missiles such as the U.S. Tomahawk can now be reprogrammed in flight, allowing them to loiter over a battlefield until given a target. In some cases, cruise missiles need not fly directly over their targets; they can disseminate chemical and biological agents from a distance upwind. Further, cruise missiles can be small and stealthy. All these factors make cruise missiles difficult to find in flight and therefore difficult to shoot down.

UAVs offer many capabilities that are similar to those of cruise missiles, and recent developments in UAV technology demonstrate their rapidly increasing military utility. Though not yet widely used as offensive weapons, UAVs are capable of carrying heavier payloads and flying longer distances for extended periods than cruise missiles. The April 2001 transpacific flight of the U.S. Global Hawk UAV nonstop from the United States to Australia demonstrated the long-range capabilities of these machines. The Global Hawk, which is capable of carrying a 900-kilogram payload and cruising at a maximum altitude of 19,800 meters, can travel a distance of 2,300 kilometers and survey a given area for 36 hours while preserving the capability to return to its initial base 2,300 kilometers away. The range of the Global Hawk increases if operators change the flight surveillance time of a given mission.

As noted, UAVs are currently used primarily for intelligence and reconnaissance missions. However, the weaponization of UAVs into unmanned combat aerial vehicles (UCAVs) is also progressing. The United States deployed a version of its Predator UAV armed with Hellfire missiles in the wars in Afghanistan and Iraq. The U.S. Army may also be using the armed Hunter UAV to combat insurgents in Iraq.[30] Furthermore, the X-45A UCAV is now under testing and is capable of releasing a precision-guided "small smart bomb."[31] The United States has also begun experiments to arm UAVs with "flying plate" weapons that can destroy steel structures and penetrate bunkers; with high-temperature incendiary devices, intended to neutralize chemical and biological agents, which can create firestorms inextinguishable with water; with high-power microwave technology that disrupts enemy communication centers; and with small diameter bombs, weighing only 250 pounds, which can penetrate up to 1.8 meters of reinforced concrete.[32]

Most important, UAVs could simply be used in the same fashion as cruise missiles, to deliver conventional, chemical, biological, or nuclear payloads. Like their cruise missile counterparts, armed UAVs are easier to launch than ballistic missiles, could be used to disseminate biological or chemical agents more effectively than ballistic missiles, can be recalled and retargeted, and would be difficult to defend against once launched. When developed, basic UAV platforms can be produced to provide a state or group with both armed and unarmed versions, giving them the capability to expand both reconnaissance capability and long-range strike capability at the same time. If, for example, the United States were to deploy an antimissile system, China could respond by developing a large fleet of long-range UAVs, providing a nuclear-strike capability difficult to detect by radar that also flies beneath the interceptor ranges of the system.

The operational effectiveness of UAVs, however, is still an issue. Though there have been many reports of the use of UAVs in Kosovo, Afghanistan, and Iraq, there is little public information on their effectiveness or, in the case of the Hellfire-equipped Predators, their kill rates. The Congressional Research Service reported in 2003 that "the current UAV accident rate is 100 times that of manned aircraft."[33] There is no doubt that the Predator still has many shortcomings, including a susceptibility to inclement weather, which often forces the vehicle to fly at altitudes so low that it is in the range of enemy air defenses.[34] Despite these questions about their effectiveness, many see UAVs as the wave of the future in aerial reconnaissance and combat. As a result, the U.S. Department of Defense is projected to spend more than $10 billion on UAVs over the course of this decade.[35]

The production and use of UAVs are already widespread. According to the Department of Defense, 32 nations manufacture more than 250 models of UAVs, and 41 countries operate about 80 different types of these vehicles.[36] Although many of the UAVs produced and deployed by other nations are no more than cameras attached to jet engines, France, Israel, Italy, and the United Kingdom possess medium-range, long-endurance UAVs.[37]

According to defense expert Dennis Gormley, "Given the explosive growth anticipated in UAV systems over the next decade, there will inevitably be increased pressure—led by the USA—to create more flexible, less restrictive, rules governing the export of unarmed UAVs and unmanned combat air vehicles."[38] In fact, this analysis has already proven to be accurate. In 2002, the United States took advantage of revised Missile Technology Control Regime (MTCR) rules to sell six Predator UAVs to Italy.[39] Complicating things even further, unarmed UAVs can be made into armed UAVs simply by changing their payload, meaning that an unarmed UAV purchased for one stated purpose could easily be converted into a weapon. In terms of their classification under the MTCR, Gormley notes that, unlike ballistic missiles, precise data on the one-way range and payload trade-off for most UAVs are not readily available. One study cited by Gormley found that more than 80 percent of unarmed UAVs appear capable of exceeding the MTCR's 300-kilometer range Category I threshold.[40]

Range/Payload Trade-Offs

The ability to make trade-offs between range and payload is critical for understanding missile and UAV nonproliferation. Iraq demonstrated this trade-off in 1987 by reducing the 1,000-kilogram payload of the 300-kilometer range Scud-B, helping to create the Al Hussein missile with more than twice the range, enough to reach Tehran.[41] Because the MTCR places special restrictions on missiles capable of delivering a 500-kilogram payload to a range of 300 kilometers, some exporters have tried to ignore the range/payload trade-off. China, for example, once claimed that its M-11 missile, which is capable of delivering an 850-kilogram payload to a range of 280 kilometers, did not have an adequate range to be restricted under the MTCR. A slightly lighter payload (well above 500 kilograms), however, would enable the M-11 to travel more than 300 kilometers. In October 1994, China formally recognized the applicability of this trade-off.[42] (When only ranges are cited in the remainder of this chapter, they apply to the most commonly cited missile payloads.)

Routes to Proliferation

States seeking ballistic or cruise missiles can acquire them in a variety of ways. They can attempt to import entire missile systems, or they can try to build them indigenously—normally using imported components and technology. States need not admit that they are building missiles. Space launch vehicles, scientific research rockets, and large defensive missiles use hardware, technology, and production facilities that are interchangeable with those of ballistic missiles. Various types of UAVs—reconnaissance drones, target drones, and remotely piloted vehicles (some already delivering insecticides for agricultural purposes)—can be converted to weapons use. Antiship cruise missiles can be converted to land-attack cruise missiles.

Missiles, especially ballistic missiles, are complex machines. The medium-range U.S. Pershing II, for example, contained 250,000 parts, each of which needed to work right the first time under high levels of acceleration, vibration, heat, and cold. Thus, the development of missiles is an expensive and time-consuming process, often resulting in an unreliable weapons system.

Moreover, the development of ballistic missiles becomes particularly difficult at a range of about 1,000 kilometers. Above that range, the missile must use two more advanced technologies: staging (firing rockets in a series, with the expended rockets reliably jettisoned from the missiles) and more sophisticated reentry vehicles (to keep the warhead in working order during its fiery descent through the atmosphere).[43] Longer ranges also put a premium on more efficient rocket engines, lighter and stronger materials, more advanced guidance systems, and lighter and more advanced warheads (which is a considerable challenge when nuclear warheads are at issue). These technical difficulties, compounded by the export controls of the MTCR and active diplomatic efforts by the United States and other concerned countries, have helped to restrain missile proliferation.

The former commander-in-chief of the U.S. Strategic Command, General Eugene Habiger, further elaborates on the problems facing would be proliferators:

> For the Taepodong II to reach the western part of the United States would require some very optimistic operational objectives. For example, the warhead would have to be no heavier than 300 kg. Now, there's a big leap of faith between developing a nuclear device—a weapon that operates in a laboratory kind of environment, in a concrete tunnel, no G-loading, no vibration, no temperature extremes—and to miniaturize something that's going to go in the nose cone of an ICBM, that is going to experience the kinds of things that I've just described. That takes a lot of technology, it takes a lot of work, and it takes a lot of time. I would submit that the miniaturization of a nuclear warhead is probably the most significant challenge that any proliferant would have to face.

Habiger pointed out that it took the United States "six to eight years of very intensive engineering development and aggressive testing" to reduce its first ICBM warheads from 5,000 to 1,000 kilograms. "The leap of faith is that the North Koreans would be able to go from a pristine laboratory weapon to 300 kg," he said.[44]

The Dangers of Missile Proliferation

From the point of view of a proliferator, missiles have certain generic advantages over manned warplanes:

- Simplicity: A "push-button war" with missiles is much easier for the less technically advanced regional powers than is the development of a trained air force with manned aircraft and a large infrastructure.
- Survivability: Airfields have known locations and are large, vulnerable targets beginning in the first minutes of a war. Manned aircraft, which generally operate from airfields, cannot be expected to last long against the United States and its allies. In contrast, hidden or mobile missiles are difficult to find and destroy.
- Defense penetration: Shooting down a ballistic or a cruise missile in flight is still a challenge even for the United States, which has until recently emphasized the role of protecting against manned aircraft for its active defenses.
- Accuracy: Cruise missiles with satellite navigation and some advanced regional ballistic missile systems are highly accurate. In contrast, the bombing accuracy of manned aircraft depends on equipment and pilot training, which can yield variable results.
- Geopolitics: Long-range and ship-launched missiles will diminish the protective effects of distance. They can project the battle to the rear in regional conflicts and some day may reach other continents.
- Blackmail or coercive diplomacy: The almost immediate ability to threaten to deliver a nuclear, chemical, or biological weapon by means of a ballistic missile can be used to achieve specific strategic or political goals. This threat can complicate the decision making of adversaries in times of crisis.

Missiles armed with conventional warheads have been used in regional conflicts since the 1970s.[45] Egypt fired a Scud at Israel at the end of the 1973 war, and in the 1982 Falklands/Malvinas War, Argentina's French-supplied Exocet cruise missiles sank the British frigate *Sheffield*. In 1986, after a U.S. air raid, Libya fired three Scuds at the Italian island of Lampadusa, missing it. The terror of missiles, however, was demonstrated in 1988 in the Iran-Iraq War, with Baghdad and Tehran receiving repeated Scud strikes over several weeks. Starting in 1989, the Soviet-backed government of Afghanistan fired more than 2,000 Scuds against rebel forces. In the 1991 Gulf War, 88 Iraqi Scuds terrorized Israeli civilians and fell around coalition military bases in Saudi Arabia. The overall military effect was negligible in spite of a strike on a U.S. barracks, which killed 28 soldiers. By contrast, during the Gulf War, the United States used three times as many Tomahawk and air-launched cruise missiles, which had significant military effects because of their high accuracy. Scuds were used again in the 1994 Yemen civil war. In 1995, Serbia used SA-2 air defense missiles in their secondary role as ballistic missiles.[46]

The record to date has been that, with conventional warheads, ballistic missiles cause terror that can affect an adversary's attitudes toward the continuation of a war, and cruise missiles cause significant damage to specific military targets. Thus far, no missiles have been used in warfare with unconventional payloads. After the Gulf War, U.N. inspectors discovered Iraqi Scud warheads with chemical and biological agents, Iraqi plans for nuclear warheads,[47] for remotely piloted vehicles to deliver biological agents,[48] and for ballistic missiles with ranges of up to 3,000 kilometers, capable of hitting all of Western Europe.[49]

During the run-up to the 2003 war in Iraq, U.N. inspectors determined that while Saddam Hussein, with some help from foreign sources, was attempting to develop liquid- and solid-propellant ballistic missiles with ranges of up to 1,000 kilometers, he had not succeeded in doing so by March 2003.[50] After the invasion, the U.S. Iraq Survey Group also concluded that Iraq had also been unsuccessful in attempts to develop a 1,000-kilometer-range cruise missile.[51]

Dealing with Missile Proliferation

The four most prominent instruments for limiting the dangers of missile proliferation are the MTCR, the International Code of Conduct Against Ballistic Missile Proliferation (ICOC), unilateral and bilateral U.S. measures, and anti-missile weapons.

The Missile Technology Control Regime

The MTCR is the oldest and most prominent international policy to attempt to limit the proliferation of missiles capable of delivering nuclear, biological, and chemical weapons. It consists of an export control policy, which bans the export of missiles with ranges over 300 kilometers and with payloads greater than 500 kilograms, and associated arrangements between member governments.[52]

The ICOC

The ICOC, also known as the Hague Code of Conduct, came into effect on November 25, 2002. It fills an important gap in the missile nonproliferation regime, and it is meant, according to the U.S. Department of State, "to supplement, not supplant, the Missile Technology Control Regime."[53] The ICOC, with 117 subscribing states as of the spring of 2005,[54] consists of a set of goals, pledges, and confidence-building measures, including

- Working to prevent the proliferation of ballistic missile systems that can carry and deliver nuclear, chemical, and biological weapons.
- Exercising restraint in domestic ballistic missile programs and seeking to reduce national holdings of these missiles.
- Attempting to ensure that any space launch vehicle (SLV) assistance is not manipulated to further a ballistic missile program.
- Declining to assist any ballistic missile program in a state where illegal nuclear, chemical, or biological programs or aspirations are present.
- Submitting an annual declaration of national ballistic missile and SLV policies, as well as information on all launches from the previous year.

- Voluntarily inviting international observers to SLV launch sites.
- Providing prelaunch notifications for both ballistic missile and SLV launches.[55]

The ICOC is a mixed bag as far as international nonproliferation agreements go. With 117 members, it is much more far reaching than the MTCR (which only has 34 members), and it goes well beyond the MTCR's export controls on missiles that exceed a certain range (300 kilometers) and payload (500 kilograms) by calling for restraint in domestic programs and by formally recognizing the links between SLV and ballistic missile technology. (Both the MTCR and ICOC call for the nonproliferation of all ballistic missiles, regardless of range and payload, if they can deliver any type of nuclear, chemical, or biological weapon). Conversely, the ICOC lacks any enforcement mechanism and is not legally binding (as a treaty would be). It also leaves much to be interpreted by the subscribing states, such as how one ensures that the sale of SLV technology does not further a ballistic missile program, or how one determines whether a country "might be developing or acquiring weapons of mass destruction."[56] The ICOC also must agree on implementation measures through consensus, ensuring that achieving the goals and commitments laid out in the code will be a slow, cumbersome process. Despite its shortcomings, however, the ICOC could prove to be a stepping stone to the adoption of stronger and more effective measures in the future.

Unilateral and Bilateral U.S. Measures

Legislatively prescribed sanctions and diplomatic inducements are commonly used in a carrot-and-stick fashion to limit the spread of missile technology. Such inducements as benefit packages can be used to help restrain proliferators, while sanctions are used as punitive measures against both those supplying the technology and those receiving it. U.S. policy toward China and North Korea throughout the 1990s made use of these tools in an attempt to limit proliferation at its source and to punish the countries and entities involved in the distribution and reception of controlled technology.

The George W. Bush administration has maintained a proactive and punitive approach to Chinese missile proliferators, if not to the Chinese government itself, particularly as they continue to assist Iran's missile development efforts. Between January 2001 and December 2004, the United States imposed sanctions on 24 different Chinese companies on 12 separate occasions. Most of these sanctions were levied under the Iran Nonproliferation Act of 2000.[57] Seven of these entities were explicitly accused of missile proliferation. The other 17 were more vaguely cited for "weapons proliferation," meaning that their activities may have involved either missiles or nuclear, biological, and/or chemical weapons and their related technologies. One organization, NORINCO, was sanctioned five times in 2003 and 2004. These sanctions last two years and include a ban on U.S. government purchases of the company's goods, a ban on U.S. government assistance and sales to the sanctioned entities, and a ban on issuing new export licenses to allow American companies to sell certain items to the sanctioned groups. In the face of such little progress, the United States continues to raise the issue of Chinese missile-technology transfers to Pakistan and Iran in bilateral meetings. China's bid to join the MTCR in 2004 failed because of its spotty missile proliferation record.

Since 1998, the United States has also attempted to use diplomatic inducements and sanctions packages in dealing with North Korean entities in an attempt to limit that country's ballistic missile proliferation activities. After scoring a qualified success in obtaining a self-imposed moratorium on missile testing from North Korea, the Bill Clinton administration used promises of presidential visits, increases in annual food aid, and offers of free launches for North Korean satellites as bargaining chips in an attempt to secure an agreement. The administration was unable to reach a final accord before the end of its second term, however. Upon its arrival in office, the Bush administration indicated that it would not pursue a "missiles-only" agreement. Instead, it stated that it would seek further progress on nuclear and conventional military force issues as well as in the realm of missile proliferation. In all likelihood, no progress will come on North Korean ballistic missile proliferation until the nuclear program is ended.

Antimissile Systems

Antimissile weapons can play a role in an integrated nonproliferation policy. Experts disagree on the exact role, with some arguing that they are the best and perhaps only defense, while others view them as a last line of defense should all other efforts fail. These systems are commonly referred to as "missile defense," but the term mistakenly implies that the systems provide an effective defense. This volume uses the more neutral term "antimissile" to refer to efforts to intercept offensive ballistic and cruise missiles.

The United States is developing antimissile systems in three basic versions: short range, medium range, and long range. Every step up represents a substantial increase in complexity and a lower probability of success. Most of the proposed systems employ hit-to-kill interceptors. That is, unlike the Patriot interceptors used in the 1991 Gulf War, which employed a proximity fuse and an explosive warhead to scatter pellet-sized fragments in the path of the intended target, the new interceptors will attempt to hit the target head-on, using the kinetic energy of the encounter to destroy the target.

The United States is the only country in the world that is devoting a considerable portion of its defense budget to antimissile weapons. Israel and Russia are the only other nations with indigenous antimissile efforts. Israel's program is largely funded by the United States (see chapter 13). Russia deployed the world's first operational antimissile system in the 1960s, a set of 100 nuclear-tipped interceptors around Moscow. The interceptors remain, though it appears that the nuclear warheads may have been removed. This was always a questionable defensive strategy mandated by the inability of the interceptors to score direct hits, and without the nuclear warheads the system is strictly symbolic. Nevertheless, in an attempt to demonstrate its military strength, Moscow tested an A-135 missile interceptor in late November 2004. Defense Minister Sergei Ivanov declared the test a success, claiming that Russia could now move forward with a life-extension program for the antimissile system.[58]

Russia has also upgraded its conventionally armed S-300 air defense missile systems to give them some capability against short-range missiles. The version known as the SA-12 is being marketed as an alternative to the U.S. Patriot system, but with few if any sales. A newer S-400 system is comparable to the U.S. Theater High-Altitude Area Defense (THAAD) system (described just below) and is intended to intercept medium-range missiles.[59] The development of an even newer system, the S-500, is currently under way.[60] Some analysts misunderstand the limited nature of Russia's systems and exaggerate their ability to provide the accurate and timely tracking of incoming warheads. This sometimes leads to erroneous claims that Russia has an operational antimissile system.

Despite the lack of progress, Russia has not given up all interest in developing some sort of functioning antimissile system. President Vladimir Putin, then–foreign minister Ivan Ivanov, Defense Minister Sergei Ivanov, and Dmitri Rogozin, the head of the international affairs committee in the lower house of the Russian Duma, have all expressed interest in building antimissile weapons.[61] Ever since the Bush administration's withdrawal from the Anti–Ballistic Missile Treaty of 1972, which limited Russian and American antimissile systems, Moscow has been cautiously interested in working with Washington to develop more advanced antimissile technology.[62]

Taiwan also figures prominently in antimissile discussions. It does not have an indigenous program, but it acquired Patriot missiles from the United States in 1997 to protect its capital, Taipei. Taiwan tested this system for the first time in June 2001.[63] The government is also seeking to upgrade to the Patriot Advanced Capabilities 3 (PAC-3) system, and an agreement has been reached with the United States as part of an $18 billion arms procurement package.[64] These defensive systems might provide some protection against Chinese short-range, conventionally armed ballistic missiles deployed across the Taiwan Strait. However, a barrage attack using some of the hundreds of missiles that China is deploying would quickly overwhelm the systems.

Finally, Japan has shown an interest in developing its own antimissile system, with the help of the United States. The Japan Defense Agency, which already possesses PAC-2 missiles, requested $1.3 billion for antimissile systems in fiscal year 2005.[65] Tokyo hopes to test, and then deploy, the Aegis destroyer-based Standard Missile-3 (SM-3) and the land-based PAC-3 antimissile systems by March 2008.[66] Japan has been very careful in saying that its systems would be solely for the protection of Japan, and that they would not be used for the defense of another country.[67] The U.S. Department of Defense hopes to deploy six radar-equipped Aegis destroyers and eleven Aegis cruisers and destroyers carrying SM-3s by the end of 2007, many patrolling near Japan.[68] These deadlines will likely prove difficult to meet, though, because weapons programs in their developmental stages, such as all of the antimissile programs, typically experience significant delays and cost overruns. As of the spring of 2005, only two ships, both with the modified Aegis Radar but none with the SM-3 antimissile interceptors, had been deployed in the Sea of Japan.[69]

SHORT-RANGE SYSTEMS. These systems attempt to intercept missiles in their terminal phase as they reenter the atmosphere and close in on a target. Terminal systems are practical only against short-range missiles, because longer-range missiles would fly in too fast for any current intercept system. The most advanced U.S. system is the improved Patriot system, or PAC-3, designed to intercept Scud-type missiles. Although the original Patriot was psychologically important in the Gulf War, it hit few if any Scuds, as later congressional and Israeli analyses confirmed. In the 2003 Iraq War, the new PAC-3 (along with an earlier upgrade of the PAC-2, the PAC-2 GEM) had mixed results. Together, the Army claims that it intercepted all nine "threatening" ballistic missiles: the relatively slow, short-range al-Samoud 2 and Ababil 100 systems. Proof of these claims was not provided by the Army. The Patriot batteries also shot down two coalition aircraft, and missed shooting down a third only because the pilot destroyed the Patriot unit.[70] These incidents resulted in the deaths of three coalition soldiers. In these incidents, the Patriot radar and computers mistook the friendly aircraft for enemy missiles.

The Navy Area-Wide program was an effort to upgrade the Aegis radar system and Standard missile on the U.S. Navy's destroyers and cruisers. It was similar in concept to the original Patriot system, but for use on ships. The navy canceled it in December 2001 after it fell badly behind schedule and over budget. The multinational Medium Extended Air Defense System (MEADS), which is in the fledgling stages of development, would employ an upgraded version of the PAC-3 system and be a cooperative program between the United States and two of its NATO allies, Germany and Italy. The Army hopes that MEADS will enter service by 2012.[71]

Without realistic tests, it is impossible to predict performance, but the Patriot and MEADS systems currently hold the only possibility for intercepting SRBMs armed with single warheads. They rely on previously developed radar and hardware systems and—because they intercept their targets within the atmosphere after any decoys would have been stripped away—they do not encounter the difficult discrimination problems that face higher, outside-the-atmosphere interceptors. Countermeasures, such as decoys and submunitions, remain a major unsolved technical barrier to effective antimissile systems, despite decades of effort. The difficulties posed by cruise missiles and low-flying aircraft in the Iraq War, however, demonstrate the serious and often fatal problems of even these short-range systems.

MEDIUM-RANGE SYSTEMS. Two systems are under development to counter medium-range missiles that travel from 1,000 to 3,500 kilometers: the army's THAAD system and the Navy Theater-Wide (Upper Tier) system, now known as Aegis Ballistic Missile Defense, which is based on Aegis ships with a new Standard-3 missile (see discussion above of Japan's antimissile ambitions). Both are now known as Midcourse Interceptor Systems because they primarily attempt to intercept missiles in their midcourse phase, after they have been boosted and are coasting outside the atmosphere.

The THAAD test record has been disappointing, missing in six of its eight attempts. All these tests occurred before 1999, and no additional flight or interceptor tests have been conducted because the missiles are being redesigned. Current Pentagon plans call for more tests of THAAD through 2008, with deployment possible (although highly unlikely) between 2006 and 2008.[72] The Navy Theater-Wide / Aegis system claims hits in five out of six tests, but most of those have been highly scripted. Though a problem with the kill vehicle prevented any tests from taking place in 2004, the system enjoyed a successful test in February 2005. Two more tests are currently planned for 2005. Finally, as discussed above, the Pentagon planned to deploy six radar-equipped vessels and eleven missile-equipped ships by the end of 2007.[73]

A third system, the Airborne Laser (ABL), is under development to test the idea of deploying a high-energy laser in a modified Boeing 747 aircraft. The plane would fly within 300 to 400 kilometers of missile launch points and attempt to destroy missiles of all ranges in their boost phase by weakening their missile skins through applied laser heat. The ABL system has run into major technical problems and serious cost overruns, however. These include delayed hardware deliveries and excessive vibration (or "jitter") that impedes the high-energy laser from maintaining its aim on the target missile. The system already exceeds its weight limit after assembling just a few of the laser modules needed to create the high-energy laser beam.[74] Furthermore, these modules have not been mated with the aircraft and nothing more than flight tests of the unequipped 747 have occurred.[75] The Pentagon hopes that the ABL will be deployed between 2008 and 2010.[76] This is probably wishful thinking.

LONG-RANGE SYSTEMS. These systems would also intercept long-range missiles outside the atmosphere in their midcourse phase, using very powerful ground-based interceptors. In 2004, several missile interceptors were placed in silos at Fort Greely, Alaska, and Vandenberg Air Force Base, California, as part of the so-called Ground Based Midcourse Defense (GMD) system. Up to 20 interceptors could be installed in Alaska and California by the end of 2005. The Bush administration, despite much opposition among experts as well as current and former military personnel, wanted to declare "limited operational defensive capability by late 2004." In its ten highly scripted and unrealistic tests as of mid-2005, the system intercepted the target on five occasions.

Although the system enjoys strong political support from the administration and Congress, there are widespread technical doubts about its feasibility. These concerns were summarized in an April 5, 2005, letter from twenty-two physicists, including nine Nobel laureates, to Congress. The scientists concluded:

> The GMD system has no demonstrated capability to defend against a real attack, even from a single warhead unaccompanied by countermeasures. It remains in an early stage of development, and the testing program has provided essentially no information about how the system would perform in a real missile attack. All flight intercept tests have been conducted under highly scripted conditions with the defense given advance information about the attack details. Until realistic tests are completed, there will be no data on which to base an assessment of how effective the system might be in an actual attack.

> At the same time, even without such tests, it is possible to understand the severe limitations of the system by analyzing the intrinsic capabilities of the system components. Even if the defense components work perfectly as designed, technical assessments demonstrate that the GMD system will be unable to counter a missile attack that includes even unsophisticated countermeasures. Numerous government reports have identified simple countermeasures that are readily available to states such as North Korea. Thus, the system will be unable to defend against a real attack, should one occur.[77]

In addition to GMD, the Bush administration has advanced the idea of using a Kinetic Energy Interceptor on land and at sea to destroy long-range missiles in their boost phase. This project is still very much in the developmental stages, and no tests will be conducted until at least 2008.[78]

The administration has also revived concepts of placing kinetic-energy interceptors in space (formerly known as Brilliant Pebbles), and it is again investigating the idea of space-based lasers. Both plans are in the early exploratory stage and are at least a decade away from testing.

Despite the lack of a consensus on the threat, technical feasibility, cost, schedule, and strategic consequences of deploying antimissile systems, they represent by far the largest financial component of U.S. nonproliferation policy, with more than $10.5 billion allocated for antimissile research in 2005.[79] By comparison, the United States allocated about $2 billion for all other nonproliferation programs in 2005,[80] including the Nunn-Lugar Cooperative Threat Reduction programs.

NOTES

1. Commission to Assess the Ballistic Missile Threat to the United States (hereafter Ballistic Missile Threat Commission), "Executive Summary of the Report of the Commission to Assess the Ballistic Missile Threat to the United States," July 15, 1998, p. 5; available at www.house.gov/hasc/testimony/105thcongress/BMThreat.htm.
2. Ballistic Missile Threat Commission, "Executive Summary," p. 7.
3. National Intelligence Council (NIC), "Foreign Missile Developments and the Ballistic Missile Threat to the United States through 2015," December 2001, p. 6.
4. Ibid., p. 8.
5. Ibid., pp. 3, 7.
6. U.S. Department of Defense (DOD), "Quadrennial Defense Review Report," Washington, September 30, 2002, pp. 6–7; available at www.defenselink.mil/pubs/qdr2001.pdf.
7. "Worldwide Threat: Converging Dangers in a Post-9/11 World," testimony of Director of Central Intelligence (DCI) George J. Tenet before the Senate Select Committee on Intelligence, February 6, 2002; available at www.cia.gov/cia/public_affairs/speeches/2002/dci_speech_02062002.html. See also "The Worldwide Threat in 2003: Evolving Dangers in a Complex World," testimony of DCI George J. Tenet before the Senate Select Committee on Intelligence, February 11, 2003; available at www.cia.gov/cia/public_affairs/speeches/2003/dci_speech_02112003.html.
8. France and the United Kingdom acquired intercontinental-range, submarine-launched ballistic missiles in 1987 and 1995, respectively.
9. Robert S. Norris and Thomas B. Cochran, *Nuclear Weapons Databook: U.S.–U.S.S.R./Russian Strategic Offensive Nuclear Forces, 1945–1996* (Washington, D.C.: Natural Resources Defense Council, 1997), p. 13.
10. Norris and Cochran, *Nuclear Weapons Databook*, p. 12.

11. Robert S. Norris and Hans M. Kristensen, "NRDC Nuclear Notebook: Russian Nuclear Forces, 2005," *Bulletin of the Atomic Scientists*, March/April 2005, pp. 70-72. See also Robert S. Norris and Hans M. Kristensen, "NRDC Nuclear Notebook: United States Nuclear Forces, 2005," *Bulletin of the Atomic Scientists*, January/February 2005, pp. 73–75.

12. Robert Norris and William Arkin, "NRDC Nuclear Notebook: French Nuclear Forces, 2001," *Bulletin of the Atomic Scientists*, July/August 2001, pp. 70–71. Also, telephone conversation with Hans M. Kristensen of the Natural Resources Defense Council, January 21, 2005.

13. International Institute for Strategic Studies (IISS), *The Military Balance, 2004–2005* (Oxford: Oxford University Press, 2004), p. 73.

14. Robert Norris and Hans M. Kristensen, "NRDC Nuclear Notebook: Chinese Nuclear Forces, 2003," *Bulletin of the Atomic Scientists,* vol. 59, no. 6, November/December 2003, pp. 77–80.

15. In 1987, there were 4,040 U.S., Russian, and Chinese long-range missiles.

16. The U.S. IRBM arsenal had long been eliminated by the time the INF Treaty entered into force. From 1958 to 1963, the United States deployed Thor IRBMs on U.K. territory in a joint agreement with the British government. These missiles were retired in 1963 following improvements in the U.S. ICBM arsenal, and no further IRBMs were produced or deployed.

17. Joseph Cirincione with Jon B. Wolfsthal and Miriam Rajkumar, *Deadly Arsenals: Tracking Weapons of Mass Destruction* (Washington, D.C.: Carnegie Endowment for International Peace, 2002), p. 72.

18. Norris and Kristensen, "Chinese Nuclear Forces, 2003," pp. 77–80. It is possible that China has deployed as many as 20 DF-4 IRBMs (which some consider to be "limited ICBMs"), according to one source. See IISS, *Military Balance, 2004–2005*, p. 170.

19. Cirincione, Wolfsthal, and Rajkumar, *Deadly Arsenals*, p. 72.

20. Norris and Kristensen, "Chinese Nuclear Forces, 2003," pp. 77–80.

21. In 1987, at the time of the signing of the INF Treaty, the United States possessed 234 Pershing II MRBMs, and the Soviet Union posessed 149 SS-4 Sandal MRBMs. China had a force of 40 DF-3 MRBMs, 48 DF-21 MRBMs, and 12 CSS N-3 sea-launched MRBMs.

22. Listed as 50 each of Jericho I and Jericho II missiles in CNS, *Nonproliferation Review*, Winter 1996, p. 201. There are approximately 100 Jericho I and II missiles, according to IISS, *Military Balance, 2004–2005*, pp. 111–12.

23. Ibid., p.121.

24. Robert S. Norris, Hans M. Kristensen, and Joshua Handler, "NRDC Nuclear Notebook: North Korea's Nuclear Program, 2003," *Bulletin of the Atomic Scientists*, March/April 2003, pp. 74–77.

25. Najmeh Bozorgmehr, "Iran's Ballistic Missile Goes Into Service," *Financial Times*, July 21, 2003. See also "Russian Expert: Iran May Field Up to 20 Shahab-3 Missiles By 2005," World News Connection/Itar-Tass, July 21, 2003.

26. The 285 number assumes the lowest estimate of Saudi CSS-2/DF3As (40), Israeli Jericho IIs (50), North Korean No Dongs (90), Chinese DF-3s, DF-21s, and CSS-N-3/JL Is (100), Indian Agni IIs (0), Pakistani Ghauris, Ghauri IIs, and Shaheen IIs (0), and Iranian Shahab IIIs (5). The 417 number assumes the highest estimate of each of these missiles (40 Saudi CSS-2/DF3As, 50 Israeli Jericho IIs, 100 North Korean No Dongs, 104 Chinese DF-3s, DF-21s, and CSS-N-3/JL-1s, and 20 Iranian Shahab IIIs, plus an additional five missiles for North Korea (Taepo Dong I), India (Agni II), and Pakistan (Ghauri, Ghauri II, or Shaheen II).

27. "Completion of Verification Work in Libya," testimony of Assistant Secretary of State for Verification and Compliance Paula A. DeSutter before the Subcommittee on International Terrorism, Non-Proliferation, and Human Rights, September 22, 2004; available at www.state.gov/t/vc/rls/rm/2004/37220.htm. See also Paul Kerr, "Libya to Keep Limited Missile Force," *Arms Control Today*, May 2004, p. 28.

28. NIC, "Foreign Ballistic Missile Developments," p. 15. With its current arsenal of mobile Scud-B, Scud-C, and SS-21 SRBMs, Syria already possesses the capability to strike deep into the territory of potential regional adversaries such as Iraq, Israel, Jordan, and Turkey.

29. Lt. Col. Phil Tissue, Lt. Col. Ron Perkins, Cdr. Darren Sawyer, and Lt. Col. Lyle Powell, "Attacking the Cruise Missile Threat," Joint Forces Staff College, Joint and Combined Warfighting School, September 8, 2003, p. 3; available at www.jfsc.ndu.edu/current_students/documents_policies/documents/jca_cca_awsp/Cruise_Missile_Defense_Final.doc.

30. Leah Rubulcaba, "Futures Center Working Two Initiatives for Troops in Iraq," Army News Service; available at www4.army.mil/ocpa/read.php?story_id_key=6412.

31. Bill Sweetman, "In the Tracks of the Predator: Combat UAV Programs Are Gathering Speed," *Jane's International Defense Review*, August 2004, pp. 48–55.
32. U.S. Office of the Secretary of Defense, "Unmanned Aerial Vehicles Roadmap: 2002–2027," December 2002, publicly released March 11, 2003; available at www.acq.osd.mil/usd/uav_roadmap.pdf.
33. Elizabeth Bone and Christopher Bolkcom, "Unmanned Aerial Vehicles: Background and Issues for Congress," Congressional Research Service, April 25, 2003, Summary.
34. Ibid., p. 24.
35. Ibid., p. 10.
36. DOD, "Unmanned Aerial Vehicles Roadmap," pp. 21–22.
37. Ibid.
38. Dennis M. Gormley, "New Developments in Unmanned Aerial Vehicles and Land Attack Cruise Missiles," Chapter Summary, in *SIPRI Yearbook 2003: Armaments, Disarmament, and International Security,* Stockholm International Peace Research Institute (Oxford: Oxford University Press, 2003); available at http://editors.sipri.se/pubs/yb03/ch12.html.
39. Ibid. See also DOD, "Unmanned Aerial Vehicles Roadmap," p. 22.
40. Veridian Pacific-Sierra Research, "Unmanned Aerial Vehicles: Technical and Operational Aspects of an Emerging Threat," 2000, cited in Dennis Gormely, *Dealing with the Threat of Cruise Missiles,* Adelphi Paper 339 (Oxford: Oxford University Press 2001), p. 34.
41. W. Seth Carus and Joseph Bermudez, "Iraq's Al-Husayn Missile Program," parts 1 and 2, *Jane's Soviet Intelligence Review,* May–June 1990.
42. U.S. Department of State, "Joint Statement of the United States of America and the People's Republic of China on Missile Proliferation," October 4, 1994, distributed by the Office of the Spokesman.
43. Aaron Karp, *Ballistic Missile Proliferation: The Politics and Technics*, Stockholm International Peace Research Institute (New York: Oxford University Press, 1996).
44. Remarks by General Eugene Habiger, "Alaska Missile Interceptor Site Has No Credibility," Carnegie Endowment Non-Proliferation Issue Brief, vol. 7, no. 14, September 29, 2004.
45. Karp, *Ballistic Missile Proliferation*, pp. 44–46.
46. Duncan Lennox, "Ballistic Missiles," *Jane's Defense Weekly*, April 17, 1996, p. 43.
47. U.N. Security Council Document S/1996/261, April 11, 1996, p. 7.
48. Barbara Starr, "Iraq Reveals a Startling Range of Toxin Agents," *Jane's Defense Weekly*, November 11, 1995, p. 4.
49. Stewart Stogel, "Missile Plans by Iraq May Aim at Europe," *Washington Times*, February 16, 1996.
50. United Nations Monitoring, Verification, and Inspection Commission. "Unresolved Disarmament Issues: Iraq's Proscribed Weapons Programmes," March 6, 2003, available at www.un.org/Depts/unmovic/new/documents/cluster_document.pdf.
51. "Comprehensive Report of the Special Advisor to the DCI on Iraq's WMD" (Duelfer Report of September 30, 2004), "Key Findings: Delivery Systems," pp. 1–2.
52. For a full discussion of the MTCR, see appendix D in the first edition of this volume: Cirincione, Wolfsthal, and Rajkumar, *Deadly Arsenals*, pp. 403–9. More information can also be found on Carnegie Nonproliferation's "Missile Proliferation" web page, at www.carnegieendowment.org/npp/weapons/index.cfm?fa=view&id=3000092.
53. U.S. Department of State, "International Code of Conduct Against Ballistic Missile Proliferation: Fact Sheet," January 6, 2004, available at www.state.gov/t/np/rls/fs/27799.htm.
54. Austrian Foreign Ministry, "Annex: List of Subscribing States to the HCOC," available at www.bmaa.gv.at/up-media/1121_hcoc_-_list_of__subscribing_states.doc.
55. "International Code of Conduct Against Ballistic Missile Proliferation," Available at www.minbuza.nl/default.asp?CMS_ITEM=MBZ460871.
56. Ibid.
57. "U.S. Slaps Sanctions on Five Chinese, North Korean 'Proliferators,'" Agence France-Presse, December 2, 2004.
58. "Russia's Anti-Missile Test Called Success," United Press International, November 29, 2004.

59. For details on these programs, see the web site of the Federation of American Scientists at www.fas.org/spp/starwars/program/soviet/index.html.
60. Nicole C. Evans, "Missile Defense: Winning Minds, Not Hearts," *Bulletin of the Atomic Scientists*, September/October 2004, pp. 48–55.
61. Wade Boese, "Russia Considers Missile Defense," *Arms Control Today*, March 2003, p. 31. See also Michael Wines, "Threats and Responses: U.S. Defense; Moscow Miffed Over Missile Shield but Others Merely Shrug," *New York Times*, December 19, 2002.
62. Evans, "Missile Defense," pp. 48–55.
63. Jason Sherman, "Taiwan Officials Prepare for Their First Missile-Defense Test," *Defense News*, June 18–24, 2001, p. 26.
64. "U.S. Official Warns of 'Repercussions' If Taiwan Fails to Approve Weapons Deal," Associated Press, October 6, 2004; available at http://taiwansecurity.org/AP/2004/AP-061004.htm.
65. "Japan Wants Fatter Budget for Missile Defense, Intelligence," Agence France-Presse, August 31, 2004.
66. "U.S. Mulls Placing Missile Defense System in Japan: Report," Agence France-Presse, April 5, 2004.
67. "Japan Would Not Use Missile Defense to Intercept Missiles Targeting Other Countries," Global Security Newswire, January 10, 2005.
68. Lieutenant General Henry A. Obering III, testimony before the Senate Committee on Armed Services, April 7, 2005. See also "U.S. Looks to Counter North Korean Missiles," Japan Times, September 1, 2004.
69. "Raytheon Delivers SM-3 Missiles," *Jane's Defense Weekly*, November 10, 2004, p. 8.
70. Dennis M. Gormley, "Missile Defence Myopia: Lessons from the Iraq War," Survival, vol. 45, no. 4, Winter 2003–4, pp. 61–86.
71. "MEADS Medium Extended Air Defense System. Germany/Italy/USA." Available at www.armytechnology.com/projects/meads.
72. Wade Boese, "U.S. Missile Defense Programs at a Glance," Arms Control Association, Fact Sheet, August 2004; available at www.armscontrol.org/factsheets/usmissiledefense.asp.
73. Obering testimony.
74. U.S. Government Accountability Office, "Missile Defense: Actions Are Needed to Enhance Testing and Accountability," April 2004, GAO-04-409, appendix III, pp. 56–66.
75. Boese, "U.S. Missile Defense Programs."
76. Ibid.
77. Letter to Senator John W. Warner, April 5, 2005, available at www.ucsusa.org/global_security/missile_defense/page.cfm?pageID=1715.
78. Ibid.
79. Wade Boese, "Congress Backs Bush's Defense Budget," *Arms Control Today*, July/August 2004, pp. 30–31. See also "Historical Funding for MDA FY 85-05," available at www.acq.osd.mil/mda/mdalink/pdf/histfunds.pdf.
80. Anthony Wier, William Hoehn, and Matthew Bunn, "Threat Reduction Funding in the Bush Administration: Claims and Counterclaims in the First Presidential Debate," Managing the Atom Project, Harvard University and Russian-American Nuclear Security Advisory Council, October 6, 2004; available at www.ransac.org. See also "Non-Proliferation Efforts in the FY 2005 Defense Authorization Bill," Center for Arms Control and Non-Proliferation, October 13, 2004; available at www.armscontrolcenter.org/archives/000878.php.

Table 5.2. **World Ballistic Missile Arsenals**

This table represents the Carnegie Endowment's best assessment of the world's ballistic missile arsenals. We count 30 nations as fielding some type of ballistic missile. Missiles reported to be in development are listed in italics. Notes and a key are provided below.[1]

Ballistic missiles differ from military rockets, such as the widely proliferated FROGs, because they have guidance systems. The development of accurate guidance systems remains one of the most challenging engineering obstacles facing states that wish to indigenously develop ballistic missiles. Only eleven nations have missiles with ranges over 1,000 kilometers; all the rest have only short-range, Scud-type missiles. Only eight nations have been able to develop nuclear weapons that could be fitted as warheads on these missiles.

Ballistic missiles are sometimes confused with cruise missiles. A ballistic missile is one whose payload reaches its target by way of an initial powered boost and then a free flight along a high arcing trajectory. Part of the flight of longer-range ballistic missiles may occur outside the atmosphere and involve the "reentry" of a warhead or the missile. A cruise missile, as defined by the Intermediate-Range Nuclear Forces Treaty, is "an unmanned, self-propelled vehicle that sustains flight through the use of aerodynamic lift over most of its flight path." Such a missile may carry either a nuclear or conventional warhead (definitions are taken from an arms control glossary provided by the U.S. State Department). The U.S. National Air Intelligence Center further stipulates that cruise missiles are "usually categorized by intended mission and launch mode," such as antiship cruise missiles, land-attack cruise missiles, air-launched cruise missiles, and submarine-launched cruise missiles.

For more resources, please visit the web pages devoted to "Missile Proliferation" and "Anti-Missile Systems" at www.ProliferationNews.org. The Carnegie Endowment welcomes your comments. If you are aware of information that could update this table, or of sources that could expand the information on this page, please contact the authors.

Country[2]	System Name	Status	Range (kilometers)	Payload (kilograms)	Origin	Notes
Afghanistan	Scud-B	O	300	1,000	USSR	Operational status questionable.
Armenia[3]	Scud-B	O	300	1,000	Russia	
Bahrain	MGM-140 (ATACMS)	O	165	560	USA	Missiles manufactured by Lockheed-Martin.
Belarus[4]	SS-21	O	120	480	USSR	
	Scud-B	O	300	1,000	USSR	

(table continues on the following page)

Table 5.2. **World Ballistic Missile Arsenals** (continued)

Country[2]	System Name	Status	Range (kilometers)	Payload (kilo-grams)	Origin	Notes
China	CSS-8	O	150–230	190	I	Two stage, first solid, second liquid. Road-mobile.
	CSS-X-7 (DF-11/M-11)	O	300	500	I	Solid-fueled. Road-mobile.
	CSS-6 (DF-15/M-9)	O	600	500	I	Solid-fueled. Road-mobile.
	CSS-2 (DF-3/3A)	O	2,650/2,900	2,150	I	Gradually being retired.[5]
	CSS-3/DF-4	O	5,500	2,200	I	
	CSS-4 (DF-5/5A	O	12,000/13,000[6]		I	Extended version (DF-5A) to be deployed in 2005.
	CSS-5 (DF-21)	O	1,800	600	I	
	DF-25	*D?*	1,700	2,000	I	May just be the first two stages of the DF-31.[7]
	CSS-9 (DF-31)	*D/T*	8,000	700	I	Deployment expected later this decade.[8]
	DF-31A[9]	*D*	12,000	800	I	Could be deployed between 2006 and 2010.[10]
	CSS-N-3 (Julang I) SLBM	O?	1,700	600	I	
	CSS-N-4 (Julang II) SLBM	D	8,000	700	I	Sea-based version of DF-31. Could be deployed by end of decade.[11]
Egypt	Scud-B	O/U	300	1,000	USSR/DPRK	
	Project T	O	450	1,000	I/DPRK	Improved Scud.
	Scud-C	O?	500	600–700	DPRK	
France	M-45 SLBM	O	6,000	1,000	I	

	M-51 SLBM	D	8,000	?	I	Will replace the M-45 SLBM. First test scheduled for 2005. Possible deployment by 2010.[12]
Greece	MGM-140 (ATACMS)	O	165	560	USA	Purchased 160 ATACMS between 1995 and 1996.
India	Prithvi-150	O	150	800–1,000	I/USSR	From Russian SA-2. Army missile.
	Prithvi-250	O	250	500–750	I/USSR	From Russian SA-2. Air Force missile.
	Dhanush (Naval Prithvi)	D/T	250	500	I	From Prithvi. Last tested November 7, 2004.[13]
	Sagarika[14]	D?	250–350	500	I	From Prithvi.
	Prithvi-350	D	350	500–1,000	I/USSR	From Russian SA-2.
	Agni	O[15]	600–750	1,000	I/USA/ France	From Scout; tested February, 18 1994.
	Agni II	O/P	2,000–2,500	1,000	I/USA/ France	Last tested August 29, 2004;[16] India says limited production has begun.[17]
	Agni III	D	3,500	1,000?	I	Test planned by the end of 2004.[18]
Iran[19]	Mushak-120	O	130	190	I	
	Mushak-160	O	160	190	I	
	Fateh-110 (NP-110)	P	200	600	I/PRC?	Last confirmed test September 6, 2002.[20]
	M-7 (CSS-8)	O	150	190	PRC	Modified SA-2.
	Scud-B	O/U	300	1,000	I/DPRK	
	Scud-C	O	500–600	500–700	I/DPRK	
	Shahab III	O/T[21]	1,300	750–800	I/DPRK	From No Dong. Last tested October 20, 2004.[22]
	Shahab IV	D/T?[23]	2,000[24]	1,000	I/Russia	Based on Russian SS-4.

(table continues on the following page)

Table 5.2. **World Ballistic Missile Arsenals** (continued)

Country[2]	System Name	Status	Range (kilometers)	Payload (kilo-grams)	Origin	Notes
	Shahab V	D?	3,000–5,500?[25]	?	I/DPRK/ Russia?	Possibly based on the North Korean Taepo-dong I and II.[26]
Iraq[27]	Al Samoud II	O/U[28]	180–200	300	I	Liquid-fuel missile. From Scud B.
	Ababil-100/Al Fatah	O[29]	160	200–300	I	Solid-fuel missile from Scud B.
Israel	Lance	O/S	130	450	USA	
	Jericho I	O	500	750-1,000	France	Road-mobile.
	Jericho II	O	1,500	1,000	France/I	Road-mobile.
	Jericho III	D?	3,000-6,500	1,000-1,300	I	Reportedly based on the Shavit Space Launch Vehicle.[30]
Kazakh-stan	Scud-B	O	300	1,000	USSR	
	Tochka-U (modified SS-21)	O	120	480	USSR	
Libya[31]	Scud-B	E	300	1,000	USSR/ DPRK	
	Al Fatah[32]	D/T	200	500	I	
North Korea[33]	Scud-B	O/P	300	1,000	USSR/ Egypt?	
	Scud-C Variant	O/P	500	600–700	I	
	No Dong	O	1,300	700–1,000	I	Single-stage, liquid fuel missile. Derived from Scud technology. Tested May 1993.
	Taepo-dong I	T	1,500–2,000	1,000	I	Combined No Dong and Scud; tested August 31, 1998.[34]
	Taepo-dong II	D	3,500–5,500	1,000	I	Reportedly ready for flight test if North Korea ends flight-test moratorium[35]

Pakistan	Hatf I	O	80	500	I	
	Hatf-II/IIA (Abdali)	D/T	180/280	500	I/PRC?[36]	First test-fired in 2002. Last tested March 31, 2005.[37]
	Hatf III (Ghaznavi /M-11)	O	280–300	500	I/PRC	2001 NIE lists the Hatf-3 to be an M-11. Last tested November 29, 2004.[38]
	Shaheen I	O/P[39]	700–750	500	I/PRC	Solid fueled. Thought to be an M-9 derivative. Last tested December 8, 2004.
	Ghauri (No Dong)	O	1,300	500–750	DPRK	2001 NIE lists the Ghauri to be a No Dong; last tested October 12, 2004.
	Ghauri II	D/T	1,500–2,300	700	I/DPRK	From No Dong; last tested April 14, 1999.[40]
	Shaheen II[41]	D/P	2,000–2,500	750–1,000	I/PRC?	Road mobile, two-stage. Last tested March 19, 2005.
	Ghauri III	D/T	2,700–3,500	?	I/DPRK	Thought to be based on the Taepodong-1. Engines have been tested, but flight test planned for June 2004 never occurred.
Russia[42]	Scud B (SS-1c Mod 1)	O	300	1,000	I	Liquid fuel.
	SS-21	O	120	480	I	Solid fuel.
	SS-18 (Satan)	O	9,000-11,000	8,800	I	Liquid fuel. Last tested December 22, 2004.[43]
	SS-19 (Stiletto)	O	10,000	4,350	I	Liquid fuel.
	SS-24 (Scalpel)	O	10,000	4,050	I	Solid fuel. Rail-mobile.
	SS-25 (Sickle)	O	10,500	1,000	I	Solid fuel. Road-mobile. Last tested November 2, 2004.[44]

(table continues on the following page)

Table 5.2. **World Ballistic Missile Arsenals** (continued)

Country[2]	System Name	Status	Range (kilometers)	Payload (kilo-grams)	Origin	Notes
	SS-27 (Topol-M)	O/P[45]	10,500	1,000–1,200	I	First road-mobile version of SS-27 expected to become operational by 2006.[46] Last tested December 24, 2004.[47]
	SS-X-26 (Iskander)	D/T	300	480	I	Solid fuel. Testing has been completed; will enter service in 2005.[48]
	Iskander-E[49]	D/T	280	480	I	For export. Solid fuel. Belarus, Iran, and Syria interested in this missile.
	SS-N-18 SLBM.	O	6,500–8,000	1,650	I	Last tested November 2, 2004.[50]
	SS-N-20 SLBM.	O	8,300	2,550	I	No longer in service.[51]
	SS-N-23 (upgraded version is known as the Sineva) SLBM.	O	8,300	2,800	I	Last tested September 2004.
	SS-N-27 (Bulava) SLBM.	D/T	10,000	1,000–1,200[52]	I	SLBM version of the SS-27; last tested September 23, 2004; will be carried by the Borey-class submarine, could be ready by 2006.
Saudi Arabia	Dong Feng-3 (CSS-2)	O	2,600	2,150	PRC	Purchased from China in 1987.
Slovak Republic[53]	SS-21	O	120	480	USSR	
South Korea	Nike-Hercules I/A	O	180	500	I/USA	Modified SAM.

	Nike-Hercules II	D/T	260–300	450-500	I/USA	Modified SAM; Tested at reduced range in 1999.[54]
	MGM-140 (ATACMS Block I/IA)	O	165/300	560	USA	Block I purchased in 1997; Block IA purchased in 2001, deployed in 2004.[55]
Syria	SS-21	O	120	480	USSR	Transferred 1983.
	Scud-B	O	300	1,000	USSR	
	Scud-C[56]	O	500–600	600–770	DPRK	Syria can now produce its own Scud-Cs.[57]
	Scud-D	T	700	500	DPRK	Based on the No Dong; last tested September 2000; Syria may now be capable of producing its own Scud-Ds.[58]
Taiwan	Ching Feng	O[59]	130	270	I/Israel	From Lance.
	Tien Chi[60]	O?[61]	300	500	I	Modified SAM. Tested in 1997.
Turkey	MGM-140 (ATACMS)	O	165	560	USA	Purchased 120 ATACMS in 1996.
	Project J[62]	D	150	150	I/PRC	Based on Chinese WS-1.
Turkmenistan	Scud-B	O	300	1,000	USSR	
Ukraine	SS-21	O	120	480	USSR	
	Scud-B	O	300	1,000	USSR	
United Arab Emirates[63]	Scud-B	O	300	1,000	Russia?	
United Kingdom	Trident II D-5	O	7,400+	2,800	USA	
United States	MGM-140 (ATACMS Block I/IA/II)	O	165/300/140	560/160/270	I	All three versions have different ranges and payloads; all three versions have been delivered to the Army.
	Minuteman III (MK-12/12A)	O	9,650+[64]	1,150	I	Last tested September 2004; service lives being extended until at least 2020.[65]

(table continues on the following page)

Table 5.2. **World Ballistic Missile Arsenals** (continued)

Country[2]	System Name	Status	Range (kilometers)	Payload (kilo-grams)	Origin	Notes
	MX Peace-keeper	O	9,650+[66]	3,950	I	All will be deactivated by 2005, although neither silos nor missiles will be destroyed.
	Trident I C-4 SLBM	O	7,400	1,500	I	Will be retired by 2007, at which time the SSBNs that carry the C-4's will carry the D-5s.
	Trident II D-5	O	7,400+[67]	2,800	I	
Vietnam	Scud-B	O	300	1,000	USSR	
Yemen	SS-21	O	120	480	USSR	Transferred 1988.
	Scud-B	O/U	300	1,000	USSR	Transferred to South Yemen in 1979.
	Scud (variant unknown)	O?	300–500	600–1,000	DPRK	Spain and the United States interdicted shipment from DPRK, but subsequently allowed it to proceed to Yemen.[68]

Key to Status

D	*in development*	E	in process of elimination
O	operational	P	in production
S	in storage	T	tested
U	used		

RANGE

SLBM submarine-launched ballistic missile
SRBM short-range ballistic missile (<1,000 km)
MRBM medium-range ballistic missile (1,000–3,000 km)
IRBM intermediate-range ballistic missile (3,000–5,500 km)
ICBM intercontinental ballistic missile (> 5,500 km)

Origin

I Indigenous

INF Treaty Intermediate-Range Nuclear Forces Treaty
SAM Surface-to-air missile

NOTES

1. The principal sources for this table include National Air Intelligence Center, *Ballistic and Cruise Missile Threat* (National Air Intelligence Center, Wright-Patterson Air Force Base, September 2000); National Intelligence Council, *Foreign Missile Developments and the Ballistic Missile Threat to the United States Through 2015,* Unclassified National Intelligence Estimate, December 2001; U.S. Department of Defense (DOD), *Proliferation: Threat and Response* (Washington, D.C.: DOD, 1997); discussions with

various U.S. government and relevant embassy officials; International Institute for Strategic Studies, *The Military Balance 2004–2005* (Oxford: Oxford University Press, 2004); various Natural Resources Defense Council (NRDC) "Nuclear Notebooks," as published in the *Bulletin of Atomic Scientists;* Congressional Research Service. Andrew Feickert, "Missile Survey: Ballistic and Cruise Missiles of Foreign Countries," March 5, 2004; Missile Defense Agency, "Ballistic Missile Capability: 2004," available at www.acq.osd.mil/mda/mdalink/pdf/BM2004.pdf; Arms Control Association, "Worldwide Ballistic Missile Inventories," May 2002, available at www.armscontrol.org/ factsheets/missiles.asp; Claremont Institute, "Ballistic Missiles of the World," available at www.missilethreat.com/missiles/; and Global Security, "Missile Proliferation Summary," available at www.globalsecurity.org/wmd/world/ missile.htm.

2. There are some questions regarding whether Argentina and Azerbaijan continue to deploy ballistic missiles. A number of sources report that Argentina tested and may have deployed the Alacran short-range ballistic missile in the late 1980s and early 1990s. The deployment of this missile cannot be confirmed, however, and the U.S. Department of State does not credit Argentina with this missile. During the Cold War, Azerbaijan imported a number of Scud-B short-range ballistic missiles from the Soviet Union. The Azeri embassy states that Azerbaijan is no longer in possession of these missiles, and very few reliable and publicly available resources credit Azerbaijan with Scud-B missiles. For these reasons, we include neither Argentina nor Azerbaijan in our final count of countries with ballistic missiles.
3. Russia is thought to have shipped 8 Scud launchers and 24 missiles to Armenia between 1992 and 1995. See Nikolai Novichkov, "Russia Details Illegal Deliveries to Armenia," *Jane's Defense Weekly,* April 16, 1997, p. 15.
4. Belarus announced that they will acquire the Iskander-E SRBM from Russia by 2010. "Belarus to Acquire Russian Multi-Warhead Missiles By 2010," *Financial Times,* November 12, 2004.
5. Robert S. Norris and Hans M. Kristensen, NRDC: Nuclear Notebook, "Chinese Nuclear Forces, 2003," *Bulletin of the Atomic Scientists,* November/December 2003, pp. 77–80.
6. 13,000 kilometers is the range of the DF-5A, which will be deployed in 2005. See Norris and Kristensen, "Chinese Nuclear Forces, 2003."
7. See Feickert, "Missile Survey: Ballistic and Cruise Missiles of Foreign Countries."
8. See the DOD's "Annual Report on the Military Power of the People's Republic of China" for FY 2004. Available at www.defenselink.mil/pubs/d20040528PRC.pdf. See also Norris and Kristensen, "Chinese Nuclear Forces, 2003."
9. The DF-31A is often confused with the now-canceled DF-41 ICBM. See Norris and Kristensen, "Chinese Nuclear Forces, 2003."
10. Ibid.
11. See the DOD's "Annual Report on the Military Power of the People's Republic of China."
12. NRDC, "Nuclear Data," available at www.nrdc.org/nuclear/nudb/datab16.asp. See also Bruno Tertrais, "Nuclear Policy: France Stands Alone," *Bulletin of Atomic Scientists,* July/August 2004, pp. 48–55.
13. The Dhanush is the naval version of the Prithvi series. "Dhanush Successfully Test Fired," Government of India, Press Information Bureau, November 8, 2004, available at http://pib.nic.in/release/release.asp?relid=4788.
14. The Indian government first acknowledged the existence of the Sagarika in October 1998, identifying it as a 250- to 350-kilometer sea-launched cruise missile derived from the Prithvi. Other sources maintained that the Sagarika program also contained a ballistic missile division. U.S. intelligence reports have classified it as an SLBM.
15. According to Indian Defense ministry officials, the military armed itself with the Agni in August 2004. See www.spacewar.com/2004/040829170937.537jwumo.html.
16. The Agni II was tested for a third time on August 29, 2004, traveling a distance of 1,200 kilometers (Agence France-Presse, "India Tests Nuclear-Capable Ballistic Missile," August 29, 2004). It traveled approximately 2,000 kilometers in a January 2001 test.
17. On May 31, 2001, the *Times of India* reported that the government had approved the induction of the Agni II and the development of a longer-range missile. In June 2001, India announced it had begun limited production of the Agni II and that it would be under the control of the army (Rahul Bedi, "Indian Army Will Control Agni II," *Jane's Defense Weekly,* August 22, 2001, p. 15).
18. See "India Begins Deploying Agni Missiles," August 31, 2004, available at www.expressindia.com/fullstory.php?newsid=35647.
19. DOD reported that Iran also produces a 200-kilometer "Zelzal" missile and a 150-kilometer "Nazeat" missile, which may be variations of its "Mushak" series. Iran has also tried to acquire a complete North Korean No Dong system and the Chinese M-9 and M-11 missiles.

(table continues on the following page)

Table 5.2. **World Ballistic Missile Arsenals** (continued)

20. Ali Akbar Dareini, "Iran Successfully Test-Fires Missile," Associated Press, September 6, 2002.
21. The Shahab III was handed over to the Revolutionary Guard on July 20, 2003. See Feickert, "Missile Survey: Ballistic and Cruise Missiles of Foreign Countries," pp. 16–17. U.S. intelligence says Iran has a "small number ... available for use in a conflict." Iranian defense minister Ali Shamkhani claimed in November 2004 that Iran could mass produce Shahab IIIs. "Iran 'Can' Mass-Produce Missiles," BBC News, November 9, 2004, available at http://news.bbc.co.uk/2/hi/middle_east/3997151.stm.
22. "Iran Conducts New Shahab III Missile Test with Observers Present: Minister," Agence France-Presse, October 20, 2004.
23. In November 2003, Iran denied that it was continuing development of the Shahab IV, but a report *in Jane's Defense Weekly* in September 2004 cited former Israeli ballistic missile defense director Uzi Rubin as saying that an August 11, 2004, test was probably a Shahab IV rather than a Shahab III. This was based on some technical differences between the missile fired on August 11 and the Shahab III. It is possible that Rubin is wrong, however, and that the missile fired was an upgraded version of the Shahab III. See Alon Ben-David, "Iran Unveils Redesigned Shahab Missile," *Jane's Defense Weekly,* September 27, 2004; available at www.janes.com/aerospace/ military/news/ jdw/jdw040927_1_n.shtml. Also, the National Council of Resistance of Iran, a dissident coalition, suggests that Iran has already tested the Shahab IV, in May and August 2002; see www.wisconsinproject.org/countries/iran/missile2004.htm.
24. Former Iranian president Hashemi Rafsanjani said that Iran had missiles with a 2,000-kilometer range in October 2004. It is possible that he was referring to the Shahab IV, but he also could have been talking about a significantly upgraded version of the Shahab III. His claims may not be accurate, though, as Iranian officials declined to comment on the Shahab-3's range after its most recent test, on October 20, 2004. See "Iran 'Increases Missile Range,'" BBC News, October 5, 2004, available at http://news.bbc.co.uk/2/hi/middle_east/3716490.stm. See also "Iran Conducts New Shahab-3 Missile Test with Observers Present: Minister," Agence France-Presse, October 20, 2004.
25. Estimates of the range of this new IRBM are only speculative, drawing upon remarks by the Iranian defense minister, who identified the missile as the "Shahab-V."
26. See Center for Defense Information, "Iran's Ambitious Missile Programs," available at www.cdi.org/program/index.cfm?programid=82.
27. According to "Iraq's Weapons of Mass Destruction: The Assessment of the British Government," Iraq illegally retained up to 20 al-Hussein missiles with a range of 650 kilometers (in violation of U.N. sanctions). See www.mod.uk/linked_files/iraq/ wmd.pdf. No al-Hussein missiles have been uncovered as of yet, however, and the Iraq Survey Group's "Comprehensive Report of the Special Advisor to the DCI on Iraq's WMD [weapons of mass destruction]" concluded that Iraq no longer retained the al-Hussein missile after 1991, having likely unilaterally destroyed them all.
28. Al-Samoud II missiles began to be destroyed under the supervision of UNMOVIC on March 1, 2003. In all, two-thirds of the missiles were eliminated when the war began on March 17, 2003. Five al-Samoud II missiles were fired at coalition forces during the war, but the system was recalled due to "failures." See United Nations Security Council, "Thirteenth Quarterly Report on the Activities of the United Nations Monitoring, Verification, and Inspection Commission," S/2003/580, May 30, 2003, pp. 28–29; available at www.unmovic.org. See also "Comprehensive Report of the Special Advisor to the DCI on Iraq's WMD" (the Duelfer Report of September 30, 2004), vol. 2, section 1, pp. 6–7.
29. See United Nations Monitoring, Verification, and Inspection Commission, "Unresolved Disarmament Issues: Iraq's Proscribed Weapons Programmes," March 6, 2003, p. 38; available at www.un.org/Depts/unmovic/new/ documents/cluster_document.pdf.

30. See the Monterey Institute's Center for Nonproliferation Studies "Weapons of Mass Destruction in the Middle East: Israel" web page, at http://cns.miis.edu/research/wmdme/israel.htm.
31. In December 2003, Libya privately pledged to the United States that it would eliminate all Missile Technology Control Regime (MTCR)–class missiles, that is, missiles that can travel over 300 kilometers with a payload of at least 500 kilograms. It was agreed, at that time, that the Scud-B missiles would be modified and kept for defensive purposes. See Paul Kerr, "Libya to Keep Limited Missile Force," *Arms Control Today,* May 2004, p. 28. However, in September 2004, Paula DeSutter, assistant secretary of state for verification and compliance, testified before the House Subcommittee on International Terrorism, Nonproliferation, and Human Rights, saying, "Libya . . . has agreed to destroy its Scud-B missiles." See "Completion of Verification Work in Libya," Testimony of Assistant Secretary of State for Verification and Compliance Paula DeSutter before the Subcommittee on International Terrorism, Nonproliferation, and Human Rights, September 22, 2004. There have also been unconfirmed reports that Libya attempted to purchase No Dongs from North Korea prior to its December 2003 decision to cease its pursuit of unconventional weapons. See www.nti.org/e_research/profiles/Libya/Missile/ 3834_3845.html.
32. Though intended to have a range of 950 kilometers, the Al Fatah has been successfully tested to only 200 kilometers. See DOD, *Proliferation: Threat and Response* (Washington, D.C.: DOD, 2001), pp. 47–48. The Al Fatah was not considered to be MTCR-class, and thus was not included as part of the deal made between Libya and the United States in December 2003.
33. *Jane's Defense Weekly* reported that North Korea was developing two new missiles, one land-based and the other sea-based, in August 2004. Both missiles are reportedly based on the Russian SS-N-6 SLBM. The report has not been confirmed. See Joseph S. Bermudez, "North Korea Deploys New Missiles," *Jane's Defense Weekly,* August 4, 2004, p. 6.
34. This was the most recent missile test of any kind conducted by North Korea. The missile impacted 1,320 kilometers from its launch point. It attempted and failed to put a small satellite into orbit, demonstrating some progress in staging technology.
35. See "The Worldwide Threat 2004: Challenges in a Changing Global Context," Testimony of Director of Central Intelligence George J. Tenet before the Senate Armed Services Committee, March 9, 2004.
36. Most believe it is based on the Chinese M-11, but one report says it is based on French motor technology. See S. Chandrashekar, "An Assessment of Pakistan's Missile Capability," *Jane's Strategic Weapon Systems,* March 1990, p. 4.
37. "Pakistan Tests Short-Range Hatf Missile; Pact with India on Test Notification Delayed," *Global Security Newswire,* March 31, 2005.
38. "Pakistan Test-Fires Missile," Agence France-Presse, November 29, 2004.
39. Pakistan announced "serial production" of this missile in October 2000.
40. Shah Alam, "Pakistan Test-Fires Long-Range Ballistic Missile in Response to India," Agence France-Presse, April 14, 1999.
41. See Atul Aneja, "Pakistan Begins Work on Shaheen-II," *The Hindu,* September 27, 1999.
42. The Russian SS-N-8 SLBM is no longer deployed and is in the process of elimination. The 12 remaining SS-N-8s are still counted in the biannual START memoranda of understanding, however, because they have not yet been eliminated. See www.state.gov/t/ac/rls/fs/2004/30816.htm.
43. "Russia Test-Fires Ballistic Missile," Agence France-Presse, December 22, 2004.
44. "Russia Test-Launches Land- and Sea-Based Ballistic Missiles," Associated Press, November 2, 2004.
45. Forty SS-27s have been produced and deployed. See Robert S. Norris and Hans M. Kristensen, NRDC Nuclear Notebook, "Russia's Nuclear Forces, 2005," *Bulletin of the Atomic Scientists,* vol. 61, no. 2, March/April 2005, pp. 70–72.

(table continues on the following page)

Table 5.2. **World Ballistic Missile Arsenals** (continued)

46. "Press Conference with Colonel General Nikolai Solovtsov, Strategic Forces Commander," Federal News Service, December 10, 2004.
47. "Russia Test-Fires Mobile Version of Its Latest Missile," Associated Press, December 24, 2004.
48. Interfax News Agency, "New Missile Launchers Will Be Shipped to Troops Next Year, Ivanov." August 27, 2004.
49. The Iskander-E is merely the export version of the SS-X-26. It has been slightly modified, with a range of just 280 kilometers, in order to comply with the 300-kilometers, 500-kilograms limit laid out by the Missile Technology Control Regime.
50. "Russia Test-Launches Land- and Sea-Based Ballistic Missiles." Associated Press.
51. Pavel Podvig, "Russian Strategic Nuclear Forces: Strategic Fleet." Available at www.russianforces.org/eng/navy/.
52. Our estimate based on the fact that the Bulava (SS-NX-30) is the SLBM version of the Topol-M (SS-27).
53. Slovakia has eliminated its Scud-B missiles. Personal conversation with a State Department official in the Office of Nonproliferation and Disarmament Fund, October 1, 2004.
54. An unidentified missile traveled 62 kilometers in a test firing on November 22, 2001. See Don Kirk, "South Korea Launches Missile In Its First Test Since Last Year," *New York Times,* November 23, 2001.
55. "South Korea Completes Deployment of New Medium-Range Missiles: Report," Agence France-Presse, October 9, 2004.
56. The *Jerusalem Post* reported the development of an advanced Syrian modification of the Scud-C (which could possibly be the Scud-D tested in September of 2000), but this report has not been confirmed by Western sources. See Arieh O'Sullivan, "Syrian Super Scud Ready Soon—Source," *Jerusalem Post,* September 16, 1999.
57. Nuclear Threat Initiative, "Syria: Missile Capabilities." Available at www.nti.org/e_research/profiles/Syria/ Missile/print/4126_4127.prt.
58. Ibid.
59. International Institute for Strategic Studies, *Military Balance 2004–2005,* p. 189.
60. This program was reportedly initiated in autumn 1995 and is based on the Sky Bow II SAM.
61. *Jane's Defense Weekly* reported on March 26, 2001, that Taiwan had deployed up to 50 Tien Chi missiles on Tungyin Island and at an undisclosed second location.
62. Jaffee Center for Strategic Studies, *The Middle East Strategic Balance, 2003–2004* (Tel Aviv: Tel Aviv University, 2004), chap. 19; available at www.tau.ac.il/jcss/balance/Turkey.pdf.
63. In 1989, the United Arab Emirates reportedly attempted to purchase 25 Hwasong-5 (Scud-B variant) missiles from North Korea. According to the Center for Nonproliferation Studies, the United Arab Emirates was not happy with the missiles and they were never operationalized. There is no publicly available evidence to confirm these reports, however. See the Monterey Institute's Center for Nonproliferation Studies, "A History of Ballistic Missile Development in the DPRK," available at http://cns.miis.edu/pubs/opapers/op2/fbmsl.htm.
64. The Minuteman III missile may have a range of up to 13,000 kilometers, but the U.S. Strategic Command officially lists its range at "greater than" 9,650 kilometers. See www.stratcom.mil/factsheetshtml/submarines.htm.
65. With the demise of START II, the United States has amended its plans to downgrade all Minuteman missiles to a single warhead. See Robert S. Norris and Hans M. Kristensen, NRDC Nuclear Notebook, "U.S. Nuclear Forces, 2004," *Bulletin of the Atomic Scientists,* May/June 2004, pp. 68–70.

66. The MX Peacekeeper may have a range of up to 11,000 kilometers, but the U.S. Strategic Command officially lists its range at "greater than" 9,650 kilometers. See www.stratcom.mil/factsheetshtml/submarines.htm.

67. The Trident II D-5 may have a range greater than 7,400 kilometers, but this is the U.S. Strategic Command's officially listed range. Available at www.stratcom.mil/factsheetshtml/submarines.htm.

68. Spain and the United States interdicted a North Korean shipment of 15 Scud missiles, warheads, and missile fuel on December 9, 2001. The shipment was eventually allowed to proceed and arrived in Yemen five days later. It is not known whether the Scuds in question were Scud-Bs or Scud-Cs. See Paul Kerr, "U.S. Stops Then Releases Shipment of N. Korean Missiles, *Arms Control Today,* January/February 2003, p. 25. See also Nuclear Threat Initiative, "Hwasong-6 (Scud-C): Overview and History," available at www.nti.org/db/profiles/dprk/msl/cap/NKILOMETER_Ch_hwaso6_GO.html.

BALLISTIC MISSILE PROLIFERATION 2005

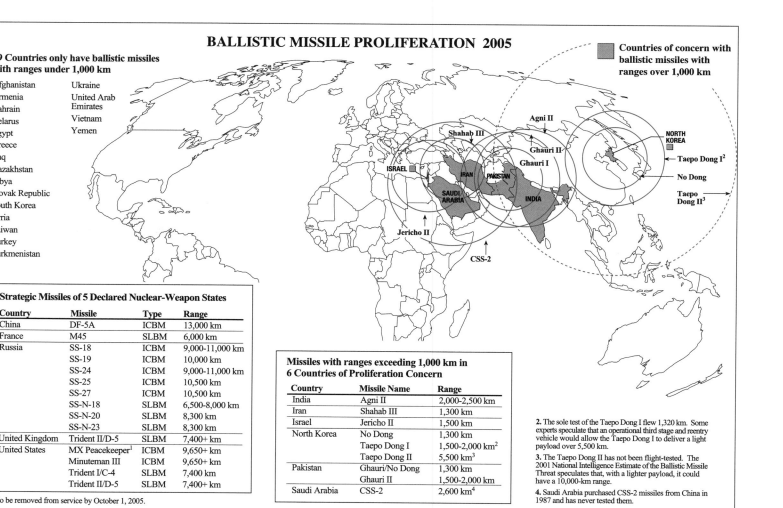

19 Countries only have ballistic missiles with ranges under 1,000 km

Afghanistan
Armenia
Bahrain
Belarus
Egypt
Greece
Iraq
Kazakhstan
Libya
Slovak Republic
South Korea
Syria
Taiwan
Turkey
Turkmenistan
Ukraine
United Arab Emirates
Vietnam
Yemen

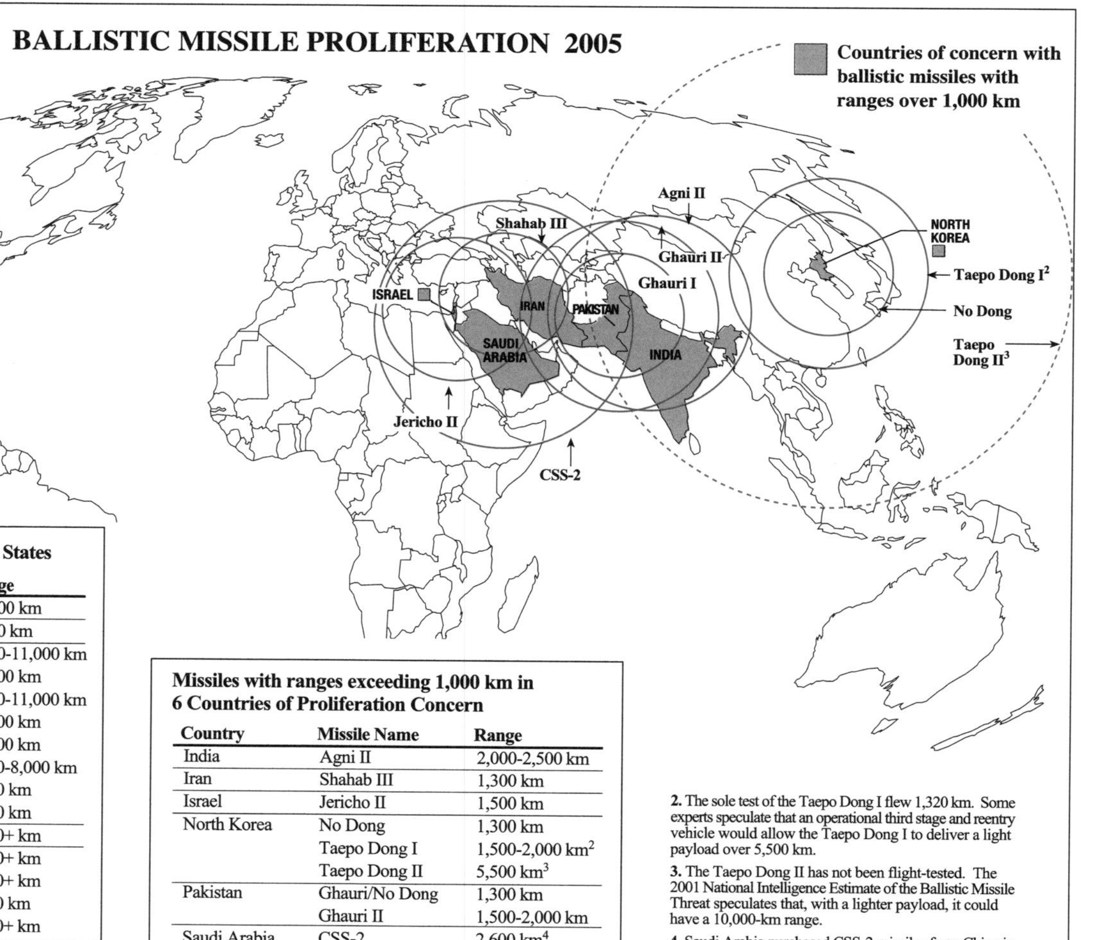

Strategic Missiles of 5 Declared Nuclear-Weapon States

Country	Missile	Type	Range
China	DF-5A	ICBM	13,000 km
France	M45	SLBM	6,000 km
Russia	SS-18	ICBM	9,000-11,000 km
	SS-19	ICBM	10,000 km
	SS-24	ICBM	9,000-11,000 km
	SS-25	ICBM	10,500 km
	SS-27	ICBM	10,500 km
	SS-N-18	SLBM	6,500-8,000 km
	SS-N-20	SLBM	8,300 km
	SS-N-23	SLBM	8,300 km
United Kingdom	Trident II/D-5	SLBM	7,400+ km
United States	MX Peacekeeper[1]	ICBM	9,650+ km
	Minuteman III	ICBM	9,650+ km
	Trident I/C-4	SLBM	7,400 km
	Trident II/D-5	SLBM	7,400+ km

1. To be removed from service by October 1, 2005.

Missiles with ranges exceeding 1,000 km in 6 Countries of Proliferation Concern

Country	Missile Name	Range
India	Agni II	2,000-2,500 km
Iran	Shahab III	1,300 km
Israel	Jericho II	1,500 km
North Korea	No Dong	1,300 km
	Taepo Dong I	1,500-2,000 km[2]
	Taepo Dong II	5,500 km[3]
Pakistan	Ghauri/No Dong	1,300 km
	Ghauri II	1,500-2,000 km
Saudi Arabia	CSS-2	2,600 km[4]

2. The sole test of the Taepo Dong I flew 1,320 km. Some experts speculate that an operational third stage and reentry vehicle would allow the Taepo Dong I to deliver a light payload over 5,500 km.

3. The Taepo Dong II has not been flight-tested. The 2001 National Intelligence Estimate of the Ballistic Missile Threat speculates that, with a lighter payload, it could have a 10,000-km range.

4. Saudi Arabia purchased CSS-2 missiles from China in 1987 and has never tested them.

PART TWO
Declared Nuclear Weapon States

There are five legally acknowledged nuclear weapon states under the terms of the Treaty on the Non-Proliferation of Nuclear Weapons (NPT). All five—China, France, Russia, the United Kingdom, and the United States—are also permanent members of the U.N. Security Council. Together, the five nations possess more than 25,000 nuclear weapons, the vast majority of which belong to the United States and Russia.

Under the terms of the NPT and the commitments taken at its five-year review meetings, the five states have agreed to an "unequivocal undertaking . . . to accomplish the total elimination of their nuclear arsenals leading to nuclear disarmament," and to "pursue negotiations in good faith on effective measures relating to cessation of the nuclear arms race at an early date and to nuclear disarmament."

The deployed arsenals of the nuclear weapon states are declining, with many thousands of nuclear weapons having been withdrawn and eliminated since the mid-1980s. Several countries, including the United States and Russia, however, still stockpile huge amounts (hundreds of metric tons) of nuclear-weapons-usable materials. This problem adds to global concern regarding the security of nuclear materials, the protection of which is of major importance in preventing the proliferation of nuclear weapons.

The following chapters on the five nuclear weapon states review the quantity of nuclear weapons and delivery systems possessed by each nation. Each chapter also looks at the issues that affect efforts to prevent the proliferation of nuclear weapons.

CHAPTER 6

Russia

Nuclear Weapons Capability

The Russian Federation is a recognized nuclear weapon state under the Treaty on the Non-Proliferation of Nuclear Weapons (NPT), and it possesses thousands of strategic and tactical nuclear weapons. Under the accounting rules of the Strategic Arms Reduction Treaty (START I), Russia maintains an accountable strategic nuclear force of 981 delivery vehicles with 4,732 associated warheads, although the actual number of deployed strategic weapons is about 3,800. Russia also is estimated to have 3,400 operational nonstrategic warheads and about 8,800 additional intact warheads retained in reserve or inactive stockpiles. Overall, Russia may possess as many as 16,000 intact nuclear weapons.

To support this arsenal, Russia maintains a massive nuclear complex that consists of ten formerly secret nuclear cities that house hundreds of metric tons of weapons-usable nuclear materials and hundreds of thousands of trained scientists and engineers with weapons-related knowledge. Russia is in the process of dramatically reducing the size of its nuclear arsenal and weapons complex owing to changed international security conditions, the negotiation of arms control agreements with the United States, and the retirement of older systems that are reaching the end of their service lives. If current trends continue, Russia may only deploy 1,989 strategic nuclear weapons by the end of the decade, although it could maintain a substantially larger nuclear arsenal given adequate resources.[1]

The Soviet Union conducted 715 nuclear weapons tests, the first on August 29, 1949, and the last on October 23, 1990. Russia has not conducted any tests since the fall of the Soviet Union. Russia has signed and ratified the Comprehensive Test Ban Treaty.

Since the end of the Cold War, the United States has provided approximately $10.3 billion to assist the states of the former Soviet Union to secure nuclear weapons and materials; eliminate aging nuclear weapon delivery systems; and find alternative, benign employment for its nuclear workforce, in addition to work on the former Soviet chemical and biological weapons complex.[2] Despite these efforts, Russia's nuclear complex continues to pose a serious proliferation risk, and much more remains to be done to adequately secure Russian nuclear materials and expertise. A failure to effectively address the proliferation challenges in Russia could result in the spread of nuclear, biological, or chemical weapons to other countries or subnational groups.

Aircraft and Missile Capabilities

As of the spring of 2005, Russia deployed 777 land- and submarine-based strategic ballistic missiles with intercontinental range, in addition to 78 strategic nuclear-capable bombers.[3] Most of the major strategic ballistic missile production facilities of the former Soviet Union were located outside Russian territory, largely in Ukraine. Russia continues to possess an advanced and accomplished, albeit currently depressed, missile design and production infrastructure.

Many of Russia's currently deployed strategic missiles are reaching the end of their service lives and are being retired, with the direct assistance of the United States under the Cooperative Threat Reduction (CTR) program (also called the Nunn-Lugar Program, after its original congressional sponsors). Russia continues to produce limited numbers of its new SS-27 land-based intercontinental ballistic missile (ICBM) (40 were deployed as of the spring of 2005). It also seeks to test and develop a new submarine-launched ballistic missile, the Bulava (SS-N-27), for deployment on its next-generation strategic submarine, also under construction.[4]

As with Russia's nuclear complex, the combination of Russia's extensive missile expertise with the economic hardships of its missile experts have raised concerns that, driven by economic necessity and profit motive, Russian equipment and technology may be finding their way into the missile programs of other countries. It appears that Russia may have had some limited missile-related contacts with Iraq before March 2003, in violation of U.N. sanctions, although this cooperation was limited to surface-to-air missiles and does not appear to have extended to ballistic missiles.[5] The United States has levied sanctions against more than a dozen Russian groups for such cooperation since 1998. Russian government officials deny that any assistance is being provided to the military missile programs of either India or Iran, and Moscow has taken significant steps to improve its export controls over missile-related technology.[6]

Biological and Chemical Weapons Capability

The Soviet Union had vast offensive chemical weapons (CW) and biological weapons (BW) programs. Today, Russia is a state party to both the Biological Weapons Convention and the Chemical Weapons Convention. However, Russia continues to possess almost 40,000 metric tons of chemical weapons, a massive stock of BW samples, and a latent BW production capability. The Soviet BW program reportedly weaponized plague, anthrax, smallpox, tularemia, brucellosis, and the Marburg virus and developed other possible agents.[7] Russia inherited the vast majority of the Soviet Union's chemical and biological weapons stocks and facilities and is responsible for the elimination of the weapons and stocks in its possession. Russia faces significant problems in complying with its commitments to eliminate these weapons, despite extensive international assistance, and it is likely to retain a considerable chemical and biological weapons stockpile for many years to come. In the meantime, there is much concern over the security of these materials as well as over the experts who are responsible for their production. The risk that chemical or biological weapons or critical production technology might leak out of Russia to proliferant states or terrorist groups remains high and will require a continued investment (domestic and international) to ensure that the Soviet chemical and biological weapons legacy does not lead to further proliferation.

Nuclear Analysis

During the Cold War, the potential, deliberate use of Soviet nuclear weapons posed the main security threat to the United States. In the aftermath of the Cold War, concern over Russia's nuclear arsenal shifted to a new set of concerns. These dangers included several risks:

- Nuclear weapons deployed in Belarus, Kazakhstan, and Ukraine might not return to Russian control.
- Russia might lose control of nuclear weapons (especially tactical nuclear weapons) in its inventory.
- Russian nuclear materials and expertise might be bought or stolen and thus assist the efforts of countries or terrorist groups in developing nuclear weapons.

Former U.S. senator Sam Nunn summed up the risk when he said:

> The old threats we faced during the Cold War, a Soviet strike or an invasion of Europe, were threats made dangerous by Soviet strength. The new threats we face today—increased Russian reliance on early launch and first use and increased reliance on tactical-battlefield nuclear weapons—are threats made dangerous by Russia's weakness. The threats of today go beyond nuclear forces and include terrorist groups. Much of Russia's nuclear, biological, and chemical weapons and materials are poorly secured; its weapons scientists and guards are poorly paid. We can't risk a world where a Russian scientist can take care of his children only by endangering ours.[8]

Those weapons deployed outside Russia when the Soviet Union dissolved have all been returned to Russia. The return of the nuclear weapons deployed in Belarus, Kazakhstan, and Ukraine was a tremendous achievement in international efforts to prevent the proliferation of nuclear weapons. The creation of three new nuclear weapon states out of the Soviet Union would have been an almost certain fatal blow to international efforts to prevent the spread of nuclear weapons (see chapter 18).

Strategic Weapons

Russia possesses a large, diverse, and advanced arsenal of strategic and tactical nuclear weapons. These weapons serve as the ultimate guarantor for Russian

Table 6.1. **Russian Strategic Nuclear Forces**

Type		START I Data, September 1990	START I Data, January 2005[1]
ICBMs	Launchers	1,064	611
	Warheads	4,278	2,436
SLBMs	Launchers	940	292
	Warheads	2,804	1,672
Bombers	Launchers	79	78
	Warheads	570	624
Totals	Launchers	2,083	981
	Warheads	7,652	4,732

ABBREVIATIONS

START I = Strategic Arms Reduction Treaty; ICBMs = intercontinental ballistic missiles; SLBMs = submarine-launched ballistic missiles.

[1]START I Memorandum of Understanding Data Exchange, U.S. Department of State, April 1, 2005. Information contained in the April 2005 data exchange is for forces accountable as of January 31, 2005.

national security. Some elements of Russia's nuclear forces have taken on an enhanced role in Russian security as its conventional military strength has faltered. Russia succeeded the Soviet Union as a nuclear weapon state and has assumed its legal obligations under arms control agreements, including the NPT, START I, and the Intermediate-Range Nuclear Forces Treaty.

Despite its continued importance to Russian security, the country's nuclear arsenal is shrinking. As the majority of Moscow's strategic weapons reach the end of their service lives and are being retired, many suffer from a lack of maintenance funds, raising questions about their long-term reliability and safety. Notwithstanding these concerns, the Russian nuclear arsenal remains formidable (see table 6.1; also see table 6.7 at the end of the chapter).

It is not yet clear to what level Russia's strategic arsenal will drop by the end of the decade. On the basis of the most optimistic assumptions of Russia's relationship with the United States, the Russian deployed strategic arsenal could drop to just under 2,000 weapons by the end of 2010. However, Russia could potentially maintain as many as 2,800 weapons by the end of 2010 (table 6.2).

Intercontinental ballistic missiles have historically made up the largest component of the Russian strategic nuclear triad. Yet of the five types of ICBMs that Russia deployed in 2005, only three (the SS-18, SS-19, and SS-27) are expected to be in service by the end of the decade. The other two systems—the SS-24 (rail and silo) and SS-25—are expected to reach the end of their serviceable lives by 2010.[9] It is also not yet clear how many of the new SS-27 land-based ICBMs Russia will produce and deploy. It has produced only limited numbers of that system, although its production capability could theoretically reach as high as

Table 6.2. **Projection of Russian Nuclear Forces**

Type		2010 Lower Limit (Launchers/ Warheads)	2010 Upper Limit (Launchers/Warheads)
ICBMs	SS-18[1]	50/500	50/500
	SS-19	30/180	30/180[2]
	SS-24	0/0	0/0
	SS-25	0/0	0/0
	SS-27	59/59[3]	70/420[4]
SLBMs	Delta III/SS-N-18	0/0	96/288[5]
	Typhoon/SS-N-20	0/0	0/0
	Delta IV/SS-N-23 (Sineva)[6]	96/384	96/384
	Borey/SS-N-27 (Bulava)[7]	0/0	24/144
Bombers[8]	Bear		
	Tu-95 H-6	27/162	32/192
	Tu-95 H-16	32/512	32/512
	Blackjack (Tu-160)	16/192	16/192
Total		230/1,989	364/2,812

ABBREVIATIONS

ICBMs = intercontinental ballistic missiles; SLBMs = submarine-launched ballistic missiles.

NOTES

1. Russia currently deploys 100 SS-18 ICBMs. The older variant is expected to be withdrawn from service in the next few years, while the newer variant is undergoing a life extension program that will allow it to remain in service until approximately 2015 or 2020.
2. It is theoretically possible that Russia, which currently deploys 130 SS-19 ICBMs, could extend the lives of these systems again (they have already been extended to 25 years), but it is much more probable that Moscow will simply retire its older SS-19s, replacing them with the 30 that it purchased from Ukraine in 2003. See www.cdi.org/russia/267-5.cfm.
3. Russia currently only has plans to purchase 4 SS-27 ICBMs in 2005, which would give Moscow a total of 44 deployed at the end of this year; experts estimate Russia's production capability to range from 3 to 9 missiles per year. In a December 2004 interview, Strategic Missile Troops Commander Nikolay Solovtsov stated that Russia could add one regiment of SS-27s every two years (or roughly 5 missiles per year). The lower-limit calculation reflects the assumption that Russia will produce and deploy 3 missiles per year from 2006 to 2010, while the upper-limit calculation reflects the assumption that Russia will produce and deploy 5 missiles each year from 2006 to 2010.
4. This assumes that each SS-27 could be MIRVed with up to six warheads. See Robert S. Norris and Hans M. Kristensen, "NRDC Nuclear Notebook: Russian Nuclear Forces, 2005," *Bulletin of the Atomic Scientists,* March/April 2005, pp. 70–72.
5. This assumes that all six Delta III nuclear ballistic missile submarines (SSBNs) could remain in service if necessary. See Norris and Kristensen, "NRDC Nuclear Notebook," pp. 70–72.
6. This estimate assumes that six Delta IV SSBNs will be deployed.
7. The lower limit assumes that no Borey class SSBNs will be deployed by 2010, while the upper limit assumes that two will be deployed by that year.
8. The lower-limit numbers depend on how many strategic bombers are converted to conventional roles. Experts speculate that some bombers will retain purely nuclear roles, while others will have the capability to carry out either nuclear or conventional missions.

50 a year with adequate funding. High-end projections suggest that Russia will have just 70 SS-27s by the end of the decade (see table 6.2).

The Russian submarine force is also in a serious state of decline. The bulk of its submarine force is slated for elimination by the end of the decade, and it is likely that Russia will deploy only eight submarines (six Delta IVs, with a seventh for testing purposes, plus one Borey-class submarine) by 2010.[10] The six Delta III submarines in the current arsenal are slated for retirement by the end of the decade, though it is possible that some could be retained if necessary. There are three Typhoon submarines in the current arsenal, but the missile they are equipped to carry, the SS-N-20, is nearing the end of its service life. One of the Typhoon subs, the *Dmitri Donskoi*, serves as a test bed for Russia's not-yet-deployed, next-generation submarine-launched ballistic missile (SLBM), the SS-N-27.[11] It is possible that some submarine launchers will remain operational in port if sufficient funds are not available for seagoing operations.

Russia is pursuing work on the next generation of strategic ballistic missile submarines, known as the Borey class. Construction began on the first boat of this class, the *Yuri Dolgoruki*, in 1996. It may be deployed by 2006. Construction of the second and third boats is under way, and both could enter service by 2012.[12]

The Russian bomber force is likely to remain the most stable component of the Russian strategic triad during the next ten years, although it too will decline in numbers as aging systems are retired. The two main bomber types in the Russian military are the Tu-160 Blackjack and the Tu-95 Bear.

STRATEGIC ARMS CONTROL AND REDUCTIONS. On July 31, 1991, the United States and the Soviet Union signed the Strategic Arms Reduction Treaty in Moscow. START I was the first arms control agreement to actually reduce the levels of deployed strategic weapons; previous agreements had served to cap the growth of existing arsenals. Under START I, the United States and Russia reduced their strategic accountable nuclear forces to 6,000 warheads each, deployed on no more than 1,600 strategic nuclear delivery vehicles—that is, ICBMs, SLBMs, and strategic bombers. The sublimits for warheads allow no more than 4,900 weapons to be deployed on either side's ICBMs and SLBMs and, of this subtotal, no more than 1,100 warheads may be deployed on mobile ICBMs. In addition, no more than 1,540 warheads may be deployed on heavy ICBMs.[13] The two countries completed their implementation of the agreement in December 2001, on schedule.

The entry into force of START I was substantially delayed because many of the systems covered by the treaty were physically deployed in non-Russian republics when the USSR fell. To address this dramatic development, the countries involved agreed that Belarus, Kazakhstan, Russia, and Ukraine would also need to ratify the agreement before the treaty would take effect. Upon the collapse of the Soviet state, Russia was almost immediately recognized by the international community as the main nuclear successor state of the Soviet Union, but obtaining agreement from the other three states required intensive diplomatic and strategic maneuvering by the United States, Russia, and the other countries involved. The result was the negotiation of the Lisbon Protocol to the START I agreement, signed on May 23, 1992, by Belarus, Kazakhstan, Russia, and Ukraine. Through the protocol, the four states agreed to participate jointly in START I as successors of the former Soviet Union and to "implement the Treaty's limits and restrictions" (article 2 of the protocol). In addition, Belarus, Kazakhstan, and Ukraine agreed to "adhere to the Treaty on the Non-Proliferation of Nuclear Weapons" as non-nuclear weapon state parties "in the shortest possible time" (article 5 of the protocol). In separate letters to President George H. W. Bush, each of the three presidents of the state parties also agreed to the elimination of all strategic nuclear arms on their territories within the seven-year START I implementation period.

In approving ratification on November 4, 1992, Russia's Supreme Soviet stipulated that Russia not exchange instruments of ratification until after the other three successor states had acceded to the NPT as non-nuclear-weapon states and carried out their other obligations under the Lisbon Protocol. The Belarusian parliament ratified START I on February 4, 1993, and Belarus formally acceded to the NPT on July 22, 1993. Kazakhstan's parliament ratified START I on July 2, 1992, and Kazakhstan formally acceded to the NPT on February 14, 1994. Ukraine's parliament approved START I and the NPT in two steps, on November 18, 1993, and on February 3, 1994, and it deposited its accession to the NPT on December 5, 1994. All nuclear weapons deployed in Belarus, Kazakhstan, and Ukraine were returned to Russia by the end of 1996 (see chapter 18).

START II. At the June 1990 Washington Summit, Presidents George H. W. Bush and Mikhail Gorbachev agreed that after the signing of START I, the two sides would begin new talks on further reductions at the earliest practical date. Those talks began in September 1991. At a subsequent summit in June 1992, Presidents Bush and Boris Yeltsin agreed on the basic principles of what was known as START II, including a ban on multiple independently targetable reentry vehicle (MIRV) land-based ICBMs. This was a significant development for two reasons. First, MIRVed ICBMs have been considered "destabilizing" weapons, posing an attractive target for a disarming first strike. Second, the majority of Russian nuclear arsenals were based on MIRVed ICBMs. Bush and Yeltsin signed the finalized START II agreement in Moscow on January 3, 1993.

START II, had it ever entered into force, would have capped the number of deployed strategic warheads in both countries at 3,500 and resulted in the elimination of all land-based MIRVed ICBMs by January 1, 2003. The U.S. Senate ratified START II on January 26, 1996. After more than six years' delay, the Russian Duma ratified the agreement on April 14, 2000.

The Russian ratification included an important caveat, however, requiring the U.S. Senate to approve protocols to the 1972 Anti–Ballistic Missile (ABM) Treaty before START II would enter into force. When the George W. Bush administration chose to withdraw from the ABM Treaty on June 13, 2002,

Moscow responded by declaring that it would no longer be bound by the limits agreed upon under START II, effectively killing the treaty.[14]

START III. At their March 20–21, 1997, Helsinki Summit, Presidents Yeltsin and Bill Clinton agreed to begin negotiations on a START III agreement immediately after START II entered into force and identified certain parameters for the new treaty. First, they agreed that the pact would limit deployed strategic forces on both sides to between 2,000 and 2,500 warheads by the end of 2007. Second, they agreed that START III would be the first strategic arms control agreement to include measures relating to the transparency of strategic nuclear warhead inventories and the actual destruction of strategic nuclear warheads. In addition, they pledged to explore measures for long-range nuclear sea-launched cruise missiles and tactical nuclear systems. These discussions were to take place apart from, but in the context of, START III negotiations.[15]

Despite several years of informal discussions between U.S. and Russian officials on issues to be addressed in the START III process, no negotiations ever took place and no agreement was ever produced.

THE TREATY OF MOSCOW (SORT). During his November 2001 summit with President Vladimir Putin, President George W. Bush announced that the United States would reduce its strategic nuclear arsenal to between 1,700 and 2,200 operationally deployed nuclear weapons over the next ten years. Bush had previously announced that this would be the level of U.S. nuclear forces. Although in 2000 Putin had declared his interest in reducing the Russian nuclear arsenal to 1,500 or fewer weapons, he did not announce a formal Russian target for reductions. In a joint press conference with Bush after their summit meeting, Putin did express his interest in having the reductions made part of a formal treaty: "For our part, [Russia is] prepared to present all our agreements in a treaty form, including the issues of verification and control."[16]

This agreement, now known as the Strategic Offensive Reductions Treaty (SORT), was signed in Moscow on May 24, 2002. The United States had previously resisted having the reductions codified in any legal agreement, but it finally accepted the Russian request to do so. The U.S. Senate ratified the pact in March 2003, and the Russian Duma followed suit in May 2003. The agreement capped the number of each side's strategic, offensively deployed, nuclear warheads at between 1,700 and 2,200 by December 31, 2012.

SORT is a significant departure from past arms control treaties. It is just two pages long, compared with the much lengthier and more detailed START agreements. It abandons the START II pledge to eliminate all MIRVed ICBMs, and its elimination and verification measures are much weaker than those under the START agreement. Whereas START I and START II called for the total, verifiable elimination of all delivery systems that were subject to strategic reductions, SORT only requires that these systems, and their corresponding warheads, not be deployed.[17] Nor does SORT follow up on the ambitious START III agenda, which considered including controls on warheads, long-range nuclear-capable cruise missiles, and tactical nuclear weapons.

Table 6.3. **Russian Tactical Nuclear Weapon Stockpiles**

Tactical Weapon Type	Totals in 1991[1]	Total to Remain under 1991 Bush–Gorbachev Agreements	Total Tactical Nuclear Weapon Stockpiles 2004[2]	Deployed Tactical Nuclear Weapons, 2005[3]
Land-based missiles	4,000	0	0	0
Artillery	2,000	0	0	0
Mines	700	0	0	0
Air defense	3,000	1,500	1,500	1,200
Air force	7,000	3,500	3,500	1,540
Navy	5,000	3,000	3,000	640
Total[4]	21,700	8,000	8,000	3,400

Notes

1. Alexei Arbatov, ed., *Yadernye Vooruzheniya Rossii* (Moscow: IMEMO, 1997), p. 56.
2. Gunnar Arbman and Charles Thornton. *Russia's Tactical Nuclear Weapons* (Stockholm: Swedish Defence Research Agency, 2003), p. 17.
3. See William M. Arkin and Hans M. Kristensen, "Russian Nuclear Forces, 2002," *Bulletin of the Atomic Scientists,* July/August 2002, pp. 71–73. The authors note in subsequent notebooks (2003, 2004, 2005) that their estimates on tactical nuclear weapons remain unchanged since 2002.
4. All totals are approximations.

THE INTERMEDIATE-RANGE NUCLEAR FORCES TREATY. U.S. and Russian nuclear deployments are also partly controlled by the Intermediate-Range Nuclear Forces Treaty (INF Treaty) signed by Presidents Gorbachev and Ronald Reagan on December 8, 1987. The INF Treaty required both countries to eliminate all nuclear-capable ground-launched ballistic and cruise missiles in their arsenals with a range of between 500 and 5,500 kilometers no later than June 1, 1991 (three years after the agreement entered into force).[18] The INF Treaty is the only pact to eliminate an entire class of nuclear weapons. Its implementation resulted, by May 1991, in the verified destruction of 846 long- and short-range U.S. INF missile systems and of 1,846 Soviet missile systems.[19] Under the terms of the agreement, implementation was completed on May 31, 2001, and the two governments announced that they would no longer need to verify the complete elimination of weapons systems covered under the agreement.

Tactical Weapons

Much less is known about the size, composition, and deployment of the Russian arsenal of tactical nuclear weapons (table 6.3). At one point during the Cold War, Russia is believed to have possessed about 30,000 tactical weapons.[20]

Russia has substantially reduced its stocks of tactical weapons, and informed estimates suggest that Russia has between 3,400 and 8,000 of these weapons.[21]

In October 1991, President Gorbachev responded to President George H. W. Bush's September initiative to dramatically reduce the deployment of tactical nuclear weapons. Gorbachev matched Bush by announcing a plan that would eliminate all Soviet nuclear artillery, short-range missile, and land-mine warheads; remove all nuclear weapons for air defense missiles from deployment areas (for storage or elimination); and remove tactical nuclear weapons from navy forces (ships, submarines, and land-based aircraft). In 1992, Russian president Yeltsin went further, announcing an end to the production of warheads for land-based tactical missiles, artillery, and land mines, as well as the decision to eliminate the stockpiles of those weapons. He also announced that Russia would eliminate one-third of its tactical sea-launched nuclear warheads, half of its tactical air-launched nuclear weapons, and half of its nuclear warheads for antiaircraft missiles.[22]

Russian tactical nuclear weapons deployed in non-Russian republics were returned to Russia in early 1992, and tactical weapons elimination is believed to have continued through the beginning of the new century. There are no formal verification procedures in place or associated with the initiatives, however, to ensure that the systems were in fact removed and destroyed. This uncertainty was reinforced in January 2001, when the *Washington Times* reported that Russia was transferring tactical nuclear weapons to Kaliningrad Oblast, which is an isolated enclave of Russian territory between Poland and Lithuania. Russia denied the claim, but in the absence of a formal inspection or other verification procedure, the truth of the allegations cannot be either confirmed or discounted.[23] Uncertainty about the elimination of tactical nuclear weapons has lingered, particularly with the general decline of Russia's conventional military forces. With that decline, tactical nuclear weapons have taken on greater importance in Russian security planning. This raises questions about whether Moscow will continue to eliminate these weapons. In late 2003, a high-ranking Russian general reaffirmed these concerns, saying that Russia would "hold onto its stockpiles" of tactical nuclear weapons.[24] In fact, it is likely that Russia is at least considering the development and deployment of new types of these weapons.[25] In October 2004, the U.S. assistant secretary of state for arms control, Stephen G. Rademaker, stated that Washington remains concerned that Russian commitments on tactical weapons in Europe have not been fulfilled.[26]

"Loose" Nuclear Weapons and Materials

There has been great concern that the security of Russia's nuclear complex since the collapse of the Soviet Union made the possible theft or unauthorized use of a Russian nuclear weapon a very real threat. As a result, the U.S. Congress started several programs to assist Russia in ensuring the security of its nuclear arsenal. U.S. assistance has been critical to improving the security of both nuclear weapons and nonweaponized nuclear materials in Russia and in other former Soviet states. Nuclear weapons generally enjoy a greater level of security than do Russian nonweaponized nuclear materials (highly enriched uranium and separated plutonium). Although Russia has never disclosed the total number of sites where nuclear weapons and materials are stored, as of the spring of 2005, the U.S. Department of Defense and the U.S. Department of Energy had identified at least 91 warhead storage sites[27] and 40 fissile material storage sites.[28]

NUCLEAR WEAPONS SECURITY. U.S.-funded programs have helped to secure the transport of Russian nuclear warheads and to develop a modern warhead accounting and tracking system. The program demonstrates an unprecedented level of cooperation between two former Cold War adversaries as well as their ability to cooperate in addressing common security threats.

Initial Russian weapons security programs, collectively known as Cooperative Threat Reduction (CTR), focused on helping to protect nuclear warheads during transit, especially those coming from the former Soviet republics to Russia. The programs also assisted with emergency planning and response in the event of an accident. For this purpose, the United States provided Russia with 4,000 Kevlar blankets, 150 supercontainers (used to carry several warheads at a time) for the physical and ballistic protection of nuclear weapons, and 117 special railcar conversion kits (100 cargo, 15 guard, and 2 prototypes) to ensure the security of warheads. In addition, the CTR programs have also provided Russia with five mobile emergency response complexes to deal with accidents. (An additional 150 supercontainers were provided by the United Kingdom in May 1997.) The railcars themselves were produced in Russia using U.S. funds and some U.S. materials; the rest of the equipment was produced in the United States. This program continues, and on November 1, 1999, the U.S. Department of Defense and the Russian Ministry of Defense signed a new memorandum for $41.7 million in additional assistance to purchase security systems for railcars. The program's aims have now shifted to the replacement of railcars that are nearing the end of their service lives.[29]

Soviet-era warhead accounting and management relied upon the manual (handwritten) tracking of its nuclear arsenal. Through the U.S. CTR program, a new automated system of tracking and accounting is being implemented in Russia. Under the program, the United States has provided Russia with 100 personal computers, as well as software and training. It is also identifying additional needs, including site preparation for the installation of permanent communication equipment. The program has certified hardware and software for the tracking system at nineteen key field and regional sites. A demonstration facility, the Security Assessment and Training Center, was completed in 2003, and installation has begun at additional sites. The program is scheduled to be completed in 2005.[30]

With shipments beginning in 1997, the U.S. Department of Defense CTR program transferred 123 "quick-fix" sets to the Russian Ministry of Defense for upgrading security at weapons storage sites. In 2002, however, the ministry indicated that it has installed only one-third of the fencing sets at 52 locations.[31] The ministry planned to install all the upgrades, but it then asked the United States for additional funding assistance. Disputes over U.S. access to Russian weapons sites have seriously stalled the upgrades. As of the spring of 2005, approximately half of the total 123 quick-fix sets had been installed.[32] At the same time, the U.S. Department of Energy has been working successfully to improve security at Russian navy sites that contain nuclear weapons. The project started in 1999, and the Energy Department expects to complete security upgrades at all 39 navy sites in 2006.[33]

NUCLEAR MATERIALS SECURITY. Even if Russia were to eliminate its nuclear weapons, the country's vast holdings of nonweaponized nuclear materials will remain a major proliferation concern for decades to come.

President Bush and President Putin have acknowledged this concern on a number of occasions. In a joint statement from November 2001, the two presidents said, "Both sides agree that urgent attention must continue to be given to improving the physical protection and accounting of nuclear materials of all possessor states, and preventing illicit nuclear trafficking."[34] President Bush stated in February 2004 that the countries of the world must do all they can to protect nuclear materials.[35]

Russia has the world's largest stocks of weapons-grade and weapons-usable nuclear materials: highly enriched uranium (HEU) and plutonium. Much of this material is not adequately protected against theft or diversion. A U.S. Department of Energy advisory group, chaired by the former Senate majority leader, Howard Baker, and the former White House counsel, Lloyd Cutler, concluded in 2000: "The most urgent unmet national security threat to the United States today is the danger that weapons of mass destruction or weapons-usable material in Russia could be stolen and sold to terrorists or hostile nation states and used against American troops abroad or citizens at home. This threat is a clear and present danger to the international community as well as to American lives and liberties." Though some progress has been made since that time, many experts believe this assessment is still correct.[36]

Reliable estimates of the total Russian nuclear material stockpile vary, but Russia is believed to have produced roughly between 180 and 185 tons of weapons-usable separated plutonium (civil and military) and close to 1,100 tons of HEU.[37] Of this material, approximately 600 to 700 metric tons are thought to be in nuclear weapons. It is not possible to be absolutely certain of the actual amount of nuclear material that Russia has produced and holds because their production cannot be fully accounted for even under the best circumstances (for example, even the United States' own nuclear production accounting system—considered vastly superior to the former Soviet system—has a margin of accounting error of almost 1 percent for plutonium).[38]

Nuclear smuggling from Russian or former Soviet facilities continues to present an acute proliferation risk, despite considerable efforts to improve the security of "loose" Russian materials. The International Atomic Energy Agency has confirmed that, from January 1993 to December 2003, seventeen cases of smuggled nuclear-weapons-usable materials occurred, many originating in the former Soviet Union. For example, in 1994 and 1995, the Czech authorities recovered small amounts of HEU that had likely originated in Obninsk, Russia. In 1999,

Kyrgystani officials arrested two persons who were attempting to sell 1.5 grams of plutonium.[39] Hundreds of similar cases have been reported and investigated during the past decade.

NUCLEAR MATERIAL PROTECTION, CONTROL, AND ACCOUNTING. U.S. programs, run primarily by the Department of Energy, work to enhance security in the Russian nuclear complex. Initial security efforts covered more than two-thirds of the total number of sites containing fissile material, and emphasized locking down the most vulnerable facilities. Even after ten years of effort, however, a majority of nonweaponized Russian nuclear materials are inadequately protected. By the end of 2004, only 26 percent of materials had received comprehensive security upgrades.[40]

Current U.S. government projects plan to complete comprehensive safeguards for all civilian and military material sites by the end of 2008.[41] Experts, however, believe that such a timetable may be unrealistic, for two reasons. First, Moscow and Washington still have unresolved issues regarding American access to Russian military sites. Consequently, much more has been done to install upgrades at civilian sites than at military sites. Upgrades at the civilian facilities had been nearly completed by the end of 2004, while a relatively small number of military sites, which hold about 83 percent of Russia's fissile material, lagged far behind.[42]

Second, the Department of Energy's current plans anticipate that 50 percent of the material will be secured in 2007 and 2008, the last two years of the program, even though it will have taken the first twelve years of the program to secure the first 50 percent. If the rate of comprehensive upgrades remains the same as it was in fiscal year (FY) 2003, then the program will not be completed until 2013.[43] Even this final level of protection, however, will be below the accepted international standards for the physical protection of nuclear materials. No plans currently exist to provide Russia with the resources needed to reach this level of physical security and accounting.

The U.S. Congress has broadly supported the Material Protection, Control, and Accounting Program (MPC&A), funding the program at the annual level requested by the Clinton administration. Despite statements of support from the George W. Bush campaign and then administration, its first budget request reduced funding for Russian nuclear material security from a little more than $170 million in 2001 to $138 million in 2002. Additional cuts in Russian nonproliferation programs, including the disposition of nuclear materials and brain drain programs (see below), totaled more than $100 million from the previous year's budget. Congressional action on the FY 2002 budget restored funding for nuclear security upgrades to 2001 levels.

After the September 11, 2001, terrorist attacks, Congress passed two supplemental appropriations for MPC&A, increasing total 2002 funding to $267 million. Budgets in the following years contained $194 million (FY 2003), $212 million (FY 2004), and $275 million (FY 2005) (see table 6.4). The Bush administration's request for FY 2006 was $246 million.[44]

In addition to protecting nuclear materials in place, the United States also funded the construction of a large nuclear material storage facility in Russia to

Table 6.4. **Funding for Materials Protection, Control, and Accounting (millions of dollars)**[1]

1993	1994	1995	1996	1997	1998	1999
2.7	3.4	10.2	85.0	112.6	137.0	139.8

2000	2001	2002	2003	2004	2005	2006
138.7	169.5	266.6[2]	193.9	212.1	275.5	245.5[3]

SOURCE

Nuclear Threat Initiative, "Interactive Threat Reduction Budget Database: FY 1992–FY 2006," available at www.nti.org/e_research/cnwm/overview/cnwm_home.asp

NOTES

1. The budgets for fiscal years 1993 to 2000 were submitted by the Bill Clinton administration. The budgets for fiscal years 2001 to 2006 were submitted by the George W. Bush administration.
2. This figure includes funding provided by supplemental appropriation passed by Congress in fiscal year 2002 in response to the September 11, 2001, terrorist attacks.
3. This is the level of funding proposed by the Bush administration in February 2005. The actual appropriation will not be made until the fall of 2005.

securely store nuclear materials released from dismantled nuclear weapons. The Fissile Material Storage Facility in Mayak was originally planned to have two wings, with each holding 25,000 canisters of nuclear material (50 tons of plutonium and 200 tons of HEU). The first wing was completed in December 2003, but Russia announced that it planned to store only 25 tons of plutonium and no HEU in the facility. No written agreement between the United States and Russia requires Moscow to store any material at Mayak, and the two states have been at odds over the need to amend agreements to include storage obligations. Additionally, the two sides have not agreed on transparency measures to verify the origin of the nuclear materials to be stored at the facility. Though they have made progress on resolving some transparency issues, disputes over measuring total mass of material remain a significant hurdle.[45] There are no current plans to construct the second wing.

Even the best long-term storage and security of nuclear materials cannot eliminate the proliferation risks associated with these huge stocks. The continued possession of large stocks of excess nuclear materials is a recognized "clear and present danger."[46] The disposal of those materials no longer required for defense purposes is vital to reduce the risk that these materials might again be used to produce nuclear weapons in Russia or in other states or by subnational groups. To this end, the United States and Russia have been cooperating on two important programs: the HEU purchase agreement and the plutonium disposition program.

The Purchase of Highly Enriched Uranium

On February 18, 1993, Presidents Clinton and Yeltsin agreed that the United States would purchase 500 metric tons of Russia's HEU from dismantled

Russian nuclear weapons.[47] The program reduces the risk of the theft of Russian nuclear material and speeds the dismantlement of Russian nuclear weapons by freeing storage space for released nuclear materials. Under the program, Russia dilutes, or "downblends," weapons-grade HEU into low-enriched uranium, which cannot be used directly in nuclear weapons. This process takes place under intrusive monitoring arrangements. Russia then ships the material to the United States for fabrication into fuel for nuclear power reactors. The entire program is designed to take place over 20 years and was originally expected to pay Russia $12 billion for the material and services. The agreement has since been renegotiated. Russia will now be paid according to market forces, which will be less than the original payment envisioned.[48]

Executing agents appointed by the two governments carry out the pact. The U.S. executive agent is the privatized United States Enrichment Corporation (USEC), and the Russian executive agent is Techsnabexport (Tenex), the commercial arm of the Russian Federal Atomic Energy Agency (Rosaton formerly Minatom). As of the spring of 2005, the United States (through USEC) had purchased the equivalent of 237 metric tons of HEU (6,974 metric tons of low-enriched uranium fuel) from Russia (enough material to produce 9,482 nuclear weapons), for which Russia received over $3.5 billion.[49]

Russia may have hundreds of additional metric tons of HEU not covered by this purchase agreement, much of which could eventually become excess to Russian military needs. Numerous nongovernmental experts have called for an expansion of the HEU agreement to include the purchase of larger amounts of HEU. The economic considerations of such a move are complicated by the fact that the private USEC lacks a financial incentive to expand its purchases. This conflict between national security and financial considerations is a major point of contention between experts and government officials. There are no firm official plans to expand the scope of the purchase agreement, although the issue is reportedly under review by the Bush administration.

Plutonium Disposition

The United States and Russia have both declared large amounts of former defense-purpose plutonium to be excess to defense needs. On March 1, 1995, President Clinton designated 50 metric tons of plutonium as excess,[50] and Boris Yeltsin declared that "up to" 50 metric tons of plutonium would be made excess through the nuclear disarmament process in 1997.[51] Collectively, this material is enough to produce 25,000 nuclear warheads, and both countries have pledged to take steps to ensure that the material is never again used for weapons.

These amounts represent significant portions of the plutonium produced in both countries. However, both countries will have large stocks of weapons-usable materials even after these amounts are dispositioned.

At the June 2000 summit in Moscow, the United States and Russia agreed to dispose of 34 metric tons each of their excess weapons plutonium. Under the agreement, the two approved methods for the disposal of this material were the irradiation of plutonium in a nuclear reactor and the immobilization of plutonium with high-level radioactive waste (in either glass or ceramic form). The agreement called on both countries to "seek to" begin the operation of "industrial-scale" facilities no later than December 2007, at a disposal rate of 2 metric tons of plutonium per year.[52]

There are several major problems looming over the implementation of the agreement, however. These include technical and political challenges to the U.S. program and a lack of financing for the Russian disposition effort. The Bush administration has decided to abandon immobilization and to pursue only reactor-based irradiation of this material.[53] The biggest remaining problem is a liability dispute, which has delayed the beginning of construction of special mixed-oxide fuel facilities in each country by at least ten months. It appears unlikely that either side will begin disposing of significant amounts plutonium by the 2007 deadline.

Russia has also stated that it does not possess the funds required to carry out the disposition alone and would simply store the material if international support were unavailable. Since the program was first funded in FY 1996, the United States has appropriated approximately $494 million for this effort.[54] Estimates now suggest that the entire Russian disposition program, including the construction and operation of facilities, could cost $2 billion.[55] Moreover, for the program to succeed, efforts to dispose of U.S. plutonium must also be sufficiently funded because Russia would be unwilling to dispose of its excess plutonium unless the United States does so as well. The 2005 budget sets funding levels for Russian disposition at $73 million, and U.S. disposition efforts at $464 million.[56]

Furthermore, both countries are hoping that third parties can assist in this essential nonproliferation endeavor. The U.S.–Russian agreement completed at the June 2000 summit in Moscow "recognizes the need for international financing and assistance" in order for Russia to implement its plutonium disposition plans.[57] The July 2000, Group of Eight (G-8) summit in Okinawa called upon the G-8 to develop an international financing plan by the 2001 meeting that was held in Genoa. Although this deadline was not met, by the spring of 2005, Canada, the European Union, France, Japan, Italy, the Netherlands, and the United Kingdom, in addition to the United States, had pledged $981 million for Russian plutonium disposition as part of the "G8 Global Partnership Against the Spread of Weapons and Materials of Mass Destruction," an initiative launched in 2002.[58] These pledges are signs of progress, but still only amount to 50 percent of the anticipated cost of the program.

Nuclear Expertise

The breakup of the Soviet Union and prolonged economic strain in Russia also pose serious nonproliferation risks in the form of Russian nuclear weapons expertise and technical know-how. International efforts to prevent the proliferation of nuclear weapons have focused not only on trying to protect Russian nuclear materials but also on preventing Russian nuclear experts from selling their skills to would-be nuclear weapon states and organizations.

Russia's nuclear complex is filled with tens of thousands of scientists, engineers, and technicians who are responsible for the construction, maintenance, and dismantlement of Russia's nuclear weapons. Counts vary, but there are approximately 35,000 excess weapons scientists and workers in the Russian nuclear complex, many of whom have direct access to weapons-usable nuclear materials.[59]

After the collapse of the Soviet Union, the employees of Russia's nuclear complex fell on hard times. Formerly the privileged inhabitants of Russia's nuclear cities, after the Soviet collapse, these nuclear elite found themselves in geographically remote locations with rapidly dropping living standards and diminishing work orders from the central government.

Collectively referred to as a brain drain, the risk that Russian nuclear experts might be forced by economic deprivation to sell their expertise or materials on hand rapidly changed the dynamics of Russian and U.S. security considerations. A 2002 National Intelligence Council study indicated that economic improvements in Russia would mitigate the problem slightly, but it also noted that officers responsible for warhead storage and maintenance receive wages that "rarely exceed $70 a month."[60] A 2003 survey of Russian scientists with weapons expertise found that 20 percent of respondents would consider working in North Korea, Syria, Iran, or Iraq.[61]

Both the U.S. Department of State and the U.S. Department of Energy are involved in efforts to help prevent the brain drain. These efforts consist of projects designed to provide grants for civilian research to scientists and institutions formerly involved in weapons development, as well as to help in the conversion and commercialization of former defense industries. The three principal programs in this area are the International Science and Technology Centers (ISTCs), the Initiatives for Proliferation Prevention (IPP), and the Nuclear Cities Initiative (NCI). In 2002, IPP and NCI were combined under the Russian Transition Initiative. In 2005, these efforts were extended to countries such as Iraq and Libya under the Global Initiatives for Proliferation Prevention.

Science Centers

The State Department manages U.S. participation in both the ISTC in Moscow and the Science and Technology Center of Ukraine (STCU). These centers are multilateral organizations designed to prevent the spread of weapons of mass destruction and missile technology expertise by providing civilian employment opportunities to former weapons scientists and engineers in the newly independent states (NIS) of the former USSR.

The ISTC was founded in Moscow in 1992. Its current members include the European Union, Canada, Japan, Norway, South Korea, and the United States as donors. Armenia, Belarus, Georgia, Kazakhstan, the Kyrgyz Republic, Russia, and Tajikstan are recipient countries.[62] To ensure the full participation of all NIS member states, branch offices of the ISTC have been established in Almaty, Kazakhstan; Yerevan, Armenia; Minsk, Belarus; Tbilisi, Georgia; and Bishkek, Kyrgyz Republic.[63] In July 1995 the STCU, a separate but parallel organization, commenced operations in Kyiv, Ukraine. Currently, under the STCU auspices, Canada, the European Union, and the United States fund projects in Ukraine, Azerbaijan, Georgia, and Uzbekistan.[64] In addition to its headquarters in Kyiv, the STCU also has field offices in the Ukrainian cities of Dnipropetrivsk, Kharkiv, and Lviv, as well as in Baku, Azerbaijan; Tbilisi, Georgia; and Tashkent, Uzbekistan.[65]

Since its inception, the ISTC has funded 2,000 projects valued at a total of $600 million. A total of 58,000 specialists at more than 765 institutions have received grants from ISTC, making it less likely that they will need to sell their services to would-be proliferators.[66]

The Initiatives for Proliferation Prevention and the Nuclear Cities Initiative

The U.S. Department of Energy manages and funds IPP and NCI. The Bush administration, however, announced in December 2001 that the programs would be merged into one, "and restructured to focus more effectively on projects to help Russia reduce its nuclear warhead complex."[67] Like the Science Centers, the IPP program aims to provide productive nonmilitary projects for former NIS weapons scientists and engineers. IPP seeks to promote the conversion of NIS defense industries to civilian production through the commercialization of technologies and the development of links between NIS institutes and U.S. industrial partners. Thus far, 22 projects have been commercialized, generating combined revenue of $24 million.[68] Unlike the ISTC and the STCU, IPP is exclusively a U.S.-NIS program and does not involve additional international partners. Since its inception, the IPP program has funded projects involving nearly 16,000 former Soviet weapons scientists at 180 institutes.[69]

In 1998, the U.S. Department of Energy launched NCI, designed to assist Russia in the development of non-defense-related industries in Russia's ten "closed" nuclear cities. Those cities, which are geographically isolated, are home to hundreds of thousands of skilled scientists, engineers, and technicians and hundreds of metric tons of weapons-usable nuclear materials. As noted before, the desperate financial situation of nuclear scientists and technicians in the Soviet Union's remote nuclear complex has sparked proliferation fears, and the NCI aims to develop paths to peaceful employment. In addition, the NCI program was designed to assist in downsizing the complex, which would reduce Russia's ability to reconstitute its Cold War nuclear arsenal rapidly, thereby strengthening strategic stability.

The NCI agreement was signed by U.S. Secretary of Energy Bill Richardson and Russian Atomic Energy Minister Yevgeny Adamov on September 22, 1998. The original concept was developed by the U.S. government in cooperation with an initiative from several nongovernmental organizations. According to the agreement, the initiative aims to "create a framework . . . that will provide new jobs for workers displaced from enterprises of the nuclear complex."[70] The U.S. Department of Energy and Minatom agreed to focus initial activities at three of the ten Russian nuclear cities: Sarov (Arzamas-16), Snezinsk (Chelyabinsk-70), and Zheleznogorsk (Krasnoyarsk-26). Minatom closed the Avangard weapons facility at Arzamas-16 in 2003, with NCI contributing to the conversion of 40 percent of the facility to nonweapons uses. In addition, Minatom has stated its intention to cease weapon-related activities at Penza-19 by 2008.[71] In September 2003, however, the NCI agreement was allowed to expire when Washington and Moscow could not work out a liability agreement that, from the United States' perspective, would sufficiently protect U.S. officials and workers. Three days before the expiration of the agreement, the United States and Russia signed a protocol that allowed the 69 ongoing NCI projects to be completed. No new projects will be taken up, however, without a new agreement.[72]

Biological and Chemical Weapons Analysis

The Soviet Union had active and large-scale chemical and biological weapons programs, the bulk of which were inherited by Russia when the Soviet Union ceased to exist in 1991 (table 6.5). Several key biological weapons facilities are located in non-Russian former Soviet republics, including Kazakhstan and Uzbekistan. Russia's stocks of chemical weapons and biological weapons samples, and the expertise it took to produce them, continue to pose serious proliferation threats. The risk that such materials or expertise might leak out of the former Soviet Union and aid countries or terrorist groups in the acquisition or use of chemical or biological weapons is a serious global security concern—a concern that has increased in the wake of the post–September 11 anthrax attacks in the United States. Weapons expert Amy Smithson told the Senate Foreign Relations Committee in March 2003, "The Soviets had a prodigious bio-weapons program involving over 65,000 weapons scientists and technicians. They weaponized contagious diseases, hardened others against antibiotic treatment, and had robust capabilities in anti-crop and anti-livestock agents. Without a doubt, this reservoir of talent is the deepest in the world, and I fear that terrorists may, indeed, go there for help."[73] Similar concerns exist for Russia's chemical weapons capabilities.

Russia continues its efforts, with the assistance of the United States and other countries, to eliminate its chemical and biological weapons capabilities in compliance with its treaty commitments. Progress to date, however, has been slow owing to inadequate funding, poor management, and bureaucratic conflicts. Moreover, the United States remains wary that Russia may not be fully complying with all of its obligations under the chemical and biological weapons conventions.[74]

Chemical Weapons

Russia possesses the largest stocks of chemical weapons in the world. Moscow's holdings include an estimated 39,280 metric tons of chemical weapons at seven storage sites. Eighty one percent of Russia's chemical weapons stockpile consists of nerve agents, including sarin, soman, and VX viral agents. The remaining 19 percent is made up of blistering agents, including lewisite, mustard, and lewisite-mustard mixtures. These materials are stored in both munition containers

Table 6.5. **Chemical Weapons by Storage Location and Form**

Chemical Weapons Storage Site	Chemical Type	Percentage of Original Stockpile[1]	Storage Form
Shchuch'ye	Nerve agent	13.6	Projectiles and rocket warheads
Popchep	Nerve agent	18.8	Air-delivered munitions
Leonidovka	Nerve agent	17.2	Air-delivered munitions
Gorny	Blister agent/mustard, lewisite, and mixture	2.9	Bulk containers
Maradykovsky	Nerve agent	17.4	Air-delivered munitions
Kizner	Blister agent/lewisite	14.2	Projectiles and rocket warheads
Kambarka	Blister agent/lewisite	15.9	Bulk containers

NOTE

1. As of the spring of 2005, approximately 1.8 percent of the total stockpile (an estimated 720 metric tons) had been destroyed at the Gorny site. See Russian Munitions Agency, Facilities of CW Stockpiling and Destruction, available at www.munition.gov.ru/eng/objects.html.

(including projectiles, rocket warheads, bombs, spray devices, and Scud missile warheads) and bulk storage containers.[75] All the nerve agents are in weaponized form, but some of the blister agents are contained in bulk storage.

Russia is a member of the Chemical Weapons Convention (CWC), which requires the elimination of all chemical weapons and the conversion of chemical weapon production facilities. Russia signed the treaty on January 13, 1993, and ratified it on November 5, 1997. There are continued suspicions, however, that Russia has not made a full and complete declaration of all its past chemical weapons activities. The terms of the treaty require that all parties eliminate their chemical weapons stockpiles in four phases, completing the destruction of portions of the national stocks within three, five, seven, and ten years of the agreement's entry into force.[76] Russia was the only one of the first four declared chemical weapon-possessing states (India, Russia, South Korea, and the United States) that failed to meet the initial April 2000 deadline for the elimination of 1 percent of its chemical weapons. (Other countries, including Syria, Israel, and North Korea, are known to have or are thought to have chemical weapons, but either they have not made official declarations or are not parties to the CWC. Since 2003, Libya and Albania have both officially declared chemical weapons stockpiles.) As of the spring of 2005, Russia had completed destruction of nearly 2 percent of its stockpile.[77] Its second deadline, to eliminate 20 percent of the stockpile, was extended five years to April 29, 2007, at the Eighth Session of the Conference of States Parties. There is little hope that Russia will meet this deadline. At the same session, the 45 percent and 100 percent deadlines were also extended "in principle" for both Russia and the United States.[78]

The Russian government's new plan for the elimination of chemical weapons was approved on July 5, 2001. Under the new plan, blister agent destruction is ongoing at Gorny, largely thanks to German funding, and is scheduled to be complete by the end of 2005. The large majority of Russia's stockpile of blister agents will be destroyed at the Kambarka facility, which is now under construction. Shchuch'ye, which is also currently under construction, will likely be the main CW destruction facility for all Russian nerve agents, building upon the support provided by the United States and Germany. Still, some press reports have indicated that Moscow may have new plans to destroy its nerve agents at the various locations where they are already stored (including Shchuch'ye).[79] A September 2003 accord between the U.S. Department of Defense and the Russian Munitions Agency determined that all nerve agents would be destroyed at Shchuch'ye, but Russian concerns about transportation make their compliance with the agreement anything but certain.[80]

Russia is receiving considerable assistance from the United States and other countries to facilitate its CW destruction. The United States has agreed to provide funds for the construction of the plant in Shchuch'ye, but it has been delayed, in part, by a U.S. Congress decision not to fund the construction in 2000 and 2001. In October 2003, the U.S. Department of Defense, which oversees the program, estimated that the facility would be up and running by July 2009.[81] In 2004, one Russian official offered a slightly accelerated timetable, stating that the facility would be complete in 2007.[82] Meanwhile, Russia has completed the destruction of "unfilled munitions and devices, and equipment specifically designed for use directly in connection with employment of chemical weapons," controlled as Category III items under the CWC. Moscow has also finished eliminating its World War I chemical agents, controlled as Category II items under the CWC.[83]

Biological Weapons

The former Soviet Union possessed the world's largest offensive BW program. The covert program continued to expand even after the USSR signed the Biological Weapons Convention in 1972 and eventually included a network of more than 50 institutes that produced vast amounts (metric tons) of biological agents, including anthrax and smallpox. The Soviet program, however, relied mainly on a surge capability to produce large amounts of weaponized agents in a time of crisis. Russia, according to U.S. and Russian officials and experts, is thought to have destroyed its stocks of offensive weapons, although this destruction cannot be independently verified and significant amounts of offensive stocks may continue to exist in Russia.

Russia is known to maintain a large quantity of biological weapons samples that could be used to grow and produce large amounts of offensive biological agents. In addition, Russia continues to maintain many of the former facilities that would have been used in the production of BW stocks, representing a latent ability to weaponize biological agents. Though this residual production capability is of concern to some, the main proliferation risks posed by the former Soviet BW capability is the risk that the samples of BW agents could be stolen or that the experts responsible for their production might sell their skills to others.

The Soviet BW program produced large amounts of many BW agents. In addition, the Soviet program developed genetically altered strains of weapons to make them resistant to common antibiotics. Thousands of samples of these agents exist in several dozen "libraries" in Russia, each sample of which could be used to grow large amounts of virulent, offensive BW agents.

The nonproliferation threats posed by the former Soviet BW program are twofold. The first is that the samples of BW agents are not adequately protected against theft. These samples are extremely portable, many consisting merely of test tubes of agents, and an adequate security and tracking system for these agents does not exist. In addition, the official closure of the former BW program by the Russian government means that tens of thousands of experts and employees have been forced to find other ways to support themselves, raising concerns that they may have migrated to help BW programs in other countries.

In response to the Russian BW threats, the United States funds a number of biothreat reduction activities, all through ISTC grants. The U.S. Department of Defense runs the Biological Weapons Proliferation Prevention program, which seeks to improve security and safety measures at institutes (in Russia and the other states of the former Soviet Union) involved in legitimate research with dangerous pathogens. Five Russian institutes and an additional eight in Kazakhstan, Uzbekistan, and Georgia have applied for assistance with security enhancements.[84] The State Department also provides employment for former bioweapons scientists through the ISTC grants.[85]

Missile Analysis

Russia's advanced missile capabilities also pose important proliferation challenges, especially given the continued economic stress in Russian society and in the Russian weapons complex. Just as Russia relied on dedicated nuclear cities in the production of its nuclear arsenal, so too did it construct a series of missile design and production enterprises. Those factories and design bureaus maintain Russia's current missile arsenal, including the only missile in production, the SS-27 ICBM. Although initial plans seemed to allow for the production of as many as 50 SS-27s per year, Russia only produced and deployed 6 new SS-27s in 2003, adding just 4 more in 2004.[86]

With the post–Cold War decline of its conventional forces, Russia has begun to rely on its nuclear forces as a source of national pride and strength. Such domestic political concerns, in addition to the desire to counter U.S. antimissile efforts, have led to a number of boastful statements, like President Putin's November 2004 claim that Russia is developing and preparing to deploy "weapons that not a single other nuclear power has, or will have in the near future."[87] Presumably, he was referring to the new mobile version of the SS-27. In this same vein, Russia is developing a maneuverable reentry vehicle that can reportedly change its flight path after separating from its missile. This would increase its ability to evade antimissile systems, such as those being developed by the United States.[88]

Despite much talk, the current level of missile production is quite low, and, as a result, there is a large body of underpaid and underemployed missile experts who must find alternative ways to make a living. This, along with the parallel concerns in the nuclear realm, has raised serious concern that Russia's missile expertise may be assisting other countries in the production of advanced ballistic missile capabilities. Chief among these concerns is the possible role of Russia in helping Iran develop long-range missiles. In addition, there continues to be concern over Russia's role in helping India develop its advanced missile and space launch capabilities, which are virtually identical to long-range missile programs. These worries remain, despite the fact that Russia became a member of the Missile Technology Control Regime in 1995 and has adopted internal reforms to tighten controls over missile-related exports. Vice Admiral Lowell Jacoby, the director of the Defense Intelligence Agency, testified in February 2004 that "Russian entities support missile and civil nuclear programs in China, Iran, India, and to a lesser degree in Syria."[89]

In a 2003 report to the U.S. Congress then–Central Intelligence Agency director George Tenet focused on Russian missile assistance to Iran, stating, "Iran's earlier success in gaining technology and materials from Russian entities helped to accelerate Iranian development of the Shahab-3 medium-range ballistic missile, and continuing Russian entity assistance has supported Iranian efforts to develop new missiles and increase Tehran's self-sufficiency in missile production."[90]

It has never been shown conclusively, however, whether the assistance to Iran is carried out by organizations within Russia operating in violation of Russian government policy and export controls, or whether the assistance is part of an official Russian government policy to aid Iran. The goal of the assistance would be to ensure Russia's relation with a key potential ally in the Middle East, especially one with which the United States has no formal relations. Russian officials vigorously deny any formal assistance to Iran's missile or nuclear weapons programs.

The United States has been highly vocal in its concern that Russian missile expertise is being exported to countries of proliferation concern. U.S. law, including Executive Order 12938 (amended in 1998) and the Iran Nonproliferation Act of 2000, authorizes the president to impose sanctions on companies that provide equipment or technology to Iran's ballistic missile program (see table 6.6). These sanctions prohibit any U.S. government assistance to, or contracts with, the sanctioned entities, and last a minimum of two years. Of the

Table 6.6. **U.S. Sanctions against Russian Entities**

Year	Organization
1998	Baltic State Technical University
	Europalace 2000 (sanctions lifted April 2004)
	Glavkosmos
	Grafit (sanctions lifted April 2004)
	INOR Scientific Center
	MOSO Company (sanctions lifted April 2004)
	Polyus Scientific Production Association
1999	Moscow Aviation Institute
	Mendeleyev University
2000	Yuri Savelyev, Director, Baltic State Technical University
2004	Baranov Engine Building Association
	Federal Scientific Research Center Altai
	Khazra Trading
	Vadim Vorobey

Sources

Sandy Berger, U.S. national security adviser, speech at Carnegie Endowment International Non-Proliferation Conference, January 12, 1999. Joseph Cirincione, ed., *Repairing the Regime: Preventing the Spread of Weapons of Mass Destruction* (New York: Routledge, 2000). Howard Diamond, "Clinton Vetoes Sanctions Bill; Sets, Imposes New Sanctions on Russia," *Arms Control Today,* June/July 1998. "U.S. Slaps Sanctions on 14 Firms, People for Arms and Missile Sales to Iran," Agence France-Presse, September 29, 2004.

fourteen Russian entities sanctioned for missile proliferation since 1998, penalties have been lifted against five (INOR and Polyus in April 2000 and Europalace, Grafit, and MOSO in April 2004). The most recent group to be targeted for sanctions was Khazra Trading in September 2004.[91]

Notes

1. See the calculations in table 6.2.
2. These calculations are based on Nuclear Threat Initiative, "Interactive Threat Reduction Budget Database: FY 1992–FY 2005," available at www.nti.org/e_research/cnwm/charts/cnm_funding_interactive_table.asp.
3. Robert S. Norris and Hans M. Kristensen, "NRDC Nuclear Notebook: Russian Nuclear Forces, 2005," *Bulletin of the Atomic Scientists*, March/April 2005, pp. 70–72.
4. Ibid.
5. Charles Duelfer, "Comprehensive Report of the Special Advisor to the DCI for Iraq's WMD," September 30, 2004, vol. 1, pp. 116–119; available at www.foia.cia.gov/duelfer/Iraqs_WMD_Vol1.pdf.

6. Jon Wolfsthal et al., eds., *Nuclear Status Report: Nuclear Weapons, Fissile Material, and Export Controls in the Former Soviet Union* (Washington, D.C.: Carnegie Endowment for International Peace and Monterey Institute, 2001), p. 175.
7. Amy Smithson, *Toxic Archipelago: Preventing Proliferation from the Former Soviet Chemical and Biological Weapons Complexes,* Report 32 (Washington, D.C.: Henry L. Stimson Center, 1999).
8. Senator Sam Nunn, Acceptance Speech at Eisenhower Institute Awards Dinner, April 26, 2001, available at www.nti.org/c_press/c1_speeches.html.
9. Wolfsthal, *Nuclear Status Report,* p. 35.
10. Norris and Kristensen, "NRDC Nuclear Notebook," pp. 70–72.
11. Ibid. See also Pavel Podvig, "Russian Strategic Nuclear Forces: Strategic Fleet," October 19, 2004, available at www.russianforces.org/eng/navy/.
12. Norris and Kristensen, "NRDC Nuclear Notebook," pp. 70–72.
13. U.S. Arms Control and Disarmament Agency, *START I Treaty.*
14. Arms Control Association, "START II and Its Extension Protocol at a Glance," Fact Sheet, January 2003; available at www.armscontrol.org/factsheets/start2.asp.
15. White House Fact Sheet, "Joint Statement on Parameters on Future Reduction in Nuclear Forces," Helsinki, March 21, 1997.
16. White House press conference transcript, November 2001.
17. Joseph Cirincione and Jon Wolfsthal, "SORT of a Treaty," Carnegie Analysis May 14, 2003, available at www.carnegieendowment.org/publications/index.cfm?fa=print&id=13823.
18. U.S. Arms Control and Disarmament Agency, *Treaty between the United States of America and the Union of Soviet Socialist Republics on the Elimination of their Intermediate-Range and Shorter-Range Missiles.*
19. Defense Threat Resolution Agency, DOD, "Onsite Inspection Operations, Intermediate-Range Nuclear Forces (INF) Treaty," available at www.dtra.mil/toolbox/directorates/osi/programs/ops/inf/index.cfm.
20. Natural Resources Defense Council, "USSR/Russian Nuclear Warheads" (table), October 23, 2001; available at www.nrdc.org/nuclear/nudb/datab10.asp.
21. Norris and Kristensen, "NRDC Nuclear Notebook," pp. 72–74. See also Amy F. Woolf, "Nonstrategic Nuclear Weapons," Congressional Research Service, September 9, 2004, p. 17.
22. Stockholm International Peace Research Institute (SIPRI), *Yearbook 1991: World Armament and Disarmament* (New York: Oxford University Press, 1992). Richard Fieldhouse et al., "Nuclear Weapon Developments and Unilateral Reduction Initiatives," chap. 2 in *Yearbook 1991*, SIPRI, p. 70. SIPRI, *Yearbook 1992: World Armament and Disarmament* (New York: Oxford University Press, 1993). Dunbar Lockwood and Jon Wolfsthal, "Nuclear Weapon Developments and Proliferation," chap. 6 in *Yearbook 1992,* SIPRI, p. 228.
23. Nikolai Sokov, "The Tactical Nuclear Weapons Scare of 2001," Monterey Institute of Strategic Studies, available at http://cns.miis.edu/pubs/reports/tnw.htm.
24. Woolf, "Nonstrategic Nuclear Weapons," p. 17.
25. Ibid., "Executive Summary."
26. Stephen G. Rademaker, assistant secretary of state for arms control, Press Roundtable at Interfax, Moscow, October 6, 2004; available at www.state.gov/t/ac/rls/rm/2004/37275.htm.
27. This figure is the sum of 52 Ministry of Defense weapons storage sites identified by the U.S. Department of Defense CTR program and 39 Russian Navy weapons storage sites identified by the National Nuclear Security Administration, U.S. Department of Energy (DOE). For Department of Defense (DOD) numbers, see U.S. Government Accountability Office (GAO), *Additional Russian Cooperation Needed to Facilitate U.S. Efforts to Improve Security at Russian Sites,* GAO-03-482 (Washington, D.C.: GAO, 2003), p. 34; available at www.gao.gov/new.items/d03482.pdf. For Navy sites, see Matthew Bunn and Anthony Wier, *Securing the Bomb: An Agenda for Action* (Washington, D.C.: Nuclear Threat Initiative and the Project on Managing the Atom, Harvard University, 2004), p. 52, footnote 51, and p. 54.
28. DOE has identified 243 buildings at 40 materials sites in Russia. These figures include both military and civilian sites. GAO, *Additional Russian Cooperation Needed,* p. 24.
29. Discussions with DOD officials, 2001. See also Wolfsthal, *Nuclear Status Report,* 2001.

30. DOD, "Cooperative Threat Reduction Annual Report to Congress, Fiscal Year 2006," p. 38, available at www.ransac.org/documents/fy06_ctr_annual_report_to_congress.pdf.
31. GAO, *Additional Russian Cooperation Needed*, p. 8.
32. DOE, *Detailed Budget Justifications, Volume 1, National Nuclear Security Administration*, pp. 447–448; available at www.mbe.doe.gov/budget/05budget/content/DEFNN/nn.pdf.
33. Bunn and Wier, *Securing the Bomb: An Agenda for Action*, pp. 52–54.
34. White House transcript, November 13, 2001.
35. White House transcript, February 11, 2004.
36. DOE, "A Report Card on the Department of Energy's Nonproliferation Programs with Russia," Secretary of Energy Advisory Board, January 10, 2000. p. 1.
37. The actual number may not even be known in Russia. This estimate includes 95 metric tons of military plutonium, 50 metric tons of plutonium in excess of defense needs, and 38.2 metric tons of separated civil plutonium. See IAEA, INFCIRC/549/Add.9/6, "Communication Received from the Russian Federation Concerning Its Policies Regarding the Management of Plutonium." See also David Albright and Kimberly Kramer, "Plutonium Watch: Tracking Plutonium Inventories," ISIS, June 2004, p. 5. See also David Albright, "Civil Inventories of Highly Enriched Uranium," Institute for Science and International Security (ISIS), June 11, 2004, p. 11. See also David Albright, "Military and Excess Stocks of Highly Enriched Uranium (HEU) in the Acknowledged Nuclear Weapon States," ISIS, June 25, 2004, p. 2. All ISIS documents are available at www.isis-online.org/global_stocks/tableofcontents.html.
38. DOE, "Plutonium: The First Fifty Years," 1994.
39. International Atomic Energy Agency, "Illicit Nuclear Trafficking: Facts and Figures," available at www.iaea.org/NewsCenter/Features/RadSources/Fact_Figures.html. See also Willaim C. Potter and Elena Sokova, "Illicit Trafficking in the NIS: What's New? What's True?" *Nonproliferation Review*, Summer 2002, available at http://cns.miis.edu/pubs/npr/vol09/92/92potsok.pdf.
40. Matthew Bunn and Anthony Wier, *Securing the Bomb 2005: New Global Imperatives* (Washington, D.C.: Nuclear Threat Initiative and the Project on Securing the Atom, May 2005), executive summary.
41. Bunn and Wier, *Securing the Bomb: An Agenda for Action*, pp. 46–47.
42. Ibid.
43. Ibid.
44. The full $150 million supplemental included funding for other programs managed by the MPC&A office, including Second Line of Defense. For more budget information, see Matthew Bunn, "Materials Protection Control and Accounting, 2003"; available at www.nti.org/e_research/cnwm/securing/mpca.asp. See also Nuclear Threat Initiative, "Interactive Threat Reduction Budget Database: Subtotals by U.S. Government Department, FY 1992–FY 2006"; available at www.nti.org/e_research/cnwm/overview/cnwm_home.asp.
45. See Matthew Bunn, "Mayak Fissile Material Storage Facility," available at www.nti.org/e_research/cnwm/securing/mayak.asp.
46. National Academy of Science, *Plutonium Disposition Report* (Washington, D.C.: National Academy of Science, 1994).
47. For a complete review of this program, refer to Wolfsthal, *Nuclear Status Report.*
48. Thomas Neff, "Privatizing U.S. National Security: the U.S.–Russian HEU Deal Risk," *Arms Control Today*, August/September 1998.
49. USEC Fact Sheet, March 31, 2005, available at www.usec.com/v2001_02/html/megatons_fact.asp.
50. President Clinton, Speech at the Nixon Center for Peace and Freedom, March 1, 1995.
51. Statement delivered by Minatom Minister Mikhailov at 41st International Atomic Energy Agency General Conference, September 26, 1997.
52. Office of Fissile Materials Disposition, DOE, "Strategic Plan," June 2000.
53. DOE, "Disposing of Surplus U.S. Plutonium," available at www.nnsa.doe.gov/na-26/pu.htm.
54. Nuclear Threat Initiative, "Interactive Threat Reduction Budget."
55. Group of Eight, "G8 Global Partnership Annual Report: G8 Senior Group, June 2004," available at www.g8usa.gov/d_060904i.htm.
56. Nuclear Threat Initiative, "Interactive Threat Reduction Budget."

57. White House Fact Sheet, June 4, 2000.
58. Strengthening the Global Partnership, "Donor Fact Sheets," available at www.sgpproject.org/Donor%20factsheets/Index.html.
59. V. Tikhonov, *Russia's Nuclear and Missile Complex* (Washington, D.C.: Carnegie Endowment for International Peace, 2001), p. 7.
60. National Intelligence Council, "Annual Report to Congress on the Safety and Security of Russian Nuclear Facilities and Military Forces," February 2002, available at www.cia.gov/nic/special_russiannucfac.html.
61. "Nonproliferation of WMD Expertise," available at www.state.gov/t/np/c12265.htm.
62. International Science and Technology Center (ISTC), "Parties," available at www.istc.ru/ISTC/sc.nsf/html/profile-parties.htm.
63. ISTC, "Branch Offices," available at www.istc.ru/ISTC/sc.nsf/html/branch-offices. Also, in accordance with U.S. policy, the United States has not funded any new projects in Belarus since 1997, although Belarus is still a party to the ISTC.
64. Science and Technology Center in Ukraine (STCU), available at www.stcu.int/info/.
65. Information about the STCU field offices is available at www.stcu.int/about/structure/offices/kyiv/index.php. Also, the decision to open the joint office in Tbilisi is contained in "Joint Statement: STCU Governing Board Meeting, December 15, 1999," available at www.stcu.int/documents/gbm/gbm9.
66. ISTC Fact Sheet, available at www.istc.ru/ISTC/sc.nsf/html/public-info-fact-sheet.htm.
67. White House Fact Sheet, December 27, 2001.
68. National Nuclear Security Administration, DOE, "Initiatives for Proliferation Prevention (IPP)," available at www.nnsa.doe.gov/na-20/ipp.shtml.
69. National Nuclear Security Administration, "Initiatives for Proliferation Prevention." Also, personal communication with DOE staff, November 2001.
70. *Agreement between the Government of the United States of America and the Government of the Russian Federation on the Nuclear Cities Initiative*, September 22, 1998.
71. Nuclear Cities Initiative home page, "Notable Successes," www.nnsa.doe.gov/na-20/nci/about_success.shtml.
72. Joe Fiorill, "U.S.-Russian Liability Dispute Could Bode Ill for Threat Reduction Programs," *Global Security Newswire*, September 22, 2003.
73. Amy Smithson, "Statement before the Senate Foreign Relations Committee," March 19, 2003.
74. Paula A. DeSutter, assistant secretary of state for verification and compliance, "Cooperative Threat Reduction," testimony before the House Armed Services Committee, March 4, 2003; available at www.state.gov/t/vc/rls/rm/18736.htm.
75. GAO, "Delays in Implementing the Chemical Weapons Convention Raise Concerns About Proliferation," GAO-04-361, March 2004, p. 20; available at www.gao.gov/new.items/d04361.pdf.
76. *Convention on the Prohibition of the Development, Production, Stockpiling and Use of Chemical Weapons*, article 4.
77. Mike Nartker, "Russian Official Outlines Detailed Schedule to Eliminate Chemical Weapons Arsenal by 2012," *Global Security Newswire,* November 19, 2004; available at www.nti.org/d_newswire/issues/2004_11_19.html#4215509C.
78. Organization for the Prohibition of Chemical Weapons, Conference on State Parties, Fifth Session Decision Document C-8/Dec. 13, October 24, 2003; available at www.opcw.org/docs/c8dec13.pdf.
79. Nartker, "Russian Official Outlines Detailed Schedule."
80. GAO, "Delays in Implementing the Chemical Weapons Convention," p. 22.
81. Ibid., pp. 21–22.
82. Nartker, "Russian Official Outlines Detailed Schedule." See also Viktor Kholstov, "Urgent Problems of Chemical Weapons Disarmament in the Russian Federation," presentation at the Green Cross National Dialogue, Moscow, November 10, 2004; available at www.globalgreen.org.
83. Organization for the Prohibition of Chemical Weapons, Conference on States Parties, First Review Conference Technical Secretariat Background Paper RC-1/S/6, April 25, 2003; available at www.opcw.org/html/global/docs_frameset.html.

84. DOD, "Cooperative Threat Reduction Annual Report to Congress for Fiscal Year 2005," pp. 67–68.

85. Bureau of Nonproliferation, U.S. Department of State, "Fact Sheet: The U.S. Bio-Chem Redirect Program," August 17, 2004; available at www.state.gov/t/np/rls/fs/32398.htm.

86. Pavel Podvig, "Changes in the Russian Strategic Forces," October 20, 2004, available at http://russianforces.org/eng/news/archive/000101.shtml.

87. Mike Eckel, "Russia Developing New Nuclear Missile Systems, Putin Says," Associated Press, November 17, 2004. For additional commentary on this issue, see Rose Gottemoeller, "Nuclear Necessity in Putin's Russia," *Arms Control Today*, April 2004.

88. Wade Boese, "Putin Boasts about Russian Military Capabilities," *Arms Control Today*, March 2004; available at www.armscontrol.org/act/2004_03/Putin.asp.

89. Vice Admiral Lowell E. Jacoby, U.S. Navy director, Defense Intelligence Agency, "Current and Projected National Security Threats to the United States," testimony before the Senate Select Committee on Intelligence, February 24, 2004; available at http://intelligence.senate.gov/0402hrg/040224/jacoby.pdf.

90. Central Intelligence Agency, "Unclassified Report to Congress on the Acquisition of Technology Relating to Weapons of Mass Destruction and Advanced Conventional Munitions, July 1–December 31, 2003"; available at www.cia.gov/cia/reports/721_reports/pdfs/721report_july_dec2003.pdf.

91. "U.S. Slaps Sanctions on 14 Firms, People for Arms and Missile Sales to Iran." Agence France-Presse, September 29, 2004.

Table 6.7. **Russian Nuclear Facilities with Weapons Materials**

Location and Name	Activity	Comments	MPC&A Status
Moscow and vicinity			
Bochvar All-Russian Scientific Research Institute of Inorganic Materials	Fuel-cycle technology research/ fissile material processing		Upgrades not yet completed; expected to be completed in 2005[1]
Institute of Medical and Biological Problems	Scientific research: medical and biological	1 research reactor, under construction	No plans to conduct upgrades
Institute of Theoretical and Experimental Physics	Research on heavy-water applications for nuclear weapon production		Upgrades not yet completed
Electrostal Machine-building Plant	HEU fuel fabrication, uranium conversion	HEU and LEU fuel production lines, 7 critical assemblies	Upgrades not yet completed, expected to be completed in late 2006[2]
Institute of Theoretical and Experimental Physics	Research on heavy-water applications for nuclear weapon production	1 decommissioned 2.5-MW heavy-water research reactor	Upgrades completed February 1998
Kurchatov Institute	Research in solid-state physics, fusion, and plasma physics	10 research and power reactors, 16 critical assemblies, 2 subcritical assemblies	Upgrades completed May 2005[3]
Moscow Engineering and Physics Institute	Educational institution	1 2.5-MW research reactor, 5 subcritical assemblies	Upgrades completed June 1998.

(table continues on the following page)

Table 6.7. **Russian Nuclear Facilities with Weapons Materials** (continued)

Location and Name	Activity	Comments	MPC&A Status
Scientific Research and Design Institute of Power Technology	Design of nuclear reactors for power generation, naval propulsion	1 inactive (50 kW) research reactor, 3 critical assemblies	Upgrades completed February 1998
Scientific Research Institute for Instruments Lytkarino	R&D of radioelectronic instruments	5 nonoperational pulsed research reactors	Upgrades not yet completed, expected to be completed in 2005[4]
Sarov (Arzamas-16)			
All-Russian Scientific Research Institute of Experimental Physics (UNIIEF)	Nuclear weapon design, research, and development, Non-Proliferation Center		Upgrades not yet completed
Avangard Electromechanical Plant	Nuclear warhead assembly and dismantlement		No ongoing upgrades, part of plant closed under the Nuclear Cities Initiative[5]
Osersk (Chelyabinsk-64)			
Mayak Production Association	Warhead component production, spent-fuel storage and reprocessing	5 nonoperational plutonium production reactors, 2 HEU fueled tritium production reactors	Upgrades not yet completed

Snezhinsk (Chelyabisnk-70)			
All-Russian Scientific Research Institute of Technical Physics (UNIITF)	Nuclear warhead research and design	3 pulse reactors	Upgrades not yet completed
Zheleznogorsk (Krasnoyarsk-26)			
Mining and Chemical Combine	Spent-fuel storage and reprocessing	1 operational plutonium production power reactor (see below)	Construction of plutonium storage facility in progress, upgrades in progress
Power reactor (part of the Mining and Chemical Combine)	Power generation for city and production of weapons grade plutonium	Shutdown planned under NNSA Elimination of Weapons Grade Plutonium Production Program[6]	
Zelenogorsk (Krasnoyark-45)			
Electrochemical Plant	Uranium enrichment, HEU downblending	Centrifuge enrichment plant	Upgrades completed in 2005[7]
Zarechnyy (Penza-19)			
START Production Association	Nuclear warhead assembly and dismantlement		No ongoing upgrades[8]
Novouralsk (Sverdlovsk-44)			
Urals Electrochemical Integrated Plant	Uranium enrichment		Upgrades completed in 2005[9]

(table continues on the following page)

Table 6.7. **Russian Nuclear Facilities with Weapons Materials** (continued)

Location and Name	Activity	Comments	MPC&A Status
Lesnoy (Sverdlovsk-45)			
Elektrokhimpribor Combine	Nuclear warhead production and dismantlement facility	Gas-centrifuge enrichment plant, HEU downblending facilities	No ongoing upgrades[10]
Seversk (Tomsk-7)			
Siberian Chemical Combine	Largest multi-function compound in the Russian nuclear complex, power generation for city and production of weapons grade plutonium; planned site of MOX fuel fabrication	2 operational plutonium production reactors (see below), a reprocessing plant, a uranium enrichment plant, plutonium pit fabrication facilities	Upgrades not yet completed[11]
Power Reactors (part of the Siberian Chemical Combine)	2 operational plutonium production power reactors	Power reactors shutdown planned under NNSA Elimination of Weapons Grade Plutonium Production Program[12]	
Trekhgorny (Zlatoust-36)			
Instrument-making Plant	Nuclear warhead assembly and dismantlement	Also produces ballistic missile reentry vehicles	No ongoing upgrades[13]
Obninsk			
Institute of Physics and Power Engineering	Research and development for nuclear power engineering	3 research reactors, 2 fast critical assemblies, up to 16 critical assemblies	Upgrades completed February 1998

Karpov Scientific Research Institute of Physical Chemistry	Research on chemical applications, medical isotope production		Upgrades completed in 1998[14]
Dubna			
Joint Institute of Nuclear Research	International scientific research center	Plutonium-fueled pulsed research reactor	Upgrades completed February 1998
Podolsk			
Luch Scientific Production Association	R&D, production and testing of high-temperature uranium fuel elements	3 research reactors, 1 central storage facility	Upgrades completed in 2003[15]
Novosibirsk			
Novosibirsk Chemical Concentrates Plant	HEU fuel fabrication for light–water reactors	HEU and LEU fuel production lines	Upgrades completed in 2004[16]
Gatchina			
Petersburg Institute of Nuclear Physics	Research on high-energy theoretical physics	Operational 18-MW research reactor, 100-MW research reactor under construction	Upgrades completed May 1998
Dimitrovgrad			
Scientific Research Institute of Atomic Reactors	Pilot plants, MOX fuel fabrication, spent-fuel reprocessing	7 operational research reactors, 2 critical assemblies	Upgrades not yet completed, expected to be completed in 2005[17]
Zarechnyy, Sverdlovsk oblast			
Scientific Research and Design Institute of Power Technology	Nuclear reactor design and development	1 research reactor, 3 critical assemblies, hot cells	Upgrades completed May 1998

(table continues on the following page)

Table 6.7. **Russian Nuclear Facilities with Weapons Materials** (continued)

Location and Name	Activity	Comments	MPC&A Status
Beloyarsky-3	Nuclear Power Plant, 560 MWe	Bn-600 fast-breeder reactor, fresh- and spent-fuel storage	Upgrades completed May or June 1998[18]
Tomsk			
Tomsk Polytechnical University	Educational institution	1 research reactor, fresh-fuel storage vault	Upgrades completed July 1998
Navy Facilities, Northern Fleet			
Ara Bay Naval Base (part of Vidyayevo Naval Base)	Operational naval base serving nuclear submarines, decommissioned nuclear submarine storage		
RTP Atomflot (2 km north of Murmansk)	Operational nuclear-powered icebreaker base, radioactive waste processing and storage		Upgrades completed September 1999
Gadzhiyevo Naval Base	Operational naval base serving nuclear submarines, decommissioned nuclear submarine storage, nuclear submarine defueling, waste management	Northern Fleet's largest SSBN base	
Gremikha-Yokanga Naval Base (near Ostrovnoy, formerly Murmansk-140)	Former naval base, nuclear submarine defueling, waste management		

Northern Machine Building Enterprise Sevmash (Severodvinsk)	START designated submarine dismantlement facility, waste management, nuclear submarine construction facility	The hull of the first Borey-class SSBN, the *Yury Dolgoruki*, was laid down at Sevmash in November 1996.	Upgrades not yet completed[20]
Olenya Bay Naval Base	Operational naval base serving nuclear submarines		Upgrades completed September 2000
Pala Bay Submarine Repair Facility (Polyarnyy)	Nuclear submarine repair, waste management		
Polyarninskiy Shipyard, formerly Shkval Naval Shipyard No. 10 (Polyarnyy)	Operational naval base serving nuclear submarines, decommissioned nuclear submarine storage, minimal submarine dismantlement activities		
Sayda Bay (near Gadzhiyevo)	Decommissioned submarine storage, waste management		
Severomorsk Naval Base	Headquarters of the Northern Fleet, Operational base serving two nuclear-powered battle cruisers		No upgrades planned
Sevmorput Naval Shipyard No. 35 (Rosta district of Murmansk)	Nuclear submarine repairs, decommissioned submarine storage, waste management		
Site 49 (Near Severomorsk)	Fresh fuel storage facility		Upgrades completed September 1999

(table continues on the following page)

Table 6.7. **Russian Nuclear Facilities with Weapons Materials** (continued)

Location and Name	Activity	Comments	MPC&A Status
Zapadnya Litsa Naval Base, consists of four facilities: Andreeva Bay, Bolshaya Lopatka, Malaya Lopatka, and Nerpicha (Zaorzersk)	Operational naval base serving nuclear submarines, decommissioned nuclear submarine storage, and waste management		
Zvezdochka State Machine Building Enterprise (Yagra Island)	START-designated submarine dismantlement facility, submarine repair, waste management		
Naval Facilities, Pacific Fleet			
Amurskiy Zavod, Leninskiy Komsomol Shipyard (Komsomolsk-na-Amure)	SSBN and SSN construction, submarine repair		
Cape Sysoyeva (Site 32, Shkotovo Peninsula)	Nuclear submarine waste storage		Upgrades completed January 2000
Chazhma Bay Repair Facility (Shkotovo Peninsula)	Fresh fuel storage (Site 34), submarine repair, refueling, and defueling, decommissioned nuclear submarine storage, dismantlement facility		Upgrades completed September 2000[21]
Gornyak Shipyard, also known as Vilyuchinskiy Shipyard #49 (Kamchatka Peninsula)	Dismantlement facility, decommissioned nuclear submarine storage, waste management, submarine repair and refueling		Upgrades completed on PM-74 ship in August 2000; no upgrades planned for rest of facility

Pavlovsk Bay (Eastern edge of Strelok Bay)	Main operational submarine base for Pacific Fleet, home port to several nuclear-powered ships, decommissioned submarine and reactor compartment storage		
Razboynik Bay	Decommissioned nuclear submarine and reactor compartment storage		
Rybachiy Nuclear Submarine Base, Krasheninnikov Bay (near Petropavlovsk, Kamchatka Peninsula)	Operational naval base serving nuclear submarines		
Zavety Ilyicha (Postavaya Bay)	Former operational naval base, decommissioned submarine storage		
Zvezda Far Eastern Shipyard (Bolshoy Kamen)	START-designated submarine dismantlement, waste management		Upgrades completed June 2001 (work done by U.S. Department of Defense as part of CTR, not by DOE as part of MPC&A)
Other Naval Facilities			
Admiralteyskiye Verfi Shipyard (St. Petersburg)	Construction of submarines and naval vessels		
Baltic Shipyard (St. Petersburg)	Construction of nuclear-propelled surface vessels		Upgrades not yet completed

(table continues on the following page)

Table 6.7. **Russian Nuclear Facilities with Weapons Materials** (continued)

Location and Name	Activity	Comments	MPC&A Status
Central Physical-Technical Institute (Sergiyev Posad, formerly Zagorsk)	Research on nuclear propulsion for naval and space vessels	At least 2 pulsed research reactors	Upgrades not yet completed[22]
Experimental Machine Building Design Bureau (Nizhniy Novgorod)	Nuclear reactor design	4 critical assemblies	
Krylov Central Scientific Research Institute (Krylov Shipbuilding Institute, St. Petersburg)	R&D of nuclear reactors for naval vessels	1 0.5-MW research reactor, 2 critical assemblies	Upgrades completed November 1998[23]

ABBREVIATIONS

CTR	Cooperative Threat Reduction program
DOE	U.S. Department of Energy
HEU	highly enriched uranium
kW	kilowatts
LEU	low-enriched uranium
MOX	mixed-oxide fuel
MPC&A	material protection, control, and accounting
MW	megawatts
MWe	megawatts electric
NNSA	National Nuclear Security Administration
R&D	research and development
SSBN	nuclear ballistic missile submarine
START	Strategic Arms Reduction Treaty
SSN	nuclear-fueled submarine

NOTES

1. Author conversation with U.S. Department of Energy (DOE) official.
2. Ibid.
3. National Nuclear Security Administration, DOE, "NNSA Completes Security Upgrades at Nuclear Site in Moscow," press release, May 6, 2005, available at www.nnsa.doe.gov.
4. Author conversation with DOE official.
5. Author conversation with DOE official; DOE, "Notable Successes," in *The Nuclear Cities Initiative,* available at www.nnsa.doe.gov/na-20/nci/about_impact.shtml.
6. National Nuclear Security Administration, DOE, "U.S. Signs Contract As Part of Effort to Permanently Shut Down Plutonium Production Reactors in Russia," press release, December 20, 2004; available at www.nnsa.doe.gov/docs/PR_NA-04-34_Contract_signed_for_electricity_plant_in_EWGPP_program-shutting_down_pu_reactors_(12-04).htm.
7. Author conversation with DOE official.
8. Ibid.
9. Ibid.
10. Ibid.
11. DOE, *Detailed Budget Justifications, Volume 1, National Nuclear Security Administration,* p. 487.
12. National Nuclear Security Administration, "U.S. Signs Contract."
13. Author conversation with DOE official.
14. National Nuclear Security Administration, DOE, MPC&A Program Strategic Plan (Washington, D.C.: DOE, 2001), appendix B; available at www.nti.org/e_research/official_docs/doe/mpca2001.pdf.
15. Author conversation with DOE official.
16. Ibid.
17. Ibid.
18. GAO, "Security of Russia's Nuclear Material Improving," p. 34. See also Jon Wolfsthal et al., eds., *Nuclear Status Report: Nuclear Weapons, Fissile Material, and Export Controls in the Former Soviet Union* (Washington, D.C.: Carnegie Endowment for International Peace and Monterey Institute, 2001).
19. The upgrades at Nerpa Shipyard were on the PM-12 nuclear fuel transfer ship, which also operates at Olenya Bay.
20. Wolfsthal, *Nuclear Status Report,* and GAO, "Security of Russia's Nuclear Material Improving," say that upgrades were completed, but the July 2001 *DOE MPC&A Strategic Plan* indicate that they would not be completed until late 2001.
21. The upgrades at Chazhma included upgrades on the PM-74 nuclear fuel service ship, which also travels to Gornyak Shipyard.
22. GAO, "Security of Russia's Nuclear Material Improving," p. 35.
23. GAO, "Security of Russia's Nuclear Material Improving," p. 34.

NORWAY
Norwegian Sea
SWEDEN
Gadzhiyevo Naval Base
Zapadnaya Litsa
Murmansk
FINLAND
Baltic Sea
Novaya Zemlya
Barents Sea
POLAND
ESTONIA
LITHUANIA
LATVIA
St. Petersburg
Kara Sea
Vypolzovo
BELARUS
Kurchatov Institute
Lytkarino
Elektrostal
Moscow
Kostroma
RUSSIA
Kozelsk
Teykovo
Obninsk/IPPE
Luch
Avangard
VNIIEF
Yurya
UKRAINE
Sarov
Yoshkar Ola
Perm
Lesnoy
Zarech
Bershet
Nizhniy Tagil
Tatishchevo
Dimitrovgrad/NIIAR
Novouralsk
Engels
Yekaterinburg
Volgograd
Osersk/Mayak
Snezhinsk/VNIITF
Chelyabinsk
Trekhgormyy
Kartaly
Dombarovskiy
Seversk
Novosibirsk
Caspian Sea
GEORGIA
Barnaul
ARMENIA
Aleysk
AZERBAIJAN
KAZAKHSTAN
Aral Sea
TURKMENISTAN
UZBEKISTAN
IRAN
CHINA
KYRGYZSTAN

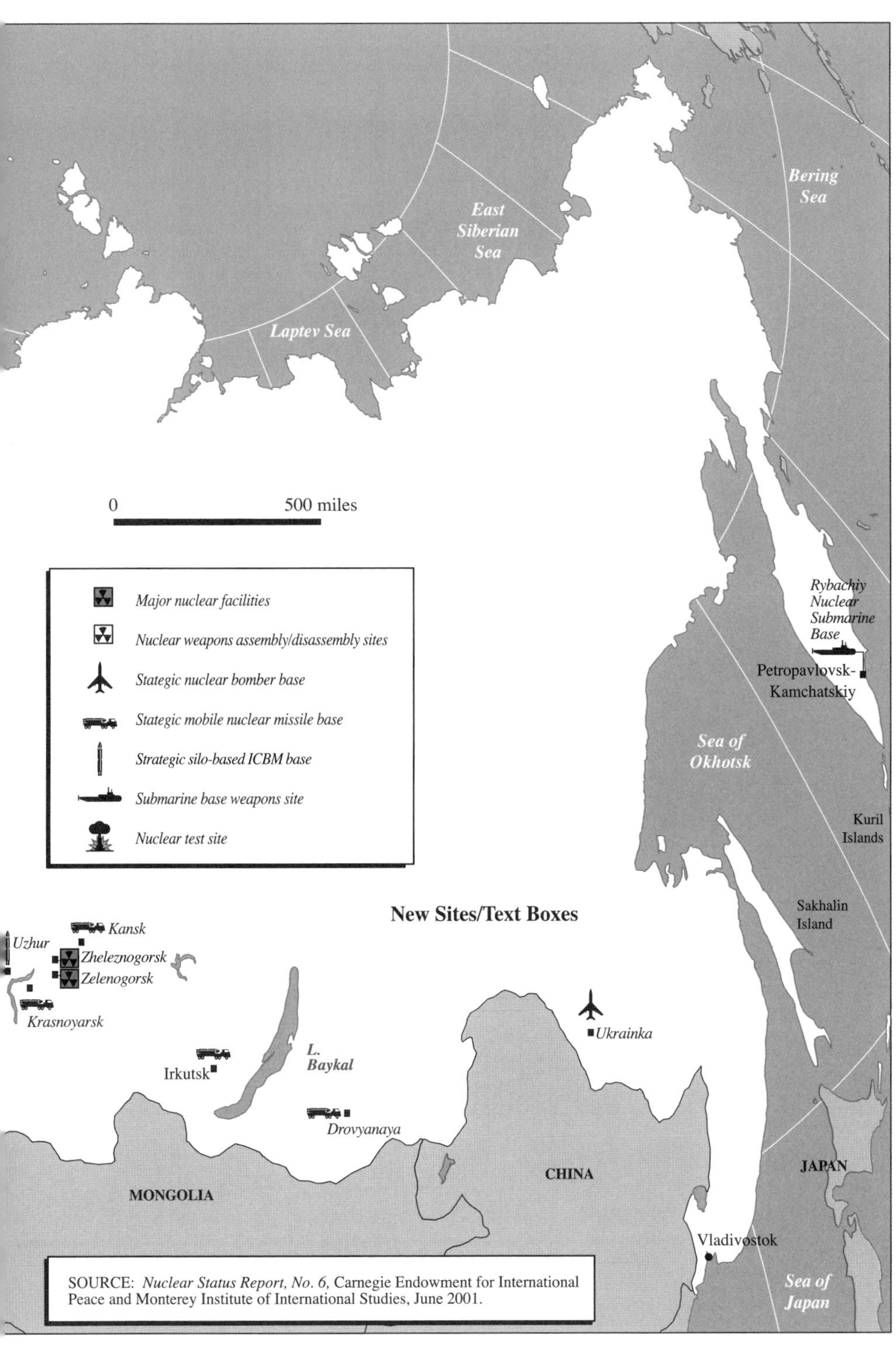

SOURCE: *Nuclear Status Report, No. 6,* Carnegie Endowment for International Peace and Monterey Institute of International Studies, June 2001.

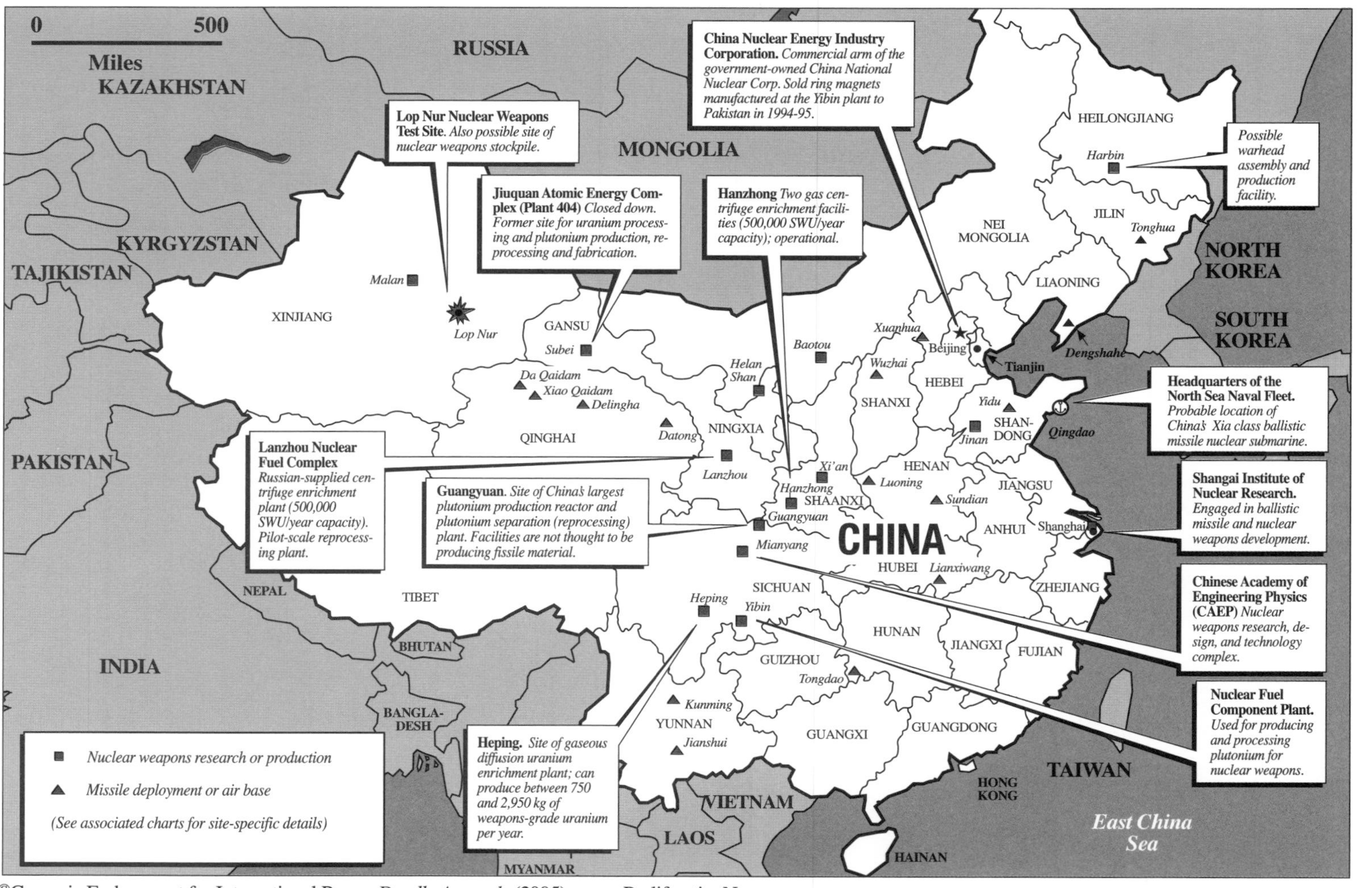
0 500
Miles
RUSSIA
KAZAKHSTAN
MONGOLIA
KYRGYZSTAN
TAJIKISTAN
PAKISTAN
INDIA
NEPAL
BHUTAN
BANGLA-DESH
MYANMAR
LAOS
VIETNAM
NORTH KOREA
SOUTH KOREA
TAIWAN
HONG KONG
HAINAN
East China Sea
CHINA
XINJIANG
GANSU
QINGHAI
TIBET
NINGXIA
NEI MONGOLIA
HEILONGJIANG
JILIN
LIAONING
HEBEI
SHANXI
SHAN-DONG
HENAN
SHAANXI
JIANGSU
ANHUI
HUBEI
SICHUAN
ZHEJIANG
HUNAN
JIANGXI
FUJIAN
GUIZHOU
YUNNAN
GUANGXI
GUANGDONG
Malan
Lop Nur
Subei
Da Qaidam
Xiao Qaidam
Delingha
Datong
Helan Shan
Lanzhou
Baotou
Xuanhua
Wuzhai
Beijing
Tianjin
Dengshahe
Harbin
Tonghua
Yidu
Jinan
Qingdao
Xi'an
Luoning
Sundian
Hanzhong
Guangyuan
Mianyang
Lianxiwang
Shanghai
Heping
Yibin
Tongdao
Kunming
Jianshui
Lop Nur Nuclear Weapons Test Site. Also possible site of nuclear weapons stockpile.
Jiuquan Atomic Energy Complex (Plant 404) Closed down. Former site for uranium processing and plutonium production, reprocessing and fabrication.
Hanzhong Two gas centrifuge enrichment facilities (500,000 SWU/year capacity); operational.
China Nuclear Energy Industry Corporation. Commercial arm of the government-owned China National Nuclear Corp. Sold ring magnets manufactured at the Yibin plant to Pakistan in 1994-95.
Possible warhead assembly and production facility.
Headquarters of the North Sea Naval Fleet. Probable location of China's Xia class ballistic missile nuclear submarine.
Shangai Institute of Nuclear Research. Engaged in ballistic missile and nuclear weapons development.
Chinese Academy of Engineering Physics (CAEP) Nuclear weapons research, design, and technology complex.
Nuclear Fuel Component Plant. Used for producing and processing plutonium for nuclear weapons.
Lanzhou Nuclear Fuel Complex Russian-supplied centrifuge enrichment plant (500,000 SWU/year capacity). Pilot-scale reprocessing plant.
Guangyuan. Site of China's largest plutonium production reactor and plutonium separation (reprocessing) plant. Facilities are not thought to be producing fissile material.
Heping. Site of gaseous diffusion uranium enrichment plant; can produce between 750 and 2,950 kg of weapons-grade uranium per year.
Nuclear weapons research or production
Missile deployment or air base
(See associated charts for site-specific details)

CHAPTER 7

China

Nuclear Weapons Capability

China is a recognized nuclear weapon state under the Non-Proliferation Treaty (NPT) and possesses enough nuclear material for hundreds of nuclear weapons (see table 7.1 at the end of the chapter). China has approximately 400 nuclear weapons and various delivery platforms, mostly short- and medium-range missiles. Approximately 20 Chinese weapons are deployed on missiles that can reach the continental United States. After developing its first nuclear weapon in 1964, China became a major supplier of sensitive nuclear and missile technology to the developing world. The United States and other countries have worked to draw China step-by-step into the international nonproliferation regime. Over three decades, these efforts have achieved important progress. Proliferation issues exist, but they are now a relatively minor aspect of the United States–China relationship.

China has not officially released details about the size or composition of its nuclear arsenal, making estimates difficult to develop. Much of the unclassified information compiled on China's forces is from unverified media reports and occasional statements by intelligence or government officials. From these, it is possible to estimate that China fields approximately 152 warheads on land- and sea-launched missiles, 130 bomber weapons, and 120 weapons on artillery, short-range missiles, and other weapons.[1] Beijing also maintains a fairly extensive nuclear weapons production and research complex. China has conducted 45 nuclear weapons tests, the first of which took place on October 16, 1964, and the last on July 29, 1996. China has signed but not yet ratified the Comprehensive Test Ban Treaty.

Aircraft and Missile Capabilities

China is in the process of modernizing its strategic missile forces, although historically its progress has been slow and has lagged well behind foreign estimates. Although China deploys several types of ballistic missiles, only the DF-5 (13,000-kilometer range) is an intercontinental ballistic missile (ICBM) by Western standards and is capable of reaching the continental United States. Currently, China deploys approximately 20 DF-5 ICBMs and 12 DF-4 intermediate-range missiles (5,500-kilometer range).[2] China is developing and may have deployed the DF-31, a mobile, three-stage solid-fueled ICBM with an estimated range of 8,000 kilometers. China conducted three flight tests of the DF-31, the last one on

January 2002.[3] One source concludes that 8 missiles were deployed in 2004.[4] Plans to develop another land-based missile, the DF-41, a solid-fueled ICBM with a range of 12,000 kilometers, appear to have been canceled in favor of an extended-range version of the DF-31, the DF-31A.[5] The U.S. Department of Defense estimates that the number of Chinese ICBMs capable of hitting the United States "could increase to around 30 by 2005 and may reach up to 60 by 2010."[6]

China's medium-range ballistic missiles include an aging force of 40 DF-3As (2,900-kilometer range) that it is phasing out after 30 years in service.[7] China also has 48 DF-21As (1,800-kilometer range), but it has converted some to conventionally armed missiles.[8] China is also developing the Julang-2, a submarine-launched ballistic missile (SLBM) based on the DF-31. China has only one ballistic missile submarine, however, which has never left coastal waters and is not operational. There are some reports that a new missile submarine may be ready to enter service in the next few years. China's bomber force consists mainly of aging H-6 aircraft based on the Soviet Tu-16 Badger bomber, with a range of 3,100 kilometers.[9] China purchased 24 Su-30 fighter aircraft and SA-20 surface-to-air missile systems from Russia in 2004, but these are not thought to have been modified for a nuclear role.[10]

Biological and Chemical Weapons Capability

China is believed by U.S. intelligence to possess chemical and biological weapons research and development programs, and some offensive chemical weapons.[11] There is no publicly available evidence of such weapons. China is a signatory to the Biological Weapons Convention and the Chemical Weapons Convention (CWC) and has denied having any biological warfare programs. It declared under the terms of the CWC that it previously had a chemical weapons program but that it destroyed those agents before joining the treaty.

Nuclear Analysis

China is of particular nonproliferation importance in two ways. As a nuclear weapon state, it has a large nuclear weapons and material production complex. These weapons and materials are of concern to its neighbors, to the United States, and other potential adversaries. Questions about the security and accountability of the weapons and materials are particularly important. China, however, has also been a major supplier of nuclear technology and equipment in the developing world, and its past behavior in the nuclear and missile fields was a significant nonproliferation concern.

Following its first nuclear test in 1964, China began a slow but steady process of developing a full-fledged nuclear weapons infrastructure and strategic and tactical nuclear arsenal.[12] Having been isolated by the West after the Communist revolution in 1949, China was also isolated from the evolving international framework of peaceful uses of nuclear energy and from the collaboration that produced the International Atomic Energy Agency (IAEA) in the 1950s, the NPT in the late 1960s, and the development of nuclear export control guidelines in the 1970s. As a Communist power during the Cold War, China was also excluded from the establishment of the Missile Technology Control Regime (MTCR), which originated in 1987 as a Western arrangement to exchange information on and restrain the exports of nuclear-capable missiles and related technology.

In the early years, the People's Republic of China adopted a posture that rhetorically *favored* nuclear weapons proliferation, particularly in the developing world, where this theme once had some appeal as a rallying point for anti-imperialism.[13] Through the 1970s, China's policy was *not to oppose* nuclear proliferation, which it still saw as limiting U.S. and Soviet power. After China began to open to the West in the 1970s, its rhetorical position gradually shifted to one that *opposes* nuclear proliferation.

China's practical approach to the export of nuclear and military goods did not, however, conform to the standards of the international nonproliferation regime. Despite China's de facto commitments in 1992, 1994, and 1998 to uphold the nonproliferation regulations of the MTCR, Chinese state-owned corporations continued to engage in illicit nuclear arms transfers to Pakistan, Iran, North Korea, and Libya.[14] Major efforts have been made over the past 25 years to persuade China to modify its approach formally, bringing it into closer alignment with the policies of the other nuclear supplier states. These efforts have produced demonstrable results, evident in China's accession to the Zangger Committee in October 1997 and to the Nuclear Suppliers Group (NSG) in May 2004 and in greatly reduced technology transfers. In October 2004, at their meeting in Seoul, the thirty-four members of the MTCR rejected China's bid to become a member, apparently over China's failure to meet fully their nonproliferation standards. Many experts believe that China's entry into the MTCR could deter it from proliferating its nuclear-related materials to countries such as Iran, Pakistan, and North Korea.[15] A domestic export control system has developed with constant U.S. encouragement, but it is still a work in progress and has not yet become completely effective.

China plays a central role in both the North Korean and Iranian proliferation crises.The United States believes that ending North Korea's nuclear program depends heavily on China's ability to pressure Pyongyang. The U.S. Department of State's former director for policy planning, Mitchell Reiss, has characterized China as the "mediator" between North Korea and the U.S. in discussions. China has, he said, "the most influence on the North. And so to get [it] on board . . . gives us much more weight in these negotiations."[16] During an April 2004 visit to China, Vice President Dick Cheney spoke approvingly of China's increased commitment to the nonproliferation regime, while urging it to make economic assistance to North Korea conditional on Pyongyang's cooperation in the six-party talks designed to end its nuclear activities.[17]

China's relationship with Iran has become a greater concern as China's economic relationship with that country grows. In November 2004, China signed oil and gas contracts with Iran worth an estimated $100 to $200 billion. (China has also signed oil deals with Brazil, Angola, and Sudan because its booming economy has stimulated a huge and growing need for natural resources.)[18] Shortly after concluding the Iran oil deal, Chinese officials announced that they would not support an effort to bring Iran to the U.N. Security Council for possible sanctions, though they did not explicitly say that they would veto such a resolution. China is not looking for a confrontation with the United States over Iran, but neither does it want U.S. actions to increase instability in areas vital to its economic development. It sees Iran and North Korea not as threats that must be confronted but as problems that can be managed through flexible and patient diplomacy.

China's Nuclear Weapons

China is slowly modernizing its strategic nuclear forces but still has the least advanced nuclear arsenal of the five declared nuclear weapon states. The Chinese doctrine is centered on the maintenance of a "minimum nuclear deterrent" capable of launching a retaliatory strike on a small number of countervalue targets (such as cities) after an adversary's nuclear attack. The design and deployment of China's nuclear forces appear consistent with the declared policy and have been shaped by two key concerns: the survival of a second-strike capability and the potential deployment of antimissile systems.

China currently has the capability to strike U.S. cities with a force of approximately 20 long-range Dong Feng–5 missiles, each armed with a single 4- to 5-megaton warhead. The 12 Dong Feng–4 missiles "are almost certainly intended as a retaliatory deterrent against targets in Russia and Asia," according to U.S. intelligence assessments, but the missiles could strike parts of Alaska and the Hawaiian island chain.[19] (China has 80–100 other missiles that could strike targets in Eurasia.) The time needed to launch these liquid-fueled ICBMs, a lack of hardened missile silos, and a lack of missile mobility have raised concern in the Chinese leadership about the survivability of these forces. In addition, China's sea-based force (one Xia submarine armed with twelve medium-range ballistic missiles) does not pose a credible threat to either Moscow or Washington. The Xia has never sailed outside China's territorial waters, is considered vulnerable to modern antisubmarine warfare techniques, and is not currently operational.[20] To overcome these concerns, China has been pursuing the development of smaller, mobile missiles with intercontinental ranges.

Because of its limited second-strike capabilities, China has historically been particularly concerned about the potential development of antimissile systems. A national antimissile system designed to counter strikes on the United States, together with advanced theater antimissile systems sold to America's Asian allies, could greatly complicate China's nuclear planning. The United States theoretically would then have the ability to destroy or defeat China's deterrent force. Should China's concerns about its security substantially increase, and if military modernization were given preference over economic modernization, it would likely increase its number of deployed warheads, increase its production of planned systems, and develop and deploy (and possibly sell) countermeasures to defeat antimissile systems.

China's concerns over the U.S. Strategic Defense Initiative announced in 1983 reportedly spurred its plans to develop multiple-warhead technology. The first Chinese test of a multiple-warhead missile took place in September 1984. While similar tests have been conducted on several missile types since then (including November 2000 and January 2002 tests of the DF-31 with decoy warheads), no missile currently deployed is thought to carry multiple independently targeted reentry vehicles (MIRVs).[21] China is thought to have been developing smaller warheads when it ended its nuclear test program before signing the Comprehensive Test Ban Treaty in 1996, and allegations over nuclear espionage by China against the United States, which erupted in 1999, were centered on China's interest in developing smaller warheads for future MIRVed missiles. China plans by 2010 to have modernized its nuclear forces by developing a new generation of strategic and possibly substrategic weapons on various delivery platforms, deploying a new-generation nuclear ballistic missile submarine, and deploying more nuclear-powered submarines. Historically, however, its progress has been slow and lagged well behind foreign estimates.

ICBMS. The planned improvements of China's land-based forces include the replacement of the aging force of DF-5s, and potentially the DF-4s, with two new land-based ICBMs.[22] The DF-31 is designed to be a solid-fueled, road-mobile missile with a range of 8,000 kilometers, capable of reaching parts of Alaska and Hawaii, though not the continental United States. Plans to develop a 12,000-kilometer land-based missile, the DF-41, appear to have been canceled in favor of a longer-range version of the DF-31, also solid-fueled and road-mobile but less developed.[23] This missile may be deployed near 2010 as the DF-5 leaves service. Some of the newer DF-5s may remain in service past that date.

Exact deployment numbers are unknown, but a 2002 U.S. National Intelligence Estimate concluded that that China could field between 75 and 100 warheads on MIRVed, solid-fueled ICBMs over the next fifteen years, both mobile and in hardened silos, and equipped with various penetration aids to defeat missile defenses.[24]

SLBMS. China does not currently have an operational submarine capable of launching ballistic missiles. Press reports on December 3, 2004, cited claims by an unnamed U.S. defense official that China had launched a Type 094 submarine with a range in excess of 4,600 miles, a development that had not been expected before 2010.[25] Each submarine could be armed with 12 JL-2 SLBMs, with a range of 8,000 kilometers and a potential MIRV capability, but the official could not confirm whether any were ready for deployment. The JL-2 is based on the DF-31 missile and has been under development since the 1980s.[26]

STRATEGIC BOMBERS. China has approximately 120 Hong-6s, its current medium-range bomber.[27] It is based on the Soviet Tu-16 Badger of 1950s vintage, and it has a range of 3,100 kilometers and can carry up to three nuclear bombs.[28] The Chinese air force flight tested a more modern medium-range bomber, the H-7, which experts now believe to have a nuclear role.[29] China purchased 24 multirole Su-30 aircraft and an Su-27/Flanker aircraft "kit" from Russia.[30] Although these multirole aircraft can be configured to have a nuclear role, there is no evidence that China made such modifications. It is unlikely that China will invest substantial resources in its airborne nuclear capability unless it is able to purchase the T-22M Backfire from Russia. China is, however, reportedly developing an air-launched cruise missile.

China's Fissile Material Stockpile

A frequently overlooked proliferation issue in China is its large stockpile of weapons-usable fissile material. Although the situation in China seems stable at present, increased political and economic strain could raise the risk of the diversion of fissile material from China's nuclear complex. Little is known about the state of China's material protection, control, and accounting (MPC&A) system.

The exact size of China's fissile material stock is unknown because Beijing has not disclosed it or the size of its nuclear weapons stockpile. Analysts estimate that China has produced between 3 and 7 metric tons of weapons-grade plutonium and between 15 and 25 metric tons of highly enriched uranium.[31] China is believed to have ended its production of plutonium for weapons in 1991 and of uranium for weapons in 1987.[32] Chinese weapons are believed to be heavily dependent on weapons-grade uranium, and it is estimated that China uses 20 to 30 kilograms per weapon. Plutonium weapons might require 3 to 4 kilograms on average.[33]

China produced weapons-usable enriched uranium from 1964 until 1987 at two sites, Lanzhou and Heping.[34] Plutonium was also produced at two sites, Jiuquan and Guangyuan, from 1968 until 1991.[35]

China presumably has stored its residual fissile material stocks at various nuclear facilities. Their locations and the amounts of China's nonweaponized fissile material, however, have not been declared and are not specifically known, nor is the level of security at the storage sites. The China National Nuclear Corporation (which has the status of a government ministry) "produces, stores, and controls all fissile material for civilian as well as military applications."[36] It is estimated that about fourteen sites associated with China's nuclear weapons program have significant quantities of weapons-usable fissile material. The primary locations of nonweaponized fissile material are believed to be China's facilities for plutonium production and uranium enrichment as well as its research institutes for nuclear weapons and other nuclear fuel cycle facilities across the country.

Information on China's MPC&A system is scarce, but the United States has been concerned about it enough to initiate discussions on China's MPC&A (among other issues) between the national nuclear laboratories in both countries. Contacts between the nuclear weapons laboratories in the United States and China were developing beginning in 1994, but they were suspended in the wake of allegations of Chinese nuclear espionage in the Wen Ho Lee case in 1999. Although China's MPC&A system is modeled after the Soviet system, an expert at one of the U.S. national laboratories ranked China's MPC&A system as better than that of the Soviet Union before it collapsed.[37] In 1996, China commissioned a computerized "national nuclear materials accounting system" at about twelve nuclear facilities to improve its ability to prevent the illegal loss, theft, or transfer of nuclear materials. Still, questions remain about the level of protection at China's nuclear facilities. China's MPC&A system is vulnerable to "insider" theft. Also, China lacks the resources to modernize its MCP&A technology. However, since the September 11, 2001, terrorist attacks, China has renewed efforts to improve international cooperation with the United States to install laboratory-to-laboratory collaboratives to coordinate advanced safeguard techniques between the nations.[38]

Alleged Chinese Nuclear and Missile Espionage

United States–China relations were rocked in 1999 by reports that China had stolen the designs of the most advanced U.S. nuclear warheads. The *New York Times* launched the scandal in a March 6, 1999, story that claimed, "Working with nuclear secrets stolen from a U.S. government laboratory, China has made a leap in the development of nuclear weapons: the miniaturization of its bombs. . . . Government investigators have identified a suspect, an American scientist at Los Alamos laboratory."[39] The story was based on leaks from a special investigative committee in the U.S. House of Representatives chaired by Representative Christopher Cox (R-Calif.). The committee released a glossy, three-volume, declassified report on May 25, 1999, that concluded:

- These thefts of nuclear secrets from our national weapons laboratories enabled the [People's Republic of China, or PRC] to design, develop and successfully test modern strategic nuclear weapons sooner than would otherwise have been possible.
- The stolen U.S. nuclear secrets give the PRC design information on thermonuclear weapons on a par with our own. . . . The stolen information includes classified information on seven U.S. thermonuclear warheads.
- The stolen U.S. secrets have helped the PRC fabricate and successfully test modern strategic thermonuclear weapons.[40]

The committee spent most of its time in 1998 investigating charges that critical technology had been transferred to China by major U.S. corporations while using Chinese rockets to launch U.S. satellites. Some political leaders believed the investigation might lead to impeachment charges against then-president Bill Clinton. Although it was a major political issue during much of 1998, it faded in 1999. The committee turned to the matter of Chinese espionage on October 21, 1998, concluded taking testimony on the issue from three witnesses on November 15, and filed its report on January 3, 1999.

The report led to sensational charges. Wen Ho Lee, a scientist at Los Alamos National Laboratories, was arrested under suspicion of espionage. Stephen Younger, then–associate director for nuclear weapons at Los Alamos, testified at Lee's bail hearing, "These codes and their associated data bases and the input file, combined with someone that knew how to use them, could, in my opinion, in the wrong hands, change the global strategic balance." He added, "They enable the possessor to design the only objects that could result in the military defeat of America's conventional forces. . . . They represent the gravest possible security risk to . . . the supreme national interest."[41]

The Cox committee report recommended that the executive branch conduct a comprehensive damage assessment on the implications of China's acquisition of U.S. nuclear weapons information. The administration did so, forming a team of officials from the intelligence and investigative agencies, including the Central Intelligence Agency (CIA), Federal Bureau of Investigation, and nuclear laboratories. An independent panel of nuclear experts, chaired by Admiral David Jeremiah and including General Brent Scowcroft and John Foster, then reviewed their damage assessment. In April 1999, the panel issued its report. This net assessment reached three critical conclusions:

- China's technical advances have been made on the basis of classified and unclassified information derived from espionage, contact with U.S. and other countries' scientists, conferences and publications, unauthorized media disclosures, declassified U.S. weapons information, and Chinese indigenous development. The relative contribution of each cannot be determined.
- Significant deficiencies remain in the Chinese weapons program. . . . To date, the aggressive Chinese collection effort has not resulted in any apparent modernization of their deployed strategic force or any new nuclear weapons deployment.
- China has had the technical capability to develop a multiple independently targetable reentry vehicle (MIRV) system for its large, currently deployed ICBM for many years, but has not done so.[42]

This assessment contradicted the central claims of the Cox report. As the political fires cooled, most experts agreed with the concerned but cautious independent assessment. The case brought against Lee, the alleged spy, was dropped in 2001 after he was held for months in solitary confinement. A criminal investigation of the charges was resolved in January 2002 with a fine against the Loral Corporation for its failure to follow proper declassification procedures before providing a report to Chinese officials who sought information on launch failures.[43] Neither the Bush administration nor the Senate or House of Representatives has raised anew any of the allegations in the Cox report.

China's Commitment to the Nonproliferation Regime

Drawing China into the nuclear and missile nonproliferation regimes has been a long-term process. Since opening a dialogue with China in the early 1970s, the United States has used a range of positive incentives and disincentives to encourage China to sign on to the various unilateral and multilateral commitments that make up the regime. During the 1980s and 1990s, China's nuclear-related exports, particularly to Pakistan, were of major international proliferation concern. China, however, made notable strides in the 1990s by joining formal arms control and nonproliferation regimes, beginning with its accession to the NPT in 1992; its signature (1993) and ratification (1997) of the Chemical Weapons Convention; its cessation of nuclear weapons explosive testing; and its signature of the Comprehensive Test Ban Treaty in September 1996. China has supported multilateral negotiations on a fissile material production cutoff convention, and it had acceded to the Biological Weapons Convention in 1984.

China has softened its stance toward "informal" multilateral control arrangements. China is a member of the Zangger Committee and acceded to the Nuclear Suppliers Group on May 28, 2004.[44] It held talks to consider joining the MTCR on Feburary 20, 2004, and again on June 1–2, 2004.[45] It is still not a full partner to the MTCR and may not be fully observant of the revised guidelines of 1993. It may also have a unilateral interpretation of certain guidelines. In the matter of chemical weapons, China has not joined the Australia Group, but in March 2004, China and the Australia Group held discussions on export control, pledging to strengthen ties with the group.[46]

Under direct U.S. pressure, China has moved to establish a domestic legal system to control sensitive nuclear exports by private or semiprivate Chinese entities. These steps, while imperfect, were sufficient by 1998 for the United States to certify that China could be trusted to safeguard U.S. sensitive nuclear technology as part of the implementation of the 1985 U.S.–China Agreement for Peaceful Nuclear Cooperation. The certification concluded that "the People's Republic of China has provided clear and unequivocal assurances to the United States that it is not assisting and will not assist any non-nuclear-weapon state, either directly or indirectly, in acquiring nuclear explosive devices or the material and components for such devices."[47]

Sensitive Nuclear Exports

The continuing nature of China's role as an international supplier of nuclear technology to weapons programs is in question. China disregarded international norms in the 1980s by selling nuclear materials to such countries as Argentina, India, Pakistan, and South Africa, without requiring the items be placed under IAEA safeguards. U.S. Intelligence officials in 2004 concluded, "Over the past several years, Beijing improved its nonproliferation posture through commitments to multilateral nonproliferation regimes, promulgation of expanded export controls, and strengthened oversight mechanisms, but the proliferation behavior of Chinese companies remains of great concern."[48] Given China's history of exports to weapons programs, any sensitive nuclear exports by China are likely to be interpreted as contradicting its pledges to conform to international standards, even if the items in question were not intended for or were diverted for nonpeaceful ends.

China's nuclear exports to two particular countries, Pakistan and Iran, have been a leading cause of concern. These exports and other issues have provoked several serious crises in United States–China relations and triggered repeated congressional demands for sanctions.

PAST EXPORTS TO PAKISTAN. China's assistance to Pakistan's nuclear program may have been critical to Pakistan's nuclear weapons breakthroughs in the 1980s. In the early 1980s, China is believed to have supplied Pakistan with the plans for one of its earlier nuclear bombs and possibly to have provided enough highly enriched uranium for two such weapons.[49] According to an August 1997 report by the U.S. Arms Control and Disarmament Agency: "Prior to China's [1992] accession [to the NPT], the United States concluded that China had assisted Pakistan in developing nuclear explosives. . . . Questions remain about contacts between Chinese entities and elements associated with Pakistan's nuclear weapons program."[50] In February 2004, Libya turned over to U.S. officials Chinese nuclear bomb designs that it had received from Pakistan's illicit nuclear black market.[51]

China also assisted Pakistan with the construction of an unsafeguarded 50- to 70-megawatt-thermal (MWt) plutonium production reactor at Khusab, and the completion of a plutonium-reprocessing facility at Chasma that had been started with French assistance in the early 1970s.[52] Since June 2000, Khusab has been producing between 8 and 10 kilograms of weapons-grade plutonium a year.[53] China pledged to the United States that it would not export heavy water for the Khusab reactor, but when reports in 1998 claimed China was transferring an excess of heavy water to the KANUPP reactor, the U.S. suspected that it may be rerouted to fuel the military reactor at Khusab.[54] China in 1995 also sold Pakistan ring magnets used on centrifuges for enriching uranium at the A. Q. Khan Research Laboratory in Kahuta.

China has also assisted Pakistan's civilian nuclear program, circumventing the nuclear trade embargo on Pakistan observed by members of the Nuclear Suppliers Group, by helping build a 300-megawatt-electric (MWe) power reactor at Chasma. This reactor will be placed under IAEA safeguards as a condition-of-supply under the existing China–Pakistan agreement for peaceful nuclear cooperation. Pakistan has not accepted full-scope safeguards as its official government policy, but it has accepted IAEA safeguards for the KANUPP power reactor, the PARR I and PARR I, and Chasma.[55] China will also proceed with plans to build the Chasma II reactor, and U.S. government officials state that IAEA safeguards will apply. The NSG allows members to fulfill agreements made before their accession to the group.[56]

China does not appear to have supplied any new weapons technology to Pakistan. China's close ties proved useful as Chinese officials played a quiet but—according to U.S. diplomats—crucial role in supporting Pakistan and coordinating with the United States after the September 11 attacks.[57]

EXPORTS TO IRAN. China has also been a principal supplier of nuclear technology to Iran. China provided Iran with three zero-power and one very small (30-kilowatt-thermal) research reactor, as well as two or three small calutrons (electromagnetic isotope separation machines). While calutrons in those numbers would not themselves produce fissile uranium in significant quantities, they would serve to train personnel in a sensitive nuclear activity.[58] China and Iran signed a ten-year nuclear cooperation agreement in 1990, and Iran agreed in 1992 to purchase two 300-MWe pressurized-water reactors from China.[59]

The United States has led an international effort to prevent the supply of nuclear technology to Iran and has placed pressure on China (and other suppliers) to cancel nuclear deals with Iran. United States pressure has made a difference. By 1995, there were signs that China's nuclear cooperation with Iran was being scaled back. Another factor in this retrenchment may have been Russia's competition as an alternative supplier. Russia agreed to supply light-water nuclear reactors to Iran and to help Iran finish construction of the Bushehr nuclear power plant, which had been abandoned by German contractors during the Iran-Iraq War. Opposition from the United States to China's reactor contract probably also played a part.[60] Iranian shortages of capital may have been a third factor. At any rate, in September 1995 China finally agreed to "suspend for the time being" its reactor sale to Iran.[61] A few months later, a Chinese Foreign Ministry spokesman acknowledged that "the implementation of the agreements between China and Iran on nuclear cooperation has ceased."[62]

China continued until 1997, however, to assist Iran in constructing a plant near Isfahan to produce uranium hexafluoride, the material fed into gas centrifuges for enrichment. Chinese technicians were assisting Iran with other parts of the nuclear fuel cycle, such as uranium mining and processing and fuel fabrication.[63] Yet it seems that these activities were carried out in accordance with the NPT and under IAEA safeguards.

In October 1997, China agreed to end cooperation with Iran on the uranium conversion facility and not to undertake any new cooperation with Iran after completion of the two existing projects—the zero-power reactor and a zirconium production plant. During a visit to these facilities by one of the authors in March 2005, the Chinese-built heavy machinery was clearly in evidence. Iranian officials expressed their frustration at the abrupt end to the Chinese assistance, which they said made their work more difficult. As of early 2005, Iran had still not been able to produce finished zirconium or uranium hexafluoride of adequate quality for use in centrifuges. U.S. intelligence assessments note that "although the Chinese appear to have lived up to these commitments, we are aware of some interactions between Chinese and Iranian entities that have raised questions about its 'no new nuclear cooperation' pledge. According to the State Department, the administration is seeking to address these questions with appropriate Chinese authorities."[64]

EXPORTS TO ALGERIA. China has also provided nuclear assistance to Algeria. The first stage of this cooperation, under an agreement that dates back to 1983, involved the secret construction of the Es Salam 15-MWt research reactor at Ain Oussera.[65] Shortly after the reactor was discovered and publicized in April 1991, Algeria agreed to place it under IAEA safeguards, and an agreement on safeguards for this purpose was signed in February 1992. Thus the reactor has been subject to IAEA inspections since its inauguration in December 1993.

In 1966, China signed agreements with Algeria that covered the second and third stages of nuclear cooperation between the countries.[66] China is helping to construct the Algerian Center of Nuclear Energy Research, which will be placed under IAEA safeguards.

Algeria has also built a hot-cell facility capable of separating plutonium and connected it by a covered canal to the Es Salam research reactor. The hot-cell facility was declared to the IAEA in 1992. If it were used in conjunction with a boosted output of the Es Salam reactor, it could produce up to 5 kilograms of plutonium a year. By the summer of 1997, IAEA inquiries appeared to satisfy U.S. officials that Algeria will operate the facility under safeguards, allow IAEA environmental sampling, and will not build up an inventory of separated plutonium from spent fuel.[67] Of additional interest is a larger facility nearby that Algeria has not declared to the IAEA as a nuclear facility, but that some Western officials believe may be intended as a large-scale reprocessing facility.

While Algeria formally acceded to the NPT in January 1995 and signed an agreement on safeguards with the IAEA in May 1996, China's nuclear cooperation with the country remains sensitive in light of Algeria's interest in reprocessing facilities and its past lack of candor.

Sensitive Missile Exports

As with its nuclear exports, China's role as a provider of missile and missile-related technology to several countries has been a controversial issue in overall relations with the United States and other countries. China reportedly has aided the missile programs of Iran, Iraq, Libya, North Korea, Pakistan, Saudi Arabia, and Syria, although the extent of that assistance has been greatly reduced in recent years. Unlike in the nuclear arena, however, there are no international treaties that prohibit the export of ballistic missiles and related equipment. China was not involved in the creation of the MTCR and for many years resisted being held to its standards. Over time—through the application of sanctions required under U.S. law for the export of missiles and equipment, and with the incentive of licensing the launch of U.S. satellites on Chinese commercial space launch vehicles—China did agree to abide by some terms of the MTCR. The CIA stated in 2003 that "although Beijing has taken some steps to educate firms and individuals on the new missile-related export regulations—offering its first national training course on Chinese export controls in February 2003—Chinese entities continued to work with Pakistan and Iran on ballistic missile-related projects during the first half of 2003." In May 2004, the Bush administration placed sanctions on thirteen foreign companies, five of which were Chinese, for exporting nuclear-related materials to Iran.[68]

PAST EXPORTS TO PAKISTAN. China was believed to have transferred key components for the short-range, nuclear-capable M-11 surface-to-surface missiles to Pakistan in the early 1990s. In June 1991, the United States imposed MTCR Category II sanctions against entities in Pakistan and China for missile technology transfers. These sanctions were lifted in March 1992 after the United States received written confirmation from China that it would abide by the MTCR "guidelines and parameters." Washington took this confirmation to mean that China would not export either the M-9 or the M-11 missile.

But reports surfaced that China had again transferred complete M-11s to Pakistan in late 1992. The Clinton administration again imposed Category II sanctions on Pakistan and China in August 1993. These sanctions were lifted in October 1994 after China again promised not to export M-11 or similar missiles, and to abide by the "guidelines and parameters" of the MTCR.

Press reports in the fall of 1996 revealed new evidence of additional Chinese transfers of complete M-11 missiles to Pakistan. One quoted a recent U.S. National Intelligence Estimate that indicated that Pakistan already had roughly three dozen M-11s stored in canisters at the Sargodha Air Force Base, west of Lahore, along with maintenance facilities and missile launchers.[69] It was said that those missiles, although not "operational," could be unpacked, mated with launchers, and made ready for launch in 48 hours. Even more disturbing in the report was the conclusion that Pakistan, using blueprints and equipment supplied by China, had begun construction of a factory in late 1995 that was capable of producing short-range, solid-fuel missiles based on the Chinese-designed M-11. The factory, located near Rawalpindi, was then expected to be operational in one or two years.[70]

A Chinese supply of complete missiles, or of the production technology for missiles covered by the MTCR would be a major violation of MTCR guidelines and, according to U.S. law, would trigger Category I sanctions—which could block all trade between the United States and Chinese aerospace and electronics firms. China and Pakistan have both denied the existence of the missile plant.[71] In April 1997, U.S. State Department official Robert Einhorn reiterated the Clinton administration's concerns over Chinese transfers of missile-related components, technology, and production technology to Pakistan.[72] He also said that the United States could not make the determination that complete, operational missiles had been transferred; such a determination would require a "high evidentiary standard" because the consequences of sanctions on U.S. firms would be highly damaging. The CIA reported in 2003 that Chinese entities continued to assist Pakistan in the "serial production of solid-propellant [short-range ballistic missiles] and supported the development of solid-propellant [medium-range ballistic missiles]."[73]

EXPORTS TO IRAN. China has been a supplier to Iran of antiship cruise missiles (Silkworms, C-801s, and C-802s), dating back to the Iran-Iraq War in the 1980s. More recently, China has also played a role in Iran's efforts to set up an indigenous ballistic missile development and production program. In June 1995, the CIA had reportedly concluded that China had delivered guidance systems, rocket fuel ingredients, and computerized machine tools to Iran to assist that country in improving imported ballistic missiles and in producing its own missiles.[74] In August 1996, the China Precision Engineering Institute reportedly agreed to sell missile guidance equipment to Iran.[75] China has transferred short-range CSS-8 ballistic missiles to Iran. In addition, China has sold ten fast-attack craft armed with C-802 antiship cruise missiles to Iran, and Iran is modifying additional fast-attack craft to launch the missiles. In 1997, China pledged to the United States that it would not export C-801s and C-802s.[76] China has improved relations with the United States by making de facto commitments to halt missile-related transfers in 1992, 1994, 1998, 2000, and 2002.[77] In 2002, China released a white paper listing a comprehensive set of export controls that reiterated many of those stated in the MTCR.[78]

Nevertheless, the United States placed sanctions on 28 Chinese companies or individuals, most recently in December 2004.[79] The CIA reported in 2003 that "ballistic missile-related cooperation from entities in the former Soviet Union, North Korea, and China over the years has helped Iran move toward its goal of becoming self-sufficient in the production of ballistic missiles. Such assistance during the first half of 2003 continued to include equipment, technology, and expertise."[80]

PAST EXPORTS TO SYRIA. Syria also has received Chinese assistance for its ballistic missile program. A 1988 deal to sell Syria the M-9 missile was apparently canceled under pressure from the United States, but China has supplied Syria with technical expertise for its missile program and ingredients for solid rocket fuel.[81] China has also sold Silkworm antiship cruise missiles to Iraq.

PAST EXPORTS TO SAUDI ARABIA. In 1988, China supplied Saudi Arabia with 30 or more DF-3 (CSS-2) intermediate-range ballistic missiles. Although China had deployed these missiles earlier in its own arsenal with nuclear warheads, Chinese and Saudi officials insist that the missiles transferred to Saudi Arabia were equipped only with conventional warheads. Several hundred Chinese technicians maintain the missiles at their bases at Al Sulayyil and Al Leel. These missiles are near the end of their operational life, and Saudi Arabia has been looking for replacements for some time.[82] U.S. missile sanctions laws could be triggered if China or Saudi Arabia were to arrange transfers of CSS-2 replacements.

Chemical and Biological Weapons Analysis

Official Chinese government statements consistently claim that China never researched, produced, or stockpiled biological weapons. It is widely believed nevertheless that the Chinese declarations are inaccurate and that China retains a limited biological warfare research capability despite Beijing's accession to the Biological Weapons Convention (BWC) in 1984. U.S. officials do not allege that China has biological weapons, only the capability to produce such weapons. China is believed to have begun its biological weapons program in the 1950s. Its current program is largely based on technology that was developed before it became a state party to the BWC. Nevertheless, China's biotechnical infrastructure and munitions production facilities are sufficient to develop, produce, and weaponize biological agents.[83] Research involving biological weapons is also allegedly "being conducted at two ostensibly civilian research facilities known to be under de facto military control."[84] Chinese sales of biological weapon–related technology from China remain a concern. According to former secretary of state Madeleine Albright, the United States has received reports that Chinese firms have supplied Iran with dual-use equipment that could be used in a biological weapons program.[85]

China is one of the few countries that has been the victim of biological warfare. In the late 1930s, Japan established a large biological warfare research and testing facility in Manchuria. Known as Unit 731, the program included human testing on Chinese prisoners. Before and during World War II, the Japanese successfully disseminated typhus rickettsia, cholera bacteria, and the plague in attacks against Chinese civilians and troops. In 1940, residents in Chuhsien, China, reportedly contracted the bubonic plague after the Japanese dropped ceramic bombs containing plague-infected fleas along with rice to attract rodents, which were infected by the fleas and then spread the disease to humans. A similar Japanese attack in Ning Bo resulted in the death of 500 villagers.[86]

In 1992, China revealed that more than 2 million chemical weapons had been abandoned in several sites on its territory, a legacy of the former Japanese army's occupation. By the end of 1945, China had suffered an estimated 10,000 fatalities and 80,000 casualties from Japan's use of chemical weapons in China.[87] Joint Chinese-Japanese efforts to destroy the stockpiles of mustard, lewisite, and phosgene munitions continue.[88]

Upon ratification of the Chemical Weapons Convention in April 1997, China acknowledged its former chemical weapons production capability but did not declare possession of a chemical weapons stockpile. There is little dispute that China retains an extensive chemical weapons capability, but it is less clear if China retains actual weapons. U.S. officials maintain that is does. There is some evidence that Beijing destroyed its stockpile of chemical weapons before signing the CWC.[89] Other reports contend that China's "current inventory is believed to include the full range of traditional chemical agents."[90] Testimony in 2003 by a U.S. Department of State official concluded that "China possesses an inventory of traditional CW agents."[91] China's chemical industry is able to manufacture numerous chemicals relevant to chemical weapons production. China also maintains a broad range of delivery systems for chemical agents, including artillery rockets, aerial bombs, land mines, mortars, and short-range and medium-range ballistic missiles.

Numerous instances of Chinese chemical weapons materials and technology sales abroad have established China as a serious proliferation concern. Many countries have sought chemicals and technology of Chinese origin. The United States has on numerous occasions sanctioned Chinese companies and individuals for chemical weapons proliferation activities. Chemical exports to Iran are of particular concern. During the summer of 1996, China reportedly delivered 400 metric tons of chemicals to Iran, including nerve agent precursors.[92] In May 1997, the United States imposed sanctions on seven Chinese entities for knowingly and materially contributing to Iran's chemical warfare program. These sanctions remained in effect at the beginning of 2002. In June 1998, China announced that it had expanded its chemical export controls to include 10 of the 20 listed by the Australia Group but not prohibited by the CWC. In 2002, China's revised list of export control regulations included all major controls outlined by the Australia Group.[93] Ostensibly, Beijing is seeking to restrain proliferation from within its borders. The results of government enforcement, however, have been mixed.

NOTES

1. "Chinese Nuclear Forces," list for 2003 at the web site of the *Bulletin of the Atomic Scientists*; available at www.thebulletin.org/issues/nukenotes/nd03nukenote.html.
2. Hans M. Kristensen, "Chinese Nuclear Forces," Stockholm International Peace Research Institute Project on Nuclear Technology and Arms Control, January 2003; available at http://projects.sipri.se/nuclear/china.pdf. See also "Chinese Nuclear Forces," *Bulletin of the Atomic Scientists*.
3. Global Security, "DF-31," available at www.globalsecurity.org/wmd/world/china/df-31.htm.
4. International Institute for Strategic Studies (IISS), *The Military Balance, 2004–2005* (Oxford: Oxford University Press, 2004).
5. "Chinese Nuclear Forces," *Bulletin of the Atomic Scientists*; IISS, *Military Balance*.
6. U.S. Department of Defense, "Annual Report on the Military Power of the People's Republic of China, 2000," available at www.fas.org/nuke/guide/china/dod-2002.pdf.
7. "Chinese Nuclear Forces," *Bulletin of the Atomic Scientists*.
8. Ibid.
9. Ibid.
10. U.S. Department of Defense, "Annual Report."
11. Paula A. DeSutter, "China's Record of Proliferation Activities," July 24, 2003, available at www.state.gov/t/vc/rls/rm/24518.htm.
12. See Robert Norris, Andrew Burrows, and Richard Fieldhouse, *Nuclear Weapons Databook, Vol. V: British, French, and Chinese Weapons* (Boulder, Colo.: Westview Press, 1994); Ming Zhang, *China's Changing Nuclear Posture* (Washington, D.C.: Carnegie Endowment for International Peace, 1999).
13. See John Wilson Lewis and Xue Litai, *China Builds the Bomb* (Stanford, Calif.: Stanford University Press, 1988), p. 36.
14. DeSutter, "China's Record."
15. Victor Zaborsky, "Does China Belong in the Missile Technology Control Regime?" *Arms Control Today*, October 2004; available at www.armscontrol.org/act/2004_10/Zaborsky.asp.
16. Paul Kerr, "U.S., North Korea Jockey for China's Support as Working Group Nuclear Talks Approach," *Arms Control Today*, May 2004; available at www.armscontrol.org/act/2004_05/NK.asp.
17. Dick Cheney, "Remarks by the Vice President at Fudan University Followed by Student Body Q&A, Fudan University of Shanghai, China," April 15, 2004; available at www.whitehouse.gov/news/releases/2004/04/20040415-1.html.
18. Howard W. French, "China's Splurge on Resources May Not Be a Sign of Strength," *New York Times*, December 12, 2004; available at www.nytimes.com/2004/12/12/weekinreview/12fren.html?oref=login.
19. Kristensen, "Chinese Nuclear Forces"; National Intelligence Council (NIC), *Foreign Missile Developments and the Ballistic Missile Threat through 2015*, Unclassified Summary of a National Intelligence Estimate (Washington, D.C.: Central Intelligence Agency, 2002), p. 9.
20. Vice Admiral Thomas Wilson, director, Defense Intelligence Agency, "Global Threats and Challenges through 2015," Statement for the Record, Senate Select Committee on Intelligence, February 7, 2001.
21. Global Security, "DF-31."; CNN, "China Tests Shield-Busting Missile, Report," February 4, 2002, available at http://archives.cnn.com/2002/WORLD/asiapcf/east/02/04/china.missile/.
22. NIC, *Foreign Missile Developments*, p. 10.
23. "Chinese Nuclear Forces," *Bulletin of the Atomic Scientists*.
24. NIC, "Foreign Missile Developments," p. 10.
25. John J. Lumpkin, "China Launches New Class of Nuclear Submarine Designed to Fire ICBMs," Associated Press, December 3, 2004. See also Harold Brown, Joseph W. Preuher and Adam Segal,

"Chinese Military Power," Council of Foreign Relations Task Force Report, December 2003, pp. 45, 52.

26. "NRDC Nuclear Notebook: Chinese Nuclear Forces, 2001," *Bulletin of the Atomic Scientists*, September/October 2001, p. 71.
27. "Chinese Nuclear Forces," *Bulletin of the Atomic Scientists.*
28. Ibid.
29. Nuclear Threat Initiative, "Bombers and Dual-Capable Aircraft," available at www.nti.org/db/china/wdsmdat.htm.
30. U.S. Department of Defense, "Annual Report."
31. David Albright and Kimberly Kramer, "Stockpiles are Still Growing," *Bulletin of the Atomic Scientists*, November/December 2004; available at www.isis-online.org/global_stocks/bulletin_albright_kramer.pdf.
32. David Albright, Frans Berkhout, and William Walker, *Plutonium and Highly Enriched Uranium 1996: World Inventories, Capabilities, and Policies* (Oxford: Oxford University Press, 1997), pp. 76–78, 128–130.
33. Ann MacLachlan and Mark Hibbs, "China Stops Production of Military HEU," *Nuclear Fuel*, November 13, 1989, p. 5. The 1987 date is based on a personal communication from Mark Hibbs, who was told the date by the head of the China Nuclear Energy Industry Corporation; cited in Albright, Berkhout, and Walker, *Plutonium and Highly Enriched Uranium 1996*, p. 126.
34. Norris, Burrows, and Fieldhouse, *Nuclear Weapons Databook Vol. V*, p. 350.
35. Wendy Frieman, "New Members of the Club: Chinese Participation in Arms Control Regimes 1980–1995," *Nonproliferation Review*, Spring–Summer 1996, p. 18.
36. Interview with U.S. National Laboratory official, June 1996.
37. Tang Bin, "China: Major Advances Realized in Nation's Nuclear Fuel Accounting System," *Zhongguo He Gongye Bao* [China Nuclear Industry News], September 11, 1996, in FBIS-CST-96-019, November 26, 1996.
38. Hui Zhang, "Evaluating China's MPC&A System," paper presented at the Institute of Nuclear Materials Management 44th Annual Meeting, Phoenix, 2003, pp. 5–6.
39. James Risen and Jeff Gerth, "Breach at Los Alamos: A Special Report"; and "China Stole Nuclear Secrets for Bombs, U.S. Aides Say," *New York Times*, March 6, 1999.
40. *Report of the Select Committee on U.S. National Security and Military/Commercial Concerns with the People's Republic of China*, vol. 1 (Washington, D.C.: U.S. Government Printing Office, 1999), pp. ii, iii, 60.
41. "Atomic Scientist Is Taking Case to Court of Public Opinion," *New York Times*, January 9, 2000; and "Excerpt from Testimony at Hearing on the Wen Ho Lee Case," *New York Times*, September 27, 2000.
42. "The Intelligence Community Damage Assessment on the Implications of China's Acquisition of U.S. Nuclear Weapons Information on the Development of Future Chinese Weapons," April 21, 1999; available at www.ceip.org/files/projects/npp/resources/ChinaDamageAssessment.htm.
43. "Loral Settles U.S. Probe for $14 Million," *Washington Post*, January 9, 2002.
44. Nuclear Threat Initiative, "China and the ZAC," available at www.nti.org/db/china/sacorg.htm; Wade Boese, "Nuclear Suppliers Pass on U.S. Proposals," Arms Control Association, July/August 2004; available at www.armscontrol.org/act/2004_07-08/NSG.asp?print.
45. Paul Kerr and Wade Boese, "China Seeks to Join Nuclear, Missile Control Groups," *Arms Control Today*, March 2004; available at www.armscontrol.org/act/2004_03/China.asp.
46. Ministry of Foreign Affairs of the People's Republic of China, "China and Multilateral Non-Proliferation Mechanisms," June 29, 2004, available at www.fmprc.gov.cn/eng/wjb/zzjg/jks/kjlc/fkswt/dbfks/t141201.htm.
47. Presidential Determination 98-10, issued by the White House, January 15, 1998.
48. Central Intelligence Agency, "Unclassified Report to Congress on the Acquisition of Technology Relating to Weapons of Mass Destruction and Advanced Conventional Munitions, 1 July through 31 December 2003," 2004.
49. Leslie Gelb, "Pakistan Link Perils U.S.–China Nuclear Pact," *New York Times*, June 22, 1984; Gelb, "Peking Said to Balk at Nuclear Pledges," *New York Times*, June 23, 1984; and Gary Milhollin and Gerard White, "A New China Syndrome: Beijing's Atomic Bazaar," *Washington Post*, May 12, 1991.

50. U.S. Arms Control and Disarmament Agency, *Adherence to and Compliance with Arms Control Agreements* (Washington, D.C.: U.S. Arms Control and Disarmament Agency, 1997), p. 80.
51. Joby Warrick and Peter Slevin, "Libyan Arms Designs Traced Back to China," *New York Times,* February 15, 2004; available at www.washingtonpost.com/ac2/wp-dyn/A42692-2004Feb14?language=printer; "Report: China Nuke Traffic Link," Associated Press, February 16, 2004; available at www.cbsnews.com/stories/2004/10/12/terror/main648733.shtml.
52. Bill Gertz, "China Aids Pakistani Plutonium Plant," *Washington Times,* April 3, 1996.
53. "Pakistan Producing Weapon-Grade Plutonium," *The Dawn,* June 14, 2000; available at www.dawn.com/2000/06/14/top8.htm.
54. Global Security, "Khushab," available at www.globalsecurity.org/wmd/world/pakistan/khushab.htm.
55. Global Security, "Chasma," available at www.globalsecurity.org/wmd/world/pakistan/chashma.htm.
56. John Wolf, "China in the Nuclear Suppliers Group," Testimony before the House International Relations Committee, May 18, 2004; available at www.state.gov/t/np/rls/rm/32570.htm.
57. Charles Hutzler, "China's Quiet, Crucial Role in the War," *Wall Street Journal,* December 18, 2001.
58. Albright, Berkhout, and Walker, *Plutonium and Highly Enriched Uranium 1996,* pp. 359–360.
59. Mark Hibbs, "Russian Industry May Be Key to Iran's Reactor Prospects," Jane's Special Report, *Nucleonics Week,* September 17, 1992, p. 3.
60. Elaine Sciolino, "Iran Says It Plans 10 Nuclear Plants But No Atom Arms," *New York Times,* May 14, 1995, p. 1.
61. "China Softens Stance against Iranian Reactors," *Washington Post,* September 30, 1995.
62. "China–Iran," Associated Press, January 9, 1996.
63. Bill Gertz, "Iran Gets China's Help on Nuclear Arms," *Washington Times,* April 17, 1996; R. Jeffrey Smith, "China Nuclear Deal with Iran Is Feared," *Washington Post,* April 17, 1995; and David Albright, "An Iranian Bomb?" *Bulletin of Atomic Scientists,* July/August 1995, p. 25.
64. Central Intelligence Agency, "Unclassified Report to Congress on the Acquisition of Technology Relating to Weapons of Mass Destruction and Advanced Conventional Munitions, 1 January through 30 June 2002," available at www.nti.org/e_research/official_docs/cia/cia041003.pdf.
65. Albright, Berkhout, and Walker, *Plutonium and Highly Enriched Uranium 1996,* pp. 363–364.
66. "Algeria Signs Nuclear Draft Agreement with China," Reuters, June 2, 1996; and "China: PRC, Algeria to Cooperate in Nuclear Energy Development," *Xinhua,* May 21, 1997, in FBIS-CHI-97-141, May 23, 1997.
67. Mark Hibbs, "Move to Block China Certification," *Nucleonics Week,* August 7, 1997, p. 11.
68. Central Intelligence Agency, "Unclassified Report to Congress on the Acquisition of Technology Relating to Weapons of Mass Destruction and Advanced Conventional Munitions, 1 July through 31 December 2003."
69. R. Jeffrey Smith, "China Linked to Pakistani Missile Plant," *Washington Post,* August 25, 1996.
70. Ibid.
71. Aurang Zeb, "Pakistan Denies It's Building Missile Factory," Reuters, August 26, 1996.
72. Senate Governmental Affairs Committee, "Weapons Proliferation in China."
73. Central Intelligence Agency, "Unclassified Report to Congress on the Acquisition of Technology Relating to Weapons of Mass Destruction and Advanced Conventional Munitions, 1 July through 31 December 2003."
74. Barbara Opall, "U.S. Queries China on Iran," *Defense News,* June 14–25, 1995; Elaine Sciolino, "CIA Report Says Chinese Sent Iran Arms Components," *New York Times,* June 21, 1995; and "Chinese Shipments Violate Controls," *Jane's Defense Weekly,* July 1, 1995, p. 3.
75. Bill Gertz, "China Sold Iran Missile Technology," *Washington Times,* November 21, 1996.
76. Nuclear Threat Initiative, "China's Missile Exports and Assistance to Iran," available at www.nti.org/db/china/miranpos.htm.
77. DeSutter, "China's Record."
78. Kerr and Boese, "China Seeks to Join Nuclear, Missile Control Groups."
79. "U.S. Imposes Sanctions on 3 Chinese Firms," Associated Press, December 2, 2004, available at www.nytimes.com/aponline/international/AP-China-US-Iran.html.

80. Central Intelligence Agency, "Unclassified Report to Congress on the Acquisition of Technology Relating to Weapons of Mass Destruction and Advanced Conventional Munitions, 1 July through 31 December 2003."
81. Elaine Sciolino, "China Said to Sell Parts for Missiles," *New York Times*, January 31, 1992; and William Safire, "China's 'Hama Rules,'" *New York Times*, March 5, 1992.
82. Philip Finnegan, "Saudis Study Missile Buy To Replace Aging Arsenal," *Defense News*, March 17–23, 1997, p. 3.
83. U.S. Department of Defense, *Proliferation: Threat and Response* (Washington, D.C.: U.S. Department of Defense, 2001), p. 15.
84. Center for Defense Information. "China," available at www.cdi.org/issues/cbw/china.html.
85. Bill Gertz, "Albright Concedes 'Concern' over China-Iran Transfers," *Washington Times*, January 24, 1997.
86. Edward Eitzen and Ernest Takafuji, "Historical Overview of Biological Warfare," in *Medical Aspects of Chemical and Biological Warfare, Part I, The Textbook of Military Medicine* (Washington, D.C.: Borden Institute, Office of the Surgeon General, 1997), p. 417; and see also Jeffrey Smart, "History of Chemical and Biological Warfare: An American Perspective," in *Medical Aspects of Chemical and Biological Warfare, Part I, The Textbook of Military Medicine*, p. 33.
87. Peter O'Meara Evans, "Destruction of Abandoned Chemical Weapons in China," Paper 13 (Bonn: Bonn International Center for Conversion, September 1997).
88. "Abandoned Chemical Weapons in China Come to Light," *Jane's Defense Weekly*, July 1, 1998, p. 7.
89. Center for Defense Information, "China."
90. Federation of American Scientists, "China: Chemical and Biological Weapons," available at www.fas.org/nuke/juide/china/cbw/index.html.
91. DeSutter, "China's Record."
92. Gertz, "China Sold Iran Missile Technology."
93. DeSutter, "China's Record."

Table 7.1. **China's Nuclear Infrastructure of Proliferation Concern**

Name/Location of Facility	Type/Status
Nuclear Weapons Complex[1]	
Jiuquan Atomic Energy Complex (Plant 404) Subei, Gansu[2]	Fabrication of fissile materials into bomb cores, and final weapons assembly, shutdown
Northwest Institute of Nuclear Technology Xi'an, Shaanxi[3]	Institute that was responsible for conducting and analyzing nuclear tests, nuclear weapons archive, currently studying CTBT verification issues
Lop Nur Nuclear Weapons Test Base Malan Xinjiang[4]	Nuclear weapons test site and possible nuclear weapons stockpile, high-level waste storage
Chinese Academy of Engineering Physics (CAEP) Mianyang, Sichuan[5]	Nuclear weapons research, design, and technology complex, called the Los Alamos Laboratory of China[6]
Institute 905 of CAEP outside Mianyang	Ordnance engineering lab for nonnuclear components of nuclear weapons, called the Chinese Sandia Laboratory[7]
Institute of Applied Physics and Computational Mathematics Beijing[8]	Conducts research on nuclear warhead design computations for CAEP
Shanghai Institute of Nuclear Research (at Fudan University) Shanghai, Zheijiang	Engaged in tomography, tests solid missile propellants, explosives, and detonation packages for nuclear weapons
Harbin Military Engineering Institute	Served to train nuclear weapon research and design personnel[9]
Harbin Heilongjiang[10]	Possible warhead assembly and production site
Plant 821 Guangyuan, Sichuan[11]	Possible nuclear weapon assembly facility, possible nuclear weapon component production facility, also site of plutonium production reactor and reprocessing plant (see below)
Plutonium Production Reactors	
Plant 821 Guangyuan, Sichuan[12]	LWGR, nat. U, 1,000 MW, operational[13] Largest plutonium producing reactor in China
Jiuquan Atomic Energy Complex (Plant 404) Subei, Gansu[14]	LWGR, nat. U, 500 MW, shutdown

Research Reactors[15]	
CARR China Institute of Atomic Energy	60 MWt, planned
Chinese Experimental Fast Reactor (CFER)	Fast-breeder, 65 MWt, under construction, expected to be completed in 2007
HTR-10 Institute of Nuclear Energy Technology, Tsinghua University Beijing[16]	High-temperature gas reactor, pebble bed, 10 MWt, operational
NHR-5 Institute of Nuclear Energy Technology, Tsinghua University Beijing	Heating prototype, LW, 5 MWt, operational
HFETR Nuclear Power Institute of China Chengdu, Sichuan	Tank, LW, HEU (90%), 125 MWt, operational
HFETR critical Nuclear Power Institute of China Chengdu, Sichuan	Critical assembly, LW, HEU (90%), 0 MWt, shutdown[17]
MJTR Nuclear Power Institute of China Chengdu, Sichuan	Pool, LW, HEU (90%), 5 MWt, operational
MNSR IAE China Institute of Atomic Energy Tuoli, near Beijing[18]	Tank in pool, LW, HEU (90%), 27 kWt (.027 MWt), operational
MNSR–SD Research Institute of Geological Sciences Jinan Shandong	Tank in pool, LW, HEU (90%), 33 kWt (.033 MWt), operational
MNSR-SH Shanghai Institute for Measurement and Testing Technology Shanghai	Tank in pool, LW, HEU (90%), 30 kWt (.03 MWt), operational
MNSR–SZ Shenzhen University Guangdong	Tank in pool, LW, HEU (90%), 30 kWt (.03 MWt), operational
Zero-Power Fast Critical Reactor China Institute of Atomic Energy Jianiang/Chengdu, Sichuan	Critical fast, HEU (90%), .05 kWt, operational

(table continues on the following page)

Table 7.1. **China's Nuclear Infrastructure of Proliferation Concern** (continued)

Name/Location of Facility	Type/Status
HWRR–II China Institute of Atomic Energy Tuoli, near Beijing	Heavy-water, LEU (3%), 15 MWt, operational Under IAEA safeguards
SPR IAE China Institute of Atomic Energy Tuoli, near Beijing	Pool, LW, LEU (10%), 3.5 MWt, operational
SPRR–300 Southwest Institute of Nuclear Physics and Chemistry Jianiang/Chengdu, Sichuan	Pool, LW, LEU (10%), 3 MWt, operational
Tsinghua Pool Institute of Nuclear Energy Technology, Tsinghua University Beijing	Pool, two cores, LW, LEU (10%), 1 MWt, operational
PPR Pulsing Reactor Nuclear Power Institute of China Chengdu, Sichuan	Pool, UZRH, HEU (20%), 1 MWt, operational
Uranium Enrichment	
Heping Uranium Enrichment Plant Heping, Sichuan[19]	Gaseous diffusion plant: able to produce 750–2,950 kg HEU/year,[20] operational
Lanzhou Nuclear Fuel Complex Lanzhou, Gansu[21]	Gaseous diffusion plant, estimated to have produced at least 150–330 kg HEU/year,[22] reportedly decommissioned in 1999[23]
Russian-supplied centrifuge enrichment plant, 25 km north of Lanzhou, Gansu[24]	Large-scale gas-centrifuge enrichment facility, part operational, part still under construction, completion expected in 2005, capacity of 1.0 million SWU/year[25]
Hanzhong, Shaanxi[26]	Two gaseous diffusion plants, operational, total capacity of up to 500,000 SWU/year
China Institute of Atomic Energy Tuoli, near Beijing[27]	Laboratory-scale gaseous diffusion facility: developed enrichment process installed at Lanzhou in 1964, no longer operational
Plutonium Reprocessing[28]	
Jiuquan Atomic Energy Complex (Plant 404) Subei, Gansu[29]	Reprocessing plant, capacity of 300–400 kg Pu/year, and pilot reprocessing plant (both use PUREX method), and nuclear fuel processing plant for refining plutonium into weapons-usable metals, shutdown

Plant 821 Guangyuan, Sichuan[30]	China's largest plutonium separation facility, capacity of 300–400 kg Pu/year
Nuclear Fuel Component Plant (Plant 812) Yibin, Sichuan[31]	Civilian light-water reactor fuel element plant (see below), plutonium fuel rod production, plutonium production and processing, reportedly no longer handles weapons-grade material, operating
Lanzhou Nuclear Fuel Complex Lanzhou, Gansu[32]	Pilot spent-fuel reprocessing plant, capacity of 100 kg/HM per year, under construction, but experiencing logistical delays, commercial-scale reprocessing plant planned[33]
Uranium Processing	
Nuclear Fuel Component Plant (202), Candu Fuel Plant Baotou, Inner Mongolia[34]	Fuel-rod fabrication, operational
Nuclear Fuel Component Plant (Plant 812) Yibin, Sichuan	Fuel-rod fabrication, being expanded to produce fuel elements for new types of power reactors, operational[35]
Jiuquan Atomic Energy Complex (Plant 404) Subei, Gansu	Nuclear Fuel Processing Plant: Converts enriched UF_6 to UF_4 for shaping into metal, shutdown
Tritium, Lithum Deuteride, and Beryllum	
Ningxia Non-ferrous Metal Research Institute (Plant 905) Helanshan, Ningxia[36]	China's main research and production site for beryllium, operational
Nuclear Fuel Component Plant (202) Baotou, Inner Mongolia	Tritium, Li-6 deuterium production, operational
Nuclear Fuel Element Plant (Plant 812) Yibin, Sichuan	Probable production of tritium and Li-6 deuterium, not operational[37]

Abbreviations

CTBT	Comprehensive Test Ban Treaty
HEU	highly enriched uranium
HM	heavy metal
kWt	thousands of watts of thermal output
LEU	low-enriched uranium
LW	light-water
LWGR	light-water graphite-moderated reactor
MNSR	miniature neutron source reactor
MW	megawatts
MWt	megawatts thermal
nat. U	natural uranium
Pu	plutonium
SWU	separative work unit
UZRH	uranium-zirconium-hydride

(table continues on the following page)

Table 7.1. **China's Nuclear Infrastructure of Proliferation Concern** (continued)

Sources

David Albright, Frans Berkhout, and William Walker, *Plutonium and Highly Enriched Uranium 1996: World Inventories, Capabilities and Policies* (Oxford: Oxford University Press, 1997). International Atomic Energy Agency, *Nuclear Research Reactors in the World,* available at www.iaea.org/worldatom/rrdb. Robert S. Norris, Andrew S. Burrows, and Richard W. Fieldhouse, *Nuclear Weapons Databook V* (Boulder, Colo.: Westview Press, 1994). Nuclear Engineering International, *World Nuclear Industry Handbook 2004* (Sidcup, U.K.: Wilmington Publishing, 2004). Nuclear Threat Initiative, "China Nuclear Non-Proliferation Database," available at www.nti.org/db/china/sec3.htm. "Nuclear Profile: China," *Risk Report* (Wisconsin Project on Nuclear Arms Control), November 1995, pp. 3–9.

Notes

1. In addition to the sites listed under Nuclear Weapons Complex, the following sites are engaged in nuclear research, although perhaps they are not explicitly weapon-related: the Atomic Research Center, Xingjiang; the Institute of Nuclear Energy Technology (INET), Tsinghua University, Beijing; the Institute of Nuclear Science and Technology, Sichuan University, Chengdu, Sichuan; the Institute of Materials and Elements at the Sichuan Institute of Nuclear Power, Chengdu, Sichuan province; the China Institute for Radiation Protection (CIRP), Yaiyuan, Shanxi; the Beijing Nuclear Engineering Research and Development Academy, Beijing; and the Nuclear Research and Development Institute, Tianjin, southeast of Beijing.
2. Nuclear Threat Initiative, "Jiuquan Atomic Energy Complex," available at www.nti.org/db/china/jiuq.htm.
3. Nuclear Threat Initiative, "Northwest Institute of Nuclear Technology," available at www.nti.org/db/china/nwint.htm.
4. Nuclear Threat Initiative, "Lop Nur Nuclear Weapons Test Base," available at www.nti.org/db/china/lopnur.htm.
5. Nuclear Threat Initiative, "Chinese Academy of Engineering Physics," available at www.nti.org/db/china/caep.htm.
6 CAEP is an identical copy of the Northwest Nuclear Weapons Research and Design Academy in Haiyan, the original Chinese weapon design facility that has since been phased out, and the work transferred to CAEP. See Norris, Burrows, and Fieldhouse, *Nuclear Weapons Databook V,* p. 338.
7 Ibid., p. 348; *and "Nuclear Profile: China," Risk Report,* p. 6.
8. Nuclear Threat Initiative, "Institute of Applied Physics and Computational Mathematics," available at www.nti.org/db/china/iapcm.htm.
9. John Wilson Lewis and Xue Litai, *China Builds the Bomb* (Stanford, Calif.: Stanford University Press, 1988), p. 264.
10. There is also a Harbin Military Engineering Institute that trains personnel in nuclear research and design. See Lewis and Litai, *China Builds the Bomb,* pp. 203–204.
11. Nuclear Threat Initiative, "Guangyuan," available at www.nti.org/db/china/guang.htm.
12. Ibid.
13. In 1999, there was speculation that the reprocessing facility at Guangyuan might be shut down as part of an effort to streamline and restructure the China National Nuclear Corporation. Western officials, however, doubt that the facility would have been shut down, because it is China's only operating military plutonium production and separation center. See Mark Hibbs, "China Said to be Preparing for Decommissioning Defense Plants," *Nuclear Fuel,* May 17, 1999.
14. Nuclear Threat Initiative, "Jiuquan Atomic Energy Complex," available at www.nti.org/db/china/jiuq.htm.

15. The primary source for this section was the International Atomic Energy Agency's "Research Reactor Database," available at www.iaea.org/worldatom/rrdb.
16. This reactor is being jointly developed with the Massachusetts Institute of Technology. See "MIT, Tsinghua U to Team on Pebble Bed R&D," *Nuclear News,* December 2003.
17. According to the International Atomic Energy Agency, this facility is shut down, although the *2004 World Nuclear Industry Handbook* states that it is still operational.
18. The China Institute for Atomic Energy is China's main nuclear research organization. In addition to this research reactor and the old gaseous diffusion pilot plant (see the uranium enrichment section), it did early research on hexafluoride (UF6) production and on boost materials for a hydrogen bomb.
19. Nuclear Threat Initiative, "Heping Uranium Enrichment Plant," available at www.nti.org/db/china/heping.htm.
20. U.S. Defense Intelligence Agency, *Soviet and Peoples' Republic of China Nuclear Weapons Employment Policy and Strategy,* TCS-65475-72 (Washington, D.C.: U.S Government Printing Office, 1972); see discussion in Albright, Berkhout, and Walker, *Plutonium and Highly Enriched Uranium 1996,* pp. 126–130. China reportedly ceased HEU production in 1987.
21. Nuclear Threat Initiative, "Lanzhou Nuclear Fuel Complex," available at www.nti.org/db/china/lanzhou.htm.
22. Ibid.
23. Ibid.
24. This facility, combined with that located at Hanzhong, is China's main uranium enrichment center. There has been some confusion as to the location of this new facility, but the most recent reports indicate that it is in fact near Lanzhou. See Mark Hibbs, "China Moved Centrifuge Complex," *Nuclear Fuel,* May 17, 1999; and Hibbs, "China Expected Soon to Request Bids for Qinshan Transport Cask," *Nuclear Fuel,* April 30, 2001. Earlier reports suggested that the facility might be located in Chengdu; see Hibbs, "China Moved Centrifuge Complex"; and "China's Centrifuge SWU Plant Up and Running, Minatom Says," *Nuclear Fuel,* January 27, 1997, p. 3.
25. The first module of the plant began operating in 1998, the second in late September 2000, and the third in November 2001. "Russian Atomic Ministry Delegation to Participate in Launch of Third Line of Gas-Centrifuge Plant in China," *Economic News,* November 13, 2001. Completion of the final module is expected around 2005. Hibbs, "China Moved Centrifuge Complex."
26. Nuclear Threat Initiative, "Lanzhou Nuclear Fuel Complex."
27. Nuclear Threat Initiative, "China Institute of Atomic Energy," available at www.nti.org/db/china/ciae.htm.
28. Additional military reprocessing facilities are thought to be located at Urumqi, Xinjiang province, and Yumen, Gansu province. "Datafile: China," *Nuclear Engineering International,* October 1993, p. 22.
29. Nuclear Threat Initiative, "Jiuquan Atomic Energy Complex." See also Hibbs, "China Said to be Preparing for Decommissioning Defense Plants."
30. See note 13.
31. Nuclear Threat Initiative, "Yibin Fuel Plant," available at www.nti.org/db/china/yibin.htm.
32. Nuclear Threat Initiative, "Lanzhou Nuclear Fuel Complex."
33. A commercial-scale facility is still provisionally planned, though China has not yet determined where it will be located. Construction is likely years away. Mark Hibbs, "Separation Plant on Drawing Board until 2006–2010 Plan, CIAE Says," *Nuclear Fuel,* November 22, 2004.
34. Nuclear Threat Initiative, "Baotou Nuclear Fuel Component Plant," available at www.nti.org/db/china/baotou.htm.
35. See Nuclear Threat Initiative, "Yibin Fuel Plant."
36. Nuclear Threat Initiative, "Ningxia Non-Ferrous Metal Research Institute," available at www.nti.org/db/china/ningxia.htm.
37. See Nuclear Threat Initiative, "Yibin Fuel Plant."

CHAPTER 8

France

Nuclear Weapons Capability

France is a nuclear weapon state recognized under the Non-Proliferation Treaty (NPT). It deploys approximately 350 nuclear weapons on 84 nuclear-capable aircraft and 48 submarine-launched ballistic missiles (SLBMs) on four nuclear submarines (3 of them carrying 16 missiles each) (see table 8.1 at the end of the chapter). In fiscal year 2005, the country appropriated $4.084 billion (20 percent of its annual defense budget) to maintain its nuclear arsenal.[1] France has conducted 210 nuclear weapons tests, the first on February 13, 1960, and the last on January 27, 1996. France produced approximately 1,110 nuclear warheads between 1960 and 1992. It has signed and ratified the Comprehensive Test Ban Treaty.

Missile and Aircraft Capability

France currently relies on a limited nuclear force consisting of four nuclear ballistic missile submarines (SSBNs) and 94 bombers, not all of which are deployed. Three of the four SSBNs are deployed at any given time, and each is capable of carrying 16 M-45 SLBMs with a total of 96 warheads. France's aircraft capability includes 24 Super Étendard bombers carrying a total of 10 warheads and 60 Mirage 2000N bombers carrying a total of 50 warheads.[2] Each bomber is capable of carrying an Air Sol Moyenne Portee (ASMP) supersonic guided missile. In 2004, France deployed 10 new Rafale bombers, all of which are nuclear capable. France plans to equip these with nuclear-armed ASMP missiles.

Biological and Chemical Weapons Capability

France does not have any research or production programs for either biological or chemical weapons. It is a member of both the Biological Weapons Convention and the Chemical Weapons Convention. Though it stockpiled chemical weapons before World War II and continued chemical weapons research in Algeria until the late 1960s, it eliminated its entire stockpile before joining the Chemical Weapons Convention.

The Strategic Context

France launched its nuclear program incrementally during the Fourth Republic (1945–1958). In this process, the 1956 Suez crisis was a key turning point. The decision to test a nuclear device was taken during the last weeks of the Fourth Republic in 1958. In February 1960, France tested its first weapon in then-French Algeria. The nuclear arsenal became operational in 1964 with the entry into active service of the first Mirage IVA nuclear bombers.[3]

During the Cold War, France developed a "three-circles" defense policy aimed at protecting its vital interests against external threats (primarily the Soviet Union) through nuclear deterrence, participation in the general defense of Western Europe within the Atlantic Alliance, and by maintaining an active role outside Europe (mainly in Africa and the Middle East).[4] For that purpose, the French arsenal grew to a triad of sea-, air-, and land-based weapons systems with a few hundred warheads, following a national policy of "sufficiency" (*suffisance*) and relying on the threat of massive retaliation.[5]

With the end of the Cold War, France reviewed its nuclear strategy. After the fall of the Soviet Union, France's 1994 defense white paper (the first since 1972) identified French security risks as being the likely increase in the weaponry and military of other nations, including the proliferation of weapons of mass destruction, and Russia's continuing strong military power in Europe.[6] The 1994 white paper also sought to emphasize a reduction in the central role of French nuclear weapons while maintaining a deterrence stance. Nuclear weapons would nevertheless continue to ensure the protection of France's "vital interests," primarily against the "resurgence of a major threat against Western Europe."[7]

In 1995–1996, the newly elected Gaullist president, Jacques Chirac, initiated the restructuring of the French nuclear arsenal. Assuming office after a period of "cohabitation" with a socialist president and a Gaullist prime minister, Chirac faced difficult defense choices.[8] He followed much of the white paper's suggestions for France's defense but changed funding priorities from nuclear weaponry to intelligence, force projection, and a professional army.[9] Against substantial international criticism, Chirac briefly resumed nuclear weapons testing with a series of six tests in 1995–1996 (after a moratorium from 1992 to 1995) and began to restructure the arsenal. He decided to dismantle two ground-to-ground missile systems: the S-3D, based in Albion, and the shorter-range Hades missiles. He continued to effect reductions in nuclear spending from the Cold War level of more than 30 percent of the procurement budget to about 20 percent. There was a debate as policy shifted from the Cold War era "weak to the strong" posture against the Soviet Union to a "strong to the weak," or "strong to the crazy," posture to counter emerging nuclear threats and proliferation of unconventional weapons. The concept, however, retained its original logic: that is, preserving French vital interests vis-à-vis all potential threats.[10] President Chirac summarized the current French nuclear doctrine in June 2001:

> Nuclear deterrence is the crux of the resources enabling France to affirm the principle of strategic autonomy from which derives our defense policy. Thanks to the continuous efforts made since the time of General de Gaulle, nuclear deterrence today is an essential foundation of our security and will remain so for many more years in the new strategic context, where it remains fully meaningful and effective.

> Nuclear deterrence is above all an important factor of global stability. It is thanks to nuclear deterrence that Europe has been protected for more than 50 years from the ravages it experienced during the twentieth century. By imposing restraint and inciting [others] to exercise reason, a credible nuclear threat commands peace.
>
> Our nuclear forces are not directed against any country, and we have always refused [to accept] that nuclear weapons should be regarded as weapons of war to be used as part of a military strategy.[11]

As suggested in this speech and in previous speeches, France has always given a European dimension to its nuclear forces. France has made several openings to Europeanize its nuclear capabilities more formally, the last mention having been for a "concerted deterrence" (1995). Besides increasing France–United Kingdom cooperation, these attempts have not, however, been very successful so far.

Nuclear Analysis

As early as the 1930s, France began working on a nuclear weapon, but efforts were slowed by a lack of nuclear scientific knowledge and a shortage of uranium. The efforts also suffered heavily from World War II (when France was occupied). French scientists, unlike their American and British colleagues, did not participate in the initial production and testing of the first nuclear weapon.[12]

In 1945, a French atomic energy commission (Commissariat à l'Énergie Atomique) was established, but it began focusing on military applications only in the mid-1950s. In 1948, uranium ore was discovered in central France. Four years later, the Parliament set out a five-year plan to produce 50 kilograms of plutonium a year, using natural uranium reactors, to fuel nuclear power plants. At the United Nations in 1946, France promised that all its nuclear efforts would be peaceful. At the U.N. General Assembly, France urged the United States and the Soviet Union to discontinue atmospheric nuclear weapons testing. It soon began a secret nuclear weapons development program, however, which became increasingly important throughout the 1950s, until 1958, when the decision to test a nuclear weapon was finally made.

In the early stages of the European Union's development, France discussed the possibility of renouncing nuclear weapons. That idea was soon rejected. After the 1956 Suez crisis, the nuclear program was accelerated, and France initiated plans for its first nuclear test to take place in 1960.[13]

In 1956, France signed the Euratom treaty, which would act as a unifier on European civilian nuclear policy, giving access to nuclear fuel to all members for peaceful purposes. There were parallel exploratory talks with Italy and Germany about military nuclear cooperation, but these were stopped at an early stage when General Charles de Gaulle came back into office in 1958.[14]

When de Gaulle became president, he confirmed the proposed nuclear test date and accelerated the nuclear program. After the 1960 test, France implemented a long-term nuclear plan, ignoring international objectors, and in particular, ignoring criticism made in conjunction with the Partial Test Ban Treaty

(1963). France continued atmospheric testing until 1974. In 1968, when other European countries were negotiating the NPT, France avoided the talks even though the treaty recognized its status as a nuclear weapon state. When the treaty was signed, however, France agreed to observe its conditions without signing it.[15] Even though France became increasingly involved in the nuclear nonproliferation regime (notably as a founding member of the Nuclear Suppliers Group), it was a longtime critic of the NPT per se. It joined the treaty only in 1992.

France has used at least nine reactors for plutonium production. It has now ceased the production of plutonium and highly enriched uranium (HEU) (plutonium in 1992; HEU in 1996) for military purposes, and it has started dismantling its fissile material production facilities (the Marcoule reprocessing plant and the Pierrelatte enrichment facility).[16] Paris also deactivated and dismantled the Plateau d'Albion missile site in southern France in 1997–1998. Last, but not least, President Chirac also decided to dismantle the South Pacific testing facilities in Mururoa and Fangataufa in 1996. Altogether, the French nuclear forces have been reduced by more than 40 percent since the end of the Cold War.[17]

Missile and Aircraft Analysis

At its peak from 1991 to 1992, France deployed an estimated total of 538 nuclear warheads. The arsenals included 80 ASMPs, which were supersonic wingless guided missiles. Of those missiles, 18 were equipped to the Mirage IVA/P, a low-altitude bomber; 42 missiles were attached to the Mirage 2000N sonic attack aircraft; and 20 armed the carrier-based naval strike aircraft, the Super Étendard. The remainder of France's arsenal included 384 warheads on M-45 submarine-based ballistic missiles; 18 land-based intermediate-range S-3 ballistic missiles; and 56 Plutons, which were mobile short-range surface ballistic missiles used by the army.[18]

France conducted its last nuclear test in 1996. That same year, President Chirac, having stopped fissile material production, decided to dismantle and discontinue various systems, such as the S-3D intermediate-range missile.[19]

Today, France operates four nuclear-powered ballistic missile submarines in two classes. The country owns three Triomphant submarines armed with the M-45 SLBM, and one L'Inflexible submarine, which also carries the M-45 SLBM. France has 48 SLBMs. It only arms 3 of its 4 nuclear ballistic missile submarines (SSBNs) at any given time. Each SSBN is capable of carrying 16 SLBMs. In January 2000, France's second Triomphant-class SSBN officially entered service, equipped with 16 M-45 SLBMs and carrying 6 TN-75–type nuclear warheads each. A third Triomphant-class submarine, *Le Vigilant*, entered into active duty in the fall of 2004 and carries M-45 SLBMs.[20] France has plans to build and deploy a fourth Triomphant submarine by 2010 and is currently testing a new missile, the M-51.[21]

The three-stage M-51 missile will replace the current French SLBM, the M-45, which first entered service in 1996. The M-51 will be deployed on all four of France's strategic nuclear submarines and will have a range of 6,000 kilometers. The system is scheduled to enter active service in 2008, with full flight tests scheduled to begin in 2005. The development of this system has sparked some criticism among non-nuclear-weapon states, some of which maintain that the development and deployment of a new nuclear weapon launcher is inconsistent with the commitment to nuclear disarmament made by the nuclear weapon states at the 2000 NPT Review Conference. Some countries view this deployment in the same light as the United States' interest in developing a new generation of nuclear weapons.[22]

As part of its airborne nuclear component, today France has 60 nuclear-capable aircraft in its air force, and 24 carrier-based nuclear-capable fighter-bombers in its navy. The Mirage 2000N and Super Étendard aircraft use ASMP air-to-surface nuclear missiles with a range of 250 to 300 kilometers and armed with warheads of the TN-81 type. France has in service 60 ASMP cruise missiles equipped with a TN-81 warhead, possibly with more inactive weapons stored on board. In early October 1999, France announced the continuation of its development program for the ASMP-A (Air-Sol Moyenne Portée-Amélioré) nuclear air-launched cruise missile program, which promises to double the range of the ASMP from 250 to 500 kilometers. The ASMP-A will also be armed with a new TNA (*tête nucléaire aéro-portée*) warhead, to be developed by simulation in France's Atomic Energy Commission laboratories. The ASMP-A is scheduled for use in 2007.[23] The ASMP-A will first be deployed on the Mirage 2000N, and later on the Rafale.[24]

Of the three squadrons of Mirage 2000N, two are stationed at Luxeuil and the other at Istres. The Mirage 2000N has some conventional capability in addition to its primary nuclear role. France also retains in service five Mirage IVPs, the Mirage 2000N's nuclear precursor, for reconnaissance missions while other retired Mirage IVPs are stored.[25] France has 50 missiles of the TN-81 type stockpiled for the Mirage 2000N and 10 TN-81 warheads stockpiled for the Super Étendard.

The Rafale (B-301) will replace the Mirage 2000N as the multirole fighter-bomber. The Rafale (B-301), armed with either the ASMP or the ASMP-A, is being designed for air defense and ground attacks. In 2001, the navy formed a squadron of Rafale M jets in Landivisiau. The air force expects to purchase 234 Rafales for operation in 2005. France has built three aircraft carriers: the *Clémenceau*, the *Foch*, and the *Charles de Gaulle*. After its commission in 1961, the *Clémenceau* was modified to carry the AN-52 nuclear gravity bomb and the Super Étendard fleet. The *Foch* began service in 1963 and was then altered to contain nuclear weapons, such as replacement ASMPs for the Super Étendard fighter jets. Both the *Clémenceau* and *Foch* have now been decommissioned. The carrier *Charles de Gaulle*, initially launched in 1994, entered active duty in October 2000. In June 2004, the first 10 Rafale bombers entered service aboard the *Charles de Gaulle* and do not yet carry the ASMP.[26] In 2006, France will deploy its first Rafale air force squadron. France's 2003–2008 defense budget projects the deployment of 234 Rafale aircraft for the armed services and 60 for the navy.[27] In February 2004, the French government decided to build a second aircraft carrier that will be conventionally powered rather than nuclear. The French plan to begin its construction by 2006 so that it will be operational by 2014.[28]

Previous Chemical Weapons Program

France does not have research or production programs for either chemical or biological weapons. It is a member of the Biological Weapons Convention and the Chemical Weapons Convention. It has declared to the Organization for the Prohibition of Chemical Weapons that it has a stockpile of old chemical weapons on its territory and has opened its facilities for inspection. It stockpiled mustard gas and phosgene before World War II and continued chemical weapons research and testing at B2-Namous in Algeria until the late 1960s. In 1988, President François Mitterrand announced before the United Nations that France had no chemical weapons and had no plans to produce chemical weapons.[29]

NOTES

1. In conversation with French government officials, December 22, 2004.
2. Hans M. Kristensen, "French Nuclear Forces, January 2003," Stockholm International Peace Research Institute Project on Nuclear Technology and Arms Control; available at http://projects.sipri.se/nuclear/france.pdf.
3. Robert Norris, Andrew Burrows, and Richard Fieldhouse, *British, French, and Chinese Nuclear Weapons, Vol. V* (Boulder, Colo.: Westview Press, 1994), pp. 183–184. On the origins of the French nuclear program, see Lawrence Scheinmann, *Atomic Energy in France under the Fourth Republic* (Princeton, N.J.: Princeton University Press, 1969); and Dominique Mongin, *La bombe atomique française, 1945–1958* (Louvain-la-Neuve, Belgium: Bruylant; and Paris: LGDJ, 1997).
4. Camille Grand, *A French Nuclear Exception*, Occasional Paper 38 (Washington, D.C.: Henry L. Stimson Center, 1998), pp. 12–14.
5. On French nuclear policy during the Cold War, see Marcel Duval and Yves Le Baut, *L'arme nucléaire française: Pourquoi et comment?* (Paris: Kronos/SPM, 1992).
6. Camille Grand, "France," in *Europe and Nuclear Disarmament: Debates and Political Attitudes in 16 European Countries*, edited by Harald Müller (Brussels: European Interuniversity Press, 1998), p. 39.
7. Grand, "France," p. 40.
8. Grand, "France," p. 35.
9. Grand, "France," p. 35.
10. Grand, "France," p. 38.
11. Transcript of President Jacques Chirac's speech before the Institute of Higher National Defence Studies in Paris, June 8, 2001.
12. Pierre Goldschmidt, "Proliferation and Non-Proliferation in Western Europe: A Historical Survey," in *A European Non-Proliferation Policy*, edited by Harald Müller (Oxford: Clarendon Press: 1987), p. 9.
13. Ibid., p. 12.
14. Ibid.
15. Ibid., p. 24.
16. Norris, Burrows, and Fieldhouse, *British, French and Chinese Nuclear Weapons*, p. 10; and Robert Norris and William Arkin, "Nuclear Notebook," *Bulletin of the Atomic Scientists*, June/July 2001, p. 70.
17. Norris and Arkin, "Nuclear Notebook," p. 70.
18. In Conversation with Hans M. Kristensen, consultant to the Natural Resources Defense Council, January 21, 2005.
19. Norris and Arkin, "Nuclear Notebook," p. 70.
20. In conversation with French government officials, December 17, 2004.

21. Ibid.
22. In conversation with the authors, 2005.
23. Norris and Arkin, "Nuclear Notebook," p. 71.
24. In conversation with French government officials.
25. Norris and Arkin, "Nuclear Notebook," p. 71.
26. In conversation with French government officials.
27. In conversation with French government officials.
28. Global Security, "Second Aircraft Carrier/ Deuxième Porte-Avions," March 20, 2004, available at www.globalsecurity.org/military/world/europe/dpa.htm.
29. Federation of Atomic Scientists web site on French chemical and biological weapons capability, available at www.fas.org/nuke/guide/france/cbw/index.html.

Table 8.1. **French Nuclear Forces, 2005**

	Submarine Type / Designation	**Launcher capacity / nuclear ballistic missile submarine (SSBN)**	**First Deployed**	**Range (kilometers)**	**Warheads × Yield (kilotons, kT)**	**Deployable Warheads**
Submarine-launched ballistic missiles (SLBMs)	Triomphant-class SSBN / M-45	48/3	1996	6,000	6 × 100 kT	192
	L'Inflexible-class SSBN / M-45	16/1	1991	5,000	6 × 150 kT	96
Subtotal, ballistic missiles	48/3[1]					288
	Launcher Type / Designation	**Launchers/ SSBNs**	**First Deployed**	**Range (kilometers)**	**Warheads × yield (kT)**	**Deployable Warheads**
Aircraft	Super Étendard / ASMP	24	1978	650	1 × 300 kT ASMP	10
	Mirage 2000N / ASMP	60	1988	2,750	1 × 300 kT ASMP	50
	Rafale / ASMP	10	2004	3,125	1 × 300 kT ASMP	0
Subtotal, aircraft		94				60
Total strategic nuclear forces		158				348

1. France has 48 submarine-launched ballistic missiles. It only arms 3 of its 4 SSBNs at a given time. Each SSBN is capable of carrying 16 SLBMs.

CHAPTER 9

The United Kingdom

Nuclear Weapons Capability

The United Kingdom is recognized under the Non-Proliferation Treaty as a nuclear weapon state. It currently maintains four nuclear-powered ballistic missile submarines, each armed with up to 16 Trident II missiles and with 48 warheads (see table 9.1 at the end of the chapter). Between 1952 and 1992, the country produced approximately 834 nuclear warheads.[1] It has conducted 44 nuclear weapons tests, the first on October 3, 1952, and the last on November 26, 1991. It has signed and ratified the Comprehensive Test Ban Treaty.

Aircraft and Missile Capability

The 1998 Strategic Defense Review (SDR) confirmed that the United Kingdom's new nuclear force structure would consist solely of the four Vanguard-class nuclear-powered ballistic missile submarines, only one of which is to be on active patrol duty at any one time. This discussion also confirmed the elimination of the country's tactical nuclear arsenal. Each Vanguard nuclear ballistic missile submarine (SSBN) can carry 16 Trident II D-5 submarine-launched ballistic missiles (SLBMs). The first submarine, the *HMS Vanguard*, went on patrol in December 1994. Each Trident II SLBM can carry up to 8 multiple independent reentry vehicles, for a maximum of 128 warheads. The actual force loadings, however, are lower than this because of the SDR, which stipulated that all Trident submarines should carry 48 warheads per boat when on deterrent patrol. The SDR stated that the future stockpile would be less than 200 operationally available warheads.[2]

Before the SDR revisions, the Royal Air Force operated eight squadrons of nuclear-capable Tornado GR1/1A bombers armed with WE-177 nuclear gravity bombs. By 1998, all the WE-177 bombs had been withdrawn from service. The aircraft concerned had been reassigned to other duties and, where appropriate, relocated.

Biological and Chemical Weapons Capability

The United Kingdom is a member of the Biological Weapons Convention and the Chemical Weapons Convention. The country has declared to the Organization for the Prohibition of Chemical Weapons that it has old chemical weapons on its territory and has opened its facilities for inspection. According to the British Ministry of Defence, the Joint Nuclear, Biological, and Chemical Regiment provides "a defence capability" for the air force, navy, and army. Its equipment includes biological and chemical monitoring devices, such as the man-portable chemical agent detector and the Integrated Biological Detection System; individual protection equipment; communication and information systems for tracking hazardous material movement and duration; medical research on countermeasures for biological or chemical exposure; and an expanded threat analysis program.[3]

The Strategic Context

During the Cold War, the United Kingdom and NATO planned for the worst—a European nuclear war with the Soviet Union and its allies. The close geographical position of the United Kingdom to the Soviet threat created a need for nuclear defense and deterrence. The United Kingdom joined NATO in combating the Soviet threat by contributing its land, air, and sea nuclear forces to the Alliance. The United Kingdom manufactured and owned the warheads for its strategic nuclear delivery systems, but other warheads were supplied by the United States under standard NATO nuclear-sharing arrangements.[4]

By 1998, the change in the size and composition of the United Kingdom's nuclear forces had significantly affected its means of implementing deterrence policies from the Cold War era. Its disarmament decision was reached unilaterally, motivated by such issues as the opportunity to reduce the cost of arsenal maintenance and the lack of an imminent Russian threat. The arsenal was reduced to a single type of warhead and a submarine delivery system. Developing a successor to the Polaris SSBN became an issue for debate during the Cold War. The British argued over the most cost-effective nuclear defense replacement system for the family of submarines and whether a replacement was necessary. Post–Cold War policies have left NATO as the ultimate defense for the United Kingdom, except for one patrolling nuclear submarine off the British coastline.[5]

Nuclear Analysis

The British were an integral part of helping the United States to develop the bomb. In 1941, the Maud Committee, a group of British scientists dedicated to fission research, estimated that the development of the bomb would take two and a half years. This scientific process slowed during World War II, but following the end of the war in 1946, work was started on plants to produce fissile material.

The United Kingdom wanted a nuclear force as leverage against the Soviets should they obtain weapons. The British also sought nuclear weapons as a way to achieve greater power after slipping in status as a world leader. The United States clearly showed no interest in sharing atomic knowledge with other countries under its Atomic Energy Act of 1946, which was another reason that the United Kingdom believed that it needed to construct its own nuclear arms. The

United States and the United Kingdom have developed a close relationship and share extensive nuclear information under their Mutual Defense Agreement. In 1952, the United Kingdom conducted its first nuclear test, called Hurricane, at the Monto Bello Islands off the Australian coast.

The "Blue Danube" was the first nuclear weapon that Britain produced. Initial models were transferred to the Royal Air Force in November 1953, using plutonium as the fissile material. The smaller and lighter "Red Beard" weapon entered into service in 1958. At the same time, the megaton fission bomb Violet Club was produced, followed by its successor, Yellow Sun Mk I. Yellow Sun Mk II was the first British thermonuclear operational gravity bomb with a yield in the megaton range. This came into service in 1962, at the same time as the thermonuclear Blue Steel air-launched cruise missiles. Both used an Anglicized version of the U.S. MK-28 warhead and remained in the stockpiles until 1970. The WE-177, the most recent family of British nuclear-gravity aircraft bombs, entered service with the Royal Air Force strategic bomber force in 1966 and was later deployed on Royal Navy and Air Force attack aircraft and helicopters. The WE-177 was decommissioned between 1992 and 1998.[6]

From the early 1960s to the mid-1990s, the U.K. nuclear stockpile of British-produced warheads was estimated to have been between 250 and 350 warheads. The British stockpile was supplemented by U.S. weapons, which were available under NATO nuclear-sharing arrangements from 1958 to 1991. Three hundred to 400 of these warheads were made available to the United Kingdom in the 1960s and 1970s, and 200 to 300 warheads in the 1980s. Lance warheads, artillery shells, and depth bombs for land-based maritime patrol aircraft were returned to the United States for dismantlement in 1991.[7]

British nuclear warheads are designed at the Aldermaston facility in Berkshire. Warheads are assembled and disassembled at Burghfield, as are weapon components. The other production facility, at Cardiff, was closed in February 1997. Disassembly of Chevaline warheads took place at the Burghfield facility and was completed in April 2002.[8]

Missile Analysis

Beginning in 1960, the United Kingdom operated a nuclear-capable land force of Lance missiles and 155-millimeter howitzers based in Germany with borrowed warheads and delivery devices from the United States under NATO nuclear-sharing arrangements. The Royal Air Force also had access to U.S. depth bombs for its long-range Nimrod aircraft. Bombers such as the Buccaneer, Jaguar, and Tornado were capable of delivering WE-177 bombs. The Royal Navy operated Sea Harriers and antisubmarine helicopters capable of carrying WE-177s.[9]

In 1968, the British deployed the first four Polaris (or Resolution-class) submarines carrying 16 A3T SLBMs supplied by the United States. The Polaris A3T missile carried a delivery system that incorporated three warheads, each believed to have a yield of 200 kilotons. The Polaris A3TK or Chevaline missile replaced the A3T in 1982 and was designed to penetrate the Soviet antiballistic missile system around Moscow. The fleet of Polaris SSBNs was phased out by the end of 1996, and it was replaced by the Vanguard SSBNs.[10]

The United Kingdom currently deploys the Trident II D-5 inertially guided SLBM, which has a greater payload capability, range, and accuracy than its precursor, the Polaris SLBM. The three-stage, solid-propellant missile has a range of more than 7,400 kilometers at full payload. The warhead carried by the Trident II D-5 reentry vehicle is believed to have a yield of 100 kilotons.[11]

By October 1991, the United Kingdom's forces were losing diversity: warheads for Lance missiles, Nimrod bombers, and nuclear artillery were transferred from Europe to the United States when NATO's nuclear forces were drastically reduced after the fall of the Soviet Union. In June 1992, the United Kingdom announced the removal of all WE-177 bombs from navy surface ships. The remaining WE-177s were planned for replacement in about 2005 with tactical air-to-surface cruise missiles, but in 1993 the British dropped the idea. In 1998, the Trident missiles aboard the Vanguard SSBNs took over the substrategic role of the WE-177 bombs.[12]

NOTES

1. Robert Norris, Andrew Burrows, and Richard Fieldhouse, *British, French, and Chinese Nuclear Weapons, Vol. V* (Boulder, Colo.: Westview Press, 1994), pp. 63.
2. Robert Norris and William Arkin, "British Nuclear Forces, 2001," *Bulletin of the Atomic Scientists*, November/December 2001, pp. 78–79.
3. Ministry of Defence, United Kingdom, available at www.mod.uk/index.php3?page=1920.
4. Darryl Howlett and John Simpson, "The United Kingdom," in *Europe and Nuclear Disarmament: Debates and Political Attitudes in 16 European Countries*, edited by Harald Müller (Brussels: European Interuniversity Press, 1998), p. 59.
5 Howlett and Simpson, *Europe and Nuclear Disarmament*, p. 60.
6. Norris, Burrows, and Fieldhouse, *British, French, and Chinese Nuclear Weapons*, pp. 54–60.
7. Ibid., pp. 63–66.
8. British Foreign and Commonwealth Office, "U.K. Actions Towards Verifiable Global Nuclear Disarmament," available at www.fco.gov.uk/servlet/Front?pagename=OpenMarket/Xcelerate/ShowPage&c=Page&cid=1087554459698.
9. Howlett and Simpson, "United Kingdom," p. 59.
10. Norris, Burrows, and Fieldhouse, *British, French, and Chinese Nuclear Weapons*, pp. 100–115.
11. Ibid., pp. 168–169.
12. Howlett and Simpson, "United Kingdom," pp. 60–61.

Table 9.1. **British Nuclear Forces, 2005**

Launcher Type / Designation		Launchers/ SSBNs	First Deployed	Warheads × Yield	Range	Deployable Warheads
SLBMs	Vanguard-class SSBN / Trident D-5 II	58/4	1994	1–3 × 100 kilotons	7,400 kilometers	200
Total				60.0 megatons		200

ABBREVIATIONS

SSBN = nuclear ballistic missile submarine; SLBM = submarine-launched ballistic missile

CHAPTER 10

The United States

Nuclear Weapons Capability

The United States was the first country to develop and test a nuclear weapon and is a recognized nuclear weapon state under the Non-Proliferation Treaty. The United States continues to maintain the world's largest force of deployed strategic nuclear weapons, although the arsenal is gradually being reduced in accordance with several arms control agreements with Russia (see table 10.1 at the end of the chapter).[1] Under the accounting rules of the Strategic Arms Reduction Treaty (START I), the United States maintains an accountable strategic nuclear force of 1,225 delivery vehicles with 5,966 associated warheads,[2] although the actual number of deployed strategic weapons is less. As of January 2005, the best independent estimate details 961 deployed delivery vehicles with 4,216 associated warheads.[3] The United States also has 780 operational nonstrategic warheads and approximately 5,000 additional intact warheads retained in reserve or inactive stockpiles, for a total of approximately 10,300 nuclear weapons. The United States plans to reduce this number by about 50 percent by 2012. The first U.S. nuclear test was conducted on July 16, 1945, after which the United States became the only country to use nuclear weapons in combat, on August 6 and 9, 1945. The last of its 1,030 nuclear weapons tests took place on September 23, 1992. The United States has signed but not ratified the Comprehensive Test Ban Treaty.

Aircraft and Missile Capability

The United States maintains a triad of nuclear forces on board land- and submarine-based missiles and a fleet of nuclear-capable long-range bomber aircraft. The United States deploys 10 MX/Peacekeeper intercontinental ballistic missiles (ICBMs) armed with ten warheads each and 500 Minuteman III ICBMs (50 armed with three warheads, 300 armed with two to three warheads, and 150 armed with one warhead each). The MX/Peacekeeper missiles are in the process of being retired, and will be completely phased out of service by October 2005. The missiles and their silos will be retained and most likely their warheads will be held in the reserve force.

In addition, Washington maintains 14 nuclear armed ballistic missile submarines. Two Ohio-class submarines are each equipped with 24 C-4 Trident I missiles, each of which is loaded with six warheads. Twelve additional Ohio-class submarines are armed with 24 D-5 Trident II missiles each, carrying six warheads per missile. Four older submarines, which formerly carried 24 C-4 Trident I missiles each are being converted to non-nuclear operations although their former 96 total missiles, with 576 associated nuclear warheads, are still accountable under START I rules.

The U.S. nuclear bomber force consists of 115 planes of two different types, the B-52 and the B-2. The 94 B-52s in the U.S. nuclear arsenal are equipped to carry nuclear air-launched cruise missiles and gravity bombs. The 21 B-2s only carry gravity bombs.[4] The 81 B-1 bombers currently in service have been converted to conventional roles, but are still accountable under START I. The United States also maintains nuclear-equipped tactical aircraft.[5]

Biological and Chemical Capability

The United States does not have research or production programs for either chemical or biological offensive weapons. It ratified the Biological Weapons Convention in 1974 and the Chemical Weapons Convention in 1997. The United States has a vast stockpile of chemical weapons that are slated for destruction on its territory and has opened its related facilities for inspection. It unilaterally destroyed its formidable arsenal of biological weapons over several years, beginning in 1969.

The Strategic Context

The United States is the most advanced nuclear weapon state in the world. It maintains a diverse arsenal of strategic and tactical nuclear weapons, as well as large stocks of weapons-grade nuclear materials. After peaking in the mid-1980s, the U.S. nuclear arsenal has been shrinking as part of a negotiated arms reduction process with the Soviet Union and its successor, Russia. Dedicated to nuclear deterrence during most of its existence, the mission for U.S. nuclear weapons has become less clear with the demise of the Soviet Union and the emergence of the United States as the global superpower. The stated goal and developing mission of U.S. nuclear forces continues to evolve. This evolution was highlighted in the Nuclear Posture Review (NPR) that was released by the Department of Defense on January 9, 2002.[6]

At the broadest level, the review stated that nuclear weapons continue to "play a critical role in the defense capabilities of the United States, its allies and friends. They provide credible military options to deter a wide range of threats, including WMD and large-scale conventional military force." Thus, a decade after the collapse of the main nuclear challenger to the United States, U.S. nuclear weapons remained central to U.S. defense efforts.

The review, which was mandated by Congress, outlined plans to implement negotiated reductions in strategic forces, to retain and improve the ability to increase these forces if necessary, to accelerate efforts to develop antimissile systems (see chapter 5), and to begin the development of new, low-yield nuclear weapons. Though the NPR's commitment to deep cuts in the nuclear arsenal was significant, it was basically a slower and less verifiable version of earlier U.S. plans, developed in the 1990s in START II and discussions for START III.

Under the Strategic Offensive Reductions Treaty (SORT) (the replacement for the STARTs, which U.S. president George W. Bush and Russian president Vladimir Putin signed in June 2002), the United States will field 1,700–2,200 operationally deployed strategic warheads by 2012. This agreement would leave both Russia and the United States with more weapons in the field than was envisioned in the arms reduction process pursued throughout the 1990s. In 1997, the United States and Russia agreed on a reduction goal of 2,000 to 2,500 deployed strategic warheads by the end of 2007 (see "The Effect of Arms Control," below). The lower number agreed to in SORT is derived by no longer counting the warheads on submarines or bombers in overhaul as being "operationally deployed." Two Trident submarines, with 192 warheads each, are usually in overhaul at any given time, as are several bombers capable of carrying dozens of weapons, thus accounting for lower numbers without changing existing nuclear force plans.

Under SORT, some warheads removed from delivery vehicles will be dismantled, but the removed systems could also be maintained in the active stockpile for potential return to delivery systems on short notice (weeks or months). This is a "responsive reserve" of warheads that can be redeployed should strategic conditions change for the worse. This position contradicts one advanced by the United States in the late 1990s, when the Bill Clinton administration, in the proposed START III, sought to require warhead dismantlement to make future reductions both transparent and irreversible. With the signing of SORT, the irreversibility of nuclear cuts is no longer a U.S. goal. According to U.S. officials, this approach provides the United States with the greatest amount of flexibility to reconfigure its nuclear forces in response to changes in the world, although it remains unclear exactly what projected developments might trigger the need for such flexibility.

In June 2004, the director of the National Nuclear Security Administration, (NNSA), Linton Brooks, announced that the United States would cut the stockpile of nuclear weapons "about in half" by 2012. The official plan is classified, but experts estimate that the current total arsenal of more than 10,000 warheads will be reduced to just under 6,000 warheads.[7] This plan reflects preexisting commitments to the retirements of certain components of most "reserve" and "inactive" warheads, many of which are already under way.

U.S. officials have noted that since the end of the Cold War, the United States has reduced its strategic nuclear systems by more than 50 percent, nonstrategic systems by more than 80 percent, and spending on strategic forces by almost 70 percent.[8] During the past ten years, the United States has:

- curtailed bomber and ICBM production;
- removed all sea-launched nuclear cruise missiles, bombs, and tactical nuclear weapons from ships and submarines;
- taken all bombers off day-to-day alert;

- eliminated the Minuteman II ICBM force;
- eliminated all nuclear short-range attack missiles from the bomber force;
- eliminated all ground-launched intermediate- and short-range nuclear weapons;
- canceled almost all new warhead research and development;
- halted underground nuclear testing;
- closed major portions of the nuclear weapons production complex; and
- converted the entire B-1 bomber force from nuclear to conventional missions.

Despite these development, the United States will retain for the foreseeable future robust, diverse, and highly capable nuclear forces. Sixty years after the invention of nuclear weapons, the role of these systems in U.S. defense policy is still hotly debated.

Some experts and former officials maintain that the new security environment—even one dominated by the war on terrorism—provides the United States and the other nuclear weapons states an opportunity to reduce their nuclear weapons and that doing so would diminish the perceived political and military utility of these weapons. Such a posture would reduce the risk that intact nuclear weapons could be acquired by terrorist groups or used without authorization and through miscalculation.[9] Reducing U.S. reliance on nuclear weapons for defense and security would also improve prospects for keeping new nations from developing or acquiring nuclear weapons. Former senator Sam Nunn argues that with the current nuclear policies, "the United States and Russia, whether they intend the message or not, are telling the world that conventional weapons are not enough to ensure security. Nuclear weapons—not only nuclear weapons but nuclear weapons ready for rapid launch—are essential."[10]

In the 2002 NPR, the George W. Bush administration concluded that there will be a need to maintain thousands of deployed nuclear weapons in a triad of bombers, submarines, and land-based missiles for the indefinite future. The diversity is required to "complicate any adversary's offensive and defense planning calculations while simultaneously providing protection against the failure of a single leg of the triad," according to the former commander-in-chief of the Strategic Command, Admiral Richard Mies. That is, U.S. forces must remain capable of withstanding a first strike and responding after the attack with an overwhelming and devastating nuclear counterattack. Mies explained the importance of each triad component:

> Intercontinental ballistic missiles continue to provide a reliable, low-cost, prompt response capability with a high readiness rate. They also promote stability by ensuring that a potential adversary takes their geographically dispersed capabilities into account if contemplating a disarming first strike. . . .
>
> The strategic submarine force is the most survivable leg of the triad, providing the United States with a powerful, assured response capability against

> any adversary. . . . The United States must preserve a sufficiently large strategic nuclear submarine force to enable two-ocean operations with sufficient assets to ensure an at-sea response force capable of deterring any adversary in a crisis. . . .
>
> Strategic bombers . . . allow force dispersal to improve survivability and aircraft recall during mission execution. The low-observable technology of the B-2 bomber enables it to penetrate heavily defended areas and hold high-value targets at risk deep inside an adversary's territory. . . . The B-52 bomber can be employed in a standoff role using long-range cruise missile to attack from outside enemy air defenses.[11]

The review also called for steps that make the use of nuclear weapons by the United States more likely, even in response to non-nuclear threats or attacks. The review stated that the United States would rely on nuclear weapons to deter and respond to threats from weapons of mass destruction, defined in the review to include not only nuclear weapons, but chemical and biological weapons and even conventional explosives. While the right to respond to chemical and biological weapons threats has been stated U.S. policy since the early 1990s, the NPR formulation was more explicit and also called for the development of new weapons to make the threat of such use more credible. Within the new nuclear use policy formulation, there are few if any military contingencies that would explicitly rule out a possible nuclear response by the United States.

Another important development in the NPR is the closer integration of conventional and nuclear force planning. The Pentagon states that by more closely linking intelligence, communication, and force operational planning for nuclear and conventional operations, conventional forces can more easily replace operations previously limited to nuclear options, making the use of nuclear weapons less likely. General James E. Cartwright, commander of the U.S. Strategic Command, testified on April 4, 2005, that "the Secretary of Defense recently assigned USSTRATCOM [the U.S. Strategic Command] responsibility for integrating and synchronizing DoD's [the Department of Defense's] efforts for combating weapons of mass destruction."[12] He continued, saying that the United States "will look at rationalizing our nuclear forces as an element of the overall force structure and the proper tailoring of nuclear effects as part of the broad spectrum of power. . . . For example, I intend to conduct experiments to better understand the value of weapons accuracy within a range of stressing environments. If modeling and testing confirm the value of such capability, this may lead to new thoughts on the balance between nuclear and conventional strike capabilities." This statement appears to suggest that nuclear and conventional weapons are increasingly seen as interchangeable, meaning that some current nuclear missions might be assigned to conventional weapons—but also opening up the alternative whereby nuclear weapons might be seen as credible replacements for conventional weapons.

These policies discussed in the NPR and implemented since raised two concerns. First, low-yield and "bunker buster" weapons, combined with greater operational integration, would contribute to lowering the nuclear threshold, making the use of nuclear weapons more acceptable. Second, by threatening the use of nuclear weapons, even against conventionally armed adversaries, Washington is actually increasing the incentive for states to acquire nuclear weapons, if for no other reason than to deter the use of such weapons by the United States.

Congress reacted to these concerns by cutting funds for the programs in 2004. The Bush administration began preliminary work on new weapons designs at the time of the NPR. In 2003, Congress had modified the Spratt-Furse amendment of 1993 (which had prohibited the development of any new, low-yield nuclear weapon) and funded a research program for low-yield nuclear weapons, known as the Advanced Nuclear Weapons Concepts Initiative, and a second program to modify existing warheads to create a Robust Nuclear Earth Penetrator. Congress denied funding for these programs in the fiscal year 2005 defense appropriations, while also reducing funding for a new facility to produce plutonium "pits" or cores for nuclear weapons, and for a program to prepare for the rapid resumption of nuclear weapons tests if needed.

In April 2005, the Bush administration appeared to take a different approach to restarting the development of nuclear weapons in the United States. NNSA administrator Linton Brooks testified that the United States needs to resume researching and possibly developing new nuclear warheads to maintain the country's scientific and engineering base and to preserve the safety and reliability of its nuclear arsenal. The safety and reliability of the nuclear arsenal is already the focal point of the Science Based Stockpile Stewardship program, which is funded at just over $6 billion each year. Brooks noted, however, that "there is another reason why it is critical that we begin now to transform the stockpile. . . . We are losing expertise. We must train the next generation of nuclear weapon designers and engineers before the last generation, which honed its skills on nuclear testing, retires." He continued that the United States should "begin concept and feasibility studies on replacement warheads and warhead components that provide the same or comparable military capabilities to existing warheads on the stockpile."[13] Congress again eliminated funds for the "bunker buster" in 2005, but supported a study on a replacement warhead.

Nuclear Analysis

The U.S. nuclear arsenal has developed greatly since its inception in 1945. Different strategies have guided the formation of nuclear forces and their possible use as international circumstances and technologies have continued to evolve. This evolution has continued with the collapse of the Eastern bloc and the dissolution of the Soviet Union, America's Cold War nuclear adversary.

From its small-scale beginnings during the Manhattan Project in World War II, the United States constructed a massive nuclear weapons production complex. This system of national laboratories, nuclear material production, and weapon assembly sites also included a large and advanced complex for the production of ballistic missiles, nuclear submarines, and long-range strategic bombers. The cost of producing and maintaining this arsenal since 1940 has been estimated at almost $6 trillion.[14]

The U.S. strategic arsenal consists of just under 6,000 accountable nuclear weapons under the terms of START I. The actual deployed, operational strategic nuclear arsenal is just over 4,200 nuclear weapons. In addition to its deployed, strategic nuclear arsenal, the United States maintains a smaller number (approximately 780) of tactical nuclear weapons, including perhaps 480 deployed in Europe.[15] The United States also maintains a large reserve of nuclear weapons in storage and inactive reserve. While no official numbers have been released on the size of the total U.S. arsenal, reliable estimates put the stockpile at more than 10,300 weapons.[16]

To produce nuclear weapons, a country or group must possess special nuclear-weapons-usable materials. During the Cold War, the United States produced an extensive stockpile of weapons-grade uranium and plutonium, a stockpile surpassed only by that of the Soviet Union. The United States ceased its production of highly enriched uranium for weapons in 1964 and ended plutonium production for weapons in 1988.

A report released by the Department of Energy in 1996 documented the past U.S. production of plutonium. The report revealed that by 1988 the United States had produced or acquired from other sources 111.4 metric tons of plutonium. Of this amount, 3.4 metric tons had been used in nuclear weapons tests and in the nuclear weapons used at the end of World War II. Additional amounts were consumed as waste products, through radioactive decay, fission, and transmutation; through inventory differences; supplied to foreign countries; or were transferred to the U.S. civilian industry.[17] The United States has declared 50 metric tons of plutonium as excess to defense needs and has programs under way, in conjunction with similar efforts in Russia, to dispose of the material. Russia and the United States agreed in 2000 to pursue joint programs to dispose of 34 tons of high-purity plutonium each.

No official inventory is available on the total stockpile of highly enriched uranium (HEU) produced by the United States. In 1994, the Department of Energy released an estimate that the nuclear complex had produced 994 metric tons of HEU. It is not clear from this information how much material might have been consumed in nuclear tests or nuclear reactors. In addition, the United States has declared 174 metric tons of HEU to be in excess to defense needs. The material will be diluted and used as fuel for light-water reactors or disposed of as waste.

The Effect of Arms Control

The United States and Russia reached an important arms control milestone on December 5, 2001, when both sides completed reductions in their strategic nuclear arsenals. Each side reduced its arsenal to 6,000 accountable warheads as required by START I. These are substantial reductions from the nuclear arsenals that both countries deployed when the agreement was signed on July 31, 1991; they demonstrate the value of negotiated, verified arms reduction agreements in U.S. security policy.

Through an extensive set of verification and data exchange procedures, as well as the assistance that the United States has provided Russia in implementing cuts to its arsenal, the United States is confident that Russia has achieved START I reductions. Russia, too, is able to verify adequately that the United States has made reductions to the 6,000 warhead level, to treaty sublimits on strategic nuclear-delivery vehicles (missiles and bombers), and to a limit on the number of accountable warheads on ballistic missiles (land- and submarine-launched). START I does not provide a totally accurate picture of the numbers of nuclear weapons deployed by each side, however, since it attributes weapons to some systems that may not reflect actual loadings. The treaty also does not address substrategic (or tactical) nuclear weapons or nondeployed weapons in storage.

START II, which was signed by President George H. W. Bush and Russian president Boris Yeltsin in January 1993, was ratified by both nations but has never entered into force. The Russian Duma ratified the treaty with the qualification that the United States honor the 1972 Anti–Ballistic Missile (ABM) Treaty. When the U.S. pulled out of the ABM Treaty in 2002, START II effectively ceased to exist. That treaty required reductions to 3,000–3,500 strategic warheads for each nation and eliminated the most destabilizing strategic nuclear systems: multiple-warhead ICBMs. Both countries now plan to retain multiple warhead missiles after the demise of START II.

At a March 1997 meeting in Helsinki, Presidents Clinton and Yeltsin agreed in general to reduce to 2,000–2,500 deployed strategic warheads in a future START III, to talks on tactical nuclear weapons, and to increased transparency and irreversibility in the reduction process. The Joint Chiefs of Staff in the United States endorsed those reductions and began planning for a smaller force, including the elimination of the ten-warhead MX missile force. The Department of Defense also planned to implement the START II reductions by the end of 2007 and to deactivate by the end of 2003 all strategic nuclear-delivery vehicles planned for elimination, "providing the benefits of a reduced force structure four years prior to the agreed 2007 date for full elimination."[18]

Clinton administration plans for START III were abandoned by the Bush administration in 2002 when Presidents Bush and Putin made unilateral statements that each country would reduce their deployed strategic nuclear arsenals to between 1,700 and 2,200 weapons. These statements were followed, after several months of hesitation by administration officials, by the negotiation, signing, and ratification of SORT, culminating in May 2003 with the Duma's ratification, and its entry into force the following month.

SORT represents a significant departure from previous U.S.-Russian arms reduction treaties on two counts. First, it is not fully verifiable. There is no mechanism written into the treaty that permits each side to confirm the required reductions made by the other side, although the two sides will continue to use the verification terms of START I until it expires in December 2009. Second, the SORT agreement does not require the irreversible elimination of the delivery systems or of the warheads themselves. Instead, it simply calls for no more than 2,200 strategic warheads to be deployed by December 31, 2012, at which point the treaty expires. Thus, if the treaty is not extended prior to that date, each side could choose to redeploy however many warheads it desired beginning January 1, 2013, creating instability in the strategic relationship between the two countries.

The Bush administration intends for SORT to be the last arms reduction treaty. Despite the impressive record of threat reduction achieved by these agreements, they are seen by the current administration as relics of the Cold War. The various agreements signed over the past three decades first regulated the arms race and then allowed Russia and the United States to make substantial progress in reducing arms from their Cold War peaks. (The Russian reductions are detailed in chapter 6.) In 1990, the United States had 10,563 START-accountable nuclear weapons on 2,246 missiles and bombers. As of January 2005, the United States had 5,966 START-accountable weapons on 1,225 launchers.[19] These numbers do not reflect the full extent of U.S. nuclear reductions, however. Although no official numbers have ever been provided, reliable estimates from nongovernmental organizations suggest that the United States had 7,657 tactical nuclear warheads in 1990, for a total stockpile of 21,000 warheads.[20] By 2005, the number of tactical weapons had dropped to an estimated 780 nuclear sea-launched cruise missiles and air-dropped bombs, with the number of deployed and stockpiled strategic and tactical weapons totaling about 10,300.[21]

Former Biological Weapons Programs

The U.S. biological warfare program was established during World War II under the direction of the War Reserve Service and the Army Chemical Warfare Service. The fledgling program was limited to research and development facilities at Camp Detrick, Maryland, testing facilities in Mississippi and Utah, and a production site in Terre Haute, Indiana. After 1945, research focused on the evaluation of such agents as anthrax, botulinum toxin, brucellosis, psittacosis, and tularemia. The Korean War (1950–1953) prompted an expansion of the program. Large-scale production began in 1954 with the advancement of fermentation, concentration, storage, and weaponization technologies. A biological weapons defense program was established in 1953 and included the development of vaccines and anti-sera to protect troops from biological attack.

Throughout the 1950s, other agents were added to the biological weapons research list: cholera, dengue fever, human glanders, plague, Q fever, shigellosis (dysentery), and Venezuelan equine encephalitis.[22] Efforts were made to develop more virulent and stable strains, agents that were easier and cheaper to produce and weaponize. The testing of agents involved both human and animal subjects. Large-scale open-air tests with live agents were performed on Johnston Atoll in the central Pacific Ocean from 1963 to 1969. American cities—Minneapolis, New York City, Saint Louis, San Francisco, and others—were also subjected to the clandestine testing of dispersal and aerosolization methods involving harmless bacterium.[23] Biological weapons facilities were expanded at Camp Detrick (renamed Fort Detrick in 1956), and in 1954 the army's main center for the production and stockpiling of biological weapons agents and munitions was opened in Pine Bluff, Arkansas.

By 1958 weaponization research yielded "the first missile to carry a BW warhead—the 762-mm Honest John rocket. With a 25-kilometer range, the warhead could deliver 356 4.5-inch (11.5-centimeter) spherical bomblets. By the early 1960s, the first long-range U.S. missile, the Sergeant, extended the warhead's reach to 120 kilometers and the payload up to 720 spherical bomblets."[24]

The U.S. biological weapons program also involved the development of antiplant and antianimal agricultural warfare agents. Bacterial pathogens, toxins, and fungal plant pathogens were developed, as well as herbicides to destroy food crops or defoliate trees, thereby depriving enemy forces of ground cover.

By 1969, the annual budget for chemical and biological warfare research was reported to be $300 million, with $5 million set aside for agricultural-agent development.[25] In November 1969, President Richard Nixon unilaterally and unconditionally renounced offensive biological weapons and ordered the destruction of all U.S. weapons stockpiles and the conversion of all production facilities to peaceful purposes. Biological research was reoriented to the development of defense measures such as vaccines and countermeasures against biological weapon attack. The destruction of the U.S. biological weapons arsenal took place between May 1971 and February 1973 at the Pine Bluff Arsenal, Rocky Mountain Arsenal, and Fort Detrick. The entire anticrop stockpile was also destroyed. The United States signed the Biological Weapons Convention in 1972.

The U.S. Army Medical Research Institute of Infectious Diseases was established in 1969 to continue research on medical defense against biological weapons. The institute's research includes the development of countermeasures, defense strategies, vaccines, and medical therapies. All the research is unclassified. After the September 11, 2001, terrorist attacks, the U.S. administration dramatically increased biodefense funding, and started construction on new defense laboratories capable of handling the most dangerous pathogens. Opponents worry that these new laboratories will unintentionally worsen the threat, both by becoming potential terrorist targets and by undermining attempts to limit or control other countries' research into biological agents.[26]

China, North Korea, and the Soviet Union accused the United States of using biological weapons during the Korean War against China and North Korea. The United States denied the allegations and asked for an impartial investigation. China and North Korea, however, rejected World Health Organization and International Red Cross efforts to intervene to mount an investigation. The allegations remain unsubstantiated.

Former Chemical Weapons Programs

The U.S. chemical warfare program was initiated with the establishment of the Chemical Warfare Service (CWS) in 1918. Early agent production focused on chlorine, chloropicrin, mustard gas, and phosgene. Throughout the 1920s and 1930s, the CWS stockpiled chemical shells, mortars, and portable cylinders. The service also began the production and weaponization of the chemical agents tabun and sarin. In 1925, the United States signed the Geneva Protocol, which banned the use of chemical and biological warfare. The U.S. Senate, however, did not ratify the protocol until 1974.

The CWS expanded rapidly during World War II, as the United States deployed more than 400 chemical battalions and companies.[27] Production and storage facilities were also expanded in more than ten states. Between 1940 and 1945, the United States manufactured more than 146,000 metric tons of chemical agents, including cyanogen chloride, hydrogen cyanide, lewisite, and mustard gas.[28] Despite the growth of the U.S. chemical warfare program, President Franklin D. Roosevelt announced a no-first-use policy for chemical weapons. An official statement issued in 1943 declared, "We shall under no circumstances resort to the use of such [chemical] weapons unless they are first used by our enemies."[29]

With the onset of the Korean War the use of chemical weapons was seriously considered, particularly as a means to offset the enemy's superior numbers. Ultimately, the United States did not change its no-first-use policy, although riot control agents were used on prisoners of war. The development, production, and stockpiling of chemical agents continued. During the 1950s, the U.S. chemical warfare program concentrated on the weaponization of sarin. For air delivery, the 1,000-pound M-34 and M-34A1 cluster bombs were developed. Each cluster contained 76 M-125 or M-125A1 ten-pound bombs, each holding 2.6 pounds of sarin.[30] In addition, the Chemical Corps (the CWS was renamed in 1946) began the research and development of the V nerve agent (VX). The VX program reached its height in the 1960s with the weaponization of artillery, rockets, and other delivery systems.

In 1969, Public Law 19-121 imposed restrictions on the testing, transport, storage, and disposal of chemical warfare agents. Combined with President Nixon's reaffirmation of the no-first-use policy for chemical weapons and the resubmission of the Geneva Protocol for Senate ratification, the U.S. chemical weapons program was substantially slowed, though efforts to produce new "binary" weapons continued through the 1980s.

The U.S. arsenal currently consists of unitary lethal chemical munitions that contain blister agents and nerve agents. More than half of the stockpile is in bulk storage containers and the remainder is stored in obsolete munitions.[31] The arsenal is now stored at eight U.S. Army sites. Public Law 99-145, passed by Congress in 1985, requires the army to destroy all obsolete chemical agents and munitions. Under the auspices of the Army's Chemical Materials Agency, three programs, the Chemical Stockpile Disposal Program, the Alternative Technology and Approaches Program, and the Non-Stockpile Chemical Materiel Program all work to dispose of the materials.[32] In 2000, the Chemical Stockpile Disposal Program completed the destruction of 6.6 percent of the American chemical weapons stockpile at the Johnston Atoll facility, located 800 miles southwest of Hawaii. The facility was shut down at the end of 2004.[33] It is now for sale.

The United States signed the Chemical Weapons Convention in 1993, pledging to dispose of its entire unitary chemical weapons stockpile, binary chemical weapons, recovered chemical weapons, and former chemical weapons production facilities by April 29, 2007. The process of destruction has been a slow one, however, due to the huge quantities of chemical weapons to be eliminated, and because of citizen concerns regarding the environmental effects of destroying the stockpiles through incineration. As a result, the United States has not met each of its incremental deadlines under the Chemical Weapons Convention, and the Organization for the Prohibition of Chemical Weapons extended the United States' deadline to destroy 45 percent of its stockpile to December 31, 2007, as well as its subsequent deadline to eliminate 100 percent of its chemical weapons by an undetermined date after December 31, 2007.[34]

NOTES

1. For further details, see Thomas B. Cochran, William M. Arkin, Milton Hoenig, *Nuclear Weapons Databook: U.S. Nuclear Forces and Capabilities* (Cambridge, Mass.: Ballinger, 1984); Steven Schwartz, ed., *Atomic Audit: The Costs and Consequences of U.S. Nuclear Weapons since 1940* (Washington, D.C.: Brookings Institution Press, 1998); and the web site of the *Bulletin of the Atomic Scientists*, www.thebulletin.org.
2. U.S. State Department, Bureau of Arms Control Fact Sheet, "START Aggregate Numbers of Strategic Offensive Arms," April 1, 2005 (for forces accountable as of January 31, 2005).
3. Robert S. Norris and Hans M. Kristensen, "NRDC Nuclear Notebook, U.S. Nuclear Forces, 2005," *Bulletin of the Atomic Scientists*, January/February 2005, pp. 73–75.
4. Ibid.
5. Ibid., pp. 74–75.
6. Excerpts from the Nuclear Posture Review can be found at www.globalsecurity.org/wmd/library/policy/dod/npr.htm.
7. Robert S. Norris and Hans M. Kristensen, "What's Behind Bush's Nuclear Cuts?" *Arms Control Today*, October 2004, pp. 6–12.
8. "Statement of Admiral Richard W. Mies, commander in chief, United States Strategic Command, before the Senate Armed Services Committee Strategic Subcommittee," Washington, D.C., July 11, 2001.
9. See George Perkovich, Jessica Mathews, Joseph Cirincione, Rose Gottemoeller, and Jon Wolfsthal, *Universal Compliance: A Strategy for Nuclear Security* (Washington, D.C.: Carnegie Endowment for International Peace, 2005), available at www.carnegieendowment.org/strategy.
10. Sam Nunn, "Remarks to the Carnegie International Non-Proliferation Conference," June 21, 2004, available at www.ceip.org/files/projects/npp/resources/2004conference/speeches/nunn.htm.
11. "Statement of Admiral Richard W. Mies."
12. General James Cartwright, testimony to the Senate Armed Services Committee Strategic Forces Subcommittee, April 4, 2005.
13. Ambassador Linton Brooks, testimony before the Senate Armed Services Committee, Strategic Forces Subcommittee, April 4, 2005.
14. Schwartz, *Atomic Audit.*
15. Norris and Kristensen, "NRDC Nuclear Notebook," pp. 73–75.
16. Ibid.
17. U.S. Department of Energy, "Plutonium: The First 50 Years," February 1996, pp. 2–3.
18. William S. Cohen, *Annual Report to the President and Congress* (Washington, D.C.: Department of Defense, January 2001), p. 91.
19. State Department, Bureau of Arms Control Fact Sheet, "START Aggregate Numbers of Strategic Offensive Arms," July 31, 2004.
20. Robert S. Norris and Thomas B. Cochran, *U.S.–USSR/Russian Strategic Offensive Nuclear Forces, 1945–1996* (Washington, D.C.: Natural Resources Defense Council, 1997), p. 54.

21. Norris and Kristensen, "NRDC Nuclear Notebook," pp. 73–75.
22. Tom Mangold and Jeff Goldberg, *Plague Wars: A True Story of Biological Warfare* (London: Macmillan, 2000), p. 34.
23. Judith Miller, Stephen Engelberg, and William Broad, *Germs: Biological Weapons and America's Secret War* (New York: Simon & Schuster, 2001), p. 42. In late 1950, public health concerns emerged following an experiment using *Serratia marcescens* in San Francisco. Investigation by the Centers for Disease Control and Prevention found no evidence that the experiments posed a public health risk.
24. Mangold and Goldberg, *Plague Wars*, pp. 37–38.
25. Federation of American Scientists, "United States: Biological Weapons," available at www.fas.org/nuke/guide/usa/cbw/bw.htm.
26. Jonathan Yang, "U.S. Biodefense Plans Worry Nonproliferation Advocates," *Arms Control Today*, September 2003; available at www.armscontrol.org/act/2003_09/Biodefense.asp.
27. Jeffery Smart, "History of Chemical and Biological Warfare: An American Perspective," in *Medical Aspects of Chemical and Biological Warfare, Part I. The Textbook of Military Medicine* (Washington, D.C.: Borden Institute, Office of the Surgeon General, 1997), p. 38.
28. Ibid.
29. Ibid., p. 44.
30. Ibid., p. 49.
31. Federation of American Scientists, "United States: Chemical Weapons," available at www.fas.org/nuke/guide/usa/cbw/cw.htm.
32. See www.cma.army.mil/aboutcma.aspx.
33. See www.cma.army.mil/state.aspx?state=Hawaii.
34. Eighth Session, Conference of the States Parties, "Decision: Extension of the Intermediate and Final Deadlines for the Destruction by the United States of America of its Category 1 Chemical Weapons," C-8 / Dec. 15, October 24, 2003; available at www.opcw.org/docs/c8dec15.pdf.

Table 10.1. **U.S. Nuclear Forces**

Deployed Systems					
Name/Type	**Launchers**	**Year Deployed**	**Range (kilometers)**	**Warheads/ Launcher**	**Total Warheads**
Intercontinental Ballistic Missiles (ICBMs)					
Minuteman III (MK-12A)	300	1979	9,650+	2–3	750
Minuteman III (MK-12)	50	1970	9,650+	3	150
Minuteman III (MK-12)	150	1970	9,650+	1	150
MX Peacekeeper[1]	10	1986	9,650+	10	100
ICBM Totals	510				1,150
Submarine-Launched Ballistic Missiles (SLBMs)					
	Launchers/ Boats				
Trident I C-4	48/2	1979	7,400	6	288
Trident II D-5	288/12				
MK-4		1992	7,400+	6	1,344
MK-5		1990	7,400+	6	384
SLBM Totals	336/14				2,016
Ballistic Missile Totals	846				3,166
Strategic Bombers					
B-52H	94	1961	14,000		850
B-2 Spirit	21	1994	9,600		200
Bomber Totals	115				1,050
Total Strategic Launchers and Warheads					
TOTAL	961				4,216
Nonstrategic Warheads					
B-61-3, -4, -10	N/A	1979			580
Tomahawk SLBM	325	1984		1	200
Nonstrategic Totals	N/A				780
Total Deployed Nuclear Weapons and Delivery Systems					
	1,286+				~5,000

Nondeployed Weapons (Hedge, Spares, Inactive)					
					~5,315
Total U.S. Nuclear Arsenal					
					~10,315

SOURCES

Derived from Robert S. Norris and Hans M. Kristensen, "NRDC Nuclear Notebook, U.S. Nuclear Forces 2005," *Bulletin of the Atomic Scientists,* January/February 2005, pp. 73–75. U.S. Strategic Command, "Fact File: Ballistic Missile Submarines," available at www.stratcom.mil/factsheetshtml/submarines.htm. U.S. Strategic Command, "Fact File: Intercontinental Ballistic Missiles." available at www.stratcom.mil/FactSheetshtml/ballistic_missiles.htm.

NOTE

1. The 10 remaining MX Peacekeeper missiles are scheduled to be withdrawn by the end of 2005, leaving the Minuteman III as the only operational, deployed U.S. ICBM. Current plans are to begin deployment of a next-generation ICBM in 2018.

PART THREE

Non-NPT Nuclear Weapon States

In addition to the five declared nuclear weapon states under the Treaty on the Non-Proliferation of Nuclear Weapons (NPT), three countries possess nuclear weapons: India, Israel, and Pakistan. None of these three countries is a member of the NPT, and all have a significant capability to produce, build, and deliver nuclear weapons.

The drive to create a universal nonproliferation regime is greatly complicated by these three countries. The NPT defines a nuclear weapon state as a country that has tested a nuclear weapon device before January 1, 1967 (article 9). None of the countries therefore qualifies under the treaty as a nuclear weapon state, despite the fact that all three possess nuclear weapons. It would be legally impossible for them to join the treaty without its being amended, which would have to be approved by the national procedures of all 187 current members, something that has generally been regarded as an unacceptable and unlikely approach.

The nuclear programs of all three countries demonstrate how regional security affects national decisions to acquire nuclear weapons. Israel's nuclear program was developed in direct response to its insecurity vis-à-vis its Arab neighbors. Pakistan's program was driven by similar concerns about India. India's decision is more complex, but perceived threats from China and Pakistan played an important role.

Efforts to reverse nuclear proliferation in the Middle East and South Asia, therefore, are directly tied to regional security and political dynamics.

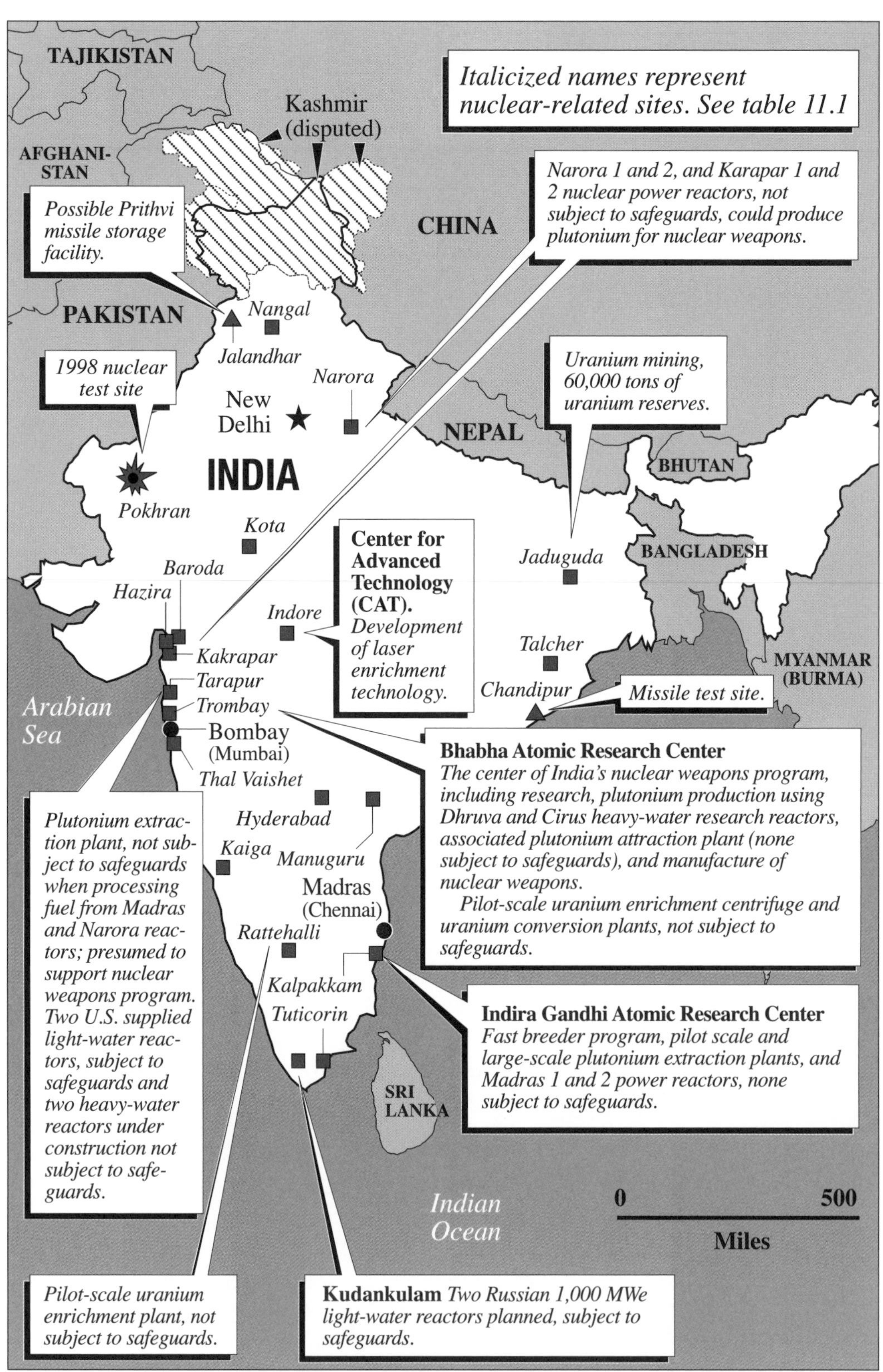
TAJIKISTAN
Italicized names represent nuclear-related sites. See table 11.1
Kashmir (disputed)
AFGHANI-STAN
Narora 1 and 2, and Karapar 1 and 2 nuclear power reactors, not subject to safeguards, could produce plutonium for nuclear weapons.
Possible Prithvi missile storage facility.
CHINA
PAKISTAN
Nangal
Jalandhar
Narora
1998 nuclear test site
Uranium mining, 60,000 tons of uranium reserves.
New Delhi
NEPAL
BHUTAN
INDIA
Pokhran
Kota
Center for Advanced Technology (CAT). Development of laser enrichment technology.
Jaduguda
BANGLADESH
Baroda
Hazira
Indore
Kakrapar
Talcher
MYANMAR (BURMA)
Tarapur
Chandipur
Missile test site.
Arabian Sea
Trombay
Bombay (Mumbai)
Bhabha Atomic Research Center
The center of India's nuclear weapons program, including research, plutonium production using Dhruva and Cirus heavy-water research reactors, associated plutonium attraction plant (none subject to safeguards), and manufacture of nuclear weapons.
Pilot-scale uranium enrichment centrifuge and uranium conversion plants, not subject to safeguards.
Thal Vaishet
Hyderabad
Plutonium extraction plant, not subject to safeguards when processing fuel from Madras and Narora reactors; presumed to support nuclear weapons program. Two U.S. supplied light-water reactors, subject to safeguards and two heavy-water reactors under construction not subject to safeguards.
Kaiga
Manuguru
Madras (Chennai)
Rattehalli
Kalpakkam
Tuticorin
Indira Gandhi Atomic Research Center
Fast breeder program, pilot scale and large-scale plutonium extraction plants, and Madras 1 and 2 power reactors, none subject to safeguards.
SRI LANKA
Indian Ocean
0
500
Miles
Pilot-scale uranium enrichment plant, not subject to safeguards.
Kudankulam Two Russian 1,000 MWe light-water reactors planned, subject to safeguards.

CHAPTER 11

India

Nuclear Weapons Capability

India possesses the components to deploy a small number of nuclear weapons within a few days or weeks, with fighter-bomber aircraft being the most likely delivery vehicle (see table 11.1 at the end of the chapter). By the end of 2005, India may have produced between 334 and 504 kilograms of weapons-grade plutonium,[1] enough to produce between 75 and 110 nuclear weapons.[2] It is not known how many actual weapons India has produced from this material, though it is most likely on the low end of the estimates. India may also be producing significant quantities of highly enriched uranium at its gas-centrifuge plant in Trombay, though precisely how much is still unknown.[3] Yet after India's "Shakti" (strength) nuclear tests, the most striking aspect of the country's weapons program has been its moderate pace. India's nuclear weapons are believed to be stored as separate components. It continues to produce nuclear materials for use in weapons, and it has not officially stated how many weapons it has or plans to produce. India is not a member of the Non-Proliferation Treaty (NPT) or a signatory of the Comprehensive Test Ban Treaty (CTBT). It conducted a test of a "peaceful" nuclear device in 1974 and five tests of nuclear weapons in May 1998.

Aircraft and Missile Capability

India has developed several types of ballistic missiles capable of carrying and delivering a nuclear payload. These are the short-range Prithvi and the medium-range Agni. Three variants of the liquid-fueled, road-mobile Prithvi exist, with ranges of 150 kilometers and payloads of 500 kilograms (the Army version); 250 kilometers and 500–750 kilograms (the Air Force version); and 350 kilometers and 500 kilograms (the Navy version). The Army and Air Force versions are in serial production. The medium-range Agni II, with a declared range of 2,000 to 2,500 kilometers, was successfully tested in April 1999, January 2001, and August 2004. As of the spring of 2005, India had deployed the short-range Prithvi missile (two versions), and the medium-range Agni I and Agni II with the Army.[4] Despite its pursuit of ballistic missiles, India's probable delivery platforms remain its fighter-bomber aircraft.[5] Of India's bomber aircraft, the most likely options are the Mirage 2000, and potentially the MiG-27, MiG-29, Su-30, and Jaguar aircraft. In a 2001 classified internal memorandum, the Indian Air Force reportedly determined that the country's fighter-bomber aircraft will remain the only feasible delivery system until the end of this decade.[6]

Biological and Chemical Weapons Capability

India is a signatory to both the Biological Weapons Convention and the Chemical Weapons Convention. Some U.S. intelligence assessments maintain, however, that India's significant biotechnical infrastructure and expertise are being used to conduct research on biological warfare defenses.[7] Under the terms of the Chemical Weapons Convention, India has pledged to destroy all its chemical agents and production facilities, but it possesses a sizable indigenous chemical industry. There is no publicly available evidence that India is pursuing either a chemical or biological offensive warfare program.

The Strategic Context

India's then–foreign minister, Jaswant Singh, has explained that with the nuclear tests of May 1998 India achieved "a degree of strategic autonomy by acquiring those symbols of power . . . which have universal currency."[8] India's acquisition of nuclear weapons and its public display of this capability can be seen as self-validation and as steps toward acquiring the power and status that the country believed was its due. Some of these perceptions are reinforced by colonial memories that still underlie a part of India's search for status and policy independence.[9] Some come from the way the country's security and political elite look at current international power equations. They note, for example, that countries that hold a permanent seat on the U.N. Security Council are all nuclear weapon states, and they note the difference in the U.S. response to Serbian atrocities in Kosovo versus Russian atrocities in Chechnya, the U.S. invasion of Iraq versus the tolerance of North Korea, and that nuclear weapons still form a central part of U.S. and NATO military strategy. They believe, therefore, that international status and power are still related to the acquisition of nuclear weapons.[10] Certainly, many members of the Bharatiya Janata Party (BJP), which was in power during the May 1998 tests, define power in terms of military power and define military power in terms of nuclear weapons capability. These views on the benefits of nuclear weapons have been as influential as military concerns in driving India's weapons program.[11]

In a letter to U.S. president Bill Clinton, India's then–prime minister, Atal Behari Vajpayee, cited the threat from China as the reason for India's nuclear testing program.[12] Indeed, pronuclear Indian strategists argue that, for India, nuclear weapons make strategic sense only vis-à-vis China. Indian government officials have publicly proclaimed the need for a credible deterrent against Chinese threats.[13] Despite improved relations since 2002, China still remains a critical factor in India's nuclear weapons objectives, particularly as the Indian security establishment considers contingencies for a China that in the future will possibly be much more powerful. In its 2002–2003 annual report assessing India's security environment, India's Ministry of Defense expressed concern that "the asymmetry in terms of nuclear forces is pronouncedly in favor of China, and is likely to get further accentuated as China responds to counter the U.S. missile defense program."[14]

The Pakistan–China nuclear and missile nexus is also a critical factor in India's strategy. China has provided major assistance to Pakistan's nuclear and missile programs—including a blueprint for a nuclear weapon, missiles, a missile production factory, a plutonium production reactor, and the technology and know-how for uranium enrichment (see chapters 7 and 12, on China and Pakistan, respectively). India's concern about China's strategic cooperation with Pakistan is intensified by a perception that the United States has not done all that it could have to stop Chinese proliferation,[15] and that the international community has done little to reprimand Pakistan on its "nuclear sabre-rattling."[16] Some analysts note that India's decision to test its nuclear weapons may have been hastened by Pakistan's April 1998 test of the 1,300-kilometer-range Ghauri missile, which demonstrated for the first time Pakistan's capability to hit deep within India's territory.[17]

Indian strategists also saw the 1995 indefinite extension of the NPT as a consolidation of the nuclear status quo, by which India was left out of the nuclear club. Those in India who were eager to test again viewed the nuclear regime as a potential stranglehold that they had to preempt. This feeling set the stage for India's rejection of the CTBT in 1996 and for the tests in 1998.[18] Despite the argument of India's pronuclear lobby, some Indian analysts argue that nuclear weapons have caused a deterioration in the country's security environment, pointing in particular to the fact that the nuclear tests neutralized its conventional weaponry advantage over Pakistan and solidified the Pakistani–Chinese nexus. They argue that the level nuclear playing field emboldened Pakistan to initiate the Kargil conflict in 1999 and constrained India's ability to respond.[19]

Relations with the United States

From India's perspective, the nuclear tests raised the country's visibility and clout in the post–Cold War era. If U.S. attention is a measure of respect and status, then the nuclear tests have ultimately achieved India's objectives. Many pronuclear Indian analysts have argued that the resulting increased attention from the sole remaining superpower proved that nuclear weapons were the only way in which to gain international relevance. President Clinton's hugely popular visit to India in March 2000 (delayed from 1997 by the collapse of the government and from 1998 by the Indian tests) set the stage for improved ties. By May 2001, with a newfound self-confidence, New Delhi had warmed to the U.S. strategic vision. The Indian government was one of the few that lauded U.S. plans to deploy antimissile systems.

The Clinton administration had set five benchmarks for the Indian and Pakistani governments to meet before the sanctions it imposed in the aftermath of the nuclear tests would be removed: (1) signing and ratifying the CTBT; (2) restraint from deploying nuclear weapons and delivery systems; (3) progress toward accepting the fissile material cutoff treaty (FMCT); (4) formal assurance that nuclear and missile technology exports would be banned; and (5) a resumption of a dialogue on Kashmir.[20] Toward the end of his administration, Clinton had already begun to lift sanctions, even though the benchmarks had not been met. The U.S. government believed that its interests in India extended beyond nonproliferation and, moreover, that sanctions were no longer effective either in deterring proliferation in South Asia or in facilitating better relations with India and Pakistan in general. India's commitment to a test moratorium, its positive record on nuclear export controls, and its expressed willingness to consider the CTBT and FMCT made it more palatable for Washington to ease sanctions in the period after the Clinton visit.

The George W. Bush administration has sought to build on the newfound camaraderie with the Indian government, and it has taken the relationship to new heights. With Republican antipathy toward the CTBT, pressure on India to sign the treaty has disappeared. Benchmarks are no longer discussed. Beyond ensuring that Kashmir does not explode, the Bush administration has decided to downplay nuclear proliferation concerns so that it can renew defense ties and establish "strategic" relations with India.[21] The two countries see eye to eye on antimissile systems. India took notice when then–deputy secretary of state Richard Armitage included New Delhi on an Asian trip to "consult" with allies in the region on deploying missile interceptors. His other stops were to visit U.S. allies Japan and South Korea. That gesture was followed by an unprecedented visit by the then–Joint Chiefs of Staff chair, Henry Shelton, who promised renewed defense ties. Thus, before September 11, 2001, India was assuming the role of America's "strategic partner" in South Asia, a potential counterweight to China, with Pakistan struggling under the weight of sanctions and isolation.

During the Bush administration's first term, the lifting of most sanctions imposed on India opened the way for hitherto unprecedented defense ties. India anticipates only a further deepening of ties in the second Bush term. High-level military meetings in December 2001 produced a joint statement that India and the United States would cooperate "to counter threats such as the spread of weapons of mass destruction, international terrorism, narcotics trafficking and piracy." The agreements that were reached reflected a U.S. willingness to sell major weapons platforms to India, something that Washington had not considered since 1984.[22] In September 2004, this new U.S. policy direction was exemplified by the Next Steps in Strategic Partnership (NSSP), a major Indo-U.S. agreement on bilateral cooperation on civilian nuclear activities, commercial space programs, high-technology trade, and missile defense. The NSSP liberalized some U.S. export controls that had been imposed after India's 1998 nuclear weapons tests. In return, India has committed to addressing U.S. concerns to ensure compliance with U.S. export controls on proliferation-sensitive items.

India was especially elated when, under the NSSP rubric, sanctions were lifted on the headquarters of the Indian Space Research Organization. A joint U.S.-Indian statement characterized the NSSP as "only the first phase in this important effort, which is a significant part of transforming our strategic relationship."[23]

Because India's quest for international status has been one of the motivating factors for its nuclear program, deeper relations between India and the United

States, the world's remaining superpower, may in fact ultimately serve to moderate New Delhi's nuclear ambitions. Though its growing economic success remains the primary variable in India's growing self-confidence, the country's foreign policy elite also perceive two other successes: the continuing development of India's nuclear and missile programs, in spite of international opprobrium and initial sanctions; and India's growing international reputation for being a "responsible" nuclear weapon state.

Nuclear Analysis

India was an early beneficiary of the United States–sponsored "Atoms for Peace" program launched in 1953. This program was intended to stem the proliferation of nuclear weapons by offering access to civilian uses of nuclear technology in exchange for pledges not to apply the technology to weapons. India's nuclear weapons program originated at the Bhabha Atomic Research Center (BARC) at Trombay, in western India. On the basis of the prevailing atmosphere of trust in the early Atoms for Peace years, in 1955 Canada supplied India with the Cirus 40-megawatts-thermal heavy-water-moderated research reactor (from which India later derived the plutonium for its 1974 "peaceful" nuclear explosion). In lieu of safeguards under the International Atomic Energy Agency (which did not exist until after the agency was founded in 1957), Canada required only written "peaceful assurances" that the reactor would be used exclusively for peaceful purposes. The United States sold India some of the heavy water needed for Cirus operations under the same assurances. There was little evidence before the mid-1950s that India had any interest in nuclear weapons.

Led by its atomic energy chief, Homi Bhabha, India recognized early the potential dual-use nature of many nuclear technologies, especially of plutonium separation. In 1958, as part of an ambitious scheme to pave the way for breeder reactors, India began to design and acquire the equipment for its Trombay plutonium-reprocessing facility. This facility was commissioned in late 1964, shortly before China detonated its first nuclear explosive device. When fully operational, the Trombay facility had an estimated capacity to separate up to 10 kilograms of plutonium annually (enough for perhaps two bombs a year). Ten years later, India detonated a nuclear device that it said was for peaceful uses only. The device used plutonium that had been generated in Cirus and separated in the Trombay reprocessing facility, demonstrating India's weapons capabilities.

After a testing hiatus of 24 years, India conducted five nuclear tests in May 1998: three on May 11 and two on May 13. The Indian government claimed that the May 11 test consisted of a fission device with a 12-kiloton yield, a thermonuclear device with a 43-kiloton yield, and a subkiloton device.[24] On May 13, India tested two more subkiloton devices with a range of between 0.2 and 0.6 kilotons. There is some controversy over whether India successfully tested a thermonuclear device, because the yield recorded and analyzed by Western seismographers was low, leading many in the scientific community to believe that the boosted-fission primary or the thermonuclear secondary did not function as designed.[25]

In its 1999–2000 report, India's Department of Atomic Energy acknowledged for the first time that it has implemented a program to develop and deploy nuclear weapons: "Following the successful nuclear tests in May 1998 at Pokharan, implementation of the program to meet the national policy of credible minimum nuclear deterrence in terms of necessary research and development as well as manufacture, is being pursued." BARC is the scientific nerve center of India's nuclear weaponization program. In April 2000, the government ended independent safety oversight at BARC.[26] Some analysts viewed this termination as an indication of accelerated weapon-related activity at BARC, though that does not appear to be the case.

There is no public information on how many nuclear weapons India may have produced. All estimates, therefore, are based on the range of material that India could have produced from its reactors, enough for 7 to 112 weapons, based on an average of 4.5 kilograms of plutonium per weapon. These are the upper limits of the possible. Given the limited test experience, the technical difficulties, and India's perceived needs, it is most likely that India has produced roughly 36 nuclear devices and unlikely that it has produced 100 or more.

In 2005, India's nuclear policy remains officially defensive. The government has cooled its early rhetorical bravado. A change in government from the right-wing BJP to the more left-leaning Congress Party has not altered India's nuclear posture. Speaking at his inaugural address, Prime Minister Manmohan Singh of the Congress-led government reaffirmed the existing nuclear policy: "We will maintain a credible minimum nuclear deterrent, along with a policy of no-first-use in our nuclear doctrine. India is a responsible nuclear power, and we will continue to work to prevent proliferation of weapons of mass destruction. At the same time, we remain committed to the goal of universal nuclear disarmament."

Prime Minister Singh's remarks reflect India's assertion that the proliferation of nuclear weapons is a global rather than regional problem, and, therefore, it must be addressed globally. As long as India's decision makers believe that the existing nuclear weapon states will not or cannot work toward disarmament, India will not countenance a rollback of its own program, regardless of the party in power.[27] Any Indian government will remain committed to weaponization, even if budget and technical realities and international political considerations continue to restrain its pace. India has maintained a self-declared moratorium on further nuclear tests, despite some domestic voices calling for their resumption. The country's testing of short- and medium-range missiles continues, however.

India's Nuclear Doctrine

A draft report of the National Security Advisory Board on Indian Nuclear Doctrine was released in August 1999, just before national elections by the then-governing BJP. After it became public, the government distanced itself from the doctrine, with then–foreign minister Singh calling it a "possible Indian Nuclear Doctrine," which was released for public debate. The doctrine, which was officially affirmed only in January 2003, calls for a "credible minimum nuclear deterrence" based on a policy of "retaliation only," whereby India "will not be the first to initiate a nuclear strike, but will respond with punitive retaliation should deterrence fail." Even during the height of tensions between India and Pakistan in 2001, India reaffirmed its no-first-use policy. However, for India a "'no-first-strike" policy does not mean that the government will not have a first strike capability. Deterrence will be a "dynamic concept," and "the "actual size, components, deployment, and employment of nuclear forces" will be determined by "the strategic environment, technological imperatives, and the needs of national security."

The doctrine further calls for nuclear forces based on a "triad of aircraft, mobile land-based missiles, and sea-based assets." For this deterrence to work, the doctrine says that India will require "sufficient, survivable, and operationally prepared nuclear forces, a robust command and control system, effective intelligence and early warning capabilities, and comprehensive planning and training for operations in line with the strategy." The doctrine makes no effort to quantify either the deterrence or associated costs.

Some experts have argued that India's doctrine is essentially "conservative" in character, because it emphasizes deterrence rather than war fighting, and because ultimately the country's nuclear force will likely be "minimum" rather than "expansive."[28] In January 2003, however, while vaguely reaffirming "credible minimum deterrence," the Indian government announced for the first time that India "will retain the option" of using nuclear weapons to retaliate against a biological or chemical weapons attack against the country.[29] This echo of U.S. doctrine narrows the definition of "no-first-strike," raising the question of the country's doctrinal commitment to not using nuclear weapons against a non-nuclear-weapon state.

India's Nuclear Command Structure

According to India's nuclear doctrine, the authority to use nuclear weapons rests with the prime minister and with a "designated successor." The nuclear doctrine also outlines a plan for the command and control of nuclear forces: "An effective and survivable command and control system with requisite flexibility and responsiveness shall be in place. An integrated operational plan, or a series of sequential plans, predicated on strategic objectives and a targeting policy, shall form part of the system."[30]

In January 2003, after much delay, India established a Nuclear Command Authority, which includes a political council and an executive council. This process was delayed by the 2001–2002 crisis with Pakistan, and interservice rivalry over the control of India's land-based missiles.

India's prime minister chairs the political council, which has the sole authority to order a nuclear strike and was set up to formulate political principles and administrative arrangements to manage India's nuclear arsenal. The national security adviser chairs the executive council, which advises the nuclear command authority and carries out orders from the political council. The Indian government also approved the appointment of a commander-in-chief of the Strategic Forces Command (SFC) to take charge of the nuclear arsenal.[31] The SFC consists of representatives from the Army, Navy, and Air Force. The commander-in-chief of the SFC will manage and administer the nuclear forces but not the nuclear warheads. The post will rotate among the three services—Army, Air Force and Navy, beginning with the Air Force.[32] Nuclear warheads remain under civilian control, in the physical custody of the Defense Research Development Organization and the Department of Energy.[33]

Two operational missile groups of the Indian Army—one armed with the 150–250-kilometer short-range Prithvi missiles and the other with the longer-version 2,500-kilometer Agni missiles—will be part of the nucleus of the new Strategic Forces Command. The Air Force will earmark some Jaguar, Mirage 2000, and Su-30MKI squadrons and the Navy will deploy some naval warships and submarines to complete the nucleus of India's first nuclear command.[34]

The creation of the Nuclear Command Authority under the political council headed by the prime minister and the SFC headed by a commander-in-chief have deliberately obscured the actual chain of command with respect to authorizing the use of India's nuclear weapons. India also created alternative nuclear command chains, arguing that it was necessary to establish them to ensure retaliation for a nuclear strike.[35]

Missile Analysis

India's missile capabilities are the result of its Integrated Guided Missile Development Program, which was begun in 1983. In 1998, one of India's prominent nuclear strategic thinkers, the retired Indian air commodore Jasjit Singh, wrote that the nuclear-capable aircraft's "limitations of range and susceptibility to interception by hostile systems make it critical that the central component of the nuclear arsenal must rest on ballistic missiles."[36] This is particularly true given China's missile capability, which is a principal driving force behind India's missile program. The *Annual Report 2002–2003* of the Ministry of Defense emphasizes: "As far as India is concerned, it cannot be ignored that every major Indian city is within reach of Chinese missiles and this capability is being further augmented to include submarine-launched ballistic missiles (SLBMs)."[37]

Given the Prithvi's range, its role would be restricted to use against Pakistan. The Prithvi and the Agni I and II are the nuclear-capable missiles in the hands of the Indian military. The Army first received the 150-kilometer-range Prithvi in 1994. Estimates of the number of Prithvis the Indian Army possesses range from 75 to 90.[38]

The Army is reportedly unenthusiastic about the Prithvi, however; never having been involved in its development, it still has questions about its guidance system.[39] Moreover, because the Prithvi is liquid-fueled, it poses significant operational liabilities as a nuclear delivery system. Prithvi units include numerous vehicles that could be detected once deployed, and hours would be required in the field to prepare the missiles for launch, which would allow interdiction by Pakistan. A nuclear war game exercise staged by the Indian Army in the summer of 2001 did not include the Prithvi.[40] There are even reports that the government has decided not to weaponize any Prithvi variant with a nuclear warhead.[41] However, India has continued its tests of the short-range ballistic missile system. The naval version, the Dhanush, has been in development since 1983 but had its first successful test only in September 2001.[42] In September 2002, India announced that the Dhanush was "ready for induction after successful trials at sea."[43] The missile was successfully test fired again in October 2004.[44] The Air Force version of the Prithvi (the Prithvi-250) was successfully tested in December 2001.[45]

The Agni medium-range program, begun in the late 1980s, was suspended in 1994 owing to technological problems and diplomatic pressure from the United States. The program resumed under the BJP government in 1998 with a second version of the missile. The Agni II medium-range ballistic missile (MRBM), which is capable of carrying a 1,000-kilogram payload, was first tested successfully in April 1999 (just before the BJP faced a no-confidence motion in the Indian Parliament), again in January 2001, and in August 2004. Nine years after receiving the Prithvi I, the Army took receipt of the 700-kilometer-range Agni I and the 1,500-kilometer-range Agni II in October 2003.[46]

The Agni II is an improvement over the "technology demonstrator" Agni I. It is a two-stage, rail- and road-mobile MRBM with a solid-fueled rocket.[47] The Agni I has a liquid-solid motor combination, with the second stage consisting of, essentially, a Prithvi. The Agni II could reach all of Pakistan, allowing India to base it deep within the country, thereby increasing the survivability factor against its western neighbor.

The Agni II could reach parts of western China, but most of northeast China, including Beijing, remains out of reach, even if the missile were based in northeast India east of Bangladesh. A Rand study argues that no upgrade of the Agni II is likely to produce a missile with the 3,500–5,000 kilometer range necessary to hold China's most valued assets at risk. Even given India's technical expertise, that range (which will also be a matter of payload) could require the development of a new ballistic missile.[48] Currently, scientists at India's Defense Research Development Organization (DRDO) are working to upgrade the Agni II to increase its accuracy. DRDO is also currently working on a new missile, the Agni III, capable of carrying an estimated 1,000-kilogram payload to a 3,500-kilometer range. Foreign assistance, particularly Russian, could allow India to develop its missile capabilities faster.

India has the technical expertise to pursue intercontinental ballistic missile (ICBM) capability, having successfully launched both the Polar Space Launch Vehicle and the Geosynchronous Space Launch Vehicle. The cadre of India's defense scientists who were influential in the nuclear tests would also like to demonstrate India's scientific capability by fielding an ICBM.[49] One member of the BJP-led National Security Advisory Board has written: "In the final analysis, a country's international standing is founded on the reach of the weapons in its armory. . . . While India has certainly boosted its image by going nuclear, it will truly emerge as an international power only when it tests its first ICBM."[50] Some Indian politicians, however, argue that an ICBM is not necessary for India's defensive needs.[51] Perhaps India will be content with an intercontinental satellite-launch-vehicle capability.[52] In 2000, then–defense minister George Fernandes informed the Indian Parliament that "in consonance with the threat perception, no ICBM development project has been undertaken."[53] In 2003, scientists at DRDO publicly reaffirmed that India did not have an ICBM program because it did not face an ICBM threat.[54] In any case, many years will be required before India has a test-proven capability to carry nuclear weapons to ranges of 5,500 kilometers or more.

Currently, India has no submarine-launched ballistic missile capability. The Sagarika SLBM project is reportedly continuing with assistance from Russia. Much like the rest of India's missile program, progress has been slow. India began the Sagarika program in 1991, and U.S. intelligence believes it will not be deployed until 2010 or later.[55]

The Advanced Technology Vessel project was begun in the late 1970s, also with Russian assistance, to develop a nuclear-powered submarine that could be equipped with nuclear-tipped missiles. The program's substantial technical, financial, and bureaucratic problems indicate that there are hurdles ahead for any submarine-based nuclear delivery system.[56] A 2000 Rand study estimated that an Indian SLBM capability was still another 10 to 20 years away.[57] Russian assistance could enable faster progress.

India's inventory of nuclear-capable aircraft consist of the Jaguar, which can carry a 1,000-kilogram warhead to a range of 900–1,400 kilometers; the Mirage 2000; and the MiG-27 and MiG-29. Russia is providing 40 nuclear-capable Su-30 aircraft and is also reportedly leasing a small number of nuclear-capable, Navy-based Tu-22 bombers.[58] India also has a variant of the Russian Tu-95 Bear, known as the Tu-142 Bear, which can carry a heavy nuclear weapon to a range of 5,000–6,000 kilometers.[59]

Biological and Chemical Weapons Analysis

India has many well-qualified scientists and numerous biological and pharmaceutical production facilities that could be used for advanced research or for the development of pathogens. U.S. intelligence assessments have maintained that India's significant biotechnical infrastructure and expertise are being used to conduct research on biological warfare defenses, although this assessment is rarely highlighted.[60] India ratified the Biological Weapons Convention in 1974.

After ratifying the Chemical Weapons Convention in 1996, India disclosed that it had a chemical weapons production program. This official acknowledgment, made in June 1997, marked the first time that India publicly admitted to be pursuing an offensive chemical warfare capability. Though it has pledged to destroy all agents and production facilities, in the past Indian firms have exported a number of items proscribed under Australia Group guidelines, including specific chemical agent precursors and dual-use equipment.[61] These are materials and items that are not themselves weapons but are used to produce chemical agents. Because India has a sizable indigenous chemical industry, its activities and sales could remain a cause for concern.

NOTES

1. This estimate is extrapolated from David Albright and Kimberly Kramer, "Fissile Materials: Stockpiles Still Growing," *Bulletin of the Atomic Scientists*, November/December 2004, pp. 14–16. Assuming the Cirus and Dhurva reactors are operating at 40 percent capacity, as Albright believes, India could produce approximately 17 kilograms of plutonium per year. See also David Albright, "India's and Pakistan's Fissile Material and Nuclear Weapons Inventories, End of 1999," Institute for Science and International Security, Washington, D.C., October 11, 2000; available at www.isis-online.org/publications/southasia/stocks1000.html.
2. Ibid. Weapon estimates are based on 4 to 5 kilograms of plutonium per weapon. For a similar estimate see, "NRDC Nuclear Notebook," *Bulletin of the Atomic Scientists*, March/April 2002.
3. Albright and Cramer, "Fissile Materials: Stockpiles Still Growing," pp. 14–16.
4. Nuclear Threat Reduction Country Profiles, www.nti.org/e_research/profiles/India/index.html; Natural Resources Defense Council, "Nuclear Data," www.nrdc.org/nuclear/nudb/datab20.asp; and Karen Yourish, "India, Pakistan Move Forward with New Weapons," *Arms Control Today*, November 2003, available at www.armscontrol.org/act/2003_11/IndiaandPakistan.asp.
5. "India Nuclear Weapon Update 2003," *Risk Report* (Wisconsin Project on Nuclear Arms Control), September–October 2003, available at www.wisconsinproject.org/countries/india/nuke2003.htm; and U.S. Department of Defense, *Proliferation: Threat and Response* (Washington, D.C.: U.S. Department of Defense, 2001), p. 23.
6. Shishir Gupta, "Down to Brasstacks," *India Today*, May 28, 2001.
7. U.S. Department of Defense, *Proliferation: Threat and Response*, p. 24.
8. Jaswant Singh, interview with National Public Radio, quoted in George Perkovich, *India's Nuclear Bomb: The Impact on Global Proliferation* (Berkeley: University of California Press, 1999). For a comprehensive discussion of India's motivations, see pp. 404–443.
9. Perkovich, *India's Nuclear Bomb*, p. 417.
10. George Perkovich, "Dystrophy of Nuclear Muscle," *Outlook India*, October 16, 2000.
11. P. R. Chari (Institute for Peace and Conflict Studies), Carnegie Proliferation Roundtable, February 16, 2001. See also P. R. Chari, "India's Nuclear Doctrine: Confused Ambitions," *Nonproliferation Review*, Fall–Winter 2000, vol. 7, no. 3.
12. Perkovich, *India's Nuclear Bomb*, p. 419.
13. "Fernandes for Maintaining Parity with China," *Times of India*, October 10, 2000.
14. Ministry of Defense of the Government of India, *Annual Report, 2002–2003*, p. 8; available at http://mod.nic.in/reports/welcome.html.
15. Brahma Chellaney, "Load Up!" *Hindustan Times*, February 13, 2001. Chellaney was one of the strategists on India's Nuclear Security Advisory Board. See also Perkovich, *India's Nuclear Bomb*, p. 421.
16. Ministry of Defense of the Government of India, *Annual Report, 2002–2003*, p. 8.
17. Perkovich, *India's Nuclear Bomb*, pp. 409–412.
18. George Perkovich, Carnegie Proliferation Roundtable, November 16, 1999.
19. Chari, Carnegie Proliferation Roundtable, February 16, 2001.
20. Karl Inderfurth, U.S. assistant secretary of state, Testimony to the U.S. Senate Foreign Relations Committee on India and Pakistan, July 13, 1998.
21. Edward Alden and Edward Luce, "A New Friend in Asia: George Bush Is Relegating Concerns about Nuclear Proliferation in Order to Win the Friendship of India as a Strategic Ally in the Region," *Financial Times*, August 21, 2001.
22. Celia Dugger, "To Strengthen Military Ties, U.S. Beats Path to India," *New York Times*, December 6, 2001.
23. "United States–India Joint Statement on Next Steps in Strategic Partnership," U.S. State Department Press Release, September 17, 2004, available at www.state.gov/r/pa/prs/ps/2004/36290.htm.
24. "Joint Statement by the Chairman of the Atomic Energy Commission and the Scientific Adviser to the Defense Minister," *The Hindu*, May 18, 1998.
25. Perkovich, *India's Nuclear Bomb*, pp. 426–427; Chari, "India's Nuclear Doctrine," pp. 128–129.

26. "Whither Nuclear Safety?" *The Hindu*, July 4, 2000.
27. Ashley J. Tellis, *India's Emerging Nuclear Posture* (Santa Monica, Calif.: Rand Corporation, 2001), p. 21.
28. Ashley Tellis, "India's Emerging Nuclear Doctrine: Exemplifying the Lessons of the Nuclear Revolution," NBR Analysis, National Bureau of Asian Research, 2001.
29. Kerry Boyd, "India Establishes Formal Nuclear Command Structure," *Arms Control Today*, January/February 2003, available at www.armscontrol.org/act/2003_01-02/india_janfeb03.asp.
30. "Draft Report of National Security Advisory Board on Indian Nuclear Doctrine," August 17, 1999, available at www.meadev.nic.in/govt/indnucld.htm.
31. Boyd, "India Establishes Formal Nuclear Command Structure."
32. "Asthana Appointed Strategic Forces Command Chief," Press Trust of India, January 10, 2003.
33. "India Consolidates its Nuclear Force," *Arms Control Today,* October 2003, available at www.armscontrol.org/act/2003_10/IndiaPakistan.asp.
34. "Missile Groups to Form Nucleus of Strategic Forces Command," Rediff.com, January 7, 2003, available at www.rediff.com/news/2003/jan/07nuke.htm, site.
35. Yourish, "India, Pakistan Move Forward."
36. Jasjit Singh, ed., *Nuclear India* (New Delhi: Institute for Defense Studies and Analyses, 1998), p. 315.
37. Ministry of Defense of the Government of India, *Annual Report, 2002–2003.*
38. Gaurav Kampani, "India's Missile Overview," Nuclear Threat Reduction Initiative, available at www.nti.org/e_research/profiles/India/Missile/index.html.
39. Pravin Sawhney, "Pakistan Scores over India in Ballistic Missile Race," *Jane's Intelligence Review*, November 2000.
40. Harinder Baweja, "Readying for Nukes," *India Today*, May 28, 2001.
41. Atul Aneja, "India Has 'Problems' Managing Nuclear Arms," *The Hindu*, August 14, 2001.
42. "Dhanush Missile Test Fired," *Times of India*, September 21, 2001.
43. Kampani, "India's Missile Overview."
44. "India Test-Fires Nuclear Capable Ballistic Missile," Agence France-Presse, October 27, 2004.
45. "IAF version of Prithvi Passes Test," *Times of India*, December 13, 2001.
46. Yourish, "India, Pakistan Move Forward."
47. Mark Hewish, "Ballistic Missile Threat Evolves," *Jane's International Defense Review*, October 2000, p. 41.
48. Gregory Jones, *From Testing to Deploying Nuclear Forces: The Hard Choices Facing India and Pakistan* Issue Paper 192 (Santa Monica, Calif.: Rand Corporation, 2000).
49. "ICBMs Any Day, Says Kalam," *Hindustan Times*, September 18, 2000.
50. Chellaney, "Load Up!" *Hindustan Times*, February 13, 2001.
51. Ibid.
52. Michael Krepon, Carnegie Proliferation Roundtable, February 16, 2001.
53. "India Reports It Has Ability to Build ICBM," Reuters, November 22, 2000.
54. "India Developing Ballistic Missiles to Counter Threats," *The Hindu,* February 10, 2003.
55. Natural Resources Defense Council, "Nuclear Data."
56. Gopi T. S. Rethiniraj and Clifford Singer, "Going Global: India Aims for a Credible Nuclear Doctrine," *Jane's Intelligence Review*, February 2001.
57. Jones, *From Testing to Deploying Nuclear Forces.*
58. Ravi Velloor, "India and Russia Ink Defence Deal; Relationship Takes on a Commercial Bent with New Trade Agreements," *Straits Times*, December 4, 2004; see also Tom Walker, David Orr, and Mark Franchetti, "India Prepares to Attack Rebel Camps," *Sunday Times* (London), June 9, 2002.
59. International Institute for Strategic Studies. *The Military Balance, 2004–2005* (Oxford: Oxford University Press, 2004), p. 152.
60. U.S. Department of Defense, *Proliferation: Threat and Response*, p. 24.
61. Ibid., p. 25.

Table 11.1. **India's Nuclear Infrastructure**

Name/Location of Facility	Type and Capacity	Completion or Target Data	IAEA Safeguards
Power Reactors: Operating			
Tarapur 1	Light-water, LEU and/or MOX, 150 MWe	1969	Yes
Tarapur 2	Light-water, LEU and/or MOX, 150 MWe	1969	Yes
Rajasthan, RAPS-1 Kota	Heavy-water, nat. U, 90 MWe	1973	Yes
Rajasthan, RAPS-2 Kota	Heavy-water, nat. U, 1871 MWe	1981	Yes
Madras, MAPS-1 Kalpakkam	Heavy-water, nat. U, 155 MWe	1984	No
Madras, MAPS-2 Kalpakkam (Tamil Nadu)	Heavy-water, nat. U, 202 MWe	1986	No
Narora 1	Heavy-water, nat. U, 202 MWe	1991	No
Narora 2	Heavy-water, nat. U, 202 MWe	1992	No
Kakrapar 1	Heavy-water, nat. U, 202 MWe	1993	No
Kakrapar 2	Heavy-water, nat. U, 202 MWe	1995	No
Kaiga 1	Heavy-water, nat. U, 202 MWe	2000	No
Kaiga 2	Heavy-water, nat. U, 202 MWe	2000	No
Rajasthan, RAPP-3 Kota	Heavy-water, nat. U, 202 MWe	2000	No
Rajasthan, RAPP-4 Kota	Heavy-water, nat. U, 202 MWe	2000	No
Power Reactors: Under Construction			
Tarapur 3	Heavy-water, nat. U, 490 MWe	2007	No

(table continues on the following page)

Table 11.1. **India's Nuclear Infrastructure** (continued)

Name/Location of Facility	Type and Capacity	Completion or Target Data	IAEA Safeguards
Tarapur 4	Heavy-water, nat. U, 490 MWe	2006	No
Kaiga 3	Heavy-water, nat. U, 202 MWe	2007	No
Kaiga 4	Heavy-water, nat. U, 202 MWe	2007	No
Kudankulam-1	Russian VVER–1000/392, Light-water, LEU 917 MWe	2007	No
Kudankulam-2	Russian VVER–1000/392, Light-water, LEU 917 MWe	2008	No
Rajasthan, RAPP-5 Kota	Heavy-water, nat. U, 202 MWe	2007	No
Rajasthan, RAPP-6 Kota	Heavy-water, nat. U, 202 MWe	2008	No
Power Reactors: Planned and Proposed[1]			
Kaiga 5	Heavy-water, nat. U, 700 MWe	–	No
Kaiga 6	Heavy-water, nat. U, 700 MWe	–	No
Rajasthan, RAPP-7 Kota	Heavy-water, nat. U, 700 MWe	–	No
Rajasthan, RAPP-8 Kota	Heavy-water, nat. U, 700 MWe	–	No
Research Reactors			
Apsara BARC, Trombay	Light-water, high-enriched uranium, pool type, 1 MWt	1956	No
Cirus BARC, Trombay	Heavy-water, nat. U, 40 MWt	1960	No
Dhruva BARC, Trombay	Heavy-water, nat. U, 100 MWt	1985	No

Kamini, IGCAR, Kalpakkam	Uranium-233, 0.03 MWt	1996	No
Zerlina BARC, Trombay	Heavy-water, variable fuel 0.1 kWt, decommissioned in 1983	1961	No
Purnima 1 BARC, Trombay	Fast neutron, critical assembly zero-power, decommissioned in 1983	1972	No
Purnima 2 BARC, Trombay	Light-water, critical assembly 0.01 kWt, decommissioned in 1986	1984	No
Purnima 3 BARC, Trombay	Light-water, uranium-233, zero-power, decomissioned in 1993	–	No
Breeder Reactors			
Fast-Breeder Test Reactor (FBTR), IGCAR Kalpakkam	Plutonium and nat. U, 40 MWt	1985	No
Prototype Fast Breeder Reactor (PFBR), IGCAR Kalpakkam	Mixed-oxide (MOX) fuel, 470 MWe, excavation work began in 2003	2009	No
Uranium Enrichment			
Trombay	Pilot-scale ultracentrifuge plant, operating	1985	No
Rattehalli Mysore	Pilot-scale ultracentrifuge plant, operating	1990	No
Center for Advanced Technology Indore	Laser enrichment research site	1993	No
Reprocessing (Plutonium Extraction)			
Trombay	Small-scale, 50 tHM/year, operating	1985	No

(table continues on the following page)

Table 11.1. **India's Nuclear Infrastructure** (continued)

Name/Location of Facility	Type and Capacity	Completion or Target Data	IAEA Safeguards
Tarapur	Medium-scale, 100 tHM/year, operating	1977	No
Kalpakkam	Medium-scale, 125 tHM/year, operating	1986	No
Kalpakkam	Large-scale,1,000 tHM/y, under construction		No
Uranium Processing			
Rakha, Surda Mosaboni	Uranium recovery plants at copper concentrator, operating	1986	No
Jaduguda	Uranium mining and milling, operating	1968	No
Hyderabad	Uranium purification (UO_2), operating		No
Hyderabad	Fuel fabrication (two facilities produce fuel for heavy-water reactors, one facility produces fuel for light-water reactors), all operating	1974 (LWR fuel fabrication, PWR fuel fabrication); 1997 (PWR-2 fuel fabrication)	Yes
Trombay	Uranium conversion (UF_6), operating	1985	No
Advanced Fuel Fabrication Facility, Tarapur	Mixed uranium-plutonium oxide (MOX) fuel fabrication, operating		No
Heavy-Water Production[2]			
Nangal	6.6 t/year, decommissioned in 2002	1962	No
Baroda	15 t/year, standby	1977	No
Tuticorin	49 t/year, operating	1978	No

Talcher, phase 1	62.5 t/year, operating	1985	No
Talcher, phase 2	72 t/year, proposed		No
Kota	85 t/year, operating	1985	No
Thal-Vaishet	78 t/year, operating	1987	No
Manuguru	185 t/year, operating, under expansion	1991	No
Hazira	80 t/year, operating	1991	No
Nuclear Weapon Test Site			
Pokharan Range	Site of nuclear tests conducted in 1998		No

Abbreviations

HEU	highly enriched uranium
IAEA	International Atomic Energy Agency
LEU	low-enriched uranium
N.A.	not applicable
nat. U	nat. uranium
MOX	mixed-oxide fuel
MWe	megawatts electric
MWt	megawatts thermal
kWt	kilowatts thermal
t	tons
tHM/yr	tons of heavy metal per year

Sources

IAEA, "Power Reactor Information System," available at www.iaea.org/programmes/a2/index.html. IAEA, "Research Reactor Database," available at www.iaea.org/worldatom/rrdb/. IAEA, "Country Nuclear Power Profiles: 2003." IAEA, "Nuclear Fuel Cycle Information System," available at www-nfcis.iaea.org/Default.asp. IAEA, "Director General's Annual Report, 2003," table A24. Nuclear Engineering International, *2004 World Nuclear Industry Handbook* (Sidcup, U.K.: Wilmington Publishing, 2004). Nuclear Threat Initiative, "India: Nuclear Facilities," available at www.nti.org/e_research/profiles/India/Nuclear/2103.html.

Notes

1. According to V. K. Chaturvedi, Managing Director of the Nuclear Power Corporation, Kaiga 5, Kaiga 6, RAPP-7, and RAPP-8 will all have 700 MWe capacity. See "RAPS-Review," Press Trust of India, October 18, 2002.
2. The nonproliferation regime does not include the application of safeguards to heavy-water production facilities, but safeguards are required on the export of heavy water.

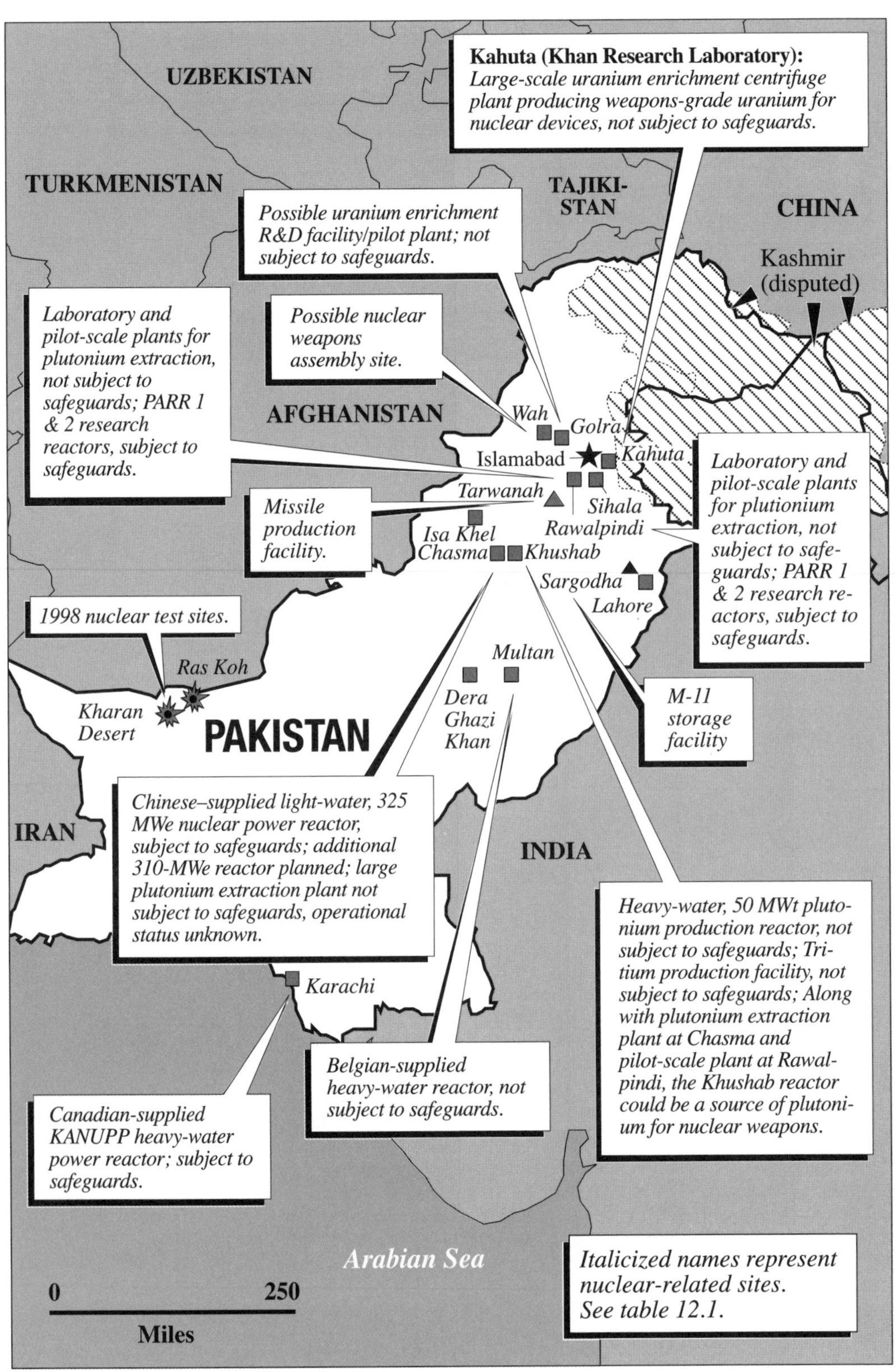

UZBEKISTAN
TURKMENISTAN
TAJIKI-
STAN
CHINA
AFGHANISTAN
IRAN
INDIA
PAKISTAN
Kashmir
(disputed)
Arabian Sea
Kahuta (Khan Research Laboratory):
Large-scale uranium enrichment centrifuge plant producing weapons-grade uranium for nuclear devices, not subject to safeguards.
Possible uranium enrichment R&D facility/pilot plant; not subject to safeguards.
Laboratory and pilot-scale plants for plutonium extraction, not subject to safeguards; PARR 1 & 2 research reactors, subject to safeguards.
Possible nuclear weapons assembly site.
Wah
Golra
Islamabad
Kahuta
Tarwanah
Sihala
Rawalpindi
Isa Khel
Chasma
Khushab
Sargodha
Lahore
Multan
Dera Ghazi Khan
Ras Koh
Kharan Desert
Karachi
Laboratory and pilot-scale plants for plutionium extraction, not subject to safe-guards; PARR 1 & 2 research re-actors, subject to safeguards.
Missile production facility.
1998 nuclear test sites.
M-11 storage facility
Chinese–supplied light-water, 325 MWe nuclear power reactor, subject to safeguards; additional 310-MWe reactor planned; large plutonium extraction plant not subject to safeguards, operational status unknown.
Heavy-water, 50 MWt pluto-nium production reactor, not subject to safeguards; Tri-tium production facility, not subject to safeguards; Along with plutonium extraction plant at Chasma and pilot-scale plant at Rawal-pindi, the Khushab reactor could be a source of plutoni-um for nuclear weapons.
Belgian-supplied heavy-water reactor, not subject to safeguards.
Canadian-supplied KANUPP heavy-water power reactor; subject to safeguards.
Italicized names represent nuclear-related sites.
See table 12.1.
0
250
Miles

CHAPTER 12

Pakistan

Nuclear Weapons Capability

Pakistan possesses the components to deploy a small number of nuclear weapons within a few days or weeks (see table 12.1 at the end of the chapter). By the end of 2005, Pakistan may have produced between 1,110 and 1,440 kilograms of weapons-grade uranium,[1] enough to produce between 50 and 110 nuclear weapons.[2] Their principal device design uses a solid core of highly enriched uranium (HEU) rather than plutonium. Pakistan's nuclear weapons are reportedly stored in component parts, with the fissile core separated from the non-nuclear explosives.[3] Where Pakistan stores its fissile material and warheads is not publicly known. Pakistan may have also produced 36 to 80 kilograms of weapons-grade plutonium by the end of 2005, or enough for 10 to 20 additional weapons.[4] Like India, Pakistan has refused to sign the Non-Proliferation Treaty. Pakistan has, however, signed but not ratified the Comprehensive Test Ban Treaty.

Aircraft and Missile Capability

Fighter-bomber aircraft are Pakistan's most likely delivery vehicles. The country also possesses missiles with ranges from 280 to 2,000 kilometers. However, it is not known if Pakistan has been able to develop nuclear warheads for its missiles.

The U.S.-supplied F-16 is likely Pakistan's primary nuclear-capable aircraft, able to carry a 1,000-kilogram bomb up to 1,600 kilometers. F-16s modified to carry nuclear weapons are deployed at Sargodha Air Force Base, 160 kilometers northwest of Lahore.[5] Other delivery vehicles possibly include the French Mirage V fighter-bombers and the Chinese A-5 Fantan.[6]

Pakistan has acquired the bulk of its missile capabilities from North Korea and China. Its surface to surface missile arsenal includes the Chinese-built and -supplied M-11; the Hatf short-range series; the North Korean, liquid-fueled Ghauri medium-range missiles; and the solid-fueled Shaheen series. The M-11 has a range of 280 to 300 kilometers. The Shaheen I, probably a derivative of the Chinese M-9 missile, has a range of 700 to 750 kilometers with a payload of 500 kilograms. The Ghauri I, the Pakistani version of the Nodong missile, has a range of 1,300 kilometers with a payload estimated at 500 to 750 kilograms and was delivered to the army in 2003.[7] Longer-range Ghauri II and Shaheen II missiles are in development and may not yet be operational.

Biological and Chemical Weapons Capability

Pakistan is not known to have any biological or chemical weapons or agents. To date, there has been no verified evidence suggesting that it has a chemical or biological weapons program. However, it does have a biotechnical infrastructure sufficient to support a limited biological weapons research and development effort.[8] Although its facilities are less well developed than those of India, they could nonetheless support the production of lethal pathogens. Pakistan is actively seeking foreign assistance to expand its civilian biological and pharmaceutical facilities. It ratified the Biological and Toxin Weapons Convention in 1974 and regularly participated in negotiations to establish an effective verification protocol for the treaty.

Pakistan is actively improving its commercial chemical industry and has imported chemicals with both commercial and weapons utility.[9] It could eventually have the capability to produce a variety of chemical agents because of the dual-use nature of its chemicals and equipment. There is some concern that it is conducting a limited chemical weapons research progam. Pakistan ratified the Chemical Weapons Convention in October 1997 and did not declare the possession of any chemical weapons.

The Strategic Context

Pakistan's quest for a nuclear deterrent has been motivated largely by fears of domination by India, whose population, economy, and military resources dwarf its own. Other factors that have also contributed to Pakistan's bid for nuclear arms include its desire for leadership and status in the Islamic world, popular nationalist sentiment, and political and bureaucratic pressures.

The country has been locked in a conflict with India since the two countries became independent from the United Kingdom in 1947 through partition. Since 1947, Pakistan has fought three full-scale wars with India, two of which have been over the disputed territory of Kashmir. The third and last of these wars, in 1971, led to the dismemberment of Pakistan; its former eastern wing became the independent state of Bangladesh. Pakistan secretly commenced its nuclear weapons program shortly thereafter, convinced that it was essential as a deterrent to ensure its survival. By the mid-1980s, Pakistan had developed a nuclear capability. However, it did not test its weapons until May 28 and 30, 1998, when it responded to India's May 11 and 13 nuclear tests by conducting tests of its own, finally declaring itself a nuclear weapon state.

Since the 1971 India-Pakistan war, relations between Islamabad and New Delhi have alternated between periods of relative peace and considerable tension. This was punctuated with crises that nearly erupted into war during the winter of 1986–1987 and the spring of 1990. During the latter crisis, international officials and experts feared that Pakistan might take steps to deploy its nascent nuclear arsenal. These concerns spurred intensive, and ultimately successful, U.S. diplomatic efforts to defuse the situation. Conflicts in Kargil in 1999 and military mobilizations after terrorist attacks on the Indian government in late 2001 and early 2002 again raised the possibility of war spiraling into a nuclear exchange between Pakistan and India.

While Pakistani scientists, engineers, and government leaders have proceeded as rapidly as possible since 1972 in developing their country's nuclear weapons capability, they have always sought to appear as though they were responding to India. General Aslam Beg, Pakistan's army chief from 1988 to 1991, has written that "Pakistan's nuclear programme was India specific and therefore it was of no consequence to Pakistan what other nuclear power nations decided for themselves."[10] In late 1995, U.S. agencies detected Indian preparations for a nuclear explosive test. This detection resulted in a major U.S.-led international effort to dissuade India from testing. Though India did decide against testing at that time, it raised the possibility of a Pakistani nuclear test. In late February 1996, then–director of the Central Intelligence Agency, John Deutch, expressed these U.S. concerns, saying, "We have judged that if India should test, Pakistan would follow."[11] Two weeks after Deutch's statement, U.S. satellite photographs reportedly revealed evidence of Pakistani nuclear test preparations at Chagai Hills, an apparent response to India's earlier preparations. However, a desire to validate the weapon design—independent of India's test preparations—is also likely to have driven Pakistan's nuclear test preparations.

In April 1998, Abdul Qadeer Khan, the self-proclaimed father of the Pakistani nuclear weapons program, declared that as soon as Pakistani scientific teams could "get permission from the government," they were ready and able to test a nuclear weapon.[12] In May 1998, following the Indian nuclear tests, the government of Nawaz Sharif finally gave its permission. On May 28, 1998, after the tests took place at Chagai Hill in western Pakistan, Sharif declared, "Today we have settled a score."[13] Pakistan's nuclear arsenal offers the country a sense of military parity with India, and it may well have emboldened Pakistan to increase its militancy in the Kashmir Valley. It is possible that Pakistan's summer 1999 military incursion into Kargil, which is located over the line of control that divides Indian- and Pakistani-held Kashmir, was a undertaken with this newfound parity in mind.[14]

Relations between India and Pakistan after the Nuclear Tests

The nuclear tests greatly raised the cost of war in South Asia, and India and Pakistan have struggled to find a measure of stability in their relations. Diplomatic initiatives have been interspersed all too frequently with nuclear brinkmanship, provocative rhetoric, and dangerous confidence in "limited war."

In February 1999, India's prime minister, Atal Behari Vajpayee, made a widely publicized bus trip to Lahore to meet Pakistan's prime minister Sharif, and the two signed the Lahore Declaration, agreeing to "intensify their efforts to resolve all issues, including the issue of Jammu and Kashmir." Both leaders recognized that "the nuclear dimension of the security environment of the two countries adds to their responsibility for avoidance of conflict between the two countries."[15] The Lahore Declaration also included a commitment to "take immediate steps for reducing the risk of accidental or unauthorized use of nuclear weapons and discuss concepts and doctrines with a view to elaborating measures for confidence building in the nuclear and conventional fields, aimed at prevention of conflict." To this effect, a Memorandum of Understanding was signed that laid out specific nuclear confidence-building measures, including prior notification of ballistic missile tests, a continuation of their unilateral moratoria on nuclear testing, and dialogue on nuclear and security issues.

The summer 1999 incursion of Pakistani troops into Kargil, however, brought this diplomatic momentum to an abrupt halt. The Kargil conflict was the first between the two neighbors after the nuclear tests of 1998, and it destroyed any illusions that the overt nuclear postures of the two countries would act as a restraint on military conflict.[16] Instead, new thinking emerged in India on "limited war," which proponents argued could be fought under a nuclear umbrella. Indeed, after the Kargil conflict, some Indian strategists proffered scenarios of limited war under the nuclear shadow, precisely because they wanted to demonstrate that their nuclear weapons did not have a restraining effect on India. Indian aircraft bombed Pakistani positions in Indian-administered Kashmir, but never over the line of control, largely because Indian political leaders did not want to risk escalation to a wider war, but partly to demonstrate that they were responsible nuclear stewards. Conversely, the nuclear tests appear to have emboldened Pakistan to launch an offensive against India. Alarmed by the potential for escalation, officials of the Bill Clinton administration intervened diplomatically. Under U.S. pressure, Sharif's government withdrew Pakistani troops from Kargil. This withdrawal contributed to his political downfall, however, when in October 1999 his government was overthrown in a military coup, bringing General Pervez Musharraf to power. Because the Indians regarded Musharraf as the chief architect of the Kargil incursion, relations between the two countries deteriorated further.

India and Pakistan held talks once again in July 2001, to set up mechanisms for future negotiations. The three-day Agra summit between Vajpayee and Musharraf ended abruptly without a joint declaration and was deemed a failure.[17] Relations took a turn for the worse in October 2001, when a militant attack on the State Assembly in Indian-administered Kashmir claimed 38 lives. This revived Indian charges against Pakistan for sponsoring cross-border terrorism.[18]

Relations between India and Pakistan took a precipitous turn after the terrorist attack on India's parliament in early December 2001. Both countries mobilized a large number of troops along the border in Kashmir, raising fears of a wider war. This massive troop buildup, combined with alarming rhetoric, once again raised the specter of a nuclear confrontation in South Asia. Most of 2002 was spent on nuclear brinkmanship, punctuated with gestures to pull back from the brink.[19]

India's brinkmanship was, in part, a means of pressuring the George W. Bush administration to expand its focus on the war on terrorism to include Pakistan's eastern border. In these efforts, however, India's Bharatiya Janata Party–led government was wary of entirely alienating Washington. Domestic compulsions notwithstanding, both countries valued their close ties with the United States and were reluctant to jeopardize that relationship. This gave the United States additional leverage to buy time and engage the two adversaries to help prevent a potential disaster.

U.S. diplomacy was helpful, and by September–October 2002, Indian forces had pulled back. Musharraf's willingness to publicly affirm that he will not "permit any territory under Pakistan's control to be used to support terrorism in any manner" was critical to pushing the process along.[20] This antiterrorism language in a January 2003 joint statement reassured the Indian government. The two countries then embarked on a "composite dialogue" process that meets India's requirements because it departs from the "centrality" of the Kashmir issue, and meets Pakistan's requirements because it keeps the Kashmir issue on the table. These South Asian semantics may seem trivial, but they were critical in getting the peace process moving. In April 2003, citing a need for a "new beginning," then–Indian prime minister Vajpayee offered to resume dialogue with Pakistan,[21] and full diplomatic ties were incrementally restored over the next few months, including a cease-fire along the line of control in Kashmir.[22] While visiting the region in May 2003, then–U.S. deputy secretary of state Richard Armitage said that he was "cautiously optimistic" that Vajpayee's diplomatic opening "could possibly lead to a step-by-step process that would eventually resolve all issues."[23]

During Armitage's May 2003 visit to Pakistan, President Musharraf reassured him that he would take action against the terrorist camps. Significantly, Pakistan banned Hizbul Mujahideen activities in Pakistan-controlled Kashmir. This group was designated a "terrorist group" by the U.S. State Department just before Armitage's visit to Islamabad. Pakistan also barred the leader of the outlawed Jaish-e-Mohammed, who was behind the December 2001 attack on India's Parliament, from entering Pakistani-controlled Kashmir. These U.S.-secured steps were essential to the return of diplomacy in South Asia.[24]

The rapprochement continued in January 2004, when President Musharraf and Prime Minister Vajpayee met for the first time since 2001. Kashmir was part of an agenda that included terrorism, drug trafficking, and economic cooperation. The two countries restored air links, exchanged ambassadors, and worked on confidence-building measures, including the details of an agreement on advance notification of missile tests and establishing a hotline.[25]

After Vajpayee's defeat in the general elections in India in April 2004, the new prime minister, Manmohan Singh, also pledged to work for peace between India and Pakistan. By the end of June 2004, as part of nuclear confidence-building measures, they had set up a hotline between their countries' foreign secretaries to avoid a nuclear confrontation, and had extended their moratorium on nuclear tests.[26] The talks and cautious optimism continued into the spring of 2005.

Nuclear Analysis

Pakistan secretly launched its nuclear weapons program in 1972. The program acquired further momentum after India' s nuclear test in May 1974. Libya and Saudi Arabia funded the program in its early years.[27] The weapon effort focused substantially on the production of highly enriched uranium with technology gained covertly during the late 1970s and 1980s. This was expedited by the return to Pakistan in 1975 of Abdul Qadeer Khan, a German-trained metallurgist who in the early 1970s was employed at the classified Urenco uranium enrichment plant at Almelo in the Netherlands. Khan brought to Pakistan personal knowledge of gas-centrifuge equipment and industrial suppliers (primarily in Europe). He was eventually put in charge of building, equipping, and operating Pakistan's Kahuta enrichment facility. He also reportedly returned to Pakistan with stolen plans for European centrifuges, which were later improved and formed the core of the black market network he headed (see below).

The Pakistani nuclear weapons effort relied on a massive smuggling program, which began with the clandestine acquisition of key technology for the Kahuta plant from the Netherlands. It included the illicit import of an entire facility from West Germany for producing uranium hexafluoride. It also involved duplicitous procurement from Canada, China, France, Italy, Switzerland, the United Kingdom, and the United States.[28]

Since 1979, Pakistan's nuclear program has repeatedly brought the country under U.S. sanctions, which have been intermittently waived as a result of developments in Afghanistan. The 1979 economic and military aid cutoff was made pursuant to the 1977 Glenn-Symington Amendment to the U.S. Foreign Assistance Act. This amendment requires the termination of assistance to any state that has imported uranium enrichment equipment or technology since 1977 and that has refused to place it under inspection by the International Atomic Energy Agency (IAEA). In 1981, in the wake of the Soviet occupation of Afghanistan, the United States suspended the application of the uranium enrichment sanctions for six years. Instead, Washington provided greatly increased military and economic assistance to Pakistan to create a bulwark against further Soviet expansion and to establish Pakistan as a strategic partner in the Cold War. Officials of Ronald Reagan's administration also argued that the restoration of aid would advance U.S. nonproliferation objectives by enhancing Pakistan's overall security, thereby reducing Islamabad's motivation to acquire nuclear arms.

Pakistan, however, continued its nuclear weapons program, which reached a key milestone in 1985, when it crossed the threshold of being able to produce weapons-grade uranium, despite numerous pledges to the United States that it would not do so. By 1986, Pakistan had apparently produced enough material to make its first nuclear device. Although the United States sought to discourage Pakistan from pursuing its nuclear program throughout this period, Washington restrained its pressure on Islamabad because of Pakistan's role in the campaign to oust Soviet forces from Afghanistan. Pakistani sources now state that the nation acquired its first nuclear explosive capability in 1987, when they were reportedly considering a first test.[29] Some Pakistani experts say that the country had acquired a capability as early as 1984.[30]

The 1985 Pressler Amendement to the Foreign Assistance Act also reflected the Afghanistan-related ambivalence of U.S. policy toward Pakistan. This legislation specified that U.S. aid and government-to-government military sales to Pakistan would be cut off unless the president certified at the beginning of each U.S. fiscal year that Pakistan did "not possess a nuclear explosive device and that the proposed U.S. assistance program would significantly reduce the risk that Pakistan will possess a nuclear explosive device." However, despite further Pakistani nuclear weapons advances through October 1989, Presidents Ronald Reagan and then George H. W. Bush made the certifications necessary to permit U.S. aid and arms sales. The 1989 certification that Pakistan did not possess a nuclear device was, reportedly, made only after Pakistan's prime minister, Benazir Bhutto, agreed to suspend the further production of weapons-grade uranium.

In late 1989 and early 1990, perhaps because of the threat of war with India, Pakistan apparently ended this freeze. The country fabricated cores for several nuclear weapons from preexisting stocks of weapons-grade uranium. By this time, the Soviet army had left Afghanistan, and in October 1990, the George H. W. Bush administration was unable or unwilling to certify that Pakistan did not possess a nuclear explosive. The United States terminated all aid and government-to-government military sales to Pakistan. At the time, 28 additional F-16s and other military hardware were on order but were never transferred because of the sanctions. Islamabad continued making payments on the purchases after October 1990, hoping to receive these armaments in the event that the prohibition against such U.S. military sales was rescinded.

In late 1991, Prime Minister Sharif reinstated the freeze on the production of weapons-grade uranium, a freeze that reportedly held until the spring of 1998.[31] Pakistan continued to produce low-enriched uranium, however, thereby enlarging its total nuclear weapons potential. Other aspects of the Pakistani nuclear program also continued to advance—including work on nuclear weapon designs; the construction of a Chinese-designed and supplied plutonium production reactor of 40 megawatts thermal at Khushab; and the enlargement of Pakistan's capacity to enrich uranium, reportedly through the construction of an enrichment plant at Golra.

Throughout the 1990s, Pakistani specialists sought to improve the Kahuta enrichment plant and to expand the country's capacity to enrich uranium. The most publicized incident was Pakistan's purchase from China of 5,000 custom-made ring magnets, a key component of the bearings that support the high-speed rotation of centrifuges. The shipments of the magnets, sized to fit the type of centrifuge at the Kahuta plant, apparently began in December 1994 and continued until the Clinton administration became aware of the transaction in August 1995. It was not clear whether the ring magnets were intended for Kahuta as a "future reserve supply," or whether they were intended to permit Pakistan to increase its number of uranium enrichment centrifuges, either at Kahuta or at another location.

During the 1990s, U.S. aid to Pakistan was limited primarily to the country's refugee and narcotics problems, although congressional amendments allowed for some military sales to Pakistan. China's ring-magnet assistance to Pakistan, however, undercut the Clinton administration's efforts to restore a measure of nonproliferation influence in its relations with Pakistan. It prevented Pakistan from receiving economic or targeted military aid, which the administration and many legislators had earlier anticipated after the 1999 Brown Amendment, which modified the Pressler Amendment's sanctions.

Under the direction of the Atomic Energy Commission, Pakistan actively pursued a plutonium production capability during the 1990s. Its efforts came to fruition in April 1998, when it announced that the Khushab reactor had begun operation. This facility is not subject to IAEA inspections and is capable of generating enough plutonium for one or two nuclear weapons annually.[32] Access to plutonium can allow Pakistan to develop smaller and lighter nuclear warheads. This, in turn, would facilitate Pakistan's development of warheads for ballistic missiles.

Nuclear Tests and Nuclear Policy

In May 1998, Pakistan conducted a series of nuclear tests. There has been no official Pakistani statement on the types of weapons tested, but they are all thought to have employed a simple fission design. The tests appear to have been successful and to have validated Pakistan's design of a nuclear device with a yield of 10 to 15 kilotons.[33] Pakistan claims to have conducted five tests on May 28. The tests, however, produced only a single seismic signal, possibly the cumulative effect of simultaneous detonations, which indicated a total yield of 6 to 13 kilotons. The single signal led U.S. scientists to question whether five detonations did take place. An addition test or tests on May 30, 1998, produced a seismic signal equivalent to a yield of 2 to 8 kilotons.[34] The tests activated Glenn-Symington Amendment sanctions once more, ending the U.S. government's economic assistance and military transfers to Pakistan. But citing the need to work with both governments in the fight against terrorism and using the authority granted him by the "Brownback II" amendment of June 1999, President George W. Bush waived sanctions for Pakistan and India on September 22, 2001.[35]

In February 2000, Pakistan established the Nuclear Command Authority (NCA), which consists of two committees to advise President Musharraf on the employment and development of nuclear weapons.[36] The Army Strategic Plan Division (SPD) was also set up to better control nuclear weapons. It functions as the secretariat to the NCA.[37] The following year, Pakistan consolidated the Khan Research Laboratories and the rival Pakistan Atomic Research Corporation into one Nuclear Defense Complex, retiring A. Q. Khan from his leadership role at the former.

Pakistan has yet to officially enunciate a nuclear doctrine. Given India's overwhelming superiority in conventional weaponry, Pakistan rejects a "no-first-use" policy. However, there are some unofficial but authoritative pointers to the broad outlines of Pakistan's nuclear policy. In 1999, three highly influential Pakistani statesmen made the case for a "credible minimum nuclear deterrence."[38] In the absence of an agreement on mutual restraints with India, they posited that "the size of Pakistan's arsenal and its deployment pattern have to be adjusted to ward off dangers of pre-emption and interception." Further, they suggested that "a high state of alert will become more necessary as India proceeds with deployment of nuclear weapons."[39] In addition, the director of Pakistan's SPD, General Khalid Kidwai, has spoken of unofficial thresholds for nuclear use, where the country's existence is considered at stake:

> Nuclear weapons are aimed solely at India. In case that deterrence fails, they will be used if
>
> - India attacks Pakistan and conquers a large part of its territory (space threshold),
> - India destroys a large part either of its land or air forces (military threshold),
> - India proceeds to the economic strangling of Pakistan (economic strangling), and
> - India pushes Pakistan into political destabilization or creates a large scale internal subversion in Pakistan (domestic destabilization).[40]

How any of these principles may translate into operational policy is unclear. Pakistani officials have said that these thresholds are "purely academic"; however, they have not disavowed the parameters.[41]

Developments since September 11, 2001, have dramatically altered the U.S. policy on nuclear-based sanctions against Pakistan, which once again became a frontline state in a U.S. battle in Afghanistan, this time against international terrorism. As a result of President Musharraf's decision to cooperate with the United States in the war against terrorism, all nuclear-related sanctions were waived. The United States also waived the democracy-related sanctions that had been imposed on Pakistan after an army coup brought Musharraf to power in October 1999.

Musharraf justified his cooperation with the United States by telling his public that Pakistan's "strategic assets" were best protected by joining the U.S. coalition against international terrorism. In the aftermath of September 11, Musharraf may have calculated that this was the best way to diminish the possibility of a U.S preemptive strike against Pakistan. After the United States began bombing Afghanistan, Pakistan immediately dispersed different components of its nuclear assets to six locations.[42] Pakistani leaders may well have feared the possibility of a U.S. strike, given that Pakistan had actively supported the Taliban and that its intelligence service was intimately involved with Al Qaeda in Afghanistan.

The potential for civil unrest and instability inside Pakistan has raised international concern over the safety of its nuclear strategic assets. Some experts have urged the United States to offer Pakistan assistance in securing its fissile material and weapons from theft by outside terrorist groups.[43] Some Pakistani officials and nuclear experts believe the more likely risk may be that militants within the military or government could seize nuclear assets or provide expertise to others.[44] This specter was raised particularly when Pakistan arrested two of its nuclear scientists for alleged connections with members of the Taliban.[45]

A. Q. Khan and the Nuclear Black Market

In late 2003, IAEA investigations into Iran's nuclear program and Libya's decision to come clean on its clandestine nuclear and chemical weapons programs exposed the A. Q. Khan–led nuclear black market. It became public knowledge that A. Q. Khan was at the center of an illegal nuclear trafficking network, whose clients included Iran, Libya, North Korea, and possibly other countries. IAEA director general Mohamed ElBaradei called it "the Wal-Mart of private proliferation."[46]

Suspicions about Pakistan's nuclear exports have long persisted. Reports of Pakistan's assistance to Iran go back to 1988, and, as early as 1979, there were reports of Pakistan providing nuclear assistance to Libya.[47] The breadth and scale of the procurement, however, was startling. "When you see things being designed in one country, manufactured in two or three others, shipped to a fourth, redirected to a fifth, that means there's lots of offices all over the world," ElBaradei said, adding, "The sophistication of the process, frankly, has surpassed my expectations."[48]

For at least twelve years, Khan led this multinational black market export operation, which netted more than $100 million from Libya alone. It provided blueprints, technical design data, specifications, components, machinery, enrichment equipment, models, and notes on first-generation P-1 and the next-generation P-2 centrifuges.[49] Khan used transit points and middlemen in Dubai in the Persian Gulf, Germany, Malaysia, South Africa, Turkey, Switzerland, and the United Kingdom, among a list of about thirty countries.[50]

In February 2004, Khan confessed (in English on Pakistani television) to his proliferation crimes and took sole responsibility, in exchange for a full pardon from President Musharraf. Musharraf maintains that Khan ran a private enterprise that had nothing to do with the government. This assertion is implausible, however, given the highly sensitive nature of the trade and the fact that Pakistan's military controls the country's nuclear assets.[51] Even if the military leaders did not formally authorize the transfers, they should have known about and stopped the transfers. And Pakistani military cargo planes transported missiles from North Korea to Pakistan—systems for which North Korea may have accepted nuclear assistance instead of hard currency—suggesting the military's complicity. Khan's nuclear black market trade spanned the civilian governments of Prime Ministers Benazir Bhutto and Nawaz Sharif and the military-led government of President Musharraf. Khan's full pardon raises the possibility that the military wanted to ensure that he did not reveal details that would have incriminated its leadership.

IAEA investigations of Iran's nuclear program reveal that Tehran acquired centrifuge equipment from Khan's black market sources. Iran purchased P-1 and P-2 centrifuge designs through the Khan network, which transferred components and weapon-related designs and drawings between 1989 and 1991.[52] Pakistani officials say Khan met personally with Iranian scientists in both Pakistan and Malaysia.[53] His personal travels are another piece of evidence that the Pakistani government was aware of at least some of his illegal activities, because all his international trips were presumably tracked.

Between 1991 and 1997, Khan supplied Libya with actual designs for nuclear weapons, along with some complete centrifuge rotor assemblies.[54] Libya's warhead blueprints were the first evidence that the black market had provided its customers with far more than just uranium enrichment technology. Libya reportedly bought those blueprints from Khan's dealers for more than $50 million.[55] The blueprints were copies of the design that China had apparently transferred to Pakistan in the 1960s and reportedly had notations in Chinese from Chinese engineers and designers.[56]

Since the discovery of North Korea's clandestine uranium enrichment program, U.S. intelligence officials have claimed that Pakistan supplied enrichment equipment to Pyongyang in exchange for Nodong missiles.[57] It was reported that North Korea ordered P-1 centrifuge components from 1997 to 2000.[58] Between 1997 and 2002, Khan reportedly made thirteen trips to North Korea. One visit occurred as late as June 2002, calling into question the Musharraf government's claims that such transfers had stopped in 2000 after the military took necessary action.[59]

Musharraf has insisted that no independent authority, including the IAEA, will be allowed to interrogate Khan. This denial of direct access to Khan has impeded a comprehensive investigation. Despite the grave consequences of Khan's activities, Musharraf's role as an ally in the war on terrorism and domestic sensitivities in Pakistan have led the United States to publicly downplay any concerns it may have that Musharraf or the government was directly involved.[60] There remains little assurance that the exports have ended permanently, in large part because the full extent of the operations is not yet known. Furthermore, Pakistan still requires imports to maintain its own nuclear weapons capability. Thus, it is possible that the country's leaders do not favorably view a permanent and full dismantling of this existing international procurement system because of Pakistan's continuing reliance on nuclear-weapon-related imports. There is also the possibility that secondary operatives might now launch their own lucrative nuclear businesses. Mohamed ElBaradei has called Khan "the tip of an iceberg," saying that Khan was not operating alone. His case "raises more questions than it answers," ElBardei has noted.[61]

U.N. Security Council Resolution 1540 and Pakistan's Export Control Law

The Khan black market network revealed both the gaping loopholes in Pakistan's domestic export control laws and the glaring gap in international law and enforcement capabilities to prosecute such illicit trade. In April 2004, the U.N. Security Council unanimously passed Resolution 1540, requiring states to criminalize such trade and prosecute their practitioners. That is, states are held fully responsible for the illicit proliferation activity that occurs within their jurisdiction.

Pakistan had passed export legislation in July 1998, February 1999, August 1999, and again in November 2000. Several loopholes and contradictions permeated these laws (for example, the military is exempted), and, facing increased international pressure, Pakistan passed a new export control bill on July 7, 2004. The National Assembly and the Senate ratified the legislation on September 19, 2004.[62]

The new law prohibits the diversion of controlled goods and technologies, including reexport, transshipment, and transit; requires licensing and record keeping; establishes export control lists and penal provisions of up to fourteen years imprisonment and a fine of PRs 5 million (about $86,500). Its jurisdiction closes some of the previous loopholes and exemptions, extending over all of Pakistan and to every Pakistani, a person in the service of Pakistan within or outside Pakistan, or any Pakistani visiting or working abroad. It would also cover any foreign national in Pakistan. The shipment and transfer of nuclear and biological technology via ground transport, ships, and aircraft registered in Pakistan is also criminalized. The act describes "technology" as a document, information in the public domain or related to basic scientific research for peaceful or provocative purpose to kill anyone.[63]

The act also calls for the creation of an oversight board to administer export control regulations, enforcement of the act, and licensing for export and reexport of nuclear- and biological-related goods and technology. Furthermore, exporters will also be required to maintain records of all transactions and report them to the designated government agencies. All agencies involved in the licensing process will be required to maintain records of all relevant recommendations and decisions. The control lists of items subject to licensing requirements will be reviewed periodically and updated as required by the government.[64]

This may well be a positive step, as long as Pakistan's civilian governments and army were not complicit in the A. Q. Khan nuclear black market and the authorities are willing and able to enforce the laws. If, however, that was the case, and state enforcement is weak, then no set of legal changes will be sufficient in a country where the rule of law is not guaranteed.

Missile and Aircraft Analysis

Throughout the 1990s, U.S. officials believed that the U.S.-supplied F-16s, which could be equipped to arm nuclear weapons in flight, were the most likely means of delivering a Pakistani nuclear weapon. There are reports that some of these have already been modified to carry nuclear weapons.[65]

The development of several mature ballistic missile systems—primarily with assistance from China and North Korea—has now given Pakistan the means to deliver nuclear weapons by missile as well.[66] Pakistan's efforts to acquire ballistic missiles began in the early 1980s and intensified in the mid-1980s when, with Chinese assistance, it launched a program to develop two short-range ballistic missile systems: the 80-kilometer-range Hatf I and the 300-kilometer-range Hatf II. Pakistan also sought to acquire from China the 280- to 300-kilometer range, nuclear-capable M-11 ballistic missile system (known in Pakistan as the Hatf III), along with associated equipment. Later, Pakistan procured longer-range systems, including the Ghauri and Shaheen systems; the former is North Korean technology and the latter Chinese.

Before 2001, Pakistan used a dual-track approach for its ballistic missile development. Competing development projects pitted the North Korean, liquid-fueled Ghauri missiles of Khan Research Laboratories against the Chinese, solid-fueled Shaheen missiles of the Pakistan Atomic Energy Commission. Rivalry between these two organizations has probably driven the country's missile program, in terms of both procurement and pace.[67]

In July 1997, on the heels of India's semideployment of the Prithvi short-range missile in Punjab, Pakistan reportedly tested the Hatf III, a nuclear-capable 300-kilometer-range ballistic missile.[68] This missile is operational, and it was tested on November 29, 2004.

On April 6, 1998, before India's nuclear tests in May, Pakistan tested the Ghauri I missile, which has a range of upward of 1,300 kilometers and carries a payload estimated at 500 to 750 kilograms.[69] The Ghauri, based on North Korea's No Dong, is Pakistan's only liquid-fueled missile, and it is launched from a road-mobile launcher.[70] In January 2003, Pakistan announced that the Ghauri had been handed over to the army.[71] The most recent Ghauri flight test occurred on October 12, 2004. Meanwhile, Pakistan continues to develop the Ghauri II, with a range of approximately 2,000 kilometers. In April 1999, after India's test of the 2,000-kilometer Agni II, Pakistan claimed to have successfully tested the Ghauri II. Finally, a third version of the Ghauri, the Ghauri III, with an unconfirmed range of 2,700 to 3,500 kilometers, is under development and was test launched on August 15, 2000. Its development has recently slowed, however, and a test launch scheduled for June 2004 never occurred.

Pakistan also successfully tested the 750-kilometer, solid-fueled, nuclear-capable Shaheen I (also called the Hatf IV) in April 1999. This missile, possibly a derivative of the Chinese M-9, is capable of carrying a 500-kilogram payload. The Pakistani Hatf III (M-11) with a 280-kilometer-range capability, would probably not be able to reach India's capital, New Delhi, from Pakistani territory. However, the Shaheen I (M-9) could target not only New Delhi but possibly also reach as far as Mumbai (Bombay), India's largest industrial city. In early 2001, Pakistan announced serial production of the Shaheen I, adding that the missile had been "inducted" into the army. It was tested on October 8, 2002;[72] a year later on October 8 and 14, 2003; and on December 8, 2004.

The Shaheen II, a solid-fueled missile, was displayed in a March 2000 parade, and it was tested for the first time in March 2004. Pakistan claims that both tests were successful.[73] The two-stage Shaheen-II medium-range missile is said by the Pakistani government to have a full range of 2,500 kilometers and to carry a 1,000-kilogram payload. Neither the Shaheen I nor II is reported to have a nuclear capability as of the spring of 2005, though they both have the potential.

In the fall of 2004, India and Pakistan agreed to develop a formal system for early notification of missile tests. The measure was a result of the high-level diplomacy over the summer between the two rivals.[74]

Foreign Assistance

Although Chinese assistance has been critical to the progress of Pakistan's ballistic missile programs, official Chinese assistance has largely petered out since 2001. Some concern continues to linger, however, over Chinese entities. The U.S. government states that assistance from Chinese entities has helped Pakistan move toward domestic serial production of the solid propellant Shaheen submarine-launched ballistic missiles and has supported Pakistan's development of solid-propellant Shaheen medium-range ballistic missiles.[75] It appears that the overall decline in Chinese assistance has left Pakistan turning to North Korea as an alternative supplier. Pakistan may have also turned to North Korea because of the above-mentioned rivalry between the Pakistan Atomic Research Corporation and the Khan Research Laboratories.[76]

North Korea's assistance has been crucial to Pakistan's medium-range Ghauri missile program.[77] The Ghauri is virtually a renamed No Dong missile. The relationship between Pyongyang and Islamabad was established between 1992 and 1995 during Prime Minister Benazir Bhutto's tenure. In 1992, Pakistani officials visited North Korea to view a No Dong prototype, and in May 1993, Pakistani engineers and scientists watched the No Dong test launch. Prime Minister Bhutto visited Pyongyang in December 1993 to set the stage for a missile deal, which was finally brokered in late 1995. Actual work on the Ghauri missile began in 1993 with North Korean assistance, after Bhutto first visited Pyongyang.[78] As part of their missile agreements, North Korea also transferred complete missile systems (the No Dong) to Pakistan.[79]

The missile cooperation became public when Pakistan first tested the Ghauri missile in April 1998 in the presence of North Koreans, who reportedly helped with the test launch. Consequently, the United States imposed Missile Technology Control Regime sanctions on the Khan Research Laboratories and on North Korea's Changgwang Sinyong Corporation. The relationship continued, however, under Prime Minister Nawaz Sharif. In 1999, Indian custom officials seized a North Korean ship off India's western coastline that was carrying missile components and metal casings to Pakistan. Indian officials also found 22 technical manuals for Scud-type missiles.[80]

The A. Q. Khan black market revelations have shed more light on long-held suspicions that this missile technology was provided in return for Pakistan's assistance with gas-centrifuge uranium enrichment technology, which was under the purview of the Khan Research Laboratories. The exchange may have also given North Korea a means of testing its missiles, even while it maintains a self-imposed moratorium on missile flight tests. This relationship has continued under the Musharraf regime, with North Korean missile experts reportedly working in Pakistan.[81]

In March 2003, the United States imposed sanctions against the Khan Research Laboratory, which produces the Ghauri systems, and against a North Korean entity, Changgwang Sinyong Corporation, "for specific missile-related transfers" that occurred in the summer of 2002.[82] The sanctions reportedly involved the transfer of fully assembled, nuclear-capable No Dong missiles from North Korea to Pakistan.[83] Despite President Musharraf's assurances that such a relationship no longer exists, it is unclear whether or not this relationship has been terminated since the fall of 2002.[84]

NOTES

1. This estimate is extrapolated from David Albright, *India's and Pakistan's Fissile Material and Nuclear Weapons Inventories, End of 1999* (Washington, D.C.: Institute for Science and International Security, 2000), available at www.isis-online.org/publications/southasia/stocks1000.html; and David Albright and Kimberly Kramer, "Fissile Materials: Stockpiles Still Growing," *Bulletin of Atomic Scientists*, November/December 2004, pp. 14–16.
2. Ibid. Weapons estimates are based on 13 to 18 kilograms of HEU per weapon. For a similar estimate based on 15–20 kilograms per weapon, see "NRDC Nuclear Notebook," *Bulletin of the Atomic Scientists*, January/February 2002, pp. 70–71.
3. Paulo Cotta-Ramusino and Maurizio Martellini, "Nuclear Safety, Nuclear Stability and Nuclear Strategy in Pakistan," a concise report of a visit by Landau Network–Centro Volta, January 21, 2002, available at www.pugwash.org/september11/pakistan-nuclear.htm; and George Perkovich, "Pakistan's Nuclear Dilemma," Carnegie Proliferation Roundtable, September 26, 2001.
4. Albright and Cramer, "Fissile Materials," pp. 14–16.
5. Natural Resources Defense Council, "Nuclear Notebook," www.nrdc.org/nuclear/nudb/datab21.asp.
6. Ibid.
7. See "Pakistan Blasts Indian Missile Test." CNN News Online, January 9, 2003.
8. Arms Control Association, "Chemical and Biological Weapons Proliferation at a Glance," September 2002, available at www.armscontrol.org/factsheets/cbwprolif.asp.
9. Ibid.
10. General Mirza Aslam Beg, "Pakistan's Nuclear Propriety," *Pakistan Observer*, April 9, 1999.
11. Testimony of John Deutch, director of central intelligence, "Current and Projected National Security Threats to the United States and Its Interests Abroad," Select Committee on Intelligence, U.S. Senate, February 22, 1996, p. 12.
12. George Perkovich, *India's Nuclear Bomb: The Impact on Global Proliferation* (Berkeley: University of California Press, 1999), p. 413.
13. Ibid., p. 433.
14. Pervez Hoodbhoy, "Nuclear Nirvana," *Carnegie Non-Proliferation Project Issue Brief*, vol. 3, no. 33, November 16, 2000; available at www.proliferationnews.org.
15. "The Lahore Declaration," February 21, 1999, available on the Carnegie Non-Proliferation web site at www.proliferationnews.org.
16. Hoodbhoy, "Nuclear Nirvana."
17. Pamela Constable, "India, Pakistan Trade Blame over Summit," *Washington Post*, July 18, 2001.
18. Rajiv Chandrasekaran, "Tension Rises in Volatile Kashmir; Pakistan Bristles at Indian Shelling; Anti-Terror Coalition Faces Challenge," *Washington Post*, October 16, 2001.
19. Amy Waldman and David Rohde, "India and Pakistan: The Dispute Burns On," *New York Times*, October 22, 2002.
20. Miriam Rajkumar, "Peace Process in South Asia," Carnegie Analysis, February 19, 2004; available at www.proliferationnews.org.
21. Amy Waldman, "Indian Leader, in Kashmir, Extends Olive Branch to Pakistan," *New York Times*, April 19, 2003.
22. Hari Kumar, "Indian and Pakistani Forces Agree to Cease-Fire in Kashmir," *New York Times*, November 26, 2003.
23. Miriam Rajkumar, "Spring Thaw in South Asia," Carnegie Analysis, May 20, 2003; available at www.proliferationnews.org.
24. Rajkumar, "Spring Thaw in South Asia."
25. B. Muralidhar Reddy, "Talks on Nuclear, Conventional CBMs from Tomorrow," *The Hindu*, December 13, 2004.
26. Rahul Bedi, "India, Pakistan Agree Nuclear Hotline," *Jane's Defense Weekly*, July 7, 2004.
27. Leonard Weiss, "Pakistan: It's Deja-Vu All Over Again," *Bulletin of the Atomic Scientists*, May/June 2004, pp. 52–59.

28. Weiss, "Pakistan." For an overview, see Leonard Spector and Jacqueline R. Smith, *Nuclear Ambitions* (Boulder, Colo.: Westview Press, 1990), chaps, 4, 7.
29. General Mirza Aslam Beg, "Pakistan's Nuclear Propriety," National Development and Security, *Friends Quarterly Journal*, 2000.
30. Ramusino and Martellini, "Nuclear Safety."
31. Gregory Jones, *From Testing to Deploying Nuclear Forces: The Hard Choices Facing India and Pakistan*, Issue Paper 192 (Santa Monica, Calif.: Rand, 2000).
32. This assumes 4 to 5 kilograms of plutonium per bomb.
33. Jones, *From Testing to Deploying Nuclear Forces.*
34. Ibid. See also William J. Broad, "Explosion Is Detected by U.S. Scientists," *New York Times*, May 29, 1998; and Michael Hirsh and John Barry, "Nuclear Jitters," *Newsweek*, June 8, 1998, p. 24.
35. Alex Wagner, "Bush Waives Nuclear-Related Sanctions on India, Pakistan," *Arms Control Today*, October 2001.
36. U.S. Department of Defense (DOD), *Proliferation: Threat and Response* (Washington, D.C.: DOD, 2001).
37. For details on this setup, see Ramusino and Martellini, "Nuclear Safety."
38. Agha Shahi, Zulfikar Ali Khan, and Abdul Sattar, "Securing Nuclear Peace," *News and Dawn*, October 5, 1999.
39. Shahi, Khan, and Sattar, "Securing Nuclear Peace."
40. Ramusino and Martellini, "Nuclear Safety."
41. Ibid.
42. M. Ijaz and R. J. Woolsey, "How Secure Is Pakistan's Plutonium? *New York Times*, November 28, 2001; and Ramusino and Martellini, "Nuclear Safety."
43. Jon Wolfsthal, "U.S. Needs a Contingency Plan for Pakistan's Nuclear Arsenal," *Los Angeles Times*, October 16, 2001. Also see Seymour Hersh, "Watching the Warheads: Pakistan's Nuclear Weapons at Risk," *New Yorker*, October 26, 2001.
44. Ramusino and Martellini, "Nuclear Safety."
45. Ibid.
46. Mark Lander, "UN Official Sees a 'Wal-Mart' in Nuclear Trafficking," *Washington Post*, January 23, 2004.
47. Weiss, "Pakistan."
48. Lander, "UN Official Sees a 'Wal-Mart' in Nuclear Trafficking."
49. Gaurav Kampani, "Proliferation Unbound: Nuclear Tales from Pakistan," Center for Nonproliferation Studies, Monterey Institute of International Studies, February 23, 2004.
50. Faye Brown, "Pakistan's Disturbing Nuclear Trail," *Christian Science Monitor*, October 27, 2004.
51. "Ending Pakistan's Nuclear Trade," *New York Times*, February 7, 2004; and Weiss, "Pakistan."
52. The "P" refers to Pakistani origin/design.
53. "A. Q. Khan: Nuclear Rogue," *India Today*, February 16, 2004, p. 32.
54. Congressional Research Service, "Weapons of Mass Destruction: Trade between North Korea and Pakistan," Report for Congress, March 11, 2004, p. 10.
55. William J. Board and David E. Sanger, "Warhead Blueprints Link Libya Project to Pakistan Figure," *New York Times*, February 4, 2004.
56. Broad and Sanger, "Warhead Blueprints."
57. Congressional Research Service, "Weapons of Mass Destruction," p. 1.
58. Ibid., p. 10.
59. "A. Q. Khan," p. 29.
60. Congressional Research Service, "Pakistan's Nuclear Proliferation Activities and the Recommendations of the 9/11 Commission: U.S. Policy Constraints and Options," Report for Congress, January 25, 2005, pp. 24–25.
61. "Pakistani Scientist Tied to Illicit Nuclear Supply Network," *Washington Post,* February 4, 2004.
62. "Export Control on Goods, Technologies, Material, and Equipment Related to Nuclear and Biological Weapons and their Delivery Systems Act." Pakistan submitted a copy to the IAEA on

November 4, 2004, available at www.iaea.org/Publications/Documents/Infcircs/2004/infcirc636.pdf.

63. "14 Years in Jail, Rs 5m Fine for N-Proliferation," *Daily Times,* May 6, 2004.

64. Shi-chin Lin, "The A. Q. Khan Revelations and Subsequent Changes to Pakistani Export Controls," Center for Nonproliferation Studies, October 2004, www.nti.org/e_research/e3_54a.html.

65. Center for Defense Information, "Summary of Pakistan's Possible Nuclear Delivery Systems," www.cdi.org/news/nuclear/nuclear-arsenals.pdf, and www.nrdc.org/nuclear/nudb/datab21.asp.

66. DOD, *Proliferation: Threat and Response,* 2001.

67. Najum Mushtaq, "Pakistan: Khan Forced Out," *Bulletin of the Atomic Scientists,* vol. 57, no. 04, July/August 2001; and R. Ramachandran, "Pakistan's Ballistic Response," *Frontline,* vol. 16, issue 9, April 24–May 7, 1999.

68. The Prithvi has since been moved to a "strategic" location, to Secunderabad in southern India.

69. "Pakistan Tests Medium-Range Missile," *Washington Post,* April 7, 1998.

70. Jones, *From Testing to Deploying Nuclear Forces.*

71. See "Pakistan Blasts Indian Missile Test," CNN News Online, January 9, 2003.

72. "India, Pakistan Conduct Missile Tests," *Arms Control Today,* November 2002.

73. Maria A. Khan with Atta ul Mohsin, "Ballistic Missile: Pakistan Test-Fires Shaheen II," *Pakistan Times,* March 10, 2004.

74. Gabrielle Kohlmeier, "India, Pakistan Seek Missile Test Pact," *Arms Control Today,* September 2004.

75. Central Intelligence Agency, "Attachment A: Unclassified Report to Congress on the Acquisition of Technology Relating to Weapons of Mass Destruction and Advanced Conventional Munitions, 1 January through 30 June 2003," available at www.cia.gov/cia/reports/721_reports/jan_jun2003.htm#17.

76. Joseph S. Bermudez Jr., "A History of Ballistic Missile Development in the DPRK," Occasional Paper 2, Center for Nonproliferation Studies, November 1999.

77. For an excellent synopsis of this relationship, see "Pakistan and North Korea: Dangerous Counter-Trades," *Strategic Comments* (International Institute for Strategic Studies), vol. 8, issue 9, November 2002.

78. Suzanne Goldenberg, "Pakistan Helped North Korea Make Bomb," *Guardian,* October 19, 2002.

79. "Pakistan and North Korea: Dangerous Counter-Trades."

80. "Pakistan and North Korea: Dangerous Counter-Trades."

81. For a good synopsis of this relationship, see "Pakistan and North Korea: Dangerous Counter-Trades."

82. Rose Gordon, "North Korea, Pakistani Lab Sanctioned for Proliferation," *Arms Control Today,* May 2003.

83. "Pakistan Nuclear Update 2003," *Risk Report* (Wisconsin Project on Nuclear Arms Control), November–December 2003.

84. "Pakistan and North Korea: Dangerous Counter-Trades."

Table 12.1. **Pakistan's Nuclear Infrastructure**

Name/Location of Facility	Type/Status	IAEA Safeguards
Nuclear Weapons Research & Development Complex		
Khan Research Laboratories (KRL) Kahuta	Fabrication of HEU into nuclear weapon	No
Ras Koh	Site of nuclear tests conducted in 1998	No
Kharan Desert	Site of nuclear tests conducted in 1998	No
Pakistan Ordnance Factory, Wah	Possible nuclear weapons assembly site	No
Power Reactors		
KANUPP Karachi	Heavy-water, nat. U, 137 MWe, operating	Yes
KANUPP-2	600 MWe, planned	Planned
Chasma-1/ Chasnupp 1	Light-water, LEU, 325 MWe, operating	Yes
Chasma-2/ Chasnupp 2	Light-water, LEU, 310 MWe, planned	Planned
Research Reactors		
Pakistan Atomic Research Reactor 1 (PARR 1) Rawalpindi	Pool-type, Light-water, originally HEU, modified to use LEU, 10 MWt, operating (may have been used clandestinely to produce tritium for advanced nuclear weapons)	Yes
PARR 2 Rawalpindi	MNSR, light-water, HEU, 30 KWt, operating	Yes
Research/Plutonium Production Reactor Khushab	Heavy-water, nat. U, 50 MWt, operating	No
Uranium Enrichment		
Khan Research Laboratories (KRL) Kahuta	Large-scale ultracentrifuge facility, operating Capacity 5,000 Swu/y will expand to 15,000	No
Sihala	Ultracentrifuge Pilot plant of 54 ultra-centrifuges, operating	No
Golra	Ultracentrifuge plant reportedly to be used as a testing facility, operational status unknown	No

Gadwal	Enrichment plant	
Reprocessing (Plutonium Extraction)		
Chasma	Partially built and terminated by France (1978), indigenous construction of the building shell may be complete, operational status unknown	No
New laboratories, SPINSTECH Rawalpindi	Pilot-scale, French design, capacity for 10-20 kg/year, operational status unclear	No
PINSTECH Rawalpindi	Experimental-scale laboratory for research on solvent extraction	No
Uranium Processing		
Baghalchar	Uranium mining, closed	No
Dera Ghazi Khan	Uranium ore processing, U308 production, operating	No
Issa Khel	Uranium ore processing, U308 production, planned	No
Qabul Khel, near Issa Khel	Uranium ore processing, operating	No
Lahore	Pilot-scale uranium mill, operating	No
Dera Ghazi Khan	Uranium conversion (UF_6), operating, annual production 23tu, capacity 30tu	No
Chasma/Kundian	Fuel fabrication, PHWR, operating	No
Heavy-Water Production[1]		
Multan	Supplied by Belgium, 13 MT/year, operating	No
Karachi	Water Upgrading plant, 15 MT/year, operating	No
Teitium		
Tritium Production Facility	Can produce 5-10 grams/day, acquired from West Germany in 1987 and tested in 1987, located 150 km south of Rawalpindi (Khushab)	No
Storage		
Hawks Bay Depot Karachi	Operating	Yes

(table continues on the following page)

Table 12.1. **Pakistan's Nuclear Infrastructure** (continued)

ABBREVIATIONS

HEU	highly enriched uranium
LEU	low-enriched uranium
nat. U	natural uranium
MWe	megawatts electric
MWt	megawatts thermal
kWt	kilowatts thermal

SOURCES

Nuclear Engineering International, *2004 World Nuclear Industry Handbook* (Sidcup, U.K.: Wilmington Publishing, 2004. International Atomic Energy Agency (IAEA), "Research Reactor Database (RRDB)," available at www.iaea.org/worldatom/rrdb/. IAEA, "Power Reactor Information System (PRIS)," available at www.iaea.org/programmes/a2/index.html. Global Security, "Pakistan Special Weapons Facilities," available at www.globalsecurity.org/wmd/world/pakistan/facility.htm. Andrew Koch and Jennifer Topping, "Pakistan's Nuclear-Related Facilities," *Nonproliferation Review,* vol. 4, no. 3, available at http://cns.miis.edu/pubs/reports/pdfs/9707paki.pdf. Anthony Cordesman and Arleigh Burke, "The Threat of Pakistani Nuclear Weapons," Center for Strategic and International Studies," November 8, 2001, available at www.csis.org/burke/hd/reports/threat_pak_nukes.pdf.

NOTE

1. The nonproliferation regime does not include the application of safeguards to heavy-water production facilities, but safeguards are required on the export of heavy water.

CHAPTER 13

Israel

Nuclear Weapons Capability

Israel has an advanced nuclear weapons capability and is thought to possess enough nuclear material for between 100 and 170 nuclear weapons. Israel is not a party to the Non-Proliferation Treaty (NPT) and has not acknowledged that it has nuclear weapons. It is, however, indisputably regarded as a de facto nuclear weapon state. The exact number of weapons Israel has assembled is unknown but is more likely on the lower end of the possible range. In all, Israel may have produced between 530 and 684 kilograms of weapons-grade plutonium from the start of its nuclear research reactor at Dimona in early 1964 through the end of 2005.* It is, however, indisputably regarded as a de facto nuclear weapon state. The exact number of weapons Israel has assembled is unknown but is more likely on the lower end of the possible range. In all, Israel may have produced between 530 and 684 kilograms of weapons-grade plutonium from the start of its nuclear research reactor at Dimona in early 1964 through the end of 2005.[1] Plutonium separated from the fuel rods in the reactor allowed Israel to complete the development of its first nuclear device by late 1966 or 1967, becoming the sixth nation in the world to do so.[2] It remains the only nation in the Middle East with nuclear weapons. It is capable of delivering nuclear weapons by aircraft, ballistic missiles, and ship- and submarine-launched cruise missiles.

Aircraft and Missile Capability

As the most capable military power in the region, Israel fields both short-range Jericho I (500 kilometers, with a 750–1,000 kilogram payload) and medium-range (1,500 kilometers) Jericho II ballistic missiles. Both missiles use solid propellant and are nuclear-capable. Israel's successful satellite launches using the Shavit space launch vehicle suggest that it could quickly develop missile platforms with much longer ranges than the Jericho II. The development of the

*This weapons estimate is based on plutonium production data provided by the Institute for Science and International Security, or ISIS; see note 1. The weapons calculation is described later in this chapter. ISIS has an alternative calculation that yields a slightly larger range of possible weapons.

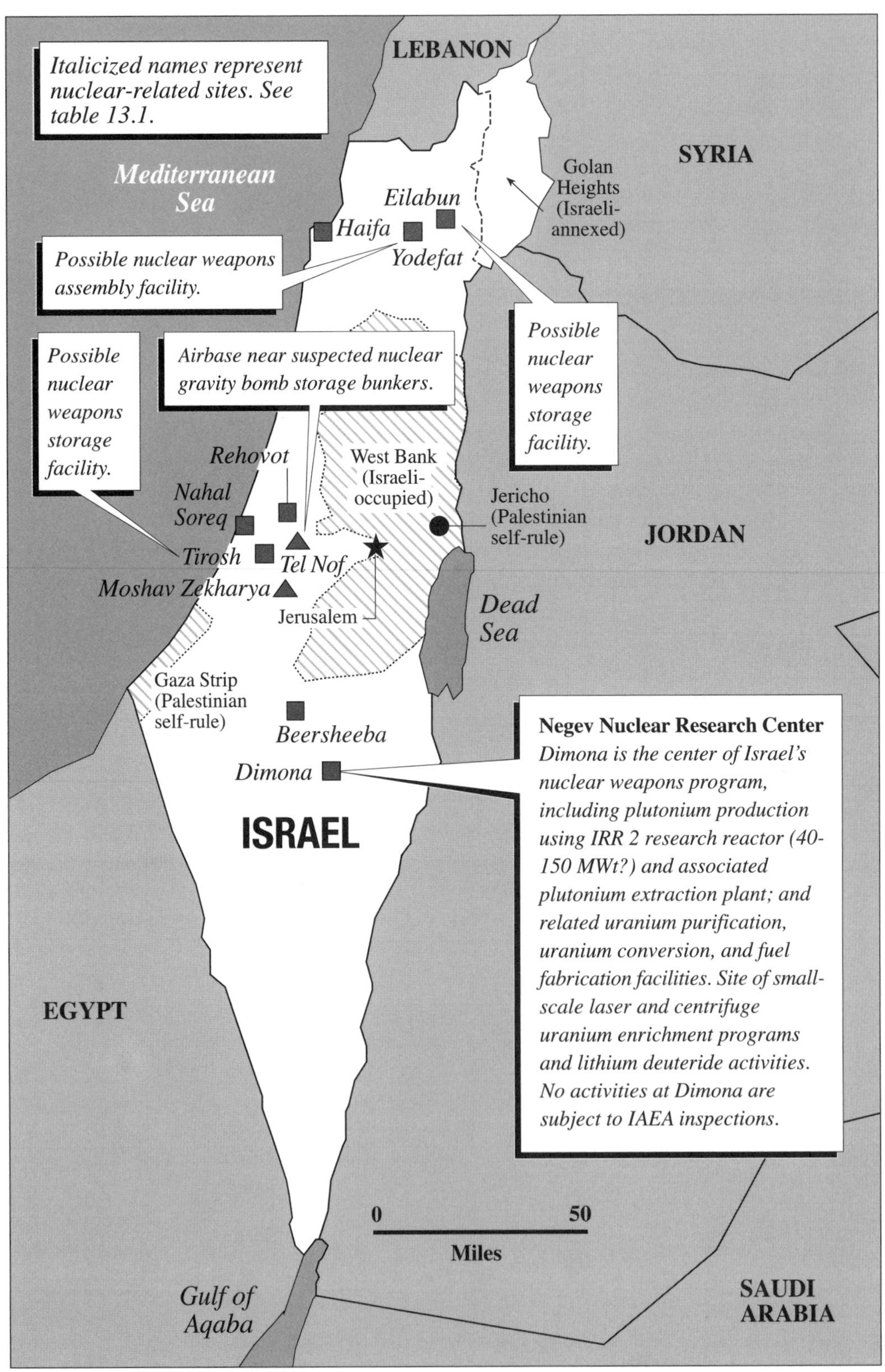
Italicized names represent nuclear-related sites. See table 13.1.
LEBANON
SYRIA
Mediterranean Sea
Golan Heights (Israeli-annexed)
Eilabun
Haifa
Yodefat
Possible nuclear weapons assembly facility.
Possible nuclear weapons storage facility.
Airbase near suspected nuclear gravity bomb storage bunkers.
Possible nuclear weapons storage facility.
Rehovot
West Bank (Israeli-occupied)
Nahal Soreq
Jericho (Palestinian self-rule)
JORDAN
Tirosh
Tel Nof
Moshav Zekharya
Jerusalem
Dead Sea
Gaza Strip (Palestinian self-rule)
Beersheeba
Dimona
Negev Nuclear Research Center
Dimona is the center of Israel's nuclear weapons program, including plutonium production using IRR 2 research reactor (40-150 MWt?) and associated plutonium extraction plant; and related uranium purification, uranium conversion, and fuel fabrication facilities. Site of small-scale laser and centrifuge uranium enrichment programs and lithium deuteride activities. No activities at Dimona are subject to IAEA inspections.
ISRAEL
EGYPT
0
50
Miles
Gulf of Aqaba
SAUDI ARABIA

single-stage Jericho I missile began in the early 1960s with French assistance, and the missile was first deployed in 1973. The development of the two-stage Jericho II began in the mid-1970s, with first deployment in 1990. The extended range and 1,000-kilogram payload of the Jericho II makes it a likely nuclear delivery vehicle. Both missiles are land- and rail-mobile. In all, Israel is believed to have deployed 100 Jericho missiles. Israel could also deliver nuclear weapons using its F-16I Falcons, F-15I Eagles, and F-4E Phantoms (now being replaced with F-16Is) and may also possess artillery-launched nuclear munitions. Israel also has a growing inventory of cruise missiles that includes the U.S.-origin Harpoon, which can be launched from an aircraft, ship, or submarine. The Harpoons can travel up to 120 kilometers with a payload of 220 kilograms. In May 2000, Israel reportedly tested a new sea-launched nuclear-capable cruise missile off Sri Lanka. The missiles are said to have hit targets at a range of 1,500 kilometers.[3]

Biological and Chemical Weapons Capability

Israel possesses advanced chemical and biological weapons (CBW) capabilities, although it is not known what type or how many offensive agents it currently has. Israel is believed to have had sophisticated CBW programs for several decades, centered at the Israel Institute for Biological Research at Ness Ziona, 10 kilometers south of Tel Aviv.

Lacking authoritative information, non-Israeli publications have made many claims about Israel's CBW capabilities, from the trivial to the sensational.[4] The government of Israel, as part of its traditional and deliberate policy of ambiguity, has neither confirmed nor denied those reports. Acknowledging the difficulty of assessing Israel's CBW programs and capabilities, Avner Cohen characterized them thus: "A near-consensus exists among experts—based on anecdotal evidence and intelligence leaks—that Israel developed, produced, stockpiled, and maybe even deployed chemical weapons at some point in its history."[5] As to biological weapons, however, Cohen is more cautious and tentative: "It would be logical—given the experience with Iraq—that Israel has acquired expertise in most aspects of weaponization, with the possible exception of testing. Although it is probable that Israel has maintained some sort of production capability, it is highly doubtful that Israel engages in the ongoing production or stockpiling of BW agents."[6]

A 1990 U.S. Defense Intelligence Agency study reported that Israel had an operational chemical warfare testing facility. In an oblique reference to Israel, the authoritative *Middle East Military Balance*, which is produced by the Jaffee Center for Strategic Studies in Tel Aviv, notes, "The chemical and biological capabilities of Syria, Iraq, and Iran are matched, according to foreign sources, by Israel's possession of a wide range of such weapons."[7] Israel has signed but not yet ratified the Chemical Weapons Convention and is not a party to the Biological Weapons Convention.

Nuclear Analysis

Unclassified estimates of Israel's nuclear capabilities are based in large part on former Israeli nuclear technician Mordechai Vanunu's revelations in October 1986.[8] On the basis of Vanunu's information about Israeli plutonium production, the London *Sunday Times* projected that Israel might have as many as 200 nuclear devices.[9] However, most experts who have attempted to harmonize Vanunu's testimony with other relevant information concluded that, given the small size of Israel's only plutonium-producing reactor, located at the Dimona research complex, Israel's nuclear inventory probably contained far fewer weapons. David Albright calculated that, depending on the power level of the Dimona reactor, Israel could have produced 510 to 650 kilograms of weapons-grade plutonium by the end of 2003.[10] The reactor can produce between 10.6 and 18.6 kilograms of plutonium a year. Assuming 4 kilograms of plutonium for each warhead, Israel could have enough material for 130 to 170 weapons at the end of 2005, with enough new material for an additional 2 to 4 new weapons a year. Assuming a more conservative 5 kilograms for each warhead would mean that Israel has enough material for 105 to 135 weapons.

Vanunu also indicated that Israel had produced tritium and lithium deuteride, suggesting that Israel may have developed "boosted" nuclear weapons, that is, weapons that use a nuclear-fusion reaction to increase their efficiency. Because Israel is not known to have conducted any nuclear tests (with the possible exception of the 1979 "flash" off South Africa,[11] it is assumed that it has not advanced to the point of producing thermonuclear weapons (hydrogen bombs). Israel is likely to rely on simple, proven designs that would require more plutonium than the intensively tested U.S. or Russian designs that use less than four kilograms.

Some experts, however, make different assumptions. A 1991 book by the American investigative journalist Seymour Hersh argued that Israel's arsenal was considerably larger and more advanced than even Vanunu's information suggested. Relying largely on interviews with U.S. intelligence analysts and Israelis knowledgeable about the country's nuclear program, Hersh concluded that Israel possessed "hundreds" of low-yield, enhanced-radiation, "neutron"-type warheads, many in the form of artillery shells and land mines, as well as full-fledged thermonuclear weapons.[12]

A 1994 report alleged plausible new details about Israel's nuclear weapons infrastructure, identifying an installation at Soreq as a research facility on nuclear weapons design. It claimed that Israel's nuclear weapons are assembled at a facility in Yodefat; that Israel has a nuclear missile base and bunker near Moshav Zekharya, a few kilometers from the town of Beit Shemesh; and that tactical nuclear weapons are stored at Eilabun.[13] Other reports suggest that gravity bomb storage bunkers are located near the Tel Nof airbase, and nuclear weapons are stored at Tirosh (see table 13.1 at the end of the chapter).[14]

A New Development: Sea-Launched Capability

Probably the most important nuclear-related development in Israel is the formation of its sea-based nuclear arm. By July 2000, Israel completed taking delivery of all three Dolphin-class submarines that it had ordered at the Thyssen-Nordseewerke shipyard in Kiel, Germany. Germany agreed to sell Israel two additional submarines in 2004.[15] In October 2003, the *Los Angeles Times* reported that U.S. and Israeli officials confirmed Israel's modification of U.S.-supplied Harpoon missiles for use with nuclear warheads. These submarine-launched cruise missiles provide Israel with a largely invulnerable second-strike nuclear capability.[16]

Since the early 1980s (and probably even earlier), the Israeli Navy (jointly with other governmental agencies) lobbied hard for building a small fleet of modern diesel submarines for "strategic purposes," an Israeli euphemism for a sea-launched nuclear capability. Because no American shipyard had the appropriate expertise in building modern diesel, electrical-powered, large submarines, Israel sought a German shipyard as a contractor for the project. After a complex series of negotiations, when a deal was almost signed in early 1990, it was vetoed by General Ehud Barak, then Israel's chief of staff, because of cost. In 1991, in the wake of Iraqi Scud attacks against Israel during the Gulf War, the German government offered to fully finance the purchase of two submarines and to share in the financing of the third to compensate for the role that the German industry had played in the development of Iraq's nonconventional weaponry. Israel immediately accepted the German offer for the first two submarines. Shortly afterward (apparently in a response to alarming reports on Iranian nuclear and missiles projects), it decided to purchase the third one as well. The cost of each submarine was estimated to be about $300 million.

The details of the specific capabilities of the submarines, named *Dolphin*, *Leviathan*, and *Tekumah*, remain highly classified. German leaks indicate that the three 1,900-metric-ton submarines are equipped with ten 21-inch multipurpose tubes, capable of launching torpedoes, mines, and cruise missiles. While the submarines were under construction in Kiel, Israel maintained tight security measures and technological oversight on the project. Many of the navigation, communication, and weapons systems in those submarines were reportedly developed, built, and assembled by the Israeli defense industries. It is also believed (but not confirmed) that the most sensitive aspect of the project, the cruise missile technology that renders the diesel submarines nuclear-capable launching platforms, was developed and built in Israel. Speaking at the ceremony for the arrival of the third submarine at its Haifa base in July 2000, the commander of the Israeli Navy, Rear Admiral Yedidya Yaari, referred to the new submarine as the finest conventional submarine of its class in the world.[17] It is reported that the Israeli-made cruise missiles have the capability of hitting targets in a range of more than 900 miles.[18]

According to one report in the London *Sunday Times*, by early 2000 Israel had carried out the first launching tests of its cruise missiles, less than two years after the first submarine, *Dolphin*, was delivered. According to that report, "Elite crews have assembled to man [the submarines]. . . . Five specially selected officers solely responsible for the warheads will be added to each vessel once the missiles are operational."[19]

A fleet of three submarines is believed to be the minimum that Israel needs to have a deployment at sea of one nuclear-armed submarine at all times. Such a survivable deterrent is perceived as essential because of Israel's unique geopolitical and demographical vulnerability to nuclear attack, and one that no potential nuclear enemy of Israel could ignore. As noted above, in 2004 Germany agreed to sell two additional submarines to Israel.

History

Israel's interest in establishing a national nuclear infrastructure, aimed at both security and energy, is as old as the state itself.[20] By 1955, in the wake of David Ben Gurion's return to power in Israel, Shimon Peres (then the director general of the Ministry of Defense) started to explore in earnest the feasibility of a nuclear weapons project. In 1956–1957, the Israeli nuclear weapons program was born as a result of Israeli–French collaboration, which reached its climax during the Suez crisis.[21] At the time, France's socialist government, led by Guy Mollet, was deeply committed to Israel's survival. The two states confronted dangers stemming from Arab nationalism, Israel because of its isolated position in the Middle East and France because of growing unrest in French Algeria. France secretly pledged to assist Israel in developing nuclear arms and agreed to supply a sizable plutonium-producing reactor to be built at Dimona, in the Negev, 40 miles from Beersheba.[22]

In mid-1957, with French Atomic Energy Commission's approval, Israel signed an agreement with the French firm St. Gobain Techniques Nouvelles for the construction of several additional facilities at the Dimona site, including the key installation (where Vanunu would subsequently work) for extracting plutonium from the Dimona reactor's spent fuel. Soon thereafter, France also gave Israel important information on the design and manufacture of nuclear weapons themselves. Francis Perrin, the scientific head of the French Atomic Energy Commission from 1951 to 1970, was intimately involved with the French–Israeli nuclear program. In an on-the-record 1986 interview with the London *Sunday Times*, Perrin acknowledged that France had supplied the Dimona reactor and the plutonium extraction plant and that, for at least two years during the late 1950s, France and Israel had collaborated on the design and development of nuclear weapons.[23]

Research by Avner Cohen concludes that by late 1966 Israel had successfully completed the research and development stage of its program. During the tense days of the crisis in late May 1967, just days before the Six-Day War, Israel improvised the assembly of two deliverable nuclear devices and placed them on "operational alert."[24]

No conclusive proof exists that Israel has ever conducted a full-scale nuclear test. Its nuclear arsenal is thought to have been developed in part through the testing of non-nuclear components and computer simulations, and through the acquisition of weapons design and test information from abroad. Israel is thought, for example, to have obtained data from France's first nuclear test, which took place in 1960.[25] It may also have obtained data from U.S. nuclear tests at approximately that time. According to a May 1989 U.S. television documentary, Israel was able to gain access to information concerning U.S. tests from the 1950s and early 1960s. The test data could have included the results of tests of U.S. boosted and thermonuclear weapons that were being developed at the time.[26]

There has been speculation, however, that a signal detected on September 22, 1979, by a U.S. VELA monitoring satellite orbiting over the South Atlantic was in fact the flash from a low-yield nuclear explosive test, possibly from a tactical nuclear weapon or from the fission trigger of a thermonuclear device. Although the official U.S. government scientific review concluded that the most likely explanation was that it was a non-nuclear event, the readings have been attributed by some to a nuclear test conducted by South Africa, and by others to Israel.

Seymour Hersh reported that "according to Israeli officials whose information about other aspects of Dimona's activities has been corroborated," the September 1979 event was indeed an Israeli nuclear weapon test and was the third of a series of tests conducted at that time.[27] The first two tests, Hersh's sources stated, were obscured by storm clouds. The claim that clouds would prevent the detection of an atmospheric nuclear detonation by a VELA satellite has been challenged, however, because the satellite is said to rely in part on infrared sensors that can penetrate cloud cover. Thus, this critical matter remains unresolved.

The Strategic Context

Israel's pursuit of the nuclear deterrent option as the basis of national survival has been founded primarily on two factors: Israel's lack of territorial strategic depth, which makes it difficult to absorb a conventional attack and respond effectively; and the "preponderance of men and equipment" enjoyed by its Arab neighbors, almost all of whom have been hostile adversaries throughout its history, and some of whom still reject Israel's right to exist. At the same time, Israel has sought to maintain a margin of qualitative conventional military superiority that would both discourage its foes from resorting to force and ensure victory without the use of nuclear arms in the event of conflict.[28] Even as Israel decided to pursue a nuclear deterrent, it did not want this decision to alienate the United States.

Out of this predicament, Israel's policy of nuclear ambiguity or nuclear opacity originated. It was first enunciated in a 1963 meeting of Shimon Peres, then Israel's deputy minister of defense, and President John F. Kennedy. Questioned about Israel's nuclear capabilities and intentions, Peres responded that "Israel would not be the first country to introduce nuclear weapons in the [Middle East]."[29]

Beginning in the early 1960s, there was continuous friction between the United States and Israel over the question of Israel's nuclear development, culminating in Israel's refusal to join the NPT in 1968.[30] In September 1969, during an official state visit to the United States, Israeli prime minister Golda Meir and President Richard Nixon for the first time reached a secret understanding on this sensitive issue that brought an end to the friction. Meir explained to Nixon why Israel had developed nuclear weapons—and hence could not sign the NPT—and why a policy of nuclear opacity (using the old formulation that "Israel will not be the first nation to introduce nuclear weapons" to the Middle East) would best serve the interests of both countries. Israel also pledged not to test nuclear weapons or publicly admit to possessing them. Nixon accepted the Israeli position, recognizing that the Israeli bomb was a fait accompli, and ended American pressure on Israel to sign the NPT.[31]

The agreement put an end to a decade of unsuccessful (and at times half-hearted) U.S. efforts to halt the Israeli nuclear program. Since then, all Israeli governments have adhered to the agreement. Likewise, while publicly calling on all states to sign the NPT, all subsequent U.S. administrations have not pressured Israel to give up its nuclear weapons. Israeli nuclear opacity was born and cultivated as a symbiotic U.S.–Israeli policy. Over the years, nuclear opacity has become Israel's most distinct contribution to the nuclear age.[32]

A refinement in Israel's defense posture was the Begin doctrine, which justified Israel's air attack on June 7, 1981, on Iraq's Osiraq research reactor. Israeli prime minister Menachem Begin then declared that Israel would block any attempt by adversaries to acquire nuclear weapons.[33]

During the 1980s, the strategic balance in the Middle East underwent significant changes. Some Arab states undertook or accelerated programs to develop or acquire unconventional weapons as well as delivery systems. By the end of the decade, Saddam Hussein was boasting about Iraq's extensive ballistic missile forces and chemical weapons capabilities by declaring (in April 1990) that, if Israel attacked any Iraqi nuclear installations, he would destroy "half of Israel" with chemical weapons. (Iraq had already used chemical weapons in the Iran-Iraq War.)[34] At the same time, Iran, Libya, and Syria were expanding their chemical weapons capabilities, and some of Israel's adversaries were also pursuing the development of biological weapons.

Although suspicion of Iraq's nuclear weapons program existed before the 1991 Gulf War, the scale and range of its efforts were not known. It was subsequently revealed that Iraq had embarked not only on a multifaceted nuclear weapons development program, but also, after its invasion of Kuwait, on a crash program to develop a single nuclear device by April 1991. The emerging threat was demonstrated during the 1991 Gulf War when Israeli cities and sites in Saudi Arabia were attacked by Iraqi extended-range Scud missiles. Although the attacking Scud missiles carried conventional warheads, it was later disclosed that Iraq had stockpiled chemical and biological warheads for such missiles. Iraq launched a total of 39 Scud missiles against Israel, causing two deaths and hundreds of injuries.[35]

The 1991 Gulf War also demonstrated the difficulties of identifying and striking facilities involved in clandestine proliferation programs. In spite of a massive air campaign, much of Iraq's nuclear weapons infrastructure remained intact. Several nuclear installations had not been identified by the United States or its partners. In some cases, attacked nuclear-related facilities suffered only slight damage, allowing the Iraqis to remove and hide equipment. It was left to the International Atomic Energy Agency (IAEA) to discover, in a painstaking effort, the magnitude of the Iraqi nuclear program. The case of Iraq raises important questions over the practicality of the Begin doctrine in the future if potential nuclear infrastructure targets are too distant, hidden too well, and too numerous to be destroyed by air attacks.[36]

A Perspective on Arms Control

The Gulf War provided an impetus for the initiation of a peace process in the region, raising the prospect of a transition to arms control.[37] The Middle East Peace Conference, which opened in Madrid on October 30, 1991, under the sponsorship of the United States and the Soviet Union, began sets of bilateral talks between Israel and its neighbors aimed at a comprehensive peace in the region. An additional multilateral component of this process was the establishment of five working groups to address regional issues of common interest, one being the Arms Control and Regional Security Working Group. However, major Israeli antagonists in the region, such as Iran and Syria, did not participate in the talks. The talks were suspended in early 1995 with very limited, if any, concrete accomplishments.

In the context of the April 1995 NPT Review and Extension Conference, the Arab states, led by Egypt, attempted but failed to pressure Israel into renouncing its nuclear option. At the fourth Preparatory Committee (PrepCom) session of the Review and Extension Conference in January 1995, Egypt, as well as Algeria, Libya, and Syria, issued statements indicating that they would consent to an indefinite extension of the NPT only after Israel had agreed to accede to the treaty.[38] Israel's response was embodied in Foreign Minister Shimon Peres' exchange with Egyptian foreign minister Amr Mussa: Peres explained that Israel would agree to a nuclear-weapon-free zone in the Middle East two years after the conclusion of a comprehensive peace accord between all states in the region, including Iran.

From Israel's point of view, security conditions deteriorated rapidly both internally and regionally after 1995. During that period, as ballistic missile threats increased, Israel accelerated its development of antimissile systems. Israel's threat assessment became more dire when Syria tested advanced 600-kilometer Scud-C missiles, a system capable of striking Israeli sites from deep within Syria, and possibly with chemical and biological weapons. Israel also saw Iran as an increasingly serious threat. In addition to its suspected stockpile of chemical weapons, a possible biological warfare program, and efforts to acquire nuclear weapons, information surfaced that Iran was developing Shahab missiles, with ranges of up to 2,000 kilometers, that would enable Iran to target Israel for the first time (see chapters 5 and 15). Moreover, Israel believed that it continued to face missile threats from Libya, Egypt, Saudi Arabia, and possibly Iraq.

At the same time, the collapse of the peace process established by the 1993 Oslo accords not only undermined efforts to resume the regional arms control talks but also created a deeply pessimistic mood among the Israeli public about peace. Efforts by Israeli prime minister Ehud Barak and Palestinian Authority chairman Yasser Arafat to negotiate an accord showed promise throughout 1999 but stalled at the end of 2000. A provocative visit by Likud Party leader

Ariel Sharon to the Temple Mount in September 2000 ignited a four-year intifada that resulted in the deaths of thousands of Palestinians and Israelis. The election in January 2005 of Mahmoud Abbas as the new president of the Palestinian Authority brought a new potential for a peaceful resolution to the conflict. The April 2005 withdrawal of Syrian troops from Lebanon, a possible shift by Hezbollah to political rather than military operations, and the pending Israeli withdrawal from Gaza contributed to a cautious optimism shared by all sides.

Treaties and Negotiations

Israel signed the Comprehensive Test Ban Treaty (CTBT) on September 25, 1996, the only one of the three non-NPT nuclear weapon states to do so. From the Israeli perspective, adherence to the CTBT and its earlier signing of the Chemical Weapons Convention demonstrated Israel's interest in arms control regimes with reliable verification systems that are not subject to abuse or frivolous requests. According to this view, Israel's arms control credentials and policies were also reflected in the active role it played in the negotiations of the CTBT as a primary participant in the drafting of the accord; in its cosponsorship of the United Nations resolution that opened the CTBT for signature; and in the fact that it was one of its first signatories.[39]

In the early 1990s, both the George H. W. Bush administration in 1991 and subsequently the Bill Clinton administration in 1993 made proposals to ban the further production of fissile materials for weapons both in the Middle East and globally. The impetus for the 1991 Bush regional proposal was the perception that the "fissban" idea, in addition to the effort to disarm Iraq, could be an important milestone toward an eventual nuclear-free zone in the Middle East. In the wake of the Gulf War, it was evident that Israel had to be a part of any effort to reduce the nuclear threat in the Middle East. In this context, advocates of a fissban argued that it offered a realistic compromise: a limited but real constraint on the Israeli nuclear program, coupled with an implicit legitimization of Israel's nuclear status.

In 1993, the Clinton administration modified the Bush proposal, calling for a global fissile material cutoff treaty that would ban the further production of plutonium and highly enriched uranium for nuclear weapons as well as the production of such materials outside IAEA safeguards. The cutoff proposal would permit the five nuclear weapon states and the three de facto nuclear powers (India, Israel, and Pakistan) to retain their existing stocks of unsafeguarded fissile material.[40]

In the early 1990s, the Israel government refrained from making an official and public response to the Bush and Clinton initiatives. Unofficially, however, Israeli officials expressed reservation about the proposals but were careful not to reject them outright. The main concern was that the constraints imposed by the fissban, together with the associated verification modalities, would put Israel on a slippery slope leading to the demise of nuclear opacity and to increased pressure to abandon its nuclear arsenal entirely.[41]

By the middle to late 1990s, following the collapse of ACRS, Israeli opposition to the fissban proposal grew firmer. In 1998, Prime Minister Benjamin Netanyahu told (and wrote to) President Clinton in unequivocal language that Israel could not accept the fissban proposal. According to Aluf Benn, *Ha'aretz's* diplomatic correspondent, in two letters and several conversations, Netanyahu told Clinton: "We will never sign the treaty, and do not delude yourselves, no pressure will help. We will not sign the treaty because we will not commit suicide."[42]

Despite India's and Pakistan's declarations of nuclear weapons in 1998 and the end of any threat from Iraq, it is unlikely that Israel will follow suit or change its policy of nuclear ambiguity. It appears that only a dramatic change in the nuclear ambitions of Iran could trigger a change in the Israeli position. Israeli decision makers will also continue to hold the view that as long as adversaries in the Middle East region maintain the capability to mount large-scale military attacks against Israel or to threaten Israeli cities with missiles carrying chemical or biological warheads, Israel will need to maintain the nuclear deterrence option.

In some respects, one Israeli observer argues, Israel's nuclear posture may have been better understood internationally as a result of its controversy with Egypt before and during the course of the 1995 Review and Extension Conference. In his view, the conflict forced Yitzhak Rabin, Peres, and other Israeli leaders to articulate for the first time "links between the maintenance of the nuclear capability and the continued threats to national survival, linked to the military, geographic and demographic asymmetries in the region."[43] From the Israeli perspective, a substantive discussion of regional arms control issues is inextricably linked to the achievement of a comprehensive Middle East peace settlement.

Missile Analysis

Israel currently deploys two nuclear-capable ballistic missile systems: the Jericho I and Jericho II. Up to 50 Jericho I solid-fueled, two-stage missiles with an approximate range of 500 kilometers are thought to be deployed in shelters on mobile launchers, possibly at a facility located midway between Jerusalem and the Mediterranean. The Jericho II solid-fueled, two-stage missile can travel an estimated 1,500 kilometers. Commercial satellite photographs indicate that the missile base between Jerusalem and the Mediterranean was enlarged between 1989 and 1993 to allow for Jericho II deployment. Furthermore, Israel is reportedly developing a third version of the Jericho missile, the Jericho III, based on the Shavit SLV, despite the fact that Tel Aviv can already reach all of its regional adversaries with the Jericho II medium-range ballistic missile. The Jericho III, whose existence cannot be confirmed, could potentially have an intermediate (greater than 3,000 km) or intercontinental (greater than 5,500 kilometer) range.[44]

Israel's anti–ballistic missile system is a joint U.S.–Israeli undertaking begun in 1988 and funded largely by the United States. The multi-billion-dollar Arrow system will attempt to intercept short-range Scud-type missiles just as they start reentering the atmosphere after reaching the highest point of their flight trajectory.

Israel has tested the Arrow II interceptor twelve times, and the entire system seven times. Two Arrow II batteries have been deployed, one near Tel-Aviv and one in Ein Shemer; a third is being developed for southern Israel.[45] The system links operations with Patriot air defense units.

Israel is also experimenting with another missile interceptor, the Moab, funded in part by the United States. This system will try to intercept Scud-like missiles soon after launch with an air-to-air missile fired from an unmanned aerial vehicle flying at high altitude. Israel is also developing jointly with the United States the Nautilus laser (also called a tactical high-energy laser system), capable of shooting down short-range artillery rockets. This system is intended for deployment in Israel's northern regions to help protect against rocket attacks on Israel from southern Lebanon and Gaza. The radar component of the Nautilus system was delivered to Israel in December of 2004, while the laser gun is undergoing development and testing in White Sands, New Mexico.[46] Israel and the United States optimistically expect the laser to be ready for deployment by 2007.[47]

Israel's unmanned aerial vehicle program has been extended to cover cruise missile development, including land-attack cruise missiles. These systems appear to be the sea-launched Harpoon cruise missile and the air- and ground-launched variants of the Delilah cruise missile. The Delilah, with a 400-kilometer range and a 450-kilogram payload, is said to have been developed with Chinese cooperation.[48] Moreover, Israel's armament industries are believed to have extensive ties, including projected cruise missile cooperation with China, India, South Korea, and Turkey. In June 2004, *Jane's Defense Weekly* reported that Israel has developed its first surface-to-surface cruise missile. Israel has sought to acquire a land-based cruise missile for almost a decade. The new Delilah GL (ground launch) is a derivation of the air-launched Delilah missile, has a range of more than 250 kilometers, and can be used for reconnaissance as well as precision attack.[49]

Notes

1. David Albright and Kimberly Kramer, "ISIS Estimates of Unirradiated Fissile Material in De Facto Nuclear Weapon States, Produced in Nuclear Weapons Programs," in *Global Fissile Material Inventories* (Washington, D.C.: Institute for Science and International Security, 2004); available at www.isis-online.org/global_stocks/de_facto_states.html. The estimate for production totals at the end of 2003 has been extended here to the end of 2005 using the institute's estimates for annual plutonium production.
2. Avner Cohen, *Israel and the Bomb* (New York: Columbia University Press, 1998), pp. 239, 273–276.
3. Uzi Mahnaimi and Matthew Campbell, "Israel Makes Nuclear Waves with Submarine Missile Test," *Sunday Times* (London), June 18, 2000.
4. Many of these sensationalist stories appeared in the *Sunday Times* (London). One of these stories cites a biologist who once held a senior post in the Israeli intelligence as saying that "there is hardly a single known or unknown form of chemical or biological weapon, which is not manufactured at the Institute." Uzi Mahnaimi, "Israeli Jets Equipped for Chemical Warfare," *Sunday Times*, October 4, 1998. See also, "Israel's Secret Institute," *Foreign Report*, August 20, 1998; "Israel's Nes[s] Ziona Mystery," *Foreign Report*, February 5, 1998.
5. Avner Cohen, "Israel and CBW: History, Deterrence, and Arms Control," *Nonproliferation Review*, Fall 2001, pp. 1–20.

6. Ibid.
7. Shai Feldman and Yiftah Shapir, eds., *The Middle East Military Balance 2000–2001*, Jaffee Center for Strategic Studies, Tel Aviv University (Cambridge, Mass.: MIT Press, 2001), p. 67.
8. "Revealed: The Secrets of Israel's Nuclear Arsenal," *Sunday Times* (London), October 5, 1986.
9. In light of what is known about Israel's nuclear infrastructure, it has long been assumed that its weapons use plutonium rather than highly enriched uranium for their cores.
10. This extrapolation is based on the assumption that the Dimona reactor has been operating reliably at a power level of between 40 and 70 megawatts thermal (MWt) and has not experienced any significant shutdowns nor extended operation at its theoretical upper limit of 150 MWt. See David Albright, Frans Berkhout, and William Walker, *Plutonium and Highly Enriched Uranium 1996: World Inventories, Capabilities, and Policies* (Oxford: Oxford University Press, 1997), pp. 259, 262; the authors assume in their calculations that Israel uses 5 kilograms of plutonium for each warhead. The authors of this volume assume that Israel uses 4 kilograms for each warhead. For the plutonium estimate through 2003, see Albright and Kramer, "ISIS Estimates of Unirradiated Fissile Material."
11. David Albright and Corey Gay, "A Flash from the Past," *Bulletin of the Atomic Scientists*, November/December 1997, pp. 15–17.
12. Seymour Hersh, *The Samson Option* (New York: Random House, 1991), pp. 291, 312, 319.
13. Harold Hough, "Israel's Nuclear Infrastructure," *Jane's Intelligence Review*, November 1994, p. 508.
14. Hans M. Kristensen and Joshua Handler, *SIPRI Yearbook 2001: Armaments, Disarmament, and International Security*, Stockholm International Peace Research Institute (Oxford: Oxford University Press, 2001), p. 484.
15. "Israel to Acquire Two More German Submarines," Maariv International, December 23, 2004.
16. Douglas Frantz, "Israel's Arsenal Is Point of Contention: Officials Confirm That the Nation Can Now Launch Atomic Weapons from Land, Sea and Air; The Issue Complicates Efforts to Rein in Iran's Ambitions," *Los Angeles Times*, October 12, 2003; available at www.latimes.com/news/nationworld/world/la-fg-iznukes12oct12.story.
17. *Ha'aretz*, July 26, 2000.
18. Mahnaimi and Campbell, "Israel Makes Nuclear Waves."
19. Ibid.
20. Cohen, *Israel and the Bomb*, pp. 9–31.
21. Ibid., pp. 41–55.
22. Cohen, *Israel and the Bomb*, chap. 4, pp. 57–68; Leonard Spector, *The Undeclared Bomb* (Cambridge, Mass.: Ballinger, 1988), pp. 165–187; Pierre Pean, *Les Deux Bombes* (Paris: Fayard, 1981), chaps. 5, 7, 8.
23. "France Admits It Gave Israel A-Bomb," *Sunday Times* (London), October 12, 1986.
24. Cohen, *Israel and the Bomb*, pp. 273–276.
25. Steven Weissman and Herbert Krosney, *The Islamic Bomb* (New York: Times Books, 1981), p. 114.
26. "Israel: The Covert Connection," *Frontline*, PBS Network, May 16, 1989.
27. Hersh, *Samson Option*, p. 271.
28. Cohen, *Israel and the Bomb*, esp. chaps. 1, 12, 17; Gerald Steinberg, "The Future of Nuclear Weapons: Israeli Perspectives," paper presented at the Ninth Amaldi Conference on Security Questions at the End of the Twentieth Century, Geneva, November 21–23, 1996; revised November 25, 1996.
29. Cohen, *Israel and the Bomb*, pp. 118–119; Barbara Opall, "Peres: Keep Nuclear Details Secret," *Defense News*, July 29–August 4, 1996, p. 3.
30. Cohen, *Israel and the Bomb*, chaps. 5–7, 9–11, 16–17.
31. Ibid., pp. 336–338; Aluf Benn, "Open Secrets: The Struggle to Keep Nuclear Capabilities Secret," *Ha'aretz*, September 14, 1999 (English Internet edition).
32. Ibid., pp. 341–344; Benn, "Open Secrets."
33. Leonard Spector, with Jacquelin Smith, *Nuclear Ambitions* (Boulder, Colo.: Westview Press, 1990), pp. 167, 188.

34. "Iraq Threatens to Use Chemical Weapons against Israeli Attack," *Financial Times*, April 3, 1990.

35. James Bruce, "Israel's Space and Missile Projects," *Jane's Intelligence Review*, vol. 7, no. 8, 1995, p. 352; and "BRF Israel Missiles," Associated Press, January 3, 1997.

36. Avner Cohen, "The Lessons of Osiraq and the American Counterproliferation Debate," in *International Perspectives on Counterproliferation*, Working Paper 99, edited by Mitchell Reiss and Harald Muller (Washington, D.C.: Woodrow Wilson Center, 1994).

37. Efraim Karsh, Efraim Inbar, and Shmuel Sandler, "Arms Control and the New Middle Eastern Environment," *Defense Analysis*, vol. 12, no. 1, 1996; reprinted in *Lessons for Arms Control in a Changing Middle East*, Security and Policy Studies 26 (Ramat Gan, Israel: BESA Center for Strategic Studies, Bar-Ilan University, June 1996), p. 40.

38. Mark Hibbs, "Last NPT PrepCom Moves toward Limited Extension," *Nucleonics Week*, February 2, 1995, p. 6.

39. Gerald Steinberg, "Deterrence and Middle East Stability: An Israeli Perspective," *Security Dialogue*, Spring 1997; Steinberg, "The Future of Nuclear Weapons: Israeli Perspectives."

40. Avner Cohen and Marvin Miller, "How to Think About—and Implement—Nuclear Arms Control in the Middle East," *Washington Quarterly*, Spring 1993, pp. 101–113; Shai Feldman, *Nuclear Weapons and Arms Control in the Middle East* (Cambridge, Mass.: MIT Press, 1997); Avner Cohen, "Nuclear Arms Control in the Middle East: Problems and Prospects," paper presented at a U.S. Institute of Peace seminar, April 8, 1998; Avner Cohen and Marvin Miller, "The U.S. and the De Facto Nuclear Weapons States: A Post–September 11 Perspective," paper prepared for the Stanley Foundation's Strategy for Peace Conference at Airlie Conference Center, Warrenton, Va., October 25–27, 2001.

41. Aluf Benn, "Senior Governmental Officials: Israel Could Live with Clinton's Arms Control Initiative," *Ha'aretz*, October 5, 1993; Cohen and Miller, "The U.S. and the De Facto Nuclear Weapons States."

42. Benn, "Open Secrets," *Ha'aretz*, March 14, 2000; Aluf Benn, "Israel Resists Pressure on Its Nuclear Policy," *Ha'aretz*, May 2, 2000; Aluf Benn, "Sharon Will Stick to Tradition of Nuclear Ambiguity," *Ha'aretz*, February 18, 2001; Cohen and Miller, "De Facto Nuclear Weapons States."

43. Gerald Steinberg, "Middle East Peace and the NPT Extension Decision," *Nonproliferation Review*, Fall 1996.

44. Andrew Feickert, "Missile Survey: Ballistic and Cruise Missiles of Foreign Countries," Congressional Research Service, March 5, 2004, p. 36. See also Center for Nonproliferation Studies, Monterey Institute, "Weapons of Mass Destruction in the Middle East: Israel"; available at http://cns.miis.edu/research/wmdme/israel.htm.

45. MissileThreat.com, "Arrow," in *Missile Defense Systems* (Claremont, Calif.: Claremont Institute, 2005); available at www.missilethreat.com/systems/arrow_israel.html.

46. Arieh O'Sullivan, "Anti-Katyusha Laser to Be Tested," *Jerusalem Post*, December 21, 2004; available at www.jpost.com/servlet/Satellite?pagename=JPost/JPArticle/ShowFull&cid=1103514262459.

47. MissileThreat.com, "Tactical High Energy Laser (THEL)," in *Missile Defense Systems*; available at www.missilethreat.com/systems/thel_usa.html.

48. Feickert, "Missile Survey," p. 36, See also International Institute for Strategic Studies, *The Military Balance, 2004–2005* (Oxford: Oxford University Press, 2004), pp. 126–127.

49. Alon Ben-David, "Israel Develops Ground-Launched Delilah Missile," *Jane's Defense Weekly*, June 16, 2004.

Table 13.1. **Israel's Nuclear Infrastructure**

Name/Location of Facility	Type/Status	IAEA Safeguards
	Nuclear Weapons Complex	
Negev Nuclear Research Center Dimona	Plutonium production research reactor and plutonium extraction facilities (see below) and other weapon-related infrastructure	No
Moshav Soreq[1]	Nuclear weapon research and design facility	No
Yodefat[2]	Possible nuclear weapon assembly facility	No
Moshav Zekharya (Zachariah)[3]	Nuclear missile base (reportedly Jericho II)	No
Sdot Micha[4]	Nuclear missile base (reportedly Jericho I), status unknown	No
Tel Nof[5]	Airbase near suspected nuclear gravity bomb storage bunkers[6]	No
Tirosh[7]	Possible nuclear weapon storage facility	No
Eilabun[8]	Possible nuclear weapon storage facility	No
	Research Reactors	
IRR-1, Nahal Soreq[9]	Light-water, pool, HEU, 5 MWt, operating	Yes
IRR-2, Dimona	Heavy-water, nat. U, 40–150 MWt, operating[10]	No
	Uranium Enrichment	
Dimona[11]	Suspected pilot-scale laser and centrifuge-enrichment programs, status unknown	No
	Reprocessing (Plutonium Extraction)	
Mochon 2 Dimona	Underground facility, uses PUREX method, converts separated plutonium into metal and shapes plutonium metal into bomb cores, operating[12]	No
Nahal Soreq	Suspected, status unknown[13]	No
	Uranium Processing[14]	
Negev area, near Beersheeba	Uranium phosphate mining, status unknown	No

(table continues on the following page)

Table 13.1. **Israel's Nuclear Infrastructure** (continued)

Haifa	Suspected yellowcake production in two phosphate plants, status unknown	No
Southern Israel	Suspected yellowcake production in phosphate plant, status unknown	No
Dimona	Uranium purification (UO_2), uranium conversion (UF_6), and fuel-fabrication facility, all operating[15]	No
Heavy-Water Processing		
Weizmann Institute (Rehovot)[16]	Suspected pilot-scale plant, status unknown	No
Tritium, Lithium Deuteride		
Dimona	Tritium may have been extracted from heavy water and/or from irradiated lithium targets,[17] irradiated lithium targets can also produce lithium deuteride,[18] status unknown	No

ABBREVIATIONS

HEU highly enriched uranium
nat. U natural uranium
MWt megawatts thermal

SOURCES

David Albright, Frans Berkhout, and William Walker, *Plutonium and Highly Enriched Uranium 1996: World Inventories, Capabilities, and Policies* (Oxford: Oxford University Press, 1997). Hans M. Kristensen and Joshua Handler, *SIPRI Yearbook 2001: Armaments, Disarmament, and International Security*, Stockholm International Peace Research Institute (Oxford: Oxford University Press, 2001). Hans M. Kristensen and Joshua Handler, "Appendix 10A: World Nuclear Forces," in *SIPRI Yearbook 2002: Armaments, Disarmament, and International Security*, Stockholm International Peace Research Institute (Oxford: Oxford University Press, 2002). Harold Hough, "Could Israel's Nuclear Assets Survive a Pre-Emptive Strike?" *Jane's Intelligence Review*, January 9, 1997; available at www.janes.com/regional_news/africa_middle_east/news/jir/jir990901_1_n.shtml. International Atomic Energy Agency, "Table A24, Facilities under Agency safeguards or containing safeguarded material on 31 December 2003"; available at www.iaea.org/Publications/Reports/Anrep2003/table_A24.pdf. Preston Mendenhall, "Israel Releases 'Atomic Prisoner,'" NBC News, April 21, 2004, available at http://msnbc.msn.com/id/4788784/.

NOTES:

1. Russian Federation Foreign Intelligence Service, "The Nuclear Potential of Individual Countries Treaty on Nonproliferation of Nuclear Weapons Problems of Extension, Appendix 2, April 6, 1995"; available at http://fas.org/irp/threat/svr_nuke.htm#israel. See also Hans M. Kristensen and Joshua Handler, "Appendix 10A: World Nuclear Forces," in *SIPRI Yearbook 2002: Armaments, Disarmament, and International Security* (Oxford: Oxford University Press, 2002), p. 42.
2. Russian Federation Foreign Intelligence Service. See also Kristensen and Handler, "Appendix 10A."
3. Hough, "Could Israel's Nuclear Assets Survive a Pre-Emptive Strike?"

4. Kristensen and Handler, "Appendix 10A."
5. Ibid.
6. Kristensen and Handler, *SIPRI Yearbook 2001.*
7. Ibid.
8. Russian Federation Foreign Intelligence Service.
9. International Atomic Energy Agency, "Nuclear Research Reactors in the World," available at www.iaea.org/worldatom/rrdb.
10. Estimates of the reactor's capacity vary widely. For a good discussion of the reactor power mystery, see Albright, Berkhout, and Walker, *Plutonium and Highly Enriched Uranium 1996,* pp. 257–264.
11. Albright, Berkhout, and Walker, *Plutonium and Highly Enriched Uranium 1996,* p. 264.
12. Ibid., p. 260.
13. According to a 1987 Pentagon study, the "Soreq Center runs the full nuclear gamut of activities . . . required for nuclear weapons design and fabrication." See Kristensen and Handler, *SIPRI Yearbook 2001.*
14. According to Albright, Berkhout, and Walker, *Plutonium and Highly Enriched Uranium 1996,* Israel produces roughly 10 tons of uranium yellowcake annually.
15. See www.globalsecurity.org/wmd/world/israel/dimona.htm.
16. Avner Cohen, *Israel and the Bomb* (Columbia University Press: New York, 1998), p. 15.
17. Albright, Berkhout, and Walker, *Plutonium and Highly Enriched Uranium 1996,* p. 263.
18. See www.globalsecurity.org/wmd/world/israel/dimona.htm.

Part Four
Two Hard Cases

Although very serious consequences are associated with the proliferation of nuclear, chemical, and biological weapons and of ballistic missiles, the number of states aggressively pursuing these capabilities is remarkably small. In fact, only two new countries—North Korea and Iran—are now moving toward producing nuclear weapons in the next decade. These two hard cases are the focus of major international nonproliferation efforts. Each of these countries is pursuing nuclear capabilities for various reasons, which need to be understood to shape effective nonproliferation policies.

The primary danger of this spread of nuclear capabilities is not that each country would use nuclear weapons to attack the United States or other nations but that its acquisition of nuclear weapons would force neighboring states to reconsider their own nuclear options. A nuclear chain reaction could spread from the Middle East or Northeast Asia, resulting in several, or perhaps many, new nuclear nations. The success or failure of nonproliferation with these two nations could decide the future of the entire nonproliferation regime.

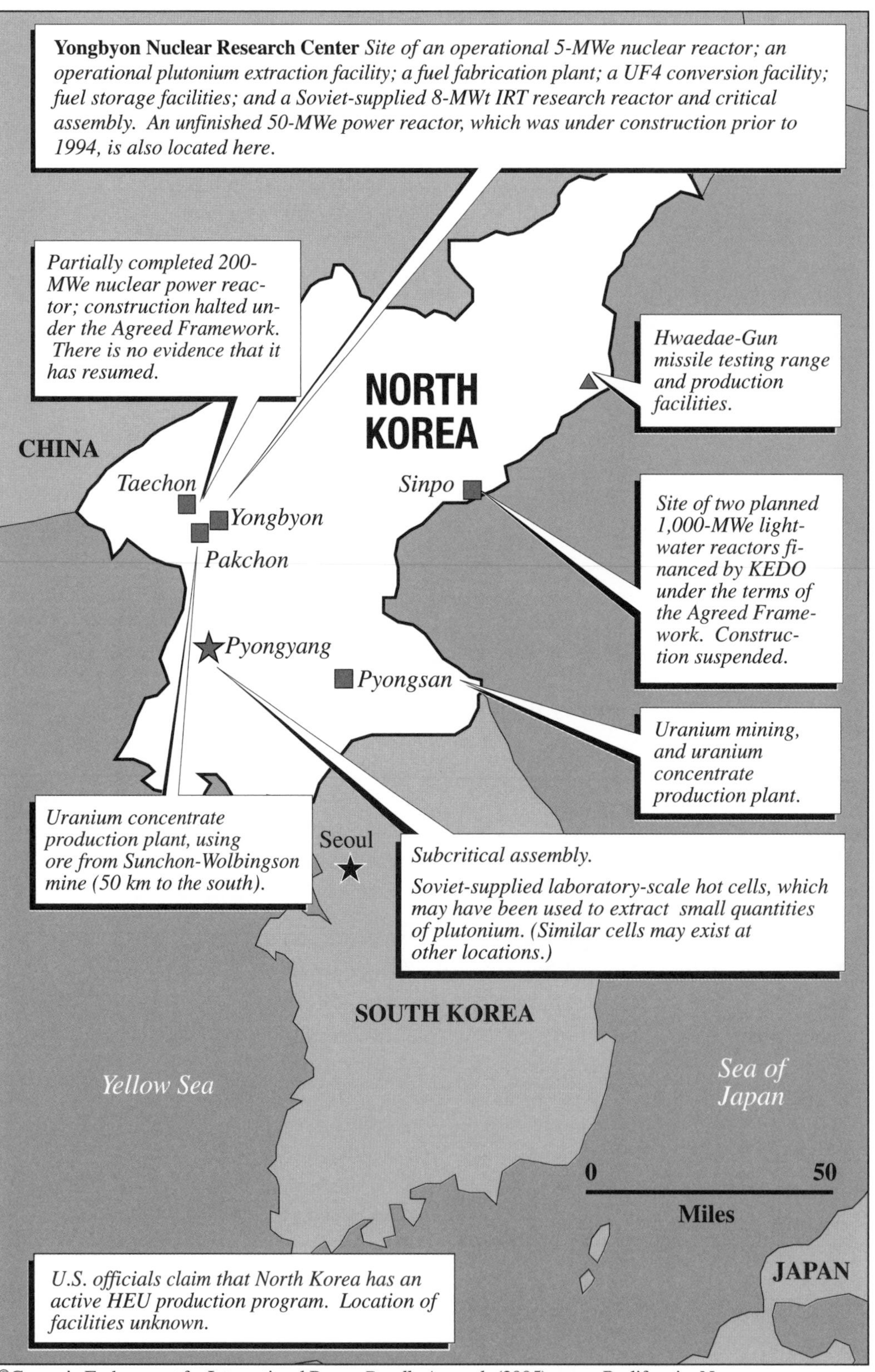
Yongbyon Nuclear Research Center Site of an operational 5-MWe nuclear reactor; an operational plutonium extraction facility; a fuel fabrication plant; a UF4 conversion facility; fuel storage facilities; and a Soviet-supplied 8-MWt IRT research reactor and critical assembly. An unfinished 50-MWe power reactor, which was under construction prior to 1994, is also located here.
Partially completed 200-MWe nuclear power reactor; construction halted under the Agreed Framework. There is no evidence that it has resumed.
NORTH KOREA
Hwaedae-Gun missile testing range and production facilities.
CHINA
Taechon
Yongbyon
Pakchon
Sinpo
Site of two planned 1,000-MWe light-water reactors financed by KEDO under the terms of the Agreed Framework. Construction suspended.
Pyongyang
Pyongsan
Uranium mining, and uranium concentrate production plant.
Uranium concentrate production plant, using ore from Sunchon-Wolbingson mine (50 km to the south).
Seoul
Subcritical assembly.
Soviet-supplied laboratory-scale hot cells, which may have been used to extract small quantities of plutonium. (Similar cells may exist at other locations.)
SOUTH KOREA
Yellow Sea
Sea of Japan
0
50
Miles
JAPAN
U.S. officials claim that North Korea has an active HEU production program. Location of facilities unknown.

CHAPTER 14

North Korea

Nuclear Weapons Capability

North Korea has an active nuclear weapon program and may already possess enough separated plutonium to produce as many as nine nuclear weapons (see table 14.1 at the end of the chapter). It is unclear how many, if any, weapons North Korea has built. U.S. intelligence agencies have stated that "in the mid-1990s North Korea had produced one possibly two, nuclear weapons,"[1] but this estimate may be based on assumptions about Pyongyang's intentions and capabilities rather than direct evidence.

North Korea continues to operate a small plutonium production reactor at the Yongbyon nuclear center that can produce enough weapons-grade plutonium for one nuclear weapon every year. In addition, there is evidence that North Korea may be pursuing a uranium enrichment centrifuge program that could increase its access to weapons-grade nuclear material in the coming years. The exact scale of the North Korean centrifuge program, however, is not publicly known, and it is unclear when North Korea will be able to begin production of weapons-grade uranium. U.S. intelligence has yet to publicly identify any centrifuge enrichment facilities in North Korea.

Aircraft and Missile Capability

North Korea has an advanced ballistic missile capability, having tested and deployed missiles with ranges of more than 1,000 kilometers and conducted a single test of a longer-range system that, if fully developed, may be able to deliver a small payload to the United States. Reliable estimates indicate that North Korea has deployed approximately 100 of its most advanced ballistic missile, the medium-range No Dong.[2] Pyongyang continues to abide by a self-declared suspension of its missile flight tests but retains the ability to resume tests at any time. North Korea is the leading exporter of short-range ballistic missiles in the world, and it has sold missiles or missile production capabilities to Egypt, Iran, Libya, Pakistan, and Syria. North Korea may also be gaining important flight test information from missiles being tested in other countries, such as Iran, and it continues to conduct ground-based testing of missile engines and components.

Biological and Chemical Weapons Capability

North Korea is believed to possess large stocks of chemical weapons and precursor chemicals, as well as an infrastructure that can be used to produce biological weapons. Although it has acceded to the Biological and Toxin Weapons Convention, it has not signed the Chemical Weapons Convention. U.S. officials believe that North Korea has pursued biological warfare capabilities since the 1960s and is able to produce sufficient quantities of biological agents for military purposes within weeks of a decision to do so.[3] The U.S. Defense Department believes that North Korea would use chemical weapons against U.S. or South Korean troops in combat.

The Strategic Context

North Korea's unchecked nuclear weapons capabilities represent a serious threat to regional security; to several key U.S. allies, including South Korea and Japan; and to the global effort to prevent the spread of nuclear weapons. This isolated and highly secretive country has developed a largely indigenous nuclear weapons and ballistic missile production capability, and in the coming decades it could produce large amounts of nuclear materials for its own weapons and possibly for export to others. Other nations possess a limited set of tools to influence North Korean behavior and convince its enigmatic leadership to abandon its unconventional weapons production and export activities, and the possible collapse of this poor and reclusive country cannot be discounted. Past efforts that have alternated between enticing and pressuring North Korea to abandon its nuclear program have been unsuccessful.

The continued military confrontation between North Korea and South Korea (and its ally the United States) represents the main source of instability in Northeast Asia—a standoff exacerbated by North Korea's pursuit of nuclear weapons and ballistic missiles. The parties remain, to this day, in a technical state of war. The United States has long-standing treaty and political commitments to defend South Korea from North Korean attack. The United States currently deploys more than 30,000 troops in South Korea, although it has plans to realign and reduce its troop presence on the peninsula in the coming years. North Korea's alleged possession of nuclear weapons and its continued production of nuclear materials threaten the United States' ability to deter North Korea actions that undermine U.S. or South Korean interests. There is increasing concern that as North Korea consolidates its nuclear position, it may become more adventurous in its attempts to extract concessions from other countries and to drive a wedge between the United States and its allies in the region. The key to the U.S. approach to stability on the Korean peninsula is to make clear to the North that any attack against the South would fail and present unacceptable costs to Pyongyang.

U.S. Policy toward North Korea

The United States has no formal diplomatic relations with North Korea. U.S. policy toward the reclusive state has alternated in the past two decades from one of open engagement to outright confrontation. In 1991, the United States began an initially cautious and then more active strategy of engagement with

Pyongyang, with the goal of ending North Korea's nuclear weapons activities and encouraging improved relations between North Korea and South Korea. This process included a high-level meeting in 1991 between then–undersecretary of state Arnold Kantor and North Korean representative Kim Yong Sun that convinced North Korea to complete the legal process of adhering to the Nuclear Non-Proliferation Treaty (NPT) in 1992.

This process continued and expanded under President Bill Clinton, which also featured several periods of crisis including one that almost led to war with North Korea. That crisis eventually resulted in the completion of the 1994 Agreed Framework, which froze North Korea's nuclear material production for eight years. The final months of the Clinton administration saw an intense negotiating effort to end North Korea's ballistic missile program, including a prolonged set of discussions dating from the mid-1990s. Then–secretary of state Madeleine Albright traveled to Pyongyang in 2000 and became the highest-ranking U.S. official ever to meet with Kim Jong Il. But the details of a missile elimination agreement could not be concluded by the time George W. Bush was inaugurated in January 2001.

Upon assuming office, the Bush administration undertook a wholesale reassessment of U.S. policy toward North Korea. Many incoming officials had actively opposed the 1994 Agreed Framework and were highly skeptical of North Korea's commitment to give up its nuclear weapon programs. Other officials, most notably Secretary of State Colin Powell, sought to "pick up where President Clinton and his administration left off" with North Korea,[4] a desire that was quickly countermanded by more conservative elements of the Bush team and the president himself. On June 6, 2001, the White House completed its policy review and issued a presidential statement announcing that the United States should "undertake serious discussions with North Korea on a broad agenda to include: improved implementation of the Agreed Framework relating to North Korea's nuclear activities; verifiable constraints on North Korea's missile programs and a ban on its missile exports; and a less threatening conventional military posture."[5]

Despite this stated desire to pursue discussions, the fabric of the U.S.–North Korean relationship was steadily deteriorating. Confronting the North Korean regime and other "rogue" states was a clear priority for the new administration even before the terrorist attacks of September 11, 2001. Attempts by South Korean president Kim Dae Jung to win President Bush's endorsement for his engagement or "sunshine" policy toward the North was bluntly rejected during a Washington summit between U.S. and South Korean leaders in March 2001. Less than a year later, President Bush included North Korea as a charter member of the "axis of evil" in his 2002 State of the Union address. The National Security Strategy Statement of the United States released in 2002 talked about the possible need to take preemptive military action against states like North Korea. These and additional statements made it clear that the Bush administration intended to pursue a more assertive policy of confronting hostile states such as North Korea; openly called for regime change in these states; and held open the possible use of nuclear weapons against North Korea, despite pledges in the Agreed

Framework to provide Pyongyang with assurances against the use of these weapons.

The situation remained tense in 2002. For more than a year, the administration made no concrete progress on its stated desire to pursue comprehensive talks with North Korea. In the summer of 2002, U.S. intelligence agencies concluded that North Korea had been secretly trying to acquire a uranium enrichment program for at least two years. The assessment was based primarily on efforts by North Korea—some successful—to buy and import enrichment-related equipment through the A. Q. Khan network of black market nuclear suppliers. The assessment, summed up in an unclassified summary submitted to Congress in 2002, also stated that the United States had recently learned that the "North had begun construction of a centrifuge facility," although no such site has been publicly identified. At the time, intelligence reports indicated that North Korea's uranium enrichment efforts stretched back to 1999 or 2000. The enrichment program violated the spirit of the 1994 Agreed Framework and the stated interpretation by the United States of that arrangement, as well as the 1992 North–South denuclearization agreement. It may also, depending on how far the program had advanced, have constituted a further violation of the NPT, which requires that all nuclear facilities be declared to the International Atomic Energy Agency (IAEA) and placed under safeguards. The intelligence findings confirmed doubts about North Korea's intentions in the minds of those government officials who were skeptical of engagement with North Korea and reinforced their desire to adopt a different approach toward Pyongyang.[6]

In October 2002, the assistant secretary of state for East Asia, James Kelly, traveled to Pyongyang for long-postponed discussions with his counterpart, Kim Gye Gwan. During the talks, Kelly confronted Kim over the North's uranium enrichment effort and informed him that any improvement in United States–North Korea relations would be conditional on the immediate and verified elimination of the enrichment program.[7] During the two days of meetings, North Korean officials consistently denied the enrichment allegation, until Kang Sok Ju, the vice foreign minister, joined the talks and, according to all U.S. participants, admitted that the enrichment effort did exist. Since then, North Korean officials have consistently denied the admission, claiming that their words were translated incorrectly. U.S. officials maintain that Kim not only admitted to the program's existence but also claimed that North Korea had the right to possess nuclear weapons because of the hostile policies of the Bush administration. Vice Minister Kang reportedly had no response when confronted with the allegation that the enrichment program predated the election of George W. Bush.

In December 2002, after having been confronted by the United States over its alleged uranium enrichment program, North Korea expelled IAEA inspectors from the country and removed all IAEA monitoring equipment and seals from its nuclear facilities, including the seals on the 8,000 fuel rods stored at Yongbyon. In addition, on January 10, 2003, North Korea announced that it was immediately withdrawing from the NPT. North Korea claimed on February 10, 2005, that it had "manufactured" nuclear weapons as a deterrent to U.S. hostility.[8] The

5-megawatt-electric (MWe) reactor at Yongbyon was restarted in 2002 and operated for more than two years. The reactor shut down in April 2005 and could provide North Korea with an additional 12 to 19 kilograms of plutonium.

Since confronting North Korea in October 2002, the United States has sought to convince the country to admit to and eliminate its uranium enrichment program, and also to eliminate all its nuclear weapons capabilities under effective verification. This process has centered on what are known as the six-party talks, which convened in August 2003 and then again in February and June 2004 in Beijing. The talks include representatives from the United States, North Korea, South Korea, China, Japan, and Russia. China was instrumental in creating the talks, and it has been influential (according to both Chinese and American officials) in persuading North Korea to participate in them.[9]

The first two rounds of the six-party talks produced little agreement. The United States has sought to use the talks largely as a vehicle to bring coordinated, international pressure on North Korea to abandon its nuclear activities and has refused to provide anything to North Korea that could be deemed as a reward for Pyongyang's participation in the talks or any interim moves on the North's nuclear program. The United States has also rejected calls to engage in any formal bilateral negotiations with North Korea, something Pyongyang has long sought and that might also be interpreted as a reward for its past behavior. North Korea, for its part, has tried to use the talks as a way of extracting concessions from the United States and other countries and has also tried to leverage the talks by demanding rewards simply for participating in them.

The U.S. posture at the talks changed significantly at their third round, which began on June 21, 2004. At the urging of South Korean and Japanese officials, the United States offered a detailed proposal for ending North Korea's nuclear program. This proposal included U.S. support for incentives for North Korea to be provided by other states—particularly South Korea and Japan, a major change from previous U.S. policy. The proposal called for a new declaration to be made by North Korea, to include all plutonium production and uranium enrichment capabilities, nuclear materials, weapons and related equipment, and for the elimination of all of these to begin after a three-month preparatory period.

In exchange for agreeing to this proposed approach, non-U.S. parties would provide North Korea with heavy fuel oil, and once the declaration was given by the North and deemed credible, the other parties would provide North Korea with multilateral security assurances, which would become more enduring as the process proceeded; begin a study on North Korea's energy requirements to see how to best meet them with non-nuclear energy programs; and begin a discussion of lifting all remaining U.S. sanctions against the North. In describing the talks before Congress, Assistant Secretary Kelly stressed that as North Korea undertook its obligation, the moves by the other parties would be temporary and "would only yield lasting benefits to [North Korea] after the dismantlement of its nuclear program had been completed."[10] No new talks have been held since the third round, as of April 2005. North Korea's February 2005 announcement that it possesses nuclear weapons and the apparent shutdown of its 5-MWe reactor at Yongbyon make an early resumption of the talks unlikely.

Nuclear Analysis

As of the spring of 2005, North Korea may have possessed enough separated plutonium to produce up to nine nuclear weapons. The 5-MWe research reactor at Yongbyon can produce enough plutonium for one more nuclear weapon each year. The United States and several other countries are also convinced that North Korea is developing the ability to produce weapons-grade uranium through centrifuge enrichment. It is unclear when North Korea might be able to start producing enriched uranium. Although there is no conclusive, public evidence that North Korea possesses any actual nuclear weapons, several top officials have stated that it already possesses such weapons. And on February 10, 2005, North Korea declared for the first time that it possesses nuclear weapons. Pyongyang is thought to be capable of building a first-generation nuclear device, given its current state of technology. North Korea's access to the A. Q. Khan black market has only enhanced the assessment that it can produce nuclear weapons. At least one other Khan customer, Libya, obtained complete and detailed nuclear warhead designs from Pakistan.

Over the long run, North Korea has the potential to become a full-fledged nuclear weapon state. Before its decisions to freeze its nuclear program in 1994, Pyongyang was on the verge of becoming a major producer of weapons-grade plutonium. Though there are no public signs that North Korea has resumed construction at other known nuclear facilities, it was previously pursuing nuclear reactors, fuel-fabrication, and spent-fuel reprocessing facilities able to produce 275 kilograms of plutonium a year, enough for 50 weapons annually.[11] This would provide it with enough nuclear materials to build its own nuclear arsenals and to export substantial quantities of plutonium to other states. It was this export capability that, as much as anything, led to the negotiation of the Agreed Framework in 1994.

Previous Plutonium Production

North Korea's nuclear research program is reported to have begun as early as the 1950s.[12] Because it was a Soviet client state, its nuclear engineers were largely trained at Soviet scientific institutes and it received a small research reactor from the USSR that began operation in 1965. Concerns over North Korea's nuclear weapons program did not fully emerge until the mid-1980s. During this period, U.S. intelligence satellites reportedly photographed the construction of a research reactor and the beginnings of a reprocessing facility at Yongbyon.[13] In 1989, open press sources indicated for the first time that North Korea possessed a plutonium production reactor and extraction capability.[14]

Also in 1989, North Korea was reported, based on intelligence sources, to have shut down its main research and plutonium production reactor for approximately 100 days.[15] This would have given it enough time to refuel the entire reactor and provide it with a source of enough nuclear material to build a nuclear device. At the time, neither the United States nor any other country took direct action in response to these activities. The strategy pursued was to press North Korea to join and then come into full compliance with its obligations under the NPT, and to make that compliance a condition of progress on diplomatic issues.

Pyongyang acceded to the NPT on April 18, 1985, after a concerted effort led by the Soviet Union, which hoped to sell North Korea light-water-power reactors (which were never built). North Korea completed the negotiation of a safeguard agreement with the IAEA within the eighteen months required by the treaty, but it was not until April 9, 1992, that Pyongyang finally approved its IAEA safeguard agreement. Initial inspections to verify the accuracy of North Korea's initial declaration began in May 1992. These long-awaited developments came after the United States signaled that it would withdraw its nuclear weapons from South Korea as part of a global tactical nuclear withdrawal in 1991. North Korea had publicly made the withdrawal of U.S. nuclear weapons from South Korea a condition of its completion of a safeguard agreement. The United States had stationed a large number (more than 700 in some years) of nuclear weapons in South Korea as part of its alliance with South Korea and its Cold War strategy of flexible response to a possible attack by the Soviet Union or its allies.

In all, six official IAEA inspection missions took place in North Korea from 1992 to 1993. The initial inspections of North Korea's nuclear facilities included tours of the completed 5-MWe reactor and of the 50-MWe plant still under construction, as well as of the incomplete "radiochemical laboratory," described by the IAEA as a plutonium-reprocessing facility. Subsequent inspections focused mainly on the plutonium-reprocessing facilities in North Korea, including some small-scale extraction equipment, referred to as hot cells.

North Korea informed the IAEA as part of this initial inspection process that it had conducted a one-time plutonium extraction experiment on "damaged" fuel rods removed from the 5-MWe reactor at Yongbyon in 1989. The IAEA was given access to the small amount separated by North Korea (approximately 90 grams,[16] or less than 1/40th of the amount required to build a nuclear device). The IAEA's chemical analysis of samples taken from the radiochemical laboratory and hot cells, however, contradicted North Korea's claims that it had previously separated only the 90 grams of plutonium on one occasion. Instead, the IAEA results indicated that the North had separated plutonium in four campaigns over a three-year period, starting in 1989.[17] The samples taken by the IAEA showed a variety of radioactive by-products that suggested numerous instances of reprocessing activities. In describing the findings, IAEA director general Hans Blix explained, "We found two gloves, a waste glove and a plutonium glove, and they don't match."[18] This means that North Korea's statements regarding its past plutonium production were not consistent with what the samples revealed and indicate that North Korea possesses more plutonium than it has declared to the IAEA or to the international community.

The findings added weight to the allegation that North Korea had removed significant amounts of fuel from its 5-MWe reactor during the observed shutdown in 1989. U.S. intelligence analysts believed that the reactor's core might have been completely replaced during a 100-day shutdown. Intelligence information provided to the IAEA also indicated that waste products from the North's plutonium extraction campaigns may have been stored at two nearby sites, which appeared to be linked to the radiochemical laboratory by underground pipes capable of transporting liquid wastes. The North Koreans had unsuccessfully camouflaged the sites and the underground pipes.

A long series of discussions and negotiations ensued over these issues, including an unusual visit to North Korea by Blix. Yet the talks did not enable the IAEA inspectors to gain the unfettered access to sites and information considered necessary to resolve the discrepancies that had been discovered. On February 11, 1993, Blix officially requested a "special inspection" of the two suspected waste sites, marking the first time in the IAEA's history that it had used its right to conduct such visits. Although these sites had been visited by the IAEA during the third inspection mission to North Korea in September 1993, North Korea did not permit full access to the sites, which were not included in its "initial declaration." Ten days later, North Korea's atomic energy minister informed Blix that the North was refusing the IAEA's special inspection request. And on March 12, in a letter to the three NPT depositary states and the other NPT members, North Korea said that it was exercising its right of withdrawal from the NPT, to take effect in 90 days as spelled out in article 10, which permits such action on 90 days' notice if a party's "supreme national interests" are jeopardized.

After a round of negotiations with the United States in June 1993, North Korea agreed to "suspend" its withdrawal one day short of the 90-day countdown. However, North Korea asserted that it was no longer a full party to the NPT and that the IAEA no longer had the right to conduct even normal routine and ad hoc inspections. During the ensuing nine months, Pyongyang severely constrained the IAEA inspection activities that are needed to preserve the "continuity of safeguards." This led Blix to declare in December 1993 that IAEA safeguards in North Korea could no longer provide "any meaningful assurances" that nuclear materials were not being diverted to weapons uses.[19]

Negotiations between the IAEA and North Korea continued. In March 1994, as part of a complicated package deal with the United States, North Korea initially agreed to an IAEA inspection of its declared facilities, but it then blocked the IAEA from taking key radioactive samples at the plutonium extraction plant at Yongbyon.[20]

More Plutonium

The crisis escalated further in mid-May 1994, when North Korea announced that it was going to defuel its 5-MWe reactor. The need for the IAEA to gain access to the fuel to be removed from this reactor immediately became of international concern, for two reasons. First, the fuel contained up to 30 kilograms of plutonium, which could be used to produce several nuclear weapons. Second, by getting access to the fuel and taking appropriate samples, the IAEA could determine whether the fuel had been in the reactor since its initial operation began in 1986 or whether the fuel was a secondary batch, indicating that North Korea had indeed removed an entire load of fuel from the reactor during the 1989 shutdown.

North Korea steadfastly refused to implement procedures demanded by the IAEA to segregate 300 carefully selected fuel rods from the 8,000-rod core, claiming that it was not a fully bound member of the NPT or of its safeguard agreement.[21] As Pyongyang accelerated and completed the defueling, Hans Blix declared in a letter to the U.N. Security Council on June 2, 1994, that the "agency's ability to ascertain, with sufficient confidence, whether nuclear material from the reactor has been diverted in the past, has been . . . lost."[22] Some controversy surrounds this point, because other ways to determine the reactor's history have since been developed and put forward.

These developments prompted the United States to circulate a proposal to the U.N. Security Council on June 15 calling for two phases of sanctions against North Korea. The first phase of the sanctions, which were to be activated after a grace period, consisted of a worldwide ban on arms imports from, and arms exports to, North Korea, along with a downgrading of diplomatic ties. In the second phase, to be triggered if the North continued to reject the IAEA's demands, a worldwide ban on financial dealings with Pyongyang would be implemented.[23] Moreover, the United States publicly began discussing plans to reinforce its military presence in South Korea, and there were growing calls for U.S. military action against North Korea to prevent it from gaining full access to the plutonium-bearing spent fuel.

The crisis eased after former U.S. president Jimmy Carter met with North Korean president Kim Il Sung on June 16 and 17. The North Korean leader agreed to freeze his country's nuclear program if the United States would resume high-level diplomatic talks. These negotiations took place in July but were suspended until early August because of the sudden death of Kim Il Sung on July 9. These talks eventually led to the negotiation of an Agreed Statement on August 12, 1994, under which, in broad terms, North Korea agreed to dismantle the elements of its nuclear program linked to the production of nuclear arms in return for the supply of two, less proliferation-prone, light-water reactors (LWRs) and a number of other energy- and security-related inducements.[24]

The Agreed Framework

The United States and North Korea engaged in several months of negotiations in the summer and fall of 1994, a process that resulted in the Agreed Framework, which was signed on October 21, 1994.[25] The deal contained a basic trade of obligations, with North Korea agreeing to freeze and eventually dismantle its nuclear facilities and eliminate its nuclear weapon capabilities in exchange for the construction of two modern nuclear power reactors and normalized relations with the United States.[26]

The agreement required North Korea to remain a member of the NPT and to come into full compliance with its IAEA safeguard agreement once a "significant portion of the LWR project is completed, but before delivery of key nuclear components." This delay postponed the question of North Korea's past production of plutonium until the final stages of the agreement's implementation, leaving open the question of North Korea's nuclear capabilities while its existing capabilities were frozen. Moreover, it established North Korea's obligation to accept whatever steps the IAEA decides are necessary to verify the accuracy of the country's nuclear declaration.

The Agreed Framework also included a U.S. pledge not to use or threaten to use nuclear weapons against the North, and a North Korean commitment to implement the 1992 North–South Joint Declaration on the Denuclearization of the Korean Peninsula, which banned uranium enrichment and plutonium reprocessing on the entire peninsula.

Uranium Enrichment

The full scope of North Korea's efforts to acquire a uranium enrichment program is unknown. As noted above, U.S. intelligence agencies concluded in the summer of 2002 that North Korea had embarked on a uranium enrichment program, was buying centrifuge equipment from outside suppliers, and had begun the construction of a uranium enrichment centrifuge facility. At the time, the Central Intelligence Agency reported to Congress that "North [Korea] is constructing a plant that could produce enough weapons-grade uranium for two or more nuclear weapons per year when fully operational—which could be as soon as mid-decade."[27] Other sources claim that North Korea was able to obtain parts for just over 2,000 centrifuges, but it was not clear if the North had acquired enough complete centrifuge kits to assemble that many units, or if it had the technical training or assistance needed to assemble and operate a full-scale uranium enrichment cascade.[28] Moreover, there is no publicly available evidence that North Korea can produce large amounts of uranium hexaflouride, which is the feed material needed to enrich uranium through the centrifuge process.

The majority of publicly available evidence surrounding North Korea's enrichment effort comes through tracking Pyongyang's foreign procurement efforts.[29] North Korea's continued refusal to publicly acknowledge that it possesses a uranium enrichment program, and the United States' inability or refusal to publicly identify uranium enrichment sites, had initially led South Korea and Chinese officials to express doubts about the U.S. claims of a uranium program by the North. These doubts have been reduced by American sharing of information with both of these countries, but many questions about the scale, progress, and eventually completion of North Korea's uranium efforts remain unanswered. It is also possible, though not yet proven, that North Korea purchases centrifuge equipment for the purpose of selling or transferring it to other customers of the A. Q. Khan network and no longer possesses any uranium enrichment equipment.

Biological and Chemical Weapons Analysis

North Korea possesses chemical weapons and a large quantity of chemical precursors for the production of such weapons. It is likely to have the ability to produce "bulk quantities of nerve, blister, choking, and blood agent."[30] Moreover, North Korea has not signed the Chemical Weapons Convention, and it has not acknowledged that it possesses chemical weapons or agreed to eliminate its holdings. North Korea is thought to possess the means to deliver chemical weapons by ballistic missile, as well as by conventional artillery or aircraft. North Korean troops have also been trained to fight in contaminated areas, according to the U.S. Defense Department.[31]

North Korea maintains facilities involved in producing or storing chemical precursors, agents, and weapons. It has at least eight industrial facilities that can produce chemical agents. The production rate and types of munitions, however, are uncertain. Presumably, adamsite, phosgene, prussic acid, sarin, tabun, and a family of mustard gases—constituting the basis of North Korea's chemical weapons—are produced there. According to the assessment of U.S. intelligence services, North Korea's reserves, accommodated at perhaps a half dozen major storage sites and in as many as 170 mountain tunnels, total at least 180 to 250 metric tons, with some estimates of chemical stockpiles running as high as 5,000 metric tons.[32]

North Korea possesses a rudimentary biological weapons capability and has engaged in biological research since the 1960s. Its biological weapons program is not nearly as advanced as its nuclear, chemical, or ballistic missile programs, but it is believed to have the basic infrastructure to produce several biological agents, including anthrax, cholera, and plague. It could deliver such weapons by several means, including artillery or possibly ballistic missiles.[33]

Missile Analysis

North Korea has an extensive ballistic missile program, based primarily on technology derived from Soviet-designed Scud-B missiles. North Korea acquired a number of Scud missiles from Egypt in the 1970s. It either successfully reverse-engineered the system (improving its range and accuracy) or received substantially more equipment and assistance from the Soviet Union than is publicly known. With substantial financing from customer states, including Iran, North Korea has developed and deployed the Scud–Mod B (with a 320- to 340-kilometer range and a 1,000-kilogram payload), the Scud–Mod C (with a 500-kilometer range and a 700-kilogram payload), and the No Dong (with a 1,000-kilometer range and a 700–1,000 kilogram payload).

In addition, North Korea tested a ballistic missile/space launch vehicle known as the Taepo Dong I on August 31, 1998. Although the third stage of the missile failed to boost its payload into orbit, the system demonstrated North Korea's accelerating ability to launch a multistage missile and to develop a system with the potential for intercontinental range. The system is believed to use a No Dong as its first stage and a Scud-B as its second stage. The third stage is thought to be a solid rocket "kick motor" of unknown origin.

North Korea is also reportedly working on a longer-range Taepo Dong II missile that could enable it to deliver a nuclear-sized payload to the continental United States. The threat from this untested missile is the main justification for the U.S. development and deployment of missile defense interceptors in Alaska and California. However, North Korea is observing a self-declared moratorium on missile flight tests, which was established as part of its discussions with the United States on a broader agreement to end Pyongyang's missile production and export activities.

North Korea is the leading exporter of ballistic missiles to the developing world, and its exports have continued despite its flight-test moratorium. States that have received missiles from North Korea include Iran, Libya, Pakistan, and Syria. Egypt may also have received some systems from Pyongyang. Iran is also believed to have received North Korean assistance in establishing its own missile production capabilities and may intend to enter the missile export market. Iran's and Pakistan's missile capabilities are thought to be highly dependent on North Korean technology and equipment.

NOTES

1. National Intelligence Council, *Foreign Missile Developments and the Ballistic Missile Threat through 2015* (Washington, D.C.: National Intelligence Council, 2001), p. 12.
2. Robert S. Norris, Hans M. Kristensen, and Joshua Handler. "North Korea's Nuclear Program, 2003," *Bulletin of the Atomic Scientists*, March/April 2003, pp. 74–77.
3. John Bolton, undersecretary of state for arms control and international security, "Remarks to the Fifth Biological Weapons Conventional Meeting," Geneva, November 19, 2001.
4. Secretary Colin L. Powell, U.S. Department of State, "Press Availability with Her Excellency Anna Lindh, Minister of Foreign Affairs of Sweden," March 6, 2001; available at www.state.gov/secretary/former/powell/remarks/2001/1116.htm.
5. "Bush Statement on Undertaking Talks with North Korea," available at www.whitehouse.gov/news/releases/2001/06/20010611-4.html.
6. The Agreed Framework contains no legal prohibitions against the construction of new nuclear facilities by North Korea. Moreover, purchasing uranium enrichment equipment does not, by itself, constitute a violation of the North–South agreement or the NPT. The start of construction of a uranium enrichment facility without providing design information to the IAEA would be a violation of safeguards and therefore the NPT. North Korea claimed at the time it was not fully bound by the NPT and was under a special status having "temporarily suspended" its withdrawal from the NPT, a status rejected by the United States.
7. For details of the controversy surrounding these issues, see Kenneth Pollack, "The United States, North Korea, and the End of the Agreed Framework," *Naval War College Review*, vol. 56, no. 3, Summer 2003, pp. 11–49.
8. KCNA, "DPRK FM on Its Stand to Suspend Its Participation in Six-Day Talks for Indeterminate Period," February 10, 2005; available at www.kcna.co.jp.
9. See Pollack, "United States, North Korea, and the End of the Agreed Framework."
10. "Dealing with North Korea's Nuclear Programs," prepared testimony of James A. Kelly before the Senate Foreign Relations Committee, July 15, 2004.
11. "Statement of Hon. Robert Gallucci, Ambassador-at-Large, to Senate Committee on Foreign Relations, December 1, 1994."
12. Mike Mazarr, *North Korea and the Bomb: A Case Study in Nonproliferation* (New York: St. Martin's Press, 1995), p. 25.
13. Don Oberdorfer, *The Two Koreas: A Contemporary History* (Lexington, Mass.: Addison-Wesley, 1997), p. 250.
14. John Fialka, "North Korea May Be Developing Ability to Produce Nuclear Weapons," *Wall Street Journal*, July 19, 1989.
15. Les Aspin, *McNeil-Lehrer Newshour*, December 1993.
16. R. Jeffrey Smith, "N. Korea and the Bomb: High-Tech Hide-and-Seek," *Washington Post*, April 27, 1993.

17. Mark Hibbs, "IAEA Special Inspection Effort Meeting Diplomatic Resistance," *Nucleonics Week*, February 18, 1993, p. 16; Smith, "N. Korea and the Bomb"; Hibbs, "U.S. Might Help North Korea Refuel Reactor," *Nuclear Fuel*, November 8, 1993, p. 1; and Smith, "West Watching Reactor for Sign of North Korea's Nuclear Intentions," *Washington Post*, December 12, 1993.
18. Smith, "N. Korea and the Bomb."
19. David Sanger, "U.N. Agency Finds No Assurance North Korea Bans Nuclear Arms," *New York Times*, December 3, 1993. For a detailed examination of the IAEA's relations with North Korea, see Leon Sigal, *Disarming Strangers: Nuclear Diplomacy with North Korea* (Princeton, N.J.: Princeton University Press, 1998).
20. R. Jeffrey Smith, "N. Korean Conduct in Inspection Draws Criticism of U.S. Officials," *Washington Post*, March 10, 1994; Smith, "Inspection of North Korea's Nuclear Facilities Is Halted," *Washington Post*, March 16, 1994; David E. Sanger, "North Korea Said to Block Taking of Radioactive Samples from Site," *New York Times*, March 16, 1994; and Michael R. Gordon, "U.S. Goes to U.N. to Increase the Pressure on North Korea," *New York Times*, March 22, 1994. For a comprehensive assessment of the March 1994 inspection, see Sigal, *Disarming Strangers*, pp. 95–108.
21. Mark Hibbs, "Fuel Readiness Means North Korea Can Start Reactors Up on Schedule," *Nucleonics Week*, April 7, 1994, p. 14; and R. Jeffrey Smith, "N. Korea Refuses Demand to Inspect Reactor Fuel," *Washington Post*, April 28, 1994.
22. "Letter from the Director General of the IAEA Addressed to the Secretary-General of the United Nations Relating to North Korea," June 2, 1994.
23. Ann Devroy, "U.S. to Seek Sanctions on N. Korea," *Washington Post*, June 3, 1994; Michael Gordon, "White House Asks for Global Sanctions on North Koreans," *New York Times*, June 3, 1994; David Ottaway, "N. Korea Forbids Inspections," *Washington Post*, June 8, 1994; and Julia Preston, "U.S. Unveils Proposal for Sanctions," *Washington Post*, June 16, 1994.
24. T. R. Reid, "Leaders of 2 Koreas Seek First Summit," *Washington Post*, June 19, 1994; and Michael Gordon, "Back from Korea, Carter Declares the Crisis Is Over," *New York Times*, June 20, 1994. For a detailed account of the Carter-Kim meeting, see Sigal, *Disarming Strangers*, pp. 150–162.
25. Mark Hibbs, "U.S., DPRK to Meet in Berlin on LWR Transfer, Spent Fuel Details," *Nucleonics Week*, September 8, 1994, p. 17; "North Korea Rejects Special Nuclear Inspections," Reuters, September 16, 1994; and "Agreed Framework between the United States of America and the Democratic People's Republic of Korea," October 21, 1994.
26. For a complete history of the negotiation and contents of the Agreed Framework, see Joel S. Wit, Daniel B. Poneman, and Robert L. Gallucci, *Going Critical: The First North Korean Nuclear Crisis* (Washington, D.C.: Brookings Institution Press, 2004).
27. "Unclassified CIA Fact Sheet," November 19, 2002.
28. Author discussions with Korean government officials.
29. Joby Warrick, "U.S. Followed the Aluminum: Pyongyang's Effort to Buy Metal Was Tip to Plans," *Washington Post*, October 18, 2002.
30. Central Intelligence Agency, "Unclassified Report to Congress on the Acquisition of Technology Relating to Weapons of Mass Destruction and Advanced Conventional Munitions, 1 July through 31 December 2003," available at www.cia.gov/cia/reports/721_reports/july_dec2003.htm#5.
31. U.S. Department of Defense, *Proliferation: Threat and Response* (Washington, D.C.: U.S. Department of Defense, 2001), pp. 11–12.
32. Federation of American Scientists, Weapons of Mass Destruction web site, www.fas.org/nuke/guide/dprk/cw/index.html.
33. U.S. Department of Defense, *Proliferation: Threat and Response*, pp. 10–11.

Table 14.1. **North Korea's Nuclear Infrastructure**

Name/Location of Facility	Type/Status	IAEA Safeguards
	Power Reactors	
Sinpo-1 Kumho[1]	Light-water, PWR, 1,040 MWe, construction suspended	No
Sinpo-2 Kumho	Light-water, 1,000 MWe, construction suspended	No
Yongbyon	Gas-graphite, nat. U, 5 MWe, operating	No
Yongbyon	Gas-graphite, nat. U, 50 MWe, construction halted, no evidence that it has resumed	No
Taechon	Gas-graphite, nat. U, 200 MWe, construction halted, no evidence that it has resumed	No
	Research Factors	
IRT Yongbyon	Pool-type, HEU (80 percent), 8 MWt, operating	No[2]
Yongbyon	Critical assembly, 0.1 MWt	No
Pyongyang	Subcritical assembly	No
	Reprocessing (Plutonium Extraction)	
Radiochemical Laboratory Yongbyon[4]	Operational[3]	No
Pyongyang	Soviet-supplied laboratory-scale hot cells, status unknown[5]	No
	Uranium Processing	
Pyongsan	Uranium ore processing, status unknown	No
Sanchon-Wolbingson mine Pakchon	Uranium ore processing, status unknown	No
Pyongsan	Uranium ore processing, status unknown	No
Pakchon	Uranium ore processing, status unknown	No
Yongbyon	Uranium purification (UO_2) facility, operating	No

Yongbyon	Fuel-fabrication facility, partially operational, partially under maintenance	No
Yongbyon	Pilot-scale fuel-fabrication facility, dismantled, according to North Korean officials	No

ABBREVIATIONS

HEU	highly enriched uranium
nat. U	natural uranium
MWe	megawatts electric
MWt	megawatts thermal
PWR	pressurized water reactor

SOURCES

IAEA, "Nuclear Fuel Cycle Information Systems." Available at www.nfcis.iaea.org/NFCISMAin.asp?Region=The%20World&Country=All&Type=All&Status=All&Scale=All&Order=2&Page=1&RightP=List&Table=1. Nuclear Engineering International, *World Nuclear Industry Handbook* (Sidcup, U.K.: Wilmington Publishing, 2004). "Visit to the Yongbyon Nuclear Scientific Research Center in North Korea, Testimony of Siegfried S. Hecker, senior fellow, Los Alamos National Laboratory, before the Senate Committee on Foreign Relations, January 21, 2004."

NOTES

1. The Sinpo-1 and Sinpo-2 light-water reactors were being constructed by the Korean Peninsula Energy Development Organization (KEDO). Construction has been suspended since the breakdown of the Agreed Framework and North Korea's withdrawal from the NPT in late 2002 and early 2003, respectively.
2. According to the IAEA, because the IRT research reactor and the critical assembly located at Yongbyon were acquired from the Soviet Union, both are subject to safeguards regardless of whether or not North Korea is a party to the NPT. (See IAEA Information Circular 66 for more). Neither of these facilities is currently under safeguards, however, because North Korea has not permitted inspectors to return to the country since expelling them at the end of 2002.
3. According to Siegfried Hecker, a senior fellow at Los Alamos National Laboratory who visited the Yongbyon nuclear facility in January 2004, North Korean officials claimed that they had successfully extracted plutonium from all 8,000 spent-fuel rods stored at Yongbyon between January and June 2003.
4. According to North Korean officials, capable of reprocessing 110 tons of spent fuel per year.
5. Jared S. Dreicer, "How Much Plutonium Could Have Been Produced in the DPRK IRT Reactor?" *Science & Global Security,* vol. 8, 2000, pp. 273–286.

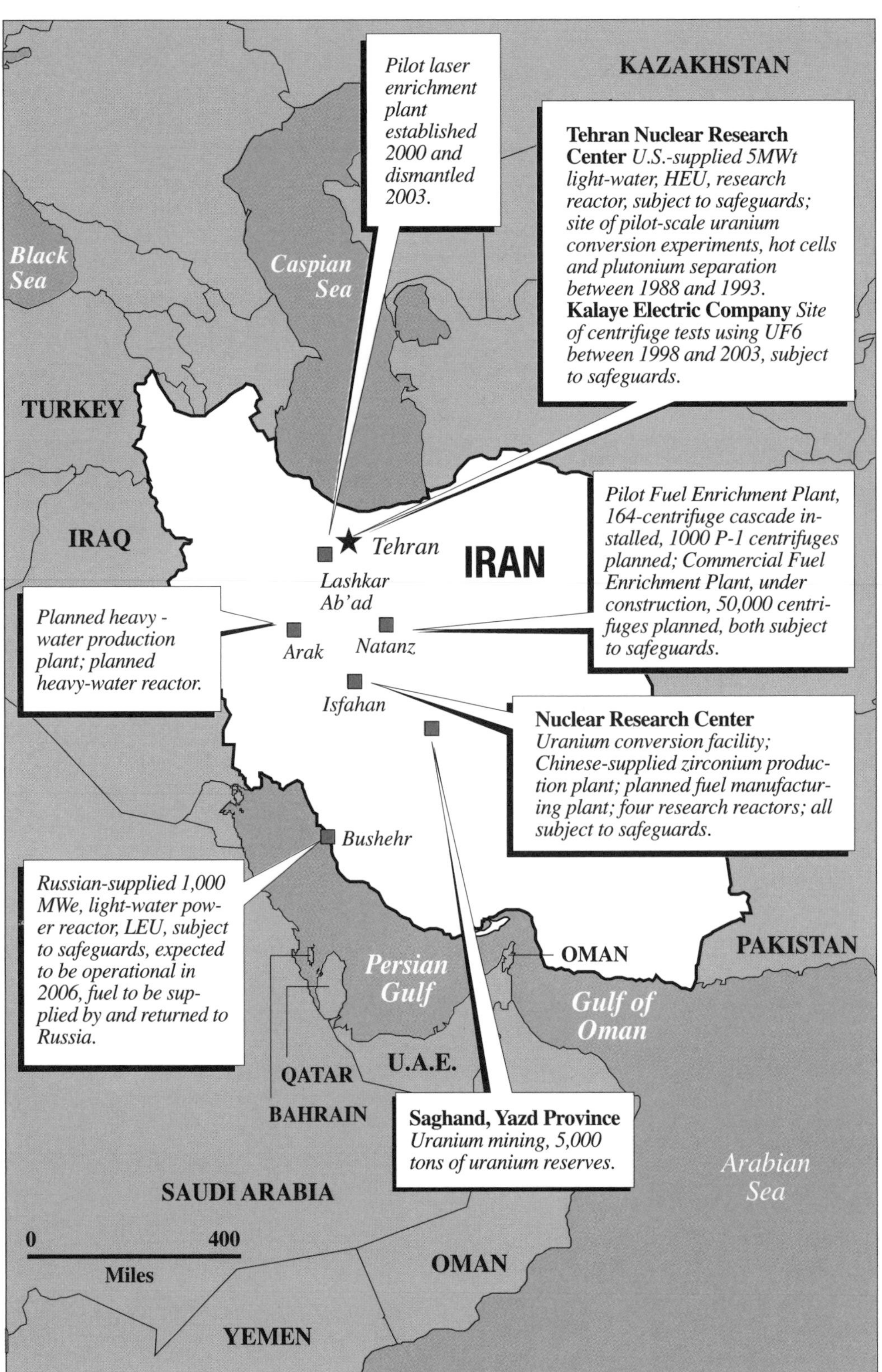
KAZAKHSTAN
Pilot laser enrichment plant established 2000 and dismantled 2003.
Tehran Nuclear Research Center U.S.-supplied 5MWt light-water, HEU, research reactor, subject to safeguards; site of pilot-scale uranium conversion experiments, hot cells and plutonium separation between 1988 and 1993.
Kalaye Electric Company Site of centrifuge tests using UF6 between 1998 and 2003, subject to safeguards.
Black Sea
Caspian Sea
TURKEY
IRAQ
Tehran
IRAN
Lashkar Ab'ad
Pilot Fuel Enrichment Plant, 164-centrifuge cascade installed, 1000 P-1 centrifuges planned; Commercial Fuel Enrichment Plant, under construction, 50,000 centrifuges planned, both subject to safeguards.
Planned heavy-water production plant; planned heavy-water reactor.
Arak
Natanz
Isfahan
Nuclear Research Center Uranium conversion facility; Chinese-supplied zirconium production plant; planned fuel manufacturing plant; four research reactors; all subject to safeguards.
Bushehr
Russian-supplied 1,000 MWe, light-water power reactor, LEU, subject to safeguards, expected to be operational in 2006, fuel to be supplied by and returned to Russia.
Persian Gulf
OMAN
PAKISTAN
Gulf of Oman
QATAR
U.A.E.
BAHRAIN
Saghand, Yazd Province Uranium mining, 5,000 tons of uranium reserves.
Arabian Sea
SAUDI ARABIA
0
400
Miles
OMAN
YEMEN

CHAPTER 15

Iran

Nuclear Weapons Capability

Iran does not possess nuclear weapons, but for more than two decades Tehran has secretly pursued the ability to produce nuclear materials that can be used in weapons. U.S. officials and intelligence services in several other nations have concluded that Iran is embarked on a nuclear weapon program, although no direct evidence of weapon activities has been made public.[1] Iran remains a party to the Non-Proliferation Treaty (NPT). Despite Iran's membership in the International Atomic Energy Agency (IAEA), that agency's Secretariat concluded in November 2004 that Iran had "failed . . . to meet its obligations under its safeguards agreement." Efforts to sanction Iran for its "failures" have been put on hold while members of the European Union attempt to negotiate an end to Iran's nuclear fuel production programs.

Past estimates about when Iran might be able to produce a nuclear weapon have proven unreliable. For example, a 1992 Central Intelligence Agency (CIA) estimate concluded that Iran would have the bomb by 2000.[2] If Iran's nuclear activities continued without outside constraint and without significant outside assistance, it could take several years for Iran to build and operate a fully functioning uranium enrichment "cascade" and an additional one to two years for that facility to produce enough weapons-grade material for the country's first nuclear device.

Missile Capability

Iran possesses up to 300 Scud-B missiles with a 300-kilometer range and with a payload of 1,000 kilograms, and perhaps 100 Scud-Cs with an approximate range of 500 kilometers with a 1,000-kilogram payload.[3] Iran has also received enough assistance from North Korea to enable the country to produce its own Scud missiles.[4]

Iran has conducted at least ten tests of the medium-range Shahab III. The system is derived from the North Korean No Dong missile, with a range of 1,300 kilometers and a payload of about 750 kilograms. The first flight test was carried out on July 22, 1998, and more recently it was tested on October 20, 2004.[5] Former Iranian president Akbar Hashemi Rafsanjani claimed on October 5, 2004, that Iran possessed a missile with a range of 2,000 kilometers, but he provided no evidence to support this claim.[6]

Both Iranian and foreign officials often claim greater progress for Tehran's missile program than tests seem to indicate. Some Western intelligence officials believe that the Shahab III, in an August 2004 test, traveled only 100 kilometers before crashing to the ground.[7]

The Shahab III has a sufficient range and payload to deliver a nuclear warhead as far as Israel and parts of southern Europe. It is not known, however, if Iran possesses the technology needed to miniaturize a nuclear warhead to deliver it by missile. Iran has built and publicly displayed prototypes of the missile, and a limited number reportedly have been deployed with units of Iran's elite Revolutionary Guard.[8] For several years, U.S. officials have assessed that Tehran could have the Shahab III on "emergency operational status."[9] In November 2004, Iranian defense minister Ali Shamkhani claimed that Iran was capable of mass producing Shahab III missiles, although this claim has not been confirmed.[10]

Iran allegedly bought six KH-55 cruise missiles from Ukraine in 2000. These Soviet-era missiles are designed to carry a 200-kiloton nuclear warhead on Russian-made Tupolev long-range bombers.[11] Iran does not possess such bombers, but it may be able to adapt its Soviet-built Su-24 strike aircraft to carry the KH-55.[12]

Biological and Chemical Weapons Capability

Although Iran is a member of the Biological Weapons Convention, U.S. intelligence reports from 2003 claim that Iran probably maintains an "offensive biological weapon program," with the capability to produce small quantities of biological weapon (BW) agents but limited ability to weaponize them. There is no independent confirmation of these claims.

In May 1998, after acceding to the Chemical Weapons Convention, Tehran acknowledged its previous chemical weapon (CW) development and production. The Iranian CW program began in the 1980s during the war with Iraq, and Iranian officials say that the program was dismantled at the war's end. The CIA, however, claims that Iran continues to seek production technology, training, and expertise from Chinese entities that could further Tehran's efforts to achieve an indigenous capability to produce chemical nerve agents. The CIA believes that Iran likely possesses both a stockpile of blister, blood, choking, and probably nerve agents and also the bombs and artillery shells to deliver them, which it had previously manufactured.[13] There is no independent confirmation of these claims.

The Strategic Context

A Persian power with a keen sense of history, Iran occupies a pivotal position straddling the Caspian Sea and the Persian Gulf, a vital maritime pathway for crude oil transport. Iran has the largest population in the Middle East and the world's third largest oil reserves and second largest natural gas reserves, and it aspires to again become the region's major power, commensurate with its history, geography, and resources. Some Iranian leaders have come to see the possession of unconventional weapons, including nuclear weapons and ballistic and cruise missiles, as critical parts of their national security and domestic political strategies.

Since the removal of Saddam Hussein from power in Iraq, Iran has likely seen unconventional weapons as a deterrent to possible U.S. military action—particularly given the large U.S. military presence in the region—and as a way to increase Tehran's power and prestige in the Persian Gulf. Iranian officials have also apparently been influenced by Israel's, India's, and Pakistan's advanced nuclear capabilities; North Korea's ability to deter U.S. coercion with its nuclear capabilities; and Israel's growing ties with Turkey to the north and India to the east. In addition, military officials in Iran may see nuclear weapons as a way to compensate for the gap between Iran's conventional military, constrained by U.S. sanctions, as compared with Gulf Arab states, which spend vast amounts of money on state-of-the-art, high-technology weaponry—often supplied by the United States.[14]

In recent years, the pursuit of civilian nuclear capabilities has become a potent domestic issue in Iran. Indeed, both conservatives and reformers support Iran's development of its nuclear fuel cycle capabilities as an inherent right accorded by the NPT. In October 2004, the parliament voted unanimously to resume uranium enrichment after a temporary suspension;[15] and in November of that year, hundreds of university students gathered outside the Atomic Energy Organization demanding that the government not concede Iran's right to peaceful nuclear technology.[16] Iran's pursuit of nuclear capabilities is seen as a source of national pride across the political spectrum, a situation that may greatly complicate efforts to convince Iranian officials to end the pursuit of their country's sensitive nuclear fuel cycle programs.

Ostensibly, Iran's nuclear program is peaceful. However, the country hid sensitive nuclear activities from the IAEA and the world for more than eighteen years, having acquired advanced uranium enrichment equipment and expertise through the nuclear black market of Pakistan's A. Q. Khan. The discovery of these clandestine activities has contributed to international suspicion about Iran's program. The successful acquisition by Iran of a fissile material production capability or of actual nuclear weapons would be a serious blow to global nonproliferation efforts. If the international community is unable or unwilling to impose penalties on Iran, and if Tehran succeeds in continuing its nuclear development, many states will question the strength and utility of the nonproliferation system. Moreover, there is serious concern that a nuclear-armed Iran would lead other states in the Gulf and Middle East to reexamine their nuclear options, including possibly Saudi Arabia, Egypt, Syria, and even Turkey, a NATO member and European Union applicant.[17] This potential wave of proliferation would seriously challenge regional and global security and undermine the worldwide effort to prevent the spread of nuclear weapons.

Iran's Nuclear History

In 1951, the democratically elected prime minister of Iran, Mohammad Mossadeq, nationalized the country's oil assets. The leaders of the United States and the United Kingdom concluded that his policies meant "that Iran was in real danger of falling behind the Iron Curtain" resulting in "a victory for the Soviets in the Cold War and a major setback for the West in the Middle East."[18] Declassified documents show that in 1953 President Dwight D. Eisenhower approved a joint British-American operation to overthrow Mossadeq, code named Operation Ajax. The CIA successfully toppled the young democratic government and installed Mohammad Raza Shah Pehlavi as the new pro-West ruler, sowing the seeds of Iran's lingering distrust of Western powers.[19]

Under the shah's autocratic rule, relations between the United States and Iran thrived. During this period, Iran began its nuclear power program, which then progressed slowly until the late 1960s. Also during this period, Iran acquired its first nuclear research reactor, a small U.S.-supplied 5-megawatt-thermal (MWt) reactor that is still in operation at the Tehran Nuclear Research Center.[20] During the 1970s, Iran developed plans to build 22 nuclear power reactors with an electrical output of 23 gigawatts. These nuclear activities were halted when the shah was toppled in 1979 and the Islamic regime led by Ayatollah Ruholla Khomeini came to power. The new revolutionary government inherited two partially completed West German–supplied nuclear power reactors at Bushehr, but Khomeini froze construction of these reactors and all other work on "Western" nuclear technologies and forced many Western-educated scientists and engineers to flee the country.[21]

Iraq's use of chemical weapons during the Iran-Iraq War in the 1980s drove Iran's more recent pursuit of nuclear technologies, chemical weapons, missile systems, and possibly biological weapons. Iranians often point out that no nation came to Iran's aid when it was invaded and attacked by Iraq with chemical weapons. U.S. relations with Iraq actually improved during this period, as U.S. officials aided the secular Saddam as a counter to what was seen as the greater threat of Iran's militant Islamic theocracy. The regime in Tehran appears to have then decided to pursue unconventional weapons as an important means of deterrence and self-defense.

Shortly after the Iran-Iraq cease-fire, Akbar Hashemi-Rafsanjani, then–speaker of the Iranian parliament and commander-in-chief of Iran's armed forces and later Iran's president, declared:

> With regard to chemical, bacteriological, and radiological weapons training, it was made very clear during the war that these weapons are very decisive. It was also made clear that the moral teachings of the world are not very effective when war reaches a serious stage and the world does not respect its own resolutions and closes its eyes to the violations and all the aggressions which are committed in the battlefield. We should fully equip ourselves both in the offensive and defensive use of chemical, bacteriological, and radiological weapons. From now on you should make use of the opportunity and perform this task.[22]

The missile programs have continued until the present day; it is unclear if other programs have as well. Iran has relied extensively on outside assistance for the acquisition of its unconventional weapons capabilities, including direct assistance from the A. Q. Khan black market network, China, North Korea, and Ukraine, and indirect assistance from Russia and countries in Europe.

Nuclear Analysis

As of the spring of 2005, there was no evidence that Iran possesses enough fissile material to produce nuclear weapons or possessed any nuclear devices.[23] Yet for the past two decades, Iran has been engaged in a secret, multifaceted program to produce nuclear materials. This has created widespread concern that Iranian leaders are committed to acquiring the means to produce nuclear weapons, if not actual weapons. In addition, there have been reports, some more reliable than others, that Iranian agents have sought to acquire nuclear materials and even weapons from other countries, including stocks of plutonium and highly enriched uranium left in Kazakhstan after the fall of the Soviet Union.

In 2002, an Iranian opposition group revealed that the country's nuclear program was much more extensive and alarming than Tehran had previously declared, or than of which the IAEA was aware (see table 15.1 at the end of the chapter). After almost two years of intensive investigations, the IAEA reported in November 2004 that it was still not "in a position to conclude that there are no undeclared nuclear materials or activities in Iran."[24] It is now known that Iran's activities include the pursuit of several nuclear material production technologies that, if mastered, could provide Tehran with the ability to produce the core materials for nuclear weapons. Iran maintains that all its nuclear activities, even those previously hidden from the IAEA, are intended for peaceful purposes; and it has agreed to place all its nuclear activities under IAEA safeguards. Moreover, in 2003 Iran signed and pledged to implement the IAEA's Additional Protocol, which includes expanded inspection rights and tools.

Uranium Enrichment

Iran has pursued at least two different methods for enriching uranium: gas centrifuges and lasers. Work on the gas-centrifuge enrichment program appears to have begun in 1985, while the laser enrichment program began under the shah in the 1970s. Work on Iran's uranium centrifuge was greatly accelerated in the 1990s after Iran gained access to centrifuge technology and material through the A. Q. Khan network, although exactly when these contacts were made remains unclear. Iran had previously tried to purchase a centrifuge facility from Russia in the 1990s, a deal that died after the United States complained to Moscow about the potential proliferation implications of such a facility.

CENTRIFUGE PROGRAM. Iran's uranium enrichment program involves the acquisition, testing, and production of two types of centrifuges, known as the P-1 and the more efficient P-2 designs (the "P" stands for the Pakistani origins of the design). All of Iran's known installed and production capabilities rely on the P-1 design, although in January 2004 Iran acknowledged that it had received advanced P-2 centrifuge drawings from foreign sources in 1995. Iran maintains that no P-2 centrifuges or components were obtained from abroad and that all P-2 components in its possession were produced domestically. Tehran claims that information about the P-2 program had not been included in previous declarations (which it had characterized as correct and complete, including its October 2003 declarations to the IAEA) due to "time constraints."

Iran has a complete pilot-scale centrifuge facility and a larger, as yet incomplete, industrial-scale centrifuge facility, both located at Natanz, approximately 200 miles south of Tehran. The site contains buildings both above and below ground and covers approximately 100,000 square meters. In August 2002, the National Council of Resistance of Iran, an opposition group based in France, publicly disclosed the existence of the site, which had previously been unknown and undeclared to the IAEA. After the disclosure, the IAEA conducted its first visit to the site in February 2003, and it has since inspected numerous times and taken more than 300 environmental samples at this and related sites.

Iran had planned to eventually install up to 1,000 P-1 centrifuges at the pilot enrichment plant. When operations were suspended in November 2004, the site contained 164 centrifuges. Between March and May 2003, the IAEA took environmental samples before uranium was officially introduced at the facility. These samples revealed particles of highly enriched uranium, the production of which Iran had previously denied. Under Iran's safeguards obligations, it is required to declare all facilities to the IAEA 180 days before the introduction of nuclear materials to the facility. Though officials in several countries, especially in the United States, thought contamination indicated that Iran was working on fissile material for nuclear weapons, Iranian officials attributed the sample results to the contamination of imported centrifuge components, which were believed to have come from Pakistan. Iran had earlier denied importing any centrifuge components, but when confronted with the evidence changed its story. The IAEA's November 2004 report concluded that this explanation appears plausible, although the IAEA had not yet been granted sufficient cooperation by Pakistan to fully confirm its findings.

In June 2003, Iran officially introduced uranium hexafluoride (UF_6) into a single centrifuge at the pilot plant for testing purposes. On August 19, 2003, Iran began testing a small, ten-machine cascade with UF_6 gas. In October 2003, Iran was finalizing installation of a test 164-machine cascade at the site, but it shut the cascade down that month as part of its agreement with the European Union. Iran does not appear either to have mastered the techniques needed to reliably operate the cascade or to have restarted tests during 2004.[25] Officials from several nations believe that Iran's attempt to produce uranium hexafluoride in November 2004 failed to produce a gas of sufficient quality that could be used in centrifuge enrichment.[26] Further cascade operations are precluded by the November 2004 suspension negotiated with the European Union and monitored by the IAEA. Centrifuge work had not restarted as of the spring of 2005.

The industrial-scale plant, which consists of three underground structures, was originally scheduled to start accepting P-1 centrifuges in 2005. The two largest buildings would house cascade halls large enough to contain approximately 50,000 centrifuge machines.[27] No centrifuges had been installed at the site when the November 2004 suspension was implemented.

Most of the known research and development of Iran's enrichment program has taken place at the Kalaye Electric Company facility. Iran initially denied, but subsequently admitted in 2003, that a small number of gas centrifuges was tested with uranium gas at the site between 1998 and 2002. These experiments reportedly involved 1.9 kilograms of UF_6. Iran claims that it did not enrich uranium beyond 1.2 percent uranium-235 (U-235).

Iran has also developed and built the full suite of supporting capabilities needed to pursue a uranium enrichment capability, including uranium mining, milling, and conversion. It is not clear that Iran's uranium reserves are sufficient, however, to provide enough material to fuel the Bushehr reactors or additional reactors, raising further questions about the peaceful nature of Iran's nuclear activities. If, as Iran claims, its goal in pursuing uranium enrichment is to become more independent of foreign supplies of fuel, then it would also need to possess a reliable domestic source of uranium. Without a large supply of indigenous uranium ore, it is difficult to justify the fuel cycle program it is pursuing on commercial or self-sufficiency grounds.

LASER ENRICHMENT. Iran's laser enrichment program, which began in the 1970s, is based on two techniques: atomic vapor laser isotope separation (AVLIS) and molecular isotope separation (MLIS). The IAEA has completed its review of the AVLIS program and has concluded that the levels of enrichment achieved matched Iran's description of the activity, that is, up to 15 percent U-235 enrichment. The IAEA did, however, determine that the equipment could have been used for the production of highly enriched uranium.[28] Iran established a pilot laser enrichment plant at a site known as Lashkar Ab'ad in 2000. Laser enrichment experiments at the site between October 2002 and January 2003 used 22 kilograms of natural uranium metal and produced small amounts (milligrams) of reactor-grade enriched uranium (3–4 percent U-235). This uranium metal was part of a 50-kilogram shipment that was undeclared and is suspected to have come from the Soviet Union in 1993. Iranian authorities claim that all equipment at Lashkar Ab'ad was dismantled in May 2003 and transferred to a storage facility at Karaj. The IAEA analyzed the environmental samples and found enrichment levels consistent with those declared by Iran.

Plutonium Facilities

Iran has also been engaged in efforts to test and develop the means to produce and separate plutonium, which can be used for both nuclear reactors and weapons. These activities were less advanced than the uranium enrichment effort at the time Iran suspended its nuclear activities in November 2004. Iran admits that it produced a small amount of plutonium outside of safeguards, a violation of its IAEA commitments. This production took place at the U.S.-supplied Tehran Research Reactor between 1988 and 1998 when Iran irradiated depleted uranium dioxide (UO_2) targets using materials previously exempted from safeguards in 1978 and later declared lost as waste. These experiments involved 7 kilograms of pressed UO_2 pellets prepared at the Isfahan Nuclear Technology Center, 3 kilograms of which were subsequently reprocessed, yielding approximately 100 milligrams of plutonium. This amount is far less than would be needed to produce a nuclear weapon but enough to validate the production and separation processes.

Iran has also been pursuing the construction of a plutonium production reactor since the 1980s. It plans to build a 40-MWt heavy-water reactor at Arak that could go into operation by 2014. The plans for the reactor were completed in 2002 and would rely on the use of natural uranium oxide as fuel. Iran has also built a heavy-water production plant at Arak and had hoped to start producing heavy water there in 2004. This project was not covered by the suspension agreement with the European Union in 2004, and work at the site is thought to be ongoing.

During the course of the 1990s, the bulk of Iran's known nuclear activities focused on the Bushehr reactor program, which was in the process of being completed by Russia. The former West Germany began construction of the facility under the shah's regime. Bonn, however, first refused to complete the project after the Iranian revolution, and then refused to repair the damaged facility after the Iran-Iraq War. In 1995, Iran signed an $800 million deal with Moscow to finish the construction of one of the reactors based on a Russian-designed reactor and to house it in the German-designed reactor facility. After years of delay, on October 14, 2004, Russia announced that the construction of the 1,000-MW reactor was complete. The facility could open in 2005 and reach full capacity by 2006. However, as a condition of supply, Russia has insisted that fuel for the facility should be provided by Russia and that spent fuel should be returned to Russia for disposal. In February 2005, Moscow and Tehran signed contracts that finalized these spent-fuel arrangements.

Sources of Technology

Despite constant claims to the contrary, almost all Iran's critical nuclear materials, equipment, and technology have been acquired from foreign suppliers. The same is true for its missile capabilities, although it has now acquired the ability to produce its own Scud-type missiles. During the past 25 years, Iran has been actively engaged in acquiring a variety of sensitive nuclear capabilities, but until recently it has been unable to effectively use much of what it has acquired. Poor management, the impact of sanctions, and a less than fully developed industrial and education base may partly explain why most estimates of when Iran might be able to acquire a nuclear capability have proven incorrect. It is also possible that Iranian leaders were ambivalent about pursuing a nuclear weapons capability, that it was not a policy priority, and therefore the leaders did not muster the necessary economic and scientific resources to accelerate the program.

It is now clear that Iran has engaged in a long-term, multifaceted program to acquire nuclear and related technology and equipment from a variety of sources and that it has benefited from the A. Q. Khan nuclear black market and from poor export controls across the globe, including Europe.

Nuclear Black Market

In 1984, in the midst of the Iran-Iraq War, Iran opened a nuclear research center in Isfahan. By 1992, press reports of Western intelligence findings indicated that Iran had established experimental programs in fissile material production at Sharif University in Tehran and possibly at other locations. Iran appears to have supported these efforts through an active but clandestine procurement network, using front companies and false end-user certificates to persuade Western European companies to provide nuclear-related, dual-use technologies. Iran also purchased a number of small companies (particularly in Germany) to serve as platforms for exporting sensitive equipment to Iran.[29]

In the spring of 1995, some details emerged on Iran's nuclear procurement activities, substantiating suspected efforts to establish a secret gas-centrifuge uranium enrichment program. Specifically, Western intelligence sources were quoted as stating that, since 1990, Iran had approached German and Swiss firms to purchase balancing machines and diagnostic and monitoring equipment—all dual-use items potentially valuable for laboratory-scale centrifuge development. In addition, Iranian agents were said to have contacted a British company to obtain samarium-cobalt magnetic equipment, potentially useful in the development of centrifuge top bearings.[30]

In January 2004, the details of Iran's successful procurement of enrichment technology and nuclear know-how from A. Q. Khan and his international nuclear black market became public.[31] This network provided Iran with key centrifuge technology and is thought to have provided Iran with a list of suppliers for essential equipment (see the fuller discussion in chapter 12 on Pakistan).

China

For a decade starting in the mid-1980s, China was a source of significant assistance to Iran's civilian nuclear program.[32] Under a ten-year agreement for cooperation signed in 1990, China reportedly trained Iranian nuclear technicians and engineers in China. China supplied Iran with two "mini" research reactors installed at Isfahan. China also supplied Iran with a calutron, the type of equipment used in Iraq's electromagnetic isotope separation enrichment program for the separation of weapons-grade uranium. Both countries claim that the aid has been used exclusively for peaceful purposes, in line with Iran's NPT obligations.

In 1992, Washington persuaded Beijing to postpone indefinitely the sale to Iran of a plutonium-producing research reactor and also convinced Argentina not to export supporting fuel cycle and heavy-water production facilities.[33] In March 1992, China agreed to supply two 300-MW-electric nuclear power reactors to Iran. In the fall of 1995, however, China's reactor sale to Iran was suspended, ostensibly because of difficulties over site selection, although the underlying cause may have been Iran's difficulties in obtaining financing. Other factors may also have been involved. Some reports indicated that China suspended or even terminated the deal because of strong U.S. pressure.[34] In addition, France, Germany, and Japan apparently had declined to supply China with essential components that it might have needed for the reactors it had offered Iran. It is also possible that Iran lost interest in the arrangement once it was confident that Russia would complete the Bushehr project.

In April 1996, the U.S. Department of Defense still regarded China as Iran's main source of nuclear assistance.[35] In the United States–China summit of October 1997, however, China made a commitment to cancel almost all its existing nuclear assistance to Iran and to provide Iran with no new nuclear assistance. By 2001, noting that "China appears to be living up to its 1997 commitments," the Department of Defense no longer viewed China as Iran's main nuclear source, although the United States continues to be concerned about some missile assistance from China to Iran.[36]

Russia

During early 1995, Russia proceeded with its contract to help Iran build a nuclear reactor at Bushehr. In March and April 1995, tensions rose with Russia when the Bill Clinton administration learned that, as part of a secret protocol to the reactor sale contract, Russia had agreed to provide Iran with a gas-centrifuge uranium enrichment facility. Such a facility, though itself under IAEA inspection and dedicated to the production of low-enriched (non-weapons-grade) uranium, could have enabled Iran to secretly build and operate a similar plant to produce weapons-grade uranium. Other disturbing elements of the protocol were an agreement in principle for Russia to supply a light-water research reactor of 30 to 50 MWt, 2,000 metric tons of natural uranium, and the training of Iranian graduates in nuclear sciences in Russia.[37]

Washington urged Moscow to halt its work on the Bushehr nuclear reactor but met with little success. U.S. concerns extended even beyond Bushehr, because Russian entities were known to also be cooperating with Iran on other projects as well.[38] Bushehr's benefits for Iran's nuclear weapons program are likely to be largely indirect. The project will augment Iran's nuclear technology infrastructure, helping Tehran's nuclear weapons research and development.[39] Iran could also benefit from the presence of the thousands of Russian nuclear scientists who are expected to take part in the Bushehr project.[40]

The United States

During the 1980s, the United States imposed a wide range of sanctions on Iran because of Tehran's support for international terrorism, its attacks in 1987 on U.S.-flagged Kuwaiti tankers, and other actions considered hostile to U.S. interests. Those sanctions blocked economic and military assistance to Iran, prohibited the importation of Iranian-origin goods, and restricted U.S. contributions to multilateral organizations that assist Iran and U.S. Export-Import Bank credits for Iran. U.S. efforts to curtail foreign nuclear sales to Iran intensified in the aftermath of the 1991 Gulf War.

The 1992 Iran-Iraq Arms Non-Proliferation Act expressly prohibited transfers of nuclear equipment and materials to Iran, as well as exports to Iran of all dual-use commodities and U.S. government and commercial arms sales. The restriction applies both to nuclear dual-use commodities (that is, those having nuclear and non-nuclear uses and that are regulated internationally by the Nuclear Suppliers Group, or NSG) and to strategic dual-use commodities (that is, those having military and nonmilitary uses, which currently are regulated under the Wassenaar Arrangement).

In 1995 and 1996, the United States tightened sanctions on Iran, aiming in part to constrain Tehran's unconventional weapons programs.[41] Legislation adopted in February 1996 provided for U.S. economic assistance to Russia to be made contingent upon presidential determination that Russia had terminated its nuclear-related assistance to Iran.[42] The legislation permitted the president to waive this restriction at six-month intervals, however, upon a determination that making U.S. funds available to Russia was in the interest of U.S. national security. Such waivers have been regularly exercised.[43]

Washington further intensified economic pressure on Iran by imposing secondary sanctions on it and Libya, through the Iran and Libya Sanctions Act of 1996 (ILSA). The law imposes sanctions on foreign enterprises that invest $20 million or more in the energy sector of Iran. By the fall of 1997, this legislation faced a serious challenge from French, Malaysian, and Russian oil companies that had signed a deal with Iran to help recover and market oil and natural gas. The Clinton administration backed away from imposing the sanctions because of the economic crisis in East Asia and in Russia in the fall of 1997 and spring of 1998, which placed larger U.S. foreign policy interests at stake. The Bush administration has not been enthusiastic about ILSA, but in the summer of 2001 Congress extended ILSA for five years.

The United States has relied on the NSG to coordinate the Western embargo on nuclear sales to Iran and has persuaded some states to withhold goods that were regulated under the NSG's core export control guidelines. NSG rules permit the sale of such items, provided they are subject to IAEA inspection in the recipient state, but Washington has convinced its Western trading partners to adopt the stricter policy in the case of Iran.

In his first State of the Union address after the September 11, 2001, terrorist attacks, President George W. Bush declared Iran a member of an "axis of evil," pursuing nuclear, chemical, and biological weapons and exporting terror.[44] Since then, U.S. officials have repeatedly charged Iran with developing such weapons and called on the members of the IAEA Board of Governors to report Iran to the U.N. Security Council for violating its NPT obligations. The Bush administration has also insisted that Iran "abandon" its nuclear fuel cycle activities.[45] On November 17, 2004, then–U.S. secretary of state Colin Powell told reporters that Iran was working to adapt missiles to deliver a nuclear weapon, citing a classified intelligence report that Iran was working on mating warheads to missiles. The report, however, remains unverified.[46] Press reports revealed that the claim was based on a single, unvetted walk-in source who provided documents purported to be Iranian drawings and technical documents, including a nuclear warhead design.

Missile Analysis

Iran's acquisition of ballistic missiles began in the 1980s when, during the Iran-Iraq War, North Korea provided Iran with about 100 Scud-Bs and with facilities that enabled Iran to produce the Scuds indigenously.[47] During the early 1990s, Iran sought to acquire ballistic missile capabilities that could be used to deliver nuclear weapons. It turned to China, Libya, and North Korea for missile systems and related technologies. In the early 1990s, Iran reportedly discussed buying the 1,300-kilometer No Dong from North Korea.[48] On March 6, 1992, the United States imposed sanctions, under the missile nonproliferation provisions of the Arms Export Control and Export Administration Acts, against the Iranian Ministry of Defense and Armed Forces Logistics and against two North Korean entities for engaging in missile proliferation activities.

In June 1995, the press cited U.S. intelligence reports that "strongly implicate[d]" China in the transfer to Iran of equipment, materials, and scientific know-how that could be used in the manufacture of short-range ballistic missiles such as the Chinese M-9 and M-11.[49] China was believed to have transferred "dozens, perhaps hundreds, of missile guidance systems and computerized machine tools" to Iran, as well as rocket propellant ingredients that could be used in its current stockpile of short-range Scud–Mod Bs and Scud–Mod Cs, as well as on Scud variants that Iran might produce in the future.[50] In the final analysis, however, the United States did not find that China's missile transactions with Iran violated China's pledges related to the Missile Technology Control Regime, and thus it declined to impose regime-related sanctions against either China or Iran.[51]

In 2001, however, the U.S. Department of Defense still determined that Chinese, along with Russian, "entities have continued to supply a wide variety of missile-related goods, technology and expertise to Iran."[52] In 1996, it became clear that North Korea was exporting missile capabilities to Iran. As a result, on May 26, 1996, the United States imposed sanctions on the Iranian Ministry of Defense Armed Forces Logistics, the Iranian State Purchasing Office, and the Korea Mining Development Trading Bureau.[53] The precise nature of the offending transactions remains classified, but U.S. officials indicated that North Korea had sold missile components, equipment, and materials to Iran, although not complete missiles, production technology, or major subsystems.

During 1997, U.S. press reports quoted U.S. and Israeli intelligence findings that Russian enterprises—including cash-strapped Russian technical institutes, research facilities, and defense-production companies—were transferring Russian SS-4 medium-range ballistic missile technologies to Iran. According to these assessments, Iran hoped to employ these technologies to develop two Iranian derivatives of the 1,000-kilometer-range North Korean No Dong missile. In September 1997, then–U.S. vice president Al Gore raised the issue in Moscow with Prime Minister Viktor Chernomyrdin, as a result of which there was a visible decline in Russian assistance until the summer of 1998.[54]

Nevertheless, U.S. officials believe Russian assistance remains critical to Iran's development of the Shahab series, helping Iran to "save years in its development of the Shahab III" and to "significantly accelerate the pace of its ballistic missile development program."[55] The Shahab III is projected to have a range of approximately 1,300 kilometers.

Iran has announced that the Shahab III is in production, as well as a new solid-propellant short-range ballistic missile, the Fateh-110, and it claims to have follow-on versions of the Shahab III in development.[56] The primary Iranian justification for the country's program is Israel's missile programs. Iranian defense minister Ali Shamkhani said in August 2004 that "the Israelis have recently tried to increase their missile capability and we will also try to upgrade our Shahab III missile in every respect."[57] An August 2004 test, for example, came just two weeks after Israel's Arrow antimissile system—designed to intercept Shahab missiles—shot down a test Scud missile for the first time.[58]

On November 5, 2003, the Iranian Defense Ministry stated that Iran did not have a program to build a Shahab IV missile. Outside experts had speculated that a Shahab IV, with an alleged 2,000-kilometer range and a 1,000-kilogram payload, could be based on the single-stage, liquid-fueled SS-4.[59] Iran is reportedly interested in two developmental North Korean intermediate-range ballistic missiles, the Taepo Dong I (TD-I) and Taepo Dong II (TD-II). These are both two-stage, liquid-fueled missiles, with theoretical ranges of 2,000 and 3,500 kilometers, respectively. A Shahab V missile program could be based on either of these missiles.[60] Yet none of these capabilities has actually surfaced, and they may simply be official aspirations or bravado.

The U.S. intelligence community has indicated that Iran will likely continue development of intermediate-range and even intercontinental ballistic missile (ICBM) systems by initially testing them as space launch vehicle (SLV) programs. The 2001 National Intelligence Estimate indicated uniform agreement among U.S. intelligence agencies that "Iran *could* attempt to launch an ICBM/SLV about mid-decade although most agencies believe Iran is *likely* to take until the last half of the decade to do so" (emphasis in original).[61] It was also noted that one agency does not find it likely that Iran will achieve a successful test of an ICBM before 2015. Since 1998, the National Intelligence Estimates have tended to overestimate the missile capabilities of developing nations. In his 2004 Worldwide Threat Assessment, Director of Central Intelligence George Tenet speculated that Iran "could begin flight testing [SLVs] in the mid- to latter-part of the decade."[62]

Biological and Chemical Weapons Analysis

Despite Iran's ratification of the Biological Weapons Convention in 1973, U.S. officials believe that Iran has pursued biological weapons under the guise of its extensive biotechnology and pharmaceutical industries. In 2001, at the Fifth Review Conference of the Biological Weapons Convention, the U.S. undersecretary of state for arms control and international security at that time, John Bolton, said that Iran had "probably" produced and weaponized BW agents.[63] In 2004, his assessment was more cautious: "Because BW programs are easily concealed, I cannot say that the United States can prove beyond a shadow of a doubt that Iran has an offensive BW program. The intelligence I have seen suggests that this is the case."[64]

In May 2003, on the basis of intelligence from the exiled National Council of Resistance of Iran (NCR), the *Washington Post* reported that Iran had begun producing biological weapons, including anthrax. Citing informants within the Iranian government, the NCR reported that the anthrax weapons were part of a program begun in 2001 intended to triple Iran's biowarfare program. Other pathogens being weaponized, the NCR said, included alfatoxin, typhus, smallpox, plague, and cholera. The group could not produce any evidence to support its claims.[65]

The United States believes that Iran also continues a chemical weapons program that seeks production technology, training, and expertise to achieve an indigenous capability to produce nerve agents.[66] Iran began its chemical weapons program to deter Iraq's use of chemical weapons during the Iran-Iraq War. During that war, Iraq employed chemical weapons, primarily mustard gas and the nerve agent tabun, against Iranian troops, with approximately 50,000 casualties reported.[67]Allegedly, Iran also employed chemical weapons late in the war, but with less success than Iraq. Iran ratified the Chemical Weapons Convention in 1997, but the CIA reports that Iran has continued to seek technology, training, and expertise from Chinese entities.[68]

NOTES

1. John Bolton, undersecretary of state for arms control and international security, "Iran's Continuing Pursuit of Weapons of Mass Destruction," statement before the House International Relations Committee Subcommittee on the Middle East and Central Asia, June 24, 2004.
2. Robert Gates, director of central intelligence, "Weapons Proliferation in the New World Order," statement before the Senate Government Affairs Committee, January 15, 1992.
3. See Jaffee Center for Strategic Studies, *The Middle East Military Balance 2003–2004* (Tel Aviv: Tel Aviv University, 2004).
4. U.S. Department of Defense (DOD), *Proliferation: Threat and Response* (Washington, D.C.: DOD, 2001), p. 38.
5. Andrew Feickert, "Missile Survey: Ballistic and Cruise Missiles of Foreign Countries," *Congressional Research Service*, March 5, 2004, p. 16. See also, "Iran Conducts New Shahab III Missile Test with Observers Present: Minister," Agence France-Presse, October 20, 2004.
6. "Iran Says It Now Has Missile with 2,000 Km Range," Agence France-Presse, October 5, 2004.
7. Conversation with authors, November 2004.
8. "Iran's Missile Update," *Risk Report* (Wisconsin Project on Nuclear Arms Control), March–April 2004. See also Feickert, "Missile Survey," pp. 16–17.
9. DOD, *Proliferation: Threat and Response* (2001), p. 38.
10. "Iran 'Can' Mass-Produce Missiles," BBC News, November 9, 2004; available at http://news.bbc.co.uk/2/hi/middle_east/3997151.stm.
11. Aleksander Vasovic, "Ukraine Missile Sales Are Alleged," *Boston Globe*, February 3, 2005.
12. Aleksander Vasovic, "Ukraine Probe Uncovers Illicit Weapons Sales," *Boston Globe*, February 5, 2005.
13. "Report to Congress on the Acquisition of Technology Relating to Weapons of Mass Destruction and Advanced Conventional Munitions, 1 January through 30 June 2003."
14. Geoffrey Kemp, presentation at Carnegie International Non-Proliferation Conference, June 2001.

15. "Iran Parliament OKs Nuke Enrichment Bill," *Washington Post*, October 31, 2004.
16. "Iran Students in Nuclear Protest," BBC News Online, November 1, 2004. Available at http://news.bbc.co.uk/1/hi/world/middle_east/3972711.stm.
17. Kurt M. Campbell, Robert J. Einhorn, and Mitchell B. Reiss, eds., *The Nuclear Tipping Point: Why States Reconsider Their Nuclear Choices* (Washington, D.C.: Brookings Institution Press, 2004).
18. Donald N. Wilber, *Clandestine Service History: Overthrow of Premier Mossadeq of Iran, November 1952–August 1953* (Washington, D.C.: Central Intelligence Agency, 1954).
19. James Risen, "Secret History of the CIA in Iran," *New York Times*, April 16, 2000.
20. "Iran: Nuclear Overview," Nuclear Threat Initiative, September 2004.
21. Shai Feldman, *Nuclear Weapons and Arms Control in the Middle East*, Harvard University's BCSIA Studies in International Studies (Cambridge, Mass.: MIT Press, 1997), p. 47.
22. Tehran Domestic Service, "Hashemi-Rafsanjani Speaks on the Future of the IRGC Iranian Revolutionary Guards Corps," October 6, 1988, FBIS-NES, October 7, 1988, p. 52.
23. This section is based on IAEA director general, "Report on 'Implementation of the NPT Safeguards Agreement in the Islamic Republic of Iran,' September 1, 2004"; and IAEA director general, "Report on 'Implementation of the NPT Safeguards Agreement in the Islamic Republic of Iran,' November 15, 2004."
24. IAEA director general, "Report on 'Implementation of the NPT Safeguards Agreement in the Islamic Republic of Iran,' September 1, 2004," p. 24.
25. David Albright and Cory Hinderstein, "Iran: Countdown to Showdown," *Bulletin of the Atomic Scientists*, November/December 2004, pp. 67–72.
26. Interviews with authors.
27. IAEA director general, "Report on 'Implementation of the NPT Safeguards Agreement in the Islamic Republic of Iran,' September 1, 2004"; and Miriam Rajkumar and Joseph Cirincione, "The IAEA's Report on Iran: No Slam Dunk," Carnegie Analysis, September 2, 2004.
28. IAEA director general, "Report on 'Implementation of the NPT Safeguards Agreement in the Islamic Republic of Iran,' September 1, 2004."
29. Mark Hibbs, "U.S. Officials Say Iran Is Pursuing Fissile Material Production Research," *Nuclear Fuel*, December 7, 1992, p. 5; "Iran and the Bomb," Frontline, PBS Network, April 13, 1993; Hibbs, "German–U.S. Nerves Frayed over Nuclear Ties to Iran," *Nuclear Fuel*, March 14, 1994, p. 9; Hibbs, "Sharif University Activity Continues Despite IAEA Visit, Bonn Agency Says," *Nuclear Fuel*, March 28, 1994, p. 10; Elaine Sciolino, "Iran Says It Plans 10 Nuclear Plants But No Atom Arms," *New York Times*, May 16, 1995.
30. Thomas Lippman, "Stepped-Up Nuclear Effort Renews Alarm about Iran," *Washington Post*, April 17, 1995; Mark Hibbs, "Investigators Deny Iran Smuggled Weapons Material from Germany," *Nucleonics Week*, February 1, 1996, p. 14.
31. Kamran Khan, "Pakistanis Exploited Nuclear Network," *Washington Post*, January 28, 2004.
32. "Iran Confirms Nuclear Cooperation with China," United Press International, November 6, 1991; R. Jeffrey Smith, "China–Iran Nuclear Tie Long Known," *Washington Post*, October 31, 1991.
33. Mark Hibbs, "Iran Sought Sensitive Nuclear Supplies from Argentina, China," *Nucleonics Week*, September 24, 1992, p. 2; Steve Coll, "U.S. Halted Nuclear Bid by Iran," *Washington Post*, November 17, 1992.
34. "Source: Nuclear Plans with China Near Collapse," *Al-Sharq Al-Awsat* (London), May 21, 1995, in FBIS-NES 95-099, May 23, 1995, p. 54; "Moscow to Proceed with Nuclear Deal with Iran," ITAR-TASS (Moscow), October 2, 1995, in FBIS-SOV 95-191, October 3, 1995, p. 22; Mark Hibbs, "Iran, China Said to Disagree Only on Site Selection for New PWRs," *Nucleonics Week*, October 5, 1995, p. 1; "China/Iran: Reactor Plans Shelved—Again?" *Nucleonics Week*, January 11, 1996, p. 9.
35. DOD, *Proliferation: Threat and Response* (Washington, D.C.: DOD, 1996), p. 14.
36. Ibid., p. 36.
37. "Clinton's Iran Embargo Initiative Impedes U.S. NPT Diplomatic Effort," *Nuclear Fuel*, May 8, 1995, p. 6; Mark Hibbs, "Countering U.S. Claims, Moscow Says Iran Nuclear Program Is Peaceful," *Nucleonics Week*, February 9, 1995, p. 4; Hibbs, "Iran's Arab Neighbors Don't Believe U.S. Has Proof of Weapons Ambitions," *Nucleonics Week*, April 20, 1995, p. 10.
38. DOD, *Proliferation: Threat and Response* (1996), p. 35.

39. Ibid.
40. Feldman, *Nuclear Weapons*, p. 48.
41. For a detailed look at the sanctions adopted, see Kenneth Katzman, "Iran: U.S. Policies and Options," Congressional Research Service Report for Congress, January 14, 2000, pp. 11–14.
42. "Russia Firm on Iran Reactor Sale; Could Mean Loss of U.S. Aid," *Post-Soviet Nuclear and Defense Monitor*, November 17, 1995, p. 4.
43. "President Clinton Says Aid to Russia Critical to National Security," *Post-Soviet Nuclear and Defense Monitor*, May 31, 1996, p. 1.
44. The president's State of the Union address, available at www.whitehouse.gov/news/releases/2002/01/20020129-11.html.
45. Bolton, "Iran's Continuing Pursuit of Weapons of Mass Destruction."
46. Robin Wright and Keith B. Richburg, "Powell Says Iran Is Pursuing Bomb," *Washington Post*, November 18, 2004; and Dana Linzer, "Nuclear Disclosures on Iran Unverified," *Washington Post*, November 19, 2004.
47. Katzman, "Iran," p. 18.
48. Ibid.
49. R. Jeffrey Smith, "Iran's Missile Technology Linked to China, Report Says," *Washington Post*, June 17, 1995; Barbara Opall, "U.S. Queries China on Iran," *Defense News*, June 19–25, 1995, p. 1.
50. Elaine Sciolino, "CIA Report Says Chinese Sent Iran Arms Components," *New York Times*, June 21, 1995; "Chinese Shipments Violate Controls," *Jane's Defense Weekly*, July 1, 1995, p. 3.
51. Katzman, "Iran," p. 16.
52. DOD, *Proliferation: Threat and Response* (1996), p. 36.
53. *Federal Register*, June 28, 1996, p. 29785; "Daily on U.S. Government Notice of Sanctions against DPRK," *Chosun Ilbo* (Seoul), June 30, 1996, in FBIS-EAS 96-127, July 3, 1996.
54. Robert Gallucci, "Iran–Russia Missile Cooperation: A U.S. View," in *Repairing the Regime: Preventing the Spread of Weapons of Mass Destruction*, edited by Joseph Cirincione (New York: Routledge, 2000), p. 187.
55. Testimony of John Lauder, director, DCI Nonproliferation Center, before the Senate Committee on Foreign Relations on Russian Proliferation to Iran's Weapons of Mass Destruction and Missile Programs, October 5, 2000.
56. "Report to Congress on the Acquisition of Technology Relating to Weapons of Mass Destruction and Advanced Conventional Munitions, 1 January through 30 June 2003."
57. "Iran Tests Missile Capable of Hitting Israel," Reuters, August 11, 2004.
58. Michael Sirak, Alon Ben-David, and Andrew Koch, "Iran, Israel Trade Barbs over New Missile Tests," *Jane's Defense Weekly*, August 16, 2004.
59. "Iran's Missile Update," *Risk Report*.
60. "Iran's Ambitious Missile Programs," Center for Defense Information, July 1, 2004.
61. National Intelligence Council, "Foreign Missile Developments and the Ballistic Missile Threat through 2015," December, 2001, p. 12.
62. "The Worldwide Threat 2004: Challenges in a Changing Global Context," testimony of Director of Central Intelligence George J. Tenet before the Senate Armed Services Committee, March 9, 2004.
63. Jenni Rissanen, "Acrimonious Opening for BWC Review Conference," *BWC Review Conference Bulletin*, November 19, 2001; available at www.acronym.org.uk/bwc/revcon1.html.
64. Bolton, "Iran's Continuing Pursuit of Weapons of Mass Destruction."
65. Joby Warrick, "Iran Said to Be Producing Bioweapons," *Washington Post*, May 15, 2003.
66. Bolton, "Iran's Continuing Pursuit of Weapons of Mass Destruction."
67. Office of Technology Assessment, U.S. Congress, *Proliferation of Weapons of Mass Destruction: Assessing the Risks* (Washington, D.C.: U.S. Government Printing Office, 1993), p. 10.
68. "Report to Congress on the Acquisition of Technology Relating to Weapons of Mass Destruction and Advanced Conventional Munitions, 1 January through 30 June 2003."

Table 15.1. **Iran's Nuclear Infrastructure**

Name/Location of Facility	Type/Status	IAEA Safeguards
Power Reactors		
Bushehr I	Light-water, LEU, 1,000 MWe, damaged by Iraqi air strikes (1987, 1988), construction completed October 2004, scheduled to be launched 2005 and reach full capacity by 2006	Yes
Bushehr II	Light-water, LEU, 1,300 MWe, damaged by Iraqi air strikes (1987, 1988), facility remains unfinished, and project is currently suspended	No
Research Reactors		
Tehran Research Reactor/ IR-0001	Light-water, HEU, 5 MWt, pool type, operating	Yes
IR-0005/MNSR Isfahan	Miniature neutron source reactor (MNSR), 900 grams of HEU fuel, 27 kWt, operating	Yes
ENTC GSCR Isfahan	Graphite-moderate subcritical assembly, Chinese-built, went critical in 1992, LEU, operating	Yes
ENTC LWSCR Isfahan	Light-water, zero-power, open tank facility fueled by uranium metal pins, Chinese-built, went critical in 1992, LEU, operating	Yes
IR-0004/ HWZPR Isfahan	Heavy-water, zero-power reactor (HWZPR), 10 kWt, LEU, operating	Yes
Uranium Encirhment		
Pilot Fuel Enrichment Plant (PFEP) Natanz	Capacity of 1,000 P-1 centrifuges, began testing a ten-machine cascade in August 2003, construction/operation suspended	Yes
Fuel Enrichment Plant (FEP) Natanz	Commercial plant, 50,000-centrifuges capacity, originally scheduled to start accepting centrifuges in 2005, construction/operation suspended	Yes
Kalaye Electric Company	Centrifuge tests using UF_6 conducted between 1998 and 2003	Yes

(table continues on the following page)

Table 15.1. **Iran's Nuclear Infrastructure** (continued)

Name/Location of Facility	Type/Status	IAEA Safeguards
Lashkar Ab'ad	Pilot laser enrichment plant established in 2000, laser enrichment experiments conducted between October 2002 and January 2003, plant dismantled in 2003	Yes
Reprocessing (Plutonium Extraction)		
Tehran Nuclear Research Center	Irradiated depleted UO_2 targets at the Tehran Research Reactor between 1988 and 1998. Also 3 kilograms of UO_2 reprocessed in three shielded boxes in a hot cell to produce at least 200 micrograms of plutonium, shielded boxes dismantled in 1992.[1]	Yes
Uranium Processing		
Isfahan Conversion Facility	Converts uranium yellowcake into UF_4 and UF_6, became operational in February 2004, operation suspended	Yes
Esfahan Fuel Manufacturing Plant	Scheduled to be commissioned 2007, capacity of 40 tons per year of UO_2 fuel	Yes
Jabr Ibn Hayan Lab—Tehran Nuclear Research Center	UF_4 converted into uranium metal, storage of UF_6, UF_4, and UO_2 from China, also storage of plutonium separated from depleted uranium at Tehran Nuclear Research Center	Yes
Saghand Yazd Province	Discovery of uranium deposits announced in 1990, 5,000 tons of uranium reserves.	No
Plutonium Production		
Arak Heavy Water Reactor (IR-40)	40 MWt heavy-water reactor, nat. U oxide as fuel, construction scheduled to begin in 2004 and reactor to go into operation in 2014, planned	Yes
Heavy-Water Production[2]		
Khondab, near Arak	Heavy-water production plant, production capacity 100 tons per year, scheduled to start producing heavy water in 2004, under construction	No

Storage		
Karaj	Equipment from Pilot Laser Enrichment plant at Lashkar Ab'ad, dismantled in May 2003, stored	Yes

Abbreviations

HEU highly enriched uranium
LEU low-enriched uranium
nat. U natural uranium
MWe megawatts electric
MWt megawatts thermal
kWt kilowatts thermal

Sources

IAEA director general, "Report on 'Implementation of the NPT Safeguards Agreement in the Islamic Republic of Iran,' September 1, 2004"; and IAEA director general, "Report on 'Implementation of the NPT Safeguards in the Islamic Republic of Iran,' November 15, 2004." Center for Nonproliferation Studies at the Monterey Institute of International Studies for Nuclear Threat Initiative, "Iran: Nuclear Facilities," available at www.nti.org/e_research/profiles/Iran/3119.html.

Notes

1. Iran claims that it produced 200 micrograms of plutonium in these experiments, but the IAEA estimates that more plutonium should have been produced. IAEA is investigating this discrepancy.
2. The nonproliferation regime does not include the application of safeguards to heavy-water production facilities, but safeguards are required on the export of heavy water.

PART FIVE
Nonproliferation Successes

One of the most striking and underappreciated facts of the nuclear age is the large number of countries that have turned away from the nuclear weapons path. This includes nations that possessed nuclear weapons but gave them up, that were pursing a nuclear capability but renounced it, or that debated developing nuclear weapons but decided not to do so.

For those countries that gave up their nuclear weapons—the states of the former Soviet Union and South Africa—the international nonproliferation regime was essential to locking in their non-nuclear status. For those states that once pursued nuclear capabilities but have since abandoned their efforts, such as Argentina and Brazil, establishing a civilian-led government was a critical factor, but the international regime drew attention to these countries' acquisition efforts and slowed their pace. In Libya, the regime failed to stop the government's clandestine pursuit of a nuclear capability but did slow it down. When Libya's leadership changed direction, the regime then provided the international tools for verifying and consolidating that change. In Iraq's case, the inspections and sanctions imposed after the 1991 war succeeded in both ending its nuclear weapons program and convincing the government not to restart it. That success, however, was not appreciated soon enough to prevent a new war to disarm Iraq in 2003.

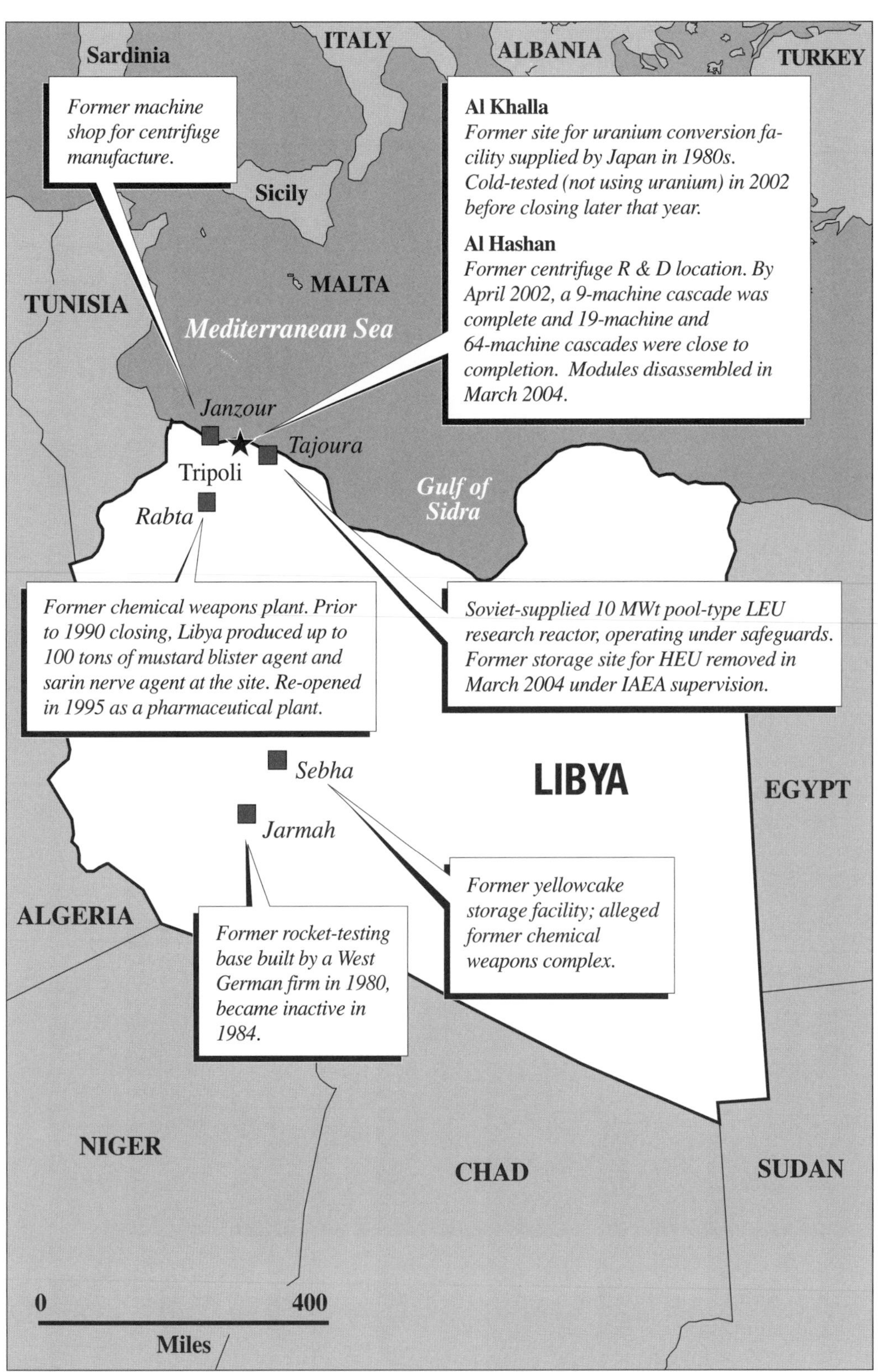

Sardinia
ITALY
ALBANIA
TURKEY
Former machine shop for centrifuge manufacture.
Al Khalla
Former site for uranium conversion facility supplied by Japan in 1980s. Cold-tested (not using uranium) in 2002 before closing later that year.
Al Hashan
Former centrifuge R & D location. By April 2002, a 9-machine cascade was complete and 19-machine and 64-machine cascades were close to completion. Modules disassembled in March 2004.
Sicily
MALTA
TUNISIA
Mediterranean Sea
Janzour
Tajoura
Tripoli
Gulf of Sidra
Rabta
Former chemical weapons plant. Prior to 1990 closing, Libya produced up to 100 tons of mustard blister agent and sarin nerve agent at the site. Re-opened in 1995 as a pharmaceutical plant.
Soviet-supplied 10 MWt pool-type LEU research reactor, operating under safeguards. Former storage site for HEU removed in March 2004 under IAEA supervision.
Sebha
LIBYA
EGYPT
Jarmah
Former yellowcake storage facility; alleged former chemical weapons complex.
ALGERIA
Former rocket-testing base built by a West German firm in 1980, became inactive in 1984.
NIGER
CHAD
SUDAN
0
400
Miles

CHAPTER 16

Libya

Nuclear Weapons Capability

After over three decades of trying to acquire a nuclear weapons capability, Libya announced that it was abandoning its clandestine nuclear program on December 19, 2003.[1] Libya's major nuclear facilities include a 10-megawatt light-water research reactor and a critical assembly (100 watts), both located at the Tajura Nuclear Research Center. In 2003, Libya permitted international officials to inspect eleven previously undisclosed nuclear sites and to remove and destroy key components of its nuclear weapons program.

Biological and Chemical Weapons Capability

Libya renounced its chemical weapons (CW) program in December 2003 and signed the Chemical Weapons Convention on January 6, 2004. In March 2004, Libya reported past production of approximately 23 tons of mustard agent between 1980 and 1990 at a CW production facility (Rabta) to the Organization for the Prohibition of Chemical Weapons (OPCW).[2] Pending the destruction of the mustard agent, the OPCW continues to monitor and inspect Libya's CW facilities. Libya also disclosed that it had produced thousands of unfilled munitions and stored the agent at two sites. The OPCW destroyed more than 3,200 unfilled CW shells. In October 2004, Libya asked the OPCW if it could convert the former weapons plant at Rabta into a plant to manufacture low-cost pharmaceuticals, and the United States supported the proposal.[3]

U.S. intelligence estimates had long held that Libya had a basic biological weapon (BW) research program. Libya denies any BW program, and U.S. and British officials investigating Libya's unconventional weapons programs found no evidence of an offensive BW program.[4] Libya has been a signatory of the Biological Weapons Convention since 1982.

Missile Capability

Libya possessed a limited and aging arsenal of Scud-B missiles (300-kilometer range, 700-kilogram payload) that it obtained from the Soviet Union in the 1970s, as well as a handful of North Korean Scud-Cs (600-kilometer range, 700-kilogram payload).[5] Libya struggled to continue its indigenous efforts to develop the 200-kilometer-range Al Fatah missile in the face of international sanctions through the 1990s. Libya does not possess any aircraft capable of delivering a nuclear payload.

In 2004, Libya agreed to eliminate ballistic missiles beyond a 300-kilometer range with a payload of 500 kilograms. By March 5, Scud-C missiles, partial missiles, missile launchers, and related equipment were flown out of the country. Libya's pledge will leave it with short-range cruise missiles, such as SS-N-2c Styx, Otomat Mk 2, and Exocet antiship cruise missiles.

The Strategic Context

On December 19, 2003, after years of negotiations capped by months of secret talks with U.S. and British officials, Libya announced its decision to dismantle its unconventional weapons capabilities and permit international verification inspections. The process has become a model for how to end a nation's nuclear weapons program by changing the behavior of even troubling regimes.

U.S. efforts to end Libya's weapons programs spanned four presidential administrations. For 30 years, Libya's mercurial leader, Colonel Mu'ammar Gadhafi, had ambitions to become the leader of the Arab world and to raise Libya's prestige among Islamic and other countries in the developing world. As part of that effort, until the late 1990s Gadhafi sought to obtain nuclear and chemical arms and remained defiant on nonproliferation and arms control issues, especially those related to Israel's nuclear capability. Despite constant international condemnation, its substantial oil wealth enabled Libya to buy the technology it needed. Its nuclear weapons and CW programs were all heavily dependent on foreign technology and expertise.

Libya is a party to the Non-Proliferation Treaty (NPT) and to the Biological Weapons Convention. In November 2001, it signed the Comprehensive Test Ban Treaty. Nonetheless, it continued its efforts to obtain nuclear and chemical arms. This pursuit, and Libya's support for terrorist groups in the 1970s and 1980s, led to economic sanctions being imposed on Libya by the United Nations and individual countries. U.N. sanctions were imposed in 1992 in response to the downing of an airliner over Lockerbie in Scotland in 1988.[6] Some U.S. sanctions were already in place by then, having been imposed in 1986 by President Ronald Reagan. More U.S. sanctions followed in 1992 and 1996.[7]

In July 1996, U.S. efforts to block the export of dual-use and military technology to Libya won approval by 33 nations of the Charter of the Wassenaar Arrangement on Export Controls for Conventional Arms and Dual-Use Goods and Technologies. The Wassenaar Arrangement is the successor regime to the Coordinating Committee for Multilateral Export Controls, which was established during the Cold War to prevent the transfer of sensitive technologies with military applications to the Soviet bloc.[8] In August 1996, President Bill Clinton signed legislation imposing sanctions on foreign companies that invest more than $40 million for future petroleum ventures in Iran and Libya, as well as companies exporting items to Libya that enhance its nuclear, biological, and chemical weapons and advanced conventional weapons programs.[9]

Decades of sanctions finally had their impact. In the late 1990s, Libya approached the Clinton administration in hopes of ending its international isolation. The administration made Libyan cooperation in the Lockerbie bombing case a prerequisite to normalizing United States–Libya relations. Libya turned over two intelligence officers who had been implicated in the Pan Am Flight 103 attack, and the United Nations suspended its sanctions in 1999. The U.S. sanctions remained in place.[10]

In March 2003, shortly before the Iraq War began, Musa Kussa, President Gadhafi's chief of intelligence, approached British M16 officials seeking to conclude negotiations for the end of its unconventional weapons programs in exchange for normalizing ties.[11] The George W. Bush administration resumed the talks with Libya but maintained the position that Libya would have to address concerns over its weapons programs before U.S. sanctions would be lifted.

The Bush administration linked Libya's turnaround to President Bush's national security strategy and the invasion of Iraq. The presence of 250,000 U.S. forces in the region undoubtedly had an impact, but it does not seem that President Gadhafi feared a U.S. invasion of Tripoli. Gadhafi seems to have concluded that he needed Western contracts and markets more than he needed chemical or nuclear weapons. He said in a January 2005 interview, "We started to ask ourselves, 'By manufacturing nuclear weapons, against whom are we going to use them?' World alliances have changed. We had no target. And then we started thinking about the cost. If someone attacks you and you use a nuclear bomb, you are in effect using it against yourself."[12]

Whether by design or by chance, the United States and the United Kingdom struck the right combination of force and diplomacy. Prime Minister Tony Blair seems to have been a decisive influence on President Bush, overcoming opposition from the U.S. Department of Defense to any "deals with dictators."[13] A former State Department official involved in the Bush administration's negotiations with Libya noted that these talks predated the war in Iraq, "The lesson is incontrovertible: to persuade a rogue regime to get out of the terrorism business and give up its weapons of mass destruction, we must not only apply pressure but also make clear the potential benefits of cooperation."[14]

A significant moment in the final negotiations seems to have been the October 2003 interception by British and American officials of a German cargo ship heading to Libya from Dubai. The ship carried a cargo of centrifuge parts reportedly based on Pakistani designs and manufactured in Malaysia. American and British spokesmen claimed that the seizure convinced Gadhafi that his programs could not escape detection. Others claimed that the Libyans alerted London and Washington to the ship as a gesture of their good faith.[15] Negotiations picked up pace after the seizure. British and U.S. officials reportedly visited ten previously secret sites and dozens of Libyan laboratories and military factories over three weeks in October and early December.[16] They searched for evidence of activity related to nuclear fuel cycles and for chemical and missile programs.[17]

The final details of the accord were hammered out in London on December 16, 2003.[18]

On December 19, 2003, Libyan foreign minister Abdel Rahman Shalqam announced that Libya would halt its unconventional weapon programs and eliminate any stockpiles of weapons under international verification and supervision. After President Gadhafi endorsed the deal through a press release, Prime Minister Blair and President Bush released press statements applauding "Qaddafi's statesmanship."[19] In the last week of December, inspectors from the International Atomic Energy Agency (IAEA) visited previously undisclosed nuclear sites in Tripoli. The IAEA's director general, Mohamed ElBaradei, stated that the facilities he visited indicated a program that was "in the initial stages of development," without any "industrial scale facility to produce highly enriched uranium."[20] ElBaradei said that it was difficult to judge with confidence but that he had a "gut feeling" that Libya was three to seven years away from producing a nuclear weapon.[21]

In early January 2004, American and British teams arrived to dismantle Libya's facilities. On January 19, the United Kingdom and the United States opened their first direct negotiations with the IAEA to determine who should be responsible for dismantling Libya's nuclear capabilities. According to news reports, the IAEA argued that it should be responsible for the dismantlement, while the United States and the United Kingdom seemed determined to retain control over the process. They ultimately reached an agreement that the United Kingdom and the United States will be responsible for dismantling the program while the IAEA will verify this process. The IAEA will also draw up an inventory detailing all aspects of Libya's nuclear program by surveying ten sites.[22] Libya joined the Chemical Weapons Convention on January 6, 2004. By January 19, it had also ratified the Comprehensive Nuclear Test Ban Treaty.

On January 27, 2004, the United States airlifted 55,000 pounds of documents and components of Libya's nuclear and ballistic programs out of the country into the United States. The cargo reportedly included uranium hexafluoride, centrifuge parts, documentation, and guidance devices for long-range missiles.[23] This was the first phase of the disarmament process. News reports said that blueprints for a warhead design, based on a first-generation Pakistani design, designed from China, were brought to the United States in late January 2004.[24] Libya's nuclear components are being held at the Oak Ridge National Laboratory in Tennessee.[25]

A delegation of seven members of Congress headed by Representative Curt Weldon (R-Pa.) arrived in Libya on January 24 on a goodwill visit, the first in 30 years.[26] Representative Tom Lantos (D-Calif.) met with Gadhafi and called for a normalization of relations the following day. Lantos had been one of the most fervent advocates of tight sanctions on Libya.

During the second phase of disarmament, Libya destroyed 3,000 chemical munitions and consolidated and secured its stocks of chemical weapon agents and precursors for destruction. The United States removed more than 1,000 metric tons of nuclear equipment, Scud-C missiles and their launchers, and more than 15 kilograms of fresh highly enriched uranium reactor fuel to Russia.[27] The United States and the United Kingdom agreed "in principle" to allow Libya to keep some of its medium-range Scud-B missiles, but these missiles must conform with range and payload limitations to which Libya agreed in December 2003.[28]

Phase three involved implementing verification mechanisms to ensure that Libya had or would definitely eliminate all its material and efforts that were related to nuclear and chemical weapons as well as all its missile programs that fell under the guidelines of the Missile Technology Control Regime. On September 22, 2004, the U.S. assistant secretary of state for verification and compliance, Paula DeSutter, told Congress that phase three of Libya's disarmament had been completed.[29]

Two days before that announcement, on September 20, President Bush lifted most remaining U.S. sanctions on Libya. The United States permitted direct air flights between the two countries and unfroze Libyan assets. Washington and Tripoli had resumed diplomatic ties in June 2004, after President Bush terminated sanctions on Libya under the 1996 Iran-Libya Sanctions Act. For the remaining disarmament work, the United States, the United Kingdom, and Libya have established a trilateral steering and cooperation committee. Libya remains subject to some sanctions because it remains on the U.S. list of state sponsors of terrorism.[30] The European Union formally ended twelve years of economic sanctions on October 12, 2004. In January 2005, Libya awarded major oil and gas exploration contracts to U.S. oil companies for the first time in 20 years.

However, in November 2004, Gadhafi voiced his disappointment that Libya had not been properly recompensed. This, he noted, provided little incentive for countries like Iran and North Korea to dismantle their nuclear programs. He said he needed more security guarantees from the United States, Europe, and Japan, as well as "civilian-use technology in return for abandoning military technology." Again in January 2005, he complained, "Libya and the whole world expected a positive response—not just words, although they were nice words—from America and Europe. Blair and Bush expressed their satisfaction. But there must be at least a declaration of a program like the Marshall Plan, to show the world that those who wish to abandon the nuclear weapon program will be helped. They promised, but we haven't seen anything yet."[31]

Nuclear Analysis

Libya's nuclear ambitions first became evident in 1970, when its attempts to buy nuclear weapons directly from China were rebuffed. In 1977 Libya reportedly turned to Pakistan, offering financial aid and supplies of uranium from Niger, apparently hoping to share in the results of Pakistan's nuclear program. But this also came to nothing, leaving Libya no option but to develop its own nuclear facilities. After Libya ratified the NPT in 1975 (it had been signed in 1969 by King Idris), the Soviet Union supplied Libya with a 10-megawatt research reactor, which began operating at Tajoura in 1979. The following year, Libya negotiated a formal safeguard agreement with the IAEA. Plans to have Russia build a power reactor near the Gulf of Sidra were subsequently dropped because of U.S. pressure on the potential supplier, Belgium, and a loss of interest by Moscow. In the 1980s, Argentina and Libya cooperated on nuclear technology and information.

At the 1995 NPT Review and Extension Conference, Libya eventually supported an indefinite extension of the treaty, despite Israel's continued refusal to sign it. Yet in January 1996, Libya's official news agency restated Gadhafi's position that the Arab states should acquire nuclear weapons to counter Israel's nuclear hegemony in the region.[32] Gadhafi has also asserted that the Arab states would be justified in possessing chemical and biological weapons to counter Israel's nuclear capability.[33] Nevertheless, Libya was among 43 African countries that signed the African Nuclear-Weapon-Free-Zone Treaty in April 1996.

The following September, Libya, along with Bhutan and India, voted against the Comprehensive Test Ban Treaty at the U.N. General Assembly, arguing that it should provide for nuclear disarmament within a specified time.[34] Nonetheless, Libya finally signed the treaty on November 13, 2001. In October 1997, Russia reopened nuclear cooperation talks with Libya,[35] and in March 1998 the Atomenergoeksport Company signed an $8 million contract involving the partial overhaul of the Tajoura research center. The possibility of cooperation in the construction of a nuclear power station was reportedly under discussion in 1999.[36] The true extent of Libya's clandestine nuclear program only became clear after its voluntary renunciation and the IAEA inspections that followed. Libya's undeclared nuclear program involved frequent movements of key equipment and nuclear material, and it relied heavily on support from foreign sources.

Between 1978 and 1991, Libya imported a total of 2,263 metric tons of yellowcake. The total amount of uranium imported by Libya was 1,587 metric tons contained in 6,367 drums. Libya conducted a series of uranium conversion experiments in a previously undeclared facility during the 1980s. In 1984, Libya ordered a modular uranium conversion facility from a foreign company. Most of the equipment was delivered in 1994, but Libyan authorities stated that one module of the facility (related to the production of uranium tetrafluoride, UF_4) was never received by Libya. Libya received two small cylinders of uranium hexafluoride (UF_6) from a foreign source (most likely Pakistan) in September 2000 and a large cylinder of UF_6 again in February 2001. The large cylinder contained natural uranium and the smaller one contained depleted uranium. Libya, however, stipulated that no fuel fabrication equipment was ever received from any sources.[37]

Libya acquired L-2 and L-1 centrifuges through various foreign sources, including the A. Q. Khan network, which are similar in design to the P-1 and P-2 centrifuges found in Iran. Libya purchased 20 preassembled L-1 centrifuges in 1997 and components for another 200. Libya managed to construct 3 different enrichment cascades, but only the smallest (using 9 cascades) was completely assembled in 2002. [38] In September 2000, Libya acquired 2 centrifuges of the more advanced L-2 type, which uses maraging steel for its rotors and can therefore spin at much faster speeds. It placed an order for another 10,000.

Libya had been developing a gas-centrifuge-based uranium enrichment facility. U.S. and British intelligence officials told Malaysian law enforcement officials in November that "a certain amount" of "enriched" UF_6 was shipped from Pakistan to Libya in 2001, according to a February 20 report from Malaysia's inspector general of police.[39] UF_6 is fed into the centrifuges, which can then produce either low-enriched uranium for civilian nuclear reactors or high-enriched uranium for nuclear weapons. Tripoli had complete centrifuges and thousands of centrifuge components, but it did not have an operating enrichment facility.

Libya also provided the IAEA with documents related to the design and fabrication of a nuclear explosive device that were provided by the A. Q. Khan network. The designs were reported to closely resemble the warheads that China had tested in the late 1960s and had passed on to Pakistan decades ago. Libyan officials have told investigators that they bought the blueprints from dealers who are part of that network, apparently for more than $50 million.[40]

Biological and Chemical Weapons Analysis

Libya's bid to acquire chemical weapons in the late 1980s has been well documented, and it once had a substantial CW stockpile. It had refused to sign the 1993 Chemical Weapons Convention, but in 1971 it became a party to the 1925 Geneva Protocol forbidding the use in war of chemical and biological weapons. Allegations that Libya used chemical weapons against Chad in 1986 have not been substantiated.

In late 1988, however, Libya finished the construction of a chemical production facility at Rabta, known as Pharma-150, with extensive foreign technical assistance.[41] It produced at least 100 metric tons of blister and nerve agents before it closed in 1990 in the face of United States–led international pressure.[42] At the same time, a similar plant, Pharma-200, was reportedly being built underground at a military base near Sebha, 650 kilometers south of Tripoli.[43] Little is known about that facility.

Most concern about Libya had focused on what the then–director of the Central Intelligence Agency (CIA), John Deutch, described as the "world's largest underground chemical weapons plant" in a mountain at Tarhuna, 40 miles southeast of Tripoli.[44] U.S. intelligence sources indicated in early 1996 that the plant would be completed "late in this decade" and would be capable of producing the ingredients for tons of poison gas daily.[45] Libya maintained that the plant was part of an irrigation system.[46] Tensions over the Tarhuna plant appeared to ease by late 1996, as reports surfaced that Libya had suspended construction,[47] following comments by U.S. defense secretary William Perry that he would not rule out the use of military force to block completion of the plant. Some Pentagon officials suggested that the United States might use a modified version of the B-61 nuclear warhead.[48] There were also reports in mid-1997 that Libya had received South African equipment for the manufacture of chemical and biological weapons. According to those reports, after the 1994 national elections in South Africa, several scientists from the South African military's CW and BW program (called Project Coast) had sold equipment and perhaps had even traveled to Libya to advise on the project.[49]

Libya declared to the Organization for the Prohibition of Chemical Weapons on March 5, 2004, that it had produced approximately 23 tons of mustard agent in one CW production facility (Rabta) between 1980 and 1990.[50] Libya also declared two storage sites to the OPCW, as well as provided a destruction plan for these weapons and production facilities. The OPCW set a deadline of April 29, 2007, for Libya to completely destroy its chemical weapons and the capacity to produce them.[51]

Libyans have already destroyed more than 3,000 chemical munitions and consolidated and secured their stocks of CW agents and precursors for destruction. Libya has also begun the process at the OPCW to seek approval to convert its former CW production facility at Rabta to produce pharmaceutical products. The United States has supported this proposal.[52]

Missile Analysis

In the late 1980s and early 1990s, Libya made several apparently unsuccessful attempts to purchase foreign missiles, such as the Soviet/Russian SS-23 and SS-21, and the Chinese DF-3A, M-9, and M-11. Libya's limited and antiquated missile arsenal includes basic Scud-Bs bought from the Soviet Union in the mid-1970s as well as North Korean Scud-Cs. Tripoli also pursued a program to develop the indigenous Al Fatah missile. On the whole, Libya's missile complex was heavily dependent upon foreign suppliers. The presence of U.N. sanctions from 1992 to 1999 was believed to have severely limited Libya's ability to maintain its Scud-B arsenal and to make further progress in its domestic ballistic missile program, though in recent years several shipments of Scud components have been intercepted en route to Libya.[53]

The CIA confirmed that Libya had received "ballistic missile-related goods and technical know-how" from Russian entities and "missile-related items, raw materials, or other help" from Chinese entities.[54] Serbian and Indian assistance to Libya's missile program was also cited in an unclassified CIA report to Congress.[55] Reports had circulated that Libya had purchased the 1,300-kilometer-range No Dong medium-range ballistic missiles from North Korea, but Western defense and intelligence sources have not confirmed such a purchase, acknowledging only that Libya had an interest in obtaining a longer-range missile capability. Since December 2003, Libya had agreed to abide by the Missile Technology Control Regime, which has meant eliminating ballistic missiles with a range exceeding 300 kilometers and a payload of 500 kilograms or more. By March 2004, Libya had relinquished five North Korean Scud-C missiles and their launchers. Libya also agreed to convert its Scud-B arsenal into shorter-range defensive missiles,[56] and it signed the Comprehensive Test Ban Treaty.[57]

NOTES

1. IAEA director general, "Report on 'Implementation of the NPT Safeguards Agreement of the Socialist People's Libyan Arab Jamahiriya,' May 28, 2004"; available at www.globalsecurity.org/wmd/library/news/libya/2004/040528-iaea.pdf.
2. Organization for the Prohibition of Chemical Weapons, "Libya Submits Initial Chemical Weapons Declaration," press release, March 5, 2004.
3. U.S. Department of State, "United States Supports Libyan Weapons Plant Conversion Plan," October 13, 2004.
4. Sharon Squassoni and Andrew Feickhert, "Disarming Libya Weapons of Mass Destruction," Congressional Research Service, April 22, 2004.
5. Ibid.
6. U.N. Security Council, Resolution 748 (1992), S/RES/748, March 31, 1992.
7. *Public Papers of the Presidents of the United States: Ronald Reagan, 1996*, Book I: January 1 to June 27, 1986 (Washington, D.C.: U.S. Government Printing Office, 1988), p. 17; and David Hoffman, "President Imposes Boycott on Business with Libya, Qadhafi's Isolation Urged," *Washington Post*, January 8, 1996.
8. "Post-Cocom 'Wassenaar Arrangement' Set to Begin New Export Control Role," *Arms Control Today*, December 1995–January 1996; *Basic Reports: Newsletter on International Security Policy*, February 21, 1996; and Jeff Erlich, "Future of Multinational Export Control Remains in Question," *Defense News*, July 22–28, 1996.
9. Iran and Libya Sanctions Act of 1996, P.L. 104-172, 50 USC 1701; and Eric Pianin, "Clinton Approves Sanctions for Investors in Iran, Libya," *Washington Post*, August 6, 1996. In 1997, the threshold investment was dropped to $20 million.
10. Flynt L. Leverett, "Why Libya Gave Up on the Bomb," *New York Times,* January 23, 2004.
11. Patrick E. Tyler, "Libyan Stagnation a Big Factor in Qaddafi Surprise," *New York Times*, January 8, 2004.
12. Scott MacLeod and Amany Radwan, "10 Questions for Muammar Gaddafi," *Time*, January 30, 2005; available at www.time.com/time/magazine/article/0,9171,1022560,00.html.
13. Private conversations between the authors and U.S. and foreign officials during 2004.
14. Leverett, "Why Libya Gave Up on the Bomb."
15. Stephen Fidler, Mark Huband, and Roula Khalaf, "Return to the Fold: How Gadaffi Was Persuaded to Give Up His Nuclear Goals," *Financial Times*, January 27, 2004.
16. Patrick E. Tyler and James Risen, "Secret Diplomacy Won Libyan Pledge on Arms," *New York Times*, December 21, 2003.
17. Fidler, Huband, and Khalaf, "Return to the Fold."
18. Ibid.
19. Glen Frankel, "A Long Slog Led to Libya's Decision," *Washington Post*, December 21, 2003.
20. Patrick E. Tyler, "Libya's Atom Bid in Early Phases," *New York Times*, December 30, 2003.
21. Ibid.
22. Mark Huband, "Nuclear Watchdog Agrees to Role in Libya," *Financial Times*, January 20, 2003.
23. Guy Dinmore, "US Praises Libya's Progress on Arms," *Financial Times*, January 28, 2004.
24. William J. Broad, "Libya's A-Bomb Blueprints Reveal New Tie to Pakistani," *New York Times*, February 9, 2003.
25. "U.S. Gains Libyan Nuclear Gear and Flies it to Knoxville, Tenn.," *New York Times*, January 28, 2004.
26. Brian Whitaker, "US Must Pay for Libya to Dismantle Weapons," *Guardian*, January 27, 2004.
27. Paula A. DeSutter, assistant secretary of state for verification and compliance, "Completion of Verification Work in Libya," testimony before the Subcommittee on International Terrorism, Nonproliferation and Human Rights, September 22, 2004; available at www.state.gov/t/vc/rls/rm/2004/37220.htm.
28. Paul Kerr, "Libya to Keep Limited Missile Force," *Arms Control Today*, May 2004.
29. DeSutter, "Completion of Verification Work in Libya."

30. Paul Kerr, "U.S. Lifts Remaining Economic Sanctions Against Libya," *Arms Control Today*, October, 2004.
31. MacLeod and Radwan, "10 Questions for Muammar Gaddafi."
32. "Arabs Must Get Nuclear Bomb to Match Israel—Libya," Reuters, January 27, 1996. Also see "Arabs Need Nuclear Bomb, Qadhafi Says," Reuters, May 17, 1995.
33. "Qadhafi Says Arabs Have Right to Germ Warfare Arms," Reuters, March 30, 1996; "Qadhafi Tunnels into Trouble Both within and without," *Jane's Defense Weekly*, September 1996, p. 24.
34. United Nations, "Assembly Adopts Comprehensive Nuclear-Test-Ban Treaty," Press Release GA/ 9083, September 10, 1996.
35. "Russia Ready to Start Talks with Libya on Nuclear Center," Interfax (Moscow), October 22, 1997.
36. "Moscow Set to Expand Trade Ties with Libya," Interfax (Moscow), April 7, 1999.
37. IAEA director general, "Report on 'Implementation of the NPT Safeguards Agreement of the Socialist People's Libyan Arab Jamahiriya,' August 30, 2004"; available at www.iaea.or.at/ Publications/Documents/Board/2004/gov2004-59.pdf; and IAEA director general, "Report on 'Implementation of the NPT Safeguards Agreement of the Socialist People's Libyan Arab Jamahiriya,' May 28, 2004."
38. Paul Kerr, "U.S. Says Libya Implementing WMD Pledge," *Arms Control Today*, March 2004.
39. Ibid.
40. William J. Broad and David E. Sanger, "Warhead Blueprints Link Libya Project to Pakistan Figure," *New York Times*, February 4, 2004.
41. Stephen Engelberg with Michael Gordon, "Germans Accused of Helping Libya Build Nerve Gas Plant," *New York Times*, January 1, 1989; R. James Woolsey, director of central intelligence, "Challenges to Peace in the Middle East," address to the Washington Institute for Near East Policy, Wye Plantation, Maryland, September 23, 1994, revised.
42. In 1990, by fabricating a fire, Libya tried to give the impression that the facility was seriously damaged. See U.S. Department of Defense, *Proliferation: Threat and Response* (Washington, D.C.: U.S. Department of Defense, 1996), p. 26.
43. "Libya," education module on chemical and biological weapons nonproliferation, available at www.sipri.org.
44. Tim Weiner, "Huge Chemical Arms Plant Near Completion in Libya," *New York Times*, February 25, 1996. See also John Diamond, "Watching China," Associated Press, February 23, 1996.
45. Weiner, "Huge Chemical Arms Plant Near Completion."
46. "Libya Denies Weapons-Factory Link," *Washington Times*, February 27, 1996; John Lancaster, "Perry Presses U.S. Charge against Libya," *Washington Post*, April 4, 1996; Lancaster, "Egypt Denies Libyan Chemical Arms Site," *Washington Post*, May 30, 1996.
47. Lancaster, "Perry Presses U.S. Charge against Libya."
48. Robert Burns, "U.S.-Libya," Associated Press, April 23, 1996; Charles Aldinger, "U.S. Lacks Conventional Arms to Destroy Libya Plant," Reuters, April 23, 1996. Also see Art Pine, "U.S. Hints It Would Bomb Libyan Facility," *Los Angeles Times*, April 19, 1996; Pine, "A-Bomb against Libya Target Suggested," *Los Angeles Times*, April 24, 1996.
49. Peta Thornycroft, "South Africa: Scientists Said to Sell CBW Technology to Libya after 1994," *Johannesburg Mail and Guardian*, February 7, 1997, in FBIS-TAC 97-007; "South Africa: Mandela Fears Chemical Arms Sales to Libya 'Tip of Iceberg,'" *Johannesburg SAPA*, February 11, 1997, in FBIS-TAC 97-007.
50. Squassoni and Feickhert, "Disarming Libya Weapons of Mass Destruction."
51. "Libya Submits Initial Chemical Weapons Declaration," press release, March 5, 2004; available at www.opcw.org/html/global/press_releases/2k4/PR8_2004.html.
52. DeSutter, "Completion of Verification Work in Libya."
53. "U.K. Warns Libya after Scud Find," BBC News, January 9, 2000. Available at http:// news.bbc.co.uk/1/hi/uk/596088.stm; and "Scud Missile Parts Intercepted," BBC News, April 12, 2000.

54. George Tenet, director of central intelligence, "Worldwide Threat 2001: National Security in a Changing World," statement before the Senate Select Committee on Intelligence, February 7, 2001.
55. CIA, "Report to Congress on the Acquisition of Technology relating to Weapons of Mass Destruction and Advanced Conventional Munitions, July–December 2000," September 7, 2001.
56. Kerr, "Libya to Keep Limited Missile Force."
57. Squassoni and Feickhert, "Disarming Libya Weapons of Mass Destruction."

CHAPTER 17

Iraq

Nuclear Weapons Capability

Iraq never successfully developed a nuclear weapon, and its nuclear program begun in the 1970s almost certainly ended in 1991. After conducting six years of inspections in Iraq, the International Atomic Energy Agency (IAEA) concluded in 1997 that its dismantling, regular monitoring, and verification efforts—along with the damage from the Gulf War—had incapacitated the country's nuclear weapons infrastructure.[1] During December 1998, U.S. and British air strikes during Operation Desert Fox inflicted further damage on Iraqi leadership offices linked to the program. But many suspected Iraq still had nuclear ambitions and retained the capability and intention to restart its program covertly.

All the available evidence indicates that Iraq did not reconstitute or maintain a nuclear program after 1991. The IAEA—charged by the U.N. Security Council with supervising nuclear disarmament and verification efforts in Iraq—was close to drawing such a conclusion in March 2003, after four months of newly restarted inspections.[2] In September 2004, Charles Duelfer, the chief of the U.S. government's Iraq Survey Group (ISG), definitively concluded in his "Comprehensive Report" that "Iraq did not possess a nuclear device, nor had it tried to reconstitute a capability to produce nuclear weapons after 1991."[3] Duelfer's predecessor at the ISG, David Kay, stated his belief that Saddam Hussein maintained an interest in acquiring nuclear weapons after 1991 but that the program "had been seriously degraded. The activities of the inspectors in the early 1990s did a tremendous amount" to prevent reconstitution.[4]

Biological and Chemical Weapons Capability

Iraq does not have an active chemical or biological weapons program or weapons stockpiles. All its related programs appear to have ended in 1992. The U.N. Security Council gave two groups the responsibility to inspect the Iraqi biological, chemical, and missile programs: the UN Special Commission on Iraq (UNSCOM, 1991–1999); and the U.N. Monitoring, Verification, and Inspection Commission (UNMOVIC, 1999–).

When UNSCOM's inspectors left Iraq in 1998, they still had many questions about Iraq's biological and chemical programs. For instance, there were justifiable suspicions that Iraq could have tons of chemical weapons hidden or enough growth media to produce tons of new biological weapon agents.[5]

Baghdad's refusal to fully disclose all the details of its past efforts led U.S. officials to conclude that it was maintaining active programs.[6]

Intensive searches by the ISG and U.S. troops after the 2003 Iraq War did not turn up any evidence of weapons stockpiles or of chemical or biological weapons programs active after 1991. Kay concluded that air strikes, sanctions, and inspections had destroyed Iraq's ability to develop stocks of these weapons. Duelfer reported in 2004: "While a small number of old, abandoned chemical munitions have been discovered, ISG judges that Iraq unilaterally destroyed its undeclared chemical weapons stockpile in 1991." He also noted, "In 1991 and 1992, Iraq appears to have destroyed its undeclared stocks of BW [biological weapons] and probably destroyed remaining holdings of bulk BW agent. . . . ISG found no direct evidence that Iraq, after 1996, had plans for a new BW program or was conducting BW-specific work for military purposes."[7]

Iraq ratified the Biological Weapons Convention in 1991. As of the spring of 2005, it had neither signed nor ratified the Chemical Weapons Convention.

Missile and Delivery System Capability

Iraq does not have an active missile or delivery system program beyond short-range systems. It did not have longer-range missiles after 1991.

Of all Iraq's alleged illicit programs, only the missile program made any advances after the 1991 Gulf War. Iraq's longest-range missiles were the 600-kilometer range Al Husseins (a modified Scud). These were destroyed after the 1991 war.[8]

Before the 2003 war, U.S. officials claimed that Iraq still possessed a force of Scud-type missiles and unmanned aerial vehicles (UAVs). U.N. inspectors did not find any Scud missiles, but under UNMOVIC's supervision, Iraq was forced to destroy Al Samoud II missiles that exceeded the permitted 150-kilometer range by 30 kilometers. By the time the war began, Iraq had destroyed two-thirds of these missiles (72) and UNMOVIC was examining Iraqi UAVs for possible chemical weapon or biological weapon (CW or BW) delivery capability.

After the war, the United States did not uncover evidence of Scud missiles or of UAVs capable of delivering chemical or biological agents. The ISG did find evidence of two cruise missile programs, of which one may have been intended to develop systems with a 1,000-kilometer range. Kay described a "substantial illegal procurement for all aspects of the missile programs," but he noted that Iraq essentially halted missile development once U.N. inspections began in 2002.

The Strategic Context

Iraq was created by the British Empire after World War I from three disparate Mesopotamian provinces of the defeated Ottoman Empire. The British ruled Iraq through an installed monarchy after they suppressed a revolt by Sunni, Shia, and Kurds in bloody counterinsurgency operations that killed tens of thousands of Arabs and more than 2,000 British troops. A military coup overthrew the monarchy in 1958 and soon established relations and arms trade with the Soviet

Union. The United States supported the Baathist Party coup that ousted the Soviet-leaning General Abdel Karim Kassem in 1963. The secular Saddam Hussein rose to assume power in 1979. After the Iranian revolution of that year, the United States generally viewed Iraq as a useful barrier to Islamic fundamentalism, and it provided arms and diplomatic support to Iraq during the 1980s.

Saddam Hussein wanted Iraq to be the predominant power in the Middle East, and throughout the 1980s he saw nuclear, chemical, and biological weapons and ballistic missiles as necessary to achieve that goal. Nuclear weapons, he believed, would ensure his victory over Iraq's regional rivals, Iran, Israel, and Turkey.[9] Israel's destruction of the Osiraq reactor in 1981 increased his determination to acquire a nuclear capability. After the Osiraq attack, according to the former Iraqi nuclear scientist Khidhir Hamza, "We went from 500 people to 7,000 in a timeframe of five years. All done in secret."[10]

The Iran-Iraq War (1980–1988) was a primary motivation for all of Iraq's unconventional weapons programs. Saddam invaded Iran on September 22, 1980, believing that it would be a quick, decisive campaign. Instead, Iranian counterattacks blocked the invasion and drove Iraqi troops back across the border in 1982. The battles developed into years of trench warfare. To break this stalemate, Iraq turned to new weapons, using chemical and missile attacks and accelerating its nuclear and biological warfare programs. Saddam increased pressure on his nuclear scientists to expand the nuclear program, including developing the capability for radiation weapons along the border with Iran.[11] The CW program went from one small-scale facility (Al Rashad) in the 1970s and early 1980s to the initial production of mustard gas in 1981 to industrial-scale production in 1983.[12] During the 1985–1990 period, the BW program grew from laboratory research on pathogens to the full-scale development and production of agents and dissemination mechanisms.[13]

After the war ended in 1988, Iraq's relations with Iran remained tense. In April 2001, for example, Iran reportedly fired between 44 and 77 Scud-B missiles against the Mujahideen Khalk Organization, an Iranian opposition group that was based in southern and eastern Iraq. Iraq characterized this "aggression" as a coordinated effort by Iran and Saudi Arabia.[14]

Saddam Hussein invaded Kuwait on August 2, 1990, and was driven back and defeated in the Gulf War of January 17 to February 27, 1991. The U.N. Security Council adopted Resolution 687 on April 3, 1991, which declared a formal cease-fire and ordered Iraq to "unconditionally accept the destruction, removal or rendering harmless under international supervision of all chemical and biological weapons and all stocks of agents and all related subsystems and component and all research, development, support and manufacturing facilities, all ballistic missiles with a range greater than 150 kilometers and related major parts and repair and production facilities. . . ." Iraq was also forbidden from acquiring or developing nuclear weapons or nuclear weapons materials or components.[15]

After several years of reluctant cooperation with this U.N. inspection process, Saddam adopted a strategy of frustrating and hindering it, forgoing more than $120 billion in oil revenues withheld by the United Nations. This appeared to be an indication of the price he was prepared to pay to keep as much of his weapons capability as possible.[16] In the fall of 1998, his defiance grew as the impact of U.N. economic sanctions generated sympathy in the Arab world, and his tactics split the U.N. Security Council. He refused to allow inspectors unfettered access inside Iraq without a firm commitment to lift all remaining sanctions. By December 15, the UNSCOM chief, Richard Butler, reported that "Iraq's conduct ensured that no progress was able to be made in the fields of disarmament."[17] This standoff led to the withdrawal of all U.N. inspection personnel on December 16, 1998, followed by military action over the next two days by the United States and the United Kingdom.

U.N. Security Council Resolution 1284, adopted in December 1999, established a follow-up inspection regime to be led by UNMOVIC and the IAEA. But Iraq refused to permit these inspections until the United Nations removed the sanctions. Without inspectors on the ground, it was difficult for the United Nations or United States to determine the state of Iraq's weapons programs.[18] The end of inspections meant not only that there were no inspectors in Iraq but also that the automated video monitoring system that the United Nations had installed at known and suspected weapons facilities was no longer operating.[19] This absence of any on-site monitoring in Iraq raised concerns that Saddam Hussein had begun to restart Iraq's nuclear and other unconventional weapons programs.

From 1999 to 2002, U.S. efforts focused on containment. Both experts and officials were concerned about the apparent erosion of the sanctions regime, and they sought new ways to restore the U.N. Security Council's ability and willingness to isolate and contain Saddam, whom many of them believed had been weakened by years of sanctions and now posed only a minor regional threat. In February 2001, for example, then–U.S. secretary of state Colin Powell stated, "Containment has been a successful policy and I think we should make sure that we continue it."[20] In July 2001, then–national security adviser Condoleezza Rice added, "We are able to keep arms from [Saddam]. His military forces have not been rebuilt. . . . This has been a successful period."[21]

There are several possible explanations for why Saddam acted as if he had weapons programs when he did not. Most likely, he sought to cooperate enough with U.N. inspections to bring about an end to the sanctions but not enough to diminish his image as a powerful, ruthless leader. Though some of his bluster may have been directed at his rival Iran, much of it may have been for the benefit of his domestic audience. His regime was weaker than many had realized before the war. Analyst Kenneth Pollack concludes:

> He may have feared that if his internal adversaries realized that he no longer had the capability to use these weapons, they would try to move against him. . . . Saddam's standing among the Sunni elites who constituted his power base was linked to a great extent to his having made Iraq a regional power—which the elites saw as a product of Iraq's unconventional arsenal. Thus openly giving up his WMD [weapons of mass destruction] could also have jeopardized his position with crucial supporters.[22]

The 2003 Iraq War

Saddam's bluff worked, but with unintended consequences. Spurred by his behavior, many national and international officials and experts began to believe that Iraq probably had research programs and hidden stores of chemical or biological weapons and was maintaining an interest in developing nuclear weapons. Beginning in 2002, these perceptions led to an international debate that was not about weapons but war. The issue was whether Iraq's residual capabilities and its failure to cooperate fully with U.N. inspections posed such a severe threat that they required military invasion and occupation.

After a determined U.S. drive to unite the U.N. Security Council on the need to disarm Iraq, on November 8, 2002, the council adopted Resolution 1441, which found that Iraq "was in material breech of its obligations under relevant resolutions, including Resolution 687" and that new enhanced inspections were necessary "with the aim of bringing to full and verified completion the disarmament process."[23]

The UNMOVIC and IAEA inspections made rapid progress, and most nations favored continuing the efforts. In March 2003, however, inspections ended when the United States led a coalition of countries to invade Iraq and topple Hussein's regime. The 2003 conflict was the world's first nonproliferation war—a war based primarily on the claimed need to prevent a nation from acquiring, using, or transferring nuclear, biological, and chemical weapons.

Foundations for the Threat Assessments

For many years, U.N. inspectors needed to resolve glaring gaps in Iraq's records before they could declare that all Iraq's chemical and biological programs and long-range missile programs had ended and that all its weapons had been destroyed. They also had concerns, but fewer questions, on its nuclear program. The IAEA had destroyed all the equipment related to the development or production of nuclear weapons, and it had concluded in 1999 that its "verification activities have revealed no indication that Iraq possesses nuclear weapons or any meaningful amounts of weapon-usable nuclear material or that Iraq has retained any practical capability (facilities or hardware) for the production of such material."[24]

There were still justifiable suspicions among the inspectors and international officials that Iraq could have tons of hidden chemical weapons or enough growth media to produce tons of new biological weapon agents. All the estimates of these quantities of weapons and media were based on those that were not accounted for when UNSCOM ended its inspections. For example, the U.S. intelligence consensus in 1999, as reported to Congress, was:

> We do not have any direct evidence that Iraq has used the period since Desert Fox to reconstitute its WMD programs, although given its past behavior, this type of activity must be regarded as likely. The United Nations assesses that Baghdad has the capability to reinitiate both its CW and BW programs within

> a few weeks to months, but without an inspection monitoring program, it is difficult to determine if Iraq has done so.[25]

These findings were repeated almost verbatim in subsequent biannual intelligence reports to Congress. A Defense Intelligence Agency (DIA) estimate from September 2002 stated:

> A substantial amount of Iraq's chemical warfare agents, precursors, munitions, and production equipment were destroyed between 1991 and 1998 as a result of Operation Desert Storm and UNSCOM (United Nations Special Commission) actions. Nevertheless, we believe Iraq retained production equipment, expertise and chemical precursors and can reconstitute a chemical warfare program in the absence of an international inspection regime. . . . There is no reliable information on whether Iraq is producing and stockpiling chemical weapons, or where Iraq has—or will—establish its chemical warfare agent production facilities.[26]

In brief, the consensus of the intelligence agencies in early 2002 was that:

- The 1991 Gulf War, U.N. inspections, and subsequent military actions had destroyed most of Iraq's nuclear, biological, and chemical weapons and long-range missile capabilities.
- Although there was no direct evidence that any chemical or biological weapons remained in Iraq, agencies judged that there were still significant stocks, and they were concerned about the possibility of renewed production.
- As Iraq rebuilt its facilities, some of the equipment purchased for civilian use could also be used to manufacture chemical or biological weapons.
- Without an inspection regime, it would be difficult to determine the status of these programs.

Rising Alarm

Starting in late 2002, however, the official statements on the threat shifted dramatically, to increased alarm and specific claims of weapons and activities. Although this shift does not appear to have been supported by concrete new evidence, these statements were picked up and amplified by U.S. congressional leaders, journalists, and some experts.

Many of the official statements on Iraq's weapons programs were supported by the U.S. National Intelligence Estimate (NIE) on Iraq, which was produced in three weeks in response to congressional requests made in September 2002.[27] The NIE was delivered to Congress ten days before the vote authorizing the use of force to compel Iraqi compliance with U.N. resolutions. The director of the Central Intelligence Agency (CIA) released an unclassified version of the NIE, *Iraq's Weapons of Mass Destruction Programs*, in October 2002. Three aspects of this NIE merit particular attention: It was produced far more quickly than is normal for such documents; it went far beyond the consensus intelligence assessments of the preceding five years; and more serious dissents were expressed about its key findings than about any other declassified NIE.

During and after this period, public government statements (including fact sheets from the State Department and the White House) increased steadily in alarm over the extent of these programs and began to assert that Saddam Hussein's regime had operational ties to al Qaeda terrorists. Some public statements went far beyond the NIE. For example, the NIE says "in the view of *most* agencies, Baghdad is reconstituting its nuclear weapons program," whereas Vice President Dick Cheney said in March 2003, "We know he's reconstituted these programs since the Gulf War. We know he's out trying once again to produce nuclear weapons and we know that he has a long-standing relationship with various terrorist groups, including the al Qaeda organization."[28]

Administration officials stated repeatedly that Iraq had a reconstituted nuclear weapons program; hundreds of tons of chemical and biological weapons; industrial facilities for the large-scale, ongoing production of even more chemical and biological weapons; dozens of Scud missiles; and a fleet of unmanned aerial vehicles capable of delivering these weapon agents. Then–secretary of state Colin Powell said in January 2003 that "Iraq continues to conceal quantities, vast quantities, of highly lethal material and weapons to deliver it."[29] Secretary of Defense Donald Rumsfeld said in March 2003 that U.S. officials knew the location of Iraq's illicit weapons: "We know where they are."[30]

Some official statements relied on unverified claims from Iraqi defectors, rather than information gathered by U.N. inspections or intelligence professionals. After the war, it became clear that several of the defectors provided by the Iraqi National Congress (headed by Ahmad Chalabi) had provided false or manufactured information. An assessment by the DIA concluded that most of the information given by Iraqi defectors was of little or no value, with much of it invented or exaggerated.[31]

With limited data, government officials said that they first had to develop an outline of a threat picture and then accumulate "bits and pieces" of information to fill in that picture. Then–national security adviser Condoleezza Rice explained in June 2003 that the White House did not have one, single assessment but rather had formed "a judgment," which was "not about a data point here or a data point there, but about what Saddam Hussein was doing. That he had weapons of mass destruction. That was the judgment." This, she said, was a picture that they developed when they "connected a lot of dots from multiple sources."[32]

Former British foreign secretary Robin Cook commented about a similar methodology in the United Kingdom that "I think it would be fair to say there was a selection of evidence to support a conclusion. I fear we got into a position in which the intelligence was not being used to inform and shape policy, but to shape policy that was already settled."[33]

Some official statements misrepresented the findings of U.N. inspections. For example, President George W. Bush said,

> The regime was forced to admit that it had produced more than 30,000 liters of anthrax and other deadly biological agents. The inspectors, however,

> *concluded* that Iraq *had likely produced* two to four times that amount. This is a massive stockpile of biological weapons that has never been accounted for, and is capable of killing millions. (emphasis added)[34]

The inspectors, however, did not say that Iraq *had likely produced* these additional amounts, only that Iraq *might have imported enough growth media to produce* these amounts. They did not know for sure either the amount or whether it had been used for this purpose. As Hans Blix explained to the U.N. Security Council in December 2003:

> Iraq declared earlier that they had produced 8,500 litres of anthrax and there was not sufficient evidence to demonstrate that it was limited to 8,500. If it was so, we must ask ourselves was there more? UNSCOM actually calculated that, with the capacity that [Iraq] had, they could have produced about three times as much, something like 24,000 litres. Then Iraq declared that they had destroyed it all and there was some evidence given that they had destroyed some of it. There was not sufficient evidence to show that all was destroyed. Hence, there is a question: is there still some anthrax in Iraq? . . . This is the kind of questions that we have on many items.[35]

In his reports to the Security Council, Blix said that though there were weapons and agents unaccounted for, "One must not jump to the conclusion that they exist. However, that possibility is also not excluded."[36] The inspectors carefully kept both possibilities open.

The U.S. assessments in the months before the war, however, did draw such conclusions. Official estimates peaked with the statement by the president to the nation on the eve of war:

> Intelligence gathered by this and other governments leaves no doubt that the Iraq regime continues to possess and conceal some of the most lethal weapons ever devised. . . . The danger is clear: using chemical, biological, or one day nuclear weapons, obtained with the help of Iraq, the terrorists could fulfill their stated ambition and kill thousands or hundreds of thousands of innocent people in our country or any other.[37]

On March 19, 2003, the main body of U.S. and British forces began the invasion of Iraq. But the search for the expected stockpiles of weapons had already begun.

The Hunt for Weapons

The initial search team, known as Task Force 20, entered Iraq covertly before fighting began. These special forces were tasked with uncovering Iraq's unconventional weapons and so-called high-value targets, such as Saddam Hussein. As major operations began, the 75th Exploitation Task Force (XTF) became the primary search team in the hunt. Site Survey Teams also joined the search as forward teams with preliminary detection equipment.

In June 2003, the Iraq Survey Group (ISG) replaced the 75th XTF. The ISG, a group of about 1,300 to 1,400 military and civilian personnel, assumed responsibility to unearth and record Iraq's weapons and uncover Saddam's human rights abuses and links to terrorist groups such as al Qaeda. The number of personnel searching for weapons far exceeded the number of original U.N. inspectors.

Neither U.N. inspectors nor U.S. forces found any of the alleged weapons beyond a few old chemical munitions. UNMOVIC found and destroyed eighteen undeclared chemical artillery shells, which appear to have been produced before 1990. Sixteen of these shells were empty, and two were filled with water.[38] A shell said to contain sarin nerve gas was apparently used as part of an improvised explosive device in an attack on U.S. forces in 2004 but caused no casualties.

None of the major statements in the NIE or in Secretary Powell's U.N. testimony were proven correct (with the exception of the NIE's finding that Saddam was unlikely to have given any weapons to terrorist groups). Most U.S. and U.K. officials recanted their claims, but they blamed the false statements on faulty intelligence provided by government agencies. In July 2004, the U.S. Senate Intelligence Committee and the Butler Commission, a British parliamentary inquiry, released reports that offered devastating critiques of both nations' intelligence failures in Iraq.[39] The March 2005 report of President Bush's commission on the intelligence failure confirmed these findings.[40] On the basis of access to the classified record and interviews with hundreds of intelligence analysts and operatives, these reports discuss in detail how top intelligence officials misrepresented and misjudged information about Iraq's suspected nuclear, biological, and chemical weapons programs. According to the Senate report, most of the key judgments in the 2002 NIE "either overstated, or were not supported by, the underlying intelligence reporting. A series of failures . . . led to the mischaracterization of the intelligence."[41] None of these reports examined how administration officials used the intelligence or influenced the development of the intelligence.

The following sections detail the history of Iraq's programs for nuclear, biological, and chemical weapons, and missile systems. The intelligence estimates are compared with prewar administration claims and with the evidence discovered in Iraq as of the spring of 2005.

Nuclear Weapons Programs

The Iraqi effort to develop nuclear weapons was the longest lasting and most significant of the weapon programs. It involved large-scale, observable facilities and operations and a clandestine procurement network.

History

Iraq ratified the Non-Proliferation Treaty (NPT) on October 29, 1969, pledging not to manufacture nuclear weapons and agreeing to place all its nuclear materials and facilities under IAEA safeguards. Iraq violated its NPT obligations, however, by secretly pursuing a multi-billion-dollar nuclear weapons program.

Iraq's efforts to produce weapons-grade uranium used virtually every feasible uranium enrichment process, including electromagnetic isotope separation (EMIS), gas centrifuges, chemical enrichment, gaseous diffusion, and laser isotope separation. The uranium enrichment program began in 1982, when authorities decided to abandon Iraq's original plan after Israel's June 7, 1981, bombing of the Osiraq research reactor.[42] Until the Israeli attack, Iraq had chosen plutonium over highly enriched uranium (HEU) as the preferred fissile material. The Osiraq reactor, which had been purchased from France in 1976, was unusually large and capable of irradiating uranium specimens to produce significant quantities of plutonium.[43]

Iraq's EMIS program went undetected because it did not rely on state-of-the-art, imported equipment whose acquisition might have given the effort away.[44] Indeed, the EMIS program might have remained hidden from the IAEA inspection teams except for the fact that it was revealed by an Iraqi nuclear engineer who had defected to U.S. forces after the 1991 war.[45] Iraq started its gas-centrifuge program for uranium enrichment after its EMIS program. It relied heavily on foreign contractors who were willing to circumvent export controls and to sell classified design information on early Western-type centrifuges and high-tensile maraging steel for the manufacture of centrifuges.[46]

Iraqi scientists also organized secret attempts to produce and separate small quantities of plutonium in IAEA-safeguarded facilities at Tuwaitha. By 1991 they had acquired a rudimentary ability to separate plutonium, producing approximately 6 grams. Without any changes to the configuration of their radiochemical laboratory, the Iraqis would have been unable to separate more than 60 grams of plutonium a year, a quantity insufficient to produce the 5 to 8 kilograms needed for a first nuclear device.[47]

Weaponization Attempts

The Iraqis focused their efforts on developing an implosion-type weapon, whose basic design involves surrounding a subcritical mass, or core, of fissile material (in this case, HEU) with conventional high-explosive charges. The charges are uniformly detonated to compress the nuclear material into a supercritical configuration.

The IAEA concluded that the original plan of the Iraqi nuclear weapons program, as set out in 1988, was to produce a small arsenal of weapons, with the first one to be ready in 1991.[48] Although the weaponization team made significant progress in designing a workable device, the original deadline could not have been met because progress in the production of HEU—using the EMIS and gas-centrifuge processes—had lagged far behind. The fact that domestically produced HEU would not have been available for some time led Iraq to undertake an accelerated program.

In September 1990, Iraq embarked on a stepped-up program to develop a nuclear device by extracting weapons-grade material from safeguarded research reactor fuel.[49] This program provided for such measures as the accelerated design and fabrication of the implosion package, the selection and construction of a test site, and the development of a delivery vehicle. The deadline for producing a weapon under this program apparently was April 1991.[50] In spite of making progress in the high-explosive testing program, Iraqi scientists were still struggling in 1991 to master the high-explosive charges that must be precisely fabricated to produce homogeneous shock waves against the core after ignition.[51]

The Gulf War and subsequent IAEA disarmament efforts ended the program. Forty-three days of bombing by coalition forces damaged but did not destroy the program's infrastructure. The IAEA removed or secured all known imported and indigenously produced uranium compounds and destroyed or removed all known single-use equipment used in enrichment research and development.[52] Inspectors dismantled all known facilities for the enrichment of fuel, and they destroyed the principal building of the Al Atheer nuclear weapons development and production plant and related equipment. The IAEA verified and accounted for the entire inventory of research reactor fuel targeted by the "crash program."[53]

In October 1997, the IAEA's assessment of Iraq's nuclear program was that "there are no indications that there remains in Iraq any physical capability for the production of amounts of weapon-usable nuclear material of any practical significance."[54] No evidence was found that Iraq had been successful in its attempt to produce nuclear weapons, and no proof was discovered that Iraq had produced more than a few grams of weapons-grade nuclear material through indigenous processes or secretly acquired weapon-usable material from abroad.[55] However, the agency was aware "that the know-how and expertise acquired by Iraqi scientists and engineers could provide an adequate base for reconstituting a nuclear-weapons-oriented program."[56] There was both natural and low-enriched uranium in Iraq under IAEA safeguards, and Iraq allowed the IAEA to inspect these materials annually in accordance with its NPT safeguard obligations.

U.S. Views before the 2003 War

Before the 2003 war, senior U.S. and U.K. officials said that Saddam Hussein was very close to having a nuclear weapon, or might already have one. Iraq's biggest challenge was to obtain sufficient fissile material for a device. Evidence cited for this included Iraqi attempts to purchase uranium from Africa and import aluminum tubes and high-strength magnets for enrichment. Vice President Cheney said, "We now know that Saddam has resumed his efforts to acquire nuclear weapons. . . . Many of us are convinced that Saddam will acquire nuclear weapons fairly soon."[57] President Bush said U.S. satellites had detected suspicious activity at nuclear-related sites in Iraq and that "Iraq has attempted to purchase high-strength aluminum tubes and other equipment needed for gas centrifuges, which are used to enrich uranium for nuclear weapons. If the Iraqi regime is able to produce, buy, or steal an amount of highly-enriched uranium a little larger than a single softball, it could have a nuclear weapon in less than a year."[58]

The official statements were supported in part by the October 2002 NIE. In the document, some agencies concluded that Iraq had restarted its nuclear weapons program, but key agencies disagreed.[59] The NIE went far beyond previous intelligence assessments that had only expressed concern that Iraq might be "attempting to acquire materials that could aid in reconstituting its nuclear weapons program." In 1997 and 1999, unclassified CIA reports on Iraq did not mention a nuclear program.[60]

U.N. Findings and Actions

The IAEA inspections from November 2002 to March 2003 found no evidence that Iraq had restarted its nuclear program.[61] The inspections were conducted by the Iraq Nuclear Verification Office and resumed on November 27, 2002, after a four-year hiatus. There were 218 inspections at 141 sites, including all those identified in overhead satellite imagery as having suspicious activity. IAEA director general Mohamed ElBaradei reported to the United Nations Security Council on March 7, 2003, that:

- There is "no indication of resumed nuclear activities . . . nor any indication of nuclear-related prohibited activities at any inspected sites."
- "There is no indication that Iraq has attempted to import uranium since 1990." The documents that indicated Iraq attempted to purchase uranium from Niger were declared "in fact not authentic."
- "There is no indication that Iraq has attempted to import aluminium tubes for use in centrifuge enrichment." Even if it had, "it was highly unlikely that Iraq could have achieved the considerable redesign needed to use them in a revived centrifuge program."
- Though the question was still under review, there was "no indication to date that Iraq has imported magnets for use in a centrifuge program."
- "During the past four years, at the majority of Iraqi sites, industrial capacity has deteriorated substantially due to the departure of the foreign support that was often present in the late '80s, the departure of large numbers of skilled Iraqi personnel in the past decade, and the lack of consistent maintenance by Iraq of sophisticated equipment. At only a few inspected sites involved in industrial research, development and manufacturing have the facilities been improved and new personnel been taken on." [62]

Postwar Conclusions

There is no evidence that there was any active Iraqi nuclear program after 1991.

In July 2003, U.S. officials said that they could not support the statement that Iraq had attempted to purchase uranium in Niger and that it should not have appeared in the president's State of the Union speech. Former ambassador Joseph Wilson revealed that in response to an administration request, he investigated the Niger claim in February 2002. Wilson had reported to the Department of State and the CIA that "it was highly doubtful that any such transaction had ever taken place."[63]

David Kay testified to Congress on October 2, 2003, that "to date we have not uncovered evidence that Iraq undertook significant post-1998 steps to actually build nuclear weapons or produce fissile material. However, Iraq did take steps to preserve some technological capability from the pre-1991 nuclear weapons program."[64]

Although Kay asserted his belief that Saddam was determined to develop nuclear weapons, he noted in interviews that there was "no doubt" that Iraq had less ability to produce fissile material than in 1991. The program, he said, "had been seriously degraded. The activities of the inspectors in the early 1990s did a tremendous amount."[65] He reported further that there were "indications that there was interest, in 2002, in reconstituting a centrifuge enrichment program," but "the evidence does not tie any activity directly to centrifuge research or development."[66]

Charles Duelfer confirmed these findings in October 2004, stating that "Iraq did not possess a nuclear device, nor had it tried to reconstitute a capability to produce nuclear weapons after 1991."[67] Although Duelfer had found no formal plans to reconstitute a nuclear weapon or any other program, he contended that "Saddam aspired to develop a nuclear capability—in an incremental fashion, irrespective of international pressure and the resulting economic risks—but he intended to focus on ballistic missile and tactical chemical warfare (CW) capabilities."[68] Published statements from several Iraqi scientists and officials indicate otherwise, though it is difficult to judge each statement's veracity.

In April 2003, for example, Mahdi Obeidi, an Iraqi scientist, came to U.S. forces with sample parts and blueprints for a nuclear centrifuge that he said he had been ordered to bury in his backyard in 1991. He said that back then, officials had planned to restart the nuclear program once and if the inspection regime collapsed. Obeidi, however, also told U.S. officials that he had never been asked to dig up the parts and plans. He said that the intercepted aluminum tubes were purchased for Iraq's rocket program, not to enrich uranium.[69] Another Iraqi nuclear scientist, Jaffar Dhai Jaffar, also told U.S. officials in July 2003 that Iraq had not reconstituted its nuclear program in the 1990s.[70] "There was no point in trying to revive this program," former bomb designer Sabah Abdul Noor told the *Associated Press* at Baghdad's Technology University in November 2003. "There was no material, no equipment, no scientists. Scientists were scattered and under the eyes of inspectors. To do a project, you have to be together."[71]

A July 2004 Senate Intelligence Committee report further concluded that almost all the NIE assertions about Iraq's nuclear program were not supported by the body of intelligence reporting. Although the report said that intelligence showed Iraq was procuring dual-use items, the evidence did not prove that Iraq had reconstituted its nuclear program or imported uranium or enrichment equipment for a nuclear program. In the case of the aluminum tubes—once the primary evidence for the administration's nuclear assertions—the report said that most NIE judgments were "incorrect" or "misleading."[72] Most experts believed then and almost all believe now that the tubes were intended for use as rockets and were not suitable for centrifuges.

Looted Materials

A remaining postwar concern is the status of Iraq's known stores of nuclear material and equipment. At Tuwaitha, the country's largest nuclear facility, Iraq stored more than 500 tons of natural uranium and almost 2 tons of low-enriched uranium. IAEA inspectors continued to verify, even after 1998, that Iraq's uranium remained sealed.[73] U.S. forces secured the Tuwaitha site on April 7, 2003, but not before Iraqis had looted the facility. In July, a small team of IAEA inspectors—who had returned to Iraq in June—reported that at least 10 kilograms of uranium compounds were missing from Tuwaitha.[74] Although the material is not suitable for a nuclear weapon, these compounds could be used in a radiological dispersal device or a so-called dirty bomb.

In July 2004, U.S. secretary of energy Spencer Abraham announced that the United States had transported 1.77 metric tons of low-enriched uranium and approximately 1,000 highly radioactive sources to the United States for research and security reasons.[75] In October 2004, the IAEA declared that it had accounted for the remaining 550 tons of nuclear materials at the Tuwaitha site.[76]

It is reported that looters damaged at least six other nuclear facilities in Iraq, including the nearby Baghdad Nuclear Research Center, which stored other radioactive isotopes, including cesium, strontium, and cobalt. Table 17.1 gives a summary of Iraq's nuclear weapons program.

Chemical Weapons Program

Iraq's chemical weapons were the only unconventional weapons actually used in combat. During the 1980s, they were produced in vast quantities in large, industrial-scale facilities.

History

Inspections by the United Nations revealed that before the Gulf War, Iraq maintained one of the most extensive chemical weapons capabilities in the developing world. Iraq's chemical weapons program began in the 1970s and accelerated during the Iran-Iraq War. Iraq developed mustard gas as well as the more sophisticated nerve agents tabun, cyclosarin, and sarin.[77] Iraq weaponized mortar shells, artillery shells, grenades, aerial bombs, and rockets for chemical use. It also deployed 50 Al Hussein missiles equipped with potent chemical warheads as part of its active forces.

Iraq first used chemical weapons, including mustard and nerve gases, during the Iran-Iraq War, resulting in approximately 50,000 Iranian casualties.[78] Iraq also used chemical weapons on its own Kurdish populations in northern Iraq. The CW attack on the city of Halabja on March 16, 1988, has been described as "the largest-scale chemical weapon attack against a civilian population in modern times."[79] During the attack, multiple chemical agents—mustard gas, tabun, sarin, and the V nerve agent (VX)—were delivered by aerial bombs. Most estimates indicate that the attack killed 5,000 and injured 10,000, while the residual effects of the weapons continue to cause abnormally high rates of disease and birth defects.[80]

Reportedly, Saddam Hussein fully intended to use chemical weapons during the 1991 Gulf War and gave local commanders the authority to use them at their discretion. Various explanations have been offered as to why Iraq did not launch a chemical or biological weapon. One is that just before the outbreak of the war, President George Bush vowed that "the American people would demand the strongest possible response . . . and [Iraq] will pay a terrible price" for the use of chemical or biological weapons against the coalition forces.[81] Another interpretation holds that the U.S. decision to halt the ground war after only four days was influenced by concerns that Iraq might use chemical or biological weapons if coalition forces closed in on Baghdad. In 1996, Iraqi officials indicated to UNSCOM that they considered their missile-based biological and chemical weapons to be "strategic" capabilities, for potential use against cities in nearby countries.

After the Gulf War, UNSCOM supervised the detection and destruction of Iraq's chemical weapons stockpiles and production facilities. U.N. specialists destroyed 760 tons of chemical weapons agents and more than 3,275 tons of chemical precursors in the Iraqi arsenal.[82] Because of the size of the Iraqi program, however, it was widely believed that significant quantities of chemical agents and precursors remain stored in secret depots. U.N. officials publicly expressed their doubts that the entire Iraqi stockpile of chemical weapons was found. UNSCOM reported to the Security Council that "the Commission has serious concerns that a full accounting and disposal of Iraq's holding of prohibited items has not been made."[83] Rough estimates concluded that Iraq might have retained up to 600 metric tons of agents, including mustard gas, VX, and sarin. Iraq did not account fully for 15,000 artillery rockets capable of delivering nerve agents and 550 artillery shells filled with mustard agents.[84]

Another major area of concern was related to VX. By 1995, UNSCOM accumulated enough circumstantial evidence to force Iraq to admit to the production of 4 tons of VX. In November 1997, UNSCOM found evidence that Iraq had developed a production capability of VX and obtained at least 750 tons of VX precursor chemicals.[85] As of June 1998, UNSCOM had no evidence that Iraq had weaponized its VX. A U.S. laboratory reported that it detected the presence of VX in samples of missile warhead remnants found by UNSCOM inspectors. Testing at French and Swiss laboratories did not confirm this report. Iraq continued to insist that it had destroyed all VX agents and precursors.[86]

In June 2003, the former executive chairman of UNSCOM, Rolf Ekeus, wrote in an article what many officials may have known, but not the general public:

> During its war against Iran, Iraq found that chemical warfare agents, especially nerve agents such as sarin, soman, tabun, and later VX, deteriorated after just a couple weeks' storage in drums or in filled chemical warfare munitions. The reason was that the Iraqi chemists, lacking access to high-quality laboratory and production equipment, were unable to make the agents pure enough. (UNSCOM found in 1991 that the large quantities of nerve agents discovered in storage in Iraq had lost most of their lethal property and were not suitable for warfare.)[87]

Table 17.1. **Summary of Iraq's Nuclear Weapons Program**

Prewar Concerns	Pre-2002 Intelligence Assessments	October 2002 NIE Assessment	UN Findings 2002–2003	Administration Statements	Evidence Since March 2003
Iraq reconstituted its nuclear program after 1998.	**PROBABLY NOT.** Consensus was that Iraq "probably continued low-level theoretical R&D."	**YES.** Iraq "probably will have a nuclear weapon during this decade." State disagreed.	**PROBABLY NOT.** No evidence Iraq had restarted a program. ElBaradei: majority of sites "deteriorated substantially."	**YES.** Saddam would acquire nuclear weapons soon. Bush: "We don't know whether or not he has a nuclear weapon."	**NO.** Duelfer: No program after 1991. Senate: claims "not supported by the intelligence."
Iraq attempted to enrich uranium for use in nuclear weapons.	**MAYBE.** "Baghdad may be attempting to acquire materials that could aid in reconstituting its nuclear weapons program."	**YES.** Iraq imported aluminum tubes and high-strength magnets. Energy and State disagreed.	**NO.** IAEA: Unlikely tubes or magnets could be used for centrifuges.	**YES.** Cheney: Iraq purchased high-strength tubes and magnets for uranium enrichment.	**NO.** Tubes were for rockets. Kay: "evidence does not tie any activity directly to centrifuge research or development." Senate: NIE "misleading."
Iraq attempted to purchase uranium from abroad.	**NO.** No pre-2002 reports mention any attempts to purchase uranium.	**YES.** "Iraq also began vigorously trying to procure uranium ore and yellowcake." State rejected reports that Iraq sought to buy uranium in Africa.	**NO.** IAEA: African uranium documents were forgeries.	**YES.** Bush: "The British government has learned that Saddam Hussein recently sought significant quantities of uranium from Africa."	**NO.** U.S. officials were aware that the evidence for the African uranium claim was unfounded. Senate: The CIA and DIA failed to find the "obvious problems" with the forged documents.

Abbreviations

NIE = National Intelligence Estimate; R&D = research and development; IAEA = International Atomic Energy Agency; CIA = Central Intelligence Agency; DIA = Defense Intelligence Agency.

Note

This table is updated from Joseph Cirincione, Jessica Mathews, and George Perkovich, *WMD in Iraq: Evidence and Implications* (Washington, D.C.: Carnegie Endowment for International Peace, 2004); available at www.ProliferationNews.org.

U.S. Views before the 2003 War

Before the war, U.S. officials said that there was no doubt that Saddam possessed a vast stockpile of chemical weapons and was engaged in the ongoing production of new weapons, emphasizing that he had used chemical weapons against both Iranians and Iraqis in the past. Secretary Powell told the United Nations, "Our conservative estimate is that Iraq today has a stockpile of between 100 and 500 tons of chemical weapons agent."[88] President Bush said, "Iraqi operatives continue to hide biological and chemical agents to avoid detection by inspectors. In some cases, these materials have been moved to different locations every 12 to 24 hours, or placed in vehicles that are in residential neighborhoods."[89]

The NIE judged that Iraq was producing and stockpiling chemical weapons: "Iraq probably has stocked at least 100 metric tons (MT) and possibly as much as 500 MT of CW agents—much of it added in the last year."[90] Previous estimates had noted a potential capability but were less definitive about whether production was under way. A September 2002 DIA report concluded, for example, that "there is no reliable information on whether Iraq is producing and stockpiling chemical weapons, or where Iraq has—or will—establish its chemical warfare agent production facilities."[91]

U.N. Findings and Actions

UNMOVIC inspections between November 2002 and March 2003 did not reveal evidence of a renewed chemical weapons program. UNMOVIC found some empty chemical munitions, including sixteen artillery shells, and it destroyed several 155-millimeter shells containing mustard gas produced more than fifteen years ago.[92] In March 2003, Iraq proposed a technical method to substantiate its claims of having destroyed its VX in 1991 and provided significant scientific data and documentation to resolve outstanding concerns regarding VX.[93] No evidence was found to substantiate claims of underground chemical facilities.[94]

Postwar Conclusions

U.S. search teams did not find chemical agents or chemical weapons in Iraq. David Kay said on October 2, 2003, that "multiple sources with varied access and reliability have told ISG that Iraq did not have a large, ongoing, centrally controlled CW program after 1991. Information found to date suggests that Iraq's large-scale capability to develop, produce, and fill new CW munitions was reduced—if not entirely destroyed—during Operations Desert Storm and Desert Fox, 13 years of UN sanctions and UN inspections. . . . Our efforts to collect and exploit intelligence on Iraq's chemical weapons program have thus far yielded little reliable information on post-1991 CW stocks and CW agent production."[95] Charles Duelfer confirmed these findings in October 2004: "ISG judges that Iraq unilaterally destroyed its undeclared chemical weapons stockpile in 1991."[96]

Some experts contend that the chemical weapons might still be hidden in some of the 130 major Iraqi weapons storage sites. However, Lieutenant General

James Conway, commander of the First Marine Expeditionary Force, said in May 2003, "It was a surprise to me then, it remains a surprise to me now, that we have not uncovered weapons. It's not for lack of trying. We've been to virtually every ammunition supply point between the Kuwaiti border and Baghdad, but they're simply not there."[97]

Some experts believe, as Charles Duelfer speculated, that "Saddam never abandoned his intentions to resume a CW effort when sanctions were lifted and conditions were judged favorable."[98] There is little evidence so far to support this belief. Table 17.2 gives a summary of Iraq's chemical weapons program.

Biological Weapons Program

Iraq began a dedicated biological weapons program in the 1970s and expanded its efforts during the war with Iran. None of the agents or delivery systems that were developed appear to have been used in combat.

History

The Iraqi BW program began in the 1970s as a basic research effort, and it proceeded haltingly until the beginning of the Iran-Iraq War. Then, Iraq's BW capability expanded and diversified at a rapid pace.[99] The BW program included a broad range of agents and delivery systems, though the first tests of a crude BW dissemination device did not occur until 1988.[100] Pathogens produced by the Iraqi program included both lethal agents (e.g., anthrax, botulinum toxin, and ricin) and incapacitating agents (e.g., aflatoxin, mycotoxins, hemorrhagic conjunctivitis virus, and rotavirus). Documents discovered by UNSCOM indicated that Iraq had produced 8,500 liters of anthrax, 20,000 liters of botulinum toxin, 2,200 liters of aflatoxin, and the biological agent ricin.[101] Iraq conducted research to examine the effects of combining biological and chemical agents and also pursued antiplant agents, such as wheat cover smut.[102]

The Iraqi BW program explored and developed a broad range of weapon delivery systems, including aerial bombs, rockets, missiles, and spray tanks. In December 1990, Iraq began the large-scale weaponization of biological agents. More than 160 R-400 aerial bombs and 25 600-kilometer-range Al Hussein missiles were filled with aflatoxin, anthrax, and botulinum toxin. The missiles were deployed in January 1991 to four sites for the duration of the Gulf War.[103]

From 1991 to 1994, Iraq consistently denied having a biological warfare program. In July 1995, it finally admitted to possessing an offensive biological warfare program. A month later, it conceded that it also had a program to weaponize biological agents.[104] Although research and development (R&D) facilities at Salman Pak and al Muthanna were known to intelligence forces, the largest R&D and production site at Al Hakam remained secret until the defection of Lieutenant General Hussein Al-Kamal, Saddam's brother-in-law, in 1995.[105]

In 1996, UNSCOM demolished all Al Hakam facilities, equipment, and materials. In addition, equipment from the Al Manal and Al Safah sites was transported to Al Hakam and dismantled, the air-handling system for high

Table 17.2. **Summary of Iraq's Chemical Weapons Program**

Prewar Concerns	Pre-2002 Intelligence Assessments	October 2002 NIE Assessment	UN Findings 2002–2003	Administration Statements	Evidence Since March 2003
Iraq had large stockpiles of chemical weapons.	**MAYBE.** Pre-2002 reports did not discuss the existence of chemical weapon stockpiles, but "Iraq may have hidden an additional 6,000 CW munitions."	**YES.** "High confidence" that Iraq had chemical weapons, probably between 100 and 500 metric tons.	**NOT SURE.** UNMOVIC uncovered several chemical warheads, but no significant stockpile. Iraq failed to prove it destroyed significant quantities of munitions and precursors.	**YES.** Certain that Iraq had vast chemical weapon stockpiles including mustard gas, sarin nerve gas, and VX, and was hiding them from inspectors.	**NO.** No chemical weapons found. Kay: "Iraq did not have a large, ongoing, centrally controlled CW program after 1991."
Iraq had covert chemical weapon production facilities.	**NOT SURE.** Iraq "rebuilt key portions of its chemical production infrastructure for industrial and commercial use."	**YES.** Iraq "has begun renewed production" of chemical agents, including mustard, sarin, cyclosarin and VX.	**PROBABLY NOT.** Inspections did not find any active production facilities or evidence of hidden production capability.	**YES.** Powell: "We know that Iraq has embedded key portions of its illicit chemical weapons infrastructure within its legitimate civilian industry."	**NO.** No open or covert chemical munitions or production facilities found. Some low-level research activity possible. Senate: Intelligence did not support claims.

ABBREVIATIONS

NIE = National Intelligence Estimate; CW = chemical weapons; UNMOVIC = U.N. Monitoring, Verification, and Inspection Commission; CIA = Central Intelligence Agency; DIA = Defense Intelligence Agency.

NOTE

This table is updated from Joseph Cirincione, Jessica Mathews, and George Perkovich, *WMD in Iraq: Evidence and Implications* (Washington, D.C.: Carnegie Endowment for International Peace, 2004); available at www.ProliferationNews.org.

containment at Al Manal was inactivated, and some of the growth media acquired by Iraq for proscribed activities were destroyed.[106] Iraq unilaterally ended UNSCOM weapons inspections and monitoring in December 1998, leaving many concerned that the Iraqi BW program could mushroom once again.

U.S. Views before the 2003 War

The U.S. administration said that Iraq was hiding a large, sophisticated BW production program, probably with hundreds of tons of agent and weapons including several mobile weapons laboratories built to deceive inspectors. The then–director of central intelligence, George Tenet, said that "Iraq's BW program includes mobile research and production facilities that will be difficult, if not impossible, for the inspectors to find. Baghdad began this program in the mid '90s, during a time when U.N. inspectors were in the country."[107] President Bush said, "Right now, Iraq is expanding and improving facilities that were used for the production of biological weapons."[108]

The NIE concluded that "all key aspects—R&D, production, and weaponization—of Iraq's offensive BW program are active and that most elements are larger and more advanced than they were before the Gulf War," and that Iraq possessed mobile biological weapons laboratories capable of producing "an amount of agent equal to the total that Iraq produced in the years prior to the Gulf War."[109] Before 2001, the assessments were less definitive, expressing concern that Iraq might still be pursuing a BW program but did not assert that any programs or weapons existed.[110]

U.N. Findings and Actions

UNMOVIC inspectors did not find any evidence of programs, production, or stockpiles of biological weapons. The 731 inspections conducted by UNMOVIC between November 27, 2002, and March 18, 2003, did not reveal any "evidence of the continuation and resumption of programs of mass destruction or significant quantities of proscribed items."[111] A total of 28 percent of the inspections were of biological sites, including laboratories and military sites.

The main problem that the inspectors reported was the absence of documentation to confirm the quantities of proscribed agents that Iraq had destroyed. Under UNMOVIC's supervision, Iraq excavated the remnants of 128 (out of the 157 declared) R-400 bombs that the Iraqis said that they had destroyed but had not previously adequately documented.[112] The biological team supervised and verified the destruction of 244.6 kilograms of declared but expired growth media and of 40 vials of expired toxin standards. In both cases, Iraq initiated the destruction request.[113] The inspectors did not find evidence to support intelligence reports regarding the existence of mobile production units for biological weapons. They noted that shortly before the suspension of inspections, Iraqi officials provided more information on vehicles that could have been mistaken for mobile laboratories, but the inspectors did not have time to investigate fully.[114]

Postwar Conclusions

U.S. search teams did not uncover any biological weapons or weaponized agents. Kay concluded that U.S. evidence "suggests Iraq after 1996 further compartmentalized its program and focused on maintaining smaller, covert capabilities that could be activated quickly to surge the production of BW agents."[115] The U.S. search teams did not find any evidence of an active weapons program, or of production facilities, though Kay reported on October 2, 2003, that Iraq had a "clandestine network of laboratories" and "concealed equipment and materials from UN inspectors," such as a "vial of live C. botulinum Okra B. from which a biological agent can be produced."

Kay's testimony and subsequent administration statements highlighted the discovery of the vial, which had been stored in an Iraqi scientist's kitchen refrigerator since 1993. This was the only suspicious biological material U.S. teams found. President Bush said that the "live strain of deadly agent botulinum" was proof that Saddam Hussein was "a danger to the world."[116] Several former U.S. bioweapons officials, U.N. inspectors, and biological experts told the *Los Angeles Times* that the sample had been purchased from the United States in the 1980s and that no country, including Iraq, has been able to use botulinum B in a weapon. Iraq had used the more deadly botulinum A in its pre-1991 weapon program, mimicking other countries' programs, including those of the Soviet Union and the United States.[117]

Kay also said he had uncovered new research on Congo Crimean Hemorrhagic Fever (CCHF) and Brucella that pointed to a new weapon program. The *Los Angeles Times* reported that both diseases are common in Iraq and that there is no evidence that the research is connected to weapons.[118] Experts note that no one has ever weaponized CCHF, and the U.N. inspectors never found evidence that Iraq had weaponized Brucella. The United States at one time had tried using Brucella in weapons but rejected it as too slow acting and too easily treated with antibiotics.[119]

In April and May 2003, U.S. troops uncovered two vehicles that a CIA report called "the strongest evidence to date" of Iraq's biological weapons capabilities, although the vehicles did not test positive for BW agents.[120] Undersecretary of Defense Stephen Cambone said on May 7, "The experts have been through it. And they have not found another plausible use for it."[121] The announcement generated headlines in the *Washington Post* and newspapers around the world. President Bush said, "We found the weapons of mass destruction. We found biological laboratories."[122]

However, in August 2003, the *New York Times* reported that engineers from the DIA who had examined the trailers had concluded in June that the vehicles were likely used to chemically produce hydrogen for artillery weather balloons, as the Iraqis had claimed.[123] Kay concluded in his testimony to Congress that the ISG had "not yet been able to corroborate the existence of a mobile BW production effort."[124]

The July 2004 Senate report similarly concluded that the majority of the NIE's conclusions on Iraq's BW program were not supported by the body of intelligence reporting. The Senate report especially criticized the intelligence community for failing to explain the "uncertainties underlying" the biological judgments, especially in relation to source reporting. The report concluded that the intelligence suggested that Iraq had a BW capability, but the NIE did not explain that Iraq's research "could have been very limited in nature, been abandoned years ago, or represented legitimate activity."[125]

Duelfer concluded: "ISG found no direct evidence that Iraq, after 1996, had plans for a new BW program or was conducting BW-specific work for military purposes. . . . ISG judges that in 1991 and 1992, Iraq appears to have destroyed its undeclared stocks of BW weapons and probably destroyed remaining holdings of bulk BW agent. However ISG lacks evidence to document complete destruction. Iraq retained some BW-related seed stocks until their discovery after Operation Iraqi Freedom (OIF)."[126] Table 17.3 gives a summary of Iraq's biological weapons program.

Missile and Delivery Programs

Before 1991, Iraq imported and developed a wide array of short-range ballistic missiles, and was also working to develop longer-range missiles. After the 1991 Gulf War, U.N. Resolution 687 prohibited Iraq from developing ballistic missiles with ranges greater than 150 kilometers. Iraq also had a program to develop unmanned aerial vehicles, though these systems never became advanced enough to deliver a nuclear, biological, or chemical payload.

History

Before the 1991 Gulf War, Iraq had extensive short-range ballistic missile capabilities—including a stockpile of Soviet-supplied, single-stage, liquid-fueled Scud-Bs (having a 300-kilometer-range and a 1,000-kilogram payload); and three indigenously produced variants of the Scud-B (the Al Hussein, the Al Hussein Short, and the Al Hijarah), all of which had an approximate range of 600 to 650 kilometers. Iraq was developing a domestic manufacturing capability for these modified Scuds, which included a sophisticated missile technology base to reverse-engineer the systems. According to Ambassador Rolf Ekeus, Iraq had the capability to produce Scud-type engines, airframes, and warheads.[127] It had also undertaken a joint venture with Argentina and Egypt to develop a two-stage, solid-fueled missile with an intended range of 750 to 1,000 kilometers, the Badr 2000.[128] UNSCOM concluded that no complete Badr 2000 missile was ever produced in Iraq. (The Argentine version was called the Condor.) Baghdad also had plans for a 2,000-kilometer-range missile called the Tammouz I,[129] which was to have a Scud-derivative first stage and an SA-2 sustainer as the second stage.

Until the 1991 Gulf War, Iraq was apparently pursuing three options. The first was tailored to the longer-term plan, initiated in 1988, to produce the first of a number of nuclear weapons in 1991. The delivery vehicle would have been based on a modification of the Al Abid satellite launcher and would have had the capability to deliver a 1,000-kilogram warhead to a distance of almost 1,200

Table 17.3. **Summary of Iraq's Biological Weapons Program**

Prewar Concerns	Pre-2002 Intelligence Assessments	October 2002 NIE Assessment	UN Findings 2002–2003	Administration Statements	Evidence Since March 2003
Iraq had current biological weapon stockpiles.	NOT SURE. "We are concerned that Iraq may again be producing BW agents."	YES. "High confidence" that Iraq had biological weapons.	NOT SURE. Inspectors did not find evidence of any BW agents or biological weapons.	YES. Bush: Iraq had "a massive stockpile of biological weapons that has never been accounted for, and capable of killing millions."	NO. No weaponized biological agents found. Senate: NIE "overstated" facts and "did not explain uncertainties."
Iraq had reconstituted its biological weapon program.	YES. December 2001 report: "Baghdad continued to pursue a BW program."	YES. Iraq had an active bioweapons program that was larger than before 1991.	NOT SURE. Inspections did not reveal evidence of a continued BW program, but Iraq did not prove it had destroyed BW agents.	YES. Bush: "Right now, Iraq is expanding and improving facilities that were used for the production of biological weapons."	NO. Duelfer: "No direct evidence that Iraq, after 1996, had plans for a new BW program." Senate: NIE "overstated" evidence.
Iraq possessed at least seven mobile biological weapon laboratories.	NO COMMENT. No pre-2002 report mentions mobile biological laboratories.	YES. Iraq had an unspecified number of mobile laboratories.	NOT SURE. UNMOVIC did not find any mobile weapon facilities.	YES. Powell: "We know that Iraq has at least seven of these mobile biological agents factories."	NO. Two vans found. DIA: most likely for producing hydrogen weather balloons." "Curveball" source discredited.

Abbreviations

NIE = National Intelligence Estimate; BW = biological weapons; UNMOVIC = U.N. Monitoring, Verification, and Inspection Commission; DIA = Defense Intelligence Agency.

Note

This table is updated from Joseph Cirincione, Jessica Mathews, and George Perkovich, *WMD in Iraq: Evidence and Implications* (Washington, D.C.: Carnegie Endowment for International Peace, 2004); available at www.ProliferationNews.org.

kilometers.[130] However, because work on the engines for the system did not begin until April 1989, it would not have been ready before 1993. The second option, a fallback position, would have been to put the nuclear warhead on an unmodified Al Hussein missile, which would have limited the range to 300 kilometers. The third option, initiated in August or September 1990 under the accelerated program, was to produce "a derivative of the Al Hussein / Al Abbas short-range missile designed to deliver a warhead of one metric ton to 650 kilometers and to accommodate a nuclear package (80 centimeters in diameter)."[131] The estimated time frame for completing the third option was six months.

Under the terms of U.N. Security Council Resolution 687, Iraq was obliged to eliminate ballistic missiles with ranges exceeding 150 kilometers. In early July 1991, UNSCOM destroyed Iraq's 48 known ballistic missiles with this range and dismantled a large part of the related infrastructure.[132] However, in March 1992 Iraq admitted that it had withheld 85 missiles from UNSCOM's controlled destruction. Iraqi officials said they had destroyed those missiles in mid-July and October 1991 in a secret operation (after the official destruction of the 48 missiles). UNSCOM inspectors confirmed that most of Iraq's remaining Scud-based missile force had been eliminated, although the clandestine character of Iraq's destruction of the 85 missiles showed that it was probably trying to preserve missiles and missile components.[133] Furthermore, after Hussein Kamel's defection, Iraqi officials admitted that Iraq had carried out R&D work on advanced rocket engines and that it had manufactured rocket engines "made of indigenously produced or imported parts and without the cannibalization of the imported Soviet-made Scud engines."[134]

By early 1995, UNSCOM believed that it had achieved a fairly complete overview of the facilities, equipment, and materials used in Iraq's former missile program. However, because Iraq repeatedly withheld and falsified information, UNSCOM still had unresolved issues, partly regarding past R&D activities and partly regarding the numerical accounting of missiles, warheads, and supporting and auxiliary equipment.[135]

In October 1997, UNSCOM finally reported that it had made significant progress in the missile area, accounting for 817 of the 819 missiles that Iraq had imported from the Soviet Union before the end of 1988. UNSCOM analyzed the remnants of those missiles that Iraq had unilaterally destroyed in July and October 1991, and it verified that 83 engines of the 85 declared missiles had in fact been destroyed.[136]

U.S. Views before the 2003 War

Bush administration officials said that Iraq had delivery systems, such as missiles and UAVs, capable of striking Israel or potentially the United States with chemical or biological payloads. President Bush said, "Iraq also possesses a force of Scud-type missiles with ranges beyond the 150 kilometers permitted by the United Nations. Work at testing and production facilities shows that Iraq is building more long-range missiles [so] that it can inflict mass death throughout the region."[137] He later said, "We've also discovered through intelligence that Iraq has a growing fleet of manned and unmanned aerial vehicles that could be used to disperse chemical and biological weapons across broad areas. We are concerned that Iraq is exploring ways of using UAVs for missions targeting the United States."[138]

The NIE said the evidence suggested that "Iraq retains a covert force of up to a few dozen Scud-variant SRBMs [short-range ballistic missiles] with ranges of 650 to 900 km." Previous assessments had noted that Iraq might use the technologies and equipment from its permitted short-range missiles to build longer-range systems if sanctions and U.N. inspections ended.

U.N. Findings and Actions

UNMOVIC inspectors found more activity in the missile programs than in any other area. Inspections carried out between November 2002 and March 2003 did not find any evidence of Scuds but did reveal that "there has been a surge of activity in the missile technology field in the past four years."[139] Iraq continued to develop two ballistic missiles after inspectors left in 1998: the Al Samoud 2 (liquid propellant) and the Al Fatah (solid propellant). UNMOVIC informed Iraq that Al Samoud 2 was proscribed and would be destroyed because it exceeded the permitted range of 150 kilometers.[140] Iraq started the destruction process on March 1, 2003, and within a week, it had destroyed 34 Al Samoud 2 missiles—including 4 training missiles, 2 combat warheads, 1 launcher, and 5 engines—under UNMOVIC supervision.[141]

By the time the war started, Iraq had destroyed two-thirds of its Al Samoud 2 missiles and one-third of the associated support equipment and logistics.[142] A decision on the Al Fatah missiles was still pending further information, when UNMOVIC withdrew from Iraq in March 2003.[143] UNMOVIC also discovered two large propellant chambers that could be used to produce rocket motors for missiles with ranges greater than 150 kilometers.[144] Iraq destroyed these in the first week of March under UNMOVIC supervision. In his report to the U.N. Security Council on March 7, 2003, Hans Blix stated: "The destruction undertaken constitutes a substantial measure of disarmament, indeed the first since the middle of the 1990's. We are not watching the breaking of toothpicks. Lethal weapons are being destroyed."[145]

In its December 8, 2002, declaration to the United Nations, Iraq claimed that it possessed a number of unmanned aerial vehicles and other smaller remotely piloted vehicles with wingspans up to 5.52 meters. UNMOVIC inspectors inspected a remotely piloted vehicle in February. By mid-February, Iraq had amended the declared wingspan of its remotely piloted vehicles to 7.4 meters. UNMOVIC had insufficient time to determine whether the vehicles were capable of chemical and biological weapons dissemination and whether their range exceeded 150 kilometers.[146]

Postwar Conclusions

U.S. troops did not find any Scud-type missiles, evidence of continued production of Scud-type missiles, or any UAVs capable of delivering chemical or

Table 17.4. **Summary of Iraq's Missile and Delivery Programs**

Prewar Concerns	Pre-2002 Intelligence Assessments	October 2002 NIE Assessment	UN Findings 2002–2003	Administration Statements	Evidence Since March 2003
Iraq possessed a covert fleet of Scuds.	**PROBABLY.** "Iraq probably retains a small, covert force of Scud-type missiles."	**PROBABLY.** Iraq had "up to a few dozen" Scud-type missiles with ranges of 650-900 km.	**PROBABLY NOT.** By 1998, UNSCOM verified destruction of all known Scud missiles. UNMOVIC did not find any evidence of Scuds.	**YES.** Bush: Iraq had a "force of Scud-type missiles."	**NO.** No Scud-type missiles found. Kay: "We have not discovered documentary or material evidence to corroborate these claims."
Iraq was developing UAVs as delivery vehicles for chemical and biological agents.	**MAYBE.** "We suspect that these refurbished trainer aircraft have been modified for delivery of chemical or, more likely, biological warfare agents."	**PROBABLY.** Iraq had a "development program" for UAVs "probably intended" to disperse biological agents – the Air Force disagreed.	**NOT SURE.** UNMOVIC did not have time to evaluate whether Iraq's UAVs could disperse biological agents.	**YES.** Bush: "Iraq has a growing fleet of manned and unmanned aerial vehicles that could be used to disperse chemical and biological weapons across broad areas."	**NO.** Air Force experts: The drones recovered are too small to disperse significant quantities of biological agents. Senate: NIE "overstated" the case.
Iraq was building missiles with 1,000 km range.	**MAYBE.** Iraq had a program to develop "longer range, prohibited missiles" of unspecified range.	**NOT EXACTLY.** Iraq was developing ballistic missile "capabilities" including a "test stand" for new missile engines.	**MAYBE, BUT . . .** UNMOVIC supervised destruction of rockets and propellant chambers that could help build longer-range missiles.	**YES.** Bush: "Iraq is building more long-range missiles [so] that it can inflict mass death."	**NO.** No evidence of such missiles. Kay: Saddam intended to develop a program.

Abbreviations

NIE = National Intelligence Estimate; UNSCOM = U.N. Special Commission on Iraq; UAV = unmanned aerial vehicle; UNMOVIC = U.N. Monitoring, Verification, and Inspection Commission.

Note

This table is updated from Joseph Cirincione, Jessica Mathews, and George Perkovich, *WMD in Iraq: Evidence and Implications* (Washington, D.C.: Carnegie Endowment for International Peace, 2004); available at www.ProliferationNews.org.

biological agents. Then, on July 18, 2003, the White House released declassified sections of the NIE that for the first time included the dissenting opinions of several agencies. The director of Air Force intelligence had disagreed with most of the administration's prewar UAV statements. The Air Force—the government agency with the most experience in UAV programs and development—concluded that Iraq's efforts to convert aircraft were unfeasible, that Iraq's latest drones were too small to carry CBW agents, and that the primary function of Iraq's UAVs was reconnaissance missions.

Recovered UAVs in Iraq confirmed the Air Force's predictions that the drones were intended for reconnaissance missions. The small size of the reported 25 to 30 UAVs recovered in Iraq in July 2003 would most likely have not allowed them to disperse significant amounts of chemical or biological agents.[147]

In October 2003, David Kay reported, "We have not discovered documentary or material evidence to corroborate these claims [of Scud-type missiles]" but that detained scientists and officials said Saddam had begun programs to develop missiles with 400- to 1,000-kilometer ranges.[148] Kay said, "One cooperative source has said that he suspected that the new large-diameter solid-propellant missile was intended to have a CW-filled warhead, but no detainee has admitted any actual knowledge of plans for unconventional warheads for any current or planned ballistic missile."

Kay reported evidence of two cruise missile programs, one of which he said was intended to develop cruise missiles with a 1,000-kilometer range. However, he noted that Iraq had halted this development once U.N. inspections began in 2002. He concluded that Iraq also had "substantial illegal procurement for all aspects of the missile programs."[149] Duelfer reached similar conclusions, noting that Saddam had tried but failed to develop long-range cruise missiles.[150] Table 17.4 gives a summary of Iraq's missile and delivery programs.

NOTES

1. IAEA, *Fourth Consolidated Report of the Director General of the International Atomic Energy Agency under Paragraph 16 of Resolution 1051 (1996)*, S/1997/779 (Vienna: IAEA, 1997), submitted to the U.N. Security Council on October 8, 1997, pp. 18–22. Also see Barbara Crossette, "Iraqis Still Defying Arms Ban, Departing U.N. Official Says," *New York Times*, June 25, 1997; and Evelyn Leopold, "France Says IAEA Should Close Nuclear File on Iraq," Reuters, October 17, 1997.
2. Mohamed ElBaradei, "Nuclear Non-Proliferation: Global Security in a Rapidly Changing World," speech to the Carnegie International Non-Proliferation Conference, June 21, 2004, p. 3; available at www.ceip.org/files/projects/npp/resources/2004conference/speeches/elbaradei.doc.
3. Charles Duelfer, "Comprehensive Report of the Special Advisor to the DCI on Iraq's WMD," September 30, 2004, hereafter referred to as the Duelfer Report; available at www.cia.gov/cia/reports/iraq_wmd_2004/index.html.
4. U.S. House of Representatives Committee on Government Reform, Minority Staff, "Iraq on the Record: The Bush Administration's Public Statements on Iraq," March 16, 2004; available at www.house.gov/reform/min/pdfs_108_2/pdfs_inves/pdf_admin_iraq_on_the_record_rep.pdf.
5. U.S. Department of Defense (DOD), *Proliferation: Threat and Response* (Washington, D.C.: DOD, 2001), p. 40.
6. John Bolton, undersecretary for arms control and international security, "Remarks to the Fifth Biological Weapons Convention RevCon Meeting," Geneva, November 19, 2001.
7. Duelfer Report.

8. Duelfer Report, vol. 2, p. 9.
9. Khidhir Hamza with Jeff Stein, *Saddam's Bombmaker: The Terrifying Inside Story of the Iraqi Nuclear and Biological Weapons Agenda* (New York: Scribner, 2000). Hamza made these comments at a Carnegie Non-Proliferation Roundtable, November 2, 2000.
10. Hamza spoke at a Carnegie Non-Proliferation Roundtable, November 2, 2000; available at www.ProliferationNews.org.
11. Ibid.
12. UNMOVIC Working Document, "Iraq's Proscribed Weapons Programs," March 6, 2003, p. 41.
13. Ibid, pp. 152, 161.
14. Amin Tarzi and Darby Parliament, "Missile Messages: Iran Strikes MKO Bases in Iraq," *Nonproliferation Review*, Summer 2001, pp. 125–33.
15. U.N. Security Council Resolution 687, April 3, 1991.
16. Rick Marshall, "Ekeus: Weapons of Mass Destruction of Higher Value to Iraq Than Oil," *USIS Washington File*, June 10, 1997.
17. Richard Butler, "Inspecting Iraq," in *Repairing the Regime: Preventing the Spread of Weapons of Mass Destruction*, edited by Joseph Cirincione (New York: Routledge, 2000), p. 181.
18. Central Intelligence Agency, "Unclassified Report to Congress on the Acquisition of Technology Relating to Weapons of Mass Destruction and Advanced Conventional Munitions 1 January through 30 June 1999," February 2000; available at www.cia.gov/cia/reports/721_reports/iraq.
19. Ibid.
20. "Media Availability with Secretary of State Colin Powell and German Foreign Minister Joschka Fischer after Bilateral Meeting," Federal News Service, February 20, 2001.
21. Interview on CNN's "Late Edition," July 29, 2001.
22. Kenneth M. Pollack, "Spies, Lies, and Weapons: What Went Wrong," *Atlantic Monthly*, January/February 2004, p. 22.
23. U.N. Security Council Resolution 1441, November 8, 2002.
24. Mohamed ElBaradei, "Seventh Consolidated Report of the Director General of the IAEA under Paragraph 16 of UNSC Resolution (1996)," April 1999; available at www.iraqwatch.org/un/IAEA/s-1999-393.htm.
25. Central Intelligence Agency, "Unclassified Report to Congress."
26. U.S. Department of State, "Defense Agency Issues Excerpt on Iraqi Chemical Warfare Program," International Information Programs, June 7, 2003; available at http://usinfo.state.gov/topical/pol/arms/03060720.htm.
27. Spencer Ackerman and John B. Judis, "The Operator," *New Republic*, September 22, 2003, p. 28; Walter Pincus, "Intelligence Report for Iraq Was 'Hastily Done,'" *Washington Post*, October 24, 2003.
28. Dick Cheney, interview on *Meet the Press*, NBC Television, March 16, 2003.
29. Colin Powell, "Iraq Weapons Inspectors' 60-Day Report: Iraqi Non-Cooperation and Defiance of the UN," briefing in Washington, January 27, 2003; available at www.state.gov/secretary/rm/2003/16921.htm.
30. Donald Rumsfeld, interview on *This Week with George Stephanopoulos*, ABC Television, March 30, 2003.
31. Bob Drogin, "U.S. Suspects It Received False Iraq Arms Tips," *Los Angeles Times*, August 28, 2003; Douglas Jehl, "Agency Belittles Information Given by Iraq Defectors," *New York Times*, September 29, 2003.
32. Condoleezza Rice, interview on *This Week with George Stephanopoulos*, ABC Television, June 8, 2003. Similarly, Vice President Cheney said before the war, "We have to assume there's more there than we know. What we know is bits and pieces we gather through the intelligence system. . . . So we have to deal with these bits and pieces and try to put them together into a mosaic to understand what's going on." Dick Cheney, interview on *Meet the Press*, NBC Television, September 8, 2002.
33. Patrick Wintour, "Short: I Was Briefed on Blair's Secret War Pact," *Guardian*, June 18, 2003; available at http://politics.guardian.co.uk/iraq/story/0,12956,979787,00.html.
34. George W. Bush, "Address on Iraq," remarks at Cincinnati Museum Center, October 7, 2003; available at www.whitehouse.gov/news/releases/2002/10/20021007-8.html.

35. Hans Blix, "Notes for Briefing the Security Council Regarding Inspections in Iraq and a Preliminary Assessment of Iraq's Declaration under Paragraph 3 of Resolution 1441 (2002)," December 19, 2002; available at www.iraqwatch.org/un/unmovic/unmovic-blix-notes-121902.htm. See also Ambassador Richard Butler's Presentation to the U.N. Security Council, June 3, 1998, available at www.fas.org/news/un/iraq/s/980603-unscom.htm: "For example, the quantity of yeast extract known-to-UNSCOM imported for Iraq's BW program by TSMID and not reported by Iraq is sufficient for 3 to 4 times more anthrax production than declared by Iraq in the FFCD."

36. Hans Blix, Briefing of the Security Council, February 14, 2003. For an example of an assessment of Iraq's weaponry that tried to convey the uncertainties, see Joseph Cirincione, "Iraq's Biological and Chemical Weapons," Carnegie Fact Sheet, April 4, 2003; available at www.ceip.org/files/projects/npp/pdf/Iraq/factsheet/Iraq-ChemBioFactSheet.pdf.

37. George W. Bush, "Address to the Nation on War with Iraq," remarks in Cross Hall, Washington, March 17, 2003; available at www.whitehouse.gov/news/releases/2003/03/20030317-7.html.

38. "Thirteenth Quarterly Report of the Executive Chairman of the United Nations Monitoring, Verification and Inspection Commission in Accordance with Paragraph 12 of Security Council Resolution 1284 (1999)," p. 30; available at www.un.org/Depts/unmovic/new/documents/quarterly_reports/s-2003-580.pdf.

39. See Joseph Cirincione, "Two Terrifying Reports: The US Senate and the 9/11 Commission on Intelligence Failures before September 11 and the Iraq War," *Disarmament Diplomacy*, July/August 2004; available at www.acronym.org.uk/dd/dd78/78jc.htm. And see Stephen Pullinger, "Lord Butler's Report on UK Intelligence, available at www.acronym.org.uk/dd/dd78/78sp.htm.

40. Commission on the Intelligence Capabilities of the United States, "Report of the Commission on the Intelligence Capabilities of the United States Regarding Weapons of Mass Destruction," March 31, 2005; available at www.wmd.gov.

41. U.S. Senate, "Senate Report on the U.S. Intelligence Community's Prewar Intelligence Assessments on Iraq," July 7, 2004; available at http://intelligence.senate.gov/iraqreport2.pdf.

42. IAEA, *Report on the Fourth IAEA On-Site Inspection in Iraq under Security Council Resolution 687*, S/22986 (Vienna: IAEA, 1991), p. 5.

43. Rodney Jones and Mark McDonough, with Toby Dalton and Gregory Koblentz, *Tracking Nuclear Proliferation: A Guide in Maps and Charts, 1998* (Washington, D.C.: Carnegie Endowment for International Peace, 1998), pp. 187–94.

44. IAEA, *Report on the Fourth IAEA On-Site Inspection*, p. 6; and IAEA, *Report on the Seventh IAEA On-Site Inspection*, S/23215 (Vienna: IAEA, 1991), annex 4, p. 4.

45. "Iraqi Defector," Associated Press, June 14, 1991; R. Jeffrey Smith, "Iraqi Nuclear Program Due Further Inspections," *Washington Post*, June 14, 1991.

46. For descriptions of the Iraqi gas-centrifuge program, see IAEA, *Report on the Fourth On-Site Inspection*, pp. 3, 9–13; IAEA, *Report on the Seventh On-Site Inspection*, pp. 17, 19, 21, and annex 4, pp. 5–10; David Albright and Mark Hibbs, "Iraq's Bomb: Blueprints and Artifacts," *Bulletin of the Atomic Scientists*, January/February 1993, pp. 39–40; Albright and Hibbs, "Iraq's Shop-till-You-Drop Nuclear Program," *Bulletin of the Atomic Scientists*, January/February 1993, pp. 27–37; Albright and Hibbs, "Iraq: Supplier-Spotting," *Bulletin of the Atomic Scientists*, January/February 1993, pp. 8–9.

47. IAEA, *Report on the Fourth On-Site Inspection*, pp. 17–19; also see IAEA, *Report on the Seventh On-Site Inspection*, pp. 23, 27; IAEA, *IAEA Inspections and Iraq's Nuclear Capabilities*, IAEA/PI/A35E (Vienna: IAEA, 1992).

48. See IAEA, *Report on the Eighth On-Site Inspection*, S/23283 (Vienna: IAEA, 1991), p. 15; and IAEA, *Report on the Eleventh IAEA On-Site Inspection*, S/23947 (Vienna: IAEA, 1992), p. 20.

49. IAEA, *Eighth Report of the Director General of the International Atomic Energy Agency on the Implementation of the Agency's Plan for Future Ongoing Monitoring and Verification of Iraq's Compliance with Paragraph 12 of Resolution 687 (1991)*, S/1995/844 (Vienna: IAEA, 1995); IAEA, *Report on the Twenty-Eighth IAEA On-Site Inspection in Iraq*, S/1995/1003 (Vienna: IAEA, 1995); IAEA, *Report on the Twenty-Ninth IAEA On-Site Inspection in Iraq under Security Council Resolution 687 (1991)*, S/1996/14 (Vienna: IAEA, 1996).

50. Mark Hibbs, "Experts Say Iraq Could Not Meet Bomb Deadline Even with Diversion"; IAEA, *Report on the Twenty-Eighth On-Site Inspection*, p. 14; and briefing by Ambassador Rolf Ekeus, "Hearings on Global Proliferation," p. 99.

51. IAEA, *First Report on the Sixth IAEA On-Site Inspection in Iraq under Security Council Resolution 687 (1991)*, S/23122 (Vienna: IAEA, 1991), p. 4; IAEA, *Report on the Seventh On-Site Inspection*, pp. 8, 9, 13.
52. Ibid., pp. 18–21.
53. Ibid.
54. Ibid.
55. Ibid., p. 21.
56. IAEA, *Second Consolidated Report of the Director General of the International Atomic Energy Agency under Paragraph 16 of Resolution 1051 (1996)*, S/1996/833 (Vienna: IAEA, 1996), p. 11.
57. Vice President Richard Cheney, "Remarks to the Veterans of Foreign Wars 103rd National Convention," August 26, 2002.
58. Bush, "Address on Iraq."
59. Director of Central Intelligence, *Key Judgments from the National Intelligence Estimate on Iraq's Continuing Programs for Weapons of Mass Destruction*, October 2002; available at www.ceip.org/files/projects/npp/pdf/Iraq/declassifiedintellreport.pdf (hereafter referred to as 2002 NIE).
60. For a detailed discussion of U.S. claims, intelligence findings and the results of inspections, see Joseph Cirincione, Jessica Mathews, and George Perkovich with Alexis Orton, *WMD in Iraq: Evidence and Implications* (Washington, D.C.: Carnegie Endowment for International Peace, 2004); available at www.ProliferationNews.org.
61. Iraq Nuclear Verification Office, "Fact Sheet: Iraq's Nuclear Weapon Programme"; available at www.iaea.org/worldatom/Programmes/ActionTeam/nwp2.html.
62. Mohamed ElBaradei, "Briefing of the Security Council," March 7, 2003, available at www.iaea.org/NewsCenter/Statements/2003/ebsp2003n006.shtml.
63. Joseph C. Wilson, "What I Didn't Find in Africa," *New York Times*, July 6, 2003.
64. Testimony of David Kay to Congress on October 2, 2003; hereafter Kay testimony.
65. David Kay, interview on *This Week with George Stephanopoulos*, ABC Television, October 5, 2003.
66. Kay testimony.
67. Duelfer Report.
68. Ibid.
69. Joby Warrick, "Iraqi Scientist Turns Over Nuclear Plans, Parts," *Washington Post*, June 26, 2003; Walter Pincus and Kevin Sullivan, "Scientists Still Deny Iraqi Arms Programs," *Washington Post*, July 31, 2003.
70. Pincus and Sullivan, "Scientists Still Deny Iraqi Arms Programs."
71. Ibid.
72. U.S. Senate, "Senate Report on the U.S. Intelligence Community's Prewar Intelligence Assessments on Iraq."
73. IAEA, "IAEA Safeguards Inspectors Begin Inventory of Nuclear Material in Iraq," IAEA Media Advisory, June 6, 2003; available at www.globalsecurity.org/wmd/library/news/iraq/2003/06/iraq-030606-iaea01.htm.
74. IAEA, "Implementation of the Safeguards Agreement between the Republic of Iraq and the International Atomic Energy Agency Pursuant to the Treaty on the Non-proliferation of Nuclear Weapons," July 14, 2003; available at www.iaea.org/NewsCenter/Focus/IaeaIraq/IraqUNSC14072003.pdf.
75. U.S. Department of Energy, "U.S. Removes Iraqi Nuclear and Radiological Materials," press release, July 6, 2004.
76. IAEA, "Security Council Statement," October 1, 2004, available at www.iaea.org/NewsCenter/Focus/IaeaIraq/OctoberReport.pdf.
77. United Nations Monitoring, Verification, and Inspection Commission, "Unresolved Disarmament Issues: Iraq's Proscribed Weapons Programmes, UNMOVIC Working Document," March 6, 2003, pp. 142–43; available at www.un.org/Depts/unmovic/documents/UNMOVIC%20UDI%20Working%20Document%206%20March%2003.pdf (hereafter referred to as "Unresolved Disarmament Issues").
78. Office of Technology Assessment, U.S. Congress, *Proliferation of Weapons of Mass Destruction: Assessing the Risks* (Washington, D.C.: U.S. Government Printing Office, 1993), p. 10.

79. Christine M. Gosden, "Chemical and Biological Weapons Threats to America: Are We Prepared?" Testimony before the Senate Select Committee on Intelligence, April 22, 1998.
80. Richard Boucher, "Anniversary of the Halabja Massacre," U.S. Department of State Press Statement, March 16, 2001; available at www.state.gov/r/pa/prs/ps/2001/1322.htm.
81. Public Papers of George Bush: Book 1, January 1 to June 30, 1991, "Statement by Press Secretary Fitzwater on President Bush's Letter to President Saddam Hussein of Iraq," January 12, 1991. Cited in Michael R. Gordon and Gen. Bernard E. Trainor, *The General's War: The Inside Story of the Conflict in the Gulf* (New York: Little Brown, 1995), p. 493.
82. "Thirteenth Quarterly Report of the Executive Chairman of the United Nations Monitoring, Verification and Inspection Commission in Accordance with Paragraph 12 of Security Council Resolution 1284 (1999)," appendix I, p. 40; available at www.un.org/Depts/unmovic/new/documents/quarterly_reports/s-2003-580.pdf.
83. UNSCOM, "First Consolidated Report of the Secretary-General Pursuant to Paragraph 9," April 11, 1996, pp. 6–8.
84. Director of Central Intelligence Report, *Iraq's Weapons of Mass Destruction Programs*, October 2002, pp. 19–22; available at www.cia.gov/cia/reports/iraq_wmd/Iraq_Oct_2002.htm.
85. Stockholm International Peace Research Institute, *Iraq: The UNSCOM Experience*, SIPRI Fact Sheet, p. 3; available at http://editors.sipri.se/pubs/Factsheet/UNSCOM.pdf (hereafter referred to as *Iraq: The UNSCOM Experience*).
86. United Nations Special Commission, *1998 Report of the Group of International Experts on VX*, October 26, 1998; available at www.un.org/Depts/unscom/s98-995.htm.
87. Rolf Ekeus, "Iraq's Real Weapons Threat," *Washington Post*, June 29, 2003.
88. Secretary of State Colin Powell, "Address to the United Nations Security Council," February 5, 2003.
89. President Bush, National Press Conference, March 6, 2003.
90. 2002 NIE.
91. Defense Intelligence Agency, *Iraq: Key WMD Facilities—An Operational Support Study;* unclassified excerpt available at http://usinfo.state.gov/topical/pol/arms/03060720.htm.
92. Ibid., p. 30.
93. Ibid., p. 25.
94. "Unresolved Disarmament Issues," pp. 12–13.
95. Kay testimony.
96. Duelfer Report.
97. Greg Miller, "Analysis of Iraqi Weapons 'Wrong,'" *Los Angeles Times*, May 31, 2003.
98. Duelfer Report.
99. UNMOVIC, "Iraq's Biological Weapons Program," UNMOVIC Working Document, March 6, 2003.
100. Ibid.
101. White House Fact Sheet, "Iraq's Program of Mass Destruction: Threatening Security of the International Community," November 14, 1997.
102. United Nations, "Report of the Secretary-General on the Status of the Implementation of the Special Commission's Plan for the Ongoing Monitoring and Verification of Iraq's Compliance with Relevant Parts of Section C of Security Council Resolution 687 (1991)," October 11, 1995.
103. Ibid.
104. *UNMOVIC 13th Quarterly Report*, p. 41.
105. Ibid.
106. *UNMOVIC 13th Quarterly Report*, p. 41.
107. Director of Central Intelligence George Tenet, "Testimony to the Senate Select Intelligence Committee," February 11, 2003.
108. President Bush, "Remarks at the United Nations General Assembly," September 12, 2002.
109. 2002 NIE.
110. See Director of Central Intelligence Report, "Unclassified Report to Congress on the Acquisition of Technology Relating to Weapons of Mass Destruction and Advanced Conventional Munitions January–June 1998"; available at www.cia.gov/cia/reports/721_reports/jan_jun1998.html#iraq.

111. Ibid., pp. 5–6.
112. Ibid., p. 21.
113. Ibid., p. 31.
114. "Unresolved Disarmament Issues," pp.12–13.
115. Kay testimony.
116. "Bush: Kay Report Vindicates Iraq War," Fox News Online, October 3, 2003; available at www.foxnews.com/story/0,2933,98995,00.html.
117. Bob Drogin, "Experts Downplay Bioagent," *Los Angeles Times*, October 17, 2003.
118. Ibid.
119. Ibid.
120. Central Intelligence Agency, "Iraqi Mobile Biological Warfare Agent Production Plants," May 28, 2003; available at www.cia.gov/cia/reports/iraqi_mobile_plants/paper_w.pdf.
121. Stephen Cambone, "Briefing on Weapons of Mass Destruction Exploitation in Iraq," May 7, 2003; available at www.defenselink.mil/transcripts/2003/tr20030507-0158.html.
122. The president continues, "You remember when Colin Powell stood up in front of the world, and he said, Iraq has got laboratories, mobile labs to build biological weapons. They're illegal. They're against the United Nations resolutions, and we've so far discovered two. And we'll find find more weapons as time goes on. But for those who say we haven't found the banned manufacturing devices or banned weapons, they're wrong. We found them." Dana Milbank, "Bush Remarks Shift in Justification of War," *Washington Post*, June 1, 2003.
123. Douglas Jehl, "Iraqi Trailers Said to Make Hydrogen, Not Biological Arms," *New York Times*, August 9, 2003.
124. Kay testimony.
125. Senate Report, the U.S. Intelligence Community's Prewar Intelligence Assessments on Iraq, July 7, 2004.
126. Duelfer Report.
127. Briefing by Ambassador Rolf Ekeus, "Hearings on Global Proliferation," p. 93.
128. DOD, *Proliferation: Threat and Response* (Washington, D.C.: DOD, 1996), p. 21; and UNSCOM, "Report of the Secretary-General on the Status of the Implementation of the Special Commission's Plan for the Ongoing Monitoring and Verification of Iraq's Compliance with Relevant Parts of Section C of Security Council Resolution 687 (1991)," S/1995/284, April 10, 1995, p. 6.
129. DOD, *Proliferation: Threat and Response* (1996).
130. DOD, *Proliferation: Threat and Response* (1996).
131. IAEA, *First Consolidated Report of the Director General of the International Atomic Energy Agency under Paragraph 16 of Resolution 1051 (1996)*, S/1996/261 (Vienna: IAEA, 1996), p. 7. Also see IAEA, *Report on the Twenty-Eighth On-Site Inspection in Iraq*, p. 15; and IAEA, *Report on the Twenty-Ninth On-Site Inspection*, p. 10.
132. *Iraq: The UNSCOM Experience*, p. 8.
133. Interview with Rolf Ekeus, Spring 1997; UNSCOM, *Report of the Secretary-General on the Activities of the Special Commission Established by the Secretary-General Pursuant to Paragraph 9 (b)(i) of Resolution 687 (1991)*, S/1997/774, October 6, 1997, p. 6.
134. UNSCOM, *Report of the Secretary-General on Iraq's Compliance*, October 11, 1995, p. 14.
135. UNSCOM, *Report of the Secretary-General on Iraq's Compliance*, April 10, 1995, p. 6; UNSCOM, *Report of the Secretary-General on Iraq's Compliance*, October 11, 1995, p. 14.
136. UNSCOM, *Report of the Secretary-General on the Activities of the Special Commission Established by the Secretary-General Pursuant to Paragraph 9 (b)(i) of Resolution 687 (1991)*, pp. 6–8.
137. Bush, "Remarks at the United Nations General Assembly."
138. Bush, "Address on Iraq."
139. "Unresolved Disarmament Issues," p. 15.
140. Ibid.
141. Hans Blix, "Briefing of the Security Council, Oral Introduction of the 12th Quarterly Report of UNMOVIC," March 7, 2003; available at www.un.org/Depts/unmovic/new/pages/security_council_briefings.asp#5.

142. *UNMOVIC 13th Quarterly Report*, p. 28.
143. "Unresolved Disarmament Issues," p. 15.
144. Ibid., p. 16.
145. Blix, "Briefing of the Security Council, Oral Introduction of the 12th Quarterly Report of UNMOVIC."
146. *UNMOVIC 13th Quarterly Report*, p. 23.
147. Dafna Linzer, "Air Force Assessment Before War Said Iraqi Drones Were Minor Threat," Associated Press, August 25, 2003; David Rogers, "Bush Oversold Drone Threat," *Wall Street Journal*, September 10, 2003.
148. Kay testimony.
149. Ibid.
150. Duelfer Report.

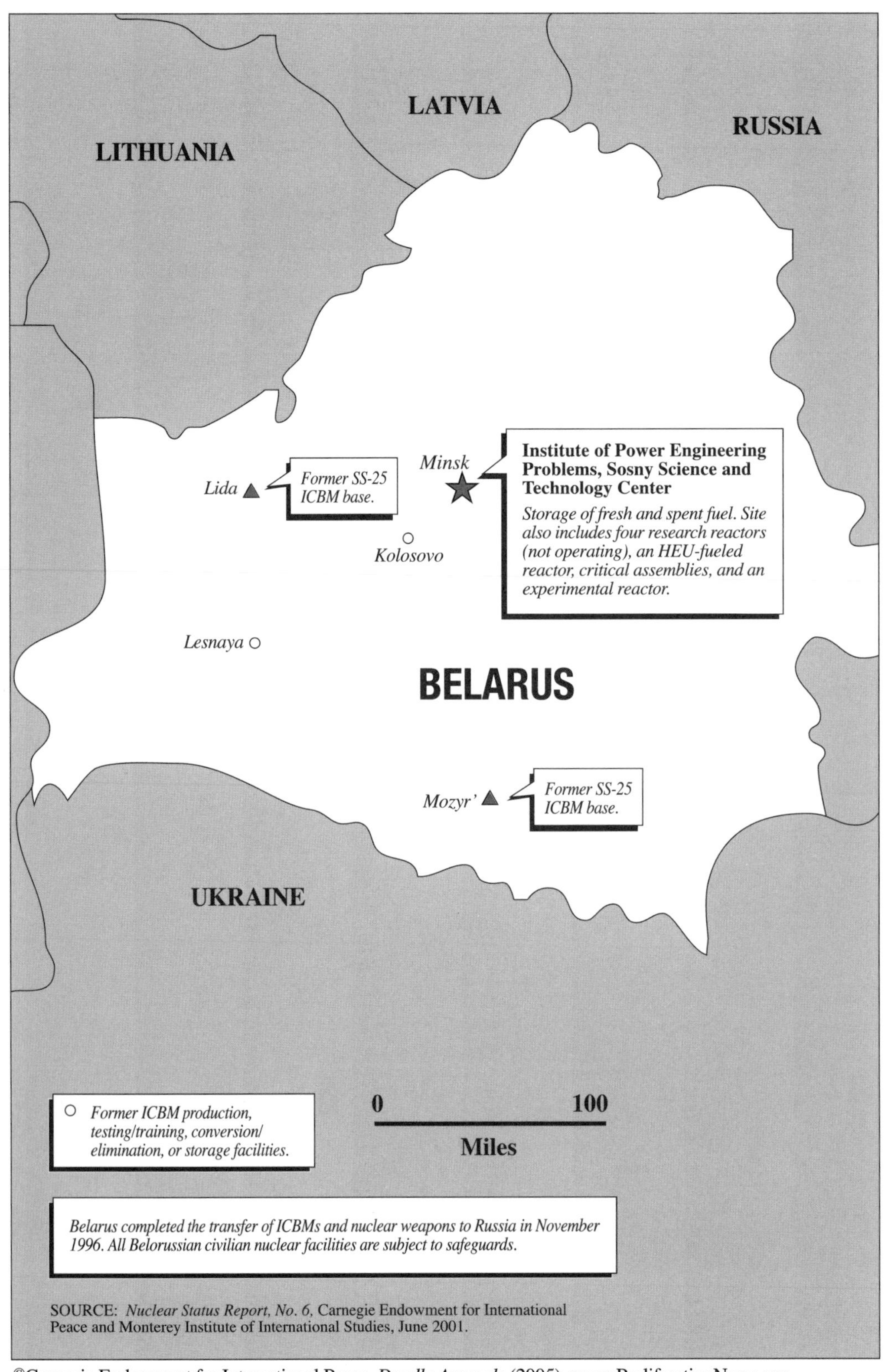
LATVIA
RUSSIA
LITHUANIA
Minsk
Institute of Power Engineering Problems, Sosny Science and Technology Center
Storage of fresh and spent fuel. Site also includes four research reactors (not operating), an HEU-fueled reactor, critical assemblies, and an experimental reactor.
Lida
Former SS-25 ICBM base.
Kolosovo
Lesnaya
BELARUS
Mozyr'
Former SS-25 ICBM base.
UKRAINE
Former ICBM production, testing/training, conversion/ elimination, or storage facilities.
0
100
Miles
Belarus completed the transfer of ICBMs and nuclear weapons to Russia in November 1996. All Belorussian civilian nuclear facilities are subject to safeguards.

SOURCE: *Nuclear Status Report, No. 6,* Carnegie Endowment for International Peace and Monterey Institute of International Studies, June 2001.

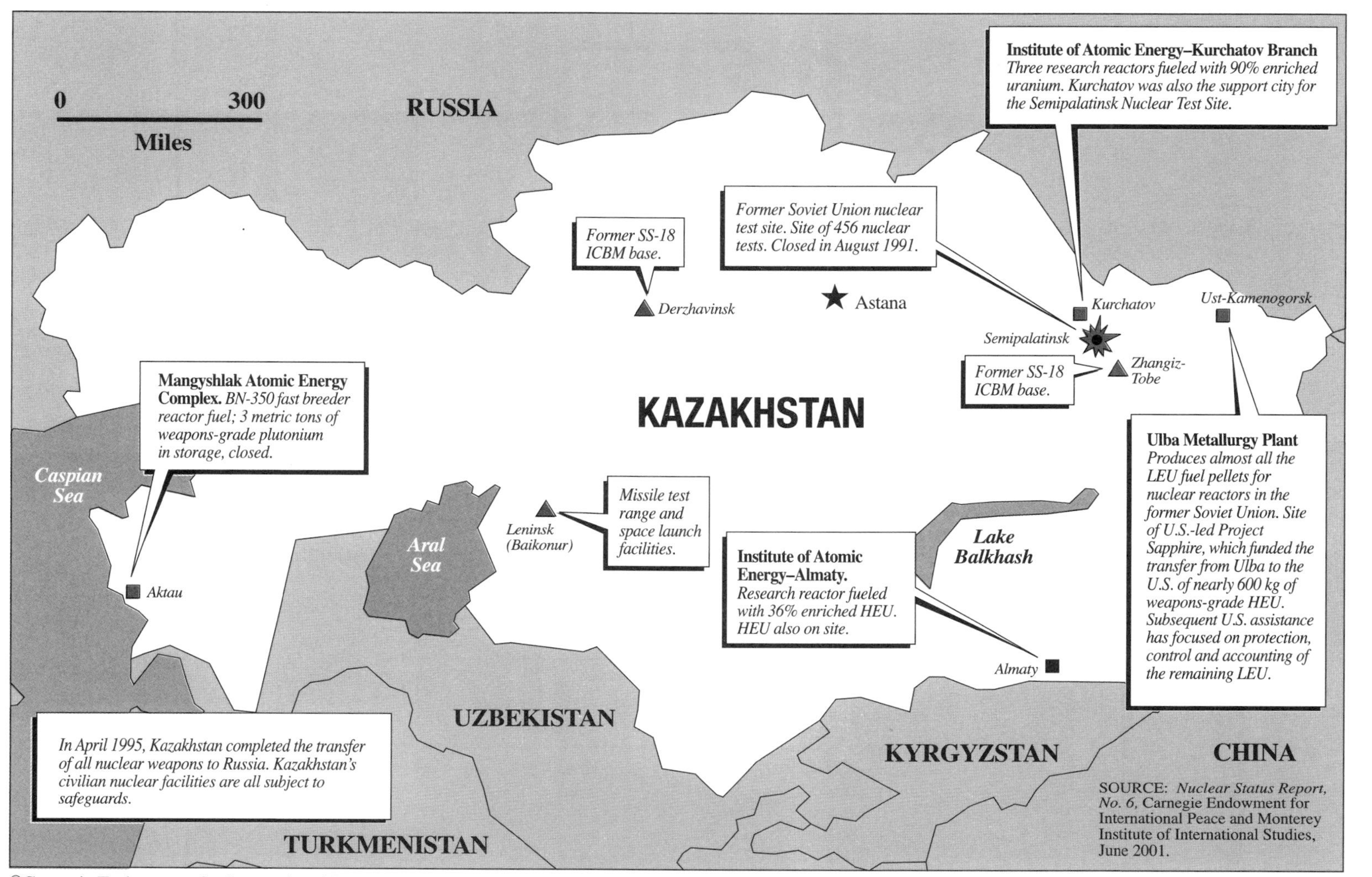

0
300
Miles
RUSSIA
Institute of Atomic Energy–Kurchatov Branch
Three research reactors fueled with 90% enriched uranium. Kurchatov was also the support city for the Semipalatinsk Nuclear Test Site.
Former Soviet Union nuclear test site. Site of 456 nuclear tests. Closed in August 1991.
Former SS-18 ICBM base.
Derzhavinsk
Astana
Kurchatov
Ust-Kamenogorsk
Semipalatinsk
Zhangiz-Tobe
Former SS-18 ICBM base.
Mangyshlak Atomic Energy Complex. BN-350 fast breeder reactor fuel; 3 metric tons of weapons-grade plutonium in storage, closed.
KAZAKHSTAN
Ulba Metallurgy Plant
Produces almost all the LEU fuel pellets for nuclear reactors in the former Soviet Union. Site of U.S.-led Project Sapphire, which funded the transfer from Ulba to the U.S. of nearly 600 kg of weapons-grade HEU. Subsequent U.S. assistance has focused on protection, control and accounting of the remaining LEU.
Caspian Sea
Missile test range and space launch facilities.
Leninsk (Baikonur)
Aral Sea
Lake Balkhash
Institute of Atomic Energy–Almaty.
Research reactor fueled with 36% enriched HEU. HEU also on site.
Aktau
Almaty
UZBEKISTAN
KYRGYZSTAN
CHINA
In April 1995, Kazakhstan completed the transfer of all nuclear weapons to Russia. Kazakhstan's civilian nuclear facilities are all subject to safeguards.
TURKMENISTAN
SOURCE: Nuclear Status Report, No. 6, Carnegie Endowment for International Peace and Monterey Institute of International Studies, June 2001.

On June 1, 1996, Ukraine completed the transfer of all nuclear weapons to Russia as agreed under the 1994 Trilateral Statement with the United States and Russia. Ukraine's civilian nuclear facilities are all subject to safeguards.
BELARUS
RUSSIA
POLAND
ROMANIA
MOLDOVA
UKRAINE
Crimea
Sea of Oziv
Black Sea
Kuznetsovsk
Sarny
Neteshin
Khmelnitskiy
Mikhaylenki
Pripyat (Chernobyl)
Kiev
Uzin
Priluki
Pomerki
Kharkiv
Dneprodzerzhinsk
Dnepropetrovsk
Pavlograd
Zheltiye Vody
Pervomaysk
Kostantinovsk
Energodar
Sevastopol
Institute of Nuclear Research Research reactor fueled by 36% and 90% HEU.
Former airbase with Blackjack strategic bombers.
Kharkiv Scientific Center Missile and missile component production.
Kharkiv Physical-Technical Institute Nuclear physics research and HEU storage.
Former airbase with Bear-H strategic bombers.
Location of several heavy-water production plants, giving Ukraine the capability to produce about 250 metric tons of heavy-water per year.
Yuzhmash Production Association Former SS-18 ICBM production facility.
Former SS-19 ICBM base.
Former SS-19 and SS-24 ICBM base.
Center of uranium mining activities in Ukraine.
Sevastopol Institute of Nuclear Energy and Industry. Research reactor and two subcritical assemblies, shutdown.
Operational nuclear power station(s).
Nuclear research institute, research reactor, storage facility, or nuclear infrastructure.
Former ICBM base, production site, or strategic bomber base.
0 100 Miles

SOURCE: *Nuclear Status Report, No. 6*, Carnegie Endowment for International Peace and Monterey Institute of International Studies, June 2001.

CHAPTER 18

Non-Russian Nuclear Successor States: Belarus, Kazakhstan, and Ukraine

Nuclear Capabilities

Belarus, Kazakhstan, and Ukraine are now all non-nuclear-weapon states, which have acceded to the Non-Proliferation Treaty (NPT). Nuclear weapons are no longer deployed on their territories. However, when the Soviet Union dissolved in 1991, four newly independent republics—Russia, Belarus, Kazakhstan, and Ukraine—had strategic nuclear weapons deployed on their territories as well as significant amounts of nuclear materials. International security and nonproliferation concerns focused immediately on the fate of the nuclear weapons deployed in the non-Russian nuclear republics. More than 8,000 strategic and tactical nuclear weapons were deployed in the non-Russian republics, the eventual fate of which was initially uncertain. Almost 800 nuclear weapons were deployed in Belarus, including 100 warheads for the road-mobile SS-25 intercontinental ballistic missiles (ICBMs) and 725 tactical nuclear weapons. A total of 1,410 strategic nuclear warheads and an undisclosed number of tactical weapons were deployed in Kazakhstan. A total of 1,900 strategic nuclear weapons and between 2,650 and 4,200 tactical nuclear weapons were deployed in Ukraine. All these weapons were eventually returned to Russia, and they and their delivery systems were repatriated or destroyed in a historic achievement for the international nonproliferation regime. If Ukraine and Kazakhstan had retained their nuclear possessions, they would have been the world's third and fourth-largest nuclear weapon states, respectively.

Belarus acceded to the NPT as a non-nuclear-weapon state on July 22, 1993. Kazakhstan's deposited its NPT instrument of ratification on February 14, 1994. Ukraine acceded to the NPT on December 5, 1994. All nuclear weapons from the non-Russian republics have been returned to Russia, and programs are being implemented to deal with the other proliferation risks remaining in those countries.

Chemical and Biological Weapons Capabilities

None of the three non-Russian republics has biological or chemical weapons development or production programs. Each is a state party to the Chemical Weapons Convention; Ukraine ratified it in 1998, Belarus in 1996, and Kazakhstan in 2000. Belarus and Ukraine are signatories of the Biological Weapons Convention (BWC); Ukraine ratified it in 1975 and Belarus in 1975. The most serious proliferation concern involves the possible presence of biological agents in the Soviet biological weapons facility in Stepnogorsk, Kazakhstan. Kazakhstan is not a state party to the BWC.

Nuclear Overview

Even after the Soviet Union ceased to exist, Russia's president and military maintained operational control over the Soviet nuclear weapons arsenal, deployed both in Russia and in the non-Russian republics. At no time did the non-Russian republics obtain operational control or the ability to launch the weapons. However, the deployment of nuclear weapons outside Russia raised the possibility that they might eventually fall under the control of the countries in which they were deployed. That risk, in turn, caused serious international concern. A failure to consolidate nuclear weapons in Russia would have provoked an unparalleled security crisis and dealt a blow to international nonproliferation efforts. As events unfolded, international nonproliferation efforts expanded to address the risks posed by stocks of weapons-usable nuclear materials in the non-Russian republics, as well as the fate of nuclear and missile experts whose knowledge could be valuable to countries or groups seeking to acquire weapons of mass destruction or their means of delivery.

A combination of political, legal, financial, and technical agreements was used to arrange the return of the nuclear weapons to Russia and to implement the terms of the Strategic Arms Reduction Treaty (START I) originally signed by the Soviet Union and the United States. That agreement was used as the legal mechanism by which the weapons systems deployed outside Russia were eliminated. The direct, concerted, and sustained efforts of the United States were critical in locking in the non-nuclear status of the non-Russian republics, ensuring the safe and secure return of the nuclear weapons to Russia, and eliminating nuclear weapons delivery systems controlled by START I.

The return of nuclear weapons to Russia from the three "possessor" states was accomplished using a set of international agreements and commitments, which included:

- *The Alma Ata Declaration*, December 1991. This declaration, made by eleven former Soviet republics, including Russia, Belarus, Kazakhstan, and Ukraine, committed the states to preserve a single control over nuclear weapons pending their consolidation and destruction. The states also committed to return tactical nuclear weapons to Russia no later than July 1, 1992, and strategic nuclear weapons by the end of 1994.

- *The Lisbon Protocol to START I*, May 23, 1992. The Lisbon Protocol codified Belarus, Kazakhstan, Russia, and Ukraine as parties to the 1991 START I as successors to the Soviet Union and to implement collectively the terms of that agreement. Belarus, Kazakhstan, and Ukraine also committed in that protocol to accede to the NPT as non-nuclear-weapon states "in the shortest possible time."[1]
- *The Treaty on the Non-Proliferation of Nuclear Weapons*, July 1, 1968. This agreement defines all countries except those that had tested nuclear weapons before January 1, 1967, as non-nuclear-weapon states. In committing to join this treaty as non-nuclear-weapon states, Belarus, Kazakhstan, and Ukraine pledged not to develop, possess, or control nuclear weapons and to accept full-scope International Atomic Energy Agency safeguards.

These agreements codified Russia's position as the sole nuclear successor state to the Soviet Union and committed the non-Russian republics to return nuclear weapons deployed on their territories to Russia. The implementation of agreements, especially the implementation of the START I, was made possible only through the significant levels of U.S. financial and technical assistance. Those efforts also address the other nonproliferation risks posed by the collapse of the Soviet Union, including the presence of poorly protected nuclear-weapons-usable materials in several non-Russian republics; important former Soviet weapons production and testing facilities located in Ukraine and Kazakhstan; and other dangerous Cold War legacies.

Belarus

Belarus is a non-nuclear-weapon state and no longer has nuclear weapons deployed on its territory. At the time of the Soviet Union's collapse, almost 800 nuclear weapons were deployed in Belarus, including almost 100 warheads for the road-mobile SS-25 ICBMs and 725 tactical nuclear weapons. Russia retained command and control over those nuclear systems, including the arming and launch codes needed to use them. Nonetheless, there was serious concern that Belarus might attempt to assert ownership and control over these nuclear arms and declare itself a nuclear weapon state (table 18.1).

Belarus signed the Lisbon Protocol to START I on May 23, 1992; ratified the decision on February 4, 1993; and acceded to the NPT as a non-nuclear-weapon state on July 22, 1993. Relations between the United States and Belarus began to deteriorate after the election of President Alexander Lukashenka in the summer of 1994, and there were hints by officials in Lukashenka's government that Belarus might retain some of the ICBMs on its territory. Despite these hints, all 54 SS-25 ICBMs and nuclear warheads in Belarus were removed to Russia by November 1996. The removal of the weapons and launchers and the elimination

Table 18.1. **Belarus' Nuclear Infrastructure and Other Sites of Proliferation Concern**

Name/Location of Facility	Type/Status	IAEA Safeguards
Nuclear Research Facilities		
Lida	former SS-25 missile base	No
Mozyr[1]	former SS-25 missile base	No
Institute of Power Engineering Problems, Sosny Science and Technology Center, Minsk	Fresh- and spent-fuel storage facility; this site also includes four research reactors, none of which are operating: one light-water, HEU-fueled reactor, two fast critical assemblies, and one experimental reactor.	Yes

Abbreviations

HEU highly enriched uranium
IAEA International Atomic Energy Agency
ICBM intercontinental ballistic missile

Note

[1]See Jon Wolfsthal et al., eds., *Nuclear Status Report: Nuclear Weapons, Fissile Material, and Export Controls in the Former Soviet Union* (Washington, D.C., and Monterey, Calif.: Carnegie Endowment for International Peace and Monterey Institute of International Studies, 2001), p. 158.

of the nuclear weapons deployment infrastructure all took place with the assistance of the U.S. Cooperative Threat Reduction (CTR) program. Increasing human rights violations, however, led to the suspension of CTR assistance to Belarus in March 1997. Equipment provided by the United States for the destruction of 81 SS-25 ICBM launch positions was withdrawn, and dismantlement work has ceased. In addition, 1,000 metric tons of liquid rocket fuel and 9,000 metric tons of oxidizer, which were slated for elimination, remain in Belarus. The status of this material is uncertain. CTR spent $77.7 million in Belarus from 1994 to 1997.[1]

Kazakhstan

Kazakhstan is a non-nuclear-weapon state, and nuclear weapons are no longer deployed on its territory. Nonproliferation concerns stemming from Kazakhstan's independence focused initially on the fate of the more than 1,400 nuclear weapons deployed in Kazakhstan (table 18.2). Attention later shifted to the significant amounts of unprotected nuclear-weapons-usable materials located in the country. Since its independence, however, Kazakhstan has been a model state, cooperating in the removal of nuclear arms from its territory and fully embracing international nuclear nonproliferation norms.

Table 18.2. **Kazakhstan's Nuclear Infrastructure and Other Sites of Proliferation Concern**

Name/Location of Facility	Type/Status	IAEA Safeguards[1]
	Nuclear Weapons Facilities	
Derzhavinsk	Former SS-18 ICBM base	No
Zhangiz Tobe	Former SS-18 ICBM base	No
Semipalatinsk	Soviet nuclear test range (closed August 1991), Soviet strategic bomber base	No
	Nuclear Research Centers	
Institute of Atomic Energy (also Institute of Nuclear Physics) Almaty	Hot cell facilities and nuclear material storage, HEU present	Yes
	Power Reactors	
Mangyshalk Atomic Energy Complex Aktau	BN-350 (sodium-cooled, fast-breeder), 90 MWe, shutdown in 1999, 3,000 Kg of Pu stored[2]	Yes
	Research Reactors	
Institute of Atomic Energy (also Institute of Nuclear Physics) Almaty	Two research reactors: WWR-K, 36% HEU, 10 MWe, operating, and critical assembly, also operating	Yes
IGR (Baikal Test Facility) Kurchatov (formerly Semipalatinsk)	Graphite-moderated, water-cooled, fueled with 90% HEU, operating	Yes
IVG-1M Kurchatov (formerly Semipalatinsk)	60 MWt reactor, 90% HEU, operating	Yes
RA Kurchatov (formerly Semipalatinsk)	0.4 MWt experimental reactor, 90% HEU, not operating, fuel has been returned to Russia[3]	Yes
	Uranium Processing	
Stepnogorsk	Uranium mining, suspended	No

(table continues on the following page)

Table 18.2. **Kazakhstan's Nuclear Infrastructure and Other Sites of Proliferation Concern** (continued)

Katco Moynkum	Uranium ore processing, operating	No
No. 6 Mining Co. Chiili	Uranium ore processing, operating	No
No. 7 Mining Co. Inkai	Uranium ore processing, operating	No
Stepnoye	Uranium ore processing, operating	No
Tsentralnoe Taukent	Uranium ore processing, operating	No
Ulba Metallurgy Plant (also known as Ulbinski Metallurgical Works) Ust-Kamenogorsk	Uranium conversion facility (UO_2) and fuel-pellet production, operating	Yes

Abbreviations

HEU highly enriched uranium
ICBM intercontinental ballistic missile
Pu plutonium
MWe megawatts electric
MWt megawatts thermal

Notes

1. As required by its adherence to the Non-Proliferation Treaty, Kazakhstan signed a full-scope safeguard agreement with the International Atomic Energy Agency (IAEA), which entered into force on August 11, 1995, that subjects all nuclear materials and activities in Kazakhstan to IAEA monitoring. The sources for this column include the IAEA director general's 2003 Annual Report, table A24, and conversations with the U.S. Department of Energy.
2. "Spent Nuclear Fuel Stays Put as U.S., Kazakhstan Quibble," Associated Press, August 29, 2004; available at http://seattletimes.nwsource.com/html/nationworld/2002019204_spentfuel29.html.
3. Though the *2004 World Nuclear Industry Handbook* states that the RA experimental research reactor is still operating, the IAEA reports that it is in "extended shutdown" and that its fuel has been returned to Russia.

In implementing its arms control and nonproliferation commitments, Kazakhstan has cooperated closely with the United States and received extensive American technical and financial assistance in eliminating its strategic nuclear weapons and delivery systems, in closing the Soviet nuclear test site at Semipalatinsk, and in securing weapons-usable nuclear materials in Kazakhstan.

Nuclear Weapons Systems

Kazakhstan emerged as an independent state in December 1991 with approximately 1,410 strategic nuclear warheads deployed on its territory, as well as a still-undisclosed number of tactical nuclear arms. The strategic warheads were deployed on 104 ten-warhead SS-18 ICBMs and on 370 single-warhead air-launched cruise missiles, the latter deliverable by Bear-H bombers.[2] The SS-18 was the most capable nuclear weapons system in the Soviet arsenal, each missile capable of carrying ten warheads over a range of 16,000 kilometers.

Kazakhstan's parliament ratified START I on July 2, 1992, and it approved Kazakhstan's accession to the NPT on December 13, 1993. Its NPT instrument of ratification was deposited on February 14, 1994. By late January 1992—four months ahead of the schedule established under the Alma-Ata Declaration on Nuclear Arms—all tactical nuclear weapons on Kazakhstan's territory had been withdrawn to Russia.[3] The last strategic nuclear weapons had been removed from Kazakhstan by April 24, 1995.[4]

The U.S. CTR program in Kazakhstan has successfully resulted in the denuclearization of what would have been the world's fourth-largest nuclear weapon state, had its nuclear possessions been consolidated. All offensive strategic arms elimination programs in Kazakhstan have been successfully completed. The CTR program resulted in the return of nuclear warheads, ICBMs, and bombers to Russia and in the destruction of 104 SS-18 silo launchers, launch control centers, and test silos located at Zhangiz-Tobe, Derzhavinsk, Semipalatinsk, and Leninsk. CTR program funds were also used to dismantle seven largely obsolete Bear bombers in Kazakhstan. Forty additional heavy strategic bombers were returned to Russia in February 1994.[5] The CTR program spent a total of $98.3 million in these efforts.

Nuclear Material Security

Beyond the elimination of weapon launchers and the return of actual weapons to Russia, the non-Russian republics also inherited stocks of weapons-usable materials. U.S. and international programs are in place to help ensure that these materials are secured and eliminated as soon as possible.

OPERATION SAPPHIRE. The U.S. government announced on November 23, 1994, that 581 kilograms (1,278 pounds) of highly enriched uranium (HEU)—previously stored behind only a padlocked door at a uranium conversion and fuel-pellet production facility at Ust-Kamenogorsk, Kazakhstan—had been airlifted secretly to the United States in a program called Operation Sapphire.[6] Although the material had been stockpiled for use as fuel in Soviet naval propulsion reactors rather than for nuclear weapons, the bulk of the HEU was in a form that could be used directly for weapon construction, or weapon fabrication with additional processing.[7] According to Bolat Nurgaliyev, then the chief of national security and arms control, Iranian government representatives had visited Ust-Kamenogorsk seeking undisclosed nuclear support or materials.[8] This situation caused Kazakh officials great concern about the material. Kazakh experts maintained that only about 5 percent of the HEU was pure enough to be used for weapons, while the rest required further processing.

The United States agreed to compensate Kazakhstan for the material. The U.S. compensation to Kazakhstan, although undisclosed, was estimated to be between $10 and $20 million, in both cash and in-kind assistance. According to a July 29, 1996, *Nuclear Fuel* report, the U.S. Enrichment Corporation (USEC) planned to sell low-enriched uranium (LEU) (on behalf of the U.S. Department of Energy) derived from the Kazakh HEU in mid-1997. After the material was shipped to the Energy Department's plant, USEC hired Babcock and Wilcox's (B&W) Naval Nuclear Fuel Division to downblend the HEU. According to B&W, roughly 90 percent of the material was in the form of uranium mixed with beryllium and a binding agent; the rest was in the form of uranium oxide or metal. The average enrichment was 89 to 90 percent. Proceeds from the sale of the blended material were to go to the U.S. Treasury.[9]

OTHER MATERIAL. A second, much larger amount of nuclear-weapons-usable material is still being stored at the former Soviet reactor complex at Aktau, Kazakhstan, on the Black Sea. The BN-350 breeder reactor located there was used in the production of "ivory-grade" plutonium for the Soviet nuclear reactor complex, and more than 3 metric tons of high-grade plutonium is stored there without any clear plan for the material's ultimate disposition. Russia has refused to accept responsibility for the material, and Kazakhstan has worked with the U.S. Department of Energy in securing the site and the material, pending a decision on where to dispose of it permanently.

The plutonium is contained in fuel rods irradiated in the reactor and has been sealed in large containers with highly radioactive spent-fuel rods to help prevent theft of the material. A total of 478 canisters with a mixture of high-grade plutonium-bearing fuel elements and highly radioactive spent fuel are now sealed and monitored by the International Atomic Energy Agency at the site. The canning project took two and one-half years and cost approximately $40 million. In addition, the Department of Energy provided Kazakhstan with $15 million in assistance to upgrade physical protection at the facility.[10] Dicussion of long-term storage options continued, but as of the spring of 2005, negotiations were stalled; Kazakhstan wants to ship the fuel to Semipalatinsk in eastern Kazakstan, while the United States argues for storage in Russia.[11]

SEMIPALATINSK NUCLEAR TEST FACILITY. The former Soviet Semipalatinsk Nuclear Test Site, located in northeastern Kazakhstan, was permanently closed to nuclear explosive tests in August 1991. One undetonated nuclear explosive device (with an expected yield of approximately 0.4 kiloton), however, was left by the Soviet Union in one of the test tunnels 130 meters below the surface of the test site. A Russian–Kazakh commission considered removing the device for dismantlement, but safety considerations precluded unearthing it. Instead, the device was destroyed with conventional explosives on May 31, 1995.[12]

The CTR program provided aid to Kazakhstan in permanently shutting the nuclear test facility at Semipalatinsk. These efforts consisted of helping to seal 13 unused nuclear test holes at the Balapan test field and 181 nuclear weapon test tunnels at the Degelen Mountain tunnel complex.[13]

Biological Weapons Concerns

The Soviet Union had the world's largest offensive biological weapons program, employing at one point 65,000 people (see the full discussion in chapter 6). Although the vast majority of production and test facilities were in Russia, several facilities were located elsewhere. One major facility was built at Stepnogorsk, Kazakhstan. This Soviet production facility "had sufficient capacity to cultivate, process and load into munitions a total of 300 metric tons a day of dry anthrax."[14] This complex of buildings, part of the joint stock company Biomedpreparat, was part of the former Soviet Biopreparat, or "civilian," side of the Soviet biological weapon production infrastructure. It is being dismantled in cooperation with the CTR program. The first several buildings in the complex were eliminated in September 2000, as part of CTR's Biological Weapons Proliferation Prevention program. By 2003, equipment has been removed from additional buildings and demolition work continued at the site.[15]

Ukraine

Ukraine is a non-nuclear-weapon state and no longer has nuclear weapons deployed on its territory. At the time of its independence in 1991, Ukraine was the deployment site for more than 1,900 strategic nuclear weapons and between 2,650 and 4,200 tactical nuclear weapons (table 18.3). Gaining operational control over those weapons would have made Ukraine the world's third-largest nuclear weapon state after Russia and the United States. Following an intensive trilateral diplomatic process with both Russian and Western involvement, however, Ukraine acceded to the NPT on December 5, 1994, as a non-nuclear-weapon state. The removal of nuclear weapons was completed in June 1996.[16]

Nuclear Weapons

Ukraine was the deployment site for 46 SS-24 ICBMs, each equipped with 10 nuclear warheads (for a total of 460 warheads), 130 SS-19 ICBMs equipped with 6 warheads each (a total of 780 warheads), 25 Bear-H16 strategic bombers, 19 Blackjack strategic bombers, and more than 600 air-launched cruise and air-to-surface missiles.[17] In addition, between 2,650 and 4,200 Soviet tactical nuclear weapons were estimated to have been deployed or stored in Ukraine when the Soviet Union collapsed.

Ukraine never acquired independent control over the strategic missiles deployed on its territory, and Russian military officers and units never relinquished the arming and targeting codes necessary to fire the missiles or detonate the warheads. Nevertheless, shortly after independence, Kyiv insisted on the right to block Russia's unilateral use of the weapons that were deployed in Ukraine. In March 1992, Ukraine considered retaining some of the weapons and temporarily halted the transfer of tactical nuclear weapons to Russia.[18] In June 1992, in the first of several steps to establish some control over the nuclear arms on its soil, Ukraine asserted "administrative control" of the strategic bombers, air-launched cruise missiles, and silo-based ICBMs and attempted to replace the Russian soldiers who were guarding them with Ukrainian forces.[19] In late 1992 and early 1993, Ukraine also publicly claimed ownership of warhead components as a means of establishing its right to financial compensation for the energy value of the plutonium and highly enriched uranium they contained. Ukraine also asserted ownership of the strategic delivery vehicles (that is, bombers and missiles). These efforts to establish control over nuclear weapons in Ukraine coincided with a highly publicized debate in the Ukrainian Rada, Ukraine's parliament, over whether the country should keep nuclear weapons to ensure its security against what many Ukrainians perceived to be a Russian threat to their still fragile independence.

LISBON PROTOCOL TO START I. On May 23, 1992, Ukrainian president Leonid Kravchuk signed the Lisbon Protocol to START I, under which Ukraine agreed to be bound by the treaty—jointly with Belarus, Kazakhstan, and Russia as successors to the obligations of the Soviet Union—and to "implement the Treaty's limits and restrictions" (article 2 of the protocol). In considering the Lisbon Protocol, the Rada passed a resolution on November 18, 1993, purportedly to ratify START I. Yet it attached qualifications and conditions, some of which attempted to undercut the Lisbon Protocol and Kravchuk's denuclearization commitment—steps unacceptable to Russia and the United States. The resolution declared that only 36 percent of the former Soviet Union's strategic delivery vehicles and 42 percent of its strategic warheads deployed on Ukrainian territory would be subject to elimination under START I, allowing Ukraine to retain the remainder on its territory indefinitely. Furthermore, the Rada made the elimination of the remaining strategic nuclear warheads and delivery vehicles conditional on Ukraine's receiving aid to cover dismantlement costs, compensation for nuclear materials to be extracted from the warheads, and complex security guarantees.

TURNING THE CORNER: THE TRILATERAL STATEMENT. Stepped-up negotiations with Ukraine resulted in a deal that satisfied some of Ukraine's practical concerns. The January 14, 1994, Trilateral Statement signed by Presidents Kravchuk, Bill Clinton, and Boris Yeltsin, reflected this deal. The statement was a key turning point that would lead, eventually, to Ukraine's fulfillment of its denuclearization and nonproliferation pledges. Under its terms, Ukraine would cooperate in the withdrawal to Russia of all remaining nuclear weapons (approximately 1,800 were still on Ukrainian soil) over a period that could not exceed seven years.[20] In Russia, the warheads would be dismantled (a process that the Ukrainians would observe), and the highly enriched uranium extracted from the warheads would be downblended to LEU. Some of the LEU, in turn, would be put in the form of pellets in fuel rods and transferred to Ukraine for use in its nuclear power reactors, in compensation for relinquishing the energy value of the uranium in the strategic warheads. In addition to power reactor fuel, Ukraine would

Table 18.3. **Ukraine's Nuclear Infrastructure and Other Sites of Proliferation Concern**

Name/Location of Facility	Type/Status	IAEA Safeguards[1]
Nuclear Weapon Bases and Support Facilities		
Pervomaysk	Former SS-19 and SS-24 missile base	No
Khmelnitskiy	Former SS-24 missile base	No
Uzin	Former strategic bomber base and former bomber conversion and elimination facility[2]	No
Priluki	Former strategic bomber base	No
Mikhaylenki	Former ICBM storage facility	No
Pavlograd Machine Plant	Former SS-24 production facility, now site of ICBM (SS-24) solid-rocket motor elimination	No
Yuzhmash Plant Dnopropetrovsk	Former SS-18 production facility, currently produces space launch vehicles based on Soviet ICBM technology, agriculture goods, etc.	No
Pomerki	Former SS-18 training facility	No
Sarny	ICBM conversion and elimination facility	No
Nuclear Research Facilities		
Institute of Nuclear Research Kyiv	Research center and nuclear material storage with HEU in fuel assemblies (see below for research reactors) and small amounts of Pu	No
Kharkov Institute of Physics and Technology Kharkov[3]	Nuclear physics research and HEU storage	Yes
Sevastopol Institute of Nuclear Energy and Industry Sevastopol	Reactor training facility and subcritical assemblies, HEU present (see "Research Reactors" for more information on the subcritical assemblies)	Yes
Power Reactors		
Chernobyl-1	LWGR (light-water), LEU, 725 MWe, shutdown in 1996	Yes
Chernobyl-2, -3, and -4	LWGR (light-water), LEU, 925 Mwe, shutdown in 1991, 2000, and 1986, respectively	Yes

((table continues on the following page)

Table 18.3. **Ukraine's Nuclear Infrastructure and Other Sites of Proliferation Concern** (continued)

Khmelnitski-1 and -2 Neteshin	VVER-1000, LEU, 950 MWe, operating	Yes
Khmelnitski-3 and -4 Neteshin	VVER-1000, LEU, 950 MWe, under construction	Yes
Rovno-1 Kuznetsovsk	VVER-440, LEU, 381 MWe, operating	Yes
Rovno-2 Kuznetsovsk	VVER-440, LEU, 376 MWe, operating	Yes
Rovno-3 and -4 Kuznetsovsk	VVER-1000, LEU, 950 MWe, operating	Yes
South Ukraine-1, -2, and -3 Kostantinovsk	VVER-1000, LEU, 950 MWe, operating	Yes
Zaporozhe-1, -2, -3, -4, -5, and -6	VVER-1000, LEU, 950 MWe, operating	Yes
Research Reactors		
WWR-M (Institute of Nuclear Research) Kyiv	Tank WWR, light-water, 36% and 90% enriched HEU, 10 MWt, operating	Yes
IR–100 (Sevastopol Institute of Nuclear Energy and Industry) Sevastopol	Pool, light-water, up to 36% enriched HEU, 200 kWt, shut down in 1995	Yes
Critical Assembly Sevastopol	Critical assembly, light-water, shut down in 1995	Yes
Subcritical Assemblies Sevastopol	2 subcritical assemblies, fresh and spent HEU fuel present, operating	Yes
Uranium Processing		
Zheltiye Vody	Uranium mining and milling, operating	No
Heavy-Water Production		
Dnepropetrovsk	Pridneprovsky Chemical Plant, can produce up to 250 metric tons of heavy water/year, status unknown	No[4]

ABBREVIATIONS

Pu	plutonium
HEU	highly enriched uranium
ICBM	intercontinental ballistic missile
LEU	low-enriched uranium
MWe	megawatts electric
MWt	megawatts thermal
kWt	kilowatts thermal

NOTES

1. Sources for this column include the International Atomic Energy Agency and author conversations with the U.S. Department of Energy.
2. Though all of Ukraine's strategic bombers have been eliminated, the U.S. Department of Defense, under the Cooperative Threat Reduction program, continues to aid Ukraine in the elimination of nonstrategic bombers and cruise missiles. This work should be completed by the end of 2005. See U.S. Department of Defense, "Cooperative Threat Reduction: Annual Report to Congress, Fiscal Year 2005," available at www.ransac.org/Official%20Documents/U.S.%20Government/Department%20of%20Defense/index.asp. Also, correspondence with Defense Threat Reduction Agency official, February 10, 2005.
3. "Kharkov" is the Russian spelling; it can also be spelled "Kharkiv."
4. The nonproliferation regime does not include the application of safeguards to heavy-water production facilities, but safeguards are required on the export of heavy water.

also receive U.S. economic aid and U.S. technical assistance for the safe and secure dismantlement of the strategic nuclear arms on its territory. Russia and the United States promised to provide security assurances to Ukraine upon Ukraine's accession to the NPT.

Acting on the deals made in the Trilateral Statement, the Rada on February 3 approved a resolution instructing Kravchuk to exchange the instruments of ratification of START I. The resolution acknowledged that article 5 of the Lisbon Protocol, which called for rapid adherence to the NPT by the three successor states as non-nuclear-weapon states, applied to Ukraine after all. The Rada also implicitly endorsed the Trilateral Statement. At that juncture, however, it did not specifically approve accession to the NPT.[21]

NPT ACCESSION AND START I'S ENTRY INTO FORCE. The summit of the Conference on Security and Cooperation in Europe (CSCE) held in Budapest on December 5, 1994, was chosen as the occasion for Russia, the United Kingdom, and the United States to convey identical security assurances to Ukraine, as well as similar assurances to Kazakhstan and Belarus. France also provided a security assurance to Ukraine at the CSCE summit in a separate document. On the same occasion, Ukraine presented its instruments of accession to the NPT. That action, together with earlier accessions by Belarus and Kazakhstan, satisfied Russia's conditions for exchanging the instruments of ratification for START I. Consequently, at the same meeting, Belarus, Kazakhstan, Russia, Ukraine, and the

United States exchanged their START I instruments of ratification, finally bringing the treaty into force.[22]

Missile Program

Ukraine also inherited important components of the Soviet missile production industrial base, which it planned to use to manufacture space launch systems for export. Ukrainian officials estimate that Ukraine's share is about 40 percent of the "Soviet space complex's production capacity."[23] This infrastructure, however, gives Ukraine the capability to produce or export strategic and theater ballistic missiles. Certain space equipment continues to be produced at the Yuzhmash Plant, formerly the SS-18 (heavy) ICBM production facility at Dnopropetrovsk. The Yuzhmash plant was the largest Soviet ICBM factory, where SS-19, SS-20, SS-23, and SS-24 missiles were built. Today, with its 2 million square feet of floor space, it is the world's largest facility of its kind. It has been reported, however, that its production of military missiles has been suspended since 1991.[24]

Although Ukraine agreed in a Memorandum of Understanding signed in Washington on May 13, 1994, to conduct its missile- and space-related exports according to the criteria and standards of the Missile Technology Control Regime (MTCR), it did not find it easy to meet all the requirements of that regime, including the elimination of its offensive missiles with ranges beyond 300 kilometers. Ukraine was finally admitted to membership in the MTCR in 1998 after it agreed to a U.S. request to cancel the planned export of electrical turbines destined for Iran's Bushehr reactor.[25] In October 2001, Ukraine finished destroying missile silos in compliance with START I. The former SS-24 production plant at Pavlograd used CTR funds to eliminate these missiles.[26]

Cooperative Threat Reduction Program Assistance

The United States has provided Ukraine with extensive assistance to implement its obligations under START I, including assistance in the elimination of ICBMs, ICBM silos, heavy bombers, and air-launched cruise missiles. Furthermore, going beyond the obligations of START I, the United States is aiding Ukraine's programs to safely dispose of liquid and solid fuel from Soviet ICBMs.

The CTR program provided Ukraine with rapid assistance in the form of $48.1 million for housing deactivated SS-19s and for the early deactivation of SS-24s, as well as providing emergency support assistance. These funds resulted in the elimination of 111 SS-19 ICBMs, 130 missile launch silos, 13 SS-19 launch control silos, and 2 SS-19 training silos.[27] Forty-six SS-24 missiles have been removed from their silos. The missiles (totaling 55 SS-24s, including 9 that were never deployed) are being stored at CTR-refurbished or CTR-built facilities at Pervomaysk and Mikhaillenki, pending rocket-motor elimination. CTR assisted Ukraine in eliminating SS-24 silo launchers in accordance with the START I Lisbon Protocol, which required the elimination of SS-24 silos by December 4, 2001. Final demolition and site work on SS-24 silos was completed on October 31, 2002.[28]

Assistance from CTR has also been provided to remove and safely eliminate solid propellant from the 55 SS-24s that were in Ukraine at the time of the Soviet breakup. CTR originally planned to fund the construction of a facility to eliminate solid propellant from SS-24 motors. In May 2003, this project was canceled, and alternate methods of propellant disposal are being considered for CTR funding. All 163 SS-24 missile motors remain in storage at Pavlograd.[29] Since 2002, the Pavlograd Chemical Plant has been engaged in eliminating these missiles and converting some solid rocket fuel into commercial high explosives.[30]

Ukrainian-based SS-19s contained 11,700 metric tons of propellant that required storage and elimination. CTR provided heavy equipment and 58 "intermodal tank" containers to Ukraine for this purpose and for the construction of a fuel-storage facility at Shevchenkovo for 60 CTR-provided fuel containers. In March 2000, the Ukraine Ministry of Defense advised that Ukraine had resolved the problem of propellant disposition. With CTR equipment provided and further assistance unnecessary, the project was terminated in May 2002.[31] In accordance with START I, Ukraine eliminated 44 heavy bombers. The CTR program assisted Ukraine with the elimination of 38 of the 44 bombers (27 Tu-95/Bears and 11 Tu-160/Blackjacks), the last of which was eliminated in May 2001.[32]

Eleven heavy bombers (3 Bears and 8 Blackjacks) were transferred to Russia in February 2000.[33] In 2002, Ukraine began dismantling TU-22 and TU-22M bombers and Kh-22 cruise missiles with US funding.[34] The projects plans to eliminate at least 40 Tu-22M bombers and 225 missiles by 2009.[35]

Conclusions

After the demise of the Soviet Union, the existence of large numbers of advance nuclear weapons and strategic delivery systems in several non-Russian republics threatened the entire international nonproliferation regime. Moreover, it could have led to the birth of four nuclear weapon states after the Soviet collapse, instead of just one. Such a situation would have irrevocably changed the international security landscape and dramatically increased the role played by nuclear weapons in global affairs.

The successful denuclearization of Belarus, Kazakhstan, and Ukraine is an unparalleled nonproliferation and security success story, and one that illustrates the value of international norms against the spread of nuclear weapons and other weapons of mass destruction. In addition, the successful implementation of nonproliferation efforts in these three countries could not have been accomplished without the provision of adequate financial, political, and technical resources to implement the removal and elimination of these weapons.

Kazakhstan and Ukraine continue to possess assets that could aid in the production of either nuclear weapons or strategic delivery systems. Nuclear materials, missile production facilities, and civil nuclear infrastructures in both countries remain sources of proliferation concern. These capabilities, however, are not unique in the industrial world. Standard approaches, including effective export controls, International Atomic Energy Agency safeguards, and material protection assistance are more than capable of addressing the residual proliferation risks in these countries.

NOTES

1. Congress obligated $77.7 million for Cooperative Threat Reduction in Belarus, but in early 1997 approximately $40 million was frozen because Belarus failed to meet international standards for human rights. "Cumulative Funding for CTR Through FY1997," August 7, 1998, available at www.nti.org/db/nisprofs/belarus/forasst/fundbel.htm.
2. START I Treaty Memorandum of Understanding (MOU) on Data; Dunbar Lockwood, "New Data from the Clinton Administration on the Status of Strategic Nuclear Weapons Deactivations," Memorandum, Arms Control Association, December 7, 1994.
3. See "Chronology of Commonwealth Security Issues," *Arms Control Today*, May 1992, p. 27.
4. "Prepared Remarks of U.S. Undersecretary of Defense for Policy Walter B. Slocombe before the Senate Armed Services Committee," May 17, 1995.
5. "All Strategic Bombers Out of Kazakhstan, Talks on Those in Ukraine," *RFE/RL News Briefs*, February 21–25, 1994.
6. R. Jeffrey Smith, "U.S. Takes Nuclear Fuel," *Washington Post*, November 23, 1994; Steven Erlanger, "Kazakhstan Thanks U.S. on Uranium," *New York Times*, November 25, 1994.
7. Interviews with U.S. government officials, December 1994.
8. Rowan Scarborough, "Tale Told of How Iran Nearly Got Nuke Gear," *Washington Post*, November 2, 1996.
9. Monterey Institute of International Studies Fact Sheet, November 21, 2001, available at cns.miis.edu/db/nisprofs/kazakst/fissmat/cfissmat/sapphire.htm.
10. "U.S. Department of Energy (DOE) and the Republic of Kazakhstan Ministry of Energy Mark the Completion of the Packaging of the BN-350 Fast Breeder Reactor Spent Fuel," DOE press release, July 12, 2001.
11. Burt Herman and Bagila Bukarbayeva, "Spent Nuclear Fuel Stays Put as U.S., Kazakhstan Quibble," Associated Press, August 29, 2004; available at http://seattletimes.nwsource.com/html/nationworld/2002019204_spentfuel29.html.
12. Bruce Pannier, "Kazakhstan Nuclear-Free," *OMRI Daily Digest*, June 1, 1995, p. 3; Douglas Busvine, "Kazakhstan to Blow up Four-Year-Old Nuclear Device," Reuters, May 25, 1995; Pannier, "Kazakhstan to Explode Nuclear Device," *OMRI Daily Digest*, May 24, 1995, p. 2; and Pannier, "Nuclear Bomb to Be Removed from Kazakhstan Test Site," *Komsomolskaya Pravda*, May 13, 1994, in FBIS-SOV-94-093, pp. 13–14.
13. CTR Kazakhstan Accomplishment web site, November 20, 2001, www.dtra.mil/ctr/project/_projkaz/ctr_nuclear_elim.html.
14. See Jonathan B. Tucker and Kathleen M. Vogal, "Preventing the Proliferation of Chemical and Biological Weapon Materials and Know-How," *Nonproliferation Review*, Spring 2000; and Judith Miller, Stephen Engelberg, and William Broad, *Germs: Biological Weapons and America's Secret War* (New York: Simon & Schuster, 2001).
15. Defense Threat Reduction Agency, *Cooperative Threat Reduction Annual Report to Congress, Fiscal Year 2005,* January 2004, available at http://armedservices.house.gov/issues/FY05CTR.pdf.
16. "Kuchma Issues Statement on Removal of Nuclear Weapons," UT-1 Television, June 1, 1996, in FBIS-SOV-96-107, June 5, 1996.
17. See *Treaty between the United States of America and the Union of Soviet Socialist Republics on the Reduction and Limitation of Strategic Offensive Arms,* signed in Moscow on July 31, 1991 (Washington, D.C.: U.S. Arms Control and Disarmament Agency, 1991). Also see Committee on Foreign Relations, U.S. Senate, "START-Related Facilities by Republic as Declared in MOU Data Exchange, September 1, 1990," Hearings on the START Treaty, 102nd Cong., 2nd Sess., February 6, 1992, p. 495.
18. "Ukraine Says Arms Transfer Delay Temporary," Reuters, March 25, 1992.
19. "Ukraine Said Seeking Command of Nuclear Forces," *Izvestiya*, June 11, 1992, in FBIS-SOV, June 11, 1992, p. 2.

20. General Roland LaJoie, special briefing on the CTR program. In congressional testimony in October 1994, Assistant Secretary of Defense Ashton Carter reported that there were 1,734 warheads in Ukraine before the initiation of the dismantlement process in January 1994 as opposed to 1,564 warheads as cited in the START I Memorandum of Understanding. See "Testimony of Assistant Secretary of Defense Ashton Carter before the Senate Foreign Relations Committee," October 4, 1994.
21. John W. R. Lepingwell, "Ukrainian Parliament Removes START I Conditions," Radio Free Europe–Radio Liberty Research Report, February 25, 1994, p. 37.
22. See "Text of Resolution Detailing NPT Reservations," Kiev Radio Ukraine World Service in Ukraine, in FM-FBIS, London, November 16, 1994; "Ukraine Joins Treaty Curbing Nuclear Arms," *Washington Post*, November 17, 1994; and "Ukraine Accedes to NPT Treaty," United Press International, December 5, 1994.
23. Gary Bertch and Victor Zaborsky, "Bringing Ukraine into the MTCR: Can U.S. Policy Succeed?" *Arms Control Today*, April 1997.
24. Ibid.
25. Office of Technology Assessment, U.S. Congress, *Technologies Underlying Weapons of Mass Destruction*, OTA-BPISC-I 15 (Washington, D.C.: U.S. Government Printing Office, 1993), p. 12; "Perry Visits Strategic Missile Unit," Moscow, ITAR-TASS, March 22, 1994, in FBIS-SOV-94-056, March 23, 1994, p. 27; Committee on Foreign Relations, U.S. Senate, "Implementation of Lisbon Protocol," Hearings on the START Treaty, 102nd Cong., 2nd Sess., June 23, 1992, p. 199.
26. "Pavlograd Mechanical Plant," *Ukraine: Missile Production/Dismantlement Facilities*, Febuary 6, 2004; available at www.nti.org/db/nisprofs/ukraine/weafacil/icbm.htm#pavmech.
27. CTR Program Plan, p. IV-5; Volodymyr Chumak and Serhey Galaka, "Programma Nann-Lugara v Ukraine" (Nunn-Lugar Program in Ukraine), Kyiv, October 1999.
28. "CTR Annual Report to Congress FY 2005," p. 43.
29. Ibid., pp. 40–41; and communication with officials of the Defense Threat Reduction Agency.
30. Nuclear Threat Initiative, "Ukraine: Missile Profile," available at www.nti.org/e_research/profiles/Ukraine/Missile/2164.html.
31. "CTR Annual Report to Congress FY 2005," pp. 40–41; and communication with officials of the Defense Threat Reduction Agency.
32. "Ukraine: Bomber Decommissioning & Transfer Development," April 30, 2003, available at www.nti.org/db/nisprofs/ukraine/weapons/hvybomr.htm.
33. "Zavershena perebroska iz Ukrainy v Rossiyu gruppirovki strategicheskikh bombardirovshchikov," Interfax, February 21, 2000, in Center for Nonproliferation Studies' NIS Nuclear Profiles Database, *Russia: Nuclear Weapons*, "Bomber/ALCM Force Developments."
34. "Ukraine: Bomber Decommissioning & Transfer Development."
35. "CTR Annual Report to Congress FY 2005," p. 40.

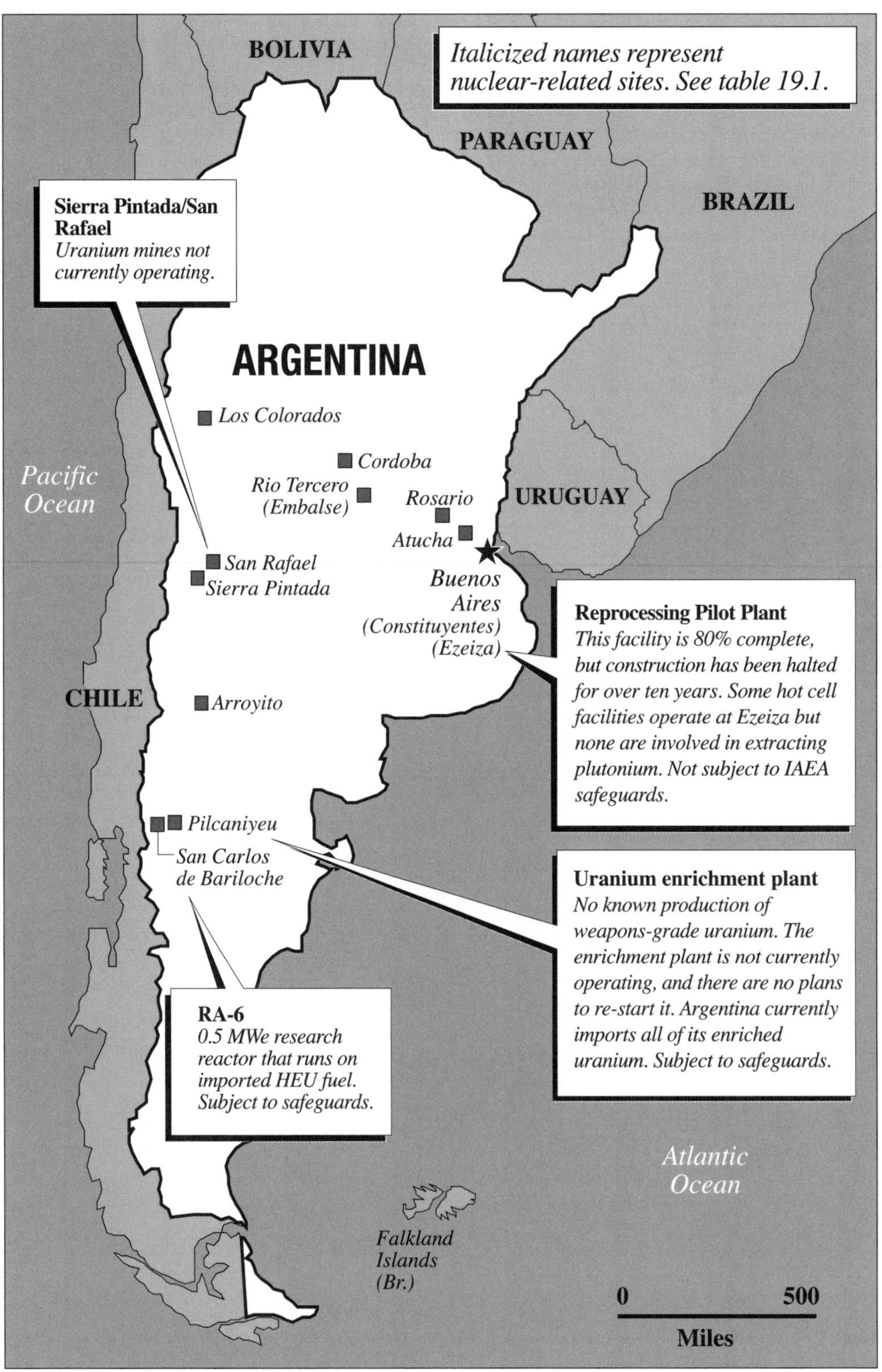

BOLIVIA
Italicized names represent nuclear-related sites. See table 19.1.
PARAGUAY
BRAZIL
Sierra Pintada/San Rafael
Uranium mines not currently operating.
ARGENTINA
Los Colorados
Cordoba
Rio Tercero (Embalse)
Rosario
Pacific Ocean
URUGUAY
Atucha
San Rafael
Sierra Pintada
Buenos Aires (Constituyentes) (Ezeiza)
Reprocessing Pilot Plant
This facility is 80% complete, but construction has been halted for over ten years. Some hot cell facilities operate at Ezeiza but none are involved in extracting plutonium. Not subject to IAEA safeguards.
CHILE
Arroyito
Pilcaniyeu
San Carlos de Bariloche
Uranium enrichment plant
No known production of weapons-grade uranium. The enrichment plant is not currently operating, and there are no plans to re-start it. Argentina currently imports all of its enriched uranium. Subject to safeguards.
RA-6
0.5 MWe research reactor that runs on imported HEU fuel. Subject to safeguards.
Atlantic Ocean
Falkland Islands (Br.)
0
500
Miles

CHAPTER 19

Argentina

Nuclear Weapons Capability

Today, Argentina does not possess nuclear weapons or unsafeguarded stocks of nuclear-weapons-usable materials, but from the 1960s to 1980s it did have a nuclear development program that many observers feared could be applied to weapons production. Argentina is among the very few countries that have been able to develop a nuclear program without becoming fully dependent on foreign technology, and it has become a significant exporter of peaceful nuclear technology in its own right. As a partner in major elements of the nuclear nonproliferation regime, Argentina has continued to develop its civil nuclear industry. Notably, Argentina joined the Nuclear Suppliers Group and curtailed its nuclear exports to high-risk nations, while still enjoying success in exporting nuclear products and services around the world. Argentina is a party to the Non-Proliferation Treaty (NPT), but has not signed the Additional Protocol to the Safeguards Agreement of the International Atomic Energy Agency (IAEA).

Biological and Chemical Weapons Capability

There is no public information to suggest that Argentina has ever had research or production programs for either chemical or biological weapons. It is a member of the Biological Weapons Convention and the Chemical Weapons Convention.

Nuclear Analysis

The Argentine nuclear program sought to realize several objectives, including the autonomous mastery of advanced technology, energy independence, regional and international prestige, and possibly to create the option to develop nculear weapons or "peaceful nuclear explosives." Argentine nuclear history was intertwined with that of neighboring rival Brazil, but the complex relationship between the two states included cooperative dimensions in nuclear affairs even at the height of political-strategic tensions in the 1970s.[1] When military rule ended in 1983, Argentina had access to sensitive technology, though it was working on weapons design. It has since curtailed activities toward that goal, with potential military applications, and it has opened all its nuclear facilities for international inspection.

In late 2001 and in the beginning of 2002, Argentina suffered an acute political-economic crisis, with deadly street riots, a succession of five presidents in just two weeks' time, and a partial default on the country's international loans. Even as of the spring of 2005, with the economy finally enjoying significant growth, more than 17 percent of Argentines were unemployed, and the question of the enormous $145 billion debt was still unresolved.[2] Yet even before conditions began to improve, there was little reason to fear a coup by the armed forces, foreign military adventurism, or any form of nuclear crisis. Argentina's commitment to nonproliferation remains firm, although it remains dependent on Brazil's actions vis-à-vis the nonproliferation regime. Argentina currently has no source of weapons-grade material, lacking both an operational plutonium separation (chemical reprocessing) plant or a uranium enrichment facility. The restructuring of the National Atomic Energy Commission (CNEA), which was established in 1950, and commercial success in Argentina's nuclear sector provides further reassurance.

By 1953, the CNEA had launched a research program and had started mining uranium.[3] Argentina's nuclear program received no outside assistance until 1958, when a U.S.-designed research reactor, the RA-1, was built at Constituyentes following the signing of a nuclear cooperation agreement in 1955.

Using the plans for RA-1, Argentina had built, unaided, three additional research reactors by 1967: the RA-0 at Cordoba, the RA-2 at Constituyentes, and the RA-3 at Ezeiza. By that time, the infrastructure to support a nuclear power plant was also in place, and in 1968 Argentina bought a natural uranium CANDU 320–megwatt electric reactor, Atucha I, from the West German firm Siemens. At the same time, it was pursuing sensitive nuclear development activities, including a laboratory-scale reprocessing facility, which it built at Ezeiza. This facility was closed in 1973, however, after intermittent operation and the extraction of less than 1 kilogram of plutonium from reprocessed spent fuel.[4]

For many years Argentina rejected the IAEA's full-scope inspection of its indigenous nuclear facilities, and only at West German insistence was the Atucha plant safeguarded. Following negotiations on the Treaty of Tlatelolco and the Nuclear Non-Proliferation Treaty (NPT) in 1967–1968, Argentina refused to join either, on the ground that the treaties would compromise its sovereignty and impose restrictions on its nuclear program (see below under "International Cooperation"). Though Argentina signed but did not ratify the Treaty of Tlatelolco, Argentine officials denounced the NPT as a discriminatory effort by the nuclear weapon states that amounted to little more than the "disarmament of the disarmed."[5] Argentina also argued that IAEA safeguards did not apply to its indigenously built facilities, and particularly not to the reprocessing laboratory at Ezeiza, even though evidence existed that an Italian firm had participated in its construction.[6]

The drive for nuclear self-sufficiency and, apparently, for a nuclear weapons option, increased after the 1976 coup, which installed a military junta. This ambition was motivated in part by Brazil's 1975 deal with West Germany to acquire the entire nuclear fuel cycle, as well as by the 1978 U.S. Nuclear Non-Proliferation Act, which called into question future supplies of uranium fuel for Argentine reactors.[7] In 1978, the CNEA began to build a second reprocessing facility at Ezeiza with a design capacity of 10 to 20 kilograms of plutonium a year. Argentina insisted that the facility would be used only for making reactor fuel, but it refused to allow IAEA inspections. Construction ceased, however, in 1990 in the face of U.S. pressure (see table 19.1 at the end of the chapter).

The most serious cause for proliferation concern in Argentina was suddenly revealed in late 1983, just before the inauguration of its first democratically elected government in ten years. The departing military junta revealed that a gaseous-diffusion uranium enrichment plant had been built since 1978 in complete secrecy at Pilcaniyeu (see the map at the beginning of the chapter). The junta's assurances that the facility was intended for peaceful purposes did not allay suspicions that it was to be part of a clandestine nuclear weapons development program.

The inauguration of Argentine president Raul Alfonsin in December 1983 led to significant policy shifts. The nuclear program, which had been directed for much of its history by retired navy admirals, was placed under civilian direction, the CNEA budget was cut, and the new government introduced legislation to prohibit the development of nuclear weapons. Nuclear confidence-building measures with Brazil were agreed upon in November 1985. That agreement culminated in reciprocal visits beginning in 1987 to the most sensitive nuclear installations in both countries (that is, those involved in reprocessing or enrichment and not subject to IAEA inspection). An extensive series of bilateral nuclear cooperation and consultation agreements were also put in place.[8]

The Pilcaniyeu plant is thought to have produced only small amounts of very-low-enriched uranium and no weapons-grade material (that is, uranium enriched to 90 percent uranium-235 or more).[9] Argentina has pledged not to produce highly enriched uranium in the future, and the plant is subject to close inspection under various international treaties (see below). Commercial decisions now drive Argentina's nuclear program; since 1997, a key concern has been privatization of the nuclear sector. Though full privatization has yet to be accomplished, the CNEA has been restructured with key functions (such as regulation and power generation) now given over to public, but independent, bodies.[10]

Argentina–Brazil Rapprochement

Rivalry for regional leadership and military suspicions has fueled the competition between Brazil and Argentina in nuclear development since the early 1950s. As explained above, cooperative elements endured even when bilateral relations were at their worst, notably in nuclear science and diplomacy, and the military governments signed formal cooperation accords in nuclear commerce in 1980.[11] Both countries pursued proliferation-sensitive enrichment and reprocessing activities, as well as civilian research and energy programs.

After the transitions from military rule in the mid-1980s, however, Brazil and Argentina took steps that definitively ended their nuclear rivalry. On July 18, 1991, the Argentine and Brazilian foreign ministers signed a bilateral agreement renouncing peaceful nuclear explosives, allowing mutual inspections of nuclear installations, and setting up the Argentine-Brazilian Accounting and Control Commission (ABACC) to implement their commitment. The Quadripartite

Safeguards Agreement to integrate the ABACC's inspection system with that of the IAEA was signed by Argentina, Brazil, the IAEA, and the ABACC in Vienna on December 13, 1991. Exchanges of nuclear material inventories and mutual inspections began in late 1992 after the ABACC's inauguration. Argentina's Congress approved the Quadripartite Safeguards Agreement in 1992, but inspections were delayed until it entered into force on March 4, 1994, following approval by Brazil's Congress in February 1994.[12] The agreement made ABACC and the IAEA responsible for undertaking an initial inventory of all nuclear materials in Argentina as a basis for inspections, a task complicated by years of unsafeguarded activities at Pilcaniyeu.[13]

During 1995, the IAEA's verification of nuclear material and facility design information was "largely completed."[14] The ABACC has also successfully implemented its program of both routine and ad hoc inspections at nuclear facilities in Argentina, conducting 79 inspections in 1996 and 66 from January 2003 to February 2004.[15] The facility of principal concern—the uranium enrichment plant at Pilcaniyeu—has been under an ABACC ad hoc inspection agreement since 1992 and subject to close monitoring and accounting procedures for its materials.[16] Developments in Brazil are magnified in Argentina and therefore will continue to have a direct impact on Argentina's nuclear policy.

International Cooperation

In January 1994, Argentina acceded to the Treaty for the Prohibition of Nuclear Weapons in Latin America and the Caribbean (the Treaty of Tlatelolco), undertaking not to acquire, manufacture, test, use, or permit the stationing of a nuclear explosive device on its territory and accepting IAEA inspections of all its nuclear activities. That same year, it joined the Nuclear Suppliers Group, accepting restrictions on the kinds of nuclear technology it could export. Argentina became a party to the NPT on February 10, 1995.

On February 29, 1996, Argentine foreign minister Guido di Tella signed a new agreement for peaceful nuclear cooperation with then–U.S. secretary of state Warren Christopher. President Bill Clinton submitted the agreement to Congress for statutory review on March 18, 1996, and it came into force on October 16, 1997. A further technical agreement, signed with the CNEA during Clinton's October 1997 trip to Argentina, promotes the exchange of information, cooperative research, and development between Argentine and U.S. nuclear laboratories.[17] The same year, a cooperation agreement with Euratom entered into force, replacing an earlier one that had lapsed in 1983.[18] Argentina also has bilateral nuclear cooperation arrangements with more than 30 other states, including a wide-ranging agreement signed in 2000 with Australia.[19]

Nuclear Exports

Argentina's comparative self-sufficiency in its nuclear program enabled it to become a major second-tier supplier of nuclear technology and equipment, first to developing nations and later to Europe and Australia. Before Argentina acceded to the NPT, that trend confounded efforts by the United States and others to prevent the spread of a nuclear weapons capability to countries such as Iran and Libya.[20] The return to democratic government in 1983 did little to change Argentina's liberal export policy, especially with respect to North Africa and the Middle East.

In 1974, Argentina concluded a deal to provide Libya with equipment for uranium mining and processing. In 1982, when Argentina was engaged in a war over the Falkland (or Malvina) Islands, Libya supplied $100 million in antiaircraft and air-to-air missiles. In exchange, Argentina may have provided information or technology for Libya's nuclear weapons program. Close nuclear cooperation is thought to have continued after the Falklands/Malvinas War, with discussions focusing on the possibility of Argentina's exporting reprocessing and enrichment technologies.[21] Reports in 1985 suggested that Argentina was prepared to supply a hot-cell facility to Libya, and that only U.S. pressure prevented the sale.[22]

In 1985, Argentina and Algeria concluded an agreement under which Argentina exported a 1-megawatt research reactor that started operating in 1989, despite the fact that Algeria was not then a NPT member and had no safeguard agreement with the IAEA. Subsequent plans to sell Algeria an isotope production reactor and hot-cell facility were not pursued.[23]

Argentina was also involved in the development of Iran's nuclear program. In 1987, the CNEA joined a consortium set up to complete the Bushehr nuclear power facility, but the project was suspended in 1995. Early in 1992, Argentina was ready to supply Iran with a fuel-fabrication facility and uranium dioxide conversion plant; only last-minute pressure, again from the United States, stopped the shipment. Though the facilities were intended for Iran's nuclear power program and would have come under IAEA safeguards, if misused they would have contributed indirectly to weapons development. Iran also sought hot-cell and heavy-water production facilities, but Argentina refused to export the equipment.[24]

Early in his first term, President Carlos Menem took dramatic steps to ally with the United States and to alleviate U.S. concerns regarding Argentine nuclear exports to questionable recipients. In 1992, he put in place a nuclear export control policy by presidential decree.[25] Two years later, Argentina became a member of the Nuclear Suppliers Group (NSG).

Exports continue to play an important role in supporting Argentina's nuclear industry. Its decision to comply with NSG guidelines has not had too serious an impact on its export opportunities. Argentina remains a major supplier of nuclear technology and training to the developing world, in particular to Latin America, and it increasingly supplies equipment and services to other customers. Recent clients have included Germany (heavy water in 1997 and 1999), Egypt (a uranium mining plant in 1998), South Korea (heavy water in 1997 and 2000), and Australia (a research reactor in 2000).

Missile Analysis

Today, Argentina has no ballistic missile program or missile stockpile, but for many years it sought to develop a potent medium-range ballistic missile, the

Condor II. Although much less reliable information on Argentine missile history exists than on its nuclear affairs, some aspects are noted here.

In the late 1970s, the Argentine air force began work on Condor I, a single-stage weather rocket that could be adapted as a short-range missile. After the change of government in 1983, missile development continued, and in 1984 Argentina concluded an agreement with Iraq and Egypt to develop the Condor II, a 1,000-kilometer, two-stage system with a potential payload of 500 kilograms. Argentina was to construct and test the missiles with Iraq providing funding through Egypt, with program managers acquiring technical expertise and equipment from a variety of European sources.[26] The United States and other members of the Missile Technology Control Regime (MTCR) identified the Condor II as being of major concern. Egypt withdrew from the project in September 1989, and in March 1990 Argentina suspended the project because of a lack of funds and canceled it the next month.[27] After much bureaucratic infighting within the Argentine government, the missile facilities were dismantled and proliferation-sensitive components of the program were physically destroyed, which cleared the way for Argentina to join the MTCR. It did so on November 29, 1994.

Since scrapping the Condor II, Argentina has not undertaken further research and development on medium-range ballistic missiles or on an indigenous space launch vehicle. In early 1997, however, Brazil and Argentina began to discuss the joint design and construction of a commercial rocket for low-altitude satellite launches.[28] Although Brazil was required to give up its development of medium-range missiles when it joined the MTCR, it was allowed to maintain its commercial space launch program.

Argentina may have retained the short-range Alacran ballistic missile, although its operational status is questionable. This missile is of little concern, however, as its range is limited to 150 kilometers.

Biological and Chemical Weapons Analysis

Argentina has no known chemical or biological weapons programs and is a party to both the Biological Weapons Convention and the Chemical Weapons Convention. It has also signed the 1991 Mendoza Accord (Joint Declaration on the Complete Prohibition of Chemical and Biological Weapons), a regional nonproliferation agreement.

NOTES

1. Michael Barletta, "Ambiguity, Autonomy, and the Atom: Emergence of the Argentine-Brazilian Nuclear Regime" (Ph.D. diss., University of Wisconsin, 2000), pp. 101–109. See also John Redick, *Nuclear Illusions: Argentina and Brazil*, Occasional Paper 25 (Washington. D.C.: Henry L. Stimson Center, December 1995). John Redick, Julio Carasales, and Paulo Wrobel, "Nuclear Rapprochement: Argentina, Brazil and the Nonproliferation Regime," *Washington Quarterly*, Winter 1994.
2. Central Intelligence Agency, "World Factbook: Argentina," available at www.cia.gov/cia/publications/factbook/geos/ar.html#People.
3. Daniel Poneman, *Nuclear Power in the Developing World* (London: Allen and Unwin, 1982), pp. 68–72.

4. Leonard Spector, *Nuclear Proliferation Today* (New York: Vintage Books, 1984), p. 203.
5. Barletta, "Ambiguity, Autonomy, and the Atom," pp. 115–117; and Julio C. Carasales, *El desarme de los desarmados: Argentina y el Tratado de No Proliferación de Armas Nucleares* (Buenos Aires: Pleamar, 1987).
6. Robert Laufer, "Argentina Looks to Reprocessing to Fill Its Own Needs Plus Plutonium Sales," *Nuclear Fuel*, November 8, 1982, p. 3.
7. Carlos Castro Madero and Esteban A. Takacs, *Política Argentina Nuclear: Avance o Retroceso?* (Buenos Aires: El Ateneo, 1991), pp. 79–80, 154–160.
8. Barletta, "Ambiguity, Autonomy, and the Atom," pp. 140–142, 337–339.
9. David Albright, Frans Berkhout, and William Walker, *Plutonium and Highly Enriched Uranium 1996: World Inventories, Capabilities and Policies* (Oxford: Oxford University Press, 1997), p. 371.
10. International Atomic Energy Agency (IAEA), "Country Nuclear Power Profiles: Argentina," available at wwwpub.iaea.org/MTCD/publications/PDF/cnpp2003/CNPP_Webpage/countryprofiles/Argentina/Argentina2003.htm.
11. Barletta, "Ambiguity, Autonomy, and the Atom," pp. 101–109, 123–126.
12. Statement by Michael McCurry, "Argentina and Brazil: Ratification of the Quadripartite Safeguards Agreement," U.S. Department of State, March 4, 1994; and John R. Redick, Julio C. Carasales, and Paulo S. Wrobel, "Nuclear Rapprochement: Argentina, Brazil, and the Non-Proliferation Regime," *Washington Quarterly*, Winter 1995, pp. 107–122.
13. Redick, *Nuclear Illusions*.
14. IAEA, *Annual Report 1995*, p. 45.
15. ABACC, *Annual Report 1996*, p. 24; *ABACC News*, January/April 1997; ABACC, *Annual Report 2003*, p. 24; *ABACC News*, February–May 2004, available at www.abacc.org/abaccnews/news2/en/noticias.asp.
16. ABACC, *Annual Report 1999*.
17. U.S. Department of Energy, "U.S.–Argentina Implementing Arrangement for Technical Exchange and Cooperation in the Area of Peaceful Uses of Nuclear Energy," press release, October 18, 1997.
18. Joint Euratom–Argentina press release, October 27, 1997.
19. U.S. Embassy, Buenos Aires. Environment, Science, and Technology Section, "Nuclear Technology Cooperation"; available at http://usembassy.state.gov/buenosaires/wwwhnuclear.html. Australian Nuclear Science and Technology Organization, press release, June 6, 2000.
20. William Potter, *International Nuclear Trade and Non-Proliferation: The Challenge of the Emerging Suppliers* (Lexington, Mass.: Lexington Books, 1990), pp. 95–109.
21. Spector, *Nuclear Proliferation Today*, p. 157, and Spector, "Brazilian Military Concern over Argentine Talks with Libya," *Correio Braziliense*, May 24, 1983, translated in FBIS/NDP, June 30, 1983, p. 8.
22. Mark Hibbs, "INVAP Seeks Thai Reactor Sale, Syria Expected to Sue for Supply," *Nucleonics Week*, October 27, 1994, p. 1.
23. Richard Kessler, "Menem Government Eyes Isotope Production Reactor for Algeria," *Nucleonics Week*, January 4, 1990, p. 11.
24. Mark Hibbs, "Iran Sought Sensitive Nuclear Supplies from Argentina, China," *Nucleonics Week*, September 24, 1992, p. 2.
25. Gary Marx, "South American Nuclear Threat Fades," *Chicago Tribune*, May 3, 1992; and Richard Kessler, "Argentina Unilaterally Adopts Nuclear, Weapons Export Controls," *Nucleonics Week*, April 30, 1992, p. 1.
26. "Nation Joins Missile Technology Control Regime," *Buenos Aires Herald*, November 30, 1994, in JPRS-TND-93-001, January 6, 1994; and Office of Technology Assessment, U.S. Congress, *Technologies Underlying Weapons of Mass Destruction*, OTA-BP-ISC-115 (Washington, D.C.: U.S. Government Printing Office, 1993), p. 224.
27. David Ottaway, "Egypt Drops Out of Missile Project," *Washington Post*, September 20, 1989; Ottaway, "Is Condor Kaput?" *U.S. News & World Report*, March 5, 1990, p. 20; and Ottaway, "Menem Says Missile Scrapped over U.S. Concern," *Clarin*, April 25, 1990, translated in FBIS-LAT, April 26, 1990.
28. Wyn Bowen, Tim McCarthy, and Holly Porteous, "Ballistic Missile Shadow Lengthens," *Jane's International Defense Review Extra*, February 1997, p. 5; "Brazil: Brazil-Argentina Discuss Building Commercial Rocket," *El Mercurio*, March 29, 1997, in FBIS-LAT-97-091, April 1, 1997.

Table 19.1. **Argentina's Nuclear Infrastructure**

Name/Location of Facility	Type/Status	IAEA Safeguards
	Power Reactors	
Atucha I Buenos Aires	Heavy-water, slightly enriched uranium (0.8–0.9%), 335 MWe, operating	IAEA/ABACC
Atucha II Buenos Aires	Heavy-water, nat. U, 600 MWe, operating	IAEA/ABACC
Embalse Cordoba Province	Heavy-water, nat. U, 692 MWe, construction halted[1]	IAEA/ABACC
	Research Reactors	
RA-0 Cordoba	Light-water, 20% enriched uranium, 0.01 kWt, operating	IAEA/ABACC
RA-1 Constituyentes	Light-water, 20% enriched uranium, 40 kWt, operating	IAEA/ABACC
RA-2 Constituyentes	Critical assembly, light-water, HEU, less than 1 MWt, shut down	IAEA/ABACC
RA-3 Ezeiza	Light-water, LEU, 4.5 MWt, operating	IAEA/ABACC
RA-4 Rosario	Light-water, 20% enriched uranium, .001 kWt, operating	IAEA/ABACC
RA-6 San Carlos de Bariloche	Light-water, HEU, 500 kWt, operating	IAEA/ABACC
RA-8 Pilcaniyeu	Critical facility, light-water, LEU, operating	IAEA/ABACC
	Uranium Enrichment	
Pilcaniyeu	Pilot plant, gaseous diffusion method, on stand by, no current plans to restart operations[2]	IAEA/ABACC
	Reprocessing (Plutonium Extraction)	
Ezeiza	Pilot plant, construction deferred[3]	No
	Uranium Processing	
Sierra Pintada/ San Rafael[4]	Uranium ore processing, stand by[5]	No
Los Colorados	Uranium ore processing, shut down	No
Cordoba	Uranium purification (UO_2) plant, on stand by[6]	IAEA/ABACC

Constituyentes[7]	Uranium conversion (UF_6) plant, operating	IAEA/ABACC
Ezeiza	Fuel fabrication plant (supplies Atucha and Embalse), operating	IAEA/ABACC
Ezeiza	Enriched uranium laboratory[8]	IAEA/ABACC
Ezeiza	Triple Altura laboratory[9]	IAEA/ABACC
Constituyentes	Research reactor fuel-fabrication plant, makes LEU silicide fuel for export, operating	IAEA/ABACC
Constituyentes	Alpha facility[10]	IAEA
Heavy-Water Production[11]		
Arroyito	Production-scale, operating[12]	ABACC
Atucha	Pilot-scale; shut down	ABACC

Abbreviations

ABACC Argentine-Brazilian Accounting and Control Commission
CNEA National Atomic Energy Commission
HEU highly enriched uranium
IAEA International Atomic Energy Agency
LEU low-enriched uranium
nat. U natural uranium
MWe megawatts electric
MWt megawatts thermal
kWt kilowatts thermal

Sources

Conversations with CNEA officials. IAEA, "Country Nuclear Power Profiles: 2003." IAEA, "Director General's Annual Report, 2003," table A24. IAEA, "Nuclear Fuel Cycle Information System," available at www-nfcis.iaea.org/Default.asp. IAEA, "Power Reactor Information System," available at www.iaea.org/programmes/a2/index.html. IAEA, "Research Reactor Database," available at www.iaea.org/worldatom/rrdb/. Nuclear Engineering International, *2004 World Nuclear Industry Handbook* (Sidcup, U.K.: Wilmington Publishing, 2004).

Notes

1. The plant is 81 percent completed. Argentina is hoping to partner with Siemens AG or Framatome ANP to complete construction. Mark Hibbs, "Argentina Puts Cost of Finishing Atucha-2 at About $200 Million," *Nucleonics Week,* December 16, 2004, p. 12.
2. According to the IAEA, the enrichment facility at Pilcaniyeu is not currently operating ("stand by" status), though the *2004 World Nuclear Industry Handbook* indicates that it is operating. According to a CNEA official, Argentina is not currently producing any enriched uranium because it is cheaper to import it. As long as this is Argentina's policy, the facility at Pilcaniyeu will remain "mothballed."
3. This facility is approximately 80 percent complete, but construction has been stopped for over ten years. According to a CNEA official, some small hot-cell facilities are operating at Ezeiza, but none are involved in extracting plutonium.

(table continues on the following page)

Table 19.1. **Argentina's Nuclear Infrastructure** (continued)

4. According to the IAEA, this facility is not currently operating ("stand by" status). A CNEA official indicated that there was some discussion in Argentina about restarting operations at Sierra Pintada in order to produce more natural uranium. This may depend on whether or not construction on Atucha II is restarted.
5. According to a CNEA official, the uranium-ore-processing facilities reported at San Rafael and Sierra Pintada are one and the same.
6. The status of the purification plant at Cordoba is subject to the same developments as the uranium-ore-processing facilities at Sierra Pintada (see note 4 above).
7. The IAEA reports that Argentina's lone uranium conversion facility is at Pilcaniyeu, though CNEA officials state that it is located at Constituyentes.
8. Listed under "Other Facilities" in IAEA, *Annual Report 2003.*
9. The Triple Altura laboratory, in operation since 1992 according to an ABACC official, is a facility used to recover enriched uranium contained in fuel element scraps.
10. The Alpha facility undertakes research on mixed-oxide fuel fuel-rod fabrication and design.
11. The international nonproliferation regime does not include the application of safeguards to heavy-water production facilities, but safeguards are required on the export of heavy water.
12. Both the IAEA and the *2004 World Nuclear Industry Handbook* report that Argentina is constructing additional heavy-water production facilities (with a combined capacity of 250 tons of heavy metal per year) at Arroyito.

CHAPTER 20

Brazil

Nuclear Weapons Capability

Brazil is a non-nuclear-weapon state and does not possess nuclear weapons or unsafeguarded stocks of weapons-usable material. Some elements in the Brazilian military previously sought the option to develop nuclear weapons or "peaceful nuclear explosives." This effort was pursued partly in competition with Argentina, which pursued a similar nuclear program during the 1970s and 1980s, but primarily in an effort to gain international prestige. Brazil changed course in the 1990s, placing all its nuclear facilities under bilateral inspections with Argentina and later accepting safeguards from the International Atomic Energy Agency (IAEA). Since that time, Brazil has assumed a leadership position in international nonproliferation efforts. The end of Brazil's nuclear weapons program is an important achievement and its continued non-nuclear-weapon status is an important element in the nonproliferation regime's preservation. Brazil is a member of the Nuclear Non-Proliferation Treaty and has signed and ratified the Comprehensive Test Ban Treaty.

Missile Capability

Brazil terminated several short-range missile programs in the 1990s. It currently has a program to develop a space launch vehicle that is theoretically capable of sending a 500-kilogram warhead up to 3,600 kilometers if it were to be converted for military purposes. Its three test flights in 1997, 1999, and 2003 failed to put satellites in orbit.

Biological and Chemical Weapons Capability

There is no public information to suggest that Brazil has ever had research or production programs for either chemical or biological weapons. It is a member of the Biological Weapons Convention and the Chemical Weapons Convention.

Nuclear Analysis

During the 1990s, Brazil renounced a previously secret military program that could have eventually produced weapons-usable material and even nuclear weapons. Since then, the Brazilian government has completed a series of steps to

VENEZUELA
COLOMBIA
GUYANA
SURINAME
FR. GUIANA
PERU
BRAZIL
URUGUAY
ARGENTINA
Pacific Ocean
Atlantic Ocean
Italicized names represent nuclear-related sites. See table 20.1.
Missile and space launch test facility.
Alcantara
Itataia
Recife
Cachimbo
Brasilia
Lagoa Real
Belo Horizonte
Pocos de Caldas
Resende
Iperó
Rio de Janeiro
Angra dos Reis
São Jose dos Campos
São Paulo (IPEN)
Cachimbo Nuclear Test Site (dismantled)
Part of nuclear program pursued by Brazil's military in the 1980s until terminated by then President Fernando Collor de Mello in 1990.
Itataia
Planned uranium mining facility.
Lagoa Real
Uranium mining facility.
Resende
Operational industrial-scale ultracentrifuge uranium enrichment plant. After some delay, Brazil reached an agreement with the IAEA in November 2004 on inspections of the facility. Under safeguards.
Resende also contains an operating fuel fabrication plant, which converts the low-enriched uranium produced at the ultracentrifuge plant into LEU fuel for the Angra I and Angra II power reactors. Under safeguards.
Aramar Research Center
Includes the first module of an industrial-scale centrifuge uranium enrichment plant, which is operating. No known production of weapons-grade uranium. Facility was apparently a key component of the now-terminated nuclear program pursued by Brazil's military in the 1980's. Brazil has declared that it will enrich uranium to no more than 20%, precluding its use for nuclear weapons. Subject to safeguards.
UF6 conversion facility under construction. For all other facilities located at the Aramar Research Center, see table 20.1.
0
500
Miles

implement binding nonproliferation commitments. Nonetheless, several decades of nuclear development, much of it through parallel civil and military programs, has given the country an impressive array of facilities covering the entire nuclear fuel cycle. Some of these—in particular, Brazil's uranium enrichment facilities—still have the technical potential to produce weapons-grade material. Some activities by the military—notably the army's effort to resurrect a research reactor project uncovered in June 1997 and the navy's resumption of its nuclear-powered submarine program in January 2000—have given rise to concerns that some in the current military may harbor nuclear ambitions that warrant continued attention. A prolonged dialogue between the IAEA and Brazil over the implementation of inspections at the uranium enrichment facility at Resende, which coincided with revelations about Iran's nuclear programs, added to international concerns about the direction of Brazil's nuclear program. Yet Brazil has unequivocally committed itself to the peaceful development of nuclear energy, and it appears unlikely that it will have any major incentives to reverse that stance in the foreseeable future.

Since 1985, Brazil has transformed itself from a cash-strapped nation under authoritarian military rule to a country with a strong market economy, democratically elected leadership, and a prominent international profile. Brazil is now a recognized member of many international nuclear organizations. The commercial prospects of its nuclear industry will figure prominently in any future developments. Brazil's second nuclear power reactor, Angra II, came on line in July 2000 after years of delay and financial difficulty, and a third reactor, Angra III, is still planned despite the fact that funding shortages and environmental concerns have delayed construction since 1986.[1] Although nuclear energy does not currently play a major role in Brazil's energy mix, it could become important in the years to come, especially since the country has the necessary supporting facilities for a nuclear power program (see table 20.1 at the end of the chapter).

Nuclear Weapons Program

The Brazilian armed forces pursued an unsafeguarded nuclear development program during the 1970s and 1980s, which aroused suspicions at home and abroad that some in the military aimed to produce nuclear weapons. Although the effort included activities of serious proliferation concern—especially the navy's development of uranium enrichment technology and the air force's construction of an apparent nuclear explosive test site—domestic and international pressures helped to isolate the narrow faction that advocated the development of a "Brazilian bomb." The available evidence does not indicate that Brazil had a program dedicated to nuclear weapons production like those of Iraq and South Africa. Instead, there was a government and military consensus only to develop the technological capacity for the *option* to build atomic weapons, and even that goal was justified within the military as a peaceful nuclear explosive (PNE) project. The military's program efforts were driven as much or more strongly, however, by nonweapon objectives, specifically to develop submarine propulsion, generally to boost Brazil's international standing and to reach technological autonomy through a mastery of nuclear energy.[2]

Brazilian military interest in sensitive nuclear technology first became evident in 1953, when the director of its National Research Council, Admiral Álvaro Alberto, went to West Germany to buy experimental ultracentrifuges. The United States blocked the centrifuge deal at the time. Brazil nevertheless signed nuclear cooperation agreements with the United States in 1955, which led in 1957 to Brazil's Comissão Nacional de Energia Nuclear, commissioning its first U.S.-supplied research reactor.

In the early 1960s, Brazil opened negotiations with France for a natural uranium-fueled power reactor, but those negotiations were dropped in 1964. Eventually, Brazil acquired its first power plant (Angra I) under a nuclear cooperation agreement signed with the United States in 1965. Brazil ordered this light-water reactor, supplied by the U.S. company Westinghouse, in 1971. Four years later, West Germany agreed to provide Brazil with ten nuclear power plants and the facilities for a complete nuclear fuel cycle, subject to IAEA safeguards. After fifteen years, however, Brazil's civilian nuclear sector had little to show for its cooperation with West Germany, apart from an unfinished reactor and an unsuccessful uranium enrichment program based on the jet-nozzle method. During that same period, however, the Brazilian military was engaged in a parallel program to acquire nuclear weapons capability.

The secret program, reportedly code-named the Solimões Project, started while Brazil was under military rule. It allegedly included research on nuclear weapons design and the excavation of a 300-meter-deep shaft for underground nuclear explosive tests at a military base near Cachimbo in the Amazon jungle. Three different methods to produce weapons-grade fissile material were pursued. Each branch of the military had its own approach, with none subject to IAEA safeguards. The navy, in cooperation with the Institute for Energy and Nuclear Research (IPEN), developed ultracentrifuges for uranium enrichment. The army chose graphite reactors suitable for plutonium production, and the air force undertook research on the laser enrichment of uranium and reportedly on nuclear weapons design and the construction of a nuclear test site.[3]

Only the navy–IPEN project succeeded, however, and the navy ultimately dominated the parallel program of the armed forces. Its installations included a laboratory-scale uranium centrifuge plant at IPEN in São Paulo, as well as the initial module of an industrial-scale plant at the navy's Aramar Research Center in Iperó. These installations could have been used to produce uranium enriched to the level needed for nuclear arms, but neither plant is believed to have produced such material.

In 1990, Brazil renounced its secret program and began a series of steps toward binding nonproliferation commitments. On September 17, 1990, then–president Fernando Collor de Mello closed the Cachimbo test site. He emphasized his decision to end Brazil's nuclear weapons option program by throwing two shovels of lime into the test shaft, symbolically to bury the program. A week later, he announced at the United Nations that Brazil was rejecting "the idea of any test that implies nuclear explosions, even for peaceful ends," which was the first time that a Brazilian president had ever renounced PNEs.[4] Brazil subsequently declared its intention to produce only low-enriched uranium, which is not readily suitable for weapons. Aramar director Admiral Othon Pinheiro da Silva declared in March 1993 that his center would not enrich uranium above 20 percent "because of a political decision."[5]

A significant milestone on the nonproliferation path came on May 30, 1994, when Brazil brought into force the Treaty for the Prohibition of Nuclear Weapons in Latin America and the Caribbean (Treaty of Tlatelolco). This treaty included commitments not to acquire, manufacture, test, use, or permit the stationing of nuclear weapons or any nuclear explosive device on a member state's territory and to accept IAEA inspections of all its nuclear activities. Though domestic political opposition delayed Brazil's signature of the Nuclear Non-Proliferation Treaty for four more years, by 1994 it had accepted the strict international supervision of its nuclear activities through the Argentine-Brazilian Accounting and Control Commission (ABACC) and the Quadripartite Safeguards Agreement (see "Brazil–Argentina Rapprochement" below).

As a sign of faith in Brazil's commitment to nonproliferation, the United States initialed with Brazil in March 1996 the text of a new nuclear cooperation accord that replaced the earlier, dormant agreement. This agreement was signed in 1997 and entered into force the following year, permitting nuclear commerce for peaceful purposes between the two countries. The United States also supported Brazil's membership in the Nuclear Suppliers Group, which Brazil joined in April 1996 during the plenary session held in Argentina.[6]

Brazil finally signed and ratified both the NPT and the Comprehensive Test Ban Treaty in 1998, following pressure from President Bill Clinton and months of domestic lobbying by President Fernando Henrique Cardoso. At a U.S. State Department ceremony marking the event on September 18, 1998, Brazilian foreign minister Luis Lampreia stressed Brazil's "unwavering commitment to the use of nuclear energy for exclusively peaceful purposes."[7]

Nuclear Complex

In July 1991, the Argentine and Brazilian foreign ministers formally established the ABACC. An agreement to integrate the ABACC's inspection system with that of the IAEA was signed by Argentina, Brazil, the IAEA, and the ABACC in Vienna on December 13, 1991. This quadripartite agreement committed the ABACC and the IAEA to establishing an initial inventory of all nuclear materials in Brazil (and Argentina) as a basis for future inspections.

The IAEA has no mandate to investigate past weapons-related activities, despite indications that Brazil undertook nuclear weapon research in the 1980s. Completing the inventory was complicated by years of unsafeguarded nuclear activities at IPEN, Iperó, and other sites that contributed to the weapons program. During 1995, however, the IAEA "largely completed" its verification of nuclear material and facility design information in Brazil.[8] Since then, regular IAEA inventory checks and inspections have been carried out to identify any potential diversion, or reversion, of nuclear materials to military use. The ABACC has also continued its ad hoc inspections, conducting 81 in 1996 and 68 between January 2003 and May 2004.[9]

Proliferation concerns were aroused in June 1997 with reports that the Brazilian army had tried to restart the Atlantic Project, involving the construction of a 0.5-megawatt experimental graphite reactor readily suitable for plutonium production in the Guaratiba natural reserve. While President Cardoso was out of the country in November 1996, Vice-President Marco Maciel authorized the project, reportedly under pressure from army officials. After the project was exposed, the army agreed to discontinue it.[10]

Although legally permitted by the NPT, Brazil's nuclear submarine propulsion program has aroused concern that uranium enrichment capabilities for submarine reactors might at some point be misused for weapons production. On February 2, 1996, navy minister Admiral Mauro Pereira announced that plans to build a nuclear-powered submarine had been suspended after seventeen years of effort. The Aramar Research Center, which houses about 1,000 ultracentrifuges, would instead turn its attention to completing the Angra II power reactor and to building conventional submarines. By then, however, $670 million had been invested at Aramar to develop enriched uranium to fuel submarines,[11] and the navy wanted to maintain its enrichment program, although it had undertaken not to produce weapons-grade material. The project therefore continued despite a series of setbacks. In 1995–1996, about half the 2,000 employees at the facility, including scientists and researchers, left.[12]

At the end of 1996, the Brazilian press publicized several accidents involving radioactive material and the contamination of personnel over the previous four years.[13] The navy insisted that the incidents had been minor, below the threshold of the IAEA's International Nuclear Events Scale.[14] In January 2000, the Brazilian government allocated funds for the navy to restart its nuclear submarine propulsion project, but the Congress subsequently cut the budget. In lobbying legislators to restore funding and to address public suspicions, the navy said that if it produced a nuclear-powered submarine, it would consider allowing the ABACC to apply seals to the onboard reactor and use remote monitoring technology to ensure that no diversion of nuclear fuel for weapons purposes took place.[15]

Though still controversial, the nuclear submarine program has begun to gain more support under the government of Ignacio Lula da Silva. In October 2003, then–science and technology minister Roberto Amaral praised the benefits of a nuclear-powered submarine, and insisted that the government would push forward on its development.[16] Even with this newfound support, however, the program has not been fully funded, and it is unlikely to be completed anytime soon.[17]

The most pressing point of concern in Brazil's nuclear complex today surrounds the new uranium enrichment facility at Resende, whose primary purpose is to produce the low-enriched uranium necessary to fuel the Angra I and Angra II (and eventually the Angra III) power reactors. The low-enriched uranium produced at Resende may also be exported.[18] Before such a facility is permitted to begin operations, it needs to be placed under IAEA safeguards. In April 2004, however, Brazilian authorities reportedly denied IAEA inspectors full access to the facility, citing concerns that the plant contained proprietary technology Brazil wanted to protect. The dialogue with the IAEA occurred just as details of A. Q. Khan's nuclear black market trade emerged, and some experts suggested that Brazil may have acquired technology through that network, technology that it was hoping to shield from IAEA inspectors.[19]

By the end of November 2004, Brasilia reached a compromise agreement with the IAEA that, according to IAEA director general Mohamed ElBaradei, "will enable [the IAEA] to do credible inspections but at the same time take care of Brazil's need to protect commercial sensitivity inside the facility."[20] The agreement, and subsequent application of safeguards, permitted Brazil to commence operations at Resende in December 2004.

Brazil–Argentina Rapprochement

Although rivalry for regional leadership and military suspicions have fueled the competition between Brazil and Argentina in nuclear development since the early 1950s, the cooperative elements of the relation endured even when bilateral relations were at their worst, notably in nuclear science and diplomacy. The military governments signed formal cooperation accords in nuclear commerce in 1980.[21] Both countries pursued proliferation-sensitive enrichment and reprocessing activities, as well as civilian research and energy programs.

After the transition from military rule in the mid-1980s, however, Brazil and Argentina took steps that definitively ended their nuclear rivalry. On July 18, 1991, the Argentine and Brazilian foreign ministers signed a bilateral agreement renouncing PNEs, allowing mutual inspections of nuclear installations, and setting up the ABACC to implement this commitment. Exchanges of nuclear material inventories and mutual inspections began in late 1992 after the ABACC's inauguration. Argentina's Congress approved the Quadripartite Safeguards Agreement in 1992, but inspections were delayed until the agreement entered into force on March 4, 1994, following approval by Brazil's Congress in February 1994.[22] The agreement made the ABACC and the IAEA responsible for performing an initial inventory of all nuclear materials in Argentina as a basis for inspections, a task complicated by years of unsafeguarded activities at Pilcaniyeu in Argentina.

The bilateral aspect is critical to both Argentina and Brazil's continued commitment to the nonproliferation regime. The ABACC's success, therefore, continues to be vital. The ABACC predates, supplements, and reinforces the work of the IAEA in these two countries. It may become even more important if Brazil has any further disagreements with the IAEA, such as it did regarding access to the enrichment facility at Resende.

Missile Analysis

Brazil developed a series of sounding rockets during the 1970s and early 1980s, some of them modified into short-range surface-to-surface missiles for export to Iraq, Libya, and Saudi Arabia. During the early 1990s, however, Brazil terminated its programs to develop more capable missiles. These missiles included the Avibras SS-300 as well as the Orbita-MB/EE-600 and -1000. With ranges of more than 300 kilometers, these missiles are subject to Missile Technology Control Regime (MTCR) restrictions. Brazil was widely criticized when the former director of the Brazilian Aerospace Technical Center, Hugo Piva, led a team of missile scientists and technicians to Iraq to assist in the development of Iraq's missile program before the 1990–1991 Persian Gulf War. Objections by the international community led Brazil to introduce export control legislation, paving the way for later adherence to MTCR export guidelines.[23]

Since 1981, Brazil has been working on a space launch vehicle (SLV) four-stage rocket, designed to place satellites in low-Earth orbit. This project largely depended on foreign missile technology, however, which is restricted under the MTCR. To obtain key missile technology, the Brazilian government announced its decision on February 11, 1994, to comply with MTCR criteria and standards. It agreed to restrict the export of missiles (and key missile components) that are capable of carrying unconventional weapons beyond the 300-kilometer threshold.[24] Though Brazil stopped exporting sensitive missile technology, it continued to import technology for its civilian space launch program. This activity, and in particular the import of carbon-fiber technology for rocket-motor casings from Russia in early 1995, was technically in violation of MTCR rules. Nevertheless, the United States sought to include Brazil in the MTCR to curb its missile program. It therefore waived sanctions relating to the Russian technology deal in return for a pledge from Brazil that it would no longer engage in such activities.[25]

Brazil was admitted to the MTCR in October 1995 and was allowed to maintain its SLV program despite its inherent military capability. The SLV, the centerpiece of the Brazilian space program, can theoretically launch a 500-kilogram warhead up to 3,600 kilometers if it were converted for military purposes. Brazil currently builds its own satellites but must launch them on foreign rockets, which are often provided by China. Brasilia hopes to launch a joint Chinese–Brazilian satellite on a Ukrainian rocket sometime after 2007.[26] The first flight of Brazil's own SLV was delayed for many years by MTCR restrictions, financing problems, and programming difficulties. In a serious setback, the maiden launch of the missile, on November 2, 1997, was terminated one minute after liftoff because of engine failure. A second attempted launch in December 1999 also failed. The third attempted launch was the program's biggest setback to date. Three days before the scheduled August 2003 test flight, one of the rocket's four boosters exploded, destroying the rocket and the two satellites it was carrying. Twenty-one technicians were killed in the accident. Despite this tragedy, Brazilian president Lula da Silva pledged to launch an SLV before the end of 2006.[27] In fact, some progress has already been made in this direction as Brazil successfully launched a less ambitious space rocket, the VSB-30 Brazilian Exploration Vehicle, in October 2004.[28]

Brazil is not a participating member of the International Code of Conduct Against Ballistic Missile Proliferation, which, among other things, formally recognizes the links between SLV and ballistic missile technology and encourages participating states to ensure that the sharing of SLV technology does not support ballistic missile programs.

Biological and Chemical Weapons Analysis

Brazil has no known chemical or biological weapons programs and is a party to both the Biological Weapons Convention and the Chemical Weapons Convention. In addition, Brazil is a signatory to the 1991 Joint Declaration on the Complete Prohibition of Chemical and Biological Weapons, a regional nonproliferation agreement also known as the Mendoza Accord.

NOTES

1. "Government to Decide on Angra III by Year-End," *Platts Power in Latin America*, November 5, 2004, p. 8.
2. Michael Barletta, "Ambiguity, Autonomy, and the Atom: Emergence of the Argentine-Brazilian Nuclear Regime" (Ph.D. diss., University of Wisconsin, 2000), pp. 213–277. Also, Barletta, "Pernicious Ideas in World Politics: 'Peaceful Nuclear Explosives,'" paper presented at the annual meeting of the American Political Science Association, August 30–September 2, 2001, pp. 29–32; available at papers.tcnj.edu/papers/019/019013BarlettaMi.pdf.
3. José Casado, "Analyst Views 'Nuclear Explosive Artifacts,'" *O Estado de São Paulo*, June 5, 1995, in FBIS-LAT-95-111, June 9, 1995, p. 30; and Helcio Costa, "CPI Sees Bomb Configuration Project at IEAv," *Gazeta Mercantil*, November 29, 1990, in JPRS-TND-91-001, January 4, 1991.
4. James Brooke, "Brazil Uncovers Plan by Military to Build Atom Bomb and Stops It," *New York Times*, October 9, 1990; David Albright, "Brazil Comes in from the Cold," *Arms Control Today*, December 1990, p. 13. But see Barletta, "Ambiguity, Autonomy, and the Atom," pp. 268–271, who reviews contradictory evidence to suggest that the allegation of a secret military plot to build the bomb may be overblown.
5. Jean Krasno, "Brazil's Secret Nuclear Program," *Orbis*, Summer 1994, p. 432.
6. U.S. Department of State, *U.S.–Brazil Agreement on Peaceful Uses of Nuclear Energy*, March 1, 1996; Wyn Bowen and Andrew Koch, "Non-Proliferation Is Embraced by Brazil," *Jane's Intelligence Review*, June 1996, p. 283.
7. U.S. State Department press release, September 18, 1998.
8. IAEA, *IAEA Annual Report 1996*, p. 46.
9. ABACC, *ABACC Annual Report 1996*, p. 24; ABACC, *Annual Report 2003*, p. 24; *ABACC News*, February–May 2004, Available at www.abacc.org/abaccnews/news2/en/noticias.asp; *ABACC News*, June–October 2004, available at www.abacc.org/abaccnews/news3/en/noticias12.asp.
10. "Brazil: Army Confirms Gas-Graphite Nuclear Reactor Project," *Jornal do Brasil*, June 5, 1997, in FBIS-LAT-97-156, June 5, 1997; and "Brazil: Ministries Term Nuclear Reactor Project 'Peaceful,'" *Jornal do Brasil*, June 5, 1997, in FBIS-TEN-97-007-L.
11. José Maria Tomazela, "Brazilian Minister: Navy Gave Up Nuclear Submarine Plans," *O Estado de São Paulo*, February 7, 1996, in FBIS-LAT-96-028, February 9, 1996, p. 12; and Philip Finnegan, "Brazil Defers Nuclear Sub Plan," *Defense News*, March 11–17, 1996, p. 4.
12. José Maria Tomazela, "Brazil: Iperó Mayor Fears Dismantling of Nuclear Center," *O Estado de São Paulo*, February 14, 1996, in FBIS-LAT-96-036, February 22, 1996, p. 50.
13. "Navy Documents Said to Confirm Leaks of Radioactive Material at Base," Rede Globo Television, December 30, 1996, in FBIS-TEN-97-001, January 23, 1997; and Jose Maria Mayrink, "Former Nuclear Plant Employees Report Frequent Past Leaks," *Jornal do Brasil*, January 1, 1997, in FBIS-TEN-97-001.
14. "Navy Communiqué on Radioactive Incidents," *Jornal do Brasil*, December 31, 1996 in FBIS–TEN–97–001.

15. José Maria Tomazela, "Government Resumes Nuclear Submarine Project," *O Estado de São Paulo*, February 1, 2000, in FBIS document FTS20000201000871; and Mark Hibbs, "Brazilian Navy to Request More Funds for Nuclear Sub," *Nucleonics Week*, July 6, 2000.
16. "Government Retains Nuclear Submarine Programme," *LatinnewsDaily*, October 1, 2003.
17. Mark Hibbs. "Shrouding of Centrifuges At Issue in Brazil's Negotiation with IAEA," *Nucleonics Week*, April 29, 2004, p. 15.
18. Carmen Gentile, "Brazil Under Nuclear Microscope—Again," United Press International, September 30, 2004.
19. Ibid.
20. "IAEA Reaches Agreement with Brazil on Inspecting Uranium Plant," Agence France-Presse, November 25, 2004.
21. Barletta, "Ambiguity, Autonomy, and the Atom," pp. 101–109, 123–126.
22. Statement by Michael McCurry, "Argentina and Brazil: Ratification of the Quadripartite Safeguards Agreement," U.S. Department of State, March 4, 1994; and John R. Redick, Julio C. Carasales, and Paulo S. Wrobel, "Nuclear Rapprochement: Argentina, Brazil, and the Non-Proliferation Regime," *Washington Quarterly*, Winter 1995, pp. 107–122.
23. Maria Helena Tachinardi, "Measures to Control Sensitive Exports Announced," *Gazeta Mercantil*, August 10, 1994, as translated in FBIS-LAT-94-162.
24. Raquel Stenzel, "Government Agrees to Comply with Missile Control Pact,"' *Gazeta Mercantil*, February 12, 1994, in JPRS-TND-94-006, March 16, 1994.
25. R. Jeffrey Smith, "U.S. Waives Objection to Russian Missile Technology Sale to Brazil," *Washington Post*, June 8, 1995.
26. Frank Braun, "Brazil in Space: A Ukrainian Connection," United Press International, September 20, 2004.
27. Ibid.
28. "Brazil Completes Its First Successful Rocket Launch Into Space," Associated Press, October 23, 2004.

Table 20.1. **Brazil's Nuclear Infrastructure**

Name/Location of Facility	Type/Status	IAEA Safeguards
Nuclear Weapons-Related Sites		
Institute of Advanced Studies, Aerospace Technical Center São Jose dos Campos	Conducted research on nuclear weapons design, shutdown[1]	No
Cachimbo	Planned nuclear weapon test site, dismantled, not operational	No
Power Reactors		
Angra I	Light-water, LEU, 626 MWe, operating	IAEA/ABACC
Angra II	Light-water, LEU, 1,275 MWe, operating	IAEA/ABACC
Angra III	Light-water, LEU, 1,309 MWe, under construction (currently deferred)[2]	No
Research Reactors[3]		
IEA-R1 São Paulo	Pool, LEU, 5 MWt, operating[4]	IAEA/ABACC
RIEN–1 (Argonauta) Rio de Janeiro	Water, 19.9% enriched uranium, 0.2 KWt, operating	IAEA/ABACC
IPR-R1 Triga Mark I Belo Horizonte	Water, 20% enriched uranium, 100 kWt, operating	IAEA/ABACC
IPEN/MB-01 Critical Assembly São Paulo	Light-water, 4.3 % enriched uranium, 0.1 kWt, operating	IAEA/ABACC
Renap reactors, Aramar Research Center Ipéro	Experimental, pressurized-water, designed for nuclear-powered submarine, program delayed[5]	IAEA/ABACC
Subcritical Assembly Rio de Janeiro	Graphite, nat. U, operating	IAEA/ABACC
Subcritical Assembly Recife	Light-water, nat. U, operating	IAEA/ABACC
Uranium Enrichment		
Resende	Pilot-scale, jet-nozzle method, completed; program canceled,[6] industrial-scale ultracentrifuge enrichment; operational[7]	IAEA/ABACC

(table continues on the following page)

Table 20.1. **Brazil's Nuclear Infrastructure** (continued)

Belo Horizonte	Laboratory-scale, jet-nozzle method, shut down	IAEA/ABACC
Aramar Research Center, Isotopic Enrichment Laboratory (LEI) Ipéro	First-stage, pilot-scale plant, ultracentrifuge method, operating,[8] a nearby pilot-plant using a carbon-fiber rotor design is also reportedly operating[9]	IAEA/ABACC
Aramar Research Center Ipéro	Centrifuge production plant, operating	No[10]
Navy Research Institute (CTMSP) São Paulo	Laboratory-scale plant, ultracentrifuge method; does small-scale tests of centrifuge cascades, operating	IAEA/ABACC
Institute of Advanced Studies (IAEv), Aerospace Technical Center São Jose dos Campos[11]	Laboratory-scale, laser method; operational[12]	IAEA/ABACC
Reprocessing (Plutonium Extraction)		
IPEN São Paulo	Laboratory-scale, shut down[13]	IAEA/ABACC
Uranium Processing[14]		
Lagoa Real	Uranium ore processing, operating	No
Pocos de Caldas	Uranium ore processing, shut down	No
Itataia	Uranium ore processing, deferred[15]	No
IPEN São Paulo[16]	Uranium-purification (UO_2) site	IAEA/ABACC
Aramar Research Center Ipéro	Uranium-purification (UO_2) facility, produces UO_2 pellets, operating	IAEA/ABACC[17]
IPEN São Paulo	Pilot-scale uranium-conversion (UF_6) facility, shut down	IAEA/ABACC
Aramar Research Center Ipéro	Uranium-conversion (UF_6) plant, under construction	IAEA/ABACC[18]
Nuclear Fuel Factory (FCN) Resende	Fuel-fabrication plant, operating[19]	IAEA/ABACC

Abbreviations

ABACC Argentine-Brazilian Accounting and Control Commission
IAEA International Atomic Energy Agency
LEU low-enriched uranium
nat. U natural uranium
MWe megawatts electric
MWt megawatts thermal
KWt kilowatts thermal

Notes

1. Though Brazil did research on nuclear weapons designs, it never produced a weapon. All evidence shows that Brazil ceased consideration of a nuclear weapons option in the 1980s.
2. The National Council of Energy Policy (CNPE) is expected to decide whether to authorize the completion of Angra III. See Joshua Schneyer, "Brazil to Decide Shortly on Finishing 1,350-MW Angra-3," *Nucleonics Week,* December 9, 2004.
3. The IAEA lists Brazil as having four research reactors: IEA-R1, RIEN-1/Argonauta, IPR-R1/Triga, and the IPEN/MB-01 critical assembly (see IAEA Research Reactor Database, www.iaea.org/worldatom/rrdb). Brazil also has experimental reactors at Ipéro and two subcritical assemblies, one at Rio de Janeiro and one at Recife.
4. The IEA-R1 research reactor used to employ highly enriched uranium. It was fully converted to low-enriched uranium through the U.S.-funded Reduced Enrichment for Research and Test Reactors program in 1998.
5. In January 2002, the Brazilian government allocated funds to restart the program, but the Congress cut the budget. Through the spring of 2005, no funding had been allocated for the program, although it has received greater support from the civilian government in recent years.
6. In March 1994, Brazil canceled its project to enrich uranium using the German jet-nozzle process. Since then, the facilities using that method at Resende and Belo Horizonte have not been operating, and the Belo Horizonte laboratory has been dismantled; George Vidor, "Jet Nozzle Uranium Enrichment Project Canceled," *O Globo,* Rio de Janeiro, March 19, 1994, in FBIS-LAT-95-056, March 23, 1994, p. 48. INB, Brazil Nuclear Industries, may sell 40 percent of the jet-nozzle enrichment equipment as junk; José Casado, "Article Views Efforts to Revive Nuclear Program," *O Estado de São Paulo,* June 4, 1995, in FBIS-TAC-95-111, June 9, 1995, p. 29.
7. In November 2004, Brazil arrived at an agreement with the IAEA, allowing for inspections of the ultracentrifuge plant at Resende. With the dispute resolved, the facility began operations in December 2004.
8. IAEA, *IAEA Annual Report, 2003,* table A24; available at www.iaea.org/Publications/Reports/Anrep2003/annex_tables.pdf.
9. David Albright, Frans Berkhout, and William Walker, *Plutonium and Highly Enriched Uranium 1996: World Inventories, Capabilities and Policies*_(Oxford: Oxford University Press, 1997), p. 375.
10. According to Marco Marzo, if the IAEA were to ask to visit a centrifuge factory (such as the one at Aramar), the inspectors would be refused because there is no nuclear material present at the site. Whether ABACC can inspect the facilities is not clear. Institute for Science and International Security and Shalheveth Freier Center for Peace, Science, and Technology, "Argentina and Brazil," pp. 51–52.
11. Laser-enrichment research and development were performed at IAEv in Sao Jose dos Campos by the air force and code named Sepila. José Casado, "Analyst Views 'Nuclear Explosive Artifacts,'" *O Estado De São Paulo,* June 5, 1995, in FBIS-LAT-95-111, June 9, 1995, p. 30; Helcio Costa, "CPI Sees Bomb Configuration Project at IAEv," Gazeta Mercantil, November 29, 1990, in JPRS-TND-91-001, January 4 1991, p. 17. The IAEA lists a laboratory for laser spectroscopy at Sao Jose dos Campos under safeguards (*Annual Report 2003,* table A24).
12. IAEA Nuclear Fuel Cycle Information System.
13. This facility was reportedly operated with plutonium simulators because Brazil did not have access to unsafeguarded spent fuel. The IAEA confirms that it has been shut down. IAEA Nuclear Fuel Cycle Facilities, Brazil.
14. Brazil reportedly has a uranium conversion agreement with Canada, whereby Brazil sends uranium yellowcake to Canada for conversion into uranium hexafluoride, which is then sent back to Brazil, where it can be enriched by centrifuges.

(table continues on the following page)

Table 20.1. **Brazil's Nuclear Infrastructure** (continued)

15. See IAEA, "IAEA Country Nuclear Power Profiles, 2003: Brazil."
16. See www.ipen.br/ipen_eng/page2-7.html.
17. This facility was commissioned and subsequently inspected by ABACC and IAEA officials in early July 1994. José Maria Tomazela, "IAEA Team Inspects Ipéro Uranium Hexafluoride Plant," *Agencia Estado,* July 29, 1994, in JPRS-TND-94-016, August 19, 1994, p. 19.
18. José Maria Tomazela, "IAEA Team Inspects Ipéro"; and Tania Malheiros, "Navy Confirms Project for Hexafluoride Conversion," *Agencia Estado,* August 4, 1994, in JPRS-TND-94-016, August 19, 1994, p. 19.
19. See IAEA, *IAEA Annual Report, 2003,* table A24. See also "IAEA Country Nuclear Power Profiles 2003: Brazil," p. 135.

CHAPTER 21

South Africa

Nuclear Weapons Capability

South Africa is a non-nuclear-weapon state and a member of the Nuclear Non-Proliferation Treaty (NPT). Since 1991, South Africa has made the transition from an undeclared possessor of nuclear weapons to a responsible participant in the nuclear nonproliferation regime. It is the first nation to develop and possess nuclear weapons and then renounce them. In a historic reform of South Africa's politics, President F. W. de Klerk ended the country's decades-long policy of racial separation and brought an end to white minority rule. Democratic elections in April 1994 brought Nelson Mandela to the presidency. Mandela's successor, Thabo Mbeki, remains committed to the NPT, which South Africa joined in 1991. The weapons-grade highly enriched uranium (HEU) that was produced during the 1970s and 1980s and used in South Africa's nuclear weapons still remains in the country under inspection by the International Atomic Energy Agency (IAEA). Despite these positive steps, however, some concerns remain. South Africa is estimated to have between 430 and 580 kilograms of HEU, most of which is weapons-grade (see table 21.1 at the end of the chapter).[1]

Biological and Chemical Weapons Capability

South Africa has disbanded its former secret biological and chemical warfare programs. It has ratified both the Biological Weapons Convention and the Chemical Weapons Convention.

Nuclear Analysis

South Africa was the first state in the world to give up its nuclear weapons capability voluntarily. When South Africa dismantled its advanced, but clandestine, nuclear weapons program and assumed a leading role in the nonproliferation regime, it reflected the country's immense political changes. On March 24, 1993, President de Klerk disclosed that South Africa had destroyed six nuclear devices that had been produced as part of its secret nuclear weapons program.[2] By 1994, the government had dismantled the entire associated weapons infrastructure under international inspection. South Africa acceded to the NPT on July 10, 1991, concluding a full-scope safeguard agreement with the IAEA the following September. All its nuclear plants and all previously produced enriched uranium were placed under IAEA safeguards. South Africa became a member of the Zangger

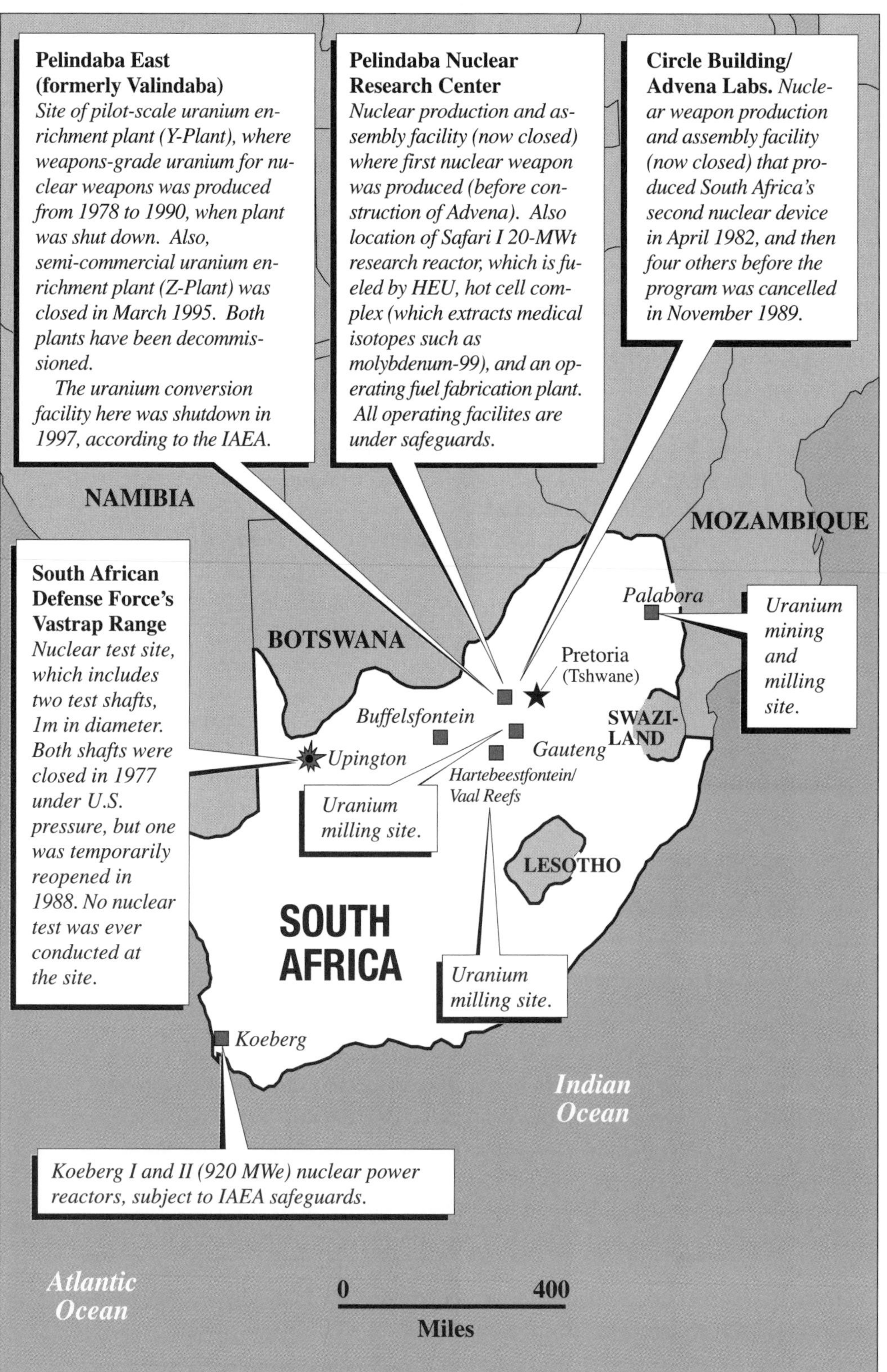
Pelindaba East (formerly Valindaba)
Site of pilot-scale uranium enrichment plant (Y-Plant), where weapons-grade uranium for nuclear weapons was produced from 1978 to 1990, when plant was shut down. Also, semi-commercial uranium enrichment plant (Z-Plant) was closed in March 1995. Both plants have been decommissioned.
The uranium conversion facility here was shutdown in 1997, according to the IAEA.
Pelindaba Nuclear Research Center
Nuclear production and assembly facility (now closed) where first nuclear weapon was produced (before construction of Advena). Also location of Safari I 20-MWt research reactor, which is fueled by HEU, hot cell complex (which extracts medical isotopes such as molybdenum-99), and an operating fuel fabrication plant. All operating facilites are under safeguards.
Circle Building/ Advena Labs. Nuclear weapon production and assembly facility (now closed) that produced South Africa's second nuclear device in April 1982, and then four others before the program was cancelled in November 1989.
NAMIBIA
MOZAMBIQUE
South African Defense Force's Vastrap Range
Nuclear test site, which includes two test shafts, 1m in diameter. Both shafts were closed in 1977 under U.S. pressure, but one was temporarily reopened in 1988. No nuclear test was ever conducted at the site.
Palabora
Uranium mining and milling site.
BOTSWANA
Pretoria
(Tshwane)
Buffelsfontein
SWAZILAND
Upington
Gauteng
Hartebeestfontein/
Vaal Reefs
Uranium milling site.
LESOTHO
SOUTH AFRICA
Uranium milling site.
Koeberg
Indian Ocean
Koeberg I and II (920 MWe) nuclear power reactors, subject to IAEA safeguards.
Atlantic Ocean
0
400
Miles

Committee in 1993 and of the Nuclear Suppliers Group in 1995. It played a leading role in the establishment of the African Nuclear Weapons Free Zone Treaty (the Treaty of Pelindaba) in 1996, becoming one of the treaty's first members in 1997. South Africa signed the Comprehensive Test Ban Treaty in 1996 and ratified it in 1999.

Although South Africa has declared its fissile material inventory to the IAEA, it has not revealed the exact figures to the public. Moreover, scientists who had previously worked on the nuclear weapons and missile programs could constitute a proliferation risk, and reports indicate that some South African scientists may have gone to work for Middle Eastern countries. Some individuals and companies in South Africa are known to have been part of the A. Q. Khan nuclear black market network. Other reports suggest that the country's Atomic Energy Corporation (AEC) secretly sold China equipment from its dismantled nuclear facilities. Until complete transparency is achieved, some questions will remain about South Africa's nuclear weapons complex, its continued enrichment activities, and the full extent of its nonproliferation commitment.

Nuclear Development

South Africa's Atomic Energy Corporation was established in Pretoria in 1948 to assess the uranium reserves in southern Africa. The AEC moved to Pelindaba when serious nuclear development began in the late 1960s under the cover of a peaceful nuclear explosives program to bolster South Africa's mining industry. In 1961, the Nuclear National Research Centre (now the Pelindaba Nuclear Institute) was established at Pelindaba, 30 kilometers west of Pretoria. South Africa's 20-megawatt Safari I nuclear research reactor, acquired from the United States under the Atoms for Peace program, began operating at the center in 1965.

Although initially devoted to peaceful research, the AEC launched a secret project in the early 1960s to develop a unique aerodynamic (vortex tube) uranium enrichment technology. The decision to build an industrial-scale pilot plant was made in 1969, and the Uranium Enrichment Corporation was set up to construct it at nearby Valindaba (later renamed Pelindaba East). The first stages of this "Y" plant were commissioned by the end of 1974, the year in which, according to President de Klerk, the government decided to develop nuclear weapons. It was at the Y plant where South Africa eventually produced the HEU for nuclear weapons. In that same year, a clandestine facility for criticality experiments was established behind a hill at Pelindaba. Subsequently, a commercial-scale "Z" plant enrichment facility was built at Pelindaba East. South Africa also conducted secret research and development on the gas-centrifuge process at Valindaba during the 1980s. Also as part of this secret program, two nuclear test shafts were completed at a site in the Kalahari Desert in 1977.[3]

In mid-1977, a Soviet observation satellite revealed preparations for an underground nuclear test at the Kalahari site, spurring Washington and Moscow to apply substantial diplomatic pressure on Pretoria, which soon abandoned the site and sealed the boreholes. Nevertheless, efforts continued to produce weapons-grade uranium and to design a nuclear device.[4] The first dummy device, without a core of HEU, was produced in August 1977, followed by a smaller version in 1978. By November 1979, once sufficient HEU had been produced, the first operational nuclear device was ready.

The South African officials involved in the program claim that the nuclear weapons were only intended to be used as part of a "three-phase nuclear strategy" to deter potential adversaries (especially Soviet-backed forces from neighboring states) and to compel Western involvement should deterrence fail. Phase 1 involved neither confirming nor denying its nuclear capability. In phase 2, if faced with imminent attack, Pretoria would reveal its capability to Western leaders to force their intervention. If that failed, phase 3 would involve overt nuclear testing to demonstrate South Africa's ability and willingness to use nuclear weapons.[5] In 1988, South Africa even took the preliminary steps necessary to put phase 3 into effect when it clandestinely reopened one of the boreholes at the Kalahari test site (and built a metal concealment shed over the shaft) as part of a contingency plan to help bring an end to the Angolan war.[6]

South Africa's nuclear weapons used the gun-type design used for the Hiroshima bomb and were designed to be delivered by aircraft. South African officials stated that great attention was given to safety, security, and reliability, which suggests that military use had not been ruled out altogether. The still-undeclared phase 4 contingency is further borne out by South Africa's substantial investment in the development and production of intermediate-range ballistic missiles to eventually be fitted with nuclear warheads, and the completion in 1989 of the Advena nuclear warhead production facility. This facility not only had a missile handling capability but was also to include a "cold implosion test facility," which was immediately adjacent to South Africa's original air-deliverable bomb production facility.[7]

De Klerk's electoral victory in September 1989 signaled the end of the nuclear weapons program. On February 26, 1990, he issued internal orders to terminate the effort and to dismantle all weapons. The shutdown and decommissioning of the Y uranium enrichment plant at Pelindaba East began in July 1990; six nuclear weapons were dismantled, and the hardware and technical documents destroyed. Both the original facility (known as the Circle building) and the adjacent Advena complex, the weapon-manufacturing site, were decontaminated and converted for commercial use (and when commercialization failed, the buildings were closed). By early September 1991, all the HEU had been recast and sent back to the AEC for permanent storage, ten days before South Africa signed the safeguard agreement with the IAEA. On August 19, 1994, after completing its inspection, the IAEA confirmed that one partial and six complete nuclear devices had been dismantled.[8]

Although the process was completed by 1992, de Klerk did not reveal the program's existence until March 1993. In his speech to parliament, he denied that South Africa had received any foreign assistance for its nuclear weapons program or that it had been involved in any nuclear weapons testing, either alone or with another country.[9] In 1979, a U.S. satellite detected a flash over the Indian Ocean that was assumed by many analysts to have been a joint Israeli–South African test, although an expert inquiry at the time was inconclusive. In

1997, however, Deputy Foreign Minister Aziz Pahad and former chief of staff General Constand Viljoen said that Israel had supported South Africa's program,[10] supplying tritium for use in boosted fission weapons in return for natural uranium.[11]

Conversion to Civilian Programs

Since 1990, the AEC has followed its 2000 Plus Plan, refocusing on commercial rather than strategic activities. It has been renamed the South African Nuclear Energy Corporation (NECSA) and receives government funding for technology development and industrialization. The Safari research reactor is now used mainly for vocational training and isotope production and is currently fueled with HEU derived from South Africa's dismantled nuclear weapons.[12] Its continued use of HEU fuel remains a bone of contention with the United States. Since June 1994, the United States has been urging a conversion to low-enriched uranium (LEU) fuel. In 1995, the U.S. Department of Energy and the AEC signed an agreement allowing the transfer of American nuclear technology to South Africa to assist in that conversion. Many South African experts and government officials believe, nevertheless, that the conversion is not economically practical. A NECSA study done in conjunction with the U.S. Argonne National Laboratory was submitted to the South African Department of Minerals and Energy in December 2001, arguing that a conversion to LEU silicide fuel would not significantly affect the reactor's production.[13]

Although the South African government has not directly responded to this study, some steps are being taken by NECSA to explore the possibility of using low-enriched uranium silicide as reactor fuel. In particular, NECSA has begun efforts to develop a prototype LEU silicide fuel fabrication facility, and, pending regulatory approval, will move forward with plans to construct two more full-scale fuel fabrication facilities. If all goes according to plan, NECSA believes that it will be producing LEU silicide fuel for potential use in the Safari reactor by April 2005.[14] Moreover, Charles Piani, the senior manager in charge of Safari, has stated that once he is given government approval, the actual reactor conversion process can begin.[15]

Meanwhile, the restructuring and dismantlement of South Africa's nuclear complex continues. The semicommercial Z enrichment plant was closed in March 1995,[16] and decommissioning was carried out from 1996 to 1999. As of January 2003, it was listed along with the Y enrichment plant as being "partially/fully decommissioned."[17] Even after the decommissioning of these facilities, however, the research and development of uranium enrichment technology continued. In February 1996, the AEC signed a contract with the French nuclear firm Cogema to develop jointly a molecular laser isotope separation (MLIS) enrichment method.[18] A demonstration-scale MLIS facility was to be built at Pelindaba East to enrich uranium for the Koeberg nuclear power plant and other reactors, but the Department of Minerals and Energy canceled that plan. The AEC then decided to build a pilot facility inside the former Z plant process building, but in December 1997 funding and technical problems led the AEC to cancel the MLIS project altogether. Currently, South Africa has no uranium enrichment capabilities. According to the IAEA, Eskom Holdings Limited, the company that owns the Koeberg power plants, procures enrichment services on the international market.[19]

Nonproliferation Concerns

Although South Africa emerged as a champion of nuclear nonproliferation at the NPT Extension Conference in 1995, concerns have been raised about the alleged role played by a number of South African individuals and entities in A. Q. Khan's black market nuclear network. Though investigations are still ongoing and much is not yet known, it is certain that South Africa, with its weakly enforced export control laws, served as a major transshipment point for nuclear weapons technology on its way to Libya, Iran, and North Korea.[20] Four individuals, some of whom were involved in the apartheid-era nuclear program, have been arrested already. According to a September 2004 report in the *Washington Post*, IAEA investigators have learned that one South African company imported equipment necessary for uranium enrichment from Europe, modified the items to meet Libyan specifications, and then shipped them to another middleman who would complete the delivery.[21]

Pretoria's dealings with Iran have also raised some proliferation questions. During the apartheid era, Iran had good relations with the now-ruling African National Congress (ANC) party. In August 1995, South Africa signed a peaceful nuclear cooperation agreement with Iran,[22] despite a United States–led international nuclear embargo. The ANC government announced in June 1996 that it had made no uranium exports to Iran during the previous five years.[23] Reports in 1997, however, alleged that AEC head Waldo Stumpf and then–minister of minerals and energy affairs Pik Botha had met in early 1996 with Gholam Reza Aghazadeh, Iran's oil minister at the time. Aghazadeh reportedly presented Stumpf with a shopping list of items needed to make nuclear weapons. Stumpf has denied that the meeting took place, but Botha confirmed it, adding that South Africa had rejected Iran's request for equipment.[24]

Reports surrounding South African-Iranian nuclear cooperation arose again in the summer of 2004, after an August meeting between Iranian defense minister Ali Shamkhani and South African defense minister Patrick Lekota. The two signed a bilateral cooperation agreement, which, according to one Israeli media source, included a deal for South Africa to sell uranium to Iran. While Pretoria denied that such a sale was part of the agreement, Lekota did publicly state that Iran had the legitimate right to pursue nuclear technology for peaceful purposes.[25] However, ongoing IAEA investigations into Iran's past and present nuclear activities have not uncovered any illegal or dubious South African *governmental* assistance to Tehran.

Last, reports in the fall of 1997 suggested that the AEC was secretly selling equipment from Pelindaba to China. Although the transfers appeared to have little relevance to China's weapons program, the secretive nature of the deal raised concerns about the autonomy of the AEC's operations.[26]

Missile Analysis

In the 1980s, South Africa's Armscor company developed a medium-range ballistic missile with Israeli assistance under the guise of a space launch vehicle program. It was tested in July 1989. The United States imposed missile proliferation sanctions on Armscor in October 1991.[27] South Africa announced in June 1993 that it was canceling the project,[28] and in October 1994 it signed an agreement with the United States pledging to eliminate its medium-range ballistic missile program and to abide by the Missile Technology Control Regime (MTCR).[29] Despite reports suggesting that in 1993 South African engineers and scientists were offering missile expertise to some Middle Eastern countries,[30] South Africa was formally admitted to the MTCR in September 1995.[31] In addition to a ballistic missile capability, South Africa has three types of unmanned aerial vehicles and is developing a land-attack cruise missile, the Torgos,[32] capable of traveling up to 300 kilometers.[33]

Biological and Chemical Weapons Analysis

South Africa pursued secret chemical and biological warfare programs during the 1980s (and abandoned them in 1993), despite having joined the Biological Weapons Convention in 1975.[34] It ratified the Chemical Weapons Convention in September 1995, although reports suggested that South African scientists were helping Libya's quest for biological and chemical weapons.[35] In October 1998, the South African Truth and Reconciliation Commission released a report containing 3,500 pages of testimony about human rights violations during the apartheid era.[36] It included a chapter on Project Coast, a clandestine government chemical and biological warfare program conducted during the 1980s and 1990s.

Project Coast started in 1983, ostensibly to produce equipment for defensive purposes, including masks and protective suits. Despite vehement assertions to the contrary, testimony showed that the program went well beyond defensive purposes. Key officials said that Project Coast sponsored the production of chocolates laced with anthrax, umbrellas with poisoned tips, screwdrivers fitted with poison-filled cylinders, and clothing infused with lethal chemicals. Biological and chemical agents were developed to make attacks appear to be the result of natural causes. Other apparently unexecuted ideas included research into drugs to render black women infertile and a plan to gradually poison Nelson Mandela.

NOTES

1. David Albright and Kimberly Kramer, "Fissile Material: Stockpiles Still Growing," *Bulletin of the Atomic Scientists*, November/December 2004, pp. 14–16.
2. "De Klerk Tells World South Africa Built and Dismantled Six Nuclear Weapons," *Nuclear Fuel*, March 29, 1993, p. 6; Helmoed-Romer Heitman, "South Africa Built Six Nuclear Weapons," *Jane's Defense Weekly*, April 10, 1993, p. 14.
3. Mark Hibbs, "South Africa's Secret Nuclear Program: From a PNE to a Deterrent," *Nuclear Fuel*, May 10, 1993, p. 3; Hibbs, "South Africa's Secret Nuclear Program: The Dismantling," *Nuclear Fuel*, May 24, 1993, p. 9; Hibbs, "Pretoria Replicated Hiroshima Bomb in Seven Years, Then

Froze Design," *Nucleonics Week*, May 6, 1993, p. 16; David Albright, "South Africa and the Affordable Bomb," *Bulletin of the Atomic Scientists*, July/August 1994, p. 37.

4. Hibbs, "South Africa: From PNE to a Deterrent," p. 3; and Albright, "South Africa and the Affordable Bomb," p. 37.
5. Albright, "South Africa and the Affordable Bomb," p. 37; Roger Jardine, J. W. de Villers, and Mitchell Reiss, "Why South Africa Gave Up the Bomb," *Foreign Affairs*, November/December 1993; Daryl Howlett and John Simpson, "Nuclearization and Denuclearization in South Africa," *Survival*, Autumn 1993.
6. Frank V. Pabian, "The South African Nuclear Weapons Program: Lessons for U.S. Non-Proliferation Policy," *Nonproliferation Review*, Fall 1995, p. 9; available at cns.miis.edu/pubs/npr/pdfs/pabian31.pdf.
7. Albright, "South Africa and the Affordable Bomb," p. 37.
8. "IAEA Confirms All South African Warheads Destroyed," Reuters, August 19, 1994; Michael Knapik, "South African AEC Head Says Stockpile of HEU Will Be Maintained for Safari," *Nuclear Fuel*, August 16, 1993, p. 5.
9. Yossi Melman, "South Africa Admits: Israel Helped Us Develop Nuclear Weapon," *Ha'aretz*, April 20, 1997. For a good recounting of the story, see David Albright and Corey Gay, "A Flash from the Past," *Bulletin of the Atomic Scientists*, November/December 1997, pp. 15–17.
10. "Israel Reportedly Helped South Africa Develop Nuclear Weapons in the Early 1980s," Associated Press, April 20, 1997.
11. Yossi Melman, "Israel–S. African Nuclear Tie," *Ha'aretz*, April 21,1997, in FBIS-NES-97-082.
12. Ann MacLachlan, "New Study Finds Little Financial Loss in Converting Safari to LEU," *Nuclear Fuel*, October 2, 2001; see also Ann MacLachlan, "Safari Operators Still Waiting for Pretoria to Approve LEU Conversion."
13. Ann MacLachlan, "New Study Finds Little Financial Loss in Converting Safari to LEU," *Platts Global Energy*, October 1, 2001.
14. Phone conversation with James Snelgrove, Reduced Enrichment for Research and Test Reactors Program, Argonne National Laboratory, U.S. Department of Energy, August 31, 2004.
15. Ann MacLachlan. "Safari Operators Still Waiting for Pretoria to Approve LEU Conversion," *Nuclear Fuel*, September 1, 2003.
16. David Albright, Frans Berkhout, and William Walker, *Plutonium and Highly Enriched Uranium 1996: World Inventories, Capabilities and Policies* (Oxford: Oxford University Press, 1997), p. 383.
17. Nuclear Liabilities Management Online, a Division of the South African Nuclear Energy Corporation, "Decommissioning of Plants and Buildings," available at www.radwaste.co.za/closed_down_plant.htm.
18. Lynda Loxton, "France, S. Africa Agree on Nuclear Cooperation," Reuters, February 29, 1996; Ann MacLachan, "Cogema to Help South Africa's AEC Develop MLIS Enrichment Process," *Nuclear Fuel*, March 11, 1996, p. 4.
19. International Atomic Energy Agency, "Country Nuclear Power Profiles, 2003."
20. Jacob Blackford, "Asher Karni Case Shows Weakness in Nuclear Export Controls," ISIS Analysis, September 8, 2004. Available at www.isis-online.org/publications/southafrica/asherkarni.html.
21. Dafna Linzer and Craig Timberg, "S. African's Arrest Seen as Key to Nuclear Black Market," *Washington Post*, September 4, 2004.
22. "S. Africa Approves Peaceful Nuclear Ties with Iran," Reuters, August 21, 1995.
23. "Energy Minister—No Uranium Sent to Iran in Last Five Years," *SAPA* (South Africa), February 21, 1996, in FBIS-TAC-96-007, June 17, 1996.
24. Al J. Venter, "Iran's Nuclear Ambition," *Jane's Intelligence Review*, September 1997, pp. 29–31.
25. "South Africa, Iran Discuss Defence Cooperation," *Jerusalem Post*, August 17, 2004; "S. Africa Says Won't Sell Uranium to Iran," *Jerusalem Post*, August 18, 2004; "S. Africa Minister Backs Iran's 'Legitimate Right' to Peaceful Nuclear Energy," BBC, August 17, 2004.
26. "National Party Condemns Nuclear Technology Sale to China," *SAPA* (South Africa), December 14, 1997, in FBIS-AFR-97-348, December 14, 1997; "China-Nuclear," Associated Press, December 16, 1997.
27. David Hoffman and R. Jeffrey Smith, "President Waives Sanctions for Israel," *Washington Post*, October 27, 1991.

28. Fred Bridgland, "South Africa Scraps Missile Plan after U.S. Pressure," *Daily Telegraph*, July 1, 1993.
29. "U.S. and South Africa Sign Missile Nonproliferation Agreement," U.S. Department of State press release, October 4, 1994.
30. Henry Sokolski, "Ending South Africa's Rocket Program: A Nonproliferation Success," unpublished paper, Non-Proliferation Education Center, August 27, 1996.
31. "South Africa Gains Entrance to MTCR," Armed Force Newswire, September 15, 1995.
32. International Institute for Strategic Studies, *The Military Balance: 2004–2005* (Oxford: Oxford University Press, 2004).
33. Andrew Feickert, "Missile Survey: Ballistic and Cruise Missiles of Foreign Countries," Congressional Research Service, March 5, 2004.
34. Paul Taylor, "Toxic S. African Arms Raise Concern," *Washington Post*, February 28, 1995.
35. James Adams, "Gadaffi Lures South Africa's Top Germ Warfare Scientists," *Sunday Times*, February 26, 1995; Alexandra Zavis, "Mandela Says Chemical Weapons Figures May Be in Libya," Associated Press, March 2, 1995; and Lynne Duke, "Drug Bust Exposes S. African Arms Probes," *Washington Post*, February 1, 1997; "Libya Was S.A.'s Closest Ally for Chemical Warfare," South African Press Association, November 23, 1999; "Basson Met With Libyan Secret Agents," South African Press Association, March 27, 2000.
36. Truth and Reconciliation Commission Final Report, presented to President Mandela, October 29, 1998.

Table 21.1. **South Africa's Nuclear Infrastructure**

Name/Location of Facility	Type/Status	IAEA Safeguards
Former Nuclear Weapon (R&D) Complex		
Pelindaba Nuclear Research Center	Nuclear weapons production and assembly facility, closed[1]	IAEA visited and verified dismantlement
Building 5000 complex (isolated buildings at Pelindaba)	Dedicated to the development and assembly of nuclear explosives, closed[2]	IAEA visited and verified dismantlement
Circle Building/ Advena Central Laboratories	Two generations of buildings involved in nuclear weapon production and assembly, closed[3]	IAEA visited and verified dismantlement
Upington (Vastrap Range) Kalahari	Nuclear test site; closed[4]	IAEA visited and verified sealing of shafts
Power Reactors		
Koeberg I	Light-water, LEU, 900 MWe, operating	Yes
Koeberg II	Light-water, LEU, 900 MWe, operating	Yes
Research Reactors		
Safari–I, Pelindaba	Tank-type, light-water, ~90% HEU, 20 MWt, operating[5]	Yes
Uranium Enrichment		
Z-Plant Pelindaba East (Valindaba)	Semi-commercial plant able to produce low-enriched uranium, jet-nozzle ("helikon") method, closed	Yes
MLIS plant Pelindaba East (Valindaba)	Demonstration-scale MLIS uranium-enrichment plant canceled,[6] nuclear materials present	Yes
Y-Plant Pelindaba East (Valindaba)	Pilot-scale facility for producing weapons-grade uranium, aerodynamic process, closed[7]	IAEA visited and verified dismantlement
Reprocessing/Plutonium Extraction		
Pelindaba	Hot-cell complex, operating[8]	Yes

Uranium Processing		
Palabora	Uranium ore processing, operating	No
Hartebeestfontein	Uranium ore processing, shut down	No
Vaal reefs-1	Uranium ore processing, shut down	No
Western Areas	Uranium ore processing, shut down[9]	No
Buffelsfontein	Uranium ore processing, decommissioned[10]	No
Central Processing Plant (Gauteng)	Uranium ore processing, operating	No
Vaal Reefs-2	Uranium ore processing, operating	No
Pelindaba East (Valindaba)	Semi-commercial-scale uranium conversion plant (UF_6), shut down[11]	Yes
Pelindaba	MTR fuel-fabrication pilot plant, operating	Yes
Pelindaba	LEU fuel-fabrication plant, shut down in 1996	Yes

Abbreviations

HEU highly enriched uranium
IAEA International Atomic Energy Agency
LEU low-enriched uranium
MLIS molecular laser isotope separation
MWe megawatts electric
MWt megawatts thermal

Sources

"South Africa" (Datafile), *Nuclear Engineering International,* January 1992. Mark Hibbs, "South Africa Reinstatement Ends 18-Year Ban from IAEA Board," *Nucleonics Week,* September 29, 1994. IAEA, *Annual Report for 1992* (Vienna: IAEA, 1993). IAEA, *Nuclear Fuel Cycle Information Systems,* available at www-nfcis.iaea.org/NFCISMAin.asp?Region=The%20World&Country=All&Type=All&Status=All&Scale=All&Order=2&Page=1&RightP=List&Table=1. IAEA, *Nuclear Research Reactors in the World,* available at www.iaea.org/worldatom/rrdb/. IAEA, *Power Reactor Information System,* available at www.iaea.org/programmes/a2/index.html. Nuclear Engineering International, *World Nuclear Industry Handbook 2004* (Sidcup, U.K.: Wilmington Publishing, 2004). Leonard S. Spector, with Jacqueline R. Smith, *Nuclear Ambitions* (Boulder, Colo.: Westview Press, 1990).

(table continues on the following page)

Table 21.1. **South Africa's Nuclear Infrastructure** (continued)

NOTES

1. South Africa's first nuclear device was produced at this facility.
2. One critical experiment was conducted at this facility; it is also the site where the first nuclear weapon was produced.
3. Five additional nuclear devices were manufactured at the Circle building between April 1982 and November 1989. When then-president De Klerk canceled the nuclear weapons program, construction of the Advena Central Laboratories had just been completed, and equipment was being moved into the facilities. The laboratories continue to conduct non-nuclear research.
4. The Kalahari test site, which was never used, consisted of two shafts of 385 meters and 216 meters in depth, both 1 meter in diameter. The shafts were sealed with concrete under IAEA supervision.
5. The reactor originally ran on 90 percent enriched fuel but was downgraded to 45 percent enriched fuel following the cutoff of fuel supplies by the United States in 1977. In the early 1990s, South Africa resumed the use of HEU in the reactor, with material from its dismantled nuclear weapons. Ann MacLachlan, "Converting Safari-I to LEU Fuel Would Be Too Costly, Study Finds," *Nuclear Fuel,* October 9, 1995, p. 10. The South African Nuclear Energy Corporation is currently awaiting government approval to convert the Safari reactor to LEU fuel, and it is taking steps to prepare for such a conversion. Ann MacLachlan, "Safari Operators Still Waiting for Pretoria to Approve LEU Conversion," *Nuclear Fuel,* September 1, 2003.
6. "South Africa: Atomic Corporation Abandons French Technology Project," *Sunday Independent,* December 14, 1997, in FBIS-AFR-97-348, December 14, 1997; "South Africa: Pilot Plant to Commercialise Uranium Enrichment Process," *Financial Mail,* November 1, 1996, in FBIS-AFR-96-212, November 1, 1996.
7. According to South Africa's declaration to the IAEA, the plant generated about 1,500 kilograms of enriched uranium while active, ranging from low-enriched uranium to weapons-grade HEU. Out of this inventory, 350 kilograms had been enriched to 90 percent U-235 and above. Each South African nuclear weapon required an estimated 55 kilograms of weapons-grade uranium. South African officials have indicated that they would like to keep at least a portion of the weapons-grade HEU to fuel the Safari-I research reactor.
8. Functions to separate Molybdenum-99 from spent fuel. Molybdenum-99 is produced for medical purposes. One reason that some in South Africa have been hesitant to convert the Safari reactor to LEU fuel is that it may make production of Molybdenum more difficult.
9. The IAEA reports that Western Areas has been shut down, though the *2004 World Nuclear Industry Handbook* states that it is operational.
10. The IAEA reports that Buffelsfontein has been decommissioned, though the *2004 World Nuclear Industry Handbook* states that it is operational.
11. The IAEA reports that the uranium conversion facility at Pelindaba East was shut down in 1997, though the *2004 World Nuclear Industry Handbook* reports that it is still operational. There are similar discrepancies for Buffelsfontein.

Appendixes

PREVIOUS PAGE: *The International Conference on the Relationship Between Disarmament and Development, held at UN Headquarters in New York, August 24, 1987.* (UN-DPI/SAW LWIN)

The Treaty on the Non-Proliferation of Nuclear Weapons

The Treaty

Signed at Washington, London, and Moscow July 1, 1968
Ratification advised by U.S. Senate March 13, 1969
Ratified by U.S. President November 24, 1969
U.S. ratification deposited at Washington, London, and Moscow March 5, 1970
Proclaimed by U.S. President March 5, 1970
Entered into force March 5, 1970

The States concluding this Treaty, hereinafter referred to as the "Parties to the Treaty,"

Considering the devastation that would be visited upon all mankind by a nuclear war and the consequent need to make every effort to avert the danger of such a war and to take measures to safeguard the security of peoples,

Believing that the proliferation of nuclear weapons would seriously enhance the danger of nuclear war,

In conformity with resolutions of the United Nations General Assembly calling for the conclusion of an agreement on the prevention of wider dissemination of nuclear weapons,

Undertaking to cooperate in facilitating the application of International Atomic Energy Agency safeguards on peaceful nuclear activities,

Expressing their support for research, development and other efforts to further the application, within the framework of the International Atomic Energy Agency safeguards system, of the principle of safeguarding effectively the flow of source and special fissionable materials by use of instruments and other techniques at certain strategic points,

Affirming the principle that the benefits of peaceful applications of nuclear technology, including any technological by-products which may be derived by nuclear-weapon States from the development of nuclear explosive devices, should be available for peaceful purposes to all Parties of the Treaty, whether nuclear-weapon or non-nuclear weapon States,

Convinced that, in furtherance of this principle, all Parties to the Treaty are entitled to participate in the fullest possible exchange of scientific information for, and to contribute alone or in cooperation with other States to, the further development of the applications of atomic energy for peaceful purposes,

Declaring their intention to achieve at the earliest possible date the cessation of the nuclear arms race and to undertake effective measures in the direction of nuclear disarmament,

Urging the cooperation of all States in the attainment of this objective,

Recalling the determination expressed by the Parties to the 1963 Treaty banning nuclear weapon tests in the atmosphere, in outer space and under water in its Preamble to seek to achieve the discontinuance of all test explosions of nuclear weapons for all time and to continue negotiations to this end,

Desiring to further the easing of international tension and the strengthening of trust between States in order to facilitate the cessation of the manufacture of nuclear weapons, the liquidation of all their existing stockpiles, and the elimination from national arsenals of nuclear weapons and the means of their delivery pursuant to a Treaty on general and complete disarmament under strict and effective international control,

Recalling that, in accordance with the Charter of the United Nations, States must refrain in their international relations from the threat or use of force against the territorial integrity or political independence of any State, or in any other manner inconsistent with the Purposes of the United Nations, and that the establishment and maintenance of international peace and security are to be promoted with the least diversion for armaments of the world's human and economic resources,

Have agreed as follows:

Article I

Each nuclear-weapon State Party to the Treaty undertakes not to transfer to any recipient whatsoever nuclear weapons or other nuclear explosive devices or control over such weapons or explosive devices directly, or indirectly; and not in any way to assist, encourage, or induce any non-nuclear weapon State to manufacture or otherwise acquire nuclear weapons or other nuclear explosive devices, or control over such weapons or explosive devices.

Article II

Each non-nuclear-weapon State Party to the Treaty undertakes not to receive the transfer from any transferor whatsoever of nuclear weapons or other nuclear explosive devices or of control over such weapons or explosive devices directly, or indirectly; not to manufacture or otherwise acquire nuclear weapons or other nuclear explosive devices; and not to seek or receive any assistance in the manufacture of nuclear weapons or other nuclear explosive devices.

Article III

1. Each non-nuclear-weapon State Party to the Treaty undertakes to accept safeguards, as set forth in an agreement to be negotiated and concluded with the International Atomic Energy Agency in accordance with the Statute of the International Atomic Energy Agency and the Agency's safeguards system, for the exclusive purpose of verification of the fulfillment of its obligations assumed under this Treaty with a view to preventing diversion of nuclear energy from peaceful uses to nuclear weapons or other nuclear explosive devices. Procedures for the safeguards required by this article shall be followed with respect to source or special fissionable material whether it is being produced, processed or used in any principal nuclear facility or is outside any such facility. The safeguards required by this article shall be applied to all source or special fissionable material in all peaceful nuclear activities within the territory of such State, under its jurisdiction, or carried out under its control anywhere.
2. Each State Party to the Treaty undertakes not to provide: (a) source or special fissionable material, or (b) equipment or material especially designed or prepared for the processing, use or production of special fissionable material, to any non-nuclear-weapon State for peaceful purposes, unless the source or special fissionable material shall be subject to the safeguards required by this article.
3. The safeguards required by this article shall be implemented in a manner designed to comply with Article IV of this Treaty, and to avoid hampering the economic or technological development of the Parties or international cooperation in the field of peaceful nuclear activities, including the international exchange of nuclear material and equipment for the processing, use or production of nuclear material for peaceful purposes in accordance with the provisions of this article and the principle of safeguarding set forth in the Preamble of the Treaty.
4. Non-nuclear-weapon States Party to the Treaty shall conclude agreements with the International Atomic Energy Agency to meet the requirements of this article either individually or together with other States in accordance with the Statute of the International Atomic Energy Agency. Negotiation of such agreements shall commence within 180 days from the original entry into force of this Treaty. For States depositing their instruments of ratification or accession after the 180-day period, negotiation of such agreements shall commence not later than the date of such deposit. Such agreements shall enter into force not later than eighteen months after the date of initiation of negotiations.

Article IV

1. Nothing in this Treaty shall be interpreted as affecting the inalienable right of all the Parties to the Treaty to develop research, production and use of nuclear energy for peaceful purposes without discrimination and in conformity with articles I and II of this Treaty.
2. All the Parties to the Treaty undertake to facilitate, and have the right to participate in, the fullest possible exchange of equipment, materials and scientific and technological information for the peaceful uses of nuclear energy. Parties to the Treaty in a position to do so shall also cooperate in contributing alone or together with other States or international organizations to the further development of the applications of nuclear energy for peaceful purposes, especially in the territories of non-nuclear-weapon States Party to the Treaty, with due consideration for the needs of the developing areas of the world.

Article V

Each party to the Treaty undertakes to take appropriate measures to ensure that, in accordance with this Treaty, under appropriate international observation and through appropriate international procedures, potential benefits from any peaceful applications of nuclear explosions will be made available to non-nuclear-weapon States Party to the Treaty on a nondiscriminatory basis and that the charge to such Parties for the explosive devices used will be as low as possible and exclude any charge for research and development. Non-nuclear-weapon States Party to the Treaty shall be able to obtain such benefits, pursuant to a special international agreement or agreements, through an appropriate international body with adequate representation of non-nuclear-weapon States. Negotiations on this subject shall commence as soon as possible after the Treaty enters into force. Non-nuclear-weapon States Party to the Treaty so desiring may also obtain such benefits pursuant to bilateral agreements.

Article VI

Each of the Parties to the Treaty undertakes to pursue negotiations in good faith on effective measures relating to cessation of the nuclear arms race at an early date and to nuclear disarmament, and on a Treaty on general and complete disarmament under strict and effective international control.

Article VII

Nothing in this Treaty affects the right of any group of States to conclude regional treaties in order to assure the total absence of nuclear weapons in their respective territories.

Article VIII

1. Any Party to the Treaty may propose amendments to this Treaty. The text of any proposed amendment shall be submitted to the Depositary Governments which shall circulate it to all Parties to the Treaty. Thereupon, if requested to do so by one-third or more of the Parties to the Treaty, the Depositary Governments shall convene a conference, to which they shall invite all the Parties to the Treaty, to consider such an amendment.

2. Any amendment to this Treaty must be approved by a majority of the votes of all the Parties to the Treaty, including the votes of all nuclear-weapon States Party to the Treaty and all other Parties which, on the date the amendment is circulated, are members of the Board of Governors of the International Atomic Energy Agency. The amendment shall enter into force for each Party that deposits its instrument of ratification of the amendment upon the deposit of such instruments of ratification by a majority of all the Parties, including the instruments of ratification of all nuclear-weapon States Party to the Treaty and all other Parties which, on the date the amendment is circulated, are members of the Board of Governors of the International Atomic Energy Agency. Thereafter, it shall enter into force for any other Party upon the deposit of its instrument of ratification of the amendment.

3. Five years after the entry into force of this Treaty, a conference of Parties to the Treaty shall be held in Geneva, Switzerland, in order to review the operation of this Treaty with a view to assuring that the purposes of the Preamble and the provisions of the Treaty are being realized. At intervals of five years thereafter, a majority of the Parties to the Treaty may obtain, by submitting a proposal to this effect to the Depositary Governments, the convening of further conferences with the same objective of reviewing the operation of the Treaty.

Article IX

1. This Treaty shall be open to all States for signature. Any State which does not sign the Treaty before its entry into force in accordance with paragraph 3 of this article may accede to it at any time.

2. This Treaty shall be subject to ratification by signatory States. Instruments of ratification and instruments of accession shall be deposited with the Governments of the United States of America, the United Kingdom of Great Britain and Northern Ireland and the Union of Soviet Socialist Republics, which are hereby designated the Depositary Governments.

3. This Treaty shall enter into force after its ratification by the States, the Governments of which are designated Depositaries of the Treaty, and forty other States signatory to this Treaty and the deposit of their instruments of ratification. For the purposes of this Treaty, a nuclear-weapon State is one which

has manufactured and exploded a nuclear weapon or other nuclear explosive device prior to January 1, 1967.

4. For States whose instruments of ratification or accession are deposited subsequent to the entry into force of this Treaty, it shall enter into force on the date of the deposit of their instruments of ratification or accession.
5. The Depositary Governments shall promptly inform all signatory and acceding States of the date of each signature, the date of deposit of each instrument of ratification or of accession, the date of the entry into force of this Treaty, and the date of receipt of any requests for convening a conference or other notices.
6. This Treaty shall be registered by the Depositary Governments pursuant to article 102 of the Charter of the United Nations.

Article X

1. Each Party shall in exercising its national sovereignty have the right to withdraw from the Treaty if it decides that extraordinary events, related to the subject matter of this Treaty, have jeopardized the supreme interests of its country. It shall give notice of such withdrawal to all other Parties to the Treaty and to the United Nations Security Council three months in advance. Such notice shall include a statement of the extraordinary events it regards as having jeopardized its supreme interests.
2. Twenty-five years after the entry into force of the Treaty, a conference shall be convened to decide whether the Treaty shall continue in force indefinitely, or shall be extended for an additional fixed period or periods. This decision shall be taken by a majority of the Parties to the Treaty.

Article XI

This Treaty, the English, Russian, French, Spanish, and Chinese texts of which are equally authentic, shall be deposited in the archives of the Depositary Governments. Duly certified copies of this Treaty shall be transmitted by the Depositary Governments to the Governments of the signatory and acceding States.

IN WITNESS WHEREOF the undersigned, duly authorized, have signed this Treaty.

DONE in triplicate, at the cities of Washington, London and Moscow, this first day of July one thousand nine hundred sixty-eight.

The Convention on the Prohibition of the Development, Production and Stockpiling of Bacteriological (Biological) and Toxin Weapons and on Their Destruction

Signed at Washington, London, and Moscow April 10, 1972
Ratification advised by U.S. Senate December 16, 1974
Ratified by U.S. President January 22, 1975
U.S. ratification deposited at Washington, London, and Moscow March 26, 1975
Proclaimed by U.S. President March 26, 1975
Entered into force March 26, 1975

The States Parties to this Convention,

Determined to act with a view to achieving effective progress towards general and complete disarmament, including the prohibition and elimination of all types of weapons of mass destruction, and convinced that the prohibition of the development, production and stockpiling of chemical and bacteriological (biological) weapons and their elimination, through effective measures, will facilitate the achievement of general and complete disarmament under strict and effective international control,

Recognizing the important significance of the Protocol for the Prohibition of the Use in War of Asphyxiating, Poisonous, or Other Gases, and of Bacteriological Methods of Warfare, signed at Geneva on June 17, 1925, and conscious also of the contribution which the said Protocol has already made, and continues to make, to mitigating the horrors of war,

Reaffirming their adherence to the principles and objectives of that Protocol and calling upon all States to comply strictly with them,

Recalling that the General Assembly of the United Nations has repeatedly condemned all actions contrary to the principles and objectives of the Geneva Protocol of June 17, 1925,

Desiring to contribute to the strengthening of confidence between peoples and the general improvement of the international atmosphere,

Desiring also to contribute to the realization of the purposes and principles of the Charter of the United Nations,

Convinced of the importance and urgency of eliminating from the arsenals of States, through effective measures, such dangerous weapons of mass destruction as those using chemical or bacteriological (biological) agents,

Recognizing that an agreement on the prohibition of bacteriological (biological) and toxin weapons represents a first possible step towards the achievement of agreement on effective measures also for the prohibition of the development, production and stockpiling of chemical weapons, and determined to continue negotiations to that end,

Determined, for the sake of all mankind, to exclude completely the possibility of bacteriological (biological) agents and toxins being used as weapons,

Convinced that such use would be repugnant to the conscience of mankind and that no effort should be spared to minimize this risk,

Have agreed as follows:

Article I

Each State Party to this Convention undertakes never in any circumstances to develop, produce, stockpile or otherwise acquire or retain:

(1) Microbial or other biological agents, or toxins whatever their origin or method of production, of types and in quantities that have no justification for prophylactic, protective or other peaceful purposes;

(2) Weapons, equipment or means of delivery designed to use such agents or toxins for hostile purposes or in armed conflict.

Article II

Each State Party to this Convention undertakes to destroy, or to divert to peaceful purposes, as soon as possible but not later than nine months after the entry into force of the Convention, all agents, toxins, weapons, equipment and means of delivery specified in article I of the Convention, which are in its possession or under its jurisdiction or control. In implementing the provisions of this article all necessary safety precautions shall be observed to protect populations and the environment.

Article III

Each State Party to this Convention undertakes not to transfer to any recipient whatsoever, directly or indirectly, and not in any way to assist, encourage, or induce any State, group of States or international organizations to manufacture or otherwise acquire any of the agents, toxins, weapons, equipment or means of delivery specified in article I of the Convention.

Article IV

Each State Party to this Convention shall, in accordance with its constitutional processes, take any necessary measures to prohibit and prevent the development, production, stockpiling, acquisition, or retention of the agents, toxins, weapons, equipment and means of delivery specified in article I of the Convention, within the territory of such State, under its jurisdiction or under its control anywhere.

Article V

The States Parties to this Convention undertake to consult one another and to cooperate in solving any problems which may arise in relation to the objective of, or in the application of the provisions of, the Convention. Consultation and cooperation pursuant to this article may also be undertaken through appropriate international procedures within the framework of the United Nations and in accordance with its Charter.

Article VI

(1) Any State Party to this Convention which finds that any other State Party is acting in breach of obligations deriving from the provisions of the Convention may lodge a complaint with the Security Council of the United Nations. Such a complaint should include all possible evidence confirming its validity, as well as a request for its consideration by the Security Council.

(2) Each State Party to this Convention undertakes to cooperate in carrying out any investigation which the Security Council may initiate, in accordance with the provisions of the Charter of the United Nations, on the basis of the complaint received by the Council. The Security Council shall inform the States Parties to the Convention of the results of the investigation.

Article VII

Each State Party to this Convention undertakes to provide or support assistance, in accordance with the United Nations Charter, to any Party to the Convention which so requests, if the Security Council decides that such Party has been exposed to danger as a result of violation of the Convention.

Article VIII

Nothing in this Convention shall be interpreted as in any way limiting or detracting from the obligations assumed by any State under the Protocol for the

Prohibition of the Use in War of Asphyxiating, Poisonous, or Other Gases, and of Bacteriological Methods of Warfare, signed at Geneva on June 17, 1925.

Article IX

Each State Party to this Convention affirms the recognized objective of effective prohibition of chemical weapons and, to this end, undertakes to continue negotiations in good faith with a view to reaching early agreement on effective measures for the prohibition of their development, production and stockpiling and for their destruction, and on appropriate measures concerning equipment and means of delivery specifically designed for the production or use of chemical agents for weapons purposes.

Article X

(1) The States Parties to this Convention undertake to facilitate, and have the right to participate in, the fullest possible exchange of equipment, materials and scientific and technological information for the use of bacteriological (biological) agents and toxins for peaceful purposes. Parties to the Convention in a position to do so shall also cooperate in contributing individually or together with other States or international organizations to the further development and application of scientific discoveries in the field of bacteriology (biology) for prevention of disease, or for other peaceful purposes.

(2) This Convention shall be implemented in a manner designed to avoid hampering the economic or technological development of States Parties to the Convention or international cooperation in the field of peaceful bacteriological (biological) activities, including the international exchange of bacteriological (biological) agents and toxins and equipment for the processing, use or production of bacteriological (biological) agents and toxins for peaceful purposes in accordance with the provisions of the Convention.

Article XI

Any State Party may propose amendments to this Convention. Amendments shall enter into force for each State Party accepting the amendments upon their acceptance by a majority of the States Parties to the Convention and thereafter for each remaining State Party on the date of acceptance by it.

Article XII

Five years after the entry into force of this Convention, or earlier if it is requested by a majority of Parties to the Convention by submitting a proposal to this effect to the Depositary Governments, a conference of States Parties to the Convention shall be held at Geneva, Switzerland, to review the operation of the Convention, with a view to assuring that the purposes of the preamble and the provisions of the Convention, including the provisions concerning negotiations on chemical weapons, are being realized. Such review shall take into account any new scientific and technological developments relevant to the Convention.

Article XIII

(1) This Convention shall be of unlimited duration.

(2) Each State Party to this Convention shall in exercising its national sovereignty have the right to withdraw from the Convention if it decides that extraordinary events, related to the subject matter of the Convention, have jeopardized the supreme interests of its country. It shall give notice of such withdrawal to all other States Parties to the Convention and to the United Nations Security Council three months in advance. Such notice shall include a statement of the extraordinary events it regards as having jeopardized its supreme interests.

Article XIV

(1) This Convention shall be open to all States for signature. Any State which does not sign the Convention before its entry into force in accordance with paragraph (3) of this Article may accede to it at any time.

(2) This Convention shall be subject to ratification by signatory States. Instruments of ratification and instruments of accession shall be deposited with the Governments of the United States of America, the United Kingdom of Great Britain and Northern Ireland and the Union of Soviet Socialist Republics, which are hereby designated the Depositary Governments.

(3) This Convention shall enter into force after the deposit of instruments of ratification by twenty-two Governments, including the Governments designated as Depositaries of the Convention.

(4) For States whose instruments of ratification or accession are deposited subsequent to the entry into force of this Convention, it shall enter into force on the date of the deposit of their instruments of ratification or accession.

(5) The Depositary Governments shall promptly inform all signatory and acceding States of the date of each signature, the date of deposit of each instrument of ratification or of accession and the date of the entry into force of this Convention, and of the receipt of other notices.

(6) This Convention shall be registered by the Depositary Governments pursuant to Article 102 of the Charter of the United Nations.

Article XV

This Convention, the English, Russian, French, Spanish and Chinese texts of which are equally authentic, shall be deposited in the archives of the Depositary

Governments. Duly certified copies of the Convention shall be transmitted by the Depositary Governments to the Governments of the signatory and acceding states.

IN WITNESS WHEREOF the undersigned, duly authorized, have signed this Convention.

DONE in triplicate, at the cities of Washington, London and Moscow, this tenth day of April, one thousand nine hundred and seventy-two.

PARTIES AND SIGNATORIES OF THE BIOLOGICAL WEAPONS CONVENTION

STATE (COUNTRY) (169)

Afghanistan
Albania
Algeria
Antigua and Barbuda
Argentina
Armenia
Australia
Austria
Azerbaijan
Bahamas
Bahrain
Bangladesh
Barbados
Belarus
Belgium
Belize
Benin
Bhutan
Bolivia
Bosnia and Herzegovina
Botswana
Brazil
Brunei Darussalam
Bulgaria
Burkina Faso
Cambodia (Kampuchea)
Canada
Cape Verde
Chile
China, People's Republic of
Colombia
Congo
Congo, Democratic People's Republic of
Costa Rica
Croatia
Cuba
Cyprus
Czech Republic
Denmark
Dominica
Dominican Republic
East Timor
Ecuador
El Salvador
Equatorial Guinea
Estonia
Ethiopia
Fiji
Finland
France
Gambia
Georgia
Germany
Ghana
Greece
Grenada
Guatemala
Guinea-Bissau
Holy See
Honduras
Hungary
Iceland
India
Indonesia
Iran
Iraq
Ireland
Italy
Jamaica
Japan
Jordan
Kenya
Korea, Democratic People's Republic of
Korea, Republic of
Kuwait
Kyrgyzstan
Laos
Latvia
Lebanon

Lesotho
Libya
Liechtenstein
Lithuania
Luxembourg
Macedonia, Former Yugoslav Republic of
Malaysia
Maldives
Mali
Malta
Mauritius
Mexico
Monaco
Mongolia
Morocco
Netherlands
New Zealand
Nicaragua
Niger
Nigeria
Norway
Oman
Palau
Pakistan
Panama
Papua New Guinea
Paraguay
Peru
Philippines
Poland
Portugal
Qatar
Romania
Russian Federation
Rwanda
St. Kitts and Nevis
St. Lucia
St. Vincent and the Grenadines
San Marino
Sao Tome and Principe
Saudi Arabia
Senegal
Serbia-Montenegro (Federal Republic of Yugoslavia)
Seychelles
Sierra Leone
Singapore
Slovakia
Slovenia
Solomon Islands
South Africa
Spain
Sri Lanka
Sudan
Suriname
Swaziland
Sweden
Switzerland
Thailand
Togo
Tonga
Tunisia
Turkey
Turkmenistan
Uganda
Ukraine
United Kingdom
United States
Uruguay
Uzbekistan
Vanuatu
Venezuela
Vietnam
Yemen
Zimbabwe

SIGNATORY COUNTRIES (16)

Burundi
Central African Republic
Côte d'Ivoire
Egypt
Gabon
Guyana
Haiti
Liberia
Madagascar
Malawi
Myanmar (Burma)
Nepal
Somalia
Syria
Tanzania
United Arab Emirates

The Chemical Weapons Convention Fact Sheet

Adapted from the U.S. Department of State, Bureau of Arms Control, Washington, November 28, 2000

The Chemical Weapons Convention is a global treaty that bans an entire class of weapons. The CWC bans the production, acquisition, stockpiling, transfer and use of chemical weapons. It entered into force on April 29, 1997.

Chemical weapons pose a threat not just to our military but to innocent civilians, as the 1995 poison gas attack in the Japanese subway showed. Certain aspects of the Chemical Weapons Convention, including its law enforcement requirements and nonproliferation provisions, strengthen existing efforts to fight chemical terrorism. The CWC is a central element of U.S. arms control and nonproliferation policy that strengthens U.S. national security and contributes to global stability.

Under the CWC, each State Party undertakes never, under any circumstances, to:

- develop, produce, otherwise acquire, stockpile or retain chemical weapons, or transfer, directly or indirectly, chemical weapons to anyone;
- use chemical weapons;
- engage in any military preparation to use chemical weapons; and
- assist, encourage or induce, in any way, anyone to engage in any activity prohibited to a State Party under this Convention.

In addition each State Party undertakes, all in accordance with the provisions of the Convention, to:

- destroy the chemical weapons it owns or possesses or that are located in any place under its jurisdiction or control;
- destroy all chemical weapons it abandoned on the territory of another State Party; and
- destroy any chemical weapons production facilities it owns or possesses or that are located in any place under its jurisdiction or control.

Chemical weapons are attractive to countries or individuals seeking a mass-destruction capability because they are relatively cheap to produce and do not demand the elaborate technical infrastructure needed to make nuclear weapons. It is therefore all the more vital to establish an international bulwark against the acquisition and use of these weapons.

The CWC is the most ambitious treaty in the history of arms control. Whereas most arms control treaties in the past have only limited weapons, the CWC requires their outright elimination. Parties to the Convention must destroy any and all chemical weapons and chemical weapons production facilities.

The CWC penalizes countries that do not join. Entry into force of the CWC served to isolate the small number of non-participating states as international pariahs and inhibit their access to certain treaty-controlled chemicals. Since many of these chemicals are not only required to make chemical weapons but have important uses in commercial industry, the hold-outs have economic as well as political incentives to join the treaty regime.

The Chemical Weapons Convention and Industry

The CWC is the first arms control treaty to widely affect the private sector. Although the United States does not manufacture chemical weapons, it does produce, process, and consume chemicals that can be used to produce chemical weapons. For example, a solvent used in ballpoint pen ink can be easily converted into mustard gas, and a chemical involved in production of fire retardants and pesticides can be used to make nerve agents. Thus, any treaty to ban chemical weapons must monitor commercial facilities that produce, process, or consume dual-use chemicals to ensure they are not diverted for prohibited purposes.

The CWC provisions covering chemical facilities were developed with the active participation of industry representatives. The verification regime is intrusive enough to give confidence that member states are complying with the treaty, yet it respects industry's legitimate interests in safeguarding proprietary information and avoiding disruption of production.

In testimony before the Senate Foreign Relations Committee, Fred Webber, president and CEO of the Chemical Manufacturers Association, said, "We have studied this treaty in great detail; we have put it to the test. We think the CWC is a good deal for American industry. . . . The Chemical Weapons Convention protects vital commercial interests. I know because we helped design the reporting forms. And I know because we helped develop inspection procedures that protect trade secrets while providing full assurance that chemical weapons are not being produced. . . . The Chemical Weapons Convention makes good business sense and good public policy."

The CWC and the Military

The CWC specifically allows Parties to maintain chemical weapon defensive programs and does not constrain non-CW military responses to a chemical weapon attack. John Shalikashvili, former chair of the Joint Chiefs of Staff, has said in Senate testimony that "Desert Storm proved that retaliation in kind is not required to deter the use of chemical weapons." He explained, "The U.S. military's ability to deter chemical weapons in a post–CW world will be predicated upon both a robust chemical weapons defense capability, and the ability to rapidly bring to bear superior and overwhelming military force in retaliation against a chemical attack." As then–Defense Secretary Cheney said during the Gulf War, and as former Defense Secretary Perry reiterated, the U.S. response to a chemical weapon attack would be "absolutely overwhelming" and "devastating."

CWC Implementation

With or without the CWC, the United States is already destroying its chemical weapons in accordance with a law passed by Congress more than a decade ago that requires the destruction of the bulk of the U.S. chemical weapon stockpile. The CWC requires that all state parties that possess chemical weapons to destroy their stockpiles by April 2007, although both the United States and Russia have been granted extensions past 2007.

The United States is a member of the executive council of the Organization for the Prohibition of Chemical Weapons, in The Hague, which will oversee the implementation of the CWC. United States citizens serve as international inspectors and in other key positions relating to the verification of the treaty.

The CWC puts into place a legally binding international standard outlawing the acquisition and possession, as well as use, of chemical weapons. The convention not only requires state parties to destroy their chemical weapon arsenals but prohibits them from transferring chemical weapons to other countries or assisting anyone in prohibited activities. Combined with restrictions on chemical trade in CWC–controlled chemicals with non-parties, these provisions increase the cost and difficulties of acquiring chemical weapons for states that choose not to participate.

Universal adherence and complete abolition of chemical weapons will not be achieved immediately, but the Convention slows and even reverses chemical weapons proliferation by isolating the small number of states that refuse to join the regime, limiting their access to precursor chemicals and bringing international political and economic pressures to bear if such states continue their chemical weapons programs.

Chemical Weapons Convention Signatories/Ratifiers

The CWC entered into force on April 29, 1997, following ratification by 65 signatories. As of the spring of 2005, 168 countries have either ratified or acceded to the CWC. Another 16 are signatories.

Afghanistan (Ratified 10/24/03)
Albania (Ratified 5/11/94)

Algeria (Ratified 8/14/95)
Andorra (Acceded 3/29/03)
Argentina (Ratified 10/2/95)
Armenia (Ratified 1/27/95)
Australia (Ratified 5/6/94)
Austria (Ratified 8/17/95)
Azerbaijan (Ratified 2/29/00)
Bahamas
Bahrain (Ratified 4/28/97)
Bangladesh (Ratified 4/25/97)
Belarus (Ratified 7/11/96)
Belgium (Ratified 1/27/97)
Belize (Acceded 12/31/03)
Benin (Ratified 5/14/98)
Bhutan
Bolivia (Ratified 8/14/98)
Bosnia and Herzegovina (Ratified 2/25/97)
Botswana (Acceded 8/31/98)
Brazil (Ratified 3/13/96)
Brunei Darussalam (Ratified 7/28/97)
Bulgaria (Ratified 8/10/94)
Burkina Faso (Ratified 7/8/97)
Burundi (Ratified 9/4/98)
Cambodia
Cameroon (Ratified 9/16/96)
Canada (Ratified 9/26/95)
Cape Verde (Ratified 11/9/03)
Central African Republic
Chad (Ratified 3/14/04)
Chile (Ratified 7/12/96)
China (Ratified 4/25/97)
Colombia (Ratified 4/5/00)
Comoros
Congo
Cook Islands (Ratified 7/15/94)
Costa Rica (Ratified 5/31/96)
Côte d'Ivoire (Ratified 12/18/95)
Croatia (Ratified 5/23/95)
Cuba (Ratified 4/29/97)
Cyprus (Ratified 8/28/98)
Czech Republic (Ratified 3/6/96)
Democratic Republic of the Congo
Denmark (Ratified 7/13/95)
Djibouti
Dominica (Ratified 2/12/01)
Dominican Republic

East Timor (Acceded 5/7/03)
Ecuador (Ratified 9/6/95)
El Salvador (Ratified 10/30/95)
Equatorial Guinea (Ratified 4/25/97)
Eritrea (Acceded 2/14/00)
Estonia (Ratified 5/26/99)
Ethiopia (Ratified 5/13/96)
Federal Republic of Yugoslavia (Acceded 4/20/00)
Fiji (Ratified 1/20/93)
Finland (Ratified 2/7/95)
Federal Yugoslav Republic of Macedonia (Acceded 6/20/1997)
France (Ratified 3/2/95)
Gabon (Ratified 9/8/00)
Gambia (Ratified 5/19/98)
Georgia (Ratified 11/27/95)
Germany (Ratified 8/12/94)
Ghana (Ratified 7/9/97)
Greece (Ratified 12/22/94)
Grenada
Guatemala (Ratified 3/14/03)
Guinea (Ratified 6/9/97)
Guinea-Bissau
Guyana (Ratified 9/12/97)
Haiti
Holy See (Ratified 5/12/99)
Honduras
Hungary (Ratified 10/31/96)
Iceland (Ratified 4/28/97)
India (Ratified 9/3/96)
Indonesia (Ratified 11/12/98)
Iran (Ratified 11/3/97)
Ireland (Ratified 6/24/96)
Israel
Italy (Ratified 12/8/95)
Jamaica (Ratified 9/8/00)
Japan (Ratified 9/15/95)
Jordan (Acceded 10/29/97)
Kazakhstan (Ratified 3/23/00)
Kenya (Ratified 4/25/97)
Kiribati (Acceded 9/7/00)
Kuwait (Ratified 5/29/97)
Kyrgyzstan (Ratified 10/29/03)
Laos (P.D.R.) (Ratified 2/25/97)
Latvia (Ratified 7/23/96)
Lesotho (Ratified 12/7/94)
Liberia

Libya (Acceded 1/6/04)
Liechtenstein (Ratified 11/24/99)
Lithuania (Ratified 4/15/98)
Luxembourg (Ratified 4/15/97)
Madagascar (Ratified 11/19/04)
Malawi (Ratified 6/11/98)
Malaysia (Ratified 4/20/00)
Maldives (Ratified 5/31/94)
Mali (Ratified 4/28/97)
Malta (Ratified 4/28/97)
Marshall Islands (Ratified 6/18/04)
Mauritania (Ratified 2/9/98)
Mauritius (Ratified 2/9/93)
Mexico (Ratified 8/29/94)
Micronesia (Ratified 6/21/99)
Monaco (Ratified 6/1/95)
Mongolia (Ratified 1/17/95)
Morocco (Ratified 12/28/95)
Mozambique (Acceded 8/15/00)
Myanmar
Namibia (Ratified 11/27/95)
Nauru (Rep of) (11/12/2001)
Nepal (Ratified 11/18/97)
Netherlands (Ratified 6/30/95)
New Zealand (Ratified 7/15/96)
Nicaragua (Ratified 11/5/99)
Niger (Ratified 4/9/97)
Nigeria (Ratified 5/19/99)
Niue (Acceded 5/21/05)
Norway (Ratified 4/7/94)
Oman (Ratified 2/8/95)
Pakistan (Ratified 10/28/97)
Palau (Acceded 3/5/03)
Panama (Ratified 10/7/98)
Papua New Guinea (Ratified 4/17/96)
Paraguay (Ratified 12/1/94)
Peru (Ratified 7/20/95)
Philippines (Ratified 12/11/96)
Poland (Ratified 8/23/95)
Portugal (Ratified 9/10/96)
Qatar (Ratified 9/3/97)
Republic of Korea (Ratified 4/28/97)
Republic of Moldova (Ratified 7/08/96)
Romania (Ratified 2/15/95)
Russian Federation (Ratified 11/5/97)
Rwanda (Ratified 4/30/04)

Saint Kitts & Nevis (Ratified 5/21/04)
Saint Lucia (Ratified 4/9/97)
Saint Vincent and The Grenadines (Ratified 10/18/02)
Samoa (Ratified 10/27/02)
San Marino (Ratified 12/10/99)
Sao Tome and Principe (Acceded 10/9/03)
Saudi Arabia (Ratified 8/9/96)
Senegal (Ratified 7/20/98)
Seychelles (Ratified 4/7/93)
Sierra Leone (Ratified 9/30/04)
Singapore (Ratified 5/21/97)
Slovak Republic (Ratified 10/27/95)
Slovenia (Ratified 6/11/97)
Solomon Islands (Acceded 9/23/04)
South Africa (Ratified 9/13/95)
Spain (Ratified 8/3/94)
Sri Lanka (Ratified 8/19/94)
Sudan (Acceded 5/24/99)
Suriname (Ratified 4/28/97)
Swaziland (Ratified 11/20/96)
Sweden (Ratified 6/17/93)
Switzerland (Ratified 3/10/95)
Tajikistan (Ratified 1/11/95)
Thailand (Ratified 12/10/02)
Togo (Ratified 4/23/97)
Tonga (Acceded 5/29/03)
Trinidad and Tobago (Acceded 6/24/97)
Tunisia (Ratified 4/15/97)
Turkey (Ratified 5/12/97)
Turkmenistan (Ratified 9/29/94)
Tuvalu (Acceded 1/19/04)
Uganda (Ratified 11/30/2001)
Ukraine (Ratified 10/16/98)
United Arab Emirates (Ratified 11/28/00)
United Kingdom of Great Britain and Northern Ireland (Ratified 5/13/96)
United Republic of Tanzania (Ratified 6/25/98)
United States of America (Ratified 4/25/97)
Uruguay (Ratified 10/6/94)
Uzbekistan (Ratified 7/23/96)
Venezuela (Ratified 12/3/97)
Viet Nam (Ratified 9/30/98)
Yemen (Ratified 10/2/00)
Zambia (Ratification 2/9/2001)
Zimbabwe (Ratified 4/25/97)

Nuclear Supplier Organizations

Two informal coalitions of nations that voluntarily restrict the export of equipment and materials that could be used to develop nuclear weapons form an important component of the nonproliferation regime. The first group, known as the Non-Proliferation Treaty (NPT) Exporters Committee (or the Zangger Committee, after its former chair, the Swiss expert Claude Zangger), was formed in the early 1970s to establish guidelines for implementing the export control provisions of article 9, paragraph 2, of the Nuclear Non-Proliferation Treaty.[1] In August 1974 the Zangger Committee adopted a set of guidelines, including a list of export items that would trigger the requirement for the application of International Atomic Energy Agency (IAEA) safeguards in recipient states. The Zangger guidelines and "trigger list" constituted the first mechanism for the uniform regulation of nuclear exports by the principal nuclear supplier states that were NPT parties.

India's nuclear test in 1974 was the catalyst for the formation in January 1976 of the Nuclear Suppliers Group (NSG), which first met in London and was called the London Group. France, not then a party to the NPT, joined the NSG. The NSG adopted guidelines that were similar to those of the Zangger Committee but went beyond the Zangger guidelines in restraining transfers of uranium-enrichment and plutonium-extraction equipment and technology.

In April 1992, in the wake of the Gulf War, the NSG expanded its export control guidelines, which until then had covered only uniquely nuclear items, to cover 65 dual-use items as well. In addition, the group added as a requirement for future exports that recipient states accept IAEA inspection on all their peaceful nuclear activities. This full-scope, or comprehensive, safeguard rule effectively precludes nuclear commerce by NSG member states with states such as India, Israel, and Pakistan, which refuse to accept IAEA safeguards on their entire nuclear infrastructure.[2]

The Zangger Committee: Formation

Shortly after the NPT came into force in 1970 several countries began consultations about the procedures and standards they would apply to nuclear fuel and equipment exports to non-nuclear-weapon states. These consultations were necessary to implement the NPT requirement that such exports and any enriched uranium or plutonium produced through their use be subject to IAEA safeguards in the recipient state. The supplier countries that were engaged in those consultations were parties to the Non-Proliferation Treaty (or have since become parties) and were also exporters or potential exporters of material and equipment for peaceful uses of nuclear energy.

In August 1974, the governments of Australia, Denmark, Canada, Finland, West Germany, the Netherlands, Norway, the Soviet Union, the United Kingdom, and the United States each informed the director general of the IAEA, by individual letters, of their intentions to require IAEA safeguards on their nuclear exports in accordance with certain procedures described in memoranda enclosed with their letters. Those memoranda were identical and included the trigger list of special nuclear materials (enriched uranium and plutonium) and items of equipment "especially designed or prepared" (EDP) for the production of those materials. The memoranda declared that these items would be exported only if the recipient agreed to place them under IAEA safeguards, agreed that they would be used only for peaceful purposes, and agreed not to retransfer such items unless under the same conditions.[3]

Soon afterward, Austria, Czechoslovakia, East Germany, Ireland, Japan, Luxembourg, Poland, and Sweden sent individual letters to the director general, referring to and enclosing memoranda identical to those transmitted by the initial group of governments.

The agreed-on procedures and trigger list represented the first major agreement on the uniform regulation of nuclear exports by current and potential nuclear suppliers. It had great significance for several reasons. It was an attempt to enforce strictly and uniformly the obligations of article 3, paragraph 2, of the NPT requiring safeguards on nuclear exports. It was intended to reduce the likelihood that states would be tempted to cut corners on safeguard requirements because of competition in the sale of nuclear equipment and fuel-cycle services. In addition, and very important in light of subsequent events, it established the principle that nuclear supplier nations should consult and agree among themselves on procedures to regulate the international market for nuclear materials and equipment in the interest of nonproliferation. Notably absent from the list of actual participants or potential suppliers, as from the list of parties to the NPT, were China, France, and India. (The current members of the Zangger Committee are listed below.)

Zangger Committee: Subsequent Developments

Because of advances in technology, the parameters of some of the items on the Zangger Committee trigger list (principally enrichment, reprocessing, and heavy-water production equipment) were subject to substantial clarifications and upgrades during the 1980s. (The Zangger Committee has also been responsible for almost all the clarification and upgrade work later taken up by the NSG.) Prompted by the discovery that Iraq was pursuing various enrichment technologies, the important changes agreed upon by the Zangger Committee in 1993 have added new forms of enrichment technology to the trigger list (including electromagnetic isotope separation and chemical or ion exchange techniques) not previously covered in the enrichment category.

Changes to the trigger list are adopted into controls on a national basis; implementation dates for member states can therefore vary depending on the bureaucratic measures required by each member. Unlike the NSG, the Zangger Committee has controls only on EDP items; it does not control dual-use equipment or technology, nor does it call on participants to exercise particular restraint in the supply of equipment to nuclear facilities that are considered sensitive (that is, reprocessing and enrichment facilities). Nor do the Zangger Committee guidelines require comprehensive IAEA safeguards as a condition of supply; single-facility arrangements are sufficient. This policy is under review.

The Zangger Committee meets in Vienna twice a year (usually in May and October, with May being considered the main plenary meeting). The United Kingdom provides secretariat services. The committee's detailed deliberations are kept confidential, as are the criteria for membership attendance at policy-making meetings (although NPT adherence, adoption of the committee's guidelines, and adherence to nonproliferation norms are among the requirements for membership).

With the 1992 agreement to harmonize the specifications of the items and equipment on the Zangger trigger list with those of the NSG (see below), some have questioned the relevance of the committee. Member governments recognize some duplication of effort and the overlap with the NSG, but the different memberships and the fact that the committee is a child of the NPT mean that no current members are (yet) willing to suggest that the group be disbanded and its work folded into the NSG.

As of Spring 2005, there were 35 members of the Zangger Committee: Argentina, Australia, Austria, Belgium, Bulgaria, Canada, China, the Czech Republic, Denmark, Finland, France, Germany, Greece, Hungary, Ireland, Italy, Japan, Republic of Korea, Luxembourg, the Netherlands, Norway, Poland, Portugal, Romania, Russian Federation, Slovak Republic, Slovenia, South Africa, Spain, Sweden, Switzerland, Turkey, Ukraine, the United Kingdom, and the United States.

The Nuclear Suppliers Group: Formation

In November 1974, within a year of the delivery of the memoranda generated in the Zangger Committee to the IAEA director general, a second series of nuclear supplier negotiations was initiated. This round, convened largely at the initiative of the United States, was a response to three developments: (1) the Indian nuclear test of May 1974, (2) mounting evidence that the pricing actions of the Organization of the Petroleum Exporting Countries were stimulating states in the developing world and other nonnuclear states to initiate or accelerate their nuclear power programs, and (3) recent contracts or continuing negotiations by France and West Germany for the supply of enrichment or reprocessing facilities to developing-world states, facilities that could provide access to weapons-usable fissile material.

The initial participants in these discussions, conducted in London, were Canada, France, West Germany, Japan, the Soviet Union, the United Kingdom, and the United States. One of the group's chief accomplishments was to persuade France to join. France, which had not joined the NPT or the Zangger Committee, could have undercut the reforms regarding nuclear supplies. The French, hesitant about becoming involved and uncertain about where the effort might lead, insisted that any meetings be kept confidential. The meetings in London were therefore held in secret. The meetings soon became known, however, which led to suspicion and exaggerated fears about their subject. The group was inaccurately referred to as a cartel. Instead, one of its purposes was to foster genuine commercial competition based on quality and prices, untainted by the bargaining away of proliferation controls.

Two major controversies arose in the series of meetings of what became known as the Nuclear Suppliers Group. These matters were resolved in a new agreement in late 1975. The first concerned whether, and under what conditions, technology and equipment for enrichment and reprocessing, the most sensitive parts of the nuclear fuel cycle from a weapons proliferation perspective, should be transferred to non-nuclear states. The United States and several other participants urged both a prohibition on such transfers and a commitment to reprocessing in multinational facilities (rather than in installations under the control of individual states). France had already signed contracts to sell reprocessing plants to Pakistan and South Korea, however, and West Germany had agreed to sell to Brazil the technology and facilities for the full fuel cycle (including enrichment and reprocessing). France and West Germany objected to any prohibition.

The second controversy concerned whether transfers should be made to states unwilling to submit all their nuclear facilities to IAEA safeguards, or whether such full-scope safeguards should be a condition of all sales. The NSG came close to reaching consensus on requiring full-scope safeguards as a condition of future supply commitments but was unable to persuade the French and the West Germans. At the time, Argentina, Brazil, India, Israel, Pakistan, and South Africa would have been barred from receiving NSG-controlled exports if the full-scope safeguard rule had been adopted, since each of those developing countries possessed or was developing nuclear installations not subject to IAEA monitoring. While not making full-scope safeguards a condition of nuclear supply, the NSG did act to expand safeguard coverage by adopting a trigger list of nuclear exports, similar to that of the Zangger Committee, which would be permitted only if the exported items were covered by IAEA safeguards in the recipient state.

On January 27, 1976, the seven participants in the NSG negotiations exchanged letters endorsing a uniform code for conducting international nuclear sales. The major provisions of the agreement required that before nuclear materials, equipment, or technology are transferred a recipient state must

1. pledge not to use the transferred materials, equipment, or technology in the manufacture of nuclear explosives of any kind;

2. accept, with no provision for termination, international safeguards on all transferred materials and facilities employing transferred equipment or technology, including any enrichment, reprocessing, or heavy-water production facility that replicates or otherwise employs transferred technology;

3. provide adequate physical security for transferred nuclear facilities and materials to prevent theft and sabotage;
4. agree not to retransfer the materials, equipment, or technology to third countries unless they also accept the constraints on use, replication, security, and transfer, and unless the original supplier nation concurs in the transactions;
5. employ "restraint" regarding the possible export of "sensitive" items (relating to uranium enrichment, spent-fuel reprocessing, and heavy-water production); and
6. encourage the concept of multilateral (in lieu of national) regional facilities for reprocessing and enrichment.[4]

The industrial states of Eastern Europe soon joined the NSG, so that it included virtually all the advanced supplier countries.

The NSG guidelines extended the Zangger Committee's requirements in several respects. First, France agreed to key points adopted by the NSG, such as the requirement that recipients pledge not to use transferred items for nuclear explosives of any kind and that safeguards on transferred items would continue indefinitely. Second, the NSG went beyond the NPT and the Zangger Committee requirements by imposing safeguards not only on the export of nuclear materials and equipment but also on nuclear technology exports. India had demonstrated the existence of this serious loophole by building its own unsafeguarded replicas of a safeguarded power reactor imported from Canada. The NSG was unable to reach agreement on the application of this reform to reactor technology, however, and so confined its recommended application to sensitive facilities built with the use of exported technology. The group's acceptance of this limited reform was facilitated by the fact that such a condition was incorporated by West Germany in its safeguard agreements for the sale of enrichment and reprocessing facilities to Brazil and by France in its safeguard agreements covering proposed sales of reprocessing plants to South Korea and Pakistan. (France subsequently canceled both contracts.)

Third, the NSG, while not absolutely prohibiting the export of these sensitive facilities, embodied the participants' agreement to "exercise restraint" in transferring them. Wherever transfers of enrichment plants are involved, the participants agreed to seek recipient-country commitments that such facilities would be designed and operated to produce only low-enriched uranium, not suitable for weapons.

Nuclear Suppliers Group: Subsequent Developments

There was a lull in NSG policy making during the 1980s. In March 1991, however, in the wake of the 1991 Gulf War, the group convened after a ten-year hiatus in The Hague and decided to adopt the clarified and upgraded specifications on the Zangger Committee trigger list. The exercise, which became known as harmonization, was completed in 1992. During 1993 the NSG added another category to its trigger list, uranium conversion plants and equipment, items that are not covered by the Zangger Committee's list.

At U.S. urging, the NSG plenary meeting in Warsaw in March and April of 1992 took a major step. The members agreed that as a condition of supply all members would insist that all contracts of EDP trigger-list items drawn up after April 1992 would require recipient states to accept full-scope safeguards on all their nuclear facilities and on any future facilities. (Previously, some NSG members, including the United States, had required full-scope safeguards as a condition of supply, but the definition of what was covered and the effective date of this requirement were not uniform.) Member states adopted this new full-scope safeguard requirement into national legislation during the first half of 1993. The new updated guidelines were issued by the IAEA in July 1993.[5] In 1993, the NSG also agreed to add to its trigger list the additional equipment used for enrichment that had been identified in the Zangger Committee. The NSG set a target date of March 1, 1993, for the implementation of the new category controls. (At the NSG plenary meeting held in Helsinki on April 5–7, 1995, the NSG reviewed the Guidelines for Nuclear Transfers, and some changes were made, particularly with respect to fuel fabrication items.[6])

In a new departure for the NSG, at The Hague meeting of March 1991, members also agreed on the need to expand controls to cover dual-use items that have legitimate non-nuclear uses. (The original NSG and Zangger Committee rules apply only to "nuclear-unique" equipment and material.) The working group established by NSG met under U.S. stewardship in Brussels in June 1991, Annapolis in October 1991, and Interlaken in January 1992 and produced agreement on a list of 65 dual-use items with detailed definitions and a series of guidelines on conditions of transfer. These were formally endorsed by the full plenary meeting of the NSG in Warsaw in April 1992. The NSG members set a target implementation date of the end of 1992 for the part 2 Guidelines, but administrative and national legislative delays have prevented some members from meeting that date.

The dual-use guidelines (known as Guidelines for Transfers of Nuclear-Related Dual-Use Equipment, Material and Related Technology and published by the IAEA in July 1992[7]) require exporting states not to ship items on the list if they are for use by non-nuclear weapon states in unsafeguarded nuclear fuel cycle facilities or in nuclear explosive activity. In addition, the dual-use guidelines require states not to transfer items on the list "when there is an unacceptable risk of diversion to such an activity, or when the transfers are contrary to the objective of averting the proliferation of nuclear weapons." Suppliers must obtain a statement from the recipient on the use to which the item will be put and where it will be located, as well as obtain assurances that it will not be used for proscribed purposes and that no retransfer will take place without the consent of the supplier. Decisions on whether a transfer should proceed are also to be guided by additional criteria, such as the recipient's nonproliferation credentials. Although decisions on whether to grant export licenses are left to national discretion, there is a system of consultation among members to ensure uniformity in the implementation of the dual-use guidelines and to guard against commercial disadvantage to a particular state if it denies a transfer request. Members are also encouraged to consult and exchange information on proliferation developments that might be relevant to licensing decisions.[8]

The Japanese (through their mission in Vienna) have taken on the role of administrative secretariat (point of contact) for the trigger list "part 2" dual-use mechanism. They are responsible for the circulation of denial notices, documents, and information to members as well as for arranging meetings. At the 1997 NSG plenary session held in Ottawa on May 8 and 9, 1997, the members agreed to new measures to speed up the sharing of information among themselves and with the point of contact. Specifically, they adopted a parallel-track approach that would combine an improved and secure U.S. computer-based bulletin board system with a European Union secure fax system proposed by France.[9]

Any state can adhere to either part of the NSG guidelines by notifying the IAEA that it has adopted the necessary legislation to control items on the NSG lists. This does not, however, confer immediate membership in the NSG or the right to attend its policy-making meetings. There are no strict criteria for membership, but potential members must satisfy the existing membership that they have proper credentials. These include a commitment to other nonproliferation norms (for example, through membership in other agreements, such as the NPT and the Chemical Weapons Convention), the adoption of the necessary legislation to bring the NSG controls into national law, and effective enforcement capabilities. Membership decisions are taken by consensus. The chairmanship of the group rotates.

As of Spring 2005, the 44 members of the NSG were Argentina, Australia, Austria, Belarus, Belgium, Brazil, Bulgaria, Canada, China, Cyprus, the Czech Republic, Denmark, Estonia, Finland, France, Germany, Greece, Hungary, Ireland, Italy, Japan, Kazakhstan, Latvia, Lithuania, Luxembourg, Malta, the Netherlands, New Zealand, Norway, Poland, Portugal, Republic of Korea, Romania, Russian Federation, Slovak Republic, Slovenia, South Africa, Spain, Sweden, Switzerland, Turkey, Ukraine, the United Kingdom, and the United States. Brazil and New Zealand are the only NSG members that do not belong to the Zangger Committee.

SOURCES

Buchanan, Ewen. "The Non-Proliferation Regime." Carnegie Endowment for International Peace, Washington, D.C. Unpublished consultant's report, March 1994.

Van Doren, Charles N. *Nuclear Supply and Non-Proliferation: The IAEA Committee on Assurances of Supply.* Report for the Congressional Research Service (Rept. 83-202-8), October 1983.

ADDITIONAL SOURCES

ACDA (U.S. Arms Control and Disarmament Agency). "Multilateral Nuclear Export Control Regimes." Fact sheet, December 17, 1996, available at www.acda.gov/factshee/exptcon/nuexpcnt.htm.

Davis, Zachary S. "Non-Proliferation Regimes: Policies to Control the Spread of Nuclear, Chemical and Biological Weapons and Missiles." Congressional Research Service, Library of Congress, Washington, D.C., February 8, 1993.

Gardner, Gary T. *Nuclear Nonproliferation: A Primer*. Boulder, Colo.: Lynne Rienner Publishers, 1994.

Office of Technology Assessment, U.S. Congress. *Nuclear Proliferation and Safeguard.* Washington, D.C.: U.S. Government Printing Office, 1977.

———. *Proliferation of Weapons of Mass Destruction: Assessing the Risks*. Washington, D.C.: U.S. Government Printing Office, August 1993.

Rauf, Tariq, James Lamson, Swawna McCartney, and Sarah Meek. *Inventory of International Nonproliferation Organizations and Regimes*. Monterey, Calif.: Monterey Institute of International Studies, 1996–1997.

Thorne, Carlton E., ed. *A Guide to Nuclear Export Controls*. Burke, Va.: Proliferation Data Services, 1997.

Timerbaev, Roland, and Lisa Moskowitz. *Inventory of International Nonproliferation Organizations and Regimes*. Monterey, Calif.: Monterey Institute of International Studies, 1994, 1995.

U.S. Department of State. "Report to the Congress Pursuant to Section 601 of the Nuclear Non-Proliferation Act of 1978." January 1979.

Notes

1. The article states: "Each State Party to the Treaty undertakes not to provide: (a) source or special fissionable material, or (b) equipment or material especially designed or prepared for the processing, use or production of special fissionable material, to any non-nuclear-weapon State for peaceful purposes, unless the source or special fissionable material shall be subject to the safeguards required by this Article." See ACDA, "Multilateral Nuclear Export Control Regimes," Factsheet, December 17, 1996 (located at www.acda.gov/factshee/exptcon/nuexpcnt.htm; accessed November 8, 1997).
2. In addition to agreeing to such full-scope safeguards, all nations importing regulated items from NSG members states must promise to furnish adequate physical security for transferred nuclear materials and facilities; pledge not to export nuclear materials and technologies to other nations without the permission of the original exporting nation or without a pledge from the recipient nation to abide by these same rules; and promise not to use any imports to build nuclear explosives. (Similar rules, apart from the full-scope safeguard requirement, apply to exports regulated by the Zangger Committee, which continues to function, although it has been partially eclipsed by the Nuclear Suppliers Group, whose export controls have, in general, been more far-reaching.)
3. The individual letters and the identical memoranda were published by the IAEA in September 1974 in IAEA, INFCIRC/209 (INFCIRC is shorthand for the series of Information Circulars distributed to IAEA members).
4. IAEA, "Guidelines for Nuclear Transfers," INFCIRC/254, part 1 (Vienna).
5. See INFCIRC/254/Rev.1/Part 1.
6. The guidelines were published in the INFCIRC 254, part 1 series; communication with U.S. State Department official, September 4, 1997.
7. INFCIRC/254/Rev.1/Part 2.
8. For further details on the development of the dual-use arrangement and the adoption of full-scope safeguards as a condition of supply, see Carlton E. Thorne, *The Nuclear Suppliers Group: A Major Success Story Gone Unnoticed,* Directors Series on Proliferation (Berkeley, Calif.: Lawrence Livermore Laboratory, 1994), p. 29.
9. In the early 1990s, the United States suggested a secure computer-based bulletin board system for information sharing that had been in use unofficially, and on a limited basis, among some NSG parties (communication with U.S. State Department official, November 5, 1997).

The Comprehensive Nuclear Test Ban Treaty

A comprehensive nuclear test ban pledge was embodied in the 1963 Partial Test Ban Treaty and was repeated as a goal in the Nuclear Non-Proliferation Treaty preamble in the following terms: "To seek to achieve the discontinuance of all test explosions of nuclear weapons for all time and to continue negotiations to that end." The U.N. General Assembly's adoption of the Comprehensive Test Ban Treaty (CTBT), on September 10, 1996, fulfilled that pledge and paved the way for a permanent ban on nuclear explosive testing to become an integral part of the nuclear nonproliferation regime.[1]

The rationale for the CTBT was that it would "constrain the development and qualitative improvement of nuclear weapons; end the development of advanced new types of nuclear weapons; contribute to the prevention of nuclear proliferation and the process of nuclear disarmament; and strengthen international peace and security."[2] Some opponents doubted that the treaty would totally prevent qualitative improvements of existing nuclear arsenals or the development of new weapon designs, given the technological capabilities of certain nuclear weapon states to experiment without fission testing. Other critics objected to the constraints that the treaty might place on the reliability of the U.S. nuclear weapons stockpile or doubted the verifiability of the treaty in other parts of the globe. Yet others have objected to the uncertainties posed by the treaty's complicated entry-into-force provisions. It is widely recognized that the CTBT will be a major advance in arresting the nuclear arms competition and inhibiting nuclear weapons proliferation.

Background

The Conference on Disarmament in Geneva negotiated the CTBT over a period of two-and-a-half years.[3] Negotiations began in January 1994 based on the mandate of a December 1993 U.N. General Assembly consensus resolution (48/70). They continued through 1994 and 1995 and concluded in mid-1996. Ambassador Jaap Ramaker of the Netherlands, chair of the Nuclear Test Ban Committee, faced a deadline to complete the CTBT negotiation in time for its signature at the outset of the 51st session of the General Assembly.[4] The key issues resolved were: the scope of the treaty; whether peaceful nuclear explosions would be permitted; the conditions for verification, including intrusive measures (for example, challenge inspections); and the terms of entry into force, EIF).

Initially, controversy surrounded the scope of the treaty. Discussions on scope centered, first, on whether the nuclear weapon states would be allowed any exemptions from the test ban to ensure the safety and reliability of their nuclear stockpiles (i.e., very low yield nuclear tests, or so-called hydronuclear experiments). They also considered China's demand that "peaceful nuclear explosions" be allowed for civil, construction, or commercial purposes. Initially seeking allowances for low-yield tests, the United States had proposed that a test "which released nuclear energy up to the equivalent of 1.8 kg (4 lbs) of TNT explosive power would not be regarded as a violation" of the CTBT.[5] Three other nuclear weapon states, France, Russia, and the United Kingdom, which lacked the sophisticated testing apparatus and techniques of the United States, proposed that any limit on permissible experiments be set at a higher yield. China officially advocated a ban on any nuclear weapons test explosion but supported an exemption for peaceful nuclear explosives.[6]

A breakthrough occurred in August 1995, when France and the United States each declared it would support a "true zero-yield" CTBT, banning any nuclear test explosion. This position would prohibit any hydronuclear experiments. The French decision was influenced by the enormous international criticism of its June 13 announcement of a final series of nuclear tests.[7] The U.S. decision followed the JASON report, commissioned by the U.S. Department of Energy, which concluded that subkiloton nuclear tests would be of little value in ensuring the reliability of the U.S. nuclear stockpile.[8] Nevertheless, in announcing the U.S. commitment to a true zero-yield test ban, President Bill Clinton explicitly reserved the right to exercise "our supreme national interest rights under a comprehensive test ban to conduct necessary testing if the safety and reliability of our nuclear deterrent could no longer be certified."[9] On September 14, 1995, the United Kingdom followed suit by announcing its support for a zero-yield ban. On October 23, in the aftermath of his Hyde Park summit meeting with President Boris Yeltsin, President Clinton announced that Russia had also agreed to seek a zero-yield CTBT.

Another important issue, in the closing stages of the CTBT negotiations in Geneva, concerned the treaty's EIF provisions. The issue arose because China, Russia, and the United Kingdom demanded that the three nuclear weapon threshold states—India, Israel, and Pakistan—become parties to the CTBT before the treaty took effect. Another group of nations, spearheaded by the United States, held a contrasting view and insisted that the EIF provisions facilitate the treaty's EIF as soon as possible, so that no nation, or group of nations, could hold its implementation hostage. After prolonged deliberations, chairman Ramaker came up with a compromise formula according to which a list of 44 nuclear-capable states (as identified by the IAEA) that were members of the expanded Conference on Disarmament, including the five nuclear weapon states and the three threshold states, would be required to ratify the treaty. If the treaty did not enter into force within three years after it was opened for signature, a conference could be held for those states that had already ratified the treaty to "decide by consensus what measures consistent with international law [could] be undertaken to accelerate the ratification process."[10]

In spite of renewed efforts in the Conference on Disarmament at the end of July to resolve outstanding differences, the full Nuclear Test Ban Ad Hoc Committee reported, on August 16, 1996, that "no consensus" could be reached, either on adopting the text of the CTBT or on formally passing it to the Conference on Disarmament, owing to objections from India. On August 22, 1996, Australia decided to move that the 50th U.N. General Assembly consider and adopt the CTBT and open the treaty for signature at the earliest possible date. On September 10, 1996, the U.N. General Assembly adopted the treaty by a vote of 158 to 3, with 5 abstentions. The treaty was opened for signature on September 24, 1996, and on that date was signed by 68 nations, including all five nuclear weapon states.

To enter into force, the CTBT requires that 44 states that were members of the Conference on Disarmament as of June 18, 1996, that had formally participated in the work of the 1996 session of the conference, and that have research or power reactors identified by the IAEA, deposit their instruments of ratification.

Synopsis of the CTBT

*Preamble.*The preamble notes that the treaty serves the goals of both nonproliferation and disarmament and reiterates the international commitment to the "ultimate goal" of eliminating nuclear weapons.

Basic obligations. The treaty parties agree "not to carry out any nuclear weapon test explosion or any other nuclear explosion." This is the zero-yield formulation that, by not defining a nuclear explosion, seeks to prohibit all of them.

Treaty organization. To implement treaty provisions, a Comprehensive Test Ban Treaty Organization (CTBTO) has been created in Vienna. The CTBTO includes an executive council, for decision making, and a technical secretariat, for implementing the treaty's verification provisions.[11]

Verification. The treaty has an extensive monitoring system that includes 24-hour-a-day data collection. The International Monitoring System (IMS) will collect four types of data: seismic, radionuclide, hydroacoustic, and infrasound. Information from these sources is collected at the International Data Center (IDC), a component of the CTBT based in Vienna. The IDC provides preliminary analysis of the information for treaty parties. When completed, the seismic data collection system will consist of about 170 seismic stations, including about 50 primary stations that send their signals to the IDC in real time. The radionuclide detection system comprises about 80 stations that collect airborne particulates and test for the presence of by-products of nuclear explosions, such as xenon. These data are relayed to the IDC on a regular basis. The hydroacoustic and infrasound systems will consist of about 70 sensors on land and underwater that detect the sonic signals produced by explosions. These sensors transmit their data in real time to the IDC. In all there will be 337 designated IMS facilities.

As of January 2004 175 stations had completed construction, with substantial progress on 57 others.

Consultation and clarification. If a treaty party has questions about "any matter which may cause concern about possible noncompliance," it may request clarification from another party or may request the executive council to investigate. In general, the clarifying nation has one or two days to respond.

On-site inspections. Any state party may request that the executive council conduct an on-site inspection to help clarify ambiguous events. After receiving such a request, the council must make a decision within 96 hours, with a majority vote of at least 30 of 50 members required to support a challenge inspection. If the council does order such an inspection, the inspection team must arrive in the suspected nation no less than six days after the inspection request was made. In making its request for an on-site inspection, a party may present information gathered both from the treaty's data collection network and from that party's own intelligence information (that is, information based on national technical means).

Confidence-building measures. To reduce the possibility of misinterpreting legal chemical explosions, such as mining charges, treaty parties are required to notify (preferably in advance) the technical secretariat of chemical blasts using more than 300 metric tons of TNT or equivalent blasting material.

Compliance. If a suspicious event is inadequately clarified through consultations or on-site inspections, the treaty parties may convene in a special session to "ensure compliance" with the treaty and "to redress and remedy" the situation. The session has three options if it determines that a party has violated the treaty: (1) it can restrict or suspend the party's rights and privileges under the treaty; (2) it can recommend that "collective measures," such as sanctions, be implemented by the remaining treaty parties; and (3), it can bring the matter before the United Nations Security Council. This final option may also be implemented by the executive council if the situation is urgent.

Entry into force. The treaty will enter into force 180 days after 44 specific nations deposit their instruments of ratification with the United Nations. The 44 nations required for EIF are Algeria, Argentina, Australia, Austria, Bangladesh, Belgium, Brazil, Bulgaria, Canada, Chile, China, Colombia, Congo (Kinshasa), Egypt, Finland, France, Germany, Hungary, India, Indonesia, Iran, Israel, Italy, Japan, Mexico, Netherlands, North Korea, Norway, Pakistan, Peru, Poland, Romania, Russia, Slovak Republic, South Africa, South Korea, Spain, Sweden, Switzerland, Turkey, Ukraine, United Kingdom, United States, and Vietnam.

Duration. The treaty is of unlimited duration. Any treaty party may withdraw from the pact, giving six-months' notice, if treaty-related events "have jeopardized its supreme interests."

Review. Review conferences will be held every ten years (or more frequently if a majority of parties agree) to examine the operation and effectiveness of the treaty and to consider new technological developments.

Test Ban Treaty Signatories

States that have ratified the treaty (121):[12]
Afghanistan, Albania, Algeria, Argentina, Australia, Austria, Azerbaijan, Bahrain, Bangladesh, Belarus, Belgium, Belize, Benin, Bolivia, Botswana, Brazil, Bulgaria, Burkina Faso, Cambodia, Canada, Chile, Costa Rica, Croatia, Cyprus, Czech Republic, Democratic Republic of the Congo, Denmark, Ecuador, El Salvador, Eritrea, Estonia, Fiji, Finland, Former Yugoslav Republic of Macedonia, France, Gabon, Georgia, Germany, Greece, Grenada, Guyana, Holy See, Honduras, Hungary, Iceland, Ireland, Italy, Ivory Coast, Jamaica, Japan, Jordan, Kazakhstan, Kenya, Kiribati, Kuwait, Kyrgyzstan, Laos, Latvia, Lesotho, Libya, Liechtenstein, Lithuania, Luxembourg, Maldives, Mali, Malta, Mauritania, Mexico, Micronesia, Monaco, Mongolia, Morocco, Namibia, Nauru, Netherlands, New Zealand, Nicaragua, Niger, Nigeria, Norway, Oman, Panama, Paraguay, Peru, Philippines, Poland, Portugal, Qatar, Republic of Korea, Romania, Russia, Rwanda, Saint Kitts and Nevis, Saint Lucia, Samoa, San Marino, Senegal, Serbia and Montenegro, Seychelles, Sierra Leone, Singapore, Slovakia, Slovenia, South Africa, Spain, Sudan, Sweden, Switzerland, Tajikistan, Togo, Tunisia, Turkey, Turkmenistan, Uganda, Ukraine, United Arab Emirates, United Kingdom, United Republic of Tanzania, Uruguay, Uzbekistan, Venezuela

[The 44 states of annex 2 whose ratification is required for entry into force:]
1. States listed in annex 2 to the treaty that have signed and ratified the treaty [33]: Algeria, Argentina, Australia, Austria, Bangladesh, Belgium, Brazil, Bulgaria, Canada, Chile, Democratic Republic of the Congo, Finland, France, Germany, Hungary, Italy, Japan, Mexico, Netherlands, Norway, Peru, Poland, Republic of Korea, Romania, Russia, Slovakia, South Africa, Spain, Sweden, Switzerland, Turkey, Ukraine, United Kingdom

2. States listed in annex 2 to the treaty that have signed but not ratified the treaty [8]: China, Colombia, Egypt, Indonesia, Iran, Israel, United States, Vietnam

3. States listed in annex 2 to the treaty which have not signed the treaty [3]: Democratic People's Republic of Korea, India, Pakistan

NOTES

1. In the mid-1970s, the United States and the Soviet Union concluded two agreements that placed ceilings on the permitted yield of an underground nuclear explosion at 150 kilotons (1 kiloton is equivalent to the explosive force of 1,000 metric tons of TNT). The 1974 Threshold Test Ban Treaty set this limit for nuclear weapon tests while the 1976 Peaceful Nuclear Explosions Treaty set this limit for peaceful nuclear explosions.

2. ACDA, "Comprehensive Test Ban Treaty," Factsheet, September 11, 1996.
3. For a detailed review and analysis of the CTBT negotiations, see Rebecca Johnson and Sean Howard, "A Comprehensive Test Ban: Disappointing Progress," *Acronym*, no. 3, September 1994; Rebecca Johnson, "Strengthening the Non-Proliferation Regime," *Acronym*, no. 6, April 1995; Johnson, "Comprehensive Test Ban Treaty: Now or Never," *Acronym*, no. 8, October 1995; Johnson, "Endgame Issues in Geneva: Can the CD Deliver the CTBT in 1996?" *Arms Control Today*, April 1996; and Joseph Cirincione, "The Signing of the Comprehensive Test Ban Treaty," ACA press briefing with Spurgeon M. Keeney Jr., Joseph Cirincione, Richard L. Garwin, Gregory E. van der Vink, and John Isaacs, *Arms Control Today*, September 1996.
4. U.N. General Assembly Resolution 50/65 was adopted by consensus on December 12, 1995.
5. Johnson, "Comprehensive Test Ban Treaty," p. 15.
6. Ibid.
7. Newly elected President Jacques Chirac announced that in September France would resume nuclear testing and conduct eight tests over the following eight months. It would then be ready to sign a CTBT in the fall of 1996. However, in light of mounting international pressure, on January 29, 1996, President Chirac terminated French nuclear testing in the South Pacific.
8. Johnson, "Comprehensive Test Ban Treaty," p. 9.
9. As cited in Johnson, "Endgame Issues in Geneva," p. 15.
10. Craig Cerniello, "India Blocks Consensus on CTB, Treaty May Still Go to U.N.," *Arms Control Today*, August 1996, p. 31.
11. The organization maintains a comprehensive web site, www.ctbto.org.
12. Accurate as of May 2005, Preparatory Commission for the Comprehensive Nuclear-Test-Ban Treaty Organization, www.ctbto.org.

Glossary

atomic bomb. A bomb whose energy comes from the fission of uranium or plutonium.

beryllium. A highly toxic steel-gray metal, possessing a low neutron absorption cross section and high melting point, which can be used in nuclear reactors as a moderator, reflector, or cladding material. In nuclear weapons, beryllium surrounds the fissile material and reflects neutrons back into the nuclear reaction, considerably reducing the amount of fissile material required. Beryllium is also used in guidance systems and other parts for aircraft, missiles, or space vehicles.

blanket. A layer of fertile nuclear material, such as uranium-238 or thorium-232, placed around the fuel core of a reactor. During operation of the reactor, material in the blanket absorbs neutrons and decays, with products forming new fissionable material.

breeder reactor. A nuclear reactor that produces somewhat more fissile material than it consumes. The fissile material is produced both in the reactor's core and when neutrons are captured in fertile material placed around the core (blanket). This process is known as breeding. Breeder reactors have not yet reached commercialization, although active research and development programs are being pursued by various countries.

CANDU (Canadian deuterium-uranium reactor). The most widely used type of heavy-water reactor. The CANDU reactor uses natural uranium as a fuel and heavy water as a moderator and a coolant.

centrifuge. See *ultracentrifuge*.

chain reaction. The continuing process of nuclear fissioning in which the neutrons that are released from a fission trigger at least one other nuclear fission. In a nuclear weapon, an extremely rapid, multiplying chain reaction causes the explosive release of energy. In a reactor, the pace of the chain reaction is controlled to produce heat (in a power reactor) or large quantities of neutrons (in a research or production reactor).

chemical processing. The chemical treatment of nuclear materials, usually in irradiated fuel, to separate specific usable constituents. Chemical reprocessing may be carried out with spent (irradiated) fuel to separate fissionable materials and other usable radioactive by-products from the residual fuel. A different kind of chemical processing may occur in preparation for uranium enrichment; natural uranium feedstock is processed chemically to convert it to gaseous form for enrichment operations.

coolant. A substance circulated through a nuclear reactor to remove or transfer heat. The most common coolants are water and heavy water.

core. The central portion of a nuclear reactor containing the fuel elements, and usually, the moderator. Also the central portion of a nuclear weapon containing highly enriched uranium or plutonium.

critical mass. The minimum amount of a concentrated fissionable material required to sustain a chain reaction. The exact mass of fissionable material needed to sustain a chain reaction varies according to the concentration (purity) and chemical form of the material, the particular fissionable isotope present, its geometric properties, and its density. When pure fissionable materials are compressed by high explosives in implosion-type atomic weapons, the critical mass needed for a nuclear explosion is reduced.

depleted uranium. Uranium having a smaller percentage of uranium-235 than the 0.7 percent found in natural uranium. It is a by-product of the uranium enrichment process, during which uranium-235 is culled from one batch of uranium, thereby depleting it, and then added to another batch to increase its concentration of uranium-235.

enrichment. The process of increasing the concentration of one isotope of a given element (in the case of uranium, increasing the concentration of uranium-235).

feedstock. Material introduced into a facility for processing.

fertile material. Nuclear material composed of atoms that readily absorb neutrons and decay into other elements, producing fissionable materials. One such element is uranium-238, which decays into plutonium-239 after it absorbs a neutron. Fertile material alone cannot sustain a fission chain reaction.

fission. The process by which a neutron strikes a nucleus and splits it into fragments. During the process of nuclear fission, several neutrons are emitted at high speed, and heat and radiation are released.

fissile material. A fissionable material that is especially amenable to fission and therefore readily usable for the core of a nuclear weapon. Uranium-235 and plutonium-239 are examples of fissile materials.

fissionable material. Material whose atoms are easily split when struck by neutrons and that can easily sustain either a controlled or explosive chain reaction, depending on concentration and other conditions of use; also commonly referred to as fissile material.

fusion. The formation of a heavier nucleus from two lighter ones (such as hydrogen isotopes) with the attendant release of energy (as in a hydrogen bomb).

gas-centrifuge process. A method of isotope separation in which heavy, gaseous atoms or molecules are separated from light ones by centrifugal force. See *ultracentrifuge.*

gaseous diffusion. A method of isotope separation based on the fact that gas atoms or molecules with different masses will diffuse through a porous barrier (or membrane) at different rates. The method is used to separate uranium-235 from uranium-238. It requires large gaseous diffusion plants and significant amounts of electric power.

gas-graphite reactor. A nuclear reactor in which a gas is the coolant and graphite is the moderator.

heavy water. Water containing significantly more than the natural proportion (1 in 6,500) of heavy hydrogen (deuterium) atoms to ordinary hydrogen atoms. (Hydrogen atoms have one proton; deuterium atoms have one proton and one neutron.) Heavy water is used as a moderator in some reactors because it slows down neutrons effectively and does not absorb them (unlike light, or normal, water) making it possible to fission natural uranium and sustain a chain reaction.

heavy-water reactor. A reactor that uses heavy water as its moderator and that typically uses natural uranium as fuel. See CANDU.

highly enriched uranium. Uranium in which the percentage of uranium-235 nuclei has been increased from the natural level of 0.7 percent to some level greater than 20 percent, usually around 90 percent.

hot cells. Lead-shielded rooms with remote handling equipment for examining and processing radioactive materials. In particular, hot cells are used for reprocessing spent reactor fuel.

hydrogen bomb. A nuclear weapon that derives its energy largely from fusion. Also known as a thermonuclear bomb.

isotope. A form of any element that is identical chemically but different in physical properties from other isotopes of the same element. Isotopes of an element have the same number of protons in the nucleus and therefore the same atomic number, but they have differing numbers of neutrons in the nucleus and therefore different atomic weights. Radioactive elements may have some isotopes that are readily fissionable and others that are not.

kilogram (kg). A metric weight equivalent to 2.2 pounds.

kiloton (KT). The energy of a nuclear explosion that is equivalent to an explosion of 1,000 metric tons of TNT.

laser enrichment method. A still-experimental process of uranium enrichment in which a finely tuned, high-power laser is used to differentially excite molecules of various nuclear isotopes. This differential excitation makes it possible, for example, to separate uranium-235 from uranium-238.

light water. Ordinary water (H_20) as distinguished from heavy water (D_20).

light-water reactor. A reactor that uses ordinary water as a moderator and coolant and low-enriched uranium as fuel.

low-enriched uranium. Uranium in which the percentage of uranium-235 nuclei has been increased from the natural level of 0.7 percent to less than 20 percent, usually 2 to 6 percent. With the increased level of fissile material, low-enriched uranium can sustain a chain reaction when immersed in light water and is used as fuel in light-water reactors.

medium-enriched uranium. Uranium in which the percentage of uranium-235 nuclei has been increased from the natural level of 0.7 percent to between 20 and 50 percent (potentially usable for nuclear weapons, but very large quantities are needed).

megawatt (MW). One million watts. Used in reference to a nuclear power plant: 1 million watts of electricity (megawatts electric, or MWe); used in reference to a research or production reactor: 1 million watts of thermal energy (megawatts thermal, or MWt).

metric ton. One thousand kilograms. A metric weight equivalent to 2,200 pounds or 1.1 tons.

milling. A process in the uranium fuel cycle by which ore containing only a very small percentage of uranium oxide (U_30_8) is converted into material containing a high percentage (80 percent) of U_3O_8, often referred to as yellowcake.

mining. Process in the uranium fuel cycle by which uranium ore is extracted from the earth.

moderator. A component (usually water, heavy water, or graphite) of some nuclear reactors that slows neutrons, thereby increasing their efficiency in splitting fissionable atoms dispersed in low-enriched or natural uranium fuel, to release energy on a controlled basis.

mixed-oxide fuels. Nuclear reactor fuel composed of plutonium and uranium in oxide form, commonly referred to as MOX fuels. The plutonium replaces some of the need for uranium to power the reactor. This is the fuel technology that the United States and Russia hope to use as part of their "Plutonium Disposition Program."

natural uranium. Uranium as found in nature, containing 0.7 percent of uranium-235, 99.3 percent of uranium-238, and a trace of uranium-234.

neutron. An uncharged elementary particle with a mass slightly greater than that of a proton, found in the nucleus of every atom heavier than hydrogen.

nuclear energy. The energy liberated by a nuclear reaction (fission or fusion) or by spontaneous radioactivity.

nuclear fuel. Basic chain-reaction material, including both fissile and fertile materials. Commonly used nuclear fuels are natural uranium and low-enriched uranium; high-enriched uranium and plutonium are used in some reactors.

nuclear fuel cycle. The set of chemical and physical operations needed to prepare nuclear material for use in reactors and to dispose of or recycle the material after its removal from the reactor. Existing fuel cycles begin with uranium as the natural resource and create plutonium as a by-product. Some future fuel cycles may rely on thorium and produce the fissionable isotope uranium-233.

nuclear fuel element. A rod, tube, plate, or other mechanical shape or form into which nuclear fuel is fabricated for use in a reactor.

nuclear fuel-fabrication plant. A facility where nuclear material (for example, enriched or natural uranium) is fabricated into fuel elements to be inserted in a reactor.

nuclear power plant. Any device or assembly that converts nuclear energy into useful power. In a nuclear electric power plant, heat produced by a reactor is used to produce steam to drive a turbine that in turn drives an electric generator.

nuclear reactor. A mechanism fueled by fissionable materials in a controlled nuclear chain reaction that releases heat, which can be used for civic purposes to generate electricity. Since reactors also produce fissionable material (for example, plutonium) in the irradiated fuel, they may be used as a source of fissile material for weapons. Nuclear reactors fall into three general categories: power reactors, production reactors (for weapons), and research reactors.

nuclear waste. The radioactive by-products formed by fission and other nuclear processes in a reactor. Most nuclear waste is initially contained spent fuel. If this material is reprocessed, new categories of waste result.

nuclear weapons. A collective term for atomic bombs and hydrogen bombs, weapons based on a nuclear explosion. Generally used throughout the text to mean atomic bombs only, unless used with reference to nuclear weapon states (all five of which have both atomic and hydrogen weapons).

plutonium-239. A fissile isotope occurring naturally in only minute quantities and manufactured artificially when uranium-238, through irradiation, captures an extra neutron. It is one of the two materials that have been used for the core of nuclear weapons, the other being highly enriched uranium.

plutonium-240. A fissile isotope produced in reactors when a plutonium-239 atom absorbs a neutron instead of fissioning. Its presence complicates the construction of nuclear explosives because of its high rate of spontaneous fission.

power reactor. A reactor designed to produce electricity, as distinguished from reactors used primarily for research or for producing radiation or fission.

production reactor. A reactor designed primarily for the large-scale production of plutonium-239 by the neutron irradiation of uranium-238.

radioactivity. The spontaneous disintegration of an unstable atomic nucleus, resulting in the emission of subatomic particles.

radioisotope. A radioactive isotope.

recycle. To reuse the remaining uranium and plutonium found in spent fuel. It occurs after those elements have been separated from unwanted radioactive waste products at a reprocessing plant.

reprocessing. The chemical treatment of spent reactor fuel to separate plutonium and uranium from unwanted radioactive waste by-products.

research reactor. A reactor designed primarily to supply neutrons for experimental purposes. It may also be used for training, the testing of materials, and the production of radioisotopes.

spent fuel. Fuel elements that have been removed from the reactor after use because they contain too little fissile material and too high a concentration of unwanted radioactive by-products to sustain reactor operation. Spent fuel is both thermally and radioactively hot.

strategic. In modern military usage, the term *strategic* usually implies a war-prosecuting plan, campaign, or combat capability that could be rapidly decisive in defeating an opponent. In the context of this book, *strategic* usually refers to those weapons—long-range offensive nuclear arms, whether missiles or bomber aircraft—that are deployed for nuclear deterrence or retaliation and to corresponding, strategically capable defensive weapons. Although the term is usually associated with *long*-range weapons and operations, in regions consisting of heavily armed small states (for example, the Middle East), even *shorter*-range offensive systems may be considered strategic if they are nuclear-equipped and capable of striking deep into an opponent's heartland with potentially crippling effects.

tactical. In modern military usage, the term *tactical* usually refers to military operations with *shorter*-range weapons systems, on the battlefield, between the front lines of opposing military forces, and to corresponding defensive systems. Tactical weapons and operations may decide the outcome of a battle but normally do not determine the outcome of a war. In this book *tactical* usually refers to *shorter*-range (nonstrategic) missiles and aircraft and to corresponding (nonstrategic) defensive systems. Weapon systems that a major power may consider tactical for its operations may be considered strategic by small states in their relations with hostile neighbors.

thermonuclear bomb. A hydrogen bomb.

thorium-232. A fertile material.

tritium. The heaviest hydrogen isotope, containing one proton and two neutrons in the nucleus, produced most effectively by bombarding lithium-6 with neutrons. In a fission weapon, tritium produces excess neutrons, which set off additional reactions in the weapon's fissile material. In this way, tritium can either reduce the amount of fissile material required or multiply (that is, boost) the weapon's destructive power as much as five times.

ultracentrifuge. A rapidly rotating cylinder that can be used for the enrichment of uranium. The spinning cylinder concentrates the heavier isotope (uranium-238) of uranium hexafluoride gas along the cylinder's walls, while the lighter isotope (uranium-235) concentrates at the center of the cylinder, where it can be drawn off separately.

uranium. A radioactive element with the atomic number 92 and, as found in natural ores, an average atomic weight of 238. The two principal natural isotopes are uranium-235 (0.7 percent of natural uranium), which is fissionable, and uranium-238 (99.3 percent of natural uranium), which is fertile.

uranium conversion. The process in which concentrated uranium (yellowcake) is converted to uranium hexafluoride for further enrichment.

uranium dioxide (UO_2). Purified uranium. The form of natural uranium used in heavy-water reactors. Also the form of uranium that remains after the fluorine is removed from enriched uranium hexafluoride (UF_6). Produced as a powder, uranium dioxide is, in turn, fabricated into fuel elements.

uranium hexafluoride (UF_6). A volatile compound of uranium and fluorine. UF_6 is a solid at atmospheric pressure and room temperature, but can be transformed into gas by heating. UF_6 gas (alone, or in combination with hydrogen or helium) is the feedstock in all uranium enrichment processes and is sometimes produced as an intermediate product in the process of purifying yellowcake to produce uranium oxide.

uranium oxide (U_3O_8). The most common oxide of uranium found in typical ores. Uranium oxide is extracted from the ore during the milling process. The ore typically contains only 0.1 percent uranium oxide; yellowcake, the product of the milling process, contains about 80 percent uranium oxide.

uranium tetrafluoride. An intermediate compound in the uranium conversion process. Uranium tetrafluoride is a solid (green salt). It is further converted to uranium hexafluoride for enrichment in ultracentrifuges.

uranium-233. A fissionable isotope bred in fertile thorium-232. Like plutonium-239, it is theoretically an excellent material for nuclear weapons but is not known to have been used for that purpose. Can be used as a reactor fuel.

uranium-235. The only naturally occurring fissionable isotope. Natural uranium contains 0.7 percent uranium-235; light-water reactors use about 3 percent; and weapons-grade, highly enriched uranium normally consists of 93 percent of this isotope.

uranium-238. A fertile material. Natural uranium is composed of approximately 99.3 percent uranium-238.

vessel. The part of a reactor that contains the nuclear fuel.

weapons-grade. Nuclear material of the type most suitable for nuclear weapons, that is, uranium enriched to 93 percent uranium-235 or plutonium that is primarily plutonium-239.

weapons-usable. Fissionable material that is weapons grade or, although less than ideal for weapons, that can still be used to make a nuclear explosive.

yellowcake. A concentrate produced during the milling process that contains about 80 percent uranium oxide (U_3O_8). In preparation for uranium enrichment, the yellowcake is converted to uranium hexafluoride gas (UF_6). In the preparation of natural uranium reactor fuel, yellowcake is processed into purified uranium dioxide. Sometimes uranium hexafluoride is produced as an intermediate step in the purification process.

yield. The total energy released in a nuclear explosion. It is usually expressed in equivalent metric tons of TNT (the quantity of TNT required to produce a corresponding amount of energy).

zirconium. A grayish-white lustrous metal that is commonly used in an alloy form (that is, zircaloy) to encase fuel rods in nuclear reactors.

SOURCES

Albright, David, Frans Berkhout, and William Walker. *World Inventory of Plutonium and Highly Enriched Uranium, 1992*. Oxford: Oxford University Press, 1993.

Cochran, Thomas B., William Arkin, Robert S. Norris, and Milton Heonig. *Nuclear Weapons Databook. Vol. 2: U.S. Nuclear Warhead Production*. Cambridge, Mass.: Ballinger, 1984.

Nero, Anthony V. Jr. *A Guidebook to Nuclear Reactors*. Berkeley: University of California Press, 1979.

Office of Technology Assessment, U.S. Congress. *Nuclear Power in an Age of Uncertainty*. Washington, D.C.: U.S. Government Printing Office, 1984.

———. *Technologies Underlying Weapons of Mass Destruction*. Washington, D.C.: U.S. Government Printing Office, 1993.

Abbreviations and Acronyms

ABACC	Argentine-Brazilian Accounting and Control Commission
ABM	anti–ballistic missile
AEC	Atomic Energy Corporation (South Africa)
ALCM	air-launched cruise missiles
BW	biological weapons
BWC	Biological and Toxin Weapons Convention
CW	chemical weapons
CIA	Central Intelligence Agency (United States)
CTBT	Comprehensive Test Ban Treaty
CTR	Cooperative Threat Reduction program
CWC	Chemical Weapons Convention
DIA	Defense Intelligence Agency (United States)
EMIS	electromagnetic isotope separation
HEU	highly enriched uranium
IAEA	International Atomic Energy Agency
ICBM	intercontinental ballistic missile
ICOC	International Code of Conduct
INF	intermediate-range nuclear forces
IPP	Initiatives for Proliferation Prevention
IRBM	intermediate-range ballistic missile
ISTC	International Science and Technology Center
LEU	low-enriched uranium
MIRV	multiple independently targeted reentry vehicle
MPC&A	material protection, control, and accounting
MRBM	medium-range ballistic missile
MTCR	Missile Technology Control Regime
NBC	Joint Nuclear, Biological, and Chemical Regiment
NCI	Nuclear Cities Initiative
NIE	National Intelligence Estimate (United States)
NPT	Non-Proliferation Treaty
NSG	Nuclear Suppliers Group
NWFZ	nuclear-weapon-free zone
OPCW	Organization for the Prohibition of Chemical Weapons
PNEs	peaceful nuclear explosives
SLBM	submarine-launched ballistic missile
SLV	space launch vehicle
SORT	Strategic Offensive Reduction Treaty

SRBM	short-range ballistic missile
SSBN	nuclear ballistic missile submarine
SSN	nuclear-fueled submarine
START	Strategic Arms Reduction Treaty
STCU	Science and Technology Centers, Ukraine
UNMOVIC	U.N. Monitoring, Verification, and Inspection Commission
UNSC	United Nations Security Council
UNSCOM	U.N. Special Commission
VX	V nerve agent
WMD	weapons of mass destruction

Maps, Figures, and Tables

Maps

Figures

Tables

Index

Page numbers in bold typeface indicate definitions or descriptions.

About the Authors

Joseph Cirincione is the director for nonproliferation at the Carnegie Endowment in Washington. One of America's best-known weapons experts, he is widely quoted in the media on international security issues. The *National Journal* named him as one of the 100 people whose ideas will shape the policy debates in Washington. He served for nine years in the U.S. House of Representatives on the professional staff of the Committee on Armed Services and the Committee on Government Operations. He is a coauthor of *Universal Compliance: A Strategy for Nuclear Security* (Carnegie Endowment, 2005) and *WMD in Iraq: Evidence and Implications* (Carnegie Endowment, 2004), the editor of *Repairing the Regime: Preventing the Spread of Weapons of Mass Destruction* (Routledge, 2000), and the author of numerous articles on defense and nuclear policy issues. He teaches at the Georgetown University School of Foreign Service.

Jon B. Wolfsthal is deputy director for nonproliferation at the Carnegie Endowment and focuses his research on the security of nuclear weapons and materials. He has written extensively on Russia's nuclear complex and its proliferation challenges, as well as on regional security and proliferation in East Asia. He served for five years as an official at the U.S. Department of Energy. He is a coauthor of *Universal Compliance: A Strategy for Nuclear Security* (Carnegie Endowment, 2005). He is a frequent media commentator and the author of numerous articles on proliferation and nuclear policy issues.

Miriam Rajkumar is an associate for nonproliferation at the Carnegie Endowment and focuses her research on political and security developments in South Asia and the Persian Gulf. She contributed to *Universal Compliance: A Strategy for Nuclear Security* (Carnegie Endowment, 2004) and is coauthor of *Iraq: What Next?* (Carnegie Endowment, 2003) She holds an M.A. in International Relations from Johns Hopkins University's Paul H. Nitze School of Advanced International Studies in Washington.

About Carnegie's Nonproliferation Resources

The Carnegie Endowment for International Peace is an internationally recognized source of information and analysis on efforts to curb the spread of nuclear, chemical, and biological weapons and missile delivery systems. Through publications, conferences, and the Internet, the Endowment's experts promote greater public awareness of these security issues and encourage effective policies to address unconventional weapons proliferation and its underlying causes.

Our publications and commentary include books, working papers, monographs, articles, and interviews. In addition, project staff maintain the extensive web site www.ProliferationNews.org. *National Journal* applauded this web site as a "top site" that "mak[es] voluminous information easily accessible." It offers daily news, analysis, documents, maps, charts, and updates to *Deadly Arsenals*, along with other key resources. Updated hourly, the web site is a prime source of information for journalists, officials, and experts worldwide. The project organizes frequent roundtables and briefings; distributes regular *Proliferation Briefs*; and provides the free biweekly *Proliferation News Service*, an e-mail summary of news and analysis.

The project also convenes the Carnegie International Non-Proliferation Conference, widely considered the premier event in the field and attended by hundreds of leading proliferation experts and officials from around the world. At the Carnegie Moscow Center, the project holds the Moscow International Non-Proliferation Conference and promotes debate on nonproliferation policies in the former Soviet Union through regular seminars with key experts and officials, major conferences, and Russian-language periodicals.

The Carnegie Endowment for International Peace

The Carnegie Endowment for International Peace is a private, nonprofit organization dedicated to advancing cooperation between nations and promoting active international engagement by the United States. Founded in 1910, Carnegie is nonpartisan and dedicated to achieving practical results.

Through research, publishing, convening, and, on occasion, creating new institutions and international networks, Endowment associates shape fresh policy approaches. Their interests span geographic regions and the relations between governments, business, international organizations, and civil society, focusing on the economic, political, and technological forces driving global change. Through its Carnegie Moscow Center, the Endowment helps to develop a tradition of public policy analysis in the states of the former Soviet Union and to improve relations between Russia and the United States. The Endowment publishes *Foreign Policy*, one of the world's leading magazines of international politics and economics, which reaches readers in more than 120 countries and in several languages.

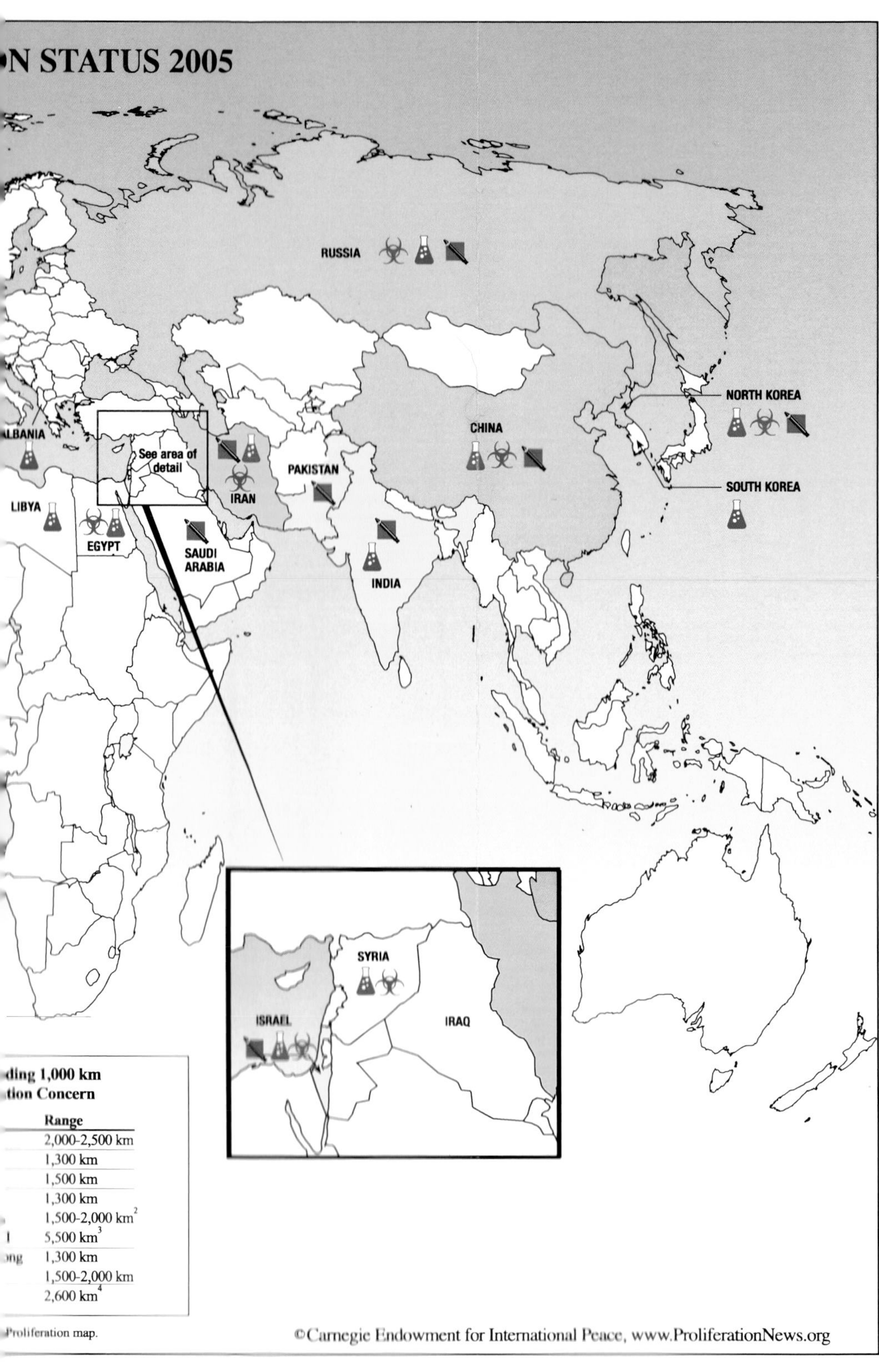
N STATUS 2005
RUSSIA
NORTH KOREA
CHINA
ALBANIA
See area of detail
PAKISTAN
IRAN
SOUTH KOREA
LIBYA
EGYPT
SAUDI ARABIA
INDIA
SYRIA
ISRAEL
IRAQ
ding 1,000 km
tion Concern
Range
2,000-2,500 km
1,300 km
1,500 km
1,300 km
1,500-2,000 km 2
5,500 km 3
1,300 km
1,500-2,000 km
2,600 km 4
Proliferation map.
©Carnegie Endowment for International Peace, www.ProliferationNews.org

PROLIFERATIC

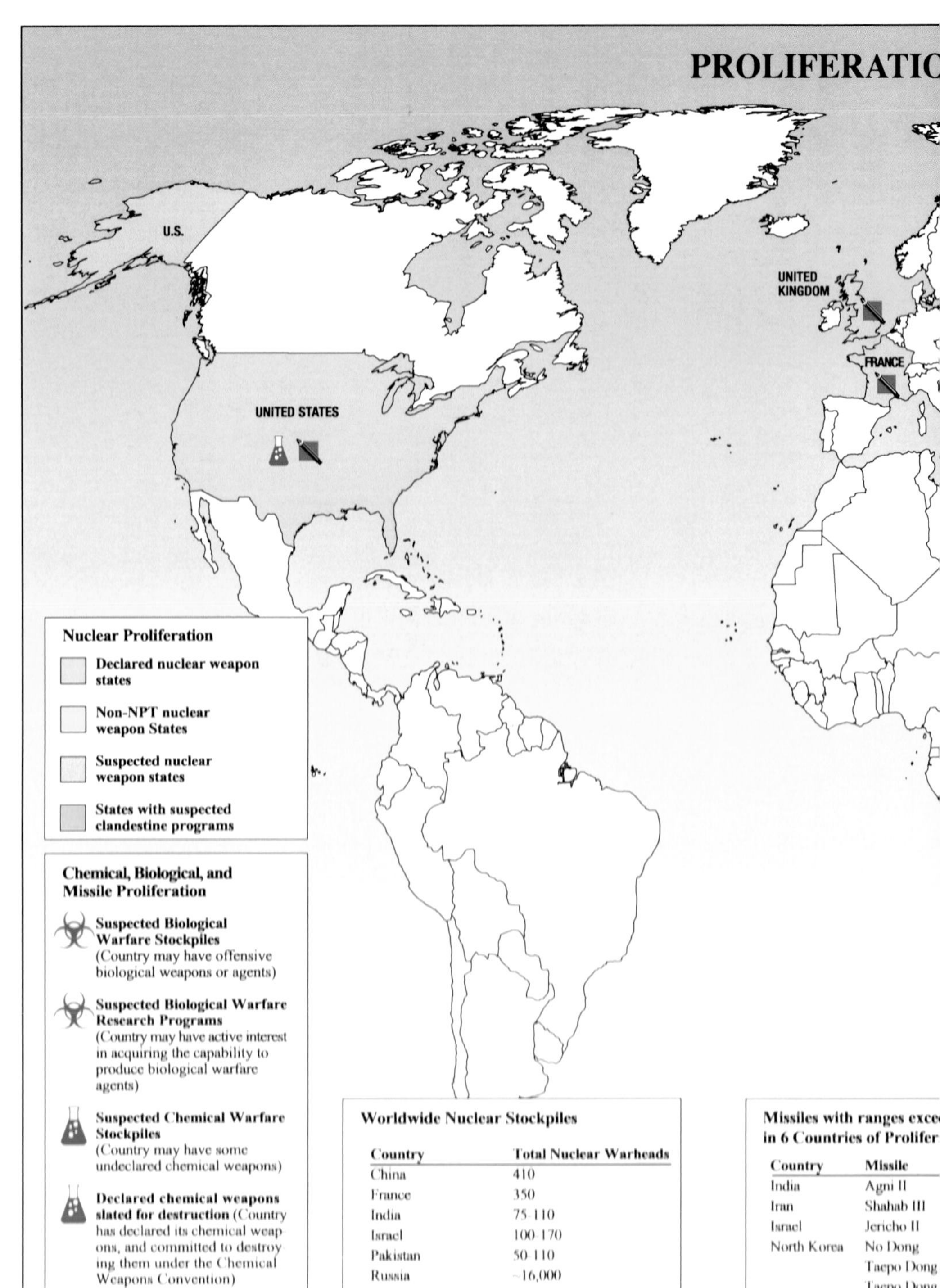

Worldwide Nuclear Stockpiles

Country	Total Nuclear Warheads
China	410
France	350
India	75-110
Israel	100-170
Pakistan	50-110
Russia	~16,000
United Kingdom	200
United States	~10,300
Total	**~27,600**

Missiles with ranges exce in 6 Countries of Prolifer

Country	Missile
India	Agni II
Iran	Shahab III
Israel	Jericho II
North Korea	No Dong
	Taepo Dong
	Taepo Dong
Pakistan	Ghauri/No D
	Ghauri II
Saudi Arabia	CSS-2

2,3,4 See notes on Ballistic Missile